FOUR MILES HIGH

JOSEPHINE SCARR

First published in 1966 by Victor Gollancz Ltd

This edition is published by The Pinnacle Club 2021

ISBN: 978-0-9513967-4-2

Website: https://pinnacleclub.co.uk/

Cover designed by Cathy Woodhead with a photograph of the author on the final ridge of Lha Shamma

DEDICATION

To my three children: Adrian, Michael and Nadine

Per ardua ad alta

CONTENTS

MAPS

LIST OF PHOTOGRAPHS

FOREWORD

In September 2016, two accomplished American mountain guides inched their way along a precarious, smooth granite fin to reach the highest point of Shigrila, so making the first ascent of this impressive 6,247 m peak in the Indian Himalaya.

They had climbed from the southeast, but near the summit were momentarily fixated by an uninterrupted view down the north-northeast ridge and its flanking east face. They were highly impressed, not only by what they could see of the terrain, but also by the audacity of the team that had almost reached the top from this direction exactly fifty-five years previously.

In 1961 two resolute British women in their early 20s bought a Land Rover, took a rudimentary maintenance course, and drove the vehicle from the UK to India to make their first expedition to the Himalaya. Their chosen destination was the Kullu (modern spelling), where straightforward access to plentiful, unclimbed, moderately technical (by today's standards) peaks would later lead to an explosion of activity that continued until the end of the 1970s.

These were no ordinary women. Jo Scarr and Barbara Spark were amongst the best British female climbers of their era and met whilst Scarr was on an extended post-university 'gap year', instructing at Plas y Brenin. Both were members of the Pinnacle Club and Scarr, a Cambridge graduate, was notably the first female to lead the globally-famous north Wales classic, *Cenotaph Corner*.

With a high degree of resourcefulness, the [British] Women's Kulu Expedition 1961 engaged two Kullu locals and defied bureaucratic difficulties to reach the Bara Shigri Glacier, from where they made first ascents of two 6,000 m peaks. Subsequently they turned their attentions to the eye-catching and then unnamed 'Peak 6,247 m', attempting it by way of the steep, difficult, rock and mixed east face. After climbing the face, they were forced to retreat from close to the top of the north-northeast ridge: there were less than three hours of daylight remaining, and the team carried no torches or equipment for a night out. The style was bold, the climbing technical, and the near-ascent highly significant for the era.

Kullu was only half of the story. After the expedition the two overwintered in India, teaching at a Delhi school, and then joined Countess Dorothea Gravina's all-woman – and all Pinnacle Club - expedition to explore the remote Jagdula/Kagmara section of the Nepalese Kanjiroba Himal in pre-monsoon 1962.

Seven years before, Monica Jackson had led the first all-female expedition to the Himalaya, climbing a high virgin summit in the Jugal region of Nepal with Sherpa support. The 1962 British Jagdula Women's expedition metaphorically followed in their footsteps by not only making the first ascent of a remote Nepalese peak, but in doing so also confirming that women could hold their own in the male dominant activity of high-altitude mountaineering. It was a fine example of exploratory alpinism in an area of Nepal that has hardly been visited since. The expedition climbed seven new peaks, including Scarr and Spark's first ascent of Lha Shamma (6,412 m), the ascent remains unrepeated to this day.

In 2021 the Pinnacle Club is 100 years old. To celebrate its centenary the club has decided to reprint Jo Scarr's wonderful book of these two expeditions, this time complete with colour images. It is an engaging account of travel, exploration, and great team spirit. Moreover, it is a book defined by Scarr's palpable enthusiasm and unfazed attitude, in an era where this sort of adventure held a significant barrier for women.

Lindsay Griffin
January 2021

10

PREFACE to 1966 edition

Expeditions to far off places and unclimbed mountains must always be the product of a co-operative effort. Although written from a personal point of view, this book recounts an exciting year for two people and a splendid three months for six, and I owe much to all those who made it possible.

Our objectives were brought within closer reach by the generous assistance we received. The Mount Everest Foundation made handsome grants to both the Kulu and Jagdula expeditions and the Royal Geographical Society lent survey instruments and provided valuable advice on map-making. John Jackson, Warden of Plas y Brenin and a very experienced Himalayan climber, was the outstanding friend and counsellor of our Kulu expedition. We were also helped by the Holt Education Trust of Liverpool and for information on our chosen areas by A E Gunther, Eve Sims and Eileen Healey on Kulu and by John Tyson on West Nepal.

The Nepal expedition was inevitably a larger, longer and more costly undertaking and we are most grateful to the members of the

Pinnacle Club, Ladies Alpine Club and many other good friends who gave their support, and in particular to Lady Rootes. To two members of the British team which conquered Everest we have special cause to be grateful - Charles Wylie who organised for us such a fine team of Sherpas and Charles Evans who gave so much help and whose name as our patron worked wonders wherever we went. Many commercial firms gave their products free or at a considerable discount. As some of these would prefer to remain anonymous, it would seem invidious to single out any from among those who so generously assisted us.

I am indebted to Barbara Spark and Nancy Smith for the use of some of their photographs and to those who helped in the preparation and typing of this book.

Like most other expeditions to the Himalayas, much has been gained from and little contributed to the delightful people of the high mountains, so as a measure of our gratitude the proceeds of this book will be given towards a small aid project in the region.

Josephine Scarr
Canberra 1966

PREFACE to 2021 edition

I was delighted when Cathy Woodhead of the Pinnacle Club suggested publishing a new edition of *Four Miles High* with colour photos to celebrate the club's centenary in 2021. It has also enabled me to bring the story up to date to some extent. Sixty years have passed since the Pinnacle Club's 1962 Jagdula Expedition to northwest Nepal, and sadly the leader Dorothea Gravina, Nancy Smith, Pat Wood and Barbara Roscoe (née Spark) are no longer alive. Their obituaries form an Appendix to this book, as do Denise's and my subsequent lives.

This book is not and never was an official account of these Himalayan expeditions. It came about because as we were saying our goodbyes in Kathmandu, Dorothea suddenly remembered that Livia Gollancz of Victor Gollancz Ltd Publishers in London had given her an advance against producing a book on the expedition. Dorothea quickly said she could not write a book so it would have to be one of us. Going round the circle it emerged that I was the only one who did not have a job or children to go back to and was therefore free, so I meekly agreed to do it. Luckily I had kept detailed diaries since leaving Wales and these formed the basis of my narrative. My lack of an income was solved by Frances Tanner, a friend of Nancy Smith, who lent me her cottage in Kirkby Lonsdale in the Lake District in which to write. I also earned a small income by becoming a lecturer on Foyles Bookstore's lecture circuit.

I have several times been asked to write my autobiography but instead this book has been expanded into a personal account of how I accidentally became a climber, how I came to join the Pinnacle Club and how I ended up on two all-women Himalayan expeditions. (The ensuing sixty years are outlined in a brief Appendix.)

By June 1963 the book was finished and was published by Gollancz in 1966, when it was translated into Hungarian as a women's liberation tract! I had never thought of myself in those terms but as pursuing a life of 'Discovery'. This has been fulfilled by my two major interests, first mountaineering and then archaeology; 'From the Heights to the Depths', as I entitled a recent public lecture for my old College.

In 1963 I emigrated to a job in Australia in order to climb in New Zealand, but ended up doing decades of archaeological fieldwork in the Australian outback. I am just finishing my seventh book on Australian Aboriginal Archaeology and rock art, writing in lockdown in Wales, where I returned in 1991.

Finally, I would like to thank all those who have helped with this new edition, especially Cathy Woodhead and Nigel Peacock on the text and John Cleare, Tony Smythe and others for editing or contributing the photographs.

Josephine Peacock (formerly Flood, née Scarr)
Llanbedr-y-Cennin, North Wales
January 2021

1 THE ROCK CEILING

My fingers were getting tired. The rock was dry and warm but very steep and I could not see how to move up from the tiny toeholds on which I was poised. The strain of standing on only a few centimetres of boot made my legs begin to shake, a sure sign that I must either move up quickly or climb down for a rest. About twenty feet below there was a ledge wide enough to stand on comfortably, and I decided to retreat down to it. The first few moves down were quite easy, but then came the place where initially I had swung across from the ledge on a sideways handhold. Try as I might, with my short reach (I was only 5 ft 3 ins tall), it was impossible to swing back the other way. Slowly came the nasty realisation that there could be no return, no rest, the only way now was up.

Quickly I regained my previous position but my legs were trembling like jelly and my fingertips numb from gripping the minute handholds. A wave of panic swept over me, then I noticed a larger handhold out to one side. Perhaps this was the key to reaching the sloping ledge above. Thankfully I gripped it, only to find that all feeling had gone from my fingers. "I'm going to fall off," I whispered.

Looking down I could see Muriel Baldwin, my fellow climber from the Pinnacle Club, sitting on the ground about eighty feet below, paying out the rope and idly chatting to Doug. Between us stretched the long white rope running through a series of snaplinks attached to spikes of rock by strong rope slings, running belays put on· to act as pulleys should the leader fall. And the leader was going to fall. Anxiously I looked at the highest one fixed to a metal peg about twenty feet below, and prayed that it would hold. Three inches of steel lay between me and an eighty-foot fall to the ground. Slowly my numb fingers uncurled and I felt myself falling; there was a strange dream-like sensation of drifting through space and then a sickening jolt on my waist as I was pulled up short, bouncing like a yo-yo on the stretchy nylon rope, about forty feet from the ground. The peg had held and was acting as a perfect pulley: as I came down Muriel had been pulled up and was now some way off the ground, with Doug hanging on to her legs.

"What do we do now?" I was wondering, when a Lancashire voice sounded below, "Ee, what's going on 'ere, 'aving fun?" It was another party of climbers who helped Doug retrieve Muriel and then lowered me to the ground.

Neither of us was hurt but a bit bruised and shaken. I profusely apologised to Muriel and we sat down for a cigarette. It was a Saturday afternoon in the Llanberis Pass and there were crowds of trippers on the road a few hundred feet below, but fortunately none of them appeared to have noticed my spectacular descent.

"You know, I'm sure that I could do it," I said, studying the sweep of rock, "it was just that I got so tired and panicked. When I've had a good rest I'd like to have another go." Doug and Muriel tried to dissuade me, but I knew that if I did not try again straight away, it would loom larger and larger in my imagination and I might never do it again. Finally we agreed that I would lead it as before, but Doug would belay on the ledge above the climb with a rope ready to drop to me if I should again become exhausted. With the confidence of these extra safety measures I climbed up without any hesitation, and could not understand why I had found it so difficult before.

Difficulty, of course, is entirely relative. This route, *Kaisergebirge Wall*, was graded extremely severe and would horrify a beginner, but to the 'hard men' would be an easy climb for an off-day. It was 1960 and the hardest route that I had ever tried to lead. It had never been led by a woman before, perhaps partly because of its strenuous nature, but mainly, I suspect, because very few girls climbed and even fewer led climbs.

I have begun with Kaisergebirge because for me it was to be a turning point. It was the first time that I had fallen off a climb, and although I went on rock-climbing and subsequently did still harder routes, it made me question just what I was doing and why, a question which was to have far-reaching consequences.

It had all begun six years before in my village of Boston Spa in Yorkshire. I was a real bookworm and one day in the village library, I picked up a thick volume called *Farthest North*, Nansen's account of his epic attempt to reach the North Pole. The story of men against those vast expanses of snow and ice fascinated me, and led me on to Shackleton, Scott, and thence to mountaineering books, but women never seemed to take part in this world of exploration and adventure. Then and there I decided that I wanted a life of Discovery.

At school I was very mediocre at games. The only sports which I enjoyed were swimming and sailing on family holidays at Abersoch. When I was allowed my first independent holiday at the age of fifteen I went sailing with two school friends on the Norfolk Broads, and the following year took a boat on the River Severn at Tewkesbury. These were chaotic expeditions with the boat frequently jammed under bridges or aground in the reeds, but they gave me a taste for independence which was later to find an outlet in mountaineering.

At this time my energies were mainly concentrated on getting into Cambridge to read Classics. (I actually wanted to study History or English, but Isobel Sayers, my head-mistress at Lowther College and an old Girtonian, persuaded me to go for the far less competitive field of Classics.) It was a relief when I was offered a place at Girton College, on the condition that I should learn a great deal more Greek in the next nine months. I was the first in my family to go to University and my father could not afford to send me but I obtained two scholarships, so was able to reassure him that it wouldn't cost him a penny.

I had left school but was only just eighteen and in the 1950s one was not allowed to go up to Cambridge until one was nineteen, so I had time to fill in. Fortunately the Classics Department of Leeds University generously allowed me to join their first-year course for two terms. Fortunately again, Leeds is only 15 miles from Boston Spa so I could drive in each day. (I had got my driver's licence at the earliest opportunity to ferry my mother around, since, like most ladies in those days, she did not drive.) My father had bought an old Morgan Plus 4 sports car for my two older brothers and me to use, but they were far away so I got the lion's share.

By a lucky chance the only person whom I knew at Leeds, a family friend, Frank Butler, was also secretary of the University climbing club which was open to both men and women. Each day I used to have lunch with Frank and his friends in the cafeteria and always the talk was of climbing, not of mountains but of cliffs, pitches, 'hanging on' and 'peeling off'. None of this meant anything to me till one afternoon when they were going out to the local millstone grit crag of Almscliff I was invited to go and watch. It was a revelation to see apparently sane people acting like monkeys, swinging up overhangs and wriggling up slimy chimneys, but it looked exciting and by the end of the afternoon in dirndl skirt and stockinged feet I was doing my first climb.

From then on once or twice a week we would roar out of Leeds to Almscliff or Ilkley for an hour or two's rock gymnastics. Frank and his particular group were all very good climbers and made few concessions to beginners. After only one or two easy routes I was expected either to follow where they led or watch from below. It was not the ideal introduction, it was not mountaineering, but it was great fun and a new world to me.

The final months at Leeds University are one of the happiest times I can remember. Almost every weekend we went up to the Lake District, me driving my red Morgan as, after his many near-misses on his own motor-bike, my father would not let me drive or ride pillion on one. We usually headed for Langdale, Gimmer Crag and the Old Dungeon Ghyll. I suppose there must have been bad days and rainy days but, in retrospect, it seems one long idyll of perpetual sunshine with not a care in the world. When it snowed we went caving in the Yorkshire Dales, discovering previously unknown caves where warm air from below had melted hollows in surface snow. I also enjoyed abseiling down into Gaping Ghyll, the largest cave chamber in Britain. (Ghyll has now become Gill and there is a pulley and chair for visitors to descend into the depths.)

When I went up to Cambridge in 1955 it was disappointing to find that the thriving Mountaineering Club was strictly men only, and although the Committee were pleasant and helpful, it was made clear that there were enough novices in the club without taking on any more. A few years earlier someone had started a women's mountaineering club, named the Magog Club after a legendary giant, but this had now almost petered out. There were so many other things to do in Cambridge that to persist against these odds seemed very contrary, but already climbing had taken such a hold on me that to give it up was unthinkable.

I have to confess that I had almost no interest in Classics, the subject I had to read for my first two years, and found I was a complete beginner compared with the men who had been studying it from the age of eight (in the 1950s at Cambridge men outnumbered women students by eleven to one). I was sure I would fail so decided to enjoy life climbing and working on the weekly University newspaper. My most memorable journalistic experience was being sent to London to report on a reception being given at the Russian embassy for the visiting leaders Bulganin and Khrushchev. Much vodka flowed and the reception turned into a drunken orgy. We had difficulty in escaping through the media mob fighting for the telephones to report their story of the drama, and I decided then and there that I did not want to become a journalist.

I expected to be sent down after my Part I exams in 1957. One of the Greek papers asked me to translate a Shakespeare sonnet into Greek verse –an impossibility for me so instead I wrote a comic version of Shakespeare's sonnet in English. However, they gave me a Third and allowed me to change subjects for Part II. I chose Classical Archaeology, a new subject for all of us students, which later led me to a fascinating career in Australian Aboriginal Archaeology (see Appendix).

At this stage I had never tried to analyse why I climbed. If questioned, I would probably have produced the stock answers - for enjoyment, excitement, good exercise and companionship in beautiful scenery away from the crowds. Yet even then after only six months climbing there was more to it than that, much more.

Everyone has their own motives, conscious or unconscious, and mixed in differing proportions at different times. Initially perhaps it was the desire for the Unknown, something exciting outside ordinary everyday life, but as I climbed I found that here at last was a field where I could hold my own with other people. At school I had discovered I had no eye for a ball and had developed an inferiority complex about sport, yet I had always wanted to get to the top in some sphere. Now this ambition was transferred into the field of mountaineering. As a sport it has the great advantage that it demands no superhuman strength or ability; all one needs is fitness, a reasonable head for heights, a sense of balance and a great deal of determination.

The desire to go on climbing was strong enough to make me restart the Women's Club, and begin to lead easy climbs. Mountains became like a drug which I had to have to survive at all. Sunday after Sunday from Cambridge I would endure ten hours' coach journey to Derbyshire and back, feeling bus-sick all the way, just for four hours' climbing on rock that was invariably wet, cold, and greasy. Occasionally, we would hire a car and go to Wales or the Lake District for a weekend, driving all night Friday and Sunday, arriving back for lectures on Monday morning dirty, tired-out, but happy. Looking back I find it difficult to credit that I could ever have been quite so fanatical, but then there seemed a great sense of urgency, as though the mountains might disappear at any moment.

During each long vacation I worked as a waitress for a month or two at the Pen-y-Gwryd hotel in Snowdonia to save like mad to go travelling and climbing in the Alps. In 1956 I went rock-climbing in the island of Skye in Scotland with Kay Baker and two other Magog friends and then abroad for the first time down through France to the Pyrenees. Our entire experience of snow and ice climbing was confined to my one fortnight in Scotland the previous winter with some CUMC climbers in Glencoe, the Cairngorms and seeing the New Year in on the snow-covered top of Ben Nevis with Scotsmen in kilts. Nevertheless, we decided 'to have a look at' a few Pyrenean peaks and climbed two 10,000-footers, climbing on snow and even crossing a small glacier.

In retrospect this Pyrenean climbing seems distinctly rash. Our mountaineering experience was woefully inadequate and our ignorance abysmal: I recall that when the guidebook described a cliff as *vertigineuse* we expected something grassy! In the Gavarnie area we climbed the Vignemale (3,298 m) and made the first ascent of the Arête d'Astazou 'sans garçons'. It was a wonderful holiday and nothing went wrong but it made me realise that if I was ever to climb larger peaks in the Alps, I must have some proper training in the techniques of snow and ice climbing. Accordingly the following year with Meg Harris, another Magog, I went to Austria on a course run by the Austrian Alpine Club. There for a fortnight we were instructed by professional guides, climbing peaks and crossing passes from one mountain hut to the next each day regardless of the weather. Two months studying Classical monuments in Greece and Italy followed, a fabulous summer of travel.

The next summer, 1958, I went to the Alps, this time with a Cambridge men's party to Switzerland. There I gained valuable experience of snow and ice climbing on the 14,000-footers around Zermatt, and we did some memorable peaks such as Monte Rosa, the traverse of the Lyskamm, the Rothorn (by the Kanzelgrat) and the Wellenkuppe-Obergabelhorn traverse. My climbing partner was Nigel Peacock, with whom I had recently been to a May Ball, but the trip nearly ended in disaster on the Lenzspitze-Nadelhorn traverse, when a snow-bridge gave way and Nigel plunged down into a very deep, bottle-shaped crevasse. Luckily my instant axe belay held with me kneeling on my ice axe in the deep snow, and Nigel was able to pendulum to and fro until he could get a purchase on the side with his axe and a crampon and climb out. We retreated to the valley below and Nigel was so embarrassed that we stopped climbing together and went our separate ways.

I began to climb more and more with other women, sharing the leading, with increased enjoyment by not always being on the bottom end of the rope. I treated all men like my older brothers and romance was not on my agenda. In Leeds University I was called 'the girl in the red Morgan', in Cambridge I was 'Fair Miss Frigidaire', as in the Bing Crosby song in 'High Society'. In search of women to climb with, especially when working at the Pen-y-Gwryd, in 1958 I joined the Pinnacle Club, the all-women climbing club with a hut at Cwm Dyli in Nant Gwynant, only a few miles from the hotel. Indeed, the Pinnacle Club had been founded by a small group of women at the Pen-y-Gwryd hotel in March 1921.

My companion for my next alpine season in 1959 was Muriel Baldwin, a Londoner whom I had met at the Pinnacle Club hut. We drove out and spent a delightful month in the French Alps and Dolomites climbing such routes as the Forbes Arête on the Aiguille du

Chardonnet and traversing Tre Cime di Lavaredo (the Three Towers of Lavaredo) in the Dolomites.

Graduation came in 1959, and the question - What now? I had hoped to do a post-graduate degree in Classical Archaeology but in the 1950s that required a First rather than my 2:1 degree. Otherwise, I had little idea of what I wanted to do apart from more and more mountaineering. I was chewing over the possibilities when I learnt there was a vacancy for the first female mountaineering instructor at a centre in North Wales. I applied, went up to Plas y Brenin in Capel Curig for an interview, and to my great delight was given the post.

Plas y Brenin is a National Recreation Centre where the Central Council of Physical Recreation (now the Sports Council) runs courses in outdoor activities both for the general public and for special groups. I was the first woman instructor, the others being men with a wide variety of interests and backgrounds; John Jackson (a Himalayan explorer), Roger Orgill (an expert canoeist and guitar-player), and Brian Grey (an ex-Marine commando).

We all instructed a wide range of activities and I found myself doing not only mountaineering, map-reading, camp-craft, skiing and canoeing, but also running courses on the history of Snowdonia and organising excavations on Roman roads and forts, such as the fort above the Pen-y-Gwryd. The composition of the courses was equally varied, one week it would be schoolboys, another a Women's Training College, industrial apprentices, youth leaders, boys from Borstal (now Young Offenders Institution) or Prison Officers. Most courses lasted only a week, but occasionally we would have a special group such as Girls Outward Bound for a month.

After so many years of academic work it was satisfying to be doing a practical outdoor job and one that I enjoyed so much. It was a congenial but exacting life, instructing six days a week in all weathers and several evenings a week doing lectures or running social activities for the courses.

Inevitably holidays were taken in the mountains, skiing in the winter and climbing in the summer. In my summer holiday in 1960 again I went to the Alps, this time with three Pinnacle Club members, Muriel Baldwin, Pat Wood and Barbara Spark. Pat and Muriel were both experienced alpinists, and Barbara, new to snow and ice climbing, proved an excellent climber. The weather was kind to us for once and we had a very good three weeks around Saas-Fee, the highlight being on the Jägigrat ridge seeing and photographing a Brocken spectre - the rare phenomenon of a shadow of oneself surrounded by a rainbow cast onto mist.

A fortnight later I fell off whilst leading *Kaisergebirge Wall*. For some time I had been doing harder and harder climbs, but Kaisergebirge made me realise that I had almost reached my physical limit in rock-climbing.

For men this problem does not arise to the same extent, if at all, for almost all the existing climbs do not require more than the strength of an average man. The limitation is more in the mind than in the body. But even for a woman I am small and not very strong, I have never yet achieved a single pull-up. Up to the Very Severe class this did not matter particularly but on the vertical walls or overhangs of the higher grades there was a very real danger of becoming exhausted and falling off. And not all routes are as safe to fall off as Kaisergebirge.

Of course there was great pleasure in doing easier routes, savouring the pure joy of rhythmic movement up rock, but if I never tried anything new or more difficult I felt I was evading the issue, rather like a diver who never goes off the top board. At the age of twenty-four I could not be satisfied with just doing things which I knew I could do. There were only two alternatives: to go on banging my head on the rock ceiling till I eventually killed myself, or to seek difficulties in fresh channels.

In instructing I seemed to have reached much the same impasse. I had learnt my job, I was doing it as well as I possibly could, but there seemed no future, no progression. This is inevitable when one is constantly teaching beginners and in spite of its limitations the life was remarkably varied, but I was too restless to stay in it year after year.

But what should I do? What could I do? The only job which I thought I might enjoy would be teaching, but after Plas y Brenin I would probably find the life very uncongenial.

I constantly puzzled over the problem, which was not eased by the fact that I was really expected to stay three years at the Centre so would have to produce a very good reason for leaving earlier. Then one day, when I was taking two engineering apprentices climbing on Tryfan, it suddenly occurred to me-why get a job at all? Why not save up and go on a trip somewhere, round the world, or climbing in the Himalayas?

2 THE END AND THE MEANS

In the autumn of 1960 Barbara Spark was the first person I approached as a possible companion for a Himalayan trip. When we had been climbing together in Switzerland she had expressed feelings of restlessness after four years' teaching in a Liverpool high school, and I knew that if she could come she would make an ideal companion. We had met through Plas y Brenin. Barbara had actually started climbing by going on a course there, had later gone back on a more advanced rock-climbing course, and then had begun to bring groups of girls up from the school where she was teaching Physical Education. Immediately I had been struck by her red-headed vitality and warm personality and, when we climbed together, by her steadiness and willingness to have a go at anything.

Barbara's reply was swift and full of enthusiasm, tempered by characteristic commonsense. The following weekend we met in Liverpool to talk it over. We were both armed with wads of travel leaflets on India, Peru and New Zealand, but it was not difficult to make up our minds where to go; we soon discovered that we could not afford the fares to either New Zealand or Peru. It seemed unlikely that we would be able to work our passages to either of these countries, whereas we could drive overland to India fairly cheaply. Barbara had not yet learnt to drive but immediately began to learn and passed her test a week before our departure.

We both wanted to do something active rather than just go sightseeing, but were uncertain whether our mountaineering experience was adequate for even walking in the foothills of the Himalayas. The only way to find out was to consult people who had been there and we agreed that I should ask John Jackson, the warden of Plas y Brenin and a very experienced Himalayan climber. During the war he had spent a year instructing at an RAF Mountain Centre in Kashmir and since then had been on four expeditions in Garhwal and Nepal, including Kanchenjunga in 1955.

The difficulty was that to consult John I would have to make known my intention of leaving Plas y Brenin. With some jobs it would not have mattered so much, but Plas y Brenin was different. In two years the place and people had become a part of me, something that I could not easily give up. If circumstances had compelled the decision it would have been easier, but how was I to explain this ill-defined compulsion that I hardly understood myself? I was afraid that John might interpret my decision as a criticism of Plas y Brenin, but I should have known him better for without any explanations he understood perfectly.

John stood with his back to the log fire, gazing out of the window at the green slopes of Moel Siabod, but in his eyes was that faraway look that always came when he talked of the Himalayas.

"You could certainly go trekking, but why not climb as well?" he said, "You know, there are hundreds, possibly thousands, of Himalayan peaks just waiting to be climbed, and some of them would be well within your capabilities. Peaks of 20,000 ft or so. And there are passes that have never been crossed, glaciers that have never been explored, there's endless scope. Just two of you is rather a small party but you wouldn't be the first party of two to climb in the Himalayas, and as long as you choose the right area you should be alright."

From this moment John gave us all possible help, advice and information, and, above all, continual encouragement which dispelled most of our doubts.

As none of our other climbing friends were free to go we decided to keep it a party of two and leave the following July 1961 as soon as Barbara's school term ended. We both handed in our resignations and began work on the detailed plans and preparations which were to occupy us most evenings and weekends for the next seven months.

First we had to choose our area. We had no particular lodestone in the Himalayas, and our choice was limited by our lack of funds and experience. There were also political restrictions, which then in the 1,500 mile-long Himalayan chain reduced the possible climbing areas for a foreign party to three alternatives: the Karakoram, Nepal, or the Kulu-Lahul area in the Indian Punjab Himalaya.

The Karakoram peaks we dismissed immediately as too large, difficult and remote, but for some time we seriously considered going to Nepal. Everything we heard and read about its fine peaks and colourful country made us want to go there, but there were innumerable difficulties. First we would have to obtain the permission of the Nepalese Government, which they were most unlikely to grant to such an unorthodox pair as us. Then, even if we were given permission, we would have to pay an expedition entry 'tariff' of about £70 and also pay, feed and clothe the compulsory liaison officer. Moreover, both the transport of equipment and food into Nepal and the hire of local porters and Sherpas would be very expensive, certainly too expensive for our slim budget.

There remained the Kulu-Lahul area, which on investigation seemed ideal for us. There were unclimbed peaks only three or four days' walk from the roadhead. They looked neither impossibly huge nor difficult, and several small expeditions had been there, including two women's parties, one trekking, the other climbing. I had met members of both these parties on Pinnacle Club meets in Wales, and at the end of November we drove down to London for a weekend to see them.

First we went to visit Eve Sims. When at last we found the flat in Putney and nervously rang the bell, Eve and her husband John gave us a wonderful welcome. Installed in huge armchairs by a roaring fire, blue and white pint mugs of tea in hand, we immediately felt at home. They had both been to Kulu, John on a RAF Expedition in 1955, and Eve in 1958 with two other women. From all they said Kulu certainly sounded the perfect area, and we came away with a mound of useful information, including Eve's expedition files.

Our next call was on Eileen Gregory, who enthusiastically showed us photographs of the Bara Shigri glacier where she had climbed as a member of Joyce Dunsheath's party in 1956.

The Bara Shigri is the largest glacier in the Kulu area and is encircled by a whole chain of beautiful peaks, ranging from 18,000 to 20,000 ft. Since the glacier lies at 14,000 ft, the scale is actually little greater than in the Alps. Moreover, the mountains looked reassuringly Alpine, as though a piece of Switzerland had been moved up 5,000 ft on to the Himalayan plane. Not only were most of the peaks unclimbed but several of the tributary glaciers were still unexplored, which meant that we might be able to tread completely new ground. It would only be exploration on a very small scale for the general outlines of the area had already been well mapped and there were no burning geographical questions to be solved, but it would be something new.

Both Eileen and Eve urged us to make ourselves into an 'official' Expedition, with headed note-paper, a patron, and a printed leaflet outlining our plans. In this way they thought we should be able to get some help with supplies from various firms, and also perhaps support from the Royal Geographical Society and the Mount Everest Foundation. We were both very dubious, feeling that to call our trip an Expedition would be rather a fraud, but when everyone whom we consulted agreed that it was a good idea, we became 'The Women's Kulu Expedition, 1961'. I often had misgivings about it, and in my own mind the word 'expedition' was always in inverted commas, but in comparison with some of the so-called Expeditions we met or heard about afterwards, we were not so very presumptuous. Before we could print a leaflet we had to finalise our plans, so in early December went down to London again to see Mr A E Gunther of the Alpine Club. He had twice been to Kulu on surveying-climbing expeditions, and had collected together all available information on the area. Soon the carpet of his study was covered with maps and photographs, on which he picked out two 20,000-foot mountains, named Lion and Central Peak.

"These are two of the finest peaks in the Bara Shigri area," he told us, "and both unclimbed. We first saw them in 1953 but could not reach them, then in 1956 Peter Holmes tried from the north and found a way to them over an 18,000-foot col, but had to turn back because they were running out of food. He tried again in 1958 from the west but went up the wrong glacier, so they're all yours. Look at this photograph."

With as much enthusiasm as if he himself were going, Gunther discussed ways and means of reaching our peaks. He also suggested that if time permitted we should try to make the first crossing of the Bara Shigri Divide by an ice-pass which he had seen and photographed, but not actually crossed.

"I'm too old to go and do these things now," he went on, "but for you to go and climb Lion and Central Peak and to cross the ice-pass will bring me as great a pleasure. And why not do a little surveying too? You don't have to be a professional surveyor to do some really useful mapping in this sort of country. You ought to get in touch with ...."

The evening went all too quickly, and we came away with heads full of peaks, passes, and glaciers. "I'm sure we're going to forget something vital," Barbara said. "Remember, it's up the Bara Shigri glacier, and the first turning on the left!"

We had now become an 'expedition', we had an area to explore, and a peak, in fact two peaks, as our objectives. All that we still required was money, food, equipment, a few documents, and a vehicle.

We had definitely decided to do the journey to India overland, for it would be much cheaper and much more interesting than going by sea. It also seemed best not to send any of our equipment or food by sea but to take it all with us overland. This would save considerable trouble and expense, especially at the Indian end, but meant that we would need a strong, capacious vehicle.

Eventually we settled on a long wheel-base Land Rover, second-hand of course. My very understanding Midland Bank Manager in Boston Spa let us buy the Land Rover on credit, and we were fortunate enough to obtain a one-year-old demonstration model from the Rover Company for half price. They also offered us a three-day Maintenance Course as guests of the Company in Solihull, and in June 1961 we found ourselves adjusting brakes, checking ignition timing, dismantling carburettors and trying to put them together again. Desperately we tried to memorise it all, but it is not easy to master the whole of motor mechanics in three days.

After explaining for half an hour how to do some vital repair, our instructor would turn to us and say, "Don't bother taking notes on this, you two, you won't have the strength to do it anyway".

Preparing for the overland journey involved much more work than we had at first anticipated. There were tools and spare parts to be procured, extra petrol cans to be fitted on the front bumper, a double roof put on the cab to save us from roasting alive inside and a partition fitted behind the front seats to hold all the luggage back. Then there were maps, visas, travellers' cheques, the appropriate currencies and documents to obtain, innumerable injections to comply with the medical regulations of thirteen different countries, and insurance to arrange, no easy task, for no one seemed to regard us as a good risk. Eventually we had to pay a premium of £30 for Third Party insurance there and back.

Looking further ahead, once we reached India and the roadhead at Manali we would need ponies to transport our stores to the glacier and porters to help us carry the loads up from there. Luckily this was fairly easy to arrange with the help of Major Banon, an Anglo-Indian hotel-keeper who for many years has helped expeditions to obtain ponies and porters. We wrote and booked six ponies and three Ladakhi porters (the local equivalent of the Sherpas of Nepal) for six weeks starting about the fifteenth of September, 1961. This allowed us six weeks for the 8,000-mile·drive, arriving in Kulu just at the end of the monsoon and climbing in the post-monsoon period when the weather promised to be fine, if cold, until the onset of the winter snows in mid-October.

With regard to food and equipment our problem was a familiar expedition one: we could not afford to buy even the bare minimum of our requirements. The only answer was to write pleading letters to the various manufacturers. We would have had no qualms if we had been writing on behalf of a good cause, but to ask purely on our own behalf went very much against the grain. However, there seemed no alternative, so very tentatively we wrote off, outlining our plans and asking if they might be prepared to help in any way. The response was amazing. All the equipment firms offered us discounts varying from 10 to 50 per cent, and almost all the food firms gave their products free, and even offered us things we had not requested. And most did not want even photographs or a report in return, although we sent these to all of them afterwards as a matter of courtesy. Barbara succeeded in cutting the cost of equipment still further by using her dressmaking talents to make sleeping bags and mountain clothing both for us and the porters.

Yet even so we found that ends were not going to meet. We had each saved up £300, a fortune in those days, but already half of this had been spent on equipment, insurance, film and so on, our ponies and porters would cost about another £100, which left less than £200 for the journey to India and back and all other expenses.

The obvious people to approach were the Mount Everest Foundation, who allocate grants to deserving mountaineering expeditions. But were we deserving? We went down to Bangor to consult Charles Evans of Everest fame and leader of the 1955 Kanchenjunga Expedition, who was on the committee of the Foundation. Charles was very much in favour of small mobile parties, had himself been to the Kulu area, and had known and encouraged our plans from the beginning. Without reservations he said that we certainly ought to apply for a grant, and also approach the Royal Geographical Society for support, moral if not financial.

In April I went down to London for an interview before these august bodies.

The night before the interview I had a nightmare. A row of men were sitting at a long table in the middle of a ballroom floor shining like glass. As I walked towards the table there was a crunch at each step; my high heels were going through the wood. When I reached the men they were all staring at a row of little holes across the floor. Then they stared at me, but I was already sinking fast through the boards.

When I was ushered into the interview room next day, the first thing I noticed was its polished floor. I tiptoed across to the table. A whole row of faces were looking at me but they looked kind and relaxed. One very old gentleman, perhaps a contemporary of Scott of the Antarctic I wildly thought, studied me carefully, and said,

"If you don't mind my saying so, you look very young and small to be going on a Himalayan expedition, my dear."

"Well, it's only a small expedition," I replied. They all laughed, and asked me to tell them about it.

A week later a letter came offering us the official support of the Royal Geographical Society and the loan of surveying instruments.

The following morning a cheque for £150 arrived from the Mount Everest Foundation.

Meanwhile Barbara had approached the Holt Education Trust in Liverpool for a grant, and just as I was going to the telephone to tell her the good news, the phone rang; it was Barbara to say that the Holt Committee had given us £100.

Now with a princely capital of £850 it seemed that our financial worries were largely solved.

3 AND NOW NEPAL

In the midst of our preparations an exciting new possibility appeared when we were unexpectedly invited to join a further expedition in the spring of 1962. Countess Dorothea Gravina, a member of the Pinnacle Club, who had decided to lead a women's expedition to Nepal, had heard of our trip and suggested the possibility of us joining her party.

Neither of us had met the Countess, and it was with considerable interest that we went along to the Pinnacle Club cottage to hear her plans. At once we were impressed by her drive, enthusiasm, vitality and obvious long experience of mountains. Two years earlier she had been a member of the International Women's Himalayan Expedition to Cho Oyu in the Everest area, and had taken over the leadership when the French leader Claude Kogan was tragically killed.

We found that as yet plans had gone no further than the idea of a party of six women exploring and climbing somewhere in Nepal. Countess Gravina was hoping to persuade Denise Evans to go as deputy leader, for Denise had an outstanding record as a climber and had already climbed in Nepal with her husband, Charles. Then it would be necessary in such remote country to have a doctor, preferably one who was also a mountaineer. If Barbara and I went, that would make five and for the sixth we suggested Pat Wood, whom we had climbed with in Switzerland the previous summer. As well as being a very competent climber, Pat's qualification as a dentist would make her a valuable asset to the party. Nothing was settled then and there, but afterwards we both agreed that it would be a wonderful experience. We had never really decided what we would do after Kulu, but vaguely planned to teach somewhere in India over the winter and then travel home by a different route in the spring. The Nepal expedition would make the whole trip much longer and more expensive, but we were not prepared to forsake our Kulu trip now. Already we were too committed and too attached to our 'baby' to even think of jettisoning it at this stage. We decided to go on both.

By May 1961 the Pinnacle Club team for Nepal was complete, with Nancy Smith as the doctor. A member of the Pinnacle Club with many years' climbing experience, she was the ideal climbing doctor for the trip, and it was a great joy when she agreed to leave her

Lancashire practice for three months to join the expedition. Nancy, like Dorothea and I, was born in Yorkshire, so half the Jagdula team were Yorkshire women – a good omen in my view.

Our objective in Nepal was finally settled as the unknown Kanjiroba Himal in the north-west, an area so unknown that it seemed almost impossible to find out anything about it at all. In June 1961 the six of us got together for the first time and spent two days trying to arrange equipment, food, finance, and a hundred and one other problems. Barbara and I would not be able to help much with the preparations once we left England in July but we were able to hand on all the information we had collected on equipment and food, and undertook to do the official photography and surveying.

The further expedition to Nepal would more than strain our finances so as a last resort I decided to approach newspapers and magazines for an advance payment against articles on our overland drive and Kulu expedition. Most of those whom I contacted were interested but too cautious to pay in advance. In the end we managed to obtain a contract with *The Observer* and also with Fleetway Publications who published several of the women's magazines. They were most enthusiastic and gave us free colour film and a £200 advance against later articles.

May, June and July 1961 were hectic months. As usual I was trying to fit a quart into a pint pot, for as well as all the expedition preparations there was often the temptation to go out rock-climbing after the day's instructing. Wales had chosen this period to have a heatwave, something so rare that it was too good to miss. I therefore decided to try to fulfil a long-held ambition – to be the first woman to lead *Cenotaph Corner* in the Llanberis Pass. I later wrote this up for the Pinnacle Club Journal (no. 10 1961-2):

> *Cenotaph Corner* 120 ft. Exceptionally severe (now graded E1 5c). A ferocious piece of work demanding exceptional strength and skill. First ascent 24 August 1952 J Brown.

> That's what the guidebook said, but guidebooks always put me off, so I only read them when absolutely necessary. With Cenotaph there was no need, for it is a beautifully direct line with no alternatives. Until Joe Brown's first ascent in 1952 it had generally been considered unclimbable, but by 1960 Cenotaph had become a fairly well-trodden route. Two or three women had been taken up it,

when in May 1960 I seconded Ron James of Ogwen Cottage, who was just 'practising' before leading clients up the route. I was very nervous, but did not find it as strenuous as I expected, for there were several good resting places, and some lovely jug-holds.

Then and there it became my ambition to lead it. With Cenotaph in mind, I had developed a technique for weak-armed climbers on strenuous routes, its essentials being to plan the route in advance in short sections of ten to fifteen feet, climb each fairly fast, and then rest. I found myself 'resting' in the most unlikely positions, but it did seem to work.

In June 1961 I was still instructing at Plas y Brenin, so most of my climbing was restricted to the evenings. In early June after an easy day instructing on Idwal Slabs we set off at 6 p.m. for Cenotaph. Tony Smythe had offered to second me, and his light-hearted optimism was a great help. "No one's been killed on it yet," he happily informed me, as I started bridging slowly upwards, and he took photos.

"You can put heaps of runners on," I had been told, but after seventy feet between me and the ground there were only two thin slings round jammed pebbles. Then with a sigh of relief I reached Geoff's boulder, a large chockstone Geoff Sutton had dropped into the crack from above. With a good runner on that I felt much happier, but I didn't relax till I actually reached the grassy ledge, and the lovely firm belay tree. I had taken an hour on the 120-foot pitch, Tony came up in ten minutes, and we retired to the Pen-y-Gwryd for celebratory drinks.

This was the culmination of my rock-climbing career and it was time to prepare for our Himalayan expedition. At the end of June the Land Rover arrived at Plas y Brenin and I drove it home to Yorkshire, where I was spending the last three weeks before departure.

These final weeks were as frantic as ever. We had vowed not to leave things till the last minute but there had been inevitable delays, and in the last week I found myself madly stuffing goose-down into the seven sleeping-bags that Barbara had made for us and the porters.

The house in Boston Spa was full of feathers, the lounge full of food and boxes, every table covered with lists and files, and outside the Land Rover blocked the drive. I don't know how my parents stood it, but once they had accepted that I had made up my mind to go to the

Himalayas and would not be dissuaded, they gradually entered into the spirit of it all. Barbara's parents in Bagillt, Holywell were the same. Neither of us would take a penny from our families towards the cost but were very glad to have some practical help. Barbara's family knitted, sewed and typed for us, and my father acted as our official agent, handling all our correspondence whilst we were away.

On 20th July I drove the Land Rover down to Plas y Brenin, then to Bagillt the next day to meet Barbara. The fifty mile journey took five hours. On the first steep hill the Land Rover stopped, belching clouds of black smoke from the exhaust pipe. Carefully I consulted my notes from the Rover Company course and the Instruction Manual but nowhere was there any mention of this contingency. Feeling very helpless I walked back to a garage a mile away where I had filled up with petrol. When I had explained the trouble the mechanic scratched his head, looking puzzled, and then said brightly, "I know, we must have put in diesel."

It was late in the evening before we were back at Plas y Brenin and able to start the great sort-out and pack, which went on throughout the night and the next day. Whilst I was in Yorkshire and Barbara still teaching in Liverpool all our food and equipment had been arriving at Capel Curig. First we had to break open the dozens of crates, then separate the food for the mountaineering from the food for the journey and sort it all into boxes of seven-day supplies. Then the boxes had to be carried down four flights of stairs from the attic to the Land Rover, put in and lashed firmly into place.

Using PyB students as Sherpas and with almost all the staff helping, by 10.30 p.m. on 22nd July the last items were in, and we were able to stagger down to John and Eileen Jackson's cottage where our farewell party had already begun.

It was a fine Plas y Brenin send-off, with wine, folk music, presents, and a farewell cake decorated with marzipan mountains, a baby Land Rover and a signpost marked 'Himalayas 8,000 miles'. Incongruously, painted on the side of our Land Rover was 'England to the Himalayas' rather than 'Wales to the Himalayas', as we thought foreigners might not have heard of Wales.

4 OLYMPUS

What is more pleasant than being cool on a very hot day? With a shady arbour of beech leaves overhead, luscious peaches, honeydew melon, crispy fresh bread and sharp crumbly cheese to hand, and soft sand and blue sea only a few yards away, this verges on paradise.

We had reached Greece and the Mediterranean after twelve days' driving, and this was the first sea we had seen since the grey gloom of the English Channel. France and Germany had been wet and flat, the Alps misty-moist with dripping green vegetation seemingly gone wild. Then came the Dolomites, their jagged towers a glorious pink in the last alpenglow, tempting a diversion just to stand and gaze at them once more if nothing else. But studiously we ignored the signpost to Cortina, and pressed on along the direct route down the centre of Jugoslavia, which was the first country entirely new to both of us. We did not linger, feeling that it was close enough to England to be saved for a few weeks' holiday another time. Abruptly a hundred miles short of the Greek frontier we ran out of tarmac, and had a rough passage through potholes and mud before entering Greece.

Greece was as friendly and colourful as I remembered it; brown hills, grey-green olive groves, whitewashed houses with mellow red tiles, tobacco hung to dry in the sun. And, never far away, the deep blue Aegean, Homer's 'wine-dark' sea.

We drove west from Thessaloniki to find a beach, and in an hour or so saw a small sign indicating the way. On the opposite side of the road an arrow was labelled 'To Olympos'. Looking up, we could just see through the heat haze the dim shape of a large mountain massif.

The beach was a tiny fishing cove, completely deserted. Blissfully we swam and lazed, and gorged ourselves on peaches bought for a halfpenny each. Stretched out in the shade I idly read the *Guide Bleu,* and just for curiosity looked up Olympus. Mytikas, the highest summit of the massif, was 9,574 ft above sea-level, and could be climbed from the nearby village of Litochoro in approximately thirteen hours.

Forgetting the heat, forgetting the fact that we were at sea-level so that every one of those 9,574 ft would have to be climbed, we decided it was the most natural thing in the world to leave our delightful beach and flog ourselves up nine thousand feet of mountain in the heat and the dust, for no better reason than 'to stretch our legs' after two weeks' driving.

Masochism? No, for when we set out we expected it to be enjoyable. And in a way it was, at least in parts. When climbers cannot justify their madness on the grounds of enjoyment or achievement, one hears the phrase "It was an experience". I think our ascent of Olympus comes into this category.

By Plas y Brenin standards it was a shambles. After two years of impressing on students the necessity of always having a map and compass on the hills and being thoroughly prepared for any contingency, we set off woefully ill-equipped. Maps were unobtainable locally, and our only guide for the route was the few short lines of description in our 1936 *Guide Bleu,* ending with the solemn warning: 'Guides, mounts, camping materials and provisions are indispensable.' We laughed this off as 'the old-fashioned approach'.

We could not find a compass. We could not find boots, anoraks, or any other mountaineering equipment, for they were all carefully packed in the bottommost recesses of the Land Rover, as items 'not wanted on the journey'. We set off at 4 p.m. in blouses, jeans and gymshoes, our provisions two peaches, some bread and cheese and a tin of fruit drops. We also had sleeping bags for we were intending to sleep out for the night halfway up, and then go on to the summit and come back down to our beach the following day.

Following the sign 'To Olympos', we drove to the small village of Litochoro where we enquired for the Monastery of Agios Dionisios, which according to the *Guide Bleu* was four hours' walk from the village. To our surprise we were directed on to a new tarmac road winding steeply uphill. In fifteen minutes we came to a monastery with whitewashed church and cobbled courtyard.

Surely this could not be the monastery? A black-habited monk assured us that it was indeed the monastery of Saint Dionisios, and when we asked for Mytikas, he pointed uphill. Repeating the question to an old man sitting by a fountain, we received the same answer. The only conclusion we could draw was that our guidebook with its 'four hours to the monastery' must be catering for aged classicists, for on foot it would not have taken us more than an hour at the most leisurely amble.

Leaving the Land Rover at the monastery we set off up a dusty mule-track winding between prickly scrub and patches of parched yellow grass. I have no idea what the temperature was for we never carried thermometers, but the heat was stifling, with that airlessness which often heralds a thunderstorm. After an hour of uphill plodding the track petered out on a broad grassy plateau where to our joy there was a spring of clear water. Our water bottles were also packed.

From here a narrow path led into green oak and pine woods which should have been cool, but proved even more stifling than the open. It was cheering to find dashes of red paint on rocks by the track, the same signs that are used all over the Alps to mark the path to a mountain hut or peak.

We decided to stop for the night as soon as we found a stream or spring, but on and on we went without hearing even the faintest trickle. Dusk gradually passed into darkness, and still there was no water. It was difficult to keep on the track (we had no torches, of course), and we had just decided to stop before we lost it for good, when there was a low snarling close at hand.

"Heavens, wolves," I shouted, and picked up some stones in lieu of any other weapons. Then they were nearly upon us, several enormous creatures. We hurled stones, shouted and punched at them; then suddenly there was a whistle and they backed off. Rather sheepishly we realised that they were not wolves but large dogs. Neither of us had been bitten, but their master, a ragged small boy, was most apologetic.

In a rapid flow of Greek he kept saying something about his father, and led us up into an open glade where some men were sitting round a campfire. Excited conversation followed, and in halting Greek I explained that we were English tourists on our way up Mytikas.

"Ah, Anglika," they said, as though that explained everything.

With traditional Greek hospitality they spread thick goatskins for us to sit on by the fire, and produced flagons of ice-cold water.

This seemed plentiful although we never discovered its source, and gratefully we drank our fill.

The glade was full of bleating, everywhere there were goats, three hundred we learnt, which were all driven into a brushwood pen through a bottle-neck where two men sat milking two goats a minute. This process was repeated at 6 a.m. next morning.

The shepherds insisted that we should share their supper of white goat's cheese, with a sharp but pleasant flavour, and hot goat's milk brewed in a large black pan. We eyed this rather dubiously and were glad to see that they let it boil; surprisingly it was absolutely delicious with a spicy flavour rather like cinnamon.

There were four men and a boy, ages ranging from twelve to eighty. They were delighted that I could speak some Greek, and we had a very happy evening by the campfire. Then they wrapped themselves in their goatskin coats, we retired to our sleeping-bags, and all bedded down amongst the dogs and the goats.

For a long time I lay awake gazing at the myriad stars above. The scene around might have belonged to the age of Homer, Theocritus, or Biblical times. Once or twice I thought I heard faint pan pipes in the distance, but a night out on the Throne of the Gods is heady stuff for a Romantic and Philhellene.

The next morning brought us down to earth again. Still the storm had not broken, the sky was ominously grey and the heat oppressively sultry. Only six hours to the summit, we consoled ourselves. But after two hours' fast level walking through the woods, we emerged to see a large group of ruined buildings below and a river cascading down from a rocky gorge.

Slowly the horrible truth dawned - this must be the monastery which the guidebook had said was four hours from Litochoro. The topography tallied exactly with the guidebook's description, which earlier we had made to fit the lower monastery by that tempting process of making the map or guidebook say what one wants it to say.

Now we were faced with another eight hours' climbing to reach the summit of Olympus. With no food or water. I am surprised that we did not turn back then and there, but we both have a very stubborn streak in this sort of situation. Fortified by a good drink of the river

Mavrolongos (the ancient Enipeus) and some wild plums, we continued up, and up, and up.

The sun hardly pierced the clouds but it was roasting hot, there was no more water, and we were bitten by horse-flies. We did not talk but kept plodding upwards, until, after four hours, by silent consent we sat down and reviewed the situation. We had no idea where we were, cloud floated over the tree-tops obscuring any view, and we had lost the red paint marks somewhere down by the river. The Olympus range is a huge wooded massif with several different summits, we might be heading for any, or none, of them.

"Do all Greek mountains grow bigger as you climb?" Barbara asked, voicing my own feelings. Talking cheered us up and we began to laugh at our own madness, but decided to go on for one more hour. Then if we were still lost, to turn back and head for the beach.

Fifty-five minutes had gone by when we struck a track with red paint dashes. A shout came from above, and we saw two figures striding down towards us, wearing boots and climbing clothes. Rarely have I been so pleased to see anyone. They were young Germans who told us that only ten minutes away was a Greek Alpine Club hut. Then we realised that they had seen us toiling upwards, and had come down from the hut especially to meet us and carry our rucksacks.

The hut was modern, clean, and blissfully cool; we collapsed at a wooden table and drank several pints of cold lemonade. Afterwards it dawned on us that we had no money, but the Germans offered to lend us some, or said that we could send the money to the hut-guardian later.

Over a salad lunch which they insisted on sharing with us, we found that Benno and Helmut were both engineers on holiday from Munich. They were obviously both experienced climbers and were rather shocked that we should have set out to climb Olympus with no map or proper guidebook; we confessed that we had done a little climbing before, but had not the face to tell them that we were en route for unclimbed 20,000-foot peaks in the Himalayas.

We learnt that Mytikas was another three hours above the hut. They had climbed it once, but were going up again in the hope of a better view from the top. We decided that we had had quite enough for one day; we would stay the night at the hut and go up Mytikas the next day. We lay on the terrace and went to sleep.

I woke later in the afternoon to find a young man with a flashing smile standing over us, proffering a plate of grapes. He introduced himself as the hut-warden. The old line, 'I fear the Greeks bringing gifts', flashed through my head, but Adonis (as we nick-named him) seemed harmless enough, if rather self-satisfied. We should have known better.

He was tall and dark, and in his early twenties must have been heroically good-looking, but already at twenty-eight his classical features were becoming slurred with sallow flabbiness. He was lonely and wanted to get married, but told us that he had not as yet found a girl who both shared his interest in climbing, was attractive, and prepared to live on Olympus 7,000 ft above the nearest shops.

Speculatively he eyed us, and asked whether we would like to go out on to the near-by rocks with him. There was no chance to consult each other, and when pathetically and insistently he told us how he never had anyone to climb with, we eventually agreed.

As we were setting out I went back to get my camera; when I caught them up five minutes later, Barbara was looking flushed and angry. When we reached the cliff she quickly organised things so that I was on the middle of the rope, next to Adonis. The cliff was small and the climbing not very steep or difficult, but I think it was the most dangerous route I have ever done. The rope was mangy hemp, which looked as though it would break if pulled too hard, and Adonis went up the cliff rather like a dog scrabbling at a hole, his flailing legs sending down a volley of stones.

When he reached a ledge he did not belay to the rock, but assuming a heroic stance, began to haul me up. The rope creaked ominously and I climbed fast, wondering whether if I slipped the rope would break before Adonis was dragged from his ledge. Arriving at the ledge I saw that he had chosen the climb carefully: the ledge was only two feet square. And I needed both hands to bring Barbara up safely. I pulled her up so fast that her feet hardly touched the rock, strong protests echoed upwards, but she grinned when I landed her like a gasping fish on the ledge and she saw the situation.

It was the familiar problem of the cannibals and the missionaries, but here there was no solution. I continued as second to Adonis, but spent our spells together telling him that unfortunately I was 'engaged', but Barbara would make him a wonderful wife. Fortunately the climb was not very long, but it's the last time either of us will go climbing with a lonely young Greek.

He did not seem the least put out by our resistance and we all spent a very convivial evening singing and drinking nectar (whisky and sugar) with Benno, Helmut, and some Athenians who had arrived.

Our sleep in the women's dormitory was undisturbed, but next morning Adonis came to wake us in nothing but his underpants. It was a cold misty morning and he tried hard to dissuade us from going up Mytikas, promising us coffee in bed and other delights, but we insisted, and escaped at 6 a.m.

First came a scree slope, then easy-angled rock, and finally ridge scrambling rather like the Snowdon horseshoe. The cold made us move fast, and we were very glad of the anoraks which the Germans had generously lent to us. In two hours we reached the top, a wet mist swirling round and the metal Greek flag eerily creaking on its rusty pole. On a fine day one would get a wonderful view from here, out over the Aegean and the hills and plains of Thessaly and Macedonia, and down the rock buttresses on the other side which are said to provide some of the finest climbing in Greece. But Zeus would not roll the veil of cloud away, and we caught only a few tantalising glimpses of the Abode of the Gods.

In six hours we were back at the monastery, foot-sore, sticky-hot and dishevelled. The monks came out to meet us, and invited us into a cool dark reception room with icons on the walls. They gave us Turkish delight and strong syrupy Turkish coffee accompanied by a glass of water. I love this but Barbara dislikes sugar in any drinks and could hardly get it down.

Meanwhile the Abbot solved the mystery about the two monasteries of Saint Dionisios: the other monastery had been destroyed by the Germans during the war, and this was a new one built to replace it. When we got up to go we asked if we might take some photographs of the monastery, whereupon the kind old Abbot disappeared and came back in his full ceremonial robes, with tall black hat and cross encrusted with jewels.

After many photographs and farewells we drove down to the beach where the two Germans were already encamped. It seemed much longer than two days since we first set off 'to stretch our legs' on Olympus, but dust, heat, thirst, and horse-flies were all forgotten as we lazed in the cool water. Supper was a huge meal of soup, onion omelette, tomatoes, green peppers, toast, peaches and coffee, which we persuaded Benno and Helmut to share with us.

Later we all strolled along to the tiny beach restaurant incongruously named the Café Honolulu, and lingered there till the early hours, sipping retsina, sampling fresh-caught fish, watching the lights of fishing boats dancing on the water, and listening to plaintive bouzouki music in the distance.

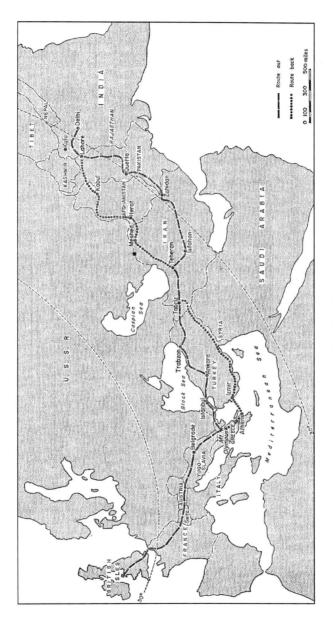

Overland route

45

5 ACROSS THE MIDDLE EAST

While there was time for the occasional stopover here and there out of the six weeks we had allowed to reach India we could not linger too long, for we wanted to make the most of the good climbing weather customary between the end of the monsoon and the beginning of winter. The most direct and straightforward route was through Ankara, along the Black Sea coast of Turkey, into Iran and down through Baluchistan to Quetta, Lahore and into India. A year later, on the way back, we were able to take just as long as we liked, and deviated through the Khyber Pass right round the north of Afghanistan, along the shores of the Caspian Sea, and round the magnificent Mediterranean coast of Turkey.

Most nights we camped, using the special home-made box tent fitted to the back of the Land Rover's canvas hood. It had just two poles and guy ropes at the outside corners and could be pulled out and erected very easily each night, giving six feet of headroom for cooking on the tail board. We cooked on primus stoves, using mainly the tinned and dried food given to us in England. The Land Rover was far too full to allow us to sleep in the back, so we bedded down on camp beds in the tent. As a deterrent to intruders, we had tried to get a revolver before leaving England but had not been able to get a licence. Perhaps it is just as well or we might have shot someone. For protection we had to make do with an ice axe and a carving knife, which fortunately we never had occasion to use.

Camping in the bigger cities was virtually impossible but in one way or another we managed, with the help of YWCA hostels and occasionally friends who put us up. Accommodation troubles were over once we reached Pakistan and India for there in each small town one finds Government Rest Houses or PWD bungalows. Originally built by the British for the use of travelling officials, they are now open to any traveller for only a few rupees a night.

In Turkey we were fortunate to be given an introduction to the Karayollari, the Turkish Highway Department, who have camps and compounds scattered throughout the country. Invariably when we reached a Karayollari camp and requested a place to camp away from crowds of onlookers, we were not even allowed to pitch our tent or cook our own food, but were entertained in the canteen and given guest rooms for the night. If such hospitality had been confined to the Karayollari we might have supposed that they were merely obeying instructions, but everywhere in Turkey we met the same helpfulness and generosity. Often people invited us into their homes, and in banks and garages we were always offered tea, served in small glasses with sugar and lemon. The only difficulty we experienced was the excessive curiosity of the local people, especially along the Black Sea coast where tourists seem comparatively rare and two girls driving a Land Rover a very strange phenomenon. Each time that we stopped for a picnic a crowd seemed to materialise from nowhere, and here as elsewhere Barbara's auburn hair attracted much envious comment from local women, unused to such colouring.

From the narrow streets and old mosques of Istanbul we had crossed the Golden Horn and climbed on to the high plateau of Anatolia with its bare rolling hills. A good tarmac road led over several passes before dropping to the fine modern city of Ankara, its tree-lined streets and gardens making it something of an oasis. Since Palaeolithic times there has been a settlement in this basin, on the junction of the main north-south and east-west ancient trade and modern road routes, and not far away lies the great Hittite capital of Hattusha.

After the glaring heat of the desolate interior ranges it was pleasant to drive down through green hills and fertile valleys to the Black Sea coast, along which Jason and the Argonauts sailed to find the Golden Fleece 3,000 years ago. The steep shores are still clad with roses, myrtle, figs, tobacco, fruit orchards and nut trees as they were in classical times, and one can still wander through the cherry orchards from which Lucullus brought the first cherry to Europe. Before turning inland one reaches Trebizond, the last capital of the Byzantine Empire. Once it boasted a thousand churches, but now only a few remain, fast disappearing beneath the brambles and fig trees.

It was sad to leave this beautiful and historic coast, but the gravel road inland took us through some spectacular mountain scenery, skirting mediaeval castles perched high on rocky towers, sliding through gorges and mud villages, and then hairpinning its way over two 9,000-foot passes before descending into the Armenian plains. The dusty grey-brownness was relieved only by the occasional village with dark green cypress trees and circles of gold where corn was being threshed and winnowed. The threshing was done by women wearing head scarves and the typical peasants' baggy trousers, riding on flat wooden sleds drawn round and round by ponderous bullocks.

A few miles from the Iran border we suddenly saw Mount Ararat, a fairy-tale snow-capped peak in a sea of undulating bareness. Remembering that it was almost 17,000 ft high and we were only at 5,000 ft, we were not tempted to climb it, even to try to find Noah's Ark which traditionally rests there.

In Iran we had our first trouble with the Land Rover when we began to get one puncture after another, including as many as five in one day. Most of them were caused by sharp stones or nails from camels' shoes and all were in the back wheels, for the Land Rover was too heavily loaded for the rough roads, which were unsurfaced and worn by the heavy lorry traffic into deep corrugations. At any speed below 45 mph we bounced and jolted over each hump individually, the hardsprung Land Rover shaking and vibrating so much that it sounded like a pneumatic drill, making all conversation impossible. Above 45 mph we skimmed along the crests with a delightful feeling of flight until we encountered a particularly large bump or deep pothole, when there would be a resounding crash and we would climb out, convinced that something must have given somewhere.

On the return journey our punctures were more evenly distributed and were caused mainly by tyre-fatigue. In our two spare tyres daylight was visible in several places. This did not perturb the Iranians who were wizards at getting the last ounce out of any tyre; first they would put pieces of old tyre inside to block up the holes, then an old inner tube as a protective sheath, and finally the proper inner tube, usually scarcely visible for patches.

We found the road between the Turkish frontier and Tehran the worst stretch on the whole journey. The country was sand-grit desert deeply corrugated like the road. As we first dropped down from Turkey it had looked like rippled sand but proved to be an endless series of dips down into dried-up river beds and steep little hills which forced us into bottom gear. The road was so dusty that each vehicle trailed an impenetrable cloud for at least a quarter of a mile behind.

Trying to overtake anyone was a horrifying business. One crept up in the swirling dust cloud, the passenger peering out to try to see what lay ahead, then with horn blaring and head-lights full on drove blindly into the cloud, just praying that no one was coming and that the road would not suddenly narrow or dip down into a river bed at the crucial moment.

On this stretch we had our worst day of the whole journey, with intolerable heat, glaring sun which burnt the eyes even through sunglasses and gritty dust that found its way into everything, borne through the open side-windows by a wind as hot as an electric hair-dryer. In addition, poor Barbara was feeling ill. And then we had a puncture. We had considerable experience of changing the wheel by now, but our jack always caused difficulties - it was so high that we invariably had to dig a small trench in the road to get it under the back axle or spring and had such a short handle that one had to lie half under the vehicle to wind it up. On one such occasion I emerged to find a large group of turbaned men with a camel encircling us. One spoke a little English and his first question was "Are you men or women?" - an understandable query, as we wore loose-fitting western shirts and jeans and they had never seen women driving a vehicle before.

An hour later we had another puncture. This was not disastrous as we had a second spare tyre, but it was packed in the back of the Land Rover and very awkward to get out. Before starting the struggle I lit a primus to make a brew of tea, for Barbara was feeling even worse now and could not face the lukewarm lemonade which was our usual midday drink. Unluckily there were some mud huts nearby, and soon men and boys began to trickle across till there was such a crowd that tea-making became impossible.

They were no help with changing the wheel but would not leave us alone. Moreover, they began to demand money and cigarettes and to try to get inside the cab. The situation was looking distinctly nasty when Barbara saw a lorry approaching and determinedly flagged it down. We could not have been luckier for the Iranian driver and his two companions were wonderful; straightaway they got rid of the locals with much fist-shaking, had the wheel changed in ten minutes, and refused even cigarettes for helping us. Fortunately, Barbara felt much better next day, and was able to enjoy two days relaxing in Tehran before we drove the thousand miles south to Pakistan.

In Tehran there was much to see, palaces, mosques, museums and bazaars, but our enjoyment was marred somewhat by a feeling that foreign women were unwelcome. Perhaps our relative freedom offended against the traditional attitude to women. Iran is a strong Muslim country and many of the Iranian women were still kept in purdah and never ventured out without wearing the chador, a long shawl draped over the head and held together to reveal little more than the eyes. In Afghanistan these purdah gowns covered the head and body completely with a gauze mesh across the face. Wearing the chador was being strongly discouraged in Iran but outside Tehran, especially in the holy cities of Meshad and Qom, it still seemed to be the rule rather than the exception. Although in Tehran we saw a few women in western clothes driving cars, elsewhere in Iran we never saw a woman driver and even inside banks and offices the girl secretaries had their heads covered. I also drew a crowd inside a bank when writing a cheque being a left-hander – apparently forbidden at that time in Pakistan. Barbara and I tried to be very discreet in what we wore, always keeping our arms covered, never wearing shorts which Muslims consider highly indecent, and in the holy cities donning head-scarves as well just for safety.

Two hundred and sixty miles south of Tehran lies Isfahan, a green oasis in the desert and architecturally the highlight of our journey to India. The whole town is full of palaces and mosques, decorated with beautiful mosaic tile-work in turquoise blue and gold. Most of them were built by Armenian craftsmen under the great Shah Abbas in the early seventeenth century, but are still perfectly preserved. Everywhere one turned there was brilliant yet subtle colour and exquisite design and craftsmanship, both in the mosques and in the covered bazaar, where bearded craftsmen sat cross-legged, delicately engraving brass, copper or filigree silver, painting and hand-printing cloth, or weaving carpets.

There was so much to see that we stayed three days in Isfahan, camping inside the compound of the British Medical Mission to whom we had been given an introduction in Tehran. The doctors and nurses were very friendly and showed us round their hospital and school for the blind. To see such worthwhile work being done made both Barbara and me feel very selfish to be spending hundreds of pounds on a trip principally for our own pleasure. This thought must occur at some stage to most travellers and mountaineers, especially in poverty-stricken countries, and we found it difficult to convince ourselves that we were doing any more than having a long holiday.

This guilt feeling was reinforced on our return journey through the wilds of Afghanistan and Turkey. We drove up the Khyber Pass to Kabul and then over the Hindu Kush to Bamiyan to see the monumental sixth century statues of Buddha carved out of the high cliffs. (Note: Tragically in 2001 they were deliberately destroyed by the Taliban as 'idols'.) We saw extreme poverty there and later on the Ionian coast of Turkey, where we visited Greek theatres and temples and the site of Troy.

For two days in southern Iran we did not see another vehicle. The desolation was eerie, especially in the salt desert of Baluchistan where not even the silhouette of a grazing camel broke the flat horizon. The only mark of man was the straight white gravel road stretching on and on. Earlier we had actually lost the road. We had come to a fork, unsignposted except for a scribble in Arabic on an old petrol can, and had chosen what appeared to be the main road only to find that it petered out in a series of sand dunes. Fighting our way out of these with four-wheel drive, we found that drifting sand had covered all our wheel marks and we could find no trace of the road. It was a frightening experience to be lost alone in that featureless waste, but when we had just calculated that we had enough water to survive for five days at least, we chanced upon the petrol can and our original road.

As we crossed into Pakistan and entered Quetta it seemed strange to find a good tarmac road, cars and camel trains keeping strictly to the left, road signs and street names in English and bungalows called 'Apple-tree Cottage' and 'Chez-Nous', yet not a European face in sight.

We had been invited to stay with Captain Niazi, a Pakistani Army officer, whose brother we had met in Ankara. As we had tea and chapattis on the terrace of his pleasant bungalow in the cantonment he told us that it would be necessary to spend some time in Quetta since both roads to Lahore were closed to all traffic. The main road was under six feet of water and would not be open again till the floods subsided; the other road was under fire from hostile tribesmen along the Afghan border.

This was bad news as it was already 1st September and we wanted to be in Kulu by the 11th, but if we were to be held up at all it was fortunate that it should happen in Quetta, one of the cooler places in Pakistan and where we had so kind a host.

At last, on 4th September, the road was declared jeepable and we set off. Dropping down from Quetta into the northern fringes of the Sind Desert, we found the heat overpowering and gradually it became more and more humid as we neared Sukkur, one of the hottest places on earth. There were three of us in the cab for we were giving a lift to Mahmud Khan, a friend of Captain Niazi. He was a big, broad-shouldered man and as we sat cramped together on the front seat perspiration ran off us in streams. Even under fans in the Rest Houses it was impossible to get cool, and our clothes were dripping wet as soon as we put them on. In the daytime we were plagued by flies, in the evening by mosquitoes. Under such conditions we had no desire to go sight-seeing but simply to reach the Himalayas as quickly as possible. Knowing that we would be covering the road from Lahore to Delhi again on our return journey, we decided to drive the rest of the way to Delhi by night to avoid the heat, and reached the Indian Customs Post at 5 p.m. This was an excellent time to arrive, for it was too early to be kept waiting till morning but too late to allow a lengthy inspection of our baggage.

En route we had encountered little difficulty at the various customs posts, being merely in transit, but we expected problems getting into India. We were uncertain whether our food and equipment was dutiable but we knew that another expedition entering by sea had had to pay £200 duty on a similar quantity.

"What have you got in the back?" the chief customs officer asked suspiciously.

"Oh, camping equipment, clothes, and so on."

"And men?" asked a grinning Sikh.

The customs officer began to undo the back flap but fortunately desisted when a dirty pan fell out and covered his white jacket in dust. Offering us tea, he then asked if we could give him a lift home to Amritsar. We had no idea how far away Amritsar was but readily agreed, whereupon he signed all documents and off we drove. On the way he obviously began to have second thoughts but it was too late then, we were safely in India.

The Grand Trunk Road was thronged with bullock carts, bicycles, and wandering animals but at last we arrived in Delhi, crawling through the crowded narrow streets of the old town into the spacious tree-lined avenues of New Delhi. Here we spent just one day collecting mail and money and completing the necessary formalities and then drove up the Grand Trunk Road again to the mountains.

It was good to leave behind the hot dusty plains and climb into the cool greenness of the hills. In gentle rain we reached Simla, the old summer headquarters of the British Raj and now a large summer resort and winter sports centre. From here the road became little better than a cart track and we saw no other traffic for several hours. We were beginning to wonder whether our road was a dead-end when a bus appeared from the opposite direction. This was a cheering sight but soon afterwards we rounded a corner to see a large river ahead but no bridge. The road led straight into the water and, presuming that the bus had crossed it, we were about to drive in when some workmen rushed up to stop us. It seemed that the buses were merely running a shuttle service to the banks from where the passengers had to wade or, if they could afford it, be carried across. The road had been closed for five weeks since the bridge was swept away in the monsoon floods.

If we could not get across it meant a 200-mile detour so we waded over to inspect the ground and see if there was any chance. Luckily a local Inspector wanted to drive his jeep across the next day so about fifty men were working to make a ford. The water was three feet deep with a fast current and shifting boulders on the bottom, but on either side there was a good ramp for entry and exit. With so many volunteers to help if we got stuck, it seemed worth trying and whilst Barbara stood in mid-stream taking photographs I drove in.

In magnificent style the Land Rover ploughed through and churned up the steep ramp to the cheers of the crowd, but then proceeded to sink in the mud on the narrow track beyond. Slowly mud oozed over the wheels, the Land Rover tilted towards the river below and the outside bank began to crumble, but just as I was about to leap out to safety the men succeeded in lifting up the whole vehicle and carrying it along to safe ground. They were rewarded with cigarettes, for fortunately we had been given, in Britain, a large supply for such eventualities.

It was with some relief that we finally reached Mandi and the last lap to Manali. From Mandi there is an extraordinary road cut out of the rock face on the side of a spectacular gorge. There is no room for two vehicles to pass so for twenty-five miles the road is one way, being open to up and down traffic in alternate four-hour shifts.

We drove up in the late afternoon and emerged into the Kulu valley as the sun was setting. On either side of green pastures rose pine-clad slopes, monsoon clouds still hung over the tops but here and there was a glimpse of icy walls, tinged pink in the sunset, our first view of the Himalayas.

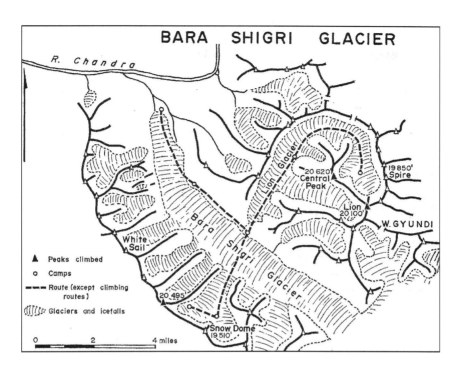

BARA SHIGRI GLACIER

R. Chandra

Lion Glacier

20 620'
Central
Peak

19 850'
Spire

Lion
20 100'

W. GYUNDI

Bara Shigri Glacier

White
Sail

▲ Peaks climbed
○ Camps
▬ ▬ Route (except climbing routes)
〰 Glaciers and icefalls

20 495'

Snow Dome
19 510'

0   2   4 miles

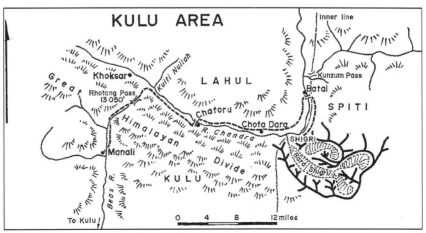

KULU AREA

Inner line

Great

Khoksar●

Kulti Nullah

LAHUL

Kunzum Pass

Batal

SPITI

Rhotang Pass
13 050'

Chatoru

Himalayan

R. Chandra

Chota Dara

SHIGRI

Bara Shigri

●Manali

Divide

KULU

Beas R.

To Kulu

0   4   8   12 miles

6   TO THE GLACIER

At the head of the Kulu valley at 6,000 ft lies the village of Manali. The village street was a dirty but picturesque clutter of open-fronted shops with cows lounging around and children playing in the dust, but above this bazaar were Alpine-style houses in green apple-orchards, and highest of all, Sunshine Orchards, Major Banon's hotel and our journey's ending.

It was a rambling old building of wood and stone, with wooden balconies and a wide overhanging roof. Below the stone terrace in front of the house was a lush green lawn, and, beyond, acres and acres of apple trees. Everywhere there were flowers, one could not be sure whether wild or cultivated, and with the wooded hillsides above and the sparkle of distant snows we might have been in Switzerland.

The manager was expecting us, in fact he reproached us for being late - two months earlier we had written that we hoped to arrive about the eleventh of September, and it was now 10 a.m. on the twelfth.

Proudly he told us that our porters and ponies would be ready to set off in two days' time. This was good news as we had expected a delay but it meant two days of very hard work, since as well as the task of sorting out all our food and equipment, there were innumerable letters to write before we left.

The next morning the manager brought along our three Ladakhi porters. As they stood in an awkward row he told us their names and 'qualifications', and each produced his testimonials from previous expeditions. Unlike Sherpas, the Ladakhis are not yet organised into a union, but no doubt this will come as more and more expeditions employ them as high altitude porters in the Kulu area instead of bringing Sherpas from Darjeeling or Kathmandu as used to be done.

Our three were all very different and none quite as I had visualised a mountain porter. Jigmet, small, wiry and very dark-skinned, came closest to my preconceived notions, but his eyes were small and he had a moustache.

Wangyal was the exact opposite. Large and broad, with a round face and permanent grin, he ambled round like a benevolent bear. Always cheerful, always shouldering the heaviest loads and doing the worst jobs, he was the personification of simple good nature, and very intelligent and full of initiative; definitely the best of the trio and quickly he became the established leader.

The third was Atchuk. With his long greased hair, flashy pointed shoes, and cigarette permanently drooping from one corner of his mouth, he looked as if he would be much more at home in a Piccadilly coffee-bar than in the Himalayas. He was older than the other two, about thirty-five I think, but this was only his second expedition. From what we could gather he had spent nine years farming in Tibet and then had worked as a photographer's assistant in Calcutta before coming to Manali. He spoke Hindi, Tibetan and the Ladakhi dialect of Urdu but only a very little English, Jigmet spoke even less and Wangyal almost none, except for a few phrases he had learnt on previous expeditions, such as 'mucky shambles'! It was a shame that we had not had time to learn Hindi and Urdu, but we picked up a great deal in the next few weeks and with this vocabulary, gestures and sketches, managed to communicate tolerably well.

Because of our difficulty in giving instructions we could not make much use of the porters to sort food and equipment, but on the morning of the fourteenth, the day before departure, they helped us pack it all into kitbags and boxes and then divide them into six pony loads of two maunds each (roughly 160 pounds). We had absolutely no reason to believe that it would split into six loads: the number was based on only the roughest of calculations made months earlier. But to our great surprise it all worked out perfectly. Until we discovered that the spring balance was weighing ten pounds light. We decided to ignore this. A torrential downpour put an end to the packing and it rained for the rest of the day, the last of the monsoon, everyone assured us.

That afternoon we went along to meet Major Banon, the owner of Sunshine Orchards. No one seemed to know exactly how old he was, but he must have been well over eighty; he was already hotel manager when General Bruce visited Manali in 1912. An Anglo-Indian, in his old age it seemed that he had turned more and more to the Indian way of life. We found him sitting in a wheel-chair in a bare Indian-style room, two women squatting at his feet. They were both dark-skinned local women, but one was old, toothless and arthritic, the other young and demure. Neither spoke English but sat quietly chatting whilst Major Banon talked to us of Lord Curzon, Younghusband, and days gone by.

When we returned to our room (a cubby-hole over the garage rented for three shillings a day), we found another visitor waiting for us, the local police officer. In his sing-song Indian English he asked us to tell him exactly where we were going and what we were going to do. Tourists are not usually interrogated like this, but this CID man had learned from the porters that we were going over the Rhotang Pass for three or four weeks and had become suspicious, since a few days walking from there in any direction would bring us to the Inner Line which foreigners are not permitted to cross. This is the Indian Government's security frontier which runs between fifty and a hundred miles inside the Indian border with Tibet.

We were well aware that no permits were now being issued to foreigners to go beyond the Inner Line, but since our objective, the Bara Shigri glacier, was only a mile on the wrong side of the Line and it seemed unlikely that a glacier which did not lead anywhere would be guarded, we were just hoping to sidle up unobserved. However, we could not tell the CID man this. Climbing peaks a few miles inside an imaginary inner frontier would hardly endanger Indian security but technically it was an offence, punishable by expulsion from the area and possibly from India.

We told the CID man that we were just going camping and bird watching. Eyeing the pile of ropes and ice axes in the corner, he told us that we must delay our departure until he had time to consult his superiors in Delhi. Our flat refusal dismayed him and without any proof of sinister intentions (he had been searching for weapons and a radio transmitter without success), he had not the confidence, or perhaps the authority, to stop us leaving. Unfortunately he hit on the obvious solution. He would come with us! He could not leave the next day, but assured us that he would follow. The trek to the Bara Shigri promised to be interesting.

10 a.m. 15th September, 1961. Departure. In accounts of other expeditions one frequently reads of the sahibs waiting impatiently for the porters, Sherpas, ponymen, camel-drivers or whoever it is; with us it was always the other way round. When at last we were ready, we

found our cavalcade had given up and set off without us. We were not even sure which way they had gone, and sheepishly had to go and ask the hotel manager. Following his directions, we found a track (obvious of course) leading down to the river, and in a few minutes saw the porters ahead. Immediately they came back and insisted on carrying our small rucksacks for us, leaving us with nothing heavier than a camera and our vividly striped golf umbrellas, purchased in Manali bazaar.

Light-heartedly we wandered along, drinking in the sunshine, the brilliant blue sky and scudding clouds, the tall deodars climbing towards dark rocky ridges, the lush meadows and sparkling river. Starting as a tiny spring just below the Rhotang Pass the River Beas surges down the Kulu valley, carves a tortuous passage through the foothills and emerges, muddy but triumphant, to roll across the Indian plains. We had crossed it north of Delhi on a mile-long pontoon bridge, we had crossed and recrossed it in the gorges of the foothills, foaming hundreds of feet below slender suspension bridges, and now we were crossing it on foot over a narrow wooden bridge, a line of coloured Buddhist prayer flags strung over the torrent to protect the passage of the devout.

I cannot remember the details of that first day. I was too full of that heady relief which comes when at last all the worry and rush of preparations are over, and for better or worse one shuts the door behind, and goes. I had known the feeling many times before, but never so intensely as this. I walked along in a dream, and of all there was to see I have only a few hazy impressions.

There was the dusty brown track, and lots of people moving in both directions; Indians in pyjama trousers and grubby shirt tails, holding huge black umbrellas, hill people driving herds of sheep and goats or caravans of laden donkeys.

There was our ponyman's puppy, a tiny Tibetan terrier with sleek black coat and long wavy tail. Several times she was nearly trampled under ponies' hooves and, after three or four miles of the dust and heat was panting as though her heart would burst. Barbara picked her up and carried her.

The first five miles were almost level, the track winding through green fields and deodar forests. Then there was open ground and the village of Koti, with an impressive new PWD bungalow above the row of shacks. The track from Manali to Koti is jeepable, and once or twice on our way up we rapidly had to scatter as PWD jeeps came bouncing along, horns blaring and dust flying. Above Koti we crossed the Beas again, and started the 6,000-foot climb up to the Rhotang Pass. This seemed endless, our legs ached and it began to rain, but at last we stopped on a dung-strewn expanse of dingy grass - our camping ground. The ponies were unloaded and set loose, the porters put up the tents and blew up our air beds, and in ten minutes had a brew of tea ready. Life began to look rather better.

Jigmet quickly showed his capabilities as a cook; he knew all about dehydrated food and pressure-cookers and in his hands ours worked properly for the first time since we left England. Whilst Jigmet cooked an excellent supper of dried meat, vegetables, and rice, Wangyal and Atchuk dug a channel round our tent to drain off the rainwater. We felt rather guilty to be so pampered but if we tried to do anything for ourselves they became most upset. They did much more than was necessary, but after a few half-hearted attempts to clean our own boots or put up our own tent we gave up and accepted our role of memsahibs.

As well as our three Ladakhis we had with us a ponyman called Rikzin, and a Tibetan donkeyman. Rikzin was small, wiry, and extremely agile. He came from Kulu but had flat Mongolian features, curly dark hair, white teeth, and eyes sparkling with devilment. He had been on several trips as a porter, but now, at the age of twenty-five, was a ghora-wallah with three ponies. If he was a rogue he was a most attractive one, and a great social asset to the party. Like the others he spoke almost no English but this did not seem to matter.

The donkeyman was a complete contrast. He kept well away from us - something we appreciated as he had fleas. He scratched and sniffed incessantly, and, unlike the others, never seemed to wash even his hands. Nor did he ever take off his battered Tibetan hat, with its embroidered crown and fur-lined ear flaps. He was a small man in an enormous baggy garment that hid his hands and feet.

The second day took us two thousand feet up, over the 13,050 ft Rhotang Pass, and three thousand feet down again to camp near Khoksar in the Chandra valley. The pass was a bleak spot in mist and a cold wind. By Himalayan standards it is quite a low pass, but has a reputation for sudden vicious storms; in one storm seventy-two porters are said to have died of exposure in less than a day. The sides of the track were strewn with the white bones of dead animals, and in one place vultures were massed around a carcass below the track.

On the summit tattered Buddhist prayer flags fluttered on poles set into a square stone monument known as a la-tso. The flags are coloured pieces of cotton on which prayers in Tibetan script are block-printed; each traveller carries a supply of them and on each pass ties one to the la-tso to ensure a safe crossing. I was reminded of a bus journey up a steep mountain road in Crete, when at the top all the Greek passengers climbed out and lit candles in a little chapel.

A little way down on the north side of the pass we dropped out of the cloud into hot sunshine. It was a different world, a mountain desert of brown and grey. In only a few miles one might have passed from the greenness of Switzerland to the desolation of Tibet. There were no trees, no vegetation, only grey scree and rock and the snow and ice peaks of Lahul. Opposite us we recognised the Kulti Nullah, which John Sims had explored with the RAF party in 1955. If we were prevented from going to the Bara Shigri the Kulti was our alternative but it would be very much a second best. John had said that it was an uninspiring area and they had climbed the only peaks conceivably worth climbing.

Winter comes early in the Kulu area and from about mid-October till the end of May the Rhotang Pass is blocked by deep snowdrifts, making all crossing impossible except on skis. Firmly Rikzin said that he must have his ponies back over the pass by the 15th October when the first winter snows would fall. This seemed unnecessarily early to us but we hesitated to argue with his local knowledge. As we dropped down the steep hillside from the pass to the river 3,000 ft below, it was easy to see what a death-trap the valley would be should winter take one by surprise there.

For the next five days we travelled eastwards up the Chandra valley. The booming of the river as it rushed between high rock walls provided constant background noise to the journey, and the sun beat relentlessly down on the boulders and rubble of long-vanished glaciers. The canyon walls shut out all but an occasional glimpse of the snow peaks above, until we came to the great bend in the river where the valley floor widened and we could see the icy ranges bordering the Bara Shigri glacier. There were no trees in the valley but here and there patches of grass by a stream or spring provided grazing and camping grounds. These were euphemistically known as meadows.

Each day we progressed from one meadow to the next, walking anything between eight and fifteen miles. On a good track and almost level ground this was not arduous but after six weeks sitting in the Land Rover we were very unfit and our feet tender. We soon had blisters. Our new rope-soled walking shoes proved lumpy and uncomfortable and our boots hot and heavy. In spite of this Barbara gaily romped along, exclaiming with delight at each new view and eagerly taking photographs, but I was not feeling at all well and walked along in a daze, feeling sick and dizzy much of the time. For me the best moment of the day came when camp was set up and we could lie in the sun and drink tea, with nothing to do for the rest of the day but sleep, eat, talk, read or write. Barbara, as always the best of companions, was very sympathetic and solicitous without making a fuss and kept optimistically reassuring me that it was merely the effects of altitude or unfitness which would soon wear off.

At Chatoru, the largest and greenest of the meadows, we crossed to the north bank of the river by a newly constructed bridge. To follow the south bank to the Bara Shigri glacier would have been a much shorter route (see map on page 55), but Rikzin would not take his ponies that way.

"No road for ponies," he replied to all our protests.

Before the Chatoru bridge had been built the south bank had been the main route, but we knew that the last two parties to take ponies to the glacier had also taken the longer northern route so perhaps, as Rikzin insisted, the short cut was too rough for laden ponies now. We were not in a strong position to argue as there were no other ponies to hire, but it seemed an obvious piece of roguery since we were paying for the ponies by the day and the northern route was two days longer. In fact our suspicions were rather unfair since a few days later I discovered that the shorter route was even worse than Rikzin had described and was very dangerous even for unladen ponies.

There are no villages in the Chandra valley above Khoksar but there are many temporary encampments and a constant coming and going along the track. The valley is a main trading route, linking the mountain provinces of Spiti, Lahul and Ladakh with the Indian plains. It was now the end of summer and of the trading season and everyone was heading homewards; the hillsmen north and eastwards, leading pony-trains laden with rice, flour, sugar, salt, tobacco and all their supplies for the long winter, the plainsmen southwards, driving their flocks of sheep and goats back from their summer grazing grounds. Each sheep and goat carried its own load - twenty pounds of wool clip slung in two little bags on its back.

Some of the people travelling south were Tibetans, the women wearing the distinctive Tibetan striped aprons, the men voluminous garments of maroon, black or undyed wool with very long sleeves, bagged over a sash round the waist. Curiously, they never appeared to be too hot, even in that glaring sun. Both men and women had wild matted hair and many beads and ornaments, and all wore the long multi-coloured wool boots of Tibet. Soles of yak hide make these very tough and waterproof and a layer of dry mosses inside acts as insulation against the cold.

Atchuk stopped and talked to all the different groups we met, and through him we learnt that some were nomadic traders but the majority were refugees. To reach that Indian valley from western Tibet the refugees must have walked well over a hundred miles across some of the most barren and difficult country in the world. Several women were carrying young babies, and one man was carrying his grandfather in a basket on his back.

They were hoping to join the other refugees in the valley who were being employed by the Indian Government to build a jeep road over into Spiti. As we walked along the track we often passed these Tibetan road gangs, the men shovelling earth, the women sitting cross legged laboriously chipping stones into piles of equal sizes. They were all very cheerful, and very curious; I suppose we were the first white women that most of them had seen. Among the boulders by the road side were their tents of black yaks' hair or undyed cotton with prayer flags fluttering between the poles. Nearby more prayer flags adorned the familiar chortens, stone monuments inscribed with prayers and pictures of Buddha.

In each encampment there was a large tent or stone shack which acted as a tea-house and hotel for travellers. We saw our porters hesitate outside the first of these; tentatively they suggested, "Chai, Memsahibs". Clearly they thought such a place might be too dirty or unhygienic for us, but actually their standards of hygiene were higher than ours in almost every respect. Our only major point of difference was on the hygienic way to blow one's nose. We didn't like their method of just pinching the nostrils and blowing, and they thought our way of using a handkerchief which we then put back into a pocket quite disgusting.

We went into the 'Hotel' for tea. Over a dung fire in the corner, tea, milk and sugar were brewed up together in a large black kettle, then poured into metal beakers and thence from the beakers into cups. I never saw the point of the beakers but they always seemed to do it this way. This was Indian tea but we also tried Tibetan tea made from solid black tea bricks mixed with salt and rancid butter. With lumps of grease floating on the surface its appearance was not inviting but it tasted much better than it looked. The sides of the smoke-blackened tent were lined with sacks of rice and flour, and we either sat on these or on striped quilts spread on the floor. Every tent had its picture of the Dalai Lama, and an altar, often an upturned box, with small brass offering cups in front of a picture of Buddha.

The last of these Tibetan encampments was at Chota Dara, and there we heard that someone had been making enquiries about us at Chatoru. It could only be the CID man. CID seems a well-known term in that part of the world, though to the porters he was always the Seedyman. They thought it all a great joke and promised to throw him in the river for us, but Barbara and I were rather worried. At Manali he had definitely said that he would follow us, but when after four days he had still not appeared, we decided it must have been just a threat. Now, however, he was at Chatoru, only a day behind, and if he were travelling light should soon overtake our slow caravan. As a CID officer he would then be bound to prevent us crossing the Inner Line to climb on the Bara Shigri, and there was no good, legal alternative climbing area.

It seemed that the end of our expedition was at hand and next morning this appeared to be a certainty when we discovered that our three donkeys had disappeared overnight and could not be found anywhere. We could not move camp without them, and gloomily resigned ourselves to the inevitable arrival of the CID man.

It was a beautiful sunny day, completely still save for thin plumes of cloud idly drifting round the distant peaks. I remember sitting outside the tent trying to imprint the scene on my memory, that line of Himalayan peaks that we would never reach. But even now I could not completely give up hope and the picture was blurred with thoughts of ways and means.

I was also becoming preoccupied with another worry. I was beginning to feel really ill. Since crossing the Rhotang Pass I had not been feeling well, but now I was feeling really sick and weak. My legs ached, and of course I thought of poliomyelitis which is so prevalent in the Himalayas. It was a great relief when later in the day one side of my face began to swell up; I had not got polio, but some sort of abscess. Barbara prescribed penicillin tablets and salt and water gargles, and although I felt no better I cheered up.

The CID man still had not arrived, and our Tibetan had retrieved his donkeys which it seemed had walked ten miles back overnight to graze on the tastier grass of our previous campsite. Perhaps it was not the end of our expedition after all, although we were not too optimistic, for it could be that the CID man had taken the short cut to the glacier and would be waiting for us there.

The next morning we tried to ford the Chandra River, but it was hopelessly deep and fast. There was no alternative but to go round by the bridge at Batal, ten miles to the north. We were afraid that the bridge might be guarded, even though it was still about two miles on the right side of the Inner Line, but when we reached it there was no one in sight. It seemed hours before the whole party was across, for it was a precarious suspension bridge that swayed in the wind and Rikzin insisted that only one pony should cross at a time.

Then we turned south and rapidly headed for cover. We skulked towards the foot of the glacier, looking around for signs of pursuit. By this time it had become a game to the porters, a game which they played with great gusto, crouching behind rocks and scouring the valley for signs of the Seedyman. At last we arrived at the glacier snout and the highest point that the ponies could reach, and still we had not been arrested or even challenged.

We put the tents out of sight of the valley, but as evening came and nothing happened all our worry and evasive tactics began to seem ludicrously melodramatic. It was a gigantic but very welcome anticlimax. Later we were to discover that the CID man had followed us to Chatoru merely to make sure that we intended to transgress the Inner Line to go to the forbidden Bara Shigri and not forbidden Tibet. He then turned a blind eye and went home.

7 IN SEARCH OF A DENTIST

My abscess was growing worse. I woke up to find that the swelling had spread to my nose, jaw and one eye. Over a breakfast of ten penicillin tablets I studied 'Hints to Travellers', that invaluable Royal Geographical Society publication which explains almost anything one needs to know. Camel-loading, dog-driving, collecting earthworms, killing snakes, it's all there and makes fascinating reading. From the dental page I diagnosed my trouble as an apical tooth abscess. The treatment: "Extract tooth. If abscess has spread to neighbouring bone and soft adjacent tissue, incise abscess as well, from inside the mouth whenever possible." It was depressing to find no mention of the possibility that the abscess might go down of its own accord or respond to penicillin. We had a scalpel and a pair of pliers but Barbara showed a marked reluctance to act as dentist. She had little faith in my diagnosis, and predicted all sorts of complications.

If there had been no alternative she would have done it, but we both knew that there was an Indian doctor at Chatoru, thirty miles away. By the short cut it would be only fifteen miles, but without ponies it would be impossible to ford the numerous nullahs, fast-flowing streams carrying snow-water down into the river. Rikzin was taking the ponies back to Manali until we were ready to leave the glacier, since there was no pasture in the Chandra valley, but normally he would return by the longer route. This meant Rikzin had to be persuaded to take his unladen ponies back the shorter way. Barbara pleaded with him and five minutes later it was all arranged. Atchuk would accompany me, while Barbara, Jigmet, and Wangyal would begin carrying loads up the glacier. The ponies were just leaving so it was a quick decision, with no time to work out what we would do if the doctor had gone, or could not cure me, or I was stopped by the CID man. Trusting to Providence, we pushed some chocolate, sweets, money and a sleeping bag into my rucksack and I set off.

My memories of that day are like a film out of focus; only occasionally is the lens adjusted and the picture sharp. I remember going to sleep lying in the sun whilst Rikzin found a place to cross the first nullah; when I awoke a huge vulture was circling round and round overhead. It thinks I'm dead, I thought, and sat up quickly. Later I found out that this was the bearded vulture, or lammergeier, with its wing span of nine feet the largest bird in the Himalayas.

Then I remember the water swirling round my legs as my pony swam across the nullah and I clung on to its mane. Later there was a very narrow path across a scree slope with a tremendous drop to the white river below, and then miles and miles of climbing over boulders. But memories are very subjective, and probably if I were to go back there I would find distances and dimensions shrunk beyond recognition as when one revisits the haunts of childhood.

Towards evening I suddenly began to feel better. Rikzin and Atchuk were touchingly pleased, and at the same time the terrain improved and we all mounted ponies. The wooden saddles were very uncomfortable but we had a gloriously exhilarating race across the gravel flats, splashing through shallow streams, shouting and laughing.

When we came to another boulder field we had to dismount and I began to feel very tired. We had been on the move since eight that morning and it was now 6 p.m. As the sun crept slowly up the valley sides until only the highest tips were tinged with pink, Atchuk and Rikzin began to murmur their evening prayers. It was strangely impressive in that setting, the hillsides gradually turning into dark silhouettes against the pale sky.

At last I saw pinpoints of light ahead. Chatoru. To reach it there was one last nullah to cross, but it was deeper, wider, and swifter than any of the others. Rikzin and the donkeyman stood on the bank shaking their heads.

"Sleep here," Rikzin said. "Tomorrow small water." I did not argue for I knew they were as anxious to get to Chatoru as I was; we had all intended to spend the night in the Tibetan hotel there so had no tents or camping equipment with us. We bivouacked on the bank, our tent a saddle-cloth strung between two boulders. Atchuk built a dry stone wall at the windward end, saddles provided seats inside, and soon we were quite warm and comfortable.

Fortunately there was enough juniper scrub around to make a fire, and Rikzin had both a cooking pot and some tea. Then the donkeyman made his only social gesture of the whole trip, producing a handful of flour from somewhere deep in the folds of his filthy coat. It looked like sawdust but Atchuk mixed it with water, slapped little balls of dough from palm to palm till they were pancake-shaped, and baked them on a flat stone on top of the fire. There was only enough flour for one chapatti each, but it tasted wonderful.

On a mattress of saddle cloths I slept extremely well, but woke up feeling ill again. We did not bother with breakfast - it would only have been a drink of hot water - but at 7 a.m. crossed the nullah which was now only a trickle, and headed for the bright lights of Chatoru. These were a bitter disappointment. In the four days since we had passed through, the place had almost vanished; everyone was packing up to leave for the winter and all we could get was tea.

I was afraid that the Indian doctor would also have left since his job was to look after the Tibetan refugees working there, but luck was with me: as I approached the tiny rest house I saw him sitting outside reading. Dropping his book, Hardy's *Return of the Native,* he rushed up to greet me. I was his first European visitor in the whole of the summer, and he was pathetically pleased to see me; he was also very reluctant to let me go. I had to discuss English literature for two hours before he would even look at my abscess. I had expected him to extract the tooth, but he said it was unnecessary - good news, as it was a front tooth. After lancing the abscess and giving some penicillin injections, he pronounced me cured, but told me not to do any strenuous exercise for a few weeks.

Escaping, I rejoined Atchuk and Rikzin in the Tibetan Hotel. After a last cup of tea we said goodbye to Rikzin who was taking the ponies back to Manali, and set off to walk the thirty miles back to the glacier. As the day wore on I felt better and better, although footsore and hungry. We managed to purchase one cold chapatti en route but that was all. There was nothing to make us linger and by nightfall we had covered the twenty-two miles to Batal, where we bivouacked again on the floor of a stone shelter. Leaving at 6 a.m. next morning, we crossed the bridge and walked south towards the glacier, watching the dawn slowly flush the highest peaks with light. The valley was still in darkness, the river a silver ribbon winding towards the distant snows.

As the first sunlight lit up one side of the valley, we reached the only nullah on our route. I began to take my shoes off to wade across but Atchuk insisted that he would carry me. I am not sure who was the more nervous as he felt for footholds in the swirling knee-deep water, chanting Buddhist prayers at top speed.

The final mile to camp seemed endless, but at last, at ten o'clock, we were there and found Barbara with a huge pan of tea ready. Jigmet and Wangyal were doing a third carry up the glacier, but she had stayed behind to watch out for us. As we wolfed biscuits and marmalade I told our story, exaggerating the hardships till she was induced to produce a tin of pears and a fruit cake from the luxury food tin.

Then gleefully Barbara told me of the horrors in store. From her descriptions the glacier sounded like something between a slag heap and a skating rink; I began to be glad that I would only have to make one journey up it. Whilst Atchuk and I had been away the three of them had done a magnificent job, for in three days they had carried up enough food and equipment to enable us all five to move up on the fourth day. We would not come back to Shigri till the 11th October, when Rikzin would be returning with three ponies to carry our equipment out before the winter snows. Tomorrow was the 25th September which gave us exactly seventeen days on the glacier, not as long as the three weeks we had originally planned, but long enough to do something, we hoped.

8 RUBBLE AND SNOW

As we packed up the tents ready to leave, Barbara began to tone down her description of the glacier, wary, perhaps, that I might ask what all the fuss had been about. She need not have worried. It was just as bad as she had suggested.

Although four previous parties had been up and down the Bara Shigri, there was not the vestige of a path; only 'an endless wilderness of rubble and blocks, oiled by mud sludge, all in potential movement on an ice surface crossed by gaping crevasses', as Gunther so well expressed it. For seven miles we jumped from one wobbly gravel-covered boulder to the next, or squeezed in between them on the dirty ice and sliding rubble. There were no continuous medial or lateral moraines the crests of which we could follow, and again and again we had to make long detours round enormous ice craters. The ice-blue lakes in the bottom of these provided the only colour in that ugly desolation. High shale walls confined the view on either side, and only occasionally did a view of gleaming snow and ice above relieve the drab greyness of the scene.

Like all Himalayan glaciers the Bara Shigri is in retreat. The glacier snout is decaying, and the lower reaches are permanently covered in debris they can no longer disgorge into the valley. As we moved up that fantastic slag heap and heard the cracking of ice and deep rumble of overturning boulders, the glacier seemed like something writhing in torment.

We rested for about ten minutes every hour. Barbara and I were pleased, and relieved, to find that our natural pace was about the same; nothing tends to mar a climbing partnership more on both sides than unequal pace, when one is constantly going slow or waiting for the other. We were also pleased to discover that we could keep up with the porters, as long as they carried fifty pounds and we only thirty. After five miles at one mph, we reached the place where Barbara, Wangyal, and Jigmet had dumped their first loads. Here we camped, levelling out platforms for the tents by moving rocks and chipping smooth the underlying ice. It was a bleak spot but inside our tents we were warm enough and, with air beds to lie on, the rough ground did not matter.

This was the only night that we spent at this transit camp for next day we moved on another two miles to the foot of what we hoped was Gunther's 'first turning on the left'. We almost missed it. There was an obvious break in the line of cliffs on our left, about a mile further up the glacier, but as we were heading for this Barbara suddenly noticed a stream emerging from a much narrower break directly opposite us. There was no sign of a tributary glacier and the break might be no more than a ravine, but it was the first turning on the left so we crossed to explore it.

We camped above the Bara Shigri on a small sandy shelf near the stream, a pleasant camp with a view across the glacier to some spectacular snow peaks on the main divide. If we can be said to have had a base camp at all I suppose this was it; we only spent two nights there, but used it as a food dump, and for a while it boasted one tent.

That afternoon whilst the porters went back for second loads, Barbara and I set off to explore above the camp. After an hour climbing up scree slopes beside the stream, we came to moraine and found ourselves clambering over yet more wobbly boulders, but without loads it was easier to balance and we made quite fast progress. Suddenly the valley widened out and we saw ice cliffs ahead - the snout of a glacier. Wildly excited we climbed up the moraines on one side of the cliffs and came out onto level snow.

Thick mist obscured the view, but it was certainly a large glacier, and on the right we could see rock buttresses in the right position for Central Peak. For half an hour we waited for the mist to clear, but without success. Yet we had seen enough to be almost sure that this was 'our glacier', untrodden and unexplored. We looked at it in awe. According to our altimeters we were at 16,000 ft, higher than Mont Blanc, higher than Monte Rosa or the Matterhorn, higher than we had ever been before. After all the worry and uncertainty of the last weeks it was a good moment. We built a cairn to mark the spot, and more on the way down to mark the route for the next day. When we reached camp the porters were back and were just setting off to look for us, as anxious as mother hens at our long absence.

Next morning we all set off with heavy loads but the going was not unpleasant with plenty of long rests in the warm sunshine. As we neared our highest point of the day before, the pace quickened and we arrived panting on the crest. The view confirmed our hopes, a broad river of ice and snow flowed smoothly down between a chain of low snow peaks and a series of steep rocky ridges leading up to what must be Central Peak.

The soft snow in the lower part of the glacier was much less tiring than the moraines, and higher up we were walking over hard crusty ice. Early in the afternoon we camped near the foot of one of the rock ridges on the lateral moraine of the glacier. Again we had to move rocks and hack the ice level for our tent, but camping on rock, even with a little ice underneath, is much warmer and more convenient than camping on snow. After a rest and a brew of tea the porters went down again, and for the first time Barbara and I were left camping on our own.

Tomorrow we would try to find a route up the upper glacier whilst the porters brought second loads up to the camp; then the next day, if all went well, we would move up again to a yet higher camp at the head of the glacier. In the meantime all we had to do was cook our supper and sleep.

We slept well, and woke to another sunny day. Breakfast was pleasantly leisurely, and not till 10 a.m. did we start up the glacier. At first it was level and the only obstacles were the deep troughs carved in the ice by glacier streams. The whole surface was dissected by channels and cauldrons, some visible, but others only detectable by a faint gurgling underneath the ice. Higher up we came to transverse crevasses, sometimes just narrow clefts which one could step or jump across, sometimes huge chasms with a curtain of icicles pointing down into shadowy blue-green depths. Zigzagging among these crevasses was awe-inspiring but quite safe as long as one could see exactly where they lay, but higher up the whole glacier surface was covered with soft snow. The only way to tell what was solid and what was space was to prod the snow before every step.

We roped together, and, whilst I cautiously moved forward, Barbara paid out the rope round her ice axe pushed deep into the snow, ready to hold me if I should break through. In soft snow checking a fall is not too difficult, for the rope cuts deep into the snow and takes most of the strain. The difficult part is getting the person out again when they are dangling on the end of the rope; harnesses did not exist at that time. Unless you are a big party you cannot haul them out, and they have to climb either up the sides of the crevasse or up the rope. Both are very difficult and completely exhausting. The thickest nylon climbing rope is less than two inches in circumference, and to climb it one has to use a system of stirrups. Two three-foot long loops of thin rope are attached to the main rope, one above the other by a special 'Prusik' knot. This knot grips when you stand in the stirrup, but when you take your weight off it, you can slide it further up the rope. Thus by standing in one stirrup whilst sliding the other one up, slowly and very laboriously you progress upwards.

We had both practised this technique on ropes dangling from Welsh trees but were not anxious to have to use it dangling in the icy depths of some bottle-necked crevasse, so decided to go on only until we could see round the corner to the head of the glacier. On our right the rocky ridges of Central Peak spread out like the spokes of a wheel with the curving glacier forming a wide outer rim. Further and further it curved to the south until at last we could see its head, a wide snow basin with a back wall of snow peaks and the rocky mass of Central Peak towering to the west. From the snow basin the glacier dropped gently towards us, and, to our relief, most of it was hard ice with the crevasses visible. They formed an intricate maze and we could not see a way through, but decided with climbers' typical optimism that there must be a way somewhere.

We got back to camp in the early afternoon and had just brewed tea and levelled a site for another tent when the porters appeared under the most enormous loads. They had brought twice as much as we had specified in order to avoid another carry. Yet they did not expect or even seem to want a rest day to recover; as soon as they arrived Wangyal pointed up the glacier, and said, "Tomorrow". To Wangyal and Jigmet, at least, being mountain porters was something more than just a way to earn a living; they really enjoyed climbing, and, like us, were always wanting to see what lay around the next corner.

It took five hours next day to make our way through the maze of crevasses to the snow basin. With the continual pauses to find a route, it was impossible to develop that rhythm whereby walking becomes completely automatic and one's mind is disembodied to range elsewhere. All I could think about was the dead weight of my load, my aching legs and dry throat. Each time we reached a crest I hopefully looked for the snow basin, but it was never there. Just when I had given up all hope we suddenly reached it, a smooth snow field with sides gently sloping down from a rim of jagged peaks. We camped almost in the centre of the basin where there was the least danger of any avalanches reaching us. Remembering John Jackson's advice about Himalayan avalanches - take what you think is a safe distance, and double it - I hoped we were out of range.

This camp was at just over 18,000 ft and that evening we began to feel the altitude. Again the porters had gone down to bring up the rest of the stores, so we were on our own. For some time we lay in our sleeping bags by the open tent door, watching the last pink glow fade from the peaks, but we both had headaches and were too tired really to appreciate the scene.

Supper took three hours to cook. A whole panful of snow melted down into only about half an inch of water, so producing one brew of tea took an hour or more. At this stage we only had one primus stove and it took another two hours to cook supper - an indigestible mess of dried meat and vegetables, spooned up off the tent floor when the pan fell off the stove. As the final touch our candle managed to burn a small hole in the tent wall.

With the unaccustomed altitude neither of us slept well, and woke up to find everything frozen and the inside of the tent covered with frosty rime from our breath. When I took an arm out of the warmth of my sleeping bag to light the primus stove, my fingers froze to the metal leaving a layer of skin behind. Then when the primus was lit, the frost on the roof began to thaw and drip down our necks.

Breakfast was not a great success. The biscuits broke into crumbs, the butter was frozen solid, and we could not unscrew the lid of the marmalade tin. For hours we melted snow to make tea, and when at last we had a pan of boiling water, Barbara knocked it over. She said it was her worst moment of the whole trip.

At 8.30 a.m. the sun reached our tent, the temperature rose rapidly and life began to improve. We drank a pint of tea each, thawed out our boots by holding them over the primus stove, and at 9 a.m. crawled out into the white world. We put on snow goggles against the glare and looked around. About a mile away to the south was the snow peak of Lion, 20,098 ft, named after its resemblance to a recumbent lion. Its summit was a round dome from which gleaming ice ridges plunged down like the corners of a pyramid. Then high above us to the west was Central Peak, five hundred feet higher than Lion, and with its steep rock walls and serrated ridges looking much more formidable. On the opposite, eastern side of the snow basin a chain of smaller peaks cast dark shadows towards our tent. One of these was a spectacular rock spire, with beautifully symmetrical ridges dropping down to cols on either side. It was 19,850 ft high, unclimbed as were all these peaks, and looked quite close to our camp. After five days of continuous glacier work we were impatient to begin climbing; this spire certainly looked worthwhile even if we did not reach the summit and it would be good training, we told ourselves.

The snow was crisp and level but it took us over an hour to reach the foot of the col to the right of the peak, only a mile from our camp. All the way we were panting and frequently had to stop for rests. Then the snow steepened and we came to the bergschrund, the giant crevasse formed where the glacier first breaks away from the mountainside. Above the bergschrund there was an ice slope, so before we tried to cross crampons had to be strapped on to the soles of our boots.

The bergschrund was very wide but in one place snow had become wedged between the two walls, forming a bridge. It was difficult to see how solid the bridge was, so with Barbara belaying me from well below the lower lip, I gingerly kicked steps across, ready to leap back if it gave way. The upper lip was steep and I had to cut a stairway of steps in the snow-ice to get up on to the ice slope above. There I took in the rope round my axe anchored in the snow, and Barbara came across. From here we estimated it to be about two ropes lengths (200 ft) to the rocks below the col. At first the angle of the slope was easy enough to climb straight up, the steel points of our crampons biting into the granular ice, but higher up it became steeper, and I began to cut steps.

One, two, three blows with the axe, and the ice chips hissed down the slope to the bergschrund below. At first out of the corner of my eye I was conscious of its gaping darkness and of Barbara anxiously watching far below, as aware as I was that she could not prevent me hurtling into it, should I fall. But concentration soon dispelled fear, anxiety, even tiredness. The world resolved itself into one gleaming slope of ice, the two-handed swing of the axe on the next step, the gentle balancing move upwards.

I was supremely happy, with the exhilaration of knowing that deliberately I was staking my whole being on my own judgement, skill and concentration. The racing-driver, bull fighter, trapeze artist or anyone who deliberately courts danger must know something of this feeling, but in mountaineering of this sort I think it reaches its height. There is no one and nothing to rely on but oneself, there is no luck or objective danger involved. It is sport for its own sake, with no reward of money or fame, no justification of social or scientific purpose. It is pointless, unnecessary, largely unjustifiable, and yet superbly satisfying. Mind and body combine to overcome difficulties deliberately sought out, and both awareness and effort are heightened by the calculated risks that must be taken.

After the ice slope (which proved to be twice as long as we had estimated), there came two hundred feet of loose, snow-covered rock. It was not steep but we moved very slowly, one at a time, whilst the other belayed round any solid rock spike that could be found. At 1 p.m. we reached the crest of the ridge and turned up towards the summit. It was a knife edge but the rock was very rotten with gigantic loose blocks that threatened at the slightest touch to slide down to the glacier a thousand feet below.

We were now at more than 19,000 ft and desperately tired. As soon as we sat down for a rest we felt full of energy, but the moment we stood up again we started panting and after a few steps would have to lean against the rock to rest. By 2 p.m. it was obvious that we would not reach the summit unless we were to spend a night out on the peak. This we did not even consider doing, for at that height with no camping equipment we would almost certainly have suffered frostbite.

With a last look up at the summit, 500 ft above us, we promised ourselves another go at the spire when we were fitter, and returned to the col. There we had a pleasant lunch snack in a little rock recess out of the wind, looking down into the West Gyundi valley to the east and across the snow basin to Lion and Central Peak to the west. Whilst we were discussing possible routes up these, we saw three specks moving round the tiny square that was our tent, looking very insignificant in that great expanse of snow. Even though the porters could not see us we did not feel quite so alone once they had arrived.

The descent took almost as long as the ascent but at last we were down and across the bergschrund, and hurrying back to the tents. Wangyal came out to meet us, with a broad grin shaking his finger to make it clear that Memsahibs should not go out climbing alone. They had watched our descent from the col, and although rather worried at the time, were clearly pleased that we really were going to do some climbing. I don't think they had ever believed it until this moment. With the five of us sitting in their two-man Meade tent, we drank tea, ate chapattis, and discussed plans for the morrow.

We had four days food and fuel with us and more could be brought up in a day from the lower camp, but our time was very limited. We therefore decided to reconnoitre the lower part of Lion the next day; it would help us to acclimatise, and looked less formidable than Central Peak. The weather did not look too promising and when we retired to our tent there was a strong wind and snow was falling. To try to get a good night's sleep we took sleeping pills and dreamily drifted off to the flapping of the tent, rhythmic as the slapping of waves against a boat.

I woke at 6 a.m. with a throbbing headache. Hopefully I looked out of the tent door to see if the weather was bad, but the wind had dropped and the sky was clear. At that moment all I wanted in the world was to snuggle down into the warmth of my sleeping bag and sleep. For ever. I began now to understand something that had puzzled me for a long time: why Himalayan climbers never seemed able to make an early start. With the short hours of daylight and danger of avalanches once the sun begins to melt the snow, an early start is obviously vital, much more vital than in the Alps where one invariably starts before 5 a.m. Yet, although they recognised the urgency, they never seemed to set off till 8 or 9 a.m. when the sun first reached the tents.

The truth is, I think, that the altitude and cold numb and almost destroy one's will-power. Everything is an immense effort, and one has no will to make the effort. If we felt this at 18,000 ft, how much worse it must be at 27,000 ft. But a large expedition does have the advantage that each climber is part of a team with other people relying on him, whereas with us there was nothing to prevent us lying in our sleeping bags all day. Nothing, that is, except the consciousness of the regret and dissatisfaction we would feel later if we wasted a day. This has always been a powerful spur to me, for I hate wasting time or opportunities, and when usually from laziness this happens, I hate myself afterwards.

We got up. By 8 a.m. Jigmet had produced tea and porridge, and by 8.30 a.m. we were ready to leave as the sun crept across the snow onto the tents. Its warmth brought us to life, and we became almost cheerful. It was good to see how excited Wangyal and Jigmet were at the prospect of a day's climbing without loads, and Atchuk too was pleased with his role of camp-guardian for the day, since he did not like climbing or more exercise than was strictly necessary.

An hour's walk over hard snow brought us up into the cwm below the east face of Lion. There was avalanche debris at the foot of the face, but on its left a snow gangway led obliquely upwards, on to a fairly easy-angled rock and snow ridge leading towards the summit.

This was the obvious route for the other right-hand ridge was very steep ice, up which we would have had to cut 1,500 ft of steps.

Already it had become clear that Jigmet and Wangyal did not understand the meaning of 'reconnaissance' or 'acclimatisation'. To them the summit must have looked very close for it was only 1,500 ft above us and they were both going very strongly. The altitude did not affect them in the least, as they were acclimatised both from going to similar heights on other expeditions and from living permanently at 16,000 ft at home in Ladakh. But to Barbara and me even the ridge crest looked impossibly remote. Our legs felt like lead, and after a dozen steps we would be doubled over our ice axes, gasping like fish out of water.

By Alpine standards the climbing was very easy, little more than a snow-plod with just a few sections of rock-scrambling. The only part of the climb that I enjoyed was one rest we had sitting out of the wind on a warm ledge, where we ate some glucose tablets, guaranteed on the packet to supply 'Instant Energy'. Wangyal and Jigmet seemed determined to reach the summit, and we began to feel the same. At least if we reached it today we would not have to go through all this toil again. Barbara and I did not even try to pretend to each other that we were enjoying it, but we both felt that Lion ought to be climbed. It was not a very interesting route and I doubt whether we would have found it particularly enjoyable even had we been more acclimatised, but if we had not reached the top this first time, we would certainly have tried again, just 'because it was there', waiting to be climbed.

Some peaks one climbs for their beautiful shape, exciting climbing, or the view from the top, but others like Lion are basically unattractive, yet attract one as strongly as an iron filing to a magnet. It is as illogical as falling in love, but just as real.

Above the rocky section there was a broad snow ridge leading up to the rounded summit which was now in sight. Wangyal pranced ahead in the lead, impatiently waiting as we slowly toiled up the final slope, but at last we were there and sank down on to the summit rocks. At first all I felt was a flood of relief, but slowly came the realisation that we were at 20,098 ft. We had climbed a 20,000-foot peak. By Himalayan standards this is a mere foothill, but for us it might have been Everest. Slowly I began to look around, across to Central Peak only 500 ft higher than us, and down on to the rest of the area, glaciers, peaks and more peaks. There were no vital topographical questions to be solved, but we did take a complete series of photographs and compass bearings in case they should be useful. Although it was only noon the afternoon clouds were already gathering and it was very cold and windy, so after ten minutes we started down again, following the same route.

The best part of the day was when we reached camp at 2.30 p.m. and collapsed into the tent where Atchuk had three pans of tea waiting for us and an enormous pile of hot onion chapattis. It was gratifying to find that even Jigmet and Wangyal were a little tired, and of their own accord suggested "Kal rest karo" (tomorrow rest). We agreed. The whole climb had only taken six hours, but to lie down and not to move felt like a new and wonderful experience.

Our rest day was delightful. It began with breakfast in bed at 9.30 a.m., another snooze, and finally out into the warm sunshine at 11 am. Our appointed task for the day was to begin surveying the glacier, which we had now named Lion Glacier. In the programme submitted to the Royal Geographical Society and the Mount Everest Foundation, we had stated our main objectives as the climbing of Central Peak and Lion and the exploration and survey of this glacier. The Royal Geographical Society had loaned us a plane table and survey instruments, and we had practised by mapping parts of north Wales.

Lion glacier had already been roughly mapped by Peter Holmes, who had seen it from a viewpoint to the east in 1956, but as the first people ever to go up the glacier we would be able to check the details. In our enthusiasm 'to extend the bounds of human knowledge' it was slightly disappointing to find that his provisional map was remarkably accurate. There was only one important error: Central Peak and Lion were much too far apart and another non-existent peak appeared in between them. To correct this we decided to survey just the upper part of the glacier.

The plan was to measure a mile-long base line on the glacier, and draw it in on the plane table sheet on a scale of two inches to the mile. The ends of the base line would be our first two survey stations and we would set up a third by putting a flag on the glacier equidistant at an angle of about 45 degrees from both of them. Finally, keeping the plane table orientated to magnetic north, from each of the three stations in turn we would draw in rays to all the surrounding peaks (by sighting along an alidade), and thus triangulate their positions by three intersecting rays.

This is a very simple type of survey, but quite adequate for our limited purposes. Accuracy largely depends on the careful measurement of the base line, but here we encountered our first difficulty: the 100-foot steel tape that we had brought for the purpose jammed halfway out of its case. We all struggled with it for a long time, but without success, so eventually decided that we would have to use a 120-foot nylon climbing rope instead. Surveyors may be shocked at this, but as long as one takes care to hold the rope taut but not to stretch it, it is not as inaccurate a method as it sounds.

Barbara, Jigmet and Wangyal started measuring eastwards from our camp in a straight line across the level snow, whilst I set up the plane table at the camp end of the base line. After a time Barbara came back to say that Jigmet and Wangyal were doing a splendid job. The next time we saw them they were still carefully measuring, halfway up the mountainside! Clearly the snow basin could not be a mile wide. Barbara went to retrieve them, put a flag at the foot of the slope to mark that end of the line, and then remeasured it all the way back again.

Meanwhile Atchuk had gone off to place a third flag about half a mile north of our camp; he returned very pleased with himself so I had not the heart to tell him that his flag was not visible. We spent all afternoon carrying the plane table and tripod round the glacier looking for flags, but at the end of the day had a map of the upper glacier that proved surprisingly accurate, agreeing with Holmes' version except in the area round Lion as we had expected.

We had decided to try to climb Central Peak the next day. We used the term 'reconnaissance', but knew that if Wangyal and Jigmet came with us, it would inevitably become a summit attempt. However, a party of four is much safer than just two, and we knew how bitterly disappointed they would be if we were to leave them in camp. I doubt, in fact, if they would ever have let us go out alone. They were too fiercely protective and too undisciplined to obey orders. All we could do was to determine to 'take a firm hand', and make them go at our pace, rather than at theirs.

To try to take the edge off their energy and to save time next morning, we suggested that they should pioneer an approach to the foot of the rocky south face. There were three possible routes, the short steep left-hand ridge, the long gradual right-hand ridge, or the rock buttresses running straight up the south face. We chose the latter, most direct route for the first attempt.

Next morning we left at 7.30 a.m. and in an hour were at the foot of the rock, thanks to Jigmet and Wangyal's route-finding of the previous afternoon. From there it was a straight rock-climb with only a few patches of snow on the wider ledges. It was wonderful to find that at last we were becoming accustomed to the altitude; we were still going slowly, but feeling infinitely better than on Lion and really enjoying ourselves.

At the time we took it for granted both that we would acclimatise and that it would be at the same rate, but later in Nepal we were to find out just how lucky we had been. All we had suffered was headaches, insomnia, and extreme tiredness, but in Nepal some of our party were really ill at 18,000 ft, and the rate of acclimatisation varied enormously.

Wangyal and Jigmet were delighted at our new energy, and we all took turns in leading the way. The rock was granite and quite sound. By English rock-climbing standards it was mostly 'Difficult', with the occasional section of 'Very Difficult'. On both sides of the buttress were ice couloirs, noisy with constant stone falls. At one point it seemed that we would be forced into one of these dangerous stonechutes when we encountered a vertical rock step extending the whole width of the buttress, but luckily we were able to by-pass it by climbing a short rock chimney round the side. After this the angle eased, and at 11.30 we reached the crest of the ridge.

It was a narrow, steep-sided ridge very like Crib Goch in Snowdonia, curving gently up to the pointed summit. We climbed it in a leisurely way, savouring the airy situation and the drop down to the glacier on either side. Like a good book, I did not want it to end, and was almost sorry when we came to the top. It was a cartoonist's summit, a sharp point capped by a small block. Precariously balancing on the top, we took a photo-panorama and compass bearings, then retired out of the cold wind to have a summit party. Miraculously, Jigmet produced from his rucksack a thermos of hot tea and we rapidly disposed of chocolate, biscuits, nuts and raisins.

The air was crisp and clear as though it were early morning and the sky quite cloudless, so that we could see for fifty or sixty miles in every direction. Range after range of mountains stretched as far as the eye could see; the snow and ice peaks of Kulu to the west and south, barren Spiti to the east, and northwards, beyond the low rock peaks of Lahul, the red-brown mountain waste of Tibet.

Below our feet Lion glacier curved smoothly round and down and we could follow our whole route back to the foot of the Bara Shigri, 8,000 ft below. It seemed scarcely credible that we had left it only nine days ago, and now we were at 20,620 ft. The altitude went to my head like champagne. I felt wonderfully happy, and so light that it seemed to be only my heavy boots that were preventing me drifting off like gossamer. I remember contemplating taking them off to see what happened.

Whilst we climbed down, we discussed plans for the next few days. It was now 3rd October, which meant that we still had a week before we must be back at Shigri. We could stay up in the snow basin, but, apart from our Spire, there was nothing really worth climbing. It would be more fun to go back to the main glacier and up one of the unexplored icefalls on the other side, perhaps to look for Gunther's ice pass or a new pass across the range.

We got back to camp at 3 p.m., at least approximately 3 p.m., for my watch stopped on the way down, and as Barbara's had broken, we had to reset mine by guesswork. We told the porters the plan to move down, and Wangyal immediately suggested that we go down that afternoon. We were surprised at their enthusiasm until we discovered that they had run out of cigarettes. This suited us very well as we were still feeling quite fresh and it would save a whole day.

After a mile or two plodding along under heavy loads we did not feel quite so fresh, but at least it was downhill. Before we turned the corner, I turned for one last look back. The snow basin glowed warm with light, long purple-black shadows crept down from Lion and Central Peak, and opposite our Spire was turned to gold, its soaring ridges clean and sharp. The glacier was no longer a featureless white glare but a sea full of ripples, each casting its own tiny shadow. Slowly the light faded from gold to palest pink, but I could stay no longer, the others had already gone on.

The last half-mile we did in complete darkness, blindly prodding ahead with our ice axes to locate the crevasses. As soon as possible we moved off the glacier on to the moraine and stumbled along amidst the boulders, looking for the food cache and tent platforms of our old campsite. It was 9 p.m. by the time we found it and had the tents up. We were too tired to bother with supper, it had been a long but very good day.

10   THE LAST PLUM

We had six days in hand, six days to do exactly what we liked. All around us were enticing unclimbed peaks and unexplored glaciers; as we examined the possibilities I felt like a child gazing in a shop window, with money to spend but spoilt for choice.

From our camp at the foot of Lion glacier we looked across the Bara Shigri to the main Dividing Range. A fine chain of high peaks formed its crest and the only ones which had been climbed were 21,148-foot White Sail at the northern end and 20,500-foot Cathedral eight miles to the south. In between lay several impressive twenty thousanders from which steep icefalls tumbled chaotically down to the main glacier. Immediately opposite our camp was a steep rock pyramid, capped by snow like thick white sauce on a pudding. Two things particularly attracted us to this peak: there was no obvious route up it, and we could not identify it on the map.

The map had been made entirely from the level of the main glacier where rock ridges curving down from the peaks restricted the view. From our vantage point a few hundred feet up it was clear that the map needed correcting both in the number and location of the plethora of peaks it showed.

There was yet one further incentive to explore this particular area: to the left, or south, of the Snow Dome was a pronounced dip in the main ridge. We had already decided that there was not enough time to reach Gunther's ice pass some miles further up the Bara Shigri, but this dip might prove to be another pass over the whole range, which had never been crossed.

After one night at base camp, memorable for the luxury of a tin of pilchards and a wash in the stream, we packed up five loads, comprising five days' food, two tents, two ropes, one primus, and the normal climbing, medical, and survey equipment. When we were almost ready to leave Atchuk suddenly said he was feeling ill and was going back to Manali. For the last few days he had certainly been coughing a little, but it had not seemed anything serious. I think the real reason was that he did not like the look of all the snow and ice where we were going. He did not enjoy climbing and obviously hankered after civilisation; this was his first, and last, summer as a mountain porter.

This was one of the rare occasions that Barbara lost her temper. After trying to reason with him in the sweet and reasonable manner of a school-mistress with a naughty child, she flew at him in a red-headed fury. This had the desired effect and meekly he shouldered his load. Usually Barbara is almost excessively considerate to anyone feeling ill, but she was convinced that Atchuk was merely making excuses. Typically however she had doubts later on, and anxiously asked, "You don't think he's really ill, do you?" To be on the safe side we agreed that after carrying to the foot of Snow Dome, four hours of laborious but straightforward rubble-trudging, he should go no higher but begin carrying the spare equipment back to Shigri. Once Atchuk knew that there would be no more ice and snow he cheered up and became co-operative again, conscientiously doing three carries down the Bara Shigri on his own whilst we were climbing above.

The nearer we approached the Snow Dome the less feasible it looked. Its rock walls were steep and smooth and were actually overhung by the dome, from which small snow avalanches frequently puffed down the face. We camped well out from its base, at the point where the icefalls which flowed round either side of the mountain met in a jumble of ice and boulders. Then Atchuk went down again, and the rest of us set off to explore as far as we could up the left-hand icefall in the remaining three hours of daylight.

Icefall, what does the word convey? To me it was little more than a geographical term associated with pictures from Everest books of men standing under large ice pinnacles. Even had I seriously tried to visualise an icefall, I could never in my wildest moments have imagined that immense torrent of ice inexorably plunging downwards. Not a sound broke the stillness, yet these towering ice cliffs and gaping crevasses seemed to exude an almost tangible hostility.

The lower part was steep but with crampons we were able to weave up through the crevasses with only a little step-cutting. Soon the sun left the snow and it was bitterly cold but on the opposite side of the valley, framed by a curtain of steely icicles, we could see the snows of Lion glacier flowing smoothly down, golden-warm in the evening sun.

Tiptoeing under overhanging seracs and across thin snow bridges we came to a point directly below the col, only to find the way barred by a series of gigantic crevasses splitting the whole icefall like slashes of a knife. On either side were vertical rock-walls, and there were no snow bridges.

In the nearest of these great craters a narrow catwalk of ice led out to a slender pinnacle in the centre. It was the most fantastic formation I have ever seen, a two-foot-wide sliver of ice with a two hundred-foot drop on each side to the crater floor. Nonchalantly, Wangyal walked along the top to the ice pinnacle, but I got down *à cheval* and worked my way along with one foot dangling into space on either side. I had thought there might be another ridge of ice extending from the other side of the pinnacle, but was rather relieved when Wangyal peered over and said, "No road". The col was tantalisingly close but clearly we were not going to reach it, and after taking a photograph for the record we retreated. (Later we discovered from Gunther's photographs that the other side would have been impassable in any case.)

Our only chance now of climbing Snow Dome or crossing the range lay up the other icefall. This looked longer but less steep than the first so to save time we decided to carry loads straight up it, in the hope that we could find a route through and camp at the top. The five loads brought from base camp now had to he split into four. Barbara and I set off carrying forty pounds and Wangyal and Jigmet sixty.

It took us seven hours to progress 1,500 ft up, yet in spite of the drag of our loads, this was one of our most enjoyable days. The weather was fine and the ice scenery exquisite, crevasses fanning out from the glistening slope like leaves from a book. Chandeliers of icicles glimmered in the blue-green depths, each ice crystal sparkled like a diamond. We had frequent rests whilst Wangyal cut steps across narrow bridges, preferring the most unlikely of routes to the long detours that Jigmet advocated.

For some reason we had expected a snow basin above the icefall so were surprised to find that the maze of crevasses continued right up to the back wall of the cwm. There was one smooth expanse of snow towards the left hand side but it was almost directly below the steep north face of Snow Dome, which looked as though its overhanging masses of ice and snow might avalanche at any moment. They did the next day, covering the area with huge blocks of avalanche debris. The right hand side of the cwm was fairly level but so criss-crossed with crevasses that we spent a long time trying to find a safe campsite. Eventually we pitched the two tents on a small snow platform with wide crevasses on three sides and a narrow jumpable one on the fourth. We just hoped this would not open up during the night.

The afternoon was cloudy with a strong wind and snow showers. Winter was definitely approaching now, the days were growing shorter and colder and almost every afternoon there was a light snowfall. The bleakness outside only emphasized the warm cosiness inside our tents as we lay in our sleeping bags beside the roaring primus.

It is curious how remote everything seemed as though we were on a different planet from the rest of the world. One might think that long hours in a small tent at high altitude would be the ideal place to discuss deep questions of philosophy, politics or religion, but it never seemed to happen. I found that my mind never felt clear, but ranged in a world of absurd fancies as though in a dream. The only things which seemed of importance were the immediate problems of how to keep snow out of the tent or dry off our socks. Incapable of reading or even sustained conversation, we spent much of that evening in the soothing occupation of beauty treatment. (We had been given various products to try out by Elizabeth Arden; found most of them excellent except for the sun cream which left indelible dark brown stains on our shirt collars).

The next morning dawned fine and cloudless and for the first time we saw the whole of the north side of Snow Dome. The view was not encouraging. The whole face was very steep and scoured by avalanches, and we could see no feasible route at all. Even to a much larger party with plenty of time and climbing equipment it would have been a formidable proposition, and for us it was clearly out of the question.

From the north of Snow Dome a high ridge curved round to the large rocky peak immediately above our campsite. This also looked steep and formidable, but on its east side rock buttresses dropped down to a low col which looked as though it should lead over on to the next icefall running down into the Bara Shigri. We set off to climb up to it with Wangyal and Jigmet. We had offered them a rest day in camp but Wangyal was eager to explore and Jigmet clearly thought it his duty to come.

An easy scramble led up to the col, the last part a breathless race to see over the other side. It was disappointing to find the view northwards blocked by the lower slopes of the rocky peak on our left, and the only means of access to the basin an impossibly sheer ice slope swooping down on to another chaotic icefall.

We sat down, ate chocolate, and discussed the situation. We could only afford one more day up here before starting down for Shigri, we had explored as much of the area as we could reach, and the only two peaks worth climbing were Snow Dome, which we had already dismissed as impracticable, and the high rocky peak above our camp. We could not identify this on the map, but decades later discovered that it was 20,495-foot (6,247 m) Shigrila.

According to our altimeters our camp lay at 17,500 ft and the col we were standing on at 18,000 ft, which meant that the summit should be less than 2,000 ft above us, a feasible distance to climb in one day. Had we known then that the peak was in fact the east face of Shigrila, the mountain erroneously marked at the head of the next icefall, I am sure we would never have attempted it, thus missing some of the best climbing of our expedition.

In blissful ignorance we set off to reconnoitre up the rock buttress which abutted on to the col. At first it was easy scrambling and we remained unroped, but higher up the angle steepened and we became conscious of the long drop to the glacier below. We roped up. The rock was reasonably sound granite and the climbing delightful, the first real rock-climbing we had done since leaving England. As we delicately traversed across airy slabs to peer round the next corner for a route, we had our first taste of the exciting rock-pioneering which absorbed the Victorian mountaineers. Often I had envied their generation's scope for exploration, for now that all the peaks in Britain and Europe have been climbed and almost all the individual cliffs have their own network of routes and guidebook, pioneering is largely confined to engineering feats on holdless walls.

For five hours we climbed up the buttress, revelling in the warm sunshine and dry rock. Wangyal also thoroughly enjoyed himself, confidently swarming up steep corners and walls in spite of his heavy build. With his long arms he looked ridiculously monkey-like, and kept us all laughing with his antics. Jigmet on the other hand was definitely not a natural rock-climber, and was patently relieved when we reached the top of the wall and found ourselves on snow again. Already it was early afternoon and our reconnaissance had taken us only a third of the way up the mountain. Clearly we would never reach the summit in a single day by our route up the buttress; the only possibility now was to try to find a more direct route on the face immediately above our camp.

From our position a thousand feet above the tents the face looked impossibly steep but slowly we zigzagged down an intricate maze of ledges. Dislodged stones whistled off into space with frightening velocity but our actual route proved surprisingly easy, and we decided to use it to try for the summit next day. As we climbed down the frost-shattered rock and scree-covered ledges we heard Wangyal muttering something which we eventually deciphered as "Mucky Shambles". Goodness knows where he picked this up, but it proved a highly appropriate unofficial name for our mountain.

Barbara and I both had headaches when we returned to camp, engendered by the altitude and glare, and felt so listless that we went to sleep at 7 p.m. without having made any plans or preparations for the morrow.

For the story of this last climb in Kulu I quote from my diary, written up the following evening.

Left camp at 6.30 a.m. Very cold. Followed our footprints to snow bridge across the wide bergschrund and up ice slope beyond on steps cut the previous day. Fast progress up the snow and lower section of rock. Lovely windless day with blue sky and hot sunshine - climbed in shirt-sleeves. When we reached our highest point of the day before the pace slowed down; route-finding was difficult and we had to kick or cut steps in the snow and ice sections. The rock-climbing also became steeper and more difficult, but luckily Barbara and I were virtually unaffected by the altitude and climbed almost as fast as if we had been in Wales.

Everything went well until we suddenly came up against a wall of rock too steep and holdless to climb. Wasted a lot of time, till Wangyal discovered a way across a steep snow gully at the side onto an easier rock rib. At 2 p.m. reached the cornice leading on to the summit ridge. The wind was whistling above and clouds fast obscuring the view so we sat down to have lunch and do some surveying. Hungrily ate all our food and shared out the thermos of tea Jigmet had carried up. Then took bearings and elevation angles whilst Wangyal began cutting a way through the overhanging cornice. The snow was so soft and powdery that he almost had to dig a tunnel through, and we found ourselves up to our waists in it.

Expected an extensive view from the ridge crest but instead there was only mist and wind-driven snow. As we ploughed up through the soft snow of the broad ridge the bitterly cold wind soon chilled us to the bone although at the same time we were sweating from the exertion of climbing-a strange sensation of being very hot and very cold simultaneously. Occasionally the mist thinned and we saw the shadowy form of the summit ahead, but gradually the ridge narrowed and progress slowed down.

At 3.15 p.m. when very close we came to an awkward section of soft snow lying on ice-covered rock, at an easy angle but with nasty void either side. Wangyal went straight up but Barbara and I were having misgivings about the lack of time, yet having come so far it would be a shame not to get to the top, and when Wangyal stopped at the top of the awkward section I couldn't forbear going to have a look.

There, about fifty yards away and fifty feet above us, I could see what seemed to be the summit, with ridges dropping away from it on the other side. The intervening ridge was clearly climbable but would necessitate about an hour's step-cutting and it was now 3.30 p.m., with only three hours of daylight left. Wangyal asked whether we should go on or not. This meant that he felt it would take too long, although he said firmly, "Memsahibs decide". I shouted back the situation to Barbara and we decided that retreat was the better part of valour, the mountain being as good as climbed. After all, what's fifty feet in 20,000? (In fact, quite a lot as we would have been faced with a further hidden ridge to reach the summit.)

Sped back along the ridge and through the cornice. Just as I had climbed down the awkward deep snow the mist blew away and it

92

looked as if we would get a view at last. Armed with cameras I went up again only to find the mist down again. Stood around for ten minutes getting colder and colder, but trying to get a view to the north and solve the problem of which peak we were on. Eventually I gave up and came down whereupon the clouds again dissolved. Wasted a lot of time going up again but still no view.

The altitude seemed to have numbed our minds and only gradually did we realise the gravity of the situation. Two thousand feet of steep cliff lay between us and our tents, there were only two hours of daylight left, and we had inadequate equipment to spend a night out in the open, with a strong danger of frostbite. All we could do was hurry down as far as possible before darkness fell.

Wangyal's snow traverse proved very tricky to get down and again we wasted a long time there, and then at 6.30 p.m., when it was getting really dark, we came to the hardest section of rock-climbing. Jigmet suggested that we should stop there and wait till morning, but the rest of us were all for going on, and we decided to abseil. Hammering a piton into a crack, we tied our ropes together, threaded them through, and one by one slid down, 120 ft in one go. Then, praying that the knot would not get stuck, we retrieved the rope by pulling one end. This manoeuvre cost us 11s. 6d. (the cost of the piton and snaplink we left behind) but was well worth it for now we were back on the easier ground we had descended the previous day.

It was a black moonless night with only a few stars. We were all wet to the skin, our hands and feet numb with cold and teeth chattering, but on we went, feeling our way down the loose scree, boulders and patches of snow. Barbara and I recognised only a few landmarks but Wangyal and Jigmet seemed to have a photographic memory of the intricate route, zigzagging along the ledges and only occasionally hesitating.

It was disconcerting to hear the stones and boulders we dislodged go whistling off into space, but as we slowly progressed downwards and realised that we might not have to spend the night out, our spirits rose and Wangyal began to sing 'It's a long way to Tipperary'. This soon became 'It's a long way down Mucky Shambles' with even Jigmet joining in. At 9 p.m. we reached the steep snow slope leading down to the bergschrund. This proved the most difficult part of the whole descent. It was impossible to see the steps cut in the ice and one just had to feel around with one's foot to find a step, knowing that any slip on that slope would be very difficult to check and that there was a large gaping crevasse at the bottom. The four of us were still roped together and very conscious that our lives depended on one another.

At last after what seemed several hours we were all safely down and across the bergschrund. Now only another half-mile to the tents. Wangyal led the way, feeling with his ice axe for hidden crevasses, but even so Jigmet fell into one. Fortunately he did not go far down and Barbara was able to haul him out again by his rucksack, but it served to wake us all up and provide some light relief.

10.30 p.m. The moment we had been longing for for seven hours. We reached the tents, exactly sixteen hours after we had left them that morning. Crowded into one tent for chai, soup and brandy. Examined our feet for frostbite but all seemed okay. Soon warm again and tired but cheerful after a very good day.

Note: In 2016 Americans Tico Gangulee and Chris Wright established a base camp on the Tos glacier on the south side of the Shigrila peaks, from where they ascended Snow Dome (19,698 ft/6,004 m), renamed Lalsura (Red Sail). They then climbed Shigrila by its south-east face (Lindsay Griffin, '55 Years of Shigrila', *Climb*, 139, 2017, pp.36-40).

11 BACK TO KULU

We had hoped to have a lie-in, but at 7 a.m. were woken by a hoarse croak at the tent door, "Chai Memsahibs." It was Wangyal, his grin as broad as ever whilst with vivid gestures he described how his voice had flown away up the mountain overnight. He treated it as a great joke and we had a hilarious breakfast, all conversing in whispers, precariously perched on ice axes stuck like shooting sticks into the snow. Of course it was Wangyal's ice axe that suddenly sank right in, leaving him and his porridge strewn on the snow.

Comedy, mainly of the slapstick type, was to be the keynote of the rest of the trip, a complete relaxation after the unconscious tension of three weeks' climbing. We were still at 17,000 ft but the dangers and difficulties were largely behind us. All we had to do now was to follow our original route back to Shigri and thence Manali.

Before we packed up this last snow camp we set about taking photographs for firms who had supplied us with equipment. In a foot of soft snow it was by no means easy, but valiantly Barbara sat in a drift rubbing Elizabeth Arden lotion on to her bare feet, followed by anti-frostbite cream. Then came socks, boots, jerseys and goggles, modelled one by one whilst Jigmet and Wangyal looked on in bewilderment.

Later, on the icefall, we did the food photographs, Barbara clicking away whilst Jigmet, Wangyal, and I sat on a photogenic rock with our peak in the background, eating chocolate, nuts, biscuits, sweets, and toffees. Jigmet joined in rather solemnly but Wangyal had really got the idea now. As he popped each goodie into his mouth, he assumed an expression of rapturous delight, a grin from ear to ear and eyes nearly popping out of his head. I have seldom laughed so much and half Barbara's photographs were blurred with camera-shake.

That evening as we camped on the glacier for the last time there was a magnificent sunset, the billowing storm clouds ablaze with fiery red light above the dark peaks. In ten minutes it had faded and snow was falling, but next morning was fine and sunny again. Everyone was in holiday spirits. We had a stone-throwing competition at an empty paraffin can; Barbara put up a most impressive show but eventually

Jigmet won, so Wangyal surreptitiously lashed a few rocks on to his load as a 'prize'.

Wangyal was in good form this morning; we discovered Pluto, my rubber mascot, tied to a boulder with an enormously thick piece of rope. Very earnestly Wangyal explained that he had been trying to go back up 'Mucky Shambles'. Later when I sat down to take a few last compass bearings and height readings, I suddenly found Wangyal sitting nearby imitating everything that I did, especially the pencil-chewing and hair-twiddling. He thought the prismatic compass was a marvellous toy, but when he discovered the bubble in the Abney spirit level he let out a whoop that brought Jigmet running from his tent. For the next six days he carried it everywhere, frequently taking it out of the case to make sure the bubble was still there.

Atchuk had already moved most of the spare equipment down to Shigri, but enough remained to give us all very heavy loads. It was a pleasant surprise when after about four miles we saw him walking up to meet us with an empty pack-frame. With lighter loads we sped down feeling fine, and reached the foot of the glacier at 4 p.m. An hour later Rikzin arrived with his three ponies, a remarkable piece of timing on both sides.

Rikzin was very agitated, talking excitedly in rapid Hindi, and eventually we gathered that he had been forced to sell his watch to pay off our donkeyman, whom we had arranged to pay in Manali but who apparently expected to be paid at the glacier. To prove his story Rikzin produced a letter written by a professional letter writer:

Dear Madams,

With due respect I beg to state that the owner of the three mules that were engaged for your good selves compelled me for payment at Manali. I was helpless to pay the aforesaid person since I am a poor man. But he threatened me, at the last I sold my wrist-watch. It is regretted that I had to suffer a great loss for the sake of your Honour and for the sake of my life, as he warned me to kill otherwise. You know these Tibetan Refugees they are rogues. So I request your honour to have a kind and favourable glance at my condition.

Thanking you in anticipation.

Rikzin Ladakhi.

Poor Rikzin really was worried, but we assured him that we would refund the price of his watch and give him some 'baksheesh' for all the trouble he had endured for our sake. When he had this in writing (not that he could read), he cheered up, and produced the extra food and paraffin he had brought from Manali and, best of all, letters from home. It was only six weeks since we had received the last mail but it seemed a lifetime.

That evening we spent in an orgy of eating. With the extra food we packed up a 'Christmas box' for our porters; amongst the contents were four packets of biscuits, a tinned fruit cake, tins of jam and cheese, six tubes of condensed milk, and a huge tin of dried meat labelled as twelve-man-days ration. All this they consumed in one evening.

The luxury menu we chose for ourselves was tinned steak and kidney pudding, carrots and rice, a tin of pears, ginger biscuits and drinking chocolate. Then came the bliss of our first real wash in hot water for three weeks, clean pyjamas, and letters to re-read before settling down to sleep.

Packing-up next morning was very slow, Wangyal and Jigmet seeming just as loath as we were to turn their backs on the mountains and bring it all to an end. Yet we had done everything we had hoped to do, and more. Our epic on the third peak had been a good end to the climbing, and there was a feeling that it was wiser to leave well alone now.

When we had been climbing the past and future had receded behind the immediate concerns of the present, but now as we started back to Manali, we began to discuss future plans. We must find jobs somewhere to tide us over the four winter months until we started for Nepal in March, but before getting jobs we very much wanted to fit in a visit to Kashmir, only two days' drive west from Manali and reputed to be the most beautiful valley in the world.

Deep in conversation Barbara and I strolled along, ahead of the rest, towards Batal. At mid-day we crossed the Batal bridge and settled down in the sun at our old campsite to wait for the ponies. We were both feeling very fit and full of energy, and planned that when camp was set up and we had had something to eat, we would climb the

2,000 ft up to the Kunzum Pass to have a look across the Inner Line into Spiti.

For an hour we dozed in the sun but still there was no sign of either ponies or porters. Then Atchuk suddenly appeared, pointing back down the river and gabbling about 'Chandra khola' and 'ghora'. At first we thought there had been an accident, but gradually realised that he was trying to explain that they had all crossed the river lower down and were camping at Choto Dara, twelve miles from Batal. It was ironic that on the way to the glacier we had tried hard to persuade Rikzin to take the ponies across the river but he had maintained that it was much too deep and swift; now on the way back he had forded it and we had walked an extra ten miles. And, of course, it was the one day that we had not bothered to pack up any lunch.

Atchuk thought it was a great joke, although he had had to walk an extra ten miles to retrieve us. Further on we met Wangyal who had walked several miles back from their camp to meet us. They both teased us non-stop but carried our rucksacks, and were most concerned when I took off my boots and found an enormous blister on each heel. All my thick socks were dirty so for our 'short day' to Batal I had put on thin socks, adequate for eight miles, but not for twenty.

At dusk we limped into camp, cold, tired, and very hungry. Jigmet fussed around, obviously feeling responsible for losing his charges, for the rest of the way he never let us out of his sight. Rikzin was most apologetic, apparently they had shouted and shouted after us, but without success. Wangyal did a lovely imitation of the scene with us walking purposefully to Batal, heads bent in earnest conversation. Gradually the stories grew taller and taller: Atchuk had retrieved us from a mountain top, from the clutches of the CID, from the Chinese. Everyone was in high spirits, and to add to the festivities another party appeared, some nomad herdsmen with a flock of sheep.

Much excited conversation ensued, then Jigmet formally asked us whether we would agree to exchange four gallons of our surplus paraffin for a sheep. It sounded a very good bargain to us. Paraffin was the only thing we had badly miscalculated, there was not much point in carrying the surplus back to Manali especially as the ponies were already overloaded, and a whole sheep for fifteen shillings' worth of paraffin did not seem an excessive price.

We were not anxious to see the slaughter done so retired into our tent. Wangyal, who never missed anything, realised that we were rather squeamish and crept round our tent making blood-curdling sheep noises. We wondered who would actually kill the sheep, since as Buddhists our Ladakhis were bound by their religion not to take life. Atchuk, however, did not take his religion so seriously that he could not kill a sheep, and next day he removed some Buddhist prayer flags and presented them to us as souvenirs.

In a surprisingly short time supper was ready and two huge platefuls of meat and rice were thrust into our tent. Tentatively we tasted it, and found it really tender and spicy, and seemingly all kidney, liver, and heart, we hoped nothing else. The next morning the headless carcass was wrapped in an old groundsheet, and lashed on to one of the ponies. We thought they must have disposed of the head until we saw a pair of horns protruding from Wangyal's rucksack, glassy eyes staring back at us. At the next camp they lit a dung fire in the lee of a boulder, and proceeded to cure it. It reappeared later, hairless, eyeless, and blackened, and then mysteriously disappeared for good.

The Chandra valley was now pleasantly green and cool, but deserted. All the Tibetans had gone, leaving only low stone walls and the remains of fires to show where their encampments had been.

We recrossed the Rhotang Pass on 15th October, the ponies struggling through five inches of fresh snow which had fallen in the night. This was the first heavy winter snowfall, arriving on the exact date that Rikzin had prophesied five weeks earlier. A few last traders were also hurrying over the pass, some of them barefoot in the snow.

Our last camp was by the clear Beas River, in a green meadow encircled by weeping willow trees. It was a lovely spot and for a long time we sat outside in the warm afternoon sun, feeling sad that this was the end. We had much to look forward to but it would be difficult to have a happier or better expedition than this had been. The porters too were unusually quiet, perhaps reflecting our mood. After supper they began to sing plaintive Ladakhi songs. Barbara, who had a very good voice, responded to their request for some English songs and the evening passed most pleasantly until a violent thunderstorm intervened.

Returning to Manali was a rather embarrassing business. As we unloaded the ponies a large crowd gathered round. The Indians stared at our sunburn and dirty clothes, and the Europeans treated us like heroines. We escaped to go and see Major Banon, who kindly gave us tea, a bag of fresh apples, and a room in the hotel.

Our room was on the ground floor and attached to it was a 'bathroom', an outhouse with concrete floor, water in buckets, and a tin tub. Sitting in a few inches of warm water in the tin tub, knees up to the chin or dangling over the side, was not exactly luxurious but an enjoyable sensation after five weeks without a bath. We both also managed to wash our hair, almost standing on our heads in the tub; at this point the lights went out. They stayed out for the next two hours, and by the light of one candle we had to try to unpack and find some respectable clothes to wear.

We had chosen to ignore expense for once and have a celebration meal in the hotel. Over dinner at the big communal table we were plied with questions about our trip, particularly by an American lecturer in Economics at Jaipur University who invited us to go and visit him and his wife, an invitation we were to take up four months later. Eventually the inevitable question came up, "What are you going to do now?" We explained our plan to find teaching jobs over the winter, whereupon from the end of the table a young Indian woman surprised us by saying, "Why not come and teach in my school?"

We thought she was joking, particularly as she looked far too young and gay to be a headmistress, but she went on to explain that with her two sisters she ran an international kindergarten in Delhi. It seemed she was short of teachers and could offer us jobs till March, teaching five mornings a week, with weekends free and a three-week Christmas holiday. The pay was the normal Indian teacher's salary, 200 rupees (£15) a month each, but she offered to find us cheap accommodation, perhaps semi-camping on the school premises.

We liked the sound of the school, and even more we liked Bim herself. Her proper name was Miss Bimla Nanda, but even at this first meeting we could not be formal with someone as young and engaging as Bim. She was small, with a warm smile and sympathetic dark eyes. Her hair was beautifully glossy and long, sometimes she wore it loose, sometimes bound up into a thick coil on top of her head. With her long dark hair, silk sari, and sandals she was wholly Indian, yet spoke perfect English without a trace of an accent.

We had little hesitation in accepting Bim's offer, for the job sounded congenial and would both keep us over the winter and allow plenty of free time. Our only reservations were that in a country as short of qualified teachers as India, we ought perhaps to teach in a secondary school of some sort rather than a pre-school. However, the Government day schools were unwilling to take teachers except for two whole terms and the boarding schools had very long winter holidays during the months that we needed jobs.

It was arranged that we should begin teaching on 5th November so that we would still have a fortnight for a much-needed rest and time to clear up the expedition correspondence before arriving in Delhi.

Before leaving for Kashmir we stayed three more days in Manali to see the beginning of the famous Kulu Dussehra. This Hindu festival celebrates the triumph of Good over Evil, symbolised by the victory of Rama, hero of the epic Ramayana, over the demon king Ravana. In Kulu the religious celebrations are accompanied by much trading, dancing, and general festivities.

The two days before the festival passed quickly but pleasantly. We sat in the garden writing letters, washed innumerable socks and clothes, cleaned all the equipment and the Land Rover inside and out, repacked it with the porters' enthusiastic help, and spent delightful evenings cooking enormous meals by the log fire in our room.

The first morning we walked down to the bazaar to send telegrams home. The Post Office was little more than a tin shack but these telegrams got through to England in one day. The Postmaster was very friendly and invited us inside. We went in only to find the CID man sitting there. He looked very stern and immediately began to cross examine us about our movements in the Chandra valley. To add to our difficulties he noticed Jigmet waiting for us outside, called him in, and proceeded to question him in Urdu and us in English simultaneously. Neither knew what story the other was telling; it would have been very funny had we not been afraid of being expelled from India. Then he asked the Postmaster for copies of the telegrams we had sent.

"Collecting flowers and watching birds?" he asked with a smile, and called for tea. With relief we realised that the 'case' was closed.

Early the following morning we went to watch the image of the local goddess, Hidimba, being carried down from the ancient wooden temple above Manali on the first stage of her twenty-four mile journey to the festival at Kulu. It was a lovely autumn morning, clear and fresh with dew sparkling on the grass. Faintly, horns sounded from among the dark deodars, then trumpeters appeared in white, red, and gold, a brilliant splash of colour against the azure sky. Finally came a gaily decked palanquin bearing Hidimba, a dazzling bronze image with hideous grin, almost smothered in orange and yellow flowers. As she was carried by, the local women and children eagerly threw yet more posies and garlands on to the palanquin.

The setting for the festival was a large grass Maidan in the centre of Kulu, similar to an English village green except that it was dotted with huge conifers. Besides the ubiquitous Tibetans, many of whom had been working in the Chandra valley when we went by and greeted us like long-lost friends, there were Lahuli women with spectacular tall head-dresses studded with turquoise beads, and Kulu women in black home-spun with different coloured head-cloths. These were rather 'biblical' in appearance; we found out later that newly-married women wore red head-dresses, matrons black, widows white, and unmarried girls went bare-headed.

Later we were fortunate enough to see some Kulu dancing. All the dancers were male, dressed in pleated white tunics and long white socks; in a line they slowly circled and turned to the discordant music of cymbals, horns, and drums.

The opening ceremony was scheduled for 4 p.m. but no one except us seemed surprised when it was two hours late. As the sun slowly withdrew up the hillsides palanquins bearing the gods and goddesses from every temple in the valley surged together in the centre of the Maidan, surrounded by a seething crowd. The greying of the mountain back-cloth only served to intensify the mass of brilliant colour.

When the local Rajah had arrived on a white horse and the image of Hidimba had been put in a carriage under a resplendent red-and-gold canopy, to a deafening blare of trumpets the procession moved forward, all the people struggling to put a hand on the rope pulling Hidimba's carriage to bring them luck in the coming year.

After several rounds of the Maidan the procession broke up, and the palanquins were carried off, each to its own tent for the night. Whilst watching one being put away with great ceremony, we saw the image begin to violently sway in spite of the apparent efforts of the bearers to keep it still. It was very eerie; if they were merely acting, it was a remarkable performance. We were told that the god sways when he is angry or has a message to impart. A crowd immediately gathered round and the image was questioned by a priest, who in a sort of trance interpreted the silent utterances of the god.

The following morning we finally left Manali, saying goodbye to all the friends we had made there. Of the porters Wangyal and Jigmet were coming with us for we had offered them a lift to Srinagar. From Manali it would have been a four-week walk for them to their homes in Ladakh, but from Srinagar it was only thirteen days. Rikzin was staying in Kulu, Atchuk was going back to his job as a photographer's assistant in Calcutta. When we said goodbye he gave us each a photograph of the Dalai Lama which he had printed himself.

There was not much room in the back for Jigmet and Wangyal but they managed to squeeze in, and when we pulled up at Kulu we found two other characters sitting on the tail board who thanked us for the ride, although they were covered in white dust from the unmade road.

Driving on down the valley we camped at dusk in a lush meadow near the river. Jigmet was not feeling well so went to bed as soon as the tents were up, but Wangyal cooked a magnificent supper. Afterwards the three of us sat outside sipping coffee, watching night gradually settling on the fields and hills. Wangyal was wonderfully at ease, and even the language barrier seemed to fade away as he told us of his home in Ladakh, his family, and his life in the winter there, looking after sheep, oxen, and yak.

His home obviously meant a great deal, but every spring he would leave on the thirty-day walk to Manali to go to the mountains again. Of our three porters Wangyal seemed the only one who really loved mountains for their own sake. We lingered a long time, filled with a wistful sadness that such a perfect time should have to end, yet happy that whatever the future should bring, no one could take away from us the memory of these weeks. Tomorrow we would leave Kulu behind; this evening was like a last fond backward glance at a treasured familiar world. I was reminded of the last lines of Lycidas :

And now the sun had stretched out all the hills,
And now was dropt into the western bay:
At last he rose, and twitch'd his mantle blue:
Tomorrow to fresh woods, and pastures new.

12 AUTUMN IN KASHMIR

The walls were green with slime, a steady shower of drips fell from the roof, and the road was a series of lakes. We were driving through the Banihal Tunnel which cuts the last few hundred feet off the 9,000-foot Banihal Pass, the only road leading from India into Kashmir. The country of Jammu south of the pass had been very beautiful but when we emerged from the tunnel's dripping blackness, the scene was breathtaking. The whole Vale of Kashmir was spread out at our feet. A riot of autumn colours, russet, orange, and acid green, led the eye down to the distant valley floor patterned with tiny rice fields, farmsteads, and silvery rivers and lakes. Encircling the whole was a high mountain chain, rising in pine-clad slopes to a rim of snow washed gold in the evening sun.

We camped overlooking the Vale, then next morning dropped into the landscape to reach its centre, Srinagar. Now the pattern broke into its individual components, slender poplars shedding a shower of yellow leaves, wooden farmsteads rising mistily above grey water and swaying reeds, pumpkins, corn, and red peppers ripening on the thatched roofs. Never had I seen autumn like this. It seemed even to be reflected in the colours of Kashmiri dress, rich brown, mustard-yellow, wine-red, orange, and muted peacock-blue.

Nothing jarred to break the spell till we entered the ugly streets of modern Srinagar. As we drove into the centre a Kashmiri cycled alongside violently waving. "It must be a one-way street," Barbara said, and pulled up quickly, but all the Kashmiri wanted was to extol the attractions of his house-boat.

"Verra good boat," he said. "Verra cheap, special price for Engleesh."

We were in fact intending to stay on a house-boat for a few days but this high-pressure salesmanship dampened our enthusiasm and we drove to the bank, our first essential call. This was right in the town centre and as soon as we stopped a seething mob surrounded us, waving Kashmiri handicrafts for sale or pictures of their house-boats. In the centre of a tight throng we pushed our way to the bank.

Fortunately only customers were allowed inside, but when we re-emerged the shouting redoubled.

Driving right out of the town, we stopped on a quiet road and read the guidebook to find the most inaccessible Rest House in Kashmir. Finally we chose Gulmarg, described as the most attractive and salubrious resort in Kashmir and situated at 8,500 ft. The last 2,000 ft could only be covered on foot, by pony or, with special permission, by jeep. To obtain a permit we had to visit the Tourist Office. We were shown into a pleasant office where the Tourist Officer signed our permit to drive to Gulmarg. When we complained about the crowds of salesmen and boat-owners he just shrugged.

"What can we do?" he asked. "They must live. It is the end of the season, and a cold winter is coming."

Elbowing our way back to the Land Rover, we drove off at high speed to the Post Office, our last call. It seemed gloriously deserted, but as we got out, one of the Tourist Office throng appeared on a bicycle. He kept waving what looked like the usual letter of recommendation, but then explained that the letter was from an English lady we had met, who had told him to look out for two young English girls in a Land Rover. Feeling very contrite, we agreed to go and look at his house-boat, with a view to spending a day or two there after Gulmarg.

With a triumphant grin he led the way on his bicycle past his friends at the Tourist Office. The house-boat was moored on the Jhelum River which runs through the centre of Srinagar; it was called the Maharajah's Palace and was enormous. There were three luxurious bedrooms, a huge drawing and dining room with thick carpet and beautiful walnut furniture, and, most impressive of all, a tiled English-style bathroom with running hot water.

We were treated, 'under no obligation', to lunch in the Palace. It was an excellent meal, but we wondered whether the standard would be maintained once we definitely agreed to stay. Over coffee the boatman tried very hard to persuade us to use the house-boat as a base to do day trips to Gulmarg and the other places we wanted to see but we would not be persuaded. We said however that we would stay a few days when we returned from Gulmarg, if he could offer a smaller but comfortable boat on one of the lakes with a good view. He obliged for the ridiculously cheap price of ten rupees a day each.

Twenty-four miles of pleasant driving took us from Srinagar to Tanmarg, a small resort at the foot of the jeepable road to Gulmarg.

The inevitable souvenir-men appeared, but we were rescued from their clutches by the Tourist Officer. His job seemed to be to make us stay in Tanmarg. He did his best to put us off Gulmarg, telling us that it was deserted, there were no shops or cafés, and the Tourist Officer there had left. It sounded ideal to us.

"Anyway the road is quite impassable now," he went on. We might have believed him, had not a jeep come down it at that moment. When we pointed this out, he replied, "Ah, it is possible to come down to Tanmarg, but not to go up." We said we would try anyway, and to our relief he gave up and let us go.

The track was muddy and steep with hairpin bends so tight that we could not get round them in one, but in four-wheel drive and low gears the Land Rover churned upwards very happily until she abruptly gave a chug and stopped. We had run out of petrol. In fact we still had more than a gallon, but it had run to the back of the tank on the steep hill.

We could not turn round or get off the track, which had a bank on the inside and a sheer drop down through the pine-woods on the outside. The only possibility was to back down again, but even with Barbara directing from behind this was none too easy on the narrow muddy track.

There was one particularly nasty moment when we came to a deep ravine, bridged by just two tree trunks for either wheel. On the 1 in 4 hill the Land Rover had gathered considerable momentum and when I tentatively touched the brake the wheels slewed in the mud and we nearly went over the edge. Wrenching her back again, we careered on backwards towards the bridge, Barbara desperately trying to direct me on to the tree trunks. There was a sickening jolt, I had a fleeting glimpse of the void below, and then we were across. A little below there was a side track leading off uphill and thankfully I ran her up it until we lost speed, then gently drifted down and came to rest on the side of the main track.

We were incredibly lucky for in less than half an hour the only other vehicle still using the Gulmarg road chanced to come up. It was an Indian army jeep and the charming Major offered to take us up to Gulmarg and bring some petrol down to the Land Rover next day. He dropped us at the Rest House, which proved to be one of the most pleasant Rest Houses that we found anywhere.

Set on a small hill amid the green meadows and pine trees, it was a long wooden bungalow with encircling verandah. No one else was staying there so we had a choice of twenty rooms. We finally settled on a corner one with two big windows, a large fireplace and colourful hand-woven curtains and bedspreads. Behind was a dressing-room which we used as a kitchen, and a bathroom with both running water, and, greatest wonder of all, a flush toilet.

Next morning I went off with the Major to fetch the Land Rover, and ten minutes later was granted an unforgettable view to 26,660-foot (8,126 m) Nanga Parbat, a glistening cone of ice soaring above the far horizon eighty miles away. Remembering the six expeditions who had tried to climb it and the thirty-one lives it had claimed before yielding at last to the fantastic solo attempt of Hermann Buhl, I looked at it with awe. Even as I gazed, clouds wreathed the summit and it disappeared from sight. Although we looked many times during our five days in Gulmarg, it obstinately remained hidden till I think Barbara doubted its existence altogether.

These were idyllic days, days of sitting writing in the warm sun and wandering through the cool deodar forests, soft pine-needles underfoot and a smell of resin in the air, collecting firewood for an evening roasting chestnuts by the fire.

The peace was undisturbed, the Army seemed to have gone, and the only other inhabitants of the meadows were a wonderful old English couple, the Phillimores. They were both over eighty but remarkably active; one morning Mrs Phillimore came trotting up on a pony to invite us to tea. Their bungalow was old and weatherbeaten but very solid, and warm and comfortable inside. As we sat down on a big sofa by the fire and were introduced to their golden spaniel in his little woollen coat, I thought how very English it all was. Then a uniformed butler came in and announced tea by ringing a silver handbell. There were home-made scones, toasted tea-cakes, neat little sandwiches and a wonderful chocolate cake, all made by their Indian cook who had been with them for decades. We ate vast quantities, watched with beaming approval by the butler and by the Phillimores, who kept pressing us to "just one more scone" until we could not manage another mouthful.

Mrs Phillimore simply could not understand how we could manage without servants or that we travelled unchaperoned. Sadly she said that she did not see how they could fit into life in modern England now, but even after fifty years in India England was still very definitely Home. Every day they listened to the BBC news and assiduously read their airmail copy of *The Times*.

A heavy snowfall drove us down from Gulmarg on the 29th October. Under its three-inch mantle of snow the meadow looked enchanting but our thoughts were on getting the Land Rover down the tortuous 2,000-foot descent to Tanmarg and the valley floor. Gingerly we headed downwards; the roof of pine trees had kept much of the snow off the track but it was a relief when we rounded the last hairpin and emerged into the Vale. It had been snowing down to about 7,000 ft but below it was raining and went on raining for the next two days.

We were glad to have the sanctuary of a house-boat, now a two-berth boat called the *Bul-Bul* moored on the shore of the Nagin Lake. Outside all we could see was lashing rain and grey water but inside the *Bul-Bul* was a haven of warmth and comfort with a wood-burning stove, deep armchairs and finely-carved furniture, its polish reflecting the soft glow of hand-painted table lamps.

A kindly old man in white turban and dhoti looked after us, producing the most delicious meals from the cook-boat next door. Our second evening was particularly memorable: after a dinner of wild duck and soufflé omelette we had our first hot baths since leaving England three months earlier.

During the continual rainstorms we would have been content never to move from our house-boat, but time was passing and before leaving Srinagar we wanted to see some of the famous handicrafts of Kashmir. We made several excursions into the town, sadly ill-equipped for the weather in our sandals and summer clothes, but the only alternative was boots and climbing trousers and at this time we were still very sensitive to the stares and comments of those around.

We saw fine carpets being woven and men embroidering 'numdas', rugs or carpets of thick felt made from goats' wool that has been sprinkled with water and then pounded underfoot. Then our boatman took us to a large woodwork factory. Starting from the pile of logs outside, we followed the whole process of manufacture through a bewildering rabbit-warren of small rooms until the *objets d'art* finally emerged into the showrooms on the top floor.

Everything was done entirely by hand, for labour is considerably cheaper than even simple machinery. The craftsmen sat cross-legged on the floor, with a tiny hammer and chisel carving out the intricate designs they had pencilled on the wood. The motifs were mainly drawn from nature, and we recognised kingfishers, herons, the jaunty crested bul-bul, lotus-flowers, roses, and, most common of all, the distinctive five-fingered leaf of the chenar tree, the special glory and symbol of Kashmir. The salerooms were a fairyland of beautiful things and to our joy the prices were very reasonable. As we purchased Christmas presents to be sent home our boatman's eyes lit up. He must have been getting commission on everything we bought.

It was so cold that we were each given a 'kangri' to hold. These are small baskets of glowing charcoal which are held between the hands. Everyone in Kashmir uses them in winter, the women holding them underneath their voluminous robes next to their bare skin. If constantly used, they leave a black burn mark. We noticed these on some men's hands, and according to our boatman the same thing happens under the women's robes. "You think our women fair, is it not?" he said, "but we know they are not so fair."

Most of the men now wear European clothes, but in the rigours of the Kashmir winter don fur hats and thick woollen blankets which they wrap around themselves like Scottish plaids. As we watched blanket-wrapped businessmen going to their offices, kangri in hand, I thought how excellent these would be for the English winter.

After two days of leaden skies we woke up to a brilliant morning. Raindrops on the trees sparkled in the sun and snow-covered mountains cast long reflections across the smooth stillness of the lake. Fresh, clear, and sunny, it was a day to be out on the water in a 'shikara' - a water taxi poled or paddled along - and we took one across the Dal Lake to the Moghul Shalimar Gardens. Only a few marigolds and bronze wallflowers still bravely bloomed but the trees were a splendour of autumn colour.

It was time to be leaving for Delhi, and the next day was our last in Kashmir. We spent it on the roof of the *Bul-Bul* being slowly poled down the lakes and river back to Dal Gate in the old part of Srinagar. As we drifted past houses and temples, the mountains, lakes and poplar trees slowly wreathed themselves in a gauze of mist and wood-smoke, becoming insubstantial as a dream, while the pole-men, chanting in soft unison, steadily propelled us back to the hubbub of ordinary life.

13 DELHI: THE OLD AND THE NEW

We saw two dead bodies on the way down the Grand Trunk road. There were several cars pulled up by the first, but the second was just lying gorily twisted in the middle of the road. It was a young boy. We slowed down to stop but then remembered Bim's last words to us: "For heaven's sake don't stop if you see a corpse or dead cow on the road." This warning had been repeated to us a dozen times, together with gruesome stories of drivers being pulled out of their cars and lynched after accidents. We drove on to the next village and told a policeman there. He did not seem particularly concerned, but said he would cycle up later on.

During our stay in India driving up and down the Grand Trunk Road became a recurrent nightmare. The traffic was chaotic and there was a continuous stream of lumbering bullock carts, wobbly trishaws and bicycles carrying as many as five of a family at once. A fair proportion of India's two hundred million cows wandered or lay on the road. Everywhere there were people, women carrying water-jars, men urinating by the roadside, naked sadhus smeared with ash. Children played in stagnant pools alongside water buffaloes, the air stank of manure and rotting vegetation, and mercilessly the sun beat down, blistering the flat grey landscape and crumbling mud huts.

In the narrow streets of Old Delhi the concentration of flies, smells, animals and sweating humanity became almost overpowering. Completely lost we crawled through at walking pace, beggars curiously peering in through the windows and lepers holding out fingerless stumps for baksheesh. At last we emerged into the open spaces of New Delhi, hot, dirty, tired and very depressed. We phoned Bim. It was cheering to hear her voice again, warm and welcoming, and immediately she invited us to join her and her sisters for lunch at a relative's house.

Driving through the tree-lined avenues of New Delhi we at last found the house, a modern white mansion in a spacious green garden. A uniformed servant opened the door, we gave our names, and without a word he ushered us through a lofty marble hall into a pillared courtyard. Here a group of middle-aged Indian women were sitting playing cards with piles of hundred-rupee notes on the table.

Diamonds sparkled at their ears and throats, and midriffs bulged over rich silk saris. We felt very awkward and out of place until a younger woman appeared from another room and said, "Ah you must be the English girls". She explained she was Padma, Bim's younger sister. There was little family resemblance for Padma was much taller than Bim with her dark hair cut fashionably short to shoulder length. Then we met Meena, the youngest sister of the three, who was not unlike Padma except for rather sharper features and a mischievous twinkle in her eyes.

At last Bim turned up and took us under her wing; there was a whirlwind round of introductions and then a sumptuous buffet lunch, with tables laden under huge dishes of hot and cold food. Most exotic of all were the sweets, including a gigantic cream soufflé covered in patterns of silver foil. It looked delicious but I could not see how one got rid of the silver foil so passed it by. Alas, Indian silver foil is edible.

It was refreshing to leave the mansion and go home with Bim. Her family lived in much homelier surroundings in the ground-floor flat of a house in Defence Colony, a mass of two-storey houses built on what was jungle a few years earlier. The land was originally granted to army officers, hence the name Defence Colony.

In this sort of house the upstairs flat usually has the use of the roof, the downstairs flat the garden. In the Nandas' flat there was a large sitting-room, a dining-room, two bedrooms with adjoining bathrooms, and a tiny kitchen where all cooking was done over charcoal fires. Like all upper-class Indian families the Nandas had servants, a bearer (general manservant-cum-butler), cook, sweeper (for all household chores), and twice a week a dhobi (washerman).

To have servants was a new experience for us but we were rather taken aback at their subservient and submissive role, and the lack of respect or even thanks which they seemed to expect.

The servants for their part were sometimes rather nonplussed by unexpected politeness and consideration from Westerners. I remember Bim telling us of a cook of theirs who had gone to work for a young American who had just moved into a new flat. There was as yet no bed in the servant's room, so the American made up his own bed for the servant and one for himself on a sofa. In horror the cook rang up Bim, "The sahib has gone mad, he will not let me sleep on the floor."

We spent a week at the Nandas' house while Bim helped us to search for accommodation. It was a very pleasant time; each morning began with 'bed-tea', then a breakfast of fruit and delicious hot chapattis spread with jam. During the day we seemed to have meals at almost hourly intervals, for the Nandas had adopted the American mid-morning coffee break and the English afternoon tea, whilst retaining the large Indian lunch and late dinner. As Hindus of course they did not eat beef, and the diet was largely vegetarian apart from chicken. Rice and chapattis provided the starch and the main vegetable was dal, a type of lentils boiled to a liquid green mush which tasted better than it looked. With the curries, cold unsweetened curd was often served, and this was something I grew to like very much.

Everyone was expected to eat large quantities and not to have a second helping was taken very amiss. Such huge quantities of starchy food were hardly conducive to a svelte appearance and Barbara and I both put on a stone in four months.

We had arrived in Delhi on 4th November to be in time for the festival of Diwali, which celebrates Rama's victorious return to his capital from exile and has come to be the Hindu 'New Year'. It is a lovely festival of lamps, for every house is lit by winking 'divas' - little earthenware lamps with a cotton wick soaked in oil - to welcome Lakshmi, a goddess symbolising wealth and prosperity. The fortunes of each household for the coming year are foretold by the length of time the lamps stay alight. When we drove around on the first evening every house and garden was lit up and even the smallest shack had a 'diva' on each side of the doorstep.

6th November was the climax of Diwali which the Nandas kept as a family festival. With present-giving and all the festivities it seemed much like our Christmas, and, like Christmas, it seemed to be all things to all people. In the afternoon there was another long gambling session. Curiously only the women seemed to play. The gambling begins two or three months before Diwali, at first two or three times a week, and then as the festival approaches, every day.

This was the very last gambling session for the year so stakes, and tension, were high. Meanwhile Bim prepared for the religious side

1   *The author on the first female lead of Cenotaph Corner*

2   *The author and Barbara Spark with their trusty Land Rover*

Preparing camp on the long drive to India

On the trek into Kulu

5 *Ladakhi porters Wangyal and Jigmet, Barbara, Jo and the ponyman, Rikzin, with the 'hotel' proprietor at the back*

6 *Crossing one of the many fast-flowing creeks*

Jo suffering f

8   *The Tibetan camp where the doctor gave Jo penicillin*

10   *Jo surveying the Lion Glacier using
the carefully-transported plane table*

Barbara with Wangyal and Jigmet on the summit of Central Peak

3   *Our third peak was 20,495 ft (6,247 m) Shigrila
        with our route indicated in red.*

14   *Overwintering in Manali with Bimla and Padma*

15   *The beautiful Nigeen Lake, Srinagar*

16   *Jagdula expedition team, L to R back Jo, Pat, Dorothea, middle row Ang Temba, Pemba Norbu 1, Mingma, Dawa, Pemba Norbu 2, front row Barbara, Denise, Pasang, Katcheri, Ang Pema, Nancy, Krishna Rana (Liaison Offi...*

7 *Base Camp at about 14,000 ft L to R: Dorothea, Nancy, Pat and Denise*

8 *Nancy Smith, our doctor, held a clinic every night at our camp, and people would walk for miles for treatment*

19   *Camp 2 (left) on Lha Shamma*

20   *View from Camp II across to the Kagmara range. Kagmara 1 (on the left*

21   *Lha Shamma seen from Kagmara Lekh, showing the camps and route*

22   *Jo, Mingma and Barbara on the summit of Lha Shamma,
looking north towards Tibet (May 13th 1962)*

23 *With their long dark hair and sheepskin clothes the men looked very fierce but could not have been friendlier.*

Denise filming the yaks from a tree

*Dorothea on one of the 'gangways' bordering
the idyllic Phoksumdo Lake*

27   *One of many 'no-good' bridges*

28   *The airport at Pokhara, from where the whole team and the Sherpas flew to Kathmandu - it was Barbara and Jo's first ever flight*

29 *Photograph taken in Turkey on the long drive home*

30 *From L to R: Barbara, Denise, Nancy, Pat and Jo outside Cwm Dyli, the Pinnacle Club hut, during the 2004 expedition reunion*

of the festival, the Tikka ceremony. At dusk she went round with a taper lighting all the divas outside, then brought in a large brass tray with a bronze figure of Lakshmi set in the centre, lit by the light of two divas. Everyone knelt round the tray, offerings and prayers were made to the goddess, and then Bim put a red tikka mark in the centre of each person's forehead, including ours, symbolising friendship and brotherhood.

The day finished with a party in another family's house. As it was an all-Indian party and Diwali the Nandas were very anxious that we should wear saris and dressed Barbara in green and me in red. It felt very awkward and insecure at first but we soon became accustomed to them, and blended in to the party much better than in European short skirts. Our hostess took it as a great compliment that we should wear saris and it seemed to ease the atmosphere all round. Many Indian women are embarrassed by the amount of bare leg exposed by Western dress. Their own legs are always discreetly covered under the sari or 'salwar-kameez', the Punjabi dress of tunic over baggy trousers, and, if they wear Western dress at all, it is slacks and never a skirt. This, of course, does not apply to the Anglo-Indians who usually dress like Westerners.

The day after Diwali we began teaching at the Playhouse School, an international pre-school. The thought of facing a class of five-year-olds that first morning made me more frightened than anything we had encountered in the Himalayas, perhaps because there I had some idea of what to expect whereas now I was faced with the absolutely unknown. Barbara, however, had some experience with this age group and was very reassuring, and when they hurtled in, they proved to be as affectionate as any children and reasonably controllable.

I began with a class of ten, three Indians, one German, two Vietnamese, and four Americans. All understood English very well except for the Vietnamese, who were there to learn it. The school was situated out of doors in a large garden with tables and chairs for each class round the side of a lawn. If the sun became too hot we would move under the shade of wide-spreading trees, havens for tame but cheeky chipmunks. On the occasional rainy days the school closed.

Indians and Americans formed the two largest groups in the school, with a sprinkling of ten other nationalities. Approximately ninety were enrolled, ranging in age from two and a half to seven years. The upbringing of the upper-class Indian children often seemed to be left largely in the hands of the servants, especially the 'ayah' (nurse). In the wealthier households there was an ayah for each child. They had no training or authority to discipline the children in any way but would slavishly follow their charges round, obeying their every command. In school the ayahs would sit round the edge of the lawn waiting to escort the children home, and children who were reproved by their teachers would invariably run to the ayahs for consolation and sweets.

The first mornings in school seemed very long and at the end of the three hours we felt quite exhausted. Then in the afternoon we usually spent another two or three hours preparing work for the next day. I could only envy Barbara's artistic ability and skill at handicrafts as she produced beautiful work for her class, and often for mine too.

After a week at the Nandas, we moved to the flat of a young American Embassy couple to look after their four-year-old daughter while they were on holiday. Our duties were nominal for there was an ayah to look after Cassi, and a cook, bearer, and sweeper. Hamadin, the cook, produced superb meals, for he had been chief chef in one of the best restaurants in Delhi until Partition in 1947 when he lost his job because he was a Muslim. Since then he had worked entirely for Western families.

When the Clarridges returned, we discovered that they had recently spent two years in Kathmandu and were able to tell us a great deal about Nepal. Dewey Clarridge had developed a keen interest in mountaineering there, and took us out to a cliff outside Delhi that he had discovered. It was an old quarry with a rock face of about two hundred feet, including a spectacular detached pinnacle. Around the foot were stone-chippers who stared open-mouthed as we roped up and began to climb. The rock was dry and sound and the climbing not difficult but we came across a giant hornets' nest and reached the top with angry hornets zooming round our heads. Peering over the other side of the pinnacle in search of an easy route down, we saw a snake-charmer sitting on the ground, piping cobras off the cliff. We did not go rock-climbing in India again.

Eventually we moved to a rooftop known as a 'barsatti' for which we paid a rent of £2 a week. It comprised a concrete terrace overlooking the rooftops of New Delhi, an unfurnished room with adjoining Indian-style lavatory and the use of the bathroom in the downstairs flat. We slept on camp beds, cooked on primus stoves set on a table of tin trunks, and kept our clothes in a wardrobe constructed from an upended charpoy and polythene ground-sheeting. Later various friends lent us carpet and other furniture and it became almost civilised. In the daytime we hardly used the room for it was warm enough to sit outside on the terrace, but the evenings were chilly and then we sat round a tiny electric fire. In fact very few evenings were spent in our room, for already we had made a large number of friends, and there was much to see and do.

Once or twice a week we used to go to Evan and Joy Charlton's house to look after their eight-year-old son whilst they were out. They were English but had been in Delhi for fifteen years and in India even longer. Evan Charlton was Editor of *The Statesman,* one of India's leading English newspapers. I remember well our first meeting with him. We were sitting talking to his wife when Evan strode in, looking very tall, distinguished, and severe.

"So you are the globe-trotters," he said, "I get dozens of them in my office every week trying to sell me their unique stories, bearded scruffs who have cycled from England or come on roller-skates from Australia or God knows where."

He looked us up and down.

"Well, you look clean enough, and you don't have beards, but I'm allergic to GTs so talk about anything but your travels."

We hardly dared to open our mouths for weeks but Evan mellowed on acquaintance and he and Joy became amongst our closest friends. Their knowledge of Delhi combined with that of the Nandas was invaluable and ensured that we missed little of what there was to see.

It is quite easy to find one's way round the inner area of New Delhi for it is carefully planned with wide straight roads radiating from two central points, the All-India War Memorial in the area of Government House, and Connaught Place, the arcaded shopping centre. Here in the official centre there is deliberate spaciousness but a few miles further out the houses crowd each other in a desperate fight for a foothold. They have not yet begun to build upwards and very few houses exceed two storeys.

On the east Delhi is bounded by the wide Jumna River, on the west by the Ridge, the escarpment of low hills from which the small British force led by Brigadier-General John Nicholson took Delhi by storm to end the Indian Mutiny in 1857. To the north lies Old Delhi, to which the new city is tied by the alignment of the Government Secretariat with the great mosque, the Jami Masjid.

Old Delhi was much more the India I had imagined, its narrow dusty streets teeming with life and noise. We would wander down Chandni Chowk, past the open-fronted shops and stalls with their lurid soft drinks and mounds of sickly sweetmeats covered in flies, past the beggars displaying their deformities on the steps of the Jami Masjid, into the fascinating markets where one could buy anything from goats to exquisite silver jewellery.

Cows roamed the streets, occasionally stopping to browse at a vegetable stall or defecate on the pavement. Stray dogs and beggars scavenged amongst the rubbish. Strident music blared from the tea-shops and the fragrance of joss sticks mingled with the smell of sewers, garbage and urine.

Beyond the shops were the shanty towns, peopled by the 400,000 refugees who poured into Delhi after Partition. There we saw shacks made of mud, old petrol cans and straw matting standing beside open sewers where dead rats floated.

After several visits to Old Delhi I knew that I could not come to India as a tourist again. If I came back it would have to be to attempt something more useful. More and more we felt guilty at our comfortable jobs, yet, even had we been able to find something more worthwhile, our meagre talents seemed hopelessly inadequate to make more than a token contribution.

As things were we spent our time trying to see as much of Indian life as possible. Our Indian friends were equally anxious that we should miss nothing. Not only did they take us out sight-seeing and to displays of Indian art, dancing and music, but also invited us to many family functions in their homes. Amongst these we attended several weddings, for the months of November and December had been declared particularly auspicious by the astrologers.

One of these weddings took place in the flat below us and we saw the whole ceremony. For more than a week beforehand the preparations went on. In the back garden we could see the cooks tirelessly working over charcoal fires, whilst in a small marquee all the women relatives and friends of the bride sang to drum music. This was directly below our bedroom window and went on for three nights. All the women were in silk saris except for the bride, who traditionally for several weeks before her wedding must dress in rags and leave her hair unkempt so that on the wedding day the contrast will make her look even more beautiful.

The astrologers are consulted to find an auspicious day and time for the wedding, which is always after sunset and usually around two o'clock or three o'clock in the morning. Whatever time the actual ceremony takes place, there is a reception first when the bridegroom arrives on the traditional white horse at the head of a procession. He used to ride from his own house to that of the bride but in 1961 in Delhi the usual system was to come by car to the nearest corner and mount a horse there.

Usually all the guests except very close friends and family leave before the actual wedding ceremony, but we were fortunate to be invited to stay on one occasion.

The bride and groom sat side by side under a flower-bedecked canopy, the groom in white and a turban, the bride wearing the traditional red sari and all her jewellery, including a pendant on her forehead and diamond nose-stud. The whole ceremony was in Sanskrit and took three hours which, we were told, was a remarkably speedy wedding. The ancient language of India meant as little to the other people there as it did to us and everyone except the bridal couple chatted among themselves. The climax came after the priest had thrown handfuls of rice on to the sacred fire. The groom led the bride seven times round the fire, imploring her to take one step for force, two steps for strength, three steps for the increase of wealth, four steps for well-being, five for offspring, six for the season and seven as a

119

friend. "Be thou faithful to me, may we have many sons, and may they attain a ripe old age." Then the groom tied the sacred thread round the bride's neck and the wedding was over.

Our first term's teaching finished on 18th December with a Christmas party as the grand climax. It was almost a grand debacle for a high wind tore at the elaborate decorations and displays of class-work, our cottonwool snowman blew away, and Santa Claus became entangled in an electrical cable when he arrived on his camel.

It was a relief when term was over and we could have a relaxed Christmas holiday seeing more of India. In a way both of us had been rather dreading Christmas for it seemed such a time for family gatherings, yet we were thousands of miles away. Fortunately we found little time to feel homesick. On Christmas morning there was church, breakfast with the Nandas who had prepared a Christmas tree especially for us, a visit to the Charltons, and then Christmas dinner at the Clarridges, where Hamadin had made a Christmas cake for the family in the form of the Taj Mahal, a perfect copy in every detail. It was a fitting end to a very international Christmas.

14 RAJASTHAN

For our fortnight's holiday we decided to drive south from Delhi into Rajasthan, a state notable for its fine scenery, temples and palaces.

We set off in holiday mood, glad to be on the road again. The air was fresh and clear, the sun warm but not too hot, and the sky a deep blue. Everything seemed brighter and cleaner, without the dusty-grey overwash of the northern plains. It was fertile country with fields of bright yellow mustard, bubbling brown irrigation streams, monkeys loping along the road, parrots dipping from tree to tree, and in the fields the startling turquoise of wild peacocks.

At intervals we passed through villages of thatched mud huts, with women gathered round the well and smoke wisping lazily from the roofs. Poverty could not have been more obvious, or more picturesque.

All the land was a network of irrigation channels, the water drawn from deep stone wells. Near Delhi we had seen Persian wells, with a camel walking round and round drawing a pole to operate a water wheel of buckets, but here the water level was too deep for that system. In some places there were tube-wells with mechanical pumping, but the usual laborious method was for the water to be drawn up in a large skin bucket by a rope running over a pulley to two bullocks, which provided the power by walking down a short steep incline. As one pair went down another pair were led back up to repeat the process.

As we went farther south the country became more arid until it was virtually desert. Ranges of rocky hills broke the flatness and the road wound up and down through spectacular gorges. Amongst the hills there was the occasional town, jarring the traveller with its noise, not noise of traffic, but noise of hundreds of people milling about, talking, arguing, shouting, bargaining, begging. The high narrow streets seemed to channel the heat, smells and flies, and it was always a relief to escape into the country again.

Sight-seeing was by no means easy. In the less-visited towns like Ajmer we were followed everywhere by beggars and small boys asking for baksheesh. In the tourist places there were fewer beggars but would-be guides were almost as much of a nuisance. Occasionally, however, we were left alone and could enjoy just standing and watching the surge of life around. There was no purposeful rush as in the West, but a constant movement. Standing in a doorway near the centre of Jaipur, we seemed the only spectators of a scene which was so colourful, so alive, as to seem hardly real to eyes used to the relative drabness of English towns. Camel trains, tongas, bullock carts and bicycles passed before a soaring pink palace, a dancing bear went through its paces, urchins darted on to the road to collect fresh cow dung, a saffron-clad Sadhu stood still in contemplation, village women walked by erect in brilliant orange, red, and yellow, the colours of Rajasthan.

Fortified hills overlooking the walled city bore witness to Rajasthan's stormy past. One of the historic warrior races of India, the Rajputs won great fame by their fierce resistance to the Muslim invasions of Akbar and his predecessors. When at last they were overcome, many fled to the Himalayas where they gave rise to a new race of warriors, the Gurkhas of Nepal.

At Chittorgarh we saw the ancient fort which was once their stronghold. Massive walls three miles long encircle a hilltop 500 ft above the plain, the only approach a steep ramp with seven gates. The city's history has been turbulent even by Rajput standards. Three times it was sacked, each time when all hope was lost the women performed 'jauhar', immolating themselves by fire in an underground cave, and the men donned their bridal robes of saffron and went out to die fighting.

Inside the fort are some fine Hindu and Jain temples, their lush decoration and profusion of sculpture a strong contrast to the severely mathematical early Muslim architecture we had seen in Delhi and the Punjab. Outstanding among the monuments were two victory towers, one 75 ft high and the other 120 ft, both covered with sculptures from base to top. The nude figures had the same full breasts and fleshiness as the more famous Khajuraho sculptures, and that provocative sensuality in which Hindu art is unmatched anywhere in the world.

Not all the Rajput strongholds are deserted and overgrown like Chittorgarh. Within the walls of Udaipur, 'City of Sunrise', are streets teeming with life, Hindu temples, and the Maharana's magnificent palace. Its bare walls and great octagonal towers present an austere appearance to the outside, but inside are gardens and spacious courts decorated with mirrors and rich inlay work. Below lies the smooth expanse of Lake Pichola, an artificial lake created in the fourteenth century and now ornamented by lake palaces of marble.

Such artificial lakes, which serve both as a town's water supply and washing place, are found widely in Rajasthan, and form a vivid splash of blue against the arid greyness beyond, for little of Rajasthan is irrigated.

Such strong contrasts were a constant reminder of India's agricultural problems and the almost Malthusian struggle of population against food production. Already much has been done to introduce better agricultural methods, but the smallholdings of villagers do not lend themselves to modern methods and many problems accompany mechanisation. An experimental state farm in Rajasthan increased its output tenfold in three years by mechanised farming but also reduced its labour force by a similar amount.

Then there is the problem of fertilising the land. The animal manure which should be ploughed back into the fields often has to be used for fuel in the absence of coal or wood. No cheap substitute for the dung has yet been found, and although several artificial fertilisers are now on the market, few peasants can afford to buy even the cheapest of these. Yet such an apparently simple problem pales to insignificance compared with the infinitely greater problems engendered by religious prejudice and tradition.

The emaciated cows which wander all over the countryside are an example of the prejudices which hold back economic progress. Because they are held to be sacred they cannot be killed, and it has been estimated that there is one cow to every two human beings in India. There is no pastureland for such great numbers so their milk yield is very poor or non-existent.

"India's five greatest problems," Prime Minister Nehru said, "are land, water, cows, capital, and babies." If one adds to these the droughts, floods and other natural disasters with which she seems so regularly to be afflicted, the magnitude of the struggle begins to be seen.

15 INDIAN SPRING

In January we moved from our rooftop to live with the Charltons. We had been child-minding for them for some time, but as they had a large spare bedroom and bathroom attached to the house, they asked if we would like to go and live there to be on the spot. It was an extremely attractive and generous suggestion, but we resisted the temptation for some time. We both felt very strongly that we must not make people feel that we needed assistance. We had come out to the Himalayas prepared to rough it, and did not want people to feel sorry for us.

It took Joy and Evan a long time to persuade us to join them and even longer to talk us into eating *en famille*. Our reluctance must have seemed ungrateful and ungracious but we were afraid of imposing on their kindness.

Their house was in Tughlak Road, a quiet area conveniently close to the Playhouse School. A large white 'colonial style' stone bungalow with pillared porch and spacious high-ceilinged rooms, in the cold weather it had been cosy with a wood fire, and in February and March was pleasantly cool when the sun became too fierce for us to sit outside. The garden was delightful; shady trees surrounded a green lawn and there were flowers everywhere, roses, pansies, brilliant purple bougainvillea and clematis, and many others we could not identify. There was also an amazing variety of birds, hoopoes and mynahs, the sleek black drongo with its elegantly forked tail, the bright magpie robin and the bronze crow-pheasant, a bird of magnificent appearance but with only a hoarse croak for song.

During the winter the unusually bad weather had aroused much speculation. In December there had been an unprecedented cold spell when many died of exposure on the streets of Old Delhi. Then there had been some sudden storms, a deluge on Republic Day, and even the phenomenon of thick fog. All this was attributed by the astrologers to the impending conjunction of eight planets, destined to take place on 3rd February. A major disaster was predicted, even the end of the world. As the day approached the fear spread and large sums were given to the priests for prayers to avert the catastrophe, but 3rd February came and went, and nothing happened. We thought that the priests and astrologers would be discredited but they proudly claimed that the great disaster had been averted by their ardent prayers.

Towards the end of February it began to get hot. Now the most pleasant time of day was the early morning before the heat haze reduced all to a featureless glare. Several times we went on breakfast picnics taking quantities of coffee and sausage sandwiches, and binoculars so that Joy and Evan could advance our meagre knowledge of birds. At the ancient fort of Tughlakabad south of Delhi we heard our first larks, and on the irrigation canals we saw three different sorts of kingfisher and the strange swimming snake-bird, looking like a miniature version of the Loch Ness monster. Behind was the River Jumna, a series of brown lagoons and muddy sandbanks populated by hundreds of wading birds.

Before the heat became too enervating we used our spare time to visit the early Hindu temples and forts outside Delhi, the Cyclopean citadel and tomb of Tughlaq Shah, and then the magnificent Moghul buildings of Akbar, Jahangir and Shah Jahan. There are few people who can remain unmoved by the beauty and craftsmanship of the best Moghul art, whether it be the grandeur of the Red Fort, the exquisite detail of miniature paintings, or the splendour of the Taj Mahal.

Deliberately we did not go to the Taj Mahal before seeing all the other Moghul buildings both in Delhi and Agra, for having seen the Taj Mahal all else suffers by comparison.

We saw it ethereal in the moonlight, we saw it in the solitude of dawn and again in the midday glare with the crowds and transistor radios. On this third visit we had the good fortune to be shown round by a craftsman in marble and inlay work. We had visited his workshop to try to see some of this work being done, and found him busy carving a miniature scale model. He insisted on showing us round the workshop, giving us tea, and then taking us to the Taj.

He was one of the most pleasant Indians we met, with a real pride in his country and his craft. The Taj Mahal needs no description, but photographs give no idea of the detailed craftsmanship around the entrance and inside the tomb. There are panels no bigger than a door which took one man fifteen years to complete, tiny wreaths of honeysuckle with each petal and stamen separately inlaid, bunches of grapes no larger than a match-head. The semi-precious stones had been brought from all over the East: cornelian from Arabia, jade from China, turquoise from Tibet, lapis lazuli from Ceylon.

Photographs again had given no impression of the true situation of the tomb, which does not stand alone in a garden as I had imagined, but is balanced between two large red sandstone buildings, a mosque and an assembly hall, at a lower level on either side. Behind, long flights of steps lead down to the River Jumna, which provides a silvery foreground to the view of the tomb from Agra Fort. Imprisoned here, after he had been deposed by his son Aurangzeb, Shah Jahan spent his last years gazing out across to the Taj Mahal, built for his Queen, Mumtaz-i-Mahal, who had died bearing their fourteenth child thirty years before.

Some of our most pleasant days at the Charltons' were spent sitting in the garden learning about India which they knew so very well, and meeting some of their friends. Among these were the painter, Sabavala, who mounted an Exhibition in Delhi whilst we were there, and Kushwant Singh, a wise, softly spoken Sikh, well-known for his deeply-felt account of the berserk bloodbath that followed Independence.

Then there was General Chaudhuri who commanded the invasion of Goa. He had worked his way up in the army under the British, suffering many injustices and indignities, some of which he recounted with humour but no trace of bitterness. With him we spent a fascinating day at the Delhi Horse Show watching his officers competing at 'tent-pegging', the modern equivalent of pig-sticking. With turbans flying and blood-curdling shouts they galloped down on tiny wooden tent-pegs; the pegs were only half-an-inch wide but somehow, at a full gallop, they managed to spear them with their long lances.

Evan also took the trouble of arranging for us to meet the President of the Himalayan Club, Lieutenant-General Sir Harold Williams. The upshot of the meeting was that we were invited to give a lecture on our Kulu expedition to the Himalayan Club, and later went to spend a weekend at the General's home in Roorkee, where he was in charge of a Building Research Institute after retiring from the Army.

Roorkee is on the edge of the Himalayan foothills of Garhwal; dense green tiger forest stretched right to the boundary of the town, above were folded grey-brown hills, and still higher a hazy line of distant snow peaks. It was enticing country but out of bounds for all foreigners, with that infuriatingly ubiquitous Inner Line.

Not far away is Rishi Kesh, a small group of shacks and white-washed temples clustered at the point where the holy river Ganges first emerges from the Siwalik Hills in a narrow gorge. It is a place of pilgrimage and was swarming with beggars, lepers, sacred monkeys and cows. Even our Hindu escort winced at the stench and quickly suggested going on to Hardwar, the main pilgrim centre a few miles downstream.

From a distance the town looked impressive with a skyline punctuated by the conical sikharas of innumerable temples and the long steps of bathing ghats lining the river banks. Army troops were busy constructing a number of pontoon bridges across the river in preparation for the great quadrennial bathing mela to be held a week later.

"There will be over a million people here for the mela," our escort told us. "Last time more than a hundred drowned when they all plunged into the water together; perhaps the same thing will happen again, but what better death is there than to die in holy Ganga?"

According to the Ramayana, when the goddess Ganga was ordered down to redeem the souls of some condemned princes, Siva let her seep out slowly through his hair as a river, lest her fall should cause undue destruction. The ashes of the princes were washed by the water and their souls ascended to heaven. Hence Hindus believe that bathing in the Ganges gives virtue and spiritual strength.

The women bathed fully-dressed with shawls covering their heads, the men in dhotis or loincloths, plunging their heads under the muddy water, gargling and spitting out. Shoals of huge sacred fish swam near the bank, jumping for breadcrumbs thrown by the pilgrims. Long-haired Sadhus, naked or in saffron robes, wandered along the ghats, children poked at bodies waiting for cremation and clambered over the red-daubed lingam stones. Cripples hawked bottles of holy water.

"You have seen enough?" our escort enquired. "I expect you think our people are unclean and superstitious, but you must admit religion is a living force in India, not dead as in the West."

We went on to the Doon School where we were to give another lecture on our Kulu expedition. The Doon is a leading Indian public school run very much on British lines. There is an English headmaster and one or two Englishmen on the staff, including the Himalayan climber Holdsworth, whom we found coaching cricket, an old pipe clenched between his teeth. In 1931, with Frank Smythe and Eric Shipton, he had reached the top of 25,447-foot Kamet, the highest peak to be climbed at that time, and had become renowned for smoking a pipe on the summit.

There is a strong mountaineering tradition at the school and it was very well represented on the 1962 Indian Everest expedition, with two masters, Gurdial Singh and Hari Dang, in the team, and one eighteen-year-old pupil.

Later we met Hari Dang in Delhi when he came to say goodbye to the Charltons before leaving for Everest. Gaily he talked of mountaineering and tiger-shooting, his two great passions, and then in more serious vein of problems and politics in India. He did extremely well on the Everest Expedition, being chosen as one of the summit pair, but bad weather thwarted their attempt only 500 ft below the top and in the course of a harrowing descent Hari got frostbite. It seemed he would lose all his toes but he flew for treatment to Europe where French doctors just managed to save them. We met again in England and found him full of plans to go back and do something for India, perhaps by entering politics.

From Roorkee we drove west across the plains towards Pathankot, where we were to meet Dewey Clarridge for a week's climbing in the hills. It was now the very end of February, the term's teaching had passed all too quickly, and we were trying to get fit before leaving on the expedition to Nepal in mid-March.

We met Dewey at Pathankot and drove up to the hill station of Dharamshala, situated at 6,000 ft above the green meadows of the Kangra valley. It was much too early in the year for mountaineering as we had halfexpected. Even to reach the Forest Rest House at 9,000 ft we had to contend with miles of waist-deep soft snow, and did not arrive till after dark. The Rest House was comfortable and well equipped and we spent a pleasant five days there, enjoying the clear air and mountain scenery. The excessively soft snow made climbing virtually impossible and we had no skis, but on our last day just for fun we went and camped out some 500 ft above the hut. It snowed heavily during the night and we almost had to swim down again, eventually arriving back in Dharamshala so wet that puddles of water formed wherever we stood.

In that sodden state we had an interview with the Dalai Lama. The Indian Government had given him a set of bungalows in the woods above Dharamshala, and had also assisted the setting up of a school for Tibetan children there.

Feeling very conscious of our boots, trousers and dripping anoraks, we were ushered in to a large dark reception lounge. As we perched nervously on the edge of a settee the Dalai Lama came in, resplendent in scarlet and yellow robes. He looked young and very serious behind his spectacles, but when he saw our bedraggled state he broke into a broad smile. We talked through an Indian interpreter, but I imagine this was principally for security purposes, since the Dalai Lama obviously understood what was said before it was translated.

He spoke with concern of the immediate problems of raising funds to build schools, feed, clothe and house the refugees until they had learnt trades whereby they could earn their own living. There were then some 38,000 Tibetans in India, about 10,000 in Sikkim and Bhutan, and 15,000 in Nepal. Neither India nor Nepal could easily provide land or employment for this great influx of refugees, but both had done a great deal to help them in conjunction with the Red Cross and other welfare organisations. The Indian Government had settled some 15,000 in the Himalayan foothills and Mysore, and employed another 10,000 on road work, of whom about 6,000 were in the Kulu valley. There were also large schools at Dharmsala, Kalimpong, Kathmandu and elsewhere where the refugee children could learn both their own language and Hindi or Nepali.

Apart from these immediate problems the Dalai Lama was especially worried about the long-term question of how the refugees could maintain their culture, religion and identity in permanent exile. As long as the Chinese remained in Tibet there would be little chance of them returning to their homeland, and in the northern mountains of Nepal and India, the only areas where the culture was predominantly Tibetan, there was not enough land for them to settle.

When we talked of the possibilities of settling refugees in Switzerland, Alaska or Patagonia, the Dalai Lama shrugged sadly. "Perhaps these mountainous countries would suit our people, but they are not Tibet."

16 ON THE MOVE AGAIN

At 7 p.m. on 12th March 1962, Dorothea and Pat arrived in their Hillman Husky. Leaping out Dorothea greeted us, "Not a single puncture since England!" Later, however, over supper we heard that there had been several adventures on the way, including a clutch burnt out while a passage was forced through snowdrifts in Turkey, and broken springs due to the inevitable overloading. The latter part of the journey had been a day and night marathon to reach Delhi on time.

The next four days were one long hectic round of activity. The stores sent by sea had to be cleared through Bombay Customs, the equipment brought by road sorted and packed. Then there were innumerable formalities to complete with the Indian and Nepalese authorities, and in between Barbara and I were trying to fit in farewell visits to our friends.

By the time Denise and Nancy arrived by plane at the end of the week we were all quite exhausted. We went along to the airport to meet them at 5.30 a.m., feeling tired and bleary-eyed after going to bed at 1.30 a.m. and then being woken up at 3 a.m. by an unusually zealous postal official bearing a Good Luck telegram.

At last in the bleak greyness before dawn two little figures appeared on the steps of the plane, unmistakable in their huge down jackets and Himalayan boots. It was wonderful to see them. Both Denise and Nancy are the sort of people who immediately inspire confidence, and once they arrived everything brightened up. "Heavens, you look well," Denise greeted Barbara and me, "but how plump you've grown!"

The Jagdula expedition was now complete. The most convenient description of the party and our aims was the leaflet prepared by Dorothea for fund-raising purposes:

Jagdula Expedition: The Party

Denise Evans, 29, has already been on two expeditions, to Greenland in 1955, and to the Himalayas in 1958 with her husband. She is the daughter of Nea Morin, also an outstanding climber and a member of the 1959 expedition to Ama Dablam. Denise is responsible for FOOD, the most important job in any expedition.

Nancy Smith, 37, our doctor, has been climbing on British mountains and in the Alps for twenty years. We are lucky to have a doctor with such a fine climbing record.

Patricia Wood, 27, is a dental surgeon. She is one of the quiet dependable types who get things done without fuss. She will need to be as she is in charge of EQUIPMENT, a harassing and responsible job packed with endless vital details. Her climbing is of the same high quality.

Josephine Scarr, 24, is a climbing instructor at Plas y Brenin, the Central Council of Physical Recreation Centre near Snowdon. Her small neat appearance hides a character of determination and ability. She and Barbara Spark will have gained invaluable experience of Himalayan climbing and conditions by the time we all meet in Delhi in March 1962.

Barbara Spark, 24, teaches physical education at a Liverpool Grammar School. Her unruffled calm and cheerfulness will go far to carry them both through all that lies ahead. They are responsible for the PHOTOGRAPHY and SURVEYING side of the expedition.

Dorothea Gravina, 56, leader in years if nothing else, has knocked round hills and mountains all her life. She was a member of the Women's Expedition to Cho Oyu in 1959. We are sponsored by the Pinnacle Club, the women's climbing club with its centre in North Wales, of which we are all members.

Aims

Our objective is the area of the Jagdula River, formed from many tributaries in the main Himalayan range to the east of Jumla, Western Nepal, near, but not too near, the frontier with Tibet. Hence the name of our expedition. This is the south-western end of the remote Kanjiroba Himal, the highest peak of which is 22,582 ft (6,883 m). There are some fine peaks in these ranges, including 21,000-foot Lha Shamma, unclimbed and mostly unmapped. From photographs taken by the Austrian climber, Dr Tichy, they look a reasonable proposition well within the competence of the party. We are planning to spend six weeks in this untrodden part of the world, exploring, climbing, and surveying; what maps exist are full of question marks, and we hope to find some of the answers.

Getting There

We shall take about three weeks walking through western Nepal to reach our area, and will be employing local porters to carry the loads, besides our six Sherpas for the climbing. We shall live off local supplies as much as possible while on the way through the country, but these may be a little thin at that time of year and we may need to rely on what we can carry with us. We should have about six weeks in our climbing area before the onset of the monsoon chases us out at the end of May.

Before driving north from Delhi to Nepalganj in West Nepal, where we proposed to leave our two vehicles, we were scheduled to have an interview with Mr Nehru. There were many questions one would have liked to ask him but he seemed anxious to talk about mountaineering. Mentioning the Indian team who were just leaving for an attempt on Everest, he said, "We have been criticised for spending so much money on this Expedition, but it will be a great thing if Indians succeed in climbing Everest. And what is £50,000 in our country of over 400 million people?"

He went on to discuss the political situation in Nepal and, in particular, the difficult situation caused by political rebels taking refuge in India and then using it as a base to stir up trouble in Nepal. "Yet we do not want to close our borders," he said, "we have too many people but still we accept and welcome refugees from Tibet and Pakistan." The great man looked much older than I had expected and very tired, with sad liquid dark eyes set very deep below his broad forehead. He talked slowly with long pauses and now and then a fatalistic shrug of the shoulders as though to say, "What are we to do against such impossible odds?"

On our second last day in Delhi a minor crisis developed when a telegram arrived from Bombay, 'Expedition luggage safely despatched 10 a.m. 18th for Raxaul.' This sounded all right until we realised that Raxaul is the railway station for Kathmandu, several hundred miles east of our destination, Nepalganj. A conscientious clerk, under the impression that all mountaineering expeditions must start from Kathmandu, had laboriously changed all the labels from Nepalganj to Raxaul.

Since trains for both Raxaul and Nepalganj pass through Lucknow, some 300 miles from Delhi, it should be possible to intercept the luggage there and redirect it to Nepalganj if only someone could reach Lucknow in time. Dorothea wanted to do an all-night drive but there were still some affairs in Delhi she had to clear up so eventually it was decided that Denise should fly over at 7 a.m. the next morning.

Dorothea followed with Barbara on a daytime marathon drive to make sure that everything was all right, while in the Land Rover Nancy, Pat and I did a more leisurely journey via Agra so that they could see the Taj Mahal. We spent the night in an isolated dak bungalow outside Agra at Fatehpur Sikri, the Emperor Akbar's first palace in India.

Barbara and I had visited Fatehpur Sikri some weeks earlier, but on a Saturday afternoon when the crowds, transistor radios and droning guides had destroyed the atmosphere of the huge red sandstone courtyards. Now with Pat and Nancy I looked round in the soft golden light of early morning; the great courts were silent, empty, peopled only by the ghosts of Moghul days.

It was almost impossible to drag Pat and Nancy away and inevitably we arrived late in Lucknow that evening. We found that the luggage had been successfully diverted, and Dorothea, Denise and Barbara had left early that morning for Nepalganj. If we left early the next morning we would only be a day behind, but our Indian hosts were anxious that we should wait a day in Lucknow since it happened to be the festival of Holi. Repeatedly they told us that it might be very dangerous to travel on Holi but would give no definite reasons, except that we might get covered in coloured water. Our handbook on Indian festivals was hardly cautious. 'Holi is a festival of colour. Riotously gay crowds fill the streets, squirting coloured water on all passers-by. All people regardless of age, caste or station participate in this fun.' We set off wearing our oldest clothes, but soon found that the guidebook's rosy description hardly applied to the villages between Lucknow and Nepalganj.

In the first village that we entered, an enormous crowd of purple stained men and boys blocked the main street. There was not a woman to be seen, and when they saw us they all came running down the street in a mass, buckets and stirrup pumps in hand. They may have been only 'riotously gay' but it looked as if it would be at our expense. Nancy noticed a side road, and pushing the Land Rover into reverse we quickly retreated down it, the mob in pursuit.

Fortunately beyond the village the track led us back on to the main road, but we were all rather worried and examined the map to see if the other villages could be avoided. But in the plains of northern India there are villages everywhere.

When we entered the next large village the street was blocked with a solid barricade and a huge crowd. There was no time to reverse for already we were surrounded by a sea of green-powdered faces and red-splashed figures. Again there was not a woman in sight. We had closed the windows and Pat had locked the passenger door but the door on my side would not lock from the inside. They were all shouting and drenching the windows in dye. Then someone wrenched open the door. As they sprayed the inside of the Land Rover I struggled to close it again, but three of them dragged me out. They daubed green powder on my face, poured a bucket of red water over me and then held me whilst an ominous murmuring spread through the crowd. But two more men pushed the others away and I scrambled back into the Land Rover. Some others quickly moved the barricade and we accelerated away, the crowd suddenly grinning and waving.

It had been an unnerving experience. We discovered later that Holi is the spring Saturnalia of the Hindus when all women except those of ill fame stay indoors. We wondered how we would be received in the other villages on the way to Nepalganj but we need not have worried as now that we had been branded there was no more trouble.

Further on we even plucked up courage to take photographs and stop for a picnic lunch, and by the time we reached the American Mission where we were to stay, on the Indian border close to Nepalganj, I had quite forgotten my bizarre appearance. The missionary, Miss Tomaseck, grasped what had happened at once. Busily assembling buckets of hot water, soap and towels, she assured me that the dyes would scrub off me, if not my clothes.

The house was a large cool stone bungalow in a very big garden, colourful with bougainvillea, clematis and pale pink tree orchids. We had expected to be camping outside but Miss Tomaseck insisted we should have rooms in her bungalow.

For twenty-five years she had been running single-handed the Mission, orphanage and dispensary which she had started. We were the first Europeans she had seen for six months.

That evening the Sherpas arrived and came on to the verandah to meet us, all grinning very shyly. They were strange faces to all except Denise, who leapt up and shook the leader's hand very warmly. This was Dawa Tensing, who was the senior Sherpa, or 'sirdar', and had been with Denise and Charles when they climbed in east Nepal on their honeymoon. Earlier he had been Charles' sirdar on Kanchenjunga, and a member of innumerable other expeditions. Immediately we all liked him; his deeply lined face was full of character, purpose, and humour, and his long hair tied back in a pigtail gave him an air of wisdom and authority. We were extremely lucky to have Dawa for he was a Himalayan veteran, with long experience not only of climbing and leading a team of Sherpas, but of coping with difficult porters and ponymen. He obviously had great respect for Denise (or Evans Memsahib as the Sherpas called her), and told us that he had come out of retirement for one last expedition when he heard she was coming; "Evans Memsahib go to mountains, Dawa go to mountains," he said very solemnly.

Dawa then introduced us to Krishna Rana, the Nepalese liaison officer, Mingma Tsering who was deputy-leader and cook, and the other five Sherpas. At this stage all seemed to look alike so it was not till they were helping us to unpack next morning that we realised there were in fact nine Sherpas altogether, instead of the seven we had requested.

Later in the day Dorothea collected everyone on Miss Tomaseck's verandah and sorted it out. In his limited English, aided by graphic gestures, Dawa explained that by mistake an extra Sherpa had come down from Sola Khumbu to Kathmandu for our expedition, and after a two-week walk they could not send him back. And another, Pasang, was a particular friend he wished to bring along.

All nine Sherpas had now travelled more than 400 miles by train to Nepalganj, but we could not afford to pay the extra two, and had no clothes, equipment or food for them. Reluctantly Dorothea decided that they would have to go back to Kathmandu, and asked Dawa who should be sent back with Pasang. Dawa pointed to another young Sherpa called Pasang Sonar.

As the two rejects sat disconsolately on the steps with the others sympathetically gathered round, it seemed this might spoil our relations with the Sherpas for the whole expedition. Denise must have been thinking this too for she asked, "Can't we compromise? Let's take them but not feed them or something?" Eagerly we all made suggestions, and eventually it was settled that they should come on half-pay (three rupees a day), and carry a porter's load of seventy pounds. They would also have to make do with what little equipment we could scrape together and the nine Sherpas would have to share the food supplies intended for seven. Everyone seemed very happy with these arrangements, and it set the expedition off on a much better note. Both we and the Sherpas realised that we were being rather soft-hearted, but there was no cause to regret the decision later for the two·extra proved very useful, especially Pasang Sonar who became kitchen boy.

We spent four days at the Mission preparing to leave on the 200 mile walk to our mountains. All the thirty-seven expedition crates had safely reached Nepalganj station. In the event all the panic had proved unnecessary since a very competent Inspector had been sent to accompany the luggage as official 'Chaser'.

Our first task was to transport the two and a half tons of crates from the station over four miles of rutted unmade road to the Nepalese frontier, where it had to be passed by the customs officer before being unpacked, sorted, and made up into pony loads. The Customs House was just a little shack by the side of the road, but fortunately the customs officer was most helpful and we were allowed to take the luggage through and unpack in a large garden put at our disposal by the Bara Hakim (District Governor) of Nepalganj.

As we saw the great mounds of food and equipment Barbara and I were very impressed but rather horrified. I had always favoured the Shipton-Tilman system of travelling light with only the barest minimum, and in Kulu we had sacrificed luxuries for mobility and ease of organisation. Of course it was easier to do this for six weeks in Kulu than it would have been for three months in Nepal.

My particular task was to sort the 5,000 pounds we were taking with us into pony loads of two equal-sized boxes or kitbags each weighing 80 pounds. Meanwhile Denise and Barbara sorted food, Pat repacked the equipment boxes, Nancy sorted the 160 pounds of medical supplies and Dorothea coped with the Customs, Bank and Post Office. Everyone worked as fast as possible but it all seemed to take an excessively long time and we became very impatient to set off.

Nepalganj was a grim place; the unmade roads were inches deep in flies. It was more primitive than any towns we had seen in India and full of mosquitoes, reputed to be of a deadly malarial type. In one street our dentist, Pat, was able to watch her Nepalese counterpart working cross-legged in the middle of the road, his instruments spread out in the dust.

By mid-day on 24th March all was packed and ready, and the ponymen began to arrive to inspect the loads. In spite of the evidence of the spring balance, at first they would not believe that the loads were all the same weight. Then, when at last they were convinced, they protested that their ponies were not all the same: "Some eeshtrong, some no eeshtrong". Eventually the difficulty was resolved by paying each ponyman for the weight his ponies carried, regardless of the number of ponies used. We therefore never knew quite how many ponies we had in our caravan and there were several spares, but on leaving Nepalganj there were about thirty-eight.

When all was arranged the Bara Hakim invited us to a farewell tea party. Handing round china tea cups and neat little wild boar sandwiches, he told us that since there were so many dacoits and political rebels in West Nepal he was sending an armed guard to accompany the expedition. I visualised a platoon of Gurkhas, but our escort proved to be two small barefoot policemen, with one rifle between them.

Departure was scheduled for early on 25th March, but Dawa thoughtfully suggested that we should have an extra day at Miss Tomaseck's and travel the first twenty miles across the flat Terai by Land Rover, catching up at the foot of the hills where the road petered out. This seemed an excellent idea for it gave us a day's grace for letter-writing and a little relaxation before setting out on the long walk ahead.

We returned to Miss Tomaseck's for our last taste of civilisation and our last bath for three and a half months. No expedition could have had a better starting point than the Mission, where Miss Tomaseck looked after us so well and entertained us with fascinating stories of her life there.

We had a delightful farewell dinner, some of the Mission orphans came in to say goodbye, we played the Messiah on the antiquated gramophone and packed ready for the morning, leaving behind a neat row of suitcases for our return. "I hope we will all come back," I thought as I added mine to the row. Illogically, we all had the feeling that we would come through, although we were going into an unknown area, completely beyond the reach of any outside help, to climb in the Himalayas where the fatality rate on expeditions was nearly one in ten.

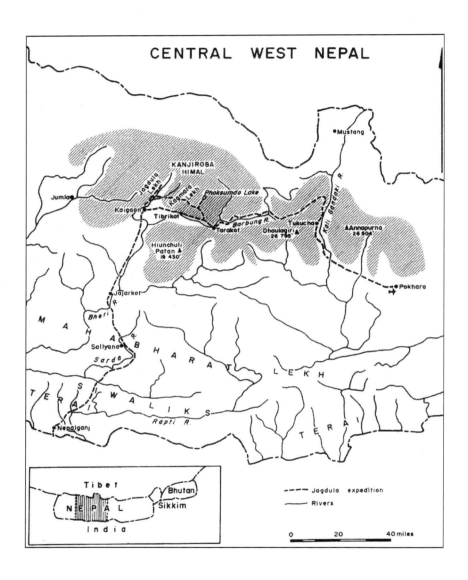

CENTRAL WEST NEPAL

KANJIROBA
HIMAL

Mustang

Jumla

Jagdula Lekh
Kaigaon
Tibrikot
Kanjara Lekh
Phoksumdo Lake
Tarakot
Barbung R.
Tukuchae
Dhaulagiri
26 795
Kali Gandaki R.
Annapurna
26 504
Hiunchuli
Patan
19 430

Pokhara

Jajarkot

Bheri R.
M A H A

Sallyana
B H A R A T   L E K H
Sarda
S   I   W A L I K S

T E R A I
Rapti R.
T E R A I
Nepalganj

Tibet
Bhutan
NEPAL
Sikkim
India

- - - - Jagdula expedition
——— Rivers

0   20   40 miles

17 STROLL TO THE HIMALAYAS

In conventional expedition terminology, our walk to the mountains was always called the Approach March or March In. This sounded impressively arduous but was in fact singularly inappropriate. Our trek to Kaigaon was a delightful saunter, wandering along with only light rucksacks, with the Sherpas busily doing all the cooking and other chores. I felt a similar twinge of guilt to be so pampered as I had in Kulu, but to resist this oriental tradition of service only causes bewilderment and unhappiness.

After a week our life assumed a very pleasant pattern, but the first few days were terrible. It was hot and dusty, we were horribly unfit, our feet were tender and soon covered in blisters, and to a greater or lesser degree most of us suffered from hill diarrhoea. We were also all trying to carry too much.

In our eagerness to get fit for the climbing we all set off with loads of thirty pounds or more, but after a few days of suffering we decided that it was stupid to spoil our enjoyment of the walk by such masochism. Thereafter we strolled up and down the hills unloaded, and only as we actually approached the mountains did we carry heavy rucksacks again, finding then that we were fit enough not to notice them.

Until the opening of Nepal to foreign expeditions in 1949 no one had been near our particular objective, the Kanjiroba Himal, except for two Indian officers of the Survey of India who skirted the southern end of the range in 1925 and 1926 when working on the first reconnaissance survey of Nepal. The result of this survey was the quarter-inch to the mile map which was still the only map of West Nepal. Then in 1952 a botanical expedition sponsored by the Natural History Museum travelled through the area and was followed in 1954 and 1956 by the oriental scholars Tucci and Snellgrove. In 1953 the Austrian mountaineer, Dr Herbert Tichy, made a few ascents in the Jagdula Lekh on his remarkable journey right across West Nepal from Kathmandu, but the first real expedition was John Tyson's in 1961.

A mountaineer and geography master at Rugby school, Tyson had organised a three-man party to explore, survey and climb in the Kanjiroba-Jagdula ranges of West Nepal. Their expedition had been highly successful but had shown that there was both a great deal still to be explored and mapped and endless scope for mountaineering, especially in the Kanjiroba range. Unfortunately Barbara and I had left England before Tyson's party returned so were unable to meet him, but he had given Dorothea all possible advice and information on the area.

The initial stage led across the twenty miles of thickly-wooded Terai to the first range of hills, the Siwaliks. The Terai region is notorious for its malarial mosquitoes, tigers and crocodiles, cobras, vipers and scorpions. It is not densely populated.

We were fortunate to be able to avoid the worst of this malarial jungle by taking the Land Rover the first fifteen miles, but after two hours of bone-shaking jolting and choking dust we would rather have faced a dozen tigers or cobras than drive an inch further. It was a great relief when the road came to an end; Miss Tomaseck's driver took the Land Rover back and we were left in the quiet of the forest. It was to be three months before we heard another engine or even saw another wheeled vehicle.

Following the imprints of Sherpa boots on the sandy path we came to their camp in an open grassy glade. Already it was dark and the glade was filled with a bewildering throng of shadowy figures, ponies and campfires, but soon we found the Sherpas clustered round a large fire with pans of tea and soup bubbling ready. It was a warm night so we did not bother with tents but slept under mosquito nets. For a long time I lay awake gazing up at the brilliant tropical moon and the million fireflies weaving silver patterns against the tall trees. Already civilisation seemed far away and the anxiety and worries of the last few days faded into the past.

It seemed only minutes later when I was awakened by a Sherpa calling "Chai, memsahibs, three o'clock." By 3.30 a.m. the ponies were loaded and we were on our way through the woods, the track a clear silver ribbon in the bright moonlight. Gradually the sky lightened and the sun came up but still it was pleasantly cool and we went on walking till 9 a.m. when a general stop was made for breakfast. Mingma produced a welcome meal of porridge, bacon and eggs, and then we lay around in the shade waiting for the last ponies to straggle in.

142

Another three hours of level walking through the oak and sal forests brought us to our campsite, a stony meadow on the edge of the River Rapti and at the foot of the Siwalik Hills which we were to cross the next day. The Rapti was a wide muddy river only about three-foot deep with a strong current, not in the least suitable for swimming but we were all so hot and sticky that we could not resist a plunge in.

Nancy, a strong swimmer, was the only one who put her head under water; it may have been merely coincidence but the next day she was struck down by an unpleasant germ causing sickness and a high temperature for several days. At this stage we were always careful to boil all drinking water or to purify it with special tablets, but higher up, when we had left the last villages behind, we were able to drink out of the mountain streams quite safely.

Leaving the Rapti we climbed up over the Siwalik Hills and down into the flat plain of Dang to camp eventually at the foot of the next much larger mountain range, the Mahabharat Lekh. The Siwaliks are the southernmost mountains of the Himalayan system, called by the ancient Aryans, 'the edge of the roof of Siva's Himalayan abode'. Their low hogbacks rise straight out of the Ganges plain without any foothills. Good tracks lead through the primeval forests but there are no settlements on the hills, for during the long dry period all the rivers run dry except for a few large ones in the wide valleys between the Siwalik and Mahabharat Ranges.

Walking across the wide plain of Dang was unpleasantly hot and dusty but we passed through some picturesque villages, and were able to have a drink of cool water drawn up by bucket from the deep communal village wells. The houses were mud-built with thatched roofs. On some of the larger ones the mud walls were covered with white plaster on which animal scenes were depicted in low relief. The dark-skinned people had markedly negroid features and wore little clothing but a great deal of jewellery including large nose rings. The women had their hair in high 'buns' and some were wearing thick-meshed black veils, the men sported ponytails tied with red ribbon.

These people are the Tharus, the only tribe of the original population of Nepal now inhabiting the Terai. They are said to survive because they have built up a resistance to the deadly awal fever which is rife there.

Most of the people we were to meet on our way northwards to the main Himalayan chain were of Indian descent, for when the Muslims invaded India in the Middle Ages, many Indians, especially the Brahmans and Kshatriyas, fled into Nepal. These Indo-Nepalese have kept their Hindu religion but speak Nepali, the official national language which was developed by the Khas class of Gurkha in Central Nepal and is related to the Hindi of the original Rajputs who invaded Gurkha in the thirteenth century.

Barbara and I had acquired a Nepali grammar in Delhi and had begun to learn the language, and it was gratifying to find that now we could make ourselves understood to some extent to the local people and the Sherpas. The Sherpas actually speak a language of their own which is related to Tibetan, but all of them also speak Nepali, and several spoke a little English learnt on previous expeditions.

It would have been interesting to spend longer among the shy Tharus who were so different from all the other Nepalese we met, but we were forced to press on in pursuit of some of our ponymen who were far ahead across the plain, intent on reaching the foot of the next range of hills before evening.

During these first days of the trek there was much confusion, with ponies far ahead and far behind and everyone giving different times and distances for the day's stage. The main trouble was that we had two distinct sets of ponies, one bunch of sturdy hill ponies who were returning to Sallyana and one very weak and slow group of plains ponies from Nepalganj. The hill ponies were accustomed to moving by night, the plains ponies by day.

We would be woken at 2 a.m. because tents had to be loaded on to the hill ponies, but when we reached camp all the food would be on the plains ponies, which would not arrive till after dark. The chaos lasted until we reorganised the loads so that our everyday requirements were carried by the hill ponies. As a further precaution Mingma and Pasang Sonar carried with them enough cooking pans and food to make breakfast, so that irrespective of the ponies' movements nobody starved.

Gradually a daily routine developed. We would be awoken by one of the Sherpas between 4 and 5 a.m. with a mug of tea, half an hour later we would have packed up, the tents would be down and the ponymen strapping the last loads on to their reluctant beasts. Then we would set off walking briskly in the chill of early morning until the sun came up about 7 a.m. Soon we would be discarding jerseys and by 9 a.m. seeking shade in which to have breakfast. This was the best part of the day, sitting in the warm sun hungrily watching Mingma cooking, with the smell of bacon wafting upwards. Breakfast was usually porridge or cereals, bacon or sausages, beans or eggs, plus biscuits and marmalade. To Barbara and me this was the height of luxury for in Kulu breakfasts had consisted of dehydrated apple and biscuits, with only one tin of sausages and beans in five weeks as a special luxury.

If there was good grazing for the ponies our breakfast stop might last as long as four hours, so sometimes we camped in the early afternoon and sometimes not till dusk. Likewise campsites were determined by the whereabouts of water and grazing, but the day's stage was usually between eight and fifteen miles.

Arriving at a campsite we would have a brew of tea while the Sherpas put up the tents and laid out our air beds and sleeping bags. Barbara and I had thought ourselves spoilt by our Ladakhis in Kulu but this was nothing compared with the Sherpas' solicitude. Dawa had assigned to each of us a personal Sherpa, and they all seemed to compete as to who could look after his memsahib the best. With all the cooking, washing, and camp chores done for us, there was ample time to sit around talking, writing diaries, reading or just simply doing nothing. Sometimes we would have to repack a few of the boxes, and each evening Denise and Barbara would have to extract some food for supper whilst I checked in the number of loads as the ponies arrived, but for all except Nancy and Pat it was a delightfully leisurely time.

Nancy and Pat as our doctor and dentist were fully employed almost every evening holding surgery for the local people. At this time there was not one doctor, dentist, clinic or hospital in the whole of West Nepal, an area of some 30,000 square miles. When the news spread that there was a foreign party travelling through, people flocked from miles around for treatment, some of them journeying for several days to meet us. It was touching but slightly surprising that they should have so much faith in white men's medicine, and should so trustingly take the pills or medicine Nancy gave them.

145

Many people were suffering from blindness, lameness and other afflictions which could have been avoided if only medical attention had been available, and there were many others whom Nancy said could have been cured with a few weeks' treatment. Goitres, eye and skin diseases were especially common. One that I particularly remember was a tiny baby boy who was clearly starving. His stomach was grotesquely distended and his arms and legs like sticks, the skin wrinkled in folds. The mother seemed quite healthy but had not been able to feed him. Nancy did what she could and gave the mother several tins of powdered milk and Complan together with careful instructions translated by Krishna, our liaison officer. As Krishna always pretended to understand more English than he actually did, one can only hope that he translated the instructions accurately and that the baby survived. Bravely Nancy coped with all these cases whilst she herself was feeling ill. For five days she kept walking in spite of constant sickness and a high temperature, determined not to hold up the rest of the party.

As we crossed the Mahabharat Range, leaving behind the low humps of the Siwaliks and the hazy flatness of the plains of India, we crested a 6,000-foot pass and had our first view of the Himalayas of Nepal.

It was everything I expected and much, much more. Ridge after ridge of forest-clad hills and deep valleys led towards the distant snow peaks, only tiny cones at that distance but we could pick out 21,132 ft (6,441 m) Hiunchuli Patan and a hundred miles away to the north-east the great massifs of Dhaulagiri and Annapurna. The scene was framed by scarlet rhododendrons, and the path led down through oak woods redolent with pink magnolia, huge tree orchids, and brilliant flame of the forest.

On the wide valley floor we found rice fields, banana trees and sugar cane, and farther north wheat and mustard were being grown. Green parrots screeched overhead and in the woods long-tailed monkeys leaped and jabbered. Following the River Sarda we came to Sital Patti, where we camped just outside the village, underneath a huge pipal tree.

At Sital Patti we had our first experience of crowds of onlookers sitting round our camp watching everything we did. They had never seen western women before and possibly not even western men so their curiosity was understandable but distinctly wearing.

To escape we climbed up to the town of Sallyana perched on a hilltop high above the valley. We had intended to have just a quiet look round but soon found ourselves the centre of an excited crowd, who bore us along to the residence of the Bara Hakim, the official Governor of the region. In a dark fly-filled office we found a charming man seated behind a desk, wearing European sports jacket and open necked shirt. He was one of the most go-ahead Nepalis that we met and most concerned about the future of his country, especially the tremendous problems of development in an area without a single road or airfield. In spite of all the difficulties a school had already been built in Sallyana and a hospital started, the materials and equipment being dropped by helicopter. The children of Sallyana had never seen a car, train, bicycle or even wheeled cart, but helicopters were a familiar sight.

The Bara Hakim was clearly very proud of the town and took us on a long, exhaustive (and exhausting!) tour. The streets were narrow and cobbled or stepped on the steeper parts for the sake of ponies, the houses two-storeyed, solidly built of stone covered with an attractive reddish-coloured plaster. All the roofs were thatched, and some of the houses had finely carved wooden balconies and doorways. We walked for miles until we had seen every house in the town and it was almost dark. Ang Temba and Krishna Rana who had accompanied us up from Sital Patti had cunningly disappeared, but met us on the way down again. With broad grins they silently handed us water bottles and biscuits.

During this excursion we acquired a black-and-white stray dog. He was a scruffy but affectionate mongrel who firmly attached himself to us for the rest of the expedition.

That evening we all went to bed early and I had been asleep for some time when suddenly I awoke to hear a tremendous commotion in the campsite with the sound of dull thuds and hysterical shouting. Peering out of the tent I could not see anything, but Dorothea and Denise had also awoken and already were striding down the field in pyjamas, armed with ice axes and torches. From the noise I visualised a pitched battle between the Sherpas and a band of marauding dacoits,

147

but it proved to be merely one drunken prowler whom our armed guard had found lurking near the expedition boxes. With wild excitement the guard had caught him and begun to beat him with his rifle, but fortunately Denise and Dorothea, together with several sleepy Sherpas in various stages of undress, had prevented serious violence and the guard had to content himself with merely tying his prisoner up for the night. Dorothea prowled round the whole circuit of the field, then sounded the all clear. The next morning the guard was most disappointed when we refused to make a charge against the prisoner and released him, but the incident made us more careful, and henceforth the Sherpas always slept close to the expedition luggage with ice axes to hand.

Whilst the new set of ponymen lashed together the loads for the next stage of our journey to Jajarkot, we took the opportunity of visiting the Sital Patti School. It was a large dark room on the upper storey of a barn-like building. From some distance away the loud chanting of children's voices could be heard through the tiny lattice windows. A wooden ladder led up to the door, and inside the children were sitting cross-legged on the floor, all holding slates from which they chanted their lessons at the tops of their voices. There was only one teacher, a retired Gurkha soldier, and his class ranged in age between four and twelve year olds. There did not appear to be any books at all, but at least the children were learning to read and write.

In 1962 schools were a comparatively recent innovation in Nepal, and the great majority of the villages we visited did not have schools of any sort, but if the government educational programme can be put into effect this will gradually be remedied.

From Sallyana it took us three days to reach the next village of any size, the hilltop settlement of Jajarkot. At first the path led up vast terraced hillsides, where maize and oats were being grown, to shady pine and rhododendron forests. Then we dropped down to the Bheri River and crossed it on a narrow suspension bridge.

On the final pull up to Jajarkot we met a long, strangely silent file of men striding down carrying evil-looking blunderbusses. From the headman we learned that they were going south to the troubled area through which we had come. Already there had been several political uprisings in West Nepal against King Mahendra's regime, and our armed escort had been intended as much as protection against political rebels as against dacoits.

This large-scale exodus of local men caused us much trouble, since north of Jajarkot the paths became too steep and narrow for ponies, and we had to engage porters instead. Dawa and Krishna Rana scoured the surrounding countryside to collect the sixty-five men we required, while we camped in the grounds of a ruined palace overlooking the town. This was built in the Kathmandu 'pagoda' style, with upturned roofs and intricately carved wooden doors and window frames.

There was plenty of room but no shade from the burning hot midday sun and no escape from the flies or the crowds of onlookers. From the moment at five o'clock in the morning when we were woken by an old woman squatting in the entrance to our tent, coughing noisily, a row of goggle-eyed giggling women and small boys was never more than a few yards away. We were certainly the first white women they had seen and they followed us everywhere round the camp and in the village. In Jajarkot we bought supplies in the last shops we were to see until we neared Pokhara, three months later and over 250 miles walk away. They were dark little shacks in which the shopkeeper sat cross-legged amidst piles of rice and flour scarcely visible under the heaving masses of flies. The crowd pressed round, some of them standing in their bare feet on the piles of grain to get a better view. Meanwhile Dawa did the bargaining, storming and shouting till he got the shopkeeper down to a reasonable price, then suddenly relaxing with a smile and handshake.

All the way through Nepal we bought local food wherever we could, but sometimes villagers had only just enough for themselves. The Sherpas' basic diet was rice and chapattis made from wheat flour, plus potatoes, meat, eggs, lentils and other vegetables whenever available. We supplemented this with tinned food, and when climbing they lived on exactly the same diet as we did, consisting mainly of dried food. This is expensive, unappetising and monotonous, but is light and compact thus saving much money in porterage costs. The tinned food which we ate below the snowline had almost all been given free to the Expedition, but by the time it had been transported from England to Nepal probably cost considerably more than the dried food. However, it provided welcome variety and we all fed extremely well and kept very healthy.

Denise had calculated the quantities so well that everything just lasted out with a surplus of only one or two items. Organising the food for a three-month expedition is by no means an easy task, especially with no idea of what, if anything, will be available locally. With a party totalling sixteen it would have been too risky to rely on purchasing local food, and in West Nepal we would certainly have gone very hungry.

Our two days at Jajarkot were highlighted by two parties, a tea party given by the headman and a birthday party to celebrate Dorothea's fifty-seventh birthday. The tea party was in the local schoolroom, a long narrow upstairs room with small wood, mullioned windows. In the centre was a large table loaded with food and set for six. The headman as a strict Hindu would not eat with us but sat at another table nearby to watch, whilst Barbara and I tried to converse with him in our limited Nepali. Tea consisted of curried chicken and sheep's liver, crisp sticks of rice bread and huge glasses of rakshi, a strong spirit brewed from rice or potatoes. Fortunately I liked the rice bread and rakshi so was able to make a great show of consuming these. At the other end of the table Dorothea, who has an iron constitution, ate platefuls of the meat but the others just picked at it, and Denise could not eat anything.

In strong contrast for Dorothea's birthday party Mingma served a special birthday supper of steak and kidney pudding, pears and chocolate sauce, fruit cake and rakshi. Dawa carved the cake with his kukri (Nepali machete knife) and, well lubricated with rakshi, everyone got very happy. Krishna Rana and the guard had been drinking all day and were distinctly drunk so we all got slightly worried when the guard began demonstrating how to load his rifle. Feeling that one of us was far more likely to get shot than any dacoits, Dawa managed to get his bullets and presented them to Dorothea as a birthday present. It was a very sheepish guard who came to ask for his bullets back next day.

Leaving Jajarkot on 7th April, for the next eight days we followed the Bheri gorge north-eastwards towards Kaigaon and the Kanjiroba Himal. North of Jajarkot the Bheri River cuts a tremendous gorge through the southern branch of the Great Himalayan Range, west of the spectacular peak of Hiunchuli Patan. At times our path led through bamboo thickets and ferns by the river side but where the gorge became too precipitous it would climb for thousands of feet over a rocky spur before descending to the river again. In sultry heat we would swim in the backwaters of the fast-flowing river or stand under waterfalls vainly trying to get cool, then in the same day climb up several thousand feet to camp amongst the conifers, azaleas and rhododendrons, the porters shivering in their cotton dhotis.

During the evenings Denise would keep us all entertained with ingenious puzzles, or sometimes Barbara would initiate gymnastic contests or games, getting the Sherpas to join in as well. We must have made a comic sight as we tried with our feet to manoeuvre a mug of water from the forehead, or took blind swipes at each other in 'Are you there, Moriarty?' These days between Jajarkot and Kaigaon stand out as some of the most delightful on the whole expedition with both the zest of new country and the joy of feeling really fit and alive. As we climbed higher towards the mountains the air grew fresh and crystal clear, there was a nip in the sunshine and the hint of snow in the distance.

We passed through several small villages en route, all with the same two-storeyed thatched houses which we had seen at ·Sallyana and Jajarkot. The people were Indo-Nepalese Hindus, wearing the typical Nepali dress of cotton skull cap, loose jacket or waistcoat, shirt, and cotton breeches fitting tightly below the knee. They seemed to be largely independent of the outside world. We saw men and women spinning their own wool with hand spindles and weaving on primitive wooden looms, making their own pottery on a slow turning wheel, weaving their own baskets from bamboo, grinding mustard in a handpress and maize in a millstone turned by water power.

Our porters from Jajarkot had carved wooden pipes, but no tobacco or matches. For tobacco they used leaf mould and for matches a smouldering piece of rag lit by placing the rag on a stone and striking a spark out of the stone with a flint. The pipes were passed round from one man to the next, the smoke being sucked in through the fingers so that the pipe never touched the lips. Alternatively they rolled cigarettes out of rhododendron leaves.

All that the porters carried with them for as long as ten days away from home was a blanket and a small bag of atta. Each night they would squat down round a campfire, cook chapattis in the embers, and then wrap themselves up in their blankets and sleep in the open. Next morning they would again shoulder their seventy-pound loads, the whole weight supported by a headband round the forehead. It seemed a tremendous weight for anyone to carry, but in Nepal both men and women carry loads from a very early age. Their neck and leg muscles become very strong and the soles of their feet as hard as leather. None of our porters wore shoes. When one of them got a crack in the sole of his foot, we saw him borrow a needle and thread and sew it up again.

They were a motley team but lively and cheerful, especially when in the hot valleys they could splash around in the rivers. We had to be very discreet as to when and where to bathe since bare legs are definitely taboo in Nepal and we never saw a woman swimming anywhere. The Sherpas suffered badly from the heat in the lower valleys but none of them had learned to swim as the glacial rivers of their native Sola Khumbu are so cold and swift that swimming is impossible. Higher up, however, when the porters were miserably shivering from the cold and altitude, the Sherpas came into their own.

Incredibly sturdy, resourceful, willing and cheerful under all conditions, the Sherpas were the best companions one could possibly have on any expedition. Coming from a variety of villages in Sola Khumbu, they had not all known each other before yet we never heard a disagreement amongst them. They were an example to us in every way.

At first Sherpas with their small build and dark Mongolian features tend to look alike and this impression is strengthened by the similarity of their names. Our party included two Pemba Norbus, two Pasangs, Ang Temba and Ang Pema. The confusion arises because Sherpas are usually named after the day of the week on which they are born, Pemba being Saturday, Pasang Friday, and so on, and the prefix Ang simply means young. But in looks and personality they are all very different and after a few days we wondered how we could ever have confused them.

On this trek we came to know Dawa better than any of the other Sherpas, for often in the evenings he would come and squat in our tent to discuss the next day's plans and problems. Sometimes he would talk about his home in Sola Khumbu or his visit to England. He loved describing the wonders he had seen there, especially the motorways, double-decker buses, and glass-bottomed beer mugs! His face, deeply wrinkled from long years in the wind and sun, was wonderfully expressive, and when he talked he used his hands to supplement his English with graphic gestures. No one could forget the diarrhoea one - Swoosh! During the day Dawa would bring up the back of the column, cheering along the lagging porters and checking the loads. Even in the Indian-style pyjamas which he wore in the lower valleys he was an imposing figure, tall and strong, with binoculars slung round his neck and his long hair tucked up under a Gurkha hat. Accompanying Dawa would be Krishna Rana, our Nepalese liaison officer from Kathmandu. His task was to liaise between us and the local people, helping in hiring porters and purchasing local food, but Dawa was so capable and experienced that Krishna had to do very little.

The porters' pace was a fast walk, almost a trot, with frequent rests. It was a difficult pace to try to follow so we usually walked well ahead or behind. Invariably Dorothea and Denise would be far ahead, having an endless competition to keep up with each other rather like two cars: Dorothea the powerful old saloon who could outdistance all else on the level and Denise the cheeky little mini-car zooming up and down without even getting hot.

In the course of this three-week walk we had become a happy, united party. From the beginning we had all been determined to get on well together, and found it very easy on this trek when one could be gregarious or solitary according to inclination. Minor irritations and disagreements were largely lost in the joy of travelling through such fascinating country, with the thought of the mountains ahead where we knew we would have to bury any differences for the common purpose. In a party of such varied ages, backgrounds and temperaments, it is perhaps surprising just how well we did all get on.

We were fortunate to have two such tolerant, unselfish, and imperturbable people as Pat and Barbara, who acted as peacemakers and a foil for the more temperamental of the rest of us. Pat was perhaps the quietest of the party, whether she was efficiently extracting teeth for the local people or organising the expedition equipment, her particular responsibility. Somehow she always managed to look neat and clean, even when she had just dived off the track into thickets in pursuit of a rare bird. Barbara shared Pat's enthusiasm for birdwatching and they spent many hours together trying to identify all the colourful species we saw.

Nancy as doctor had more to do than anyone else on our trek to the mountains, yet she surprised us all once by referring to the expedition as a holiday! She had not had more than a fortnight a year away from her Lancashire practice for ten years. Nancy had had to bear the heavy expense of flying to India, so was determined to make the very most of her three months in Nepal. Denise was in the same position, since family responsibilities looked like making it her last visit for a long time. Always full of energy and joie de vivre, she would race on ahead to film the porters or ponies, or devilishly disappear to see round the next corner, reappearing with a garland of rhododendrons or a huge boutonnière. Denise was a great asset to the party in keeping up everyone's moral and preventing any disagreements getting out of proportion. Half-French, a gifted linguist and very musical, in the evenings she would one minute be arguing heatedly with Dorothea about religion, the next singing madrigals or Italian arias.

Striding along swinging her umbrella, Dorothea would head the column, often at such a pace that Pat, Barbara and I almost had to jog-trot to keep up. At stops she would be restless and impatient to be off, in the evenings still full of energy, checking supplies and a hundred other details, or showing us all up in general knowledge quizzes.

Inspired by the example of her three sons, Dorothea had taken up mountaineering at the age of forty-eight. Six years later, after some seasons in the Alps, she had been a member of the French Himalayan expedition to Cho Oyu. It then became her ambition to lead her own Himalayan team as a 'swan song' and our Jagdula expedition was born.

The last days of the trek tend to merge in my memory into one long pleasant stroll, in which only a few incidents stand out clearly. First a porter strike, when the porters had suffered a very cold night and there was little firewood to build warming fires. It took an hour's cajoling and threatening, plus a bribe of biscuits and cigarettes to make them go on, but the next night Mingma cleverly found a campsite near a disused barn where they were able to shelter.

Then Pemba Norbu, one of the older Sherpas, developed a nasty abscess on the sole of his foot. Nancy gave him penicillin injections which cured it eventually but for several days he could hardly walk. One day on an easy section of the track we managed to hire a pony for him, but most of the way the path was too steep, narrow and rocky for a pony and he either hopped along with a crutch or the other Sherpas carried him.

Finally there was the exciting climb up through birch woods and green meadows dotted with primulas and irises to the last col and the first view of our mountains. We could not identify the different peaks with any certainty, but their spectacular spires and icy ridges looked well worth a 200-mile walk.

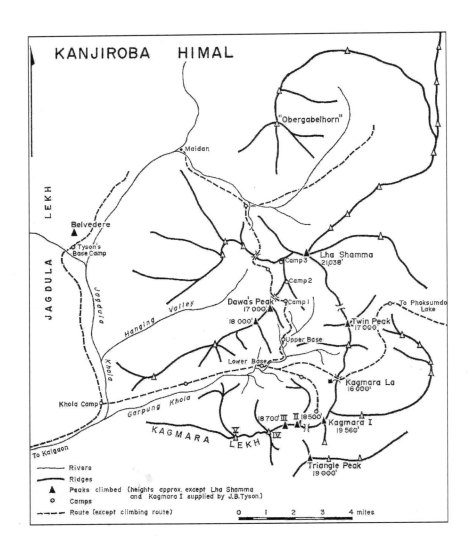

KANJIROBA HIMAL

"Obergabelhorn"

• Maidan

LEKH

Belvedere ▲

○ Tyson's
Base Camp

JAGDULA   LEKH

Jagdula

Hanging   Valley

Khola

Camp 3
Lha Shamma
21,038'

Camp 2

Dawa's Peak
17 000' ▲   ○Camp I

18 000'

To Phoksumdo
Lake

Twin Peak
17 000'

Upper Base

Lower Base

Kagmara La
16 000'

Khola Camp ○

Garpung   Khola

To Kaigaon

KAGMARA   LEKH

18 700' III   II 18 500'

IV

Kagmara I
19 560'

Triangle Peak
19 000'

——— Rivers
▬▬▬ Ridges
▲ Peaks climbed (heights approx. except Lha Shamma
  and Kagmara I supplied by J.B.Tyson.)
○ Camps
– – – Route (except climbing route)

0   1   2   3   4 miles

156

Below us lay a deep valley with ploughed fields and flat green meadows beside a foaming mountain river. Dropping down through mud and snow drifts we came to the fifteen flat-roofed houses of Kaigaon. As we walked down muddy alleys between the houses Tibetan mastiffs created an uproar on the rooftops and people came rushing out from all corners to give us an enthusiastic welcome. John Tyson's party had spent several days in Kaigaon the previous year and had employed some of the local men as mountain porters, paying them well and making generous gifts of medicine and clothing. As they crowded round we were able to recognise the headman and some of the others from Tyson's photographs, and Dorothea handed out the presents and photographs he had sent out for them. These caused great excitement for none of them had seen a photograph of themselves before.

For the next two days they never left our camp as we sorted out food and equipment and supplies to be left in Kaigaon ready for our return journey. We had a beautiful campsite on the bank of the Ilagarh River beneath some weeping willow trees, but the weather was bad and in the few periods when it was not raining we were plagued by flies. Although it was in the mountains, Kaigaon was not a healthy place. The children playing naked amongst the yak dung had sores on their heads and their faces covered in flies and many of the men and women had eye troubles, goitres, and racking tubercular coughs. Even in the pouring rain they hopefully squatted round Nancy's tent waiting for medicine and she did what she could, but it was a heart-rending business.

Kaigaon geographically lies within the inner Himalayan region which is inhabited by Buddhists of Tibetan origin. But although the houses were of the flat-roofed Tibetan style the people were mainly Hindus, since the Kaigaon valley has been penetrated by Indo-Nepalese people from the south and west. It was not until we moved eastwards on our way back from the mountains that we came into the Buddhist Himalaya proper.

To celebrate our arrival at the mountains we had a party the second night at Kaigaon, beginning with a dinner of goats' meat and rakshi and ending with a wild song and dance session. Barbara was energetically demonstrating a Cossack dance when she pulled a calf muscle; for the next few days she could only hobble painfully along, and as a result missed the first exciting reconnaissance of the expedition.

The Kanjiroba Himal lies roughly north-east of Kaigaon, and the southern part of the range is drained by two rivers, the Jagdula Khola to the west and the Garpung Khola to the south. When John Tyson had visited the area the previous year he had tried to force a way up the Jagdula Khola into the Kanjiroba Himal but after a week spent fighting vertical vegetation and steep rotten rock he had to abandon the attempt and climb exclusively west of the gorge. The whole area east of the Jagdula Khola was therefore untouched, unexplored, unsurveyed, and every peak unclimbed. Towering above all else in this range was a spectacular ice spire called Lha Shamma (modern spelling is Lhashamma), a local name meaning 'peak festooned with hanging glaciers'. John Tyson estimated its height at 22,000 ft, but his survey results later showed it to be 21,038 ft (6,412 m). He had shown Dorothea and Denise photographs of it taken from opposite on the Jagdula Lekh and suggested that a hanging valley near the bottom of the Jagdula Khola might provide a feasible approach route. The alternative was the valley of the Garpung Khola on the other side of the range, but as the hanging valley seemed nearer to Kaigaon we decided to explore it first.

We left on 17th April under a grey sky and heavy rain. A narrow path led up through pine and birch trees to the summer pastures of Kaigaon but petered out at the foot of the gorge where we camped amidst the dripping trees, just above the roaring Jagdula Khola. This Khola camp, as we called it, was wet and gloomy with mist blocking any view up the valley. Most of the evening was spent discussing how the reconnaissance of the hanging valley should be carried out. Eventually it was decided that Denise and Nancy as the two fittest should carry out a quick lightweight reconnaissance, accompanied by Ang Temba, who had been to this area the previous year with Tyson's party, and Mingma and Ang Pema, two of the most experienced climbers among the Sherpas. Their group was to go towards Tyson's old base camp and look for an approach to the hanging valley, while the rest of us would explore the western side of the Jagdula Khola to familiarise ourselves with the general topography of the area.

The sky was overcast again next day and the gorge oppressively sultry. Here and there were traces of a path made by local deer hunters but much of the way we were clambering over mossy tree trunks, wading through streams or scrambling up steep earth and juniper slopes. The sides of the gorge were very steep and at one point cliffs dropped directly into the water. We found a series of narrow grass ledges with tree trunks here and there acting as bridges or ladders, but as we climbed and crawled along, the river roaring three hundred feet below, we wondered how the porters would manage this section with their seventy-pound loads.

Gradually the path led up away from the gorge and as dusk came we emerged above the tree line. Here we camped on a small grassy platform between snow drifts. We lit a large fire of birchwood to indicate our whereabouts to Denise and Nancy, and eventually heard Denise's yodel from somewhere on the other side of the deep nullah below our camp. They had set off on their lightweight reconnaissance two hours before us that morning and were now camping at the site of Tyson's Base Camp about a mile ahead of us.

Our party consisted of Dorothea, Pat and me; Barbara had been forced to stay down at Khola camp to rest her pulled muscle. With us were two of the younger Sherpas, Katcheri and Pemba Norbu 2, and one of the oldest and most experienced climbers, Pemba Norbu 1. They were all fairly quiet, especially Katcheri who was my particular Sherpa. A facial disfigurement suffered as a child when he rolled into a campfire perhaps added to his diffidence, but he was extremely tough and willing and as the expedition progressed he gradually became more communicative.

When we awoke next morning we were greeted with a view out eastwards over the deep gorge of the Jagdula Khola to the icy peaks of the southern Kanjiroba Range, and westwards across the grassy uplands to the more rounded chain of the Jagdula Lekh. At 7 a.m. we saw the others leaving Tyson's Base Camp for the upper reaches of the Jagdula Khola. Then I felt a sharp pang of envy, but our job for the day was almost equally exciting: we were to climb as high as possible up the Jagdula Lekh to study the opposite side of the gorge for possible approaches to the peaks above.

Passing the huge boulder which sheltered Tyson's Base Camp, we set off up the long grassy spur of a 16,000-foot peak, the Belvedere. The view from the top was well worth the climb, but the opposite side of the Jagdula Khola looked horribly steep and inaccessible. We could see no sign of Tyson's hanging valley (it was actually much nearer the bottom of the gorge and therefore invisible from here), and the only possible line of approach seemed to be a side valley dropping into the Jagdula Khola from the east about three miles north of us. In the apex, at the junction of two rivers, there appeared to be a flat expanse of grass and trees which we named the Maidan. This would make a perfect base camp we thought, and above it towered a magnificent ice peak very similar in shape to the Obergabelhorn in Switzerland. To the south and east of the 'Obergabelhorn' loomed even larger peaks, including Lha Shamma, the fine spire which dominated the whole of this part of the range, so it seemed that if we reached the Maidan there would be plenty of scope for exploration and climbing. From our viewpoint it looked as if about four miles of contouring round slopes of grass and scree would bring us to the Maidan, and we wondered whether the others would reach it that day, forgetting that Tyson had spent a week trying to reach the same point.

The next day Dorothea went back down towards Khola camp to make contact with Dawa, Barbara and the porters, whilst Pat and I moved our camp up to Tyson's Base Camp ready to meet Denise and Nancy and move on up the gorge. We had expected them towards evening but at 11 a.m. we saw five small figures trudging over the horizon. They yodeled across to us, but when they arrived Ang Temba shook his head sadly and said "No road". Over tea and omelettes we heard the whole story. Nancy later wrote in the Pinnacle Club Journal:

There were no paths, not even a bear track, and we ploughed through deep snow in birch thickets where the valley side faced north, and through thorn bushes, azaleas, brambles and loose rock where the steep slope faced south. Across a steep snow slope Ang Temba lost his footing and went tumbling down on to the scrub at the bottom. Finally the going became so steep and hard that we left our considerable loads with Ang Pema and climbed on without them, trying to reach what seemed to be a more level place at the head of the valley.

We hadn't long enough to hack a way through for our porters. There was no easy access anywhere, and the steep V -shaped ravines on the eastern side of the gorge were even worse. 'No Road' the Sherpas had said all the way up. Now we knew it was true and reluctantly turned back, not knowing if the prospects were any better on the east side of the range where no one had ever been.

After hearing their tale of horrors it was obvious that the Jagdula Khola would certainly not be practicable for laden porters even if we could make our way up it. Since the Jagdula Lekh had already been well explored by Herbert Tichy and John Tyson, it seemed that the best thing would be to return to Khola camp and try to reach the Kanjiroba peaks from the other side of the range.

Halfway down we met Dorothea, Barbara and the other Sherpas bringing the porters up. Fortunately they wholeheartedly agreed with our decision and the porters were not at all disappointed to turn back. They had found it very difficult carrying their boxes on the steep sections of rock scrambling, and one had slipped on a sloping boulder and might have toppled right down into the gorge had not Dawa just managed to grab him in time. It was too late for them to go right back to Khola camp that night so we camped under some rocks by a stream. It was pouring with rain but by a lucky chance there were some caves where the porters could keep dry.

Next morning whilst the sun was drying our tents Mingma, Denise and I went ahead to put fixed ropes on the steep part of the descent. It was great fun banging in pitons and fixing a series of handrails and when the porters arrived they seemed most impressed. Even with the ropes it took a long time for them all to get down, and when a few steadfastly refused to carry their loads across, three of the strongest had to make several journeys. One of the older ones caused an uproar by leaving his load behind and then carrying an enormous baulk of wood down to use as a ploughshare. His whole passage was accompanied by a flood of abuse from Dawa, undoubtedly rich in flavour from the grins it brought to the other porters.

At Khola camp Dorothea decided that again a light reconnaissance party should forge ahead to try to find an approach route to the high peaks and a suitable spot for a base camp. Dorothea felt it her duty to stay with the main party and Pat had not been feeling too well, so the choice fell on Barbara and me, much to our delight.

We left at 6 a.m. next morning with three days lightweight rations and the minimum of equipment. We were pleased to have with us Katcheri, Mingma and Ang Temba, all extremely capable and enterprising. Mingma was one of our best climbers and also expedition cook. On the trek to the mountains he had always been in the lead, looking for a good breakfast place or campsite. He had an uncanny gift for finding firewood and water in the most unlikely places, and was adept at lighting fires out of wet juniper in pouring rain. Wearing his Gurkha hat at a jaunty angle, a bright scarf inside his shirt and neat little shorts above his shapely legs, Mingma would effortlessly stroll up the hills, joking, laughing, teasing, and telling stories of Sola Khumbu or other expeditions. He was perhaps the most handsome of the Sherpas, with beautiful bone structure and a dazzling smile; he also spoke quite good English and quickly picked up a great deal more in the course of the expedition.

Ang Temba's English was much more limited but he was a delightfully lively companion, a resourceful handyman and accomplished flute player. Invariably as he sauntered along he would be whittling a piece of wood or trilling on his bamboo flute like a Pied Piper. Tall and lean with very flat Mongolian features, he was not as strong as some of the other Sherpas but his local knowledge gained the previous year with Tyson's party proved invaluable.

Crossing the Jagdula Khola by a natural bridge where huge boulders were jammed above the water, we climbed through pine woods until we reached the main track leading up the Garpung Khola from Kaigaon. Soon the pine woods were left behind and the path wound across steep grassy slopes with the Garpung Khola foaming far below and ahead snow peaks lying beyond a grassy saddle. After three hours' steady walking we stopped by a tiny stream, where Mingma built a juniper fire and cooked a delicious breakfast of porridge, omelettes, tea and chapattis. Nearby we discovered some large caves, so we built a little cairn on the path and left a note in it for Dorothea, suggesting that the caves might make a good overnight shelter for the porters.

The path meandered on upwards and then crossed the Garpung Khola by a small wooden bridge and ascended a steep slope on the other side covered in soft deep snow. Most of the way we were up to our knees in it and wondered how the barefoot porters would fare. For a few months in the summer this path, locally known as the Tibetan track, is used by local people travelling over the pass of the Kagmara La between Kaigaon and the Phoksumdo Lake area, but we were the first people to use it this year.

Whilst the river pounded through the deep gorge on our left we zigzagged up and up towards the col, with each step wondering more and more anxiously what we would see over the other side. Seldom have I raced up a slope so fast but just below the crest I found myself hesitating, almost loath to know the truth. Slowly we walked the last few yards and looked over. After the impassable jungle of the Jagdula Khola we could hardly believe our eyes. Below stretched a broad grassy valley leading directly to high snow peaks ahead.

When we dropped into the valley bottom we found it covered with dense juniper scrub but still progress was quite fast and by 2 p.m. we had reached the head of the valley where cliffs compressed the river into another canyon. Just before the mouth of the canyon there was a wide expanse of grass below a cliff. As we approached, a herd of deer raced away up the hillside. With water nearby and juniper scrub for firewood this grassy flat was an ideal campsite, and at the base of the cliff there was even a cave where the porters could shelter for the night. We all had a very welcome mug of tea here and then, while Mingma and Katcheri established camp, Barbara, Ang Temba and I set off to explore still farther up the valley.

On both sides the hillsides dropped very steeply to the lip of the canyon, but on the west bank deer tracks led upwards, winding among the cliffs high above the river. The terrain was difficult and thick mist obscured any view but after about half a mile we glimpsed a valley forking off leftwards into the range. We were very tired, it was now getting late and raining hard, but we had to go on to see a little farther up this unknown valley. Dropping down to the junction of the two rivers we could see the Tibetan track leading up to the right towards a col on the other side of the Garpung Khola, but on our left was the other valley, its exit blocked by a steep gorge through which the river rushed and roared. For a moment it seemed that an approach to the mountains was to be stymied again, but looking up above the gorge we saw a steeply angled, but passable, grass slope leading into the valley. There was no time to go any farther but it looked promising and in high spirits we raced back to camp to tell Mingma and Katcheri. We did not expect the others to arrive till the following afternoon so the next morning Barbara, Mingma and I set off again to explore up our valley whilst Ang Temba went down to meet the others and escort them to our camp and Katcheri cut timber for firewood.

Leaving at 8 a.m. we were able to follow the river bed through the canyon as far as the junction, crossing and recrossing the torrent on snow bridges. Even at this hour of the morning, when the sun had not touched the snow, some of these bridges seemed of doubtful security with sinister holes through which we could see the swirling current, but it was a much quicker route than the laborious traverse we had done the previous day. Half an hour brought us to the fork, then leaving the river bed we climbed several hundred feet up the valley side and contoured round through juniper scrub and across several ravines filled with deep snowdrifts.

It was a fine cloudless day but we could see no more than the hillside dipping and rising ahead and the river thundering below until, abruptly, we rounded a spur and found ourselves on the lip of a wide grassy valley with the magnificent ice spire of Lha Shamma soaring from its head and mountains all round. If we ourselves had designed the ideal climbing area it could not have been better: a pleasant green valley with water and firewood, and a host of mountains of all sizes and degrees of difficulty.

Finding a site for a base camp was not too easy since at this time all the flatter part of the valley floor was covered in snow, but the steepness of the valley sides would necessitate cutting out platforms for tents. In search of the ideal site we went right up to the head of the valley, laboriously traversing two miles of loose scree slopes and soft snow patches to the corner where the valley swung westwards. There we climbed up a grassy ridge to obtain a better view of Lha Shamma, but after a thousand feet of clambering up steep slippery grass, panting after Mingma who seemed to have a built-in engine, we were relieved when we came to waist-deep soft snow which persuaded even Mingma that we had gone far enough.

Following the same route back we stopped for a snack at our provisional base camp, where to our surprise Mingma lay down and fell asleep. For the first time since we left Nepalganj it really seemed that he could become a little tired. I climbed up a gully behind to fetch icicles for us to suck, and then followed Mingma's example much to Barbara's dismay, who had not acquired this knack of going to sleep at any opportunity. Then slowly we made our way down again, building small cairns on the way to mark the route, and arrived at camp to find the others already installed. They seemed very pleased with the site, and had successfully managed to coax twenty porters up to it even though they had had to cross half a mile of snow in their bare feet.

Since leaving Kaigaon we had been on the move for seven days so a rest day seemed in order before moving up to establish base camp in the higher valley. Unselfishly Dorothea then made a day's journey down to Kaigaon with the porters returning for second loads, whilst the rest of us and Dawa moved up into the higher valley next day.

Now that we knew the route it only took an hour and a half from lower base to upper base, as they became known. By 9 a.m. we had chosen a campsite, had breakfast, and were all ready to begin exploring the area and climbing our first peaks.

19 TWO LITTLE PEAKS

Our camp was at about 14,000 ft on the west side of the valley, near a tributary stream which ran down into the main river just before it plunged into the gorge above its junction with the Garpung Khola. From the map it will be seen that the river drains a horseshoe of mountains dominated by the high peak of Lha Shamma. With its great icefall streaming down from a long knife edge crest, this spire dominated the whole area and had become 'Our Peak' from the moment we first entered the valley. Like a giant octopus it stretched ridges in all directions, enclosing our valley with two great tentacles. From its east side a ridge dropped steeply to a 16,000-foot col at the head of the valley, snaked along with a few 17,000-foot summits to drop again to the Kagmara La and then rise to the icy chain of the Kagmara Lekh. On the west it threw out another long ridge which formed west wall to our valley, nowhere much below 17,000 ft, dipping and rising to form a line of attractive small peaks.

Our camp was situated at the foot of a spur descending from one of this western chain of peaks, and on our first day there we decided to climb halfway up it to gain a better view of the whole valley and especially our mountain. We were pleased when Dawa chose to come with us, leaving the other Sherpas to level platforms for the tents and have a good rest after all their load carrying.

The lower part of the ridge was steep mud and scree alternating with buttresses of loose rock. Higher up there was very soft snow. At every step we sunk in up to our knees and every few yards up to our waists. When we reached a small knoll with a good view we rested. Behind us was the great wall of the Kagmara Lekh and ahead a possible route up Our Peak. At last we were in the Kanjiroba Himal. We were much too excited to think of turning back even though we had not come prepared for more than an exploratory scramble.

From the knoll our ridge dipped westwards to form a low col between two large snow basins, then rose up to a rocky little peak. We were all very tired and panting with the altitude but Dawa did most of the 'road-making' and now a peak was in sight we were determined to reach the top. It was hard work and the rock scrambling drained our remaining energy but at last we were on the top with the altimeters

166

reading 16,800 ft. We built a cairn to mark our first ascent and agreed to call it Dawa's Peak. Mist was swirling round but we caught exciting glimpses of a deep valley on the other side of the chain and ridges leading off north and south.

Coming down took just as long as going up. In the hot afternoon sun the snow had grown even softer and we almost had to swim through it, rolling sideways down the hill. It was an immense effort to climb out of the big holes we made but we found each others' contortions very comical. We arrived at camp hot, tired, and wet through, but very happy to have climbed our first Nepalese peak.

The next day we began the survey of our area. Unfortunately it had not been possible to bring out extra surveying equipment and we had to make do with the few instruments we had used in Kulu and to confine the survey to a simple plane table map supplemented by photo panoramas. Our upper base valley was just long and flat enough to run a baseline up it parallel to the river. For convenience we used Base Camp as one end of the line, building a large cairn to mark the spot, and then worked up the valley measuring a mile with a hundred-foot steel tape. The terrain was by no means easy. Sometimes we were measuring across boulder fields or steep scree slopes, sometimes we had to stretch the tape across the top of wide snow-filled gullies. It was a laborious business and Barbara, Pat and I spent three mornings just measuring.

Before beginning the attempt on the big peak we decided to do another training climb on the other side of the valley. Dorothea had now returned with the second group of porters so all six of us were at upper base. The Sherpas and some of the Kaigaon porters were busy ferrying food and paraffin up from the lower base so we decided to climb the Twin Peak, as we called it, on our own.

Snow conditions were still very bad so an early start was essential in order to get back before the sun melted the snow into an impassable morass. At 3 a.m. Mingma woke us up with mugs of tea and porridge. It was bitterly cold and gloomy in the greyness before dawn, but as we toiled upwards gradually the stars paled, the greyness turned darkest blue and a deep pink glow suffused each peak in turn. Even as one watched, the pink spread into a golden glow which quickly crept down the mountain side until at last it touched us, throwing out long shadows like moonlight. With boots crunching on the virgin snow, frosty air in our lungs and the sun warm on our backs it was really great to be alive. Only Nancy and Pat did not enjoy the climb, for Pat had been sick in the night and now Nancy was also feeling unwell, possibly as a result of the unaccustomed altitude. They turned back after an hour or so.

When we reached the long exposed ridge leading to the summit Dorothea and I roped together and took turns to make the way up a mixture of soft snow and rock. It was an exhilarating climb even though our lack of acclimatisation made us pant at each step and stop frequently for rests. Twin rock pinnacles formed the summit, the higher one covered with such a precarious dome of snow that we had to push it off with our ice axes before we could reach the top. When Denise and Barbara arrived they accused us of vandalism. There was barely room for the four of us to crouch there, especially when we tried to take photographs and compass bearings.

It had taken us seven hours to come about two miles from camp and 3,000 ft up. Now it was midday and the snow so soft that for much of the way down the only way to progress was to sit down and slide. Barbara devised a most ingenious 'toboggan' in the form of a polythene 'nappy' and these became standard equipment on future descents. "Oh, for a pair of skis," Denise kept saying, but because of the difficulty of transporting them we had brought none.

The lower slopes were not steep enough for sliding and we just had to flounder through thigh-deep snow. I was in front following the tracks we had made on the way up and didn't notice when the others branched off another way to try to avoid some of the snow. When I found myself on my own I could not raise the energy to go back to join them so went on alone. This would have been alright but as I was going downhill sinking in two or three feet deep at each step I suddenly caught one foot in a hole and fell forward face downward. When skiing I had often found myself in this position but then one has sticks to lean on and become upright again, now in the soft snow my short ice axe was useless and no amount of wriggling would release my foot. After ten minutes struggling I was still lying prone in the snow, only now a little deeper than before. Grimly I reflected that it would probably be at least three hours before the others arrived back in search, by which time if I had not suffocated in the snow I would certainly have frostbite. The only chance was to hack my foot out with the ice axe. I was too exhausted for the strikes to be very effective and I kept hitting my leg with the sharp point. When at last I reached the foot which was jammed under a block of ice the snow was specked with blood.

Surprised to find myself still in one piece, I slowly hobbled back to camp, half expecting to meet a search party, but to my astonishment I was the first back. This was distinctly worrying especially when Pat and Nancy had turned back so long ago, but just as the Sherpas were getting ready to go and look for them, all four arrived. They had had an equally worrying descent down steep scree and loose rock, and after we had exchanged stories we agreed that under no circumstances would we split up again on these mountains.

20 LHA SHAMMA

The attempt on Lha Shamma was the climax of our expedition, the culmination of a year's preparation and planning. It was a fine peak, the highest in the area and, if we succeeded in climbing it, the highest peak ever ascended by an all-women party.

The two weeks we spent on it were among the happiest days of our three months in Nepal. Dorothea and Denise as leader and deputy leader made the ultimate decisions but with maximum consultation so that we all felt part of the enterprise. Inevitably we·had our petty irritations and grumbles but on the important points, the siting of camps, the safest route and the general organisation, we all agreed. Our initial task was to establish and stock a series of three or four camps up the mountain until we were within striking distance of the summit, some 7,000 ft above our Upper Base Camp.

On 30th April Dorothea and Nancy set off with the Sherpas to carry the first loads up, and dumped them on a provisional site for Camp I. Our expedition dog had to be restrained from going up with them. They returned to camp in high spirits, Nancy informing us that she had had a wonderful day and then producing cut hands, torn anorak and trousers and a host of purple bruises, all acquired when she had gone head over heels down a gully on the descent. Dorothea described how she had suddenly seen Nancy's red balaclava hurtling down the steep ice and mud and thought she was done for, only to see her staggering to her feet again seventy feet below, picking up scattered belongings, including a battered toothbrush!

The following day Denise and I went up to continue the reconnaissance. With us were Mingma and the elder Pemba Norbu, both strong, reliable and extremely experienced climbers. Initially the route to Camp I was the same route by which we had climbed Dawa's Peak, but when we came to the snowy col below the final rock ridge we descended into the undulating snow basin to the north and laboriously trudged through soft snow to a flat-topped knoll on the other side, just below the icefall flowing down from Lha Shamma.

This knoll was the provisional site for Camp I and seemed ideal, being fairly sheltered and well out of the way of any possible avalanches or rock falls. We put up the three small tents close together in a row with the Sherpas' tent in the middle so that they could pass food to either Denise or me without getting out of the tent. We had set off early to avoid the very soft afternoon snow so it was now only midday, and after a good rest we set off to explore.

The camp was situated at the foot of the icefall, and only about 500 ft below the long ridge which dipped up and down and then broadened into a steep triangle of ice which eventually curved in a long icy crest up to the summit. When we had studied the mountain from the Twin Peak on the opposite side of the valley we had planned to put a second camp at the foot of the triangular ice slope. Both the icefall and the long ridge led up to this point, but neither looked particularly safe routes. The icefall was heavily crevassed and threatened both by avalanches from the slopes above and stone falls from the side of the ridge. The ridge top looked narrow and just below the ice slope was crowned by some jagged rock pinnacles, but in the hope that there might be an easy way round the side of these pinnacles we decided to try the ridge route first.

The way on to it proved straightforward, floundering through deep snow, and then to our delight a hard ice slope led up on to the crest. The angle was just easy enough to walk up in crampons without cutting steps, so it needed no preparation for the full-scale reconnaissance in the morning, and we turned back, climbing up to the col behind the camp instead for a view over the other side of the ridge. When we had looked down in that direction from the top of Dawa's Peak the view had been blocked by mist, but now there was a clear blue sky and we could see right out over the Jagdula Khola to the peaks of the Jagdula Lekh. Below us was a bare valley which was obviously the hanging valley. It was gratifying to see that even if we had succeeded in reaching it from the Jagdula Khola it would have proved a much longer and more difficult route to the mountain.

It began to snow as we got back to camp and Denise and I quickly huddled into her small tent and consumed the soup which Mingma had ready for us, and a very good meal of dried meat, vermicelli and vegetables. We never ceased to wonder at the delicious meals the Sherpas unfailingly produced under the most cramped and difficult conditions. As we ate a hailstorm started, with hailstones the size of plovers' eggs lashing the tent. Then came the thunder and lightning with flashes so close that we could see them through the thick tent walls. Our camp, in a wide snow basin at the foot of a rocky rib was not ideally situated for thunderstorms. As Denise remarked,

"It's just the sort of rib that lightning runs down."

If the storm had grown worse I suppose we might have vacated the tents but already I think we were slightly affected by high-altitude lethargy and the comfortable feeling - 'it won't happen to us'. Deciding that it might be soothing to smoke we both lit cigarettes, forgetting that there was no ventilation in the tent. In a few minutes Mingma and Pemba Norbu were roaring with laughter as they heard us coughing and spluttering whilst we fumbled to get the sleeve door open. We were almost asphyxiated when at last it was open and we poked our heads out into the hailstorm. By the time the tent was clear of smoke it was half full of hailstones, but Mingma provided the solution by tying the two sleeve entrances together so that we had a sort of tunnel between the two tents with a gap for ventilation in the centre.

The next day we set off at 7 a.m. and made fast progress up the crisp snow. As this was merely a reconnaissance Denise and I had only very light rucksacks, but Mingma insisted on carrying up a thirty pound load as the first lift to the next camp. Pemba Norbu followed his lead, with the result that very soon Denise and I were well ahead. We cramponned across an ice slope to reach the ridge crest only to look back and see them cutting steps on a different line lower down. There was a frigid silence when we all joined up. The Sherpas were annoyed that we had led the way, we were annoyed that they would not follow our route or use the steps we had cut.

The ridge crest was several yards wide but topped with a fine cornice-wave of unstable snow. On either side steep slopes dropped into the white distance. It was obviously time to rope up; as Mingma got out the two ropes Denise suggested a rope of four, and I suggested two ropes of one Sherpa and one memsahib. Both suggestions met with stony silence and without a word Mingma and Pemba Norbu roped up together and set off along the ridge.

"Well of all the ... cheek," Denise exclaimed, "if they think we are paying them to have all the fun of climbing this mountain whilst we just meekly follow, they're darned well mistaken." Seething with rage we followed their footsteps, and found them at the foot of the rock gendarmes.

Pemba Norbu was out of sight trying to find a route round the side with Mingma belaying him. Then Pemba Norbu came back, firmly saying "No road", but Mingma went to have a look. After going the full extent of the rope he returned, pronouncing "Too difficult, rock no good, snow no good". They began to pack up, obviously intending to go back down the ridge, but Denise decided that she wanted to see for herself. Whilst I belayed her and the Sherpas sat in stormy silence Denise spent half an hour trying to find a safe route across the pinnacles. And when she came back she insisted that I should go to have a look as well, although seeing the set expression on the Sherpas' faces I was reluctant to waste any more time.

The steep smooth rock gendarmes crowned the ridge like giant teeth on a comb. There was no way over the top or along the sheer right-hand side but on the left a narrow gangway of snow led round below them. Following the others' footsteps I gingerly crept along this unstable snow and then wriggled under an overhanging rock roof. Here the gangway petered out and there were only sloping flakes of rock for hand and footholds, covered with loose snow. Two hundred feet beyond I could see an easy snow ridge leading up to the foot of the ice triangle but the pinnacles were a formidable obstacle. Both Denise and I thought that we could cross them but it would need pitons and fixed rope to make them safe for laden Sherpas. Whilst there we thought it worth while to see if the rotten slate-like rock would take any pitons so Denise set off again, armed with hammer and a jangling bunch of ironmongery. Meanwhile the Sherpas were looking more and more annoyed, and eventually Mingma turned to me and said,

"If Sherpas not necessary, we go down look for other route."

"Sherpas very necessary," I assured him, "but memsahibs like climbing too."

At this point the banging noises stopped and Denise reappeared. She had not been able to get a single piton into the rock so we decided to abandon this ridge route unless the icefall proved completely impassable. Mingma wanted to branch off the ridge and go back to camp down the icefall to try to find a route ready for the next day, but I said I was too tired and in any case we felt the snow would be dangerously soft by now. The Sherpas left their loads on the ridge and we all went back down our original route.

My admission of tiredness had slightly mollified their wounded pride but in camp there was still a somewhat strained atmosphere. However, Nancy and Pat had now arrived so it was not too glum a party. With them were Ang Pema and Katcheri, both young, sturdy and incredibly tough. On his first expedition a year earlier Ang Pema had succeeded in reaching the top of 25,700-foot Nuptse, one of the most difficult peaks yet to have been climbed in the Himalayas. With his cherubic round face and grin from ear to ear, Ang Pema was as talkative and cheerful as Katcheri was quiet and serious.

In the early afternoon I set up a tripod and took a series of survey photographs. Usually by midday the peaks were wreathed in clouds but this afternoon was remarkably clear with a fine view out across our valley to the Kagmara Lekh. Whilst I was surveying one of my special fur-lined snow gloves which I had put down beside me went zooming off down the snow. In a flash it was over the edge and streaking like a small torpedo down one snow basin, over the lip, and down into another, where at last it came to rest, a tiny grey speck on the snow hundreds of feet below. I was much too tired even to think of going to fetch it, but Ang Pema had seen it go and told Katcheri who insisted on getting it for me. Two hours later he was back, tired but triumphantly bearing the lost mitten.

During the evening we determined to have a mass assault on the icefall next day, carrying enough gear to establish another camp up there, if possible at the foot of the ice triangle.

The icefall was huge but with only a sprinkling of crevasses and the route was a surprisingly straightforward snow plod until the steep heavily-crevassed face below the ice triangle. This was threatened both by rock falls from the gendarmes on the left and by avalanches rolling down from the summit ridge, but carefully the Sherpas picked a safe way through and at last we emerged on to the ridge just above the rock gendarmes. Here we found a perfect campsite on a level shoulder of snow in the lee of the ridge. Above us the wind roared and screamed across the crest but in the shelter of the snow hump our tents barely rustled. The view was magnificent. We could see not only the whole of the Jagdula and Kagmara area but in the far distance, some seventy miles away to the south-east, the great massif of Dhaulagiri. One should normally erect a tent with its back to the prevailing wind, especially in the Himalayas where winds can reach a hundred miles per hour, but on this occasion Denise and I decided to rely on our sheltered position for protection and set ours with its entrance to the view.

Then the others all descended again to Camp I, and Denise and I, Mingma and Pemba Norbu left for a reconnaissance of the lower part of the ice triangle. It was much longer and steeper than it had first appeared. The angle must have been about 50 degrees. The snow overlying the ice was very soft and we had first to kick steps and then cut out footholds in the ice. Progress was execrably slow. Whilst doing the road-making one became sweat-soaked and exhausted in about five minutes but as soon as someone else took over the lead, the perspiration froze, teeth began to chatter and hands and toes went numb. I was glad when dusk came and we could retreat to the tents.

There was still a strained atmosphere between the Sherpas and us which we found most depressing so we determined that somehow or other an end must be put to it that evening. After supper therefore I went and squatted outside their tent and in halting Nepali apologised for being angry the day before, trying to explain that we wanted to climb together with the Sherpas, not merely be taken up by them.

Slowly in simple English and Nepali we sorted it all out. It seemed that they had been annoyed because we had taken the lead when they regarded it as their job, and then unhappy because we were unhappy.

"Memsahibs naramailo chhan, Sherpas naramailo chhan," Mingma whispered sweetly.

They were obviously puzzled that we should want to do the hard work of leading the way when they were quite prepared to do it for us.

The urge to lead rather than always to follow was not easy to explain, so I used the argument that we would climb the mountain more quickly if the Sherpas carried heavy loads (which we could not do), and we broke the trail. They accepted this and from then on we took turns in step-cutting and route-finding. Later when we climbed with the younger less experienced Sherpas we had none of this difficulty for they were quite happy to follow us, but Mingma was either too chivalrous or too proud to take easily to being led by a woman.

Next day Denise woke up feeling sick with a splitting headache. We were both very surprised that she should be affected by the altitude for although we were at the critical height of 18,000 ft where altitude begins to have its effect; she had been up to 20,000 ft on her last visit to Nepal with no trouble. Barbara and I had the advantage of being more recently acclimatised on our Kulu trip.

Manfully Denise struggled into boots and anorak and we all set off for the ice triangle, but after only a few hundred feet she felt sick again and had to return to camp. We watched her trudging down to the tents and then pressed on up the slope, kicking and cutting steps. Near the top the triangle narrowed and a series of rock ribs stretched down from the apex like skeletal fingers. We tried to climb up one of these but the rock was very rotten and we soon moved back on to the steep ice. Four hours after leaving camp we reached the apex of the triangular ice slope and the beginning of the summit ridge proper.

It was a cold and windy day and on the long slow ascent my feet had gone completely numb. To try to get some feeling back into them I sat down and beat them with my ice axe. I was wearing only ordinary Alpine boots plus canvas overboots to keep out the wet snow, but Mingma and Pemba Norbu were well shod in large high altitude Everest boots lent by Charles Evans. I was also having trouble with my special snow gloves. These were fur-lined and beautifully warm but the plastic outer froze up when wet. The glove with which I had been holding my ice axe had frozen in a clenched position. For five minutes Mingma hit it and kicked it before I could move my hand.

The ridge was several feet wide in this earlier section with only a slight cornice overhanging the fluted ice face below. Moving together we made good time along it and in an hour reached a place where the crest widened out slightly, providing a possible campsite.

This was only a reconnaissance so we were not carrying any tents, but we marked the spot and then went on up the ridge to see if a better place presented itself higher up. From the knoll above the campsite we could see the whole of the ridge, telemarking in a wide curve towards the summit about two miles away and perhaps 1,500 ft above us. To our relief it was entirely ice and snow with no rock gendarmes, but there were some alarming looking ice pinnacles capping the crest and the entire ridge appeared to be knife-edged.

The snow was horribly soft and at each step great balls of it slid from under our feet to go shooting down the face. The only possible route was right along the foot-wide crest; kicking steps along the side was as hopeless as trying to make a path in a sand dune. If one of us should slip the only way to stop a fall would be for the next on the rope to jump over the other side so we moved along very carefully, keeping a close watch on each other.

We progressed about half a mile without finding anywhere where one could even dig out a platform for a tent. The ridge ahead looked no more promising and the weather was getting worse so we went back to the first place we had picked as a possible campsite. It was not as far along the ridge as we had hoped to place Camp III but at least was a safe and fairly sheltered spot. Driving snow had filled all the steps we had so laboriously cut up the ice triangle so the descent took a long time, but at last we were back in Camp II where we were glad to find Denise feeling much better.

Nancy, Pat, Ang Pema and Katcheri had also come up from Camp I, and were installed in two more tents. Unluckily Pat was suffering badly from the altitude and was sick during the night. Next morning it was obvious that she was too weak to come any higher at present. Pat generously urged Nancy to go on up to Camp III with Denise and me for a first attempt on the summit. Nancy was very fit and eager to climb higher but would not leave Pat until she saw Dorothea and Barbara on their way up from Camp I.

The four Sherpas carried tents and stores up to Camp III with us. To make the route safer for their return we fixed a three hundred-foot rope on the steepest part of the ice triangle, suspending it from an aluminium snow stake driven deep into the snow at the top. Slogging up through the new snow was hard work and when we reached the

177

campsite we all flopped down into the snow for ten minutes before we could raise the energy to trample out platforms for the tents. At last they were up, anchored with snow stakes and ice axes, we said goodbye to Ang Pema and Katcheri who were going down again, and settled down as comfortably as possible to spend our first night at 20,000 ft.

The degree of comfort was not high. With three of us inside a two-man tent there was no room to move and nowhere to put wet clothes and boots. With deft sleight of hand Denise manoeuvred herself into the centre position with an outsize air bed so that Nancy and I found ourselves compressed between this monster and the cold wet tent walls.

We passed the afternoon doing puzzles and telling stories, Nancy giving a magnificent rendering of the annals of Albert Ramsbottom in an authentic Lancashire accent. Then came the usual dehydrated supper which would have tasted quite good if our lips had not been so cracked and sore that it was very painful to eat. Despite threats and curses, Denise could not get one mouthful down.

From 8 p.m. till 6 a.m. we tried to sleep. We were all desperately tired, we took strong sleeping pills and we were not cold inside our down jackets and trousers and thick sleeping bags, but still sleep did not come. The tent flapped like a loose piece of corrugated iron and strong gusts tore at the guy ropes until we were sure we would be plucked from the ridge any moment. There was also a tear in the tent's sleeve entrance and soon a small snowdrift covered our feet. We tossed and turned and I dreamt I was in a small boat being run down by a liner. By the end of the night Nancy had christened Denise 'the Battleship', me 'the Hurricane', and pronounced camping at 20,000 ft 'hellish fun'.

At last the first grey glimmer of dawn came. The Sherpas had not slept much either and had been brewing tea since 3 a.m. At 6 a.m. they produced a good breakfast of porridge and biscuits. Then we spent an hour thawing out our frozen boots over a primus stove and struggled into our windproofs. We emerged into a cold grey world, with mist reducing visibility to the thin line of the ridge top curving round and up into the distance. Slowly, numbly, we made our way along the narrow crest of soft snow, all roped up together. Gradually icicles formed on our noses and eyebrows, the wind strengthened and the clouds came swirling up.

For four hours we kept moving along, kicking steps, sometimes on the crest, sometimes a few feet down one side, until we came to a place where the ridge widened. But at this point the clouds boiled up to envelop us completely in a white-out. Snow and sky blended into a single featureless glare so that we could not distinguish solid ground from empty space. In these conditions it is only too easy to step over into nothingness. We sat down to wait for the clouds to lift.

We waited for half an hour with no success; each time when we were about to give up the clouds would suddenly seem to be dissolving and we would say, "Let's wait another five minutes," but at last we decided that there was no hope and turned back along the ridge. We could hardly see our footsteps and very warily had to feel our way along, trying to keep alert in case anyone slipped over the edge. It was a great relief when after three hours we glimpsed the dark shapes of our tents in the whiteness ahead. The entrances were half buried in snow and we had to dig before we could get inside. We were so tired that all we wanted to do was sleep. Taking two strong sleeping pills each we dropped off almost straight away. Again the wind got up overnight, savagely tearing at the tents, but we were too tired to worry any more.

Next morning a mere suspicion of greyness told us that another day had dawned. Still the wind buffeted the tents which were half buried in snow. In these conditions another sortie along the summit ridge was out of the question, and we had insufficient food and paraffin to spend another night up there. Fastening the tents down with as many snow stakes as we could muster, we headed down for Camp II. As we descended the storm abated slightly. The fixed rope on the ice triangle was deeply buried but we managed to free it and with this as a handrail we got down quite rapidly. Dorothea and Dawa came out to meet us; they had seen us set off along the summit ridge and had been anxiously watching through binoculars all morning. It was a happy reunion to sit in the large Mont Cler tent, exchanging stories over mugs of tea and soup. Then we picked up on our tiny transistor radio one of the special weather bulletins broadcast for us from Delhi. This indicated that the bad weather would last for several days, and since none of the camps was sufficiently stocked to allow us to remain high for any length of time, reluctantly we went down to base again. By the time we reached the valley floor we were very tired after descending 6,000 ft in one day, but it was good to be on grass again, to wash, put on clean clothes and rest.

It was still snowing on the second rest day (9th May), but Pat and Barbara started up to Camp I to give Pat a chance to acclimatise more slowly. Dorothea planned for the rest of us to go direct to Camp II the following day, but unfortunately during the last few days she herself had developed a nasty cold and cough. At first she had refused to acknowledge it but when Nancy took her temperature and found it to be 101 degrees she was at last persuaded to go to bed and accept some medicine. Dorothea was too·enthusiastic a climber to be an easy patient, casting doubts on the value of Nancy's pills and medicines but simultaneously demanding an instant cure. Unselfishly she told Nancy to go up to Camp II with Denise and me where she would join us as soon as she was fit. Nancy agreed with some misgivings when we pointed out that from Camp II she could get down to base in half a day and there would be a constant coming and going of Sherpas carrying loads who could take messages to and fro.

It was a mistake to try to go from Base Camp up to Camp II in a single day. As usual distances and difficulties had diminished in retrospect, and we had forgotten just how tired we had been last time when we had covered barely half the distance. We were carrying only about twenty pounds each but, as we wearily staggered into Camp I, I wondered how we would ever raise the energy to climb the icefall. We were tempted to change our plans and stop there for the night but there was only one tent and very little food or paraffin.

Reluctantly we plodded on, going more and more slowly and sitting down to rest every ten minutes. Each time we were almost overcome by the dangerous euphoria of rest and it was only by a great deal of mutual encouragement that we hauled ourselves to our feet to go on. At one point we even sat down under an avalanche-threatened slope hoping for a merciful release .... At last Camp II was in sight and somehow we crawled up the last few hundred feet, stopping every few steps to lean gasping over our ice axes.

"Never again," said Denise, "if we don't climb this b ... mountain this time, we're not coming up here again. It's now or never." With feeling Nancy and I agreed.

We spent the afternoon trying to sort out how we should tackle the summit. Denise felt that she was not going well enough to be in the first pair, and in any case as climbing leader should remain lower down to co-ordinate and back-up our efforts. Nancy was the obvious choice to replace her since she had gone very well on the first summit attempt, but we knew that she ought to stay within reach of Dorothea at Base Camp, and it is better to keep one's doctor on the middle of the mountain, ready to rush up or down should any accidents occur. Pat was still suffering from altitude sickness although much less severely than on her first visit to Camp II, so the choice fell on Barbara and me. In her quiet way Barbara had been going faster and better than anyone and seemed to have retained her acclimatisation from Kulu. We were delighted at the prospect of climbing together but there was a risk no one would reach the summit of the big peak besides 'The Women's Kulu Expedition'.

As discussions ranged round and round I suddenly realised that I genuinely did not care whether I was one of the summit party or not, it just did not matter any more. No longer did I have to try to suppress ambition and the desire to reach the top, they had suddenly dissolved into thin air. A wonderful feeling of freedom accompanied this catharsis, and I began to understand why Buddhists believe that the uprooting of all desires is the end of misery.

In a very feminine way all of us volunteered to stand down so that at one stage it seemed that there would be no summit attempt at all. Eventually Denise decided that we should try the summit in two waves, the first to be Barbara and me, the second Nancy, herself, and Pat if she was well enough. Then Dawa came into the tent and made everyone happy by suggesting that we should all five go up to Camp III the next day and then see who was fit enough to try for the top.

During the night there was a heavy snowfall and we woke next morning to find a mild blizzard blowing, putting a very definite stop to our plans. There was nothing to do except lie in our tents. The day passed very slowly and in the afternoon I grew so restless that I went out and dug for an hour, constructing a flight of steps between the tents which filled with driving snow as fast as I dug. Again it snowed all night and, although the morning was fine, the two feet of fresh snow made movement so difficult that we had to postpone our ascent to Camp III for yet another day. After breakfast Dawa and Katcheri set off to flounder down to base with a message to Dorothea outlining our plans, and Barbara and I set up a survey station on the knoll above our camp. Meanwhile, Denise suggested a 'road-making' party should tackle the ice triangle. Barbara was keen to go as she had not yet been above Camp II but I elected to stay behind to finish the surveying and also just to be on my own for a while. Not being as naturally gregarious as the others I found I treasured occasional opportunities for solitude.

Happily I pottered round camp and then climbed up to the knoll but whilst I was taking a photographic panorama I suddenly heard shouts from the ice slope. I couldn't distinguish the words but saw a figure being lowered down on the rope. I climbed up a little way towards them and shouted to Nancy who was at the bottom. She shouted back that Pat had fainted but was all right. I quickly got back to camp and melted snow to make tea for her, but when she arrived she was pale but just as calm and cheerful as usual. It seemed she had suddenly felt dizzy and had not been able to see anything. Barbara had grabbed her whilst Denise had hacked out a ledge where she could sit down. Then when she had recovered slightly Mingma and Pemba Norbu had lowered her down again on a tight rope. (Climbing harnesses did not exist in those days so it was simply a bowline knot round the waist.) It had been a frightening experience for all of them and Pat spent most of the rest of the day in bed.

As sunset approached there were the most glorious mountain views with clouds massing in the valleys and bubbling up over the ridges. I was still feeling rather solitary and stood alone on the knoll, absorbing the splendour of sunset and clouds. As I gazed I suddenly noticed a tiny figure plodding up the ice fall below. It was Katcheri carrying a load and moving very slowly. With typical thoughtfulness Ang Temba went down to meet him and help him up the last lap. They arrived just as it was getting dark, Katcheri bearing a message from Dorothea.

We foregathered in the large tent, feeling that it must be something very serious for Dorothea to send Katcheri all the way back up to Camp II on his own so late in the day. However it proved to be merely a solemn admonition not to do anything rash and not to all five attempt the summit at the same time. She said she herself was feeling considerably better and hoped to come up in one or two days' time.

This was good news and next morning we all set off for Camp III in high spirits, especially Nancy who no longer had qualms about deserting a patient. We found the tents almost completely buried under all the fresh snow and had to re-erect them. Then Barbara and I settled down in our two-man tent to rest ready for the morrow whilst the others went out road-making on the first part of the ridge. They returned with the encouraging news that the high winds seemed to have consolidated the snow on the ridge crest and the conditions were much better than on our first sortie a week earlier. The weather was bad with clouds enveloping the ridge and the usual gusts buffeting the tents, but in spite of the flapping canvas Barbara and I managed to get a reasonably good night's sleep. The other three were not so lucky, for Pat had a bad headache and Denise was feverish.

At 5 a.m. Mingma woke Barbara and me with a breakfast of tea, dried apple and biscuits. The tea had been boiling on the primus a minute before but boiling point is so low at high altitude that it was only lukewarm.

Slowly we dressed, wondering how many layers to put on. It was very cold but we knew it would be quite hot as soon as the sun came up. Eventually I settled on woollen ski tights, tracksuit trousers, windproof over-trousers, two vests, shirt, light jersey, tracksuit top, down jacket and anorak, plus two pairs of thick socks, boots, canvas over-boots and crampons, balaclava, snow goggles, silk gloves, woollen mittens and windproof overgloves. Except for the addition of down jacket and tracksuit trousers this was my normal Himalayan attire and worked out perfectly for I felt about the right temperature almost the whole time. Barbara was similarly clad and at 5.30 a.m. we emerged from the tent with only overboots and crampons to put on. We had kept our climbing boots inside our sleeping bags overnight to prevent them freezing but our canvas over-boots were solid blocks of ice. Somehow we struggled into them and then spent twenty minutes trying to do up our frozen crampon straps. Meanwhile our lukewarm tea froze in the mugs.

It was the 13th May and the coldest morning I remember, with a stinging wind blowing across the ridge. Fortunately we were all feeling fine and snow conditions were remarkably good with the knife edge crest packed hard underfoot. On the snow pinnacles where we had floundered before we now had to cut steps, but in two hours we had reached our furthest point of our previous sortie and could actually see the summit only about half a mile ahead. It was exhilarating crunching along on the hard knife edge, great fluted ice faces dropping away on either side. On the narrowest parts of the ridge there was almost no cornice but higher up where the ridge was three or four feet wide we had to pick our way very carefully across the 45-degree slope, keeping a safe distance below the overhanging snow. To our dismay as we neared the summit we found a towering ice pinnacle some fifty feet high straddling the whole ridge crest. An overhanging face of smooth gleaming ice leant menacingly towards us, appearing to block all access to the snow humps of the summit beyond.

It would have been fun to do an artificial route up the overhanging face, using ice pitons, screws, etriers and all the other paraphernalia we had brought up to Camp III for just such a contingency, so I was almost disappointed to find when we reached its foot that we could traverse round the side.

The last quarter of a mile was a race against the clouds which were boiling up from below, threatening to envelop us as they had done the last time. We had been going steadily for three hours without any stops and even Mingma and Pemba Norbu were beginning to tire, but on we went, promising ourselves a long rest on the top. Over one snow pinnacle and then suddenly there was the summit, a small snow cone capping a snow hump. At first sight it was remarkably unspectacular a top to so steep a mountain but when we trod steps up the cone I suddenly put my foot through into space and found myself dramatically looking down into nothingness. We managed to take some impressive summit photographs with the cloud swirling up behind, then retired into a more sheltered spot to take some compass bearings and Abney level readings on the few peaks which were still visible. Everything in sight was lower than us. It was bitterly cold and when Barbara tried to change the film in her camera the film had become so brittle that it broke. The Abney level had also frozen, making it very difficult to use, and my hands were so numb that it was almost impossible to hold the compass steady. With all these preoccupations we had little time to remember that we were on the summit of our first 21,000-foot mountain, the first women ever to climb a peak of that height.

We managed to eat some chocolate and biscuits and sucked a little condensed milk out of a tube, then turned round to go down again. The clouds were now swishing round the ridge and driving snow was rapidly filling our footsteps so we sped down as fast as possible and in two and a half hours stumbled into camp again. Nancy greeted us from the Sherpas' tent where she was brewing tea; Denise and Pat were still in their sleeping bags. Casually Nancy asked how we had got on, taking it for granted that the bad weather had turned us back again: Equally casually but with a broad grin Mingma replied, "Today tuppa". When they realised that we really had reached the top Denise and Pat came to life and excitedly asked for the whole story. They all made a great fuss of us, and we could hardly contain the joy of having climbed this beautiful mountain so spectacularly towering above all else in the area.

Pat was only suffering slightly from the altitude now, but Denise was really ill. This was a real blow to such a fine climber. Overnight her temperature had gone soaring up to 103 degrees. She was slightly better now but still very weak and feverish, with what Nancy diagnosed as a touch of either pneumonia or bronchitis. Since altitude aggravates any illness it was obvious that we must get her down to Camp II before she became any worse. Fortunately at this point Ang Pema, Katcheri and the younger Pemba Norbu turned up bringing more food and paraffin from Camp II on Dorothea's instructions. This meant that Barbara and I, Mingma and the two Pemba Norbus could take Denise down whilst Nancy, Pat, Ang Pema and Katcheri stayed at Camp III for another night and tried for the summit next day.

Shakily Denise went down in the middle of the rope with Mingma firmly belaying from above. She managed very well but it was a relief when at 2 p.m. we reached the foot of the ice triangle and Camp II came into sight. There Dorothea, Dawa, Ang Temba and

Pasang were waiting, completely mystified by our antics. We had obviously not given up the peak altogether since not everyone was coming down, but through binoculars they could see that it was the summit party who were descending. The one possibility that apparently never occurred to them was that we had already reached the summit. When Mingma and Pemba Norbu shouted down the news there was a stunned silence and then wild yells from the Sherpas. Dorothea and Dawa came running up to meet us and there were handshakes all round and a flood of questions.

Coming down two thousand feet had made Denise feel considerably better and, the best tonic of all, there were letters from home waiting for all three of us, fetched from the Post Office at Jumla seven days walk away by Pasang and Krishna Rana. This was the only mail we received in three months. Later in the day we heard on our radio that a spell of fine weather was on the way.

The next morning was fine and sunny and through binoculars four tiny dots could be seen moving towards the summit. We could follow them much of the way and it seemed almost certain they would make it. Nancy and Pat with Ang Pema and Katcheri cut our time by a third. They also had a much clearer view from the summit and were able to see that our peak, Lha Shamma, was indeed the highest in the whole area. At 3 p.m. they arrived down in Camp II, tired but triumphant. Nancy was dancing with joy and Pat's usual calm almost disappeared in jubilation. Denise had already gone on down to Base Camp with some of the Sherpas; Dorothea had tried to come up to Camp III the previous day with Dawa but had been forced back by the snowstorm. She decided therefore that now two parties had climbed the mountain we would pack up all the camps and go down to base to climb on the Kagmara Lekh on the other side of the valley.

Barbara and I were keen to climb on the Kagmaras but were also full of another plan to go and explore the unknown valleys lying north-west of our mountain. The 17,000-foot col above Camp I appeared to lead into the first of these valleys so the obvious course was to do this survey trip now before going back to base. Tentatively I broached the subject to Dorothea and was delighted when she agreed, allowing us four days food and paraffin and one Sherpa, Ang Temba.

Before leaving Camp II, I climbed the knoll for the last time for a view westwards to the valleys, peaks, and passes we were going to explore. They looked gloriously mysterious and remote, attracting one with that irresistible magnetism which mountaineers cannot define but only accept. In the words of the poet-mountaineer, William Bell:

> Even there he would desire
> the distant ridge, would sigh for these
> ranges further to the north,
> colder, sharper, more immense;
> every morning setting forth
> to reach a higher waste of snows.

21 UNTRODDEN VALLEYS

From the col above Camp I we descended westwards into a new world, into valleys which neither local people nor outsiders had ever penetrated or even seen. There is nothing more fascinating than this sort of exploration, and for Barbara and me the five days we spent on this survey trip were almost the highlight of the whole expedition.

We set off from Camp I on a fine cloudless morning with warm golden sunlight making the peaks look friendly and close. The snow was unusually crisp and near the col it was so slippery that we had to cut steps. We had met so little hard snow or ice on the expedition that after some discussion we had decided not to take crampons, but now we began to wonder whether we had not made a bad mistake. From the col we looked over the other side, praying for an easy slope down into the hanging valley, but all we could see was a steep slope of hard snow plunging downwards to end in a line of cliffs. Below the cliffs were great piles of avalanche debris. It hardly looked promising but this col of 16,700 ft was the only dip on the whole south ridge of Lha Shamma and so the only means of access into both the hanging valley and other unknown valleys beyond. (See map on p.156.)

We were determined to explore this area but to attempt a descent down the hard snow without crampons would have been horribly dangerous. Barbara gallantly went back to Camp I to fetch them whilst I took photographs and bearings for the survey and Ang Temba had a good rest. His tall, lean frame was bowed under a load of more than 50 pounds and Barbara and I both had about 40 pounds for, as well as food and paraffin for four days, a tent, rope and camping equipment, we had several heavy survey instruments.

Barbara returned after an hour and a half and when we had strapped on crampons we began the descent, Ang Temba on the bottom of the rope to find the way, Barbara in the middle and me at the top to act as backstops should he slip under his heavy load. The snow was just soft enough in places to kick steps down but it took us two hours to descend a thousand feet. There were cliffs at the foot of the snow slope as we had suspected and at first we thought we would have to traverse right across the avalanche slopes above them before we could find a way down, but in the centre was a slight break where the angle eased. Here we were able to cut steps in the ice between the rocks. Halfway down Ang Temba slipped on an ice-covered rock. His huge load fell over his head and dragged him down. Another rock stopped him sliding further before his weight came on the rope but he could not get up until we went and lifted the load off. Altogether it was a great relief when we safely reached the bottom, swearing firmly that on no account were we going back up that slope. We would just have to find another way out of the valley.

We had dropped down some two thousand feet to reach the floor of the hanging valley, and now were faced with a long upward traverse to reach the next col at the valley head. The wide valley floor was filled with soft snow, the sides covered with avalanche debris. Climbing over the great piles of tumbled ice blocks was an exhausting business, but with the possibility of another avalanche roaring down on to us at any moment we did not rest till at 5 p.m. we reached the safety of a large snow hump just below the second col. This hump stood out like a large island among the debris, and encamped on its top we felt safe from any enormous avalanche Lha Shamma cared to hurl down at us.

We could not afford the weight of two tents so had brought only the little Guinea. Barbara and I were quite happy to have Ang Temba in with us but at first he was very shy and wanted both to cook and eat out in the snow. Even when we persuaded him to come inside he insisted on sleeping with his head at the door end and in the morning we found him with his head half out of the tent in the snow. Fortunately he soon overcame these inhibitions and settled down happily.

From our camp an easy snow slope led up to the second col. Mountaineers are great optimists and it scarcely occurred to Barbara or me that the col might be impassable, so we were more pleased than particularly surprised when we reached the crest and saw a series of gentle snow basins leading down the other side. On the right a ridge led up from the col to Lha Shamma, on the left a series of small peaks dropped down towards the Jagdula Khola. Ahead, almost due north of the col, soared the steep snow cone of the 'Obergabelhorn', at its foot lay a transverse valley with a river running towards the Jagdula Khola. Immediately below us was a wide snow cirque feeding a small river which joined the main river at the foot of the 'Obergabelhorn'. This T-junction seemed the ideal place to site a camp for exploring the transverse valley in both directions and happily we headed down the snow basins towards it.

Joking, laughing, and singing we plunged downwards but the descent was not to be quite as straightforward as we expected. Halfway down we came to the edge of a great semi-circle of cliffs three or four hundred feet high. In the centre the line was broken where a huge frozen waterfall poured over the lip but our only chance of finding a way down seemed to be some grass ledges and sloping rock slabs at the western end. Very gingerly we zigzagged down the slippery grass, but then were faced with two hundred feet of rock slabs covered in mud and ice. Roping up, I belayed Barbara whilst she reconnoitred a route down the first hundred feet to a ledge, and then one by one we ferried the loads down. The second hundred feet were steeper and icier but Ang Temba proved very sure-footed without his load and managed to find a way round the side into a snow-filled gully. We lowered our packs down and then climbed down a muddy thirty-foot rock wall into the gully. It was not an easy climb and as I had been belaying at the top I had to climb down last. Ang Temba stood ready to catch me if I slipped but all went well with Barbara talking me down step by step.

At the bottom a thick, firm layer of snow covering the river provided an easy corridor down towards the junction. It was a delightful green spot with silver birches growing up the hillsides and grassy flats by the sparkling river, with plenty of juniper bushes for firewood. For the first time since leaving our Lower Base Camp seven days before we camped on grass instead of snow and the evening was warm enough to sit outside round a campfire. We had dropped from 17,000 ft to only 12,000 ft. We only hoped that we could find another way out of the valley so that we did not have to climb up those 5,000 ft again.

There were two possibilities for an alternative route back: to reach the Maidan and force a route down the Jagdula Khola, or to find a col leading out of the valley eastwards to join up with the Tibetan track and thence back over the Kagmara La to Base Camp. We had only sufficient food and paraffin to be away four days, it would take us two days to return from here by the route we had come and probably longer by any other, and if we did not get back on the fifth day at the latest we knew that the others would abandon their own climbing on the Kagmara Lekh to mount a search party. This meant that we could only afford one day's exploration from our camp at the junction before starting back. It was difficult to decide which way to go, so eventually we compromised by asking Ang Temba to go down to the Maidan and see if he could find a way down the Jagdula Khola whilst we followed the river eastwards in search of a col out of the valley.

With no loads to weigh us down we set off in lighthearted mood the next morning. There is a very special joy in treading new ground and when this ground is an enchanting flower-filled valley, joy verges on ecstasy. Following the clear rushing stream we walked amongst clumps of silver birch and dark green conifers and over banks of primulas. We saw no animals but many birds: wagtails, dippers, and ram chukars (red-legged partridge) which screamed out of the bushes as we approached.

The going was rough and after a time the greenness gave way to scree and then glacial moraine. On our left towered the 'Obergabelhorn', radiating ridges like points of a star, on our right a long chain of peaks dropped down from Lha Shamma but there was nothing that looked an even faintly possible crossing place of the range. The river valley curved in a semi-circle round the base of the 'Obergabelhorn' and must once have been a large glacier. As we climbed over the piles of loose boulders or skirted enormous craters we were reminded of the horrors of the Bara Shigri in Kulu.

We saw no active glaciers in the Kanjiroba range and this was the only valley where we found extensive glacial debris. It seems that West Nepal has never been so heavily glaciated as the east of the country and for a long time now all the glaciers have been in retreat.

At 2 p.m. we reached the head of the valley and could see that there was not a single break or even low dip in the chain of high peaks which ran in the shape of a question mark from Lha Shamma to the 'Obergabelhorn'. It was disappointing but at least instructive to have our hopes shattered so definitely. As we were coming back down the valley we suddenly noticed something very odd: there was a huge cloud of smoke billowing round the corner from the direction of our camp. Soon it had filled the valley bottom and was even obscuring some of the 18,000-foot peaks above. Since we were the only people for many miles around we came to the conclusion that Ang Temba must have succeeded in setting fire to our camp and thence to the whole valley.

When we neared the corner the smoke drove us down to the edge of the river and we were wondering if we would even be able to reach the wreckage of our camp when we suddenly saw a figure sitting on a rock. It was Ang Temba, sheepishly waiting for us.

"Look, he's burned himself," Barbara exclaimed as she saw Ang Temba rubbing one knee, but when we reached him we found that he was unhurt, but very upset at what had happened. His little English had almost deserted him in this crisis but we gathered that on his way down to the Jagdula Khola he had been forced to cross the river, so on the other side had lit a small fire to dry his socks. A gust of wind had come just at the wrong moment and the little fire had gone roaring up the hillside. With the profusion of dry juniper and trees the whole hillside was ablaze in a moment, and now the fire reached 3,000 ft up to the snowline.

"But camp okay," Ang Temba added as an afterthought. It seemed the fire was confined to the other side of the river from our camp, but he had come up to meet us in case we should try to come back on that side. The route we had taken was one roaring holocaust, with fiery clouds of smoke obscuring the sun, but on the other side of the river we suffered nothing worse than waves of choking smoke. Ang Temba looked so dismayed that we could not help laughing and teasing him about his little fire. To add to his chagrin, half a mile from camp his nose suddenly began to bleed. With smoke swirling round and flames leaping on the other side we laid him out by the river and splashed cold water over him but it would not stop.

It was a very miserable Ang Temba who plodded into camp, clutching a bloody handkerchief to his nose, and muttering, "Ang Temba no good Sherpa. Bara Memsahib very angry." When we assured him that we would not tell either Dorothea (Bara Memsahib) or Dawa he cheered up, and we spent a very pleasant evening cooking and talking by the campfire, with the last of the sun slowly dying away on the peaks and a bright moon rising. The knowledge that tomorrow we would have to leave this idyllic campsite and start back to rejoin the bustle of Base Camp lent poignancy to the evening. The beauty and perfection of the scene gave me that same feeling of joyful sadness as the soaring strains of a Beethoven symphony.

Ang Temba had had no more luck than we in trying to find another route back to Base Camp, but before we retraced our steps we were determined to go down to the Maidan to have a look at the upper reaches of the Jagdula Khola. The Maidan was only three miles from our camp but it took us three hours to reach it, struggling through thick scrub, traversing steep scree slopes above the gorge, and crossing and recrossing the swirling river on dubious snow bridges. We finally had to leave the river where it plunged down a hundred feet between overhanging rock walls, and eventually reached the Maidan by climbing up steep earth and loose rock with only tree roots and juniper bushes as handholds.

When we had first seen the Maidan from the ridge of the Belvedere from above Tyson's Base Camp, it had appeared to be the perfect campsite, a flat expanse of grass and trees between the two rivers. Now we discovered that it was five hundred feet above both rivers which roared through deep cut gorges at this point, and there was no other water supply.

It was a fantastic spot with exotic vegetation and great dead trees lying grotesquely twisted like some primeval jungle. There was the eeriness of knowing that we were the first human beings ever to set foot here, and I would not have been surprised to see a prehistoric monster, or at least the yeti. Movement in a nearby thicket made us jump, but it was only some deer. The upper reaches of the Jagdula gorge looked even more formidable than the lower part. From the upper edge of the Maidan the valley narrowed again and both sides were very steep. The west side looked completely impassable, but on our side we thought that there might be a way across the top of the cliffs to a place where again the valley widened and there was a wooded flat by the riverside.

It was horribly frustrating to be at the foot of such an exciting unexplored gorge and to have no time to go up it. No one before had penetrated so far into the Kanjirobas. We were tempted to forget all other considerations and just go. We could eke out our food for several more days, especially now we had found some wild rhubarb, but we knew that the others were expecting us back that day. Even if we turned back now we would be a day late, and if we had not returned by the following evening they would certainly call off their climbing on the Kagmara Lekh to send a search party for us. There was no alternative but to turn back.

We reached Base Camp on the evening of the sixth day after a gruelling but uneventful climb over the two cols. We had run out of food and paraffin by this time so all we had to eat or drink for the day were handfuls of snow. At base we found Nancy and Pat with a signal up ready to recall Dorothea and Denise if we did not arrive that evening, so it was just as well we had turned back.

It was good to sit down, drink mug after mug of tea and eat roast potatoes whilst Pat and Nancy fussed round exclaiming how thin and worn we all looked. With nothing more energetic than washing planned for the morrow, we sat around the campfire for a long time exchanging stories and talking of those unknown valleys which already seemed more dream than reality.

22 KAGMARA LEKH

Ever since Denise first entered the valley, she had been attracted by Kagmara I, the largest and most impressive of the Kagmara Lekh which rose in a steep icy wall immediately opposite our Lower Base Camp. We estimated the height of Kagmara I to be about 20,000 ft but Tyson's survey brought it down to 19,560 ft. Almost in preference to the higher and more spectacular Lha Shamma, Denise had talked so often of climbing Kagmara I that it had become known as Denise's Peak. Now the chance had come and she and Dorothea had set off to climb it, come what may. They were both fully recovered, and intent on making up for not having reached the summit of Lha Shamma.

Nancy, Pat, and Ang Pema hurried up to join them the morning after Barbara and I returned to base. Meanwhile we had a busy rest day having our first washing session for a fortnight, and consuming the gigantic meals prepared by Pasang Sonar, our tough little cookboy and Mingma's brother-in-law. Pasang Sonar was one of the extra two Sherpas for whom we had no climbing equipment. He had been climbing on several previous expeditions so must have found it frustrating to be confined to Base Camp, yet he was unfailingly cheerful and willing. Each morning, however cold or wet, he appeared at our tent door with a broad grin, bearing piping-hot tea and porridge. He was always busy, whether squatting by the fire cooking or arriving back in camp with his tousled head barely visible above an enormous pile of firewood. Everyone was very keen that Pasang Sonar should have a chance to climb. Denise had lent him a spare pair of boots and we borrowed enough equipment for him to come up to the Kagmaras after we had finished surveying in the valley.

Luckily the next day dawned clear and cloudless, and we were able to complete the last two plane table stations on the east side of the Garpung Khola. It was a beautiful sunny morning and without a load I really enjoyed climbing up out of the valley. Katcheri came to help with the plane table and tripod. He was too shy and silent to be lively company but obviously enjoyed a leisurely day out with only the lightest of loads. From one point we saw seven little figures toiling up towards the foot of Kagmara I on their way to set up a second camp ready to make an attempt on the following day. Strangely I felt no pangs not to be with them climbing a new peak - surveying and exploration seemed an equal challenge.

At noon next day we reached their lower camp, one small tent almost lost in a wide snow basin. From here we had a brief glimpse of the other two parties approaching the top of the face of Kagmara I before cloud came down and enveloped the whole mountain. It seemed almost certain that they would reach the summit now, in which case when they descended again they might well pack up camp and come down. None of us were at all enthusiastic about going on up in the soft afternoon snow, but if we were to have any influence on plans for the next few days it seemed essential that we rendezvous with them that afternoon. It was desperately hard work in the thigh-deep snow but not as far as we expected, and we reached the camp just fifteen minutes before the main party arrived back from Kagmara I. They were all thrilled with the climb and seemed to have had a wonderful day. Over tea we heard the full story which I quote from Nancy's article in the *Pinnacle Club Journal*:

Next morning Pat and I plodded up to the new Camp I. Dorothea and Denise had gone on up to the col to the south of Kagmara I but had had to turn back on the ridge, again prevented by a gendarme of dangerous loose rock. They were talking about a terrific-looking route up the north face direct. Would it go? We all went up with heavy loads and established Camp II at about 18,000 ft on the Kagmara glacier at the foot of the north face. In the afternoon Mingma and Pemba Norbu climbed up the lower part of the face and put a fixed rope on the steepest part of the ice. Avalanches were falling on both sides of them and twice their thundering roar brought us leaping out of the tents to see if our Sherpas were still there. On 23rd May two parties set off to climb the north face of Kagmara I. Dorothea, Denise, Pembu Norbu and Mingma were the first assault party. Pat, Ang Pema and I, as the second team, kept ourselves at a respectful distance behind. This was a real Alpine climb on ice and snow all the way. A grand route and we reached the summit and lingered there as it was not so cold as on Our Peak. Pemba Norbu fell off, last man of the first party on the way down, but was held by Dorothea and when our turn came to negotiate this bit, Pat spent ages hacking out new ice steps and ice handholds too, it was so steep.

Looking up at the 2,000-foot face of steep snow and ice which they had climbed, Barbara and I were most impressed, yet it hardly occurred to any of us to reflect that at fifty-seven Dorothea had put up an extraordinary performance on this high peak. Her energy bore no relation to her age.

The Sherpas had obviously very much enjoyed this climb but after two long hard days had now had enough and wanted to go down to base. Dorothea and Pat also decided to go down the next day after one more smaller climb, but Denise and Nancy and, of course, Barbara and I were keen to stay up for as long as possible. Our three young Sherpas, Ang Temba, Katcheri and Pasang Sonar were also very anxious to climb, so we persuaded the three more experienced Sherpas returning to the valley to hand over their sleeping bags and high altitude equipment.

We all six squeezed into one two-man tent that evening to eat our dried egg omelette and mashed potato and discuss plans for the next few days. It was now the 23rd May and there was no sign of the monsoon arriving to spoil the perfect weather. We had originally planned to stay in the climbing area till the beginning of June but now that we had climbed the two major peaks in the area Dorothea felt it would be sensible to start the long walk out to Pokhara. Eventually a compromise was reached that we would spend three more days exploring and climbing in the Kagmaras before leaving the area.

The next morning Dorothea and Pat set off early to climb the small peak of Kagmara II before going down, whilst the rest of us packed up the camp ready to move it up onto the col between Kagmara I and II as a base for the next two days' climbing. I was so eager to be off that eventually I set off alone. At first the snow was quite crisp and I made good progress, but soon I was breaking through the softening snow up to my knees at every step. It was a most exhausting business, and I kept saying to myself, "I'll just go to that hump and sit down and wait for the others to arrive and take over the road-making" or "I'll stop after a hundred steps", but they were a long way behind and each time the thought of the snow getting softer every minute got me to my feet again.

Then the actual col was in sight. Another 385 steps, resting every twentieth step, and I was on its crest with a magnificent view out on to the eastern side of the range. The col was a broad windswept snow platform with a steep snow slope on the other side dropping about five hundred feet down on to a very wide flat snow field. A mile away across this rose the beautiful triangular peak which I had admired so often that it had become known as 'Jo's Peak'. This was the last outpost of the Kagmara Lekh, and beyond lay the wooded valleys of the upper Bheri River which we were to follow back right round the north of the Dhaulagiri massif.

We levelled three platforms for the tents before the Sherpas arrived, and then quickly erected them just as it began to snow. Nancy was feeling very listless and slightly sick so lay dozing in her tent with Denise, whilst Barbara and I whiled the afternoon away reading. Outside a strong wind heaped snow against the tent and thunder echoed ominously in the distance, but inside the tent we lay snug in our sleeping bags. Barbara was reading *The Humbler Creation* by Pamela Hansford Johnson and I was on Henry James' *Washington Square*. Our twelve expedition paperbacks were not carefully chosen but a strange random collection. In Kulu we had made the mistake of taking too serious a type of book, in Nepal we found we had veered in the other direction. Our two most popular books were *Doctor Zhivago* and *The Moon and Sixpence,* plus a general knowledge quiz book from Woolworth's. The snowstorm had stopped next morning and at 6 a.m. we set off to try to climb the 19,000-foot Triangle Peak, as we had named my peak. Nancy was still not well so stayed behind in camp with Katcheri, who also was not at his best. The other two Sherpas, Ang Temba and Pasang Sonar, were very keen to climb a mountain and would have hated to be left behind. Both of them were about twenty-eight and had been on several expeditions before but had never reached a summit. It was a glorious morning with the air fresh and clear and the sun slowly creeping down the symmetrical ridges of Triangle Peak till it covered the whole snow basin in warm golden light. We all took turns to make the route, and in an hour and a half had reached the foot of the narrow snow ridge leading to the summit. There we roped up and at first Ang Temba and I took turns to lead the way, with Denise having a great time filming from behind. The ridge was steep and corniced on one side, providing exhilarating climbing without being too difficult or dangerous. We were a very light-hearted party with everyone thoroughly enjoying themselves, and it was fun to have such gay young Sherpas who were very competent but quite happy for us to lead much of the time. When it came to the last few rope-lengths up to the top, we let Pasang Sonar go in front. He was so delighted at the prospect of his first summit that he almost ran along the ridge, with poor Denise on the other end of the rope puffing like a grampus in her desperate effort to keep up.

The summit was very tiny and rather unstable. Three of us sat on it very happily but Denise firmly maintained that it was a circular cornice like a mushroom of snow on a slender stalk. From it we had an excellent view of the whole Kagmara chain. We had given the peaks provisional numbers, working south from Kagmara I, and decided the next day to climb Kagmara III, either by the ridge from Kagmara II or via the snow field, which looked a fairly easy snow climb. From Kagmara III a narrow ridge led up to the more impressive Kagmara IV. If time permitted we hoped to try this as well, but tomorrow was our last day so we also had to get right down to base, a descent of 7,000 ft.

As we sat on the small summit and gazed across at that range of unclimbed, untouched peaks so tantalisingly close, we were very tempted just to disregard the time limit and take an extra day or two to move a camp into the snow basin from which we could try not only Kagmara III and IV but also V, the spectacular pointed peak on the southern end of the chain and visible from Kaigaon. Even Nancy, who had the greatest incentive to try to leave the area quickly in order to make sure of catching her plane from Pokhara, was desperately keen to go on climbing. She was still not feeling well when we got back to camp but had recovered sufficiently next day to come on an attempt at Kagmara III.

I was very anxious to obtain a good photographic panorama of the whole area from the Kagmaras so suggested climbing Kagmara II first to make sure of this before the clouds came up at midday, and then traversing the ridge from there on to Kagmara III. The others readily agreed, and I set off up the ridge with Pasang Sonar whilst they went round by the snow field. Kagmara II is a comparatively small hump on the chain but from the top we had a fine view out to the Jagdula Lekh, the 'Obergabelhorn', Lha Shamma, the deep wooded valley beyond the Kagmara La, Kagmara I, and in the other direction the snow pyramid of Kagmara III.

We then descended the south ridge which was still untrodden since Pat and Dorothea had not gone over that side. It was a steep knife edge with a very long convex slope dropping down to the snow field. Underneath the new snow was hard ice, but our crampons gripped well enough to avoid cutting steps. When we reached the bottom the others were nearing the top of Kagmara III, which was a straightforward snow slog. Using the steps they had kicked we reached the top not long after them.

It was an anti-climax; westward an exciting ridge led off towards Kagmara IV but there was no time to go farther. Sadly we realised that this was the end of the high peaks and further exploration, and we must hurry down to base.

The descent was miserable. All of us were very tired and heavily loaded with tents and equipment, and we fell into one snow drift after another with a biting wind driving snow into our faces. The lower slopes were so soft that the only way to progress was to sit down and roll. On the snow we had to push ourselves down, but near the bottom the snow abruptly changed to ice. Barbara was just ahead of me at this point and went zooming straight into a pile of rocks. Luckily she was only bruised and we picked our way down the rocks and grass till we were faced with another ice slope. I was hardly on it when in a flash my feet slid from under me and I was hurtling down the ice on my back. Desperately I tried to brake with my ice axe and in the process hit myself on the head with it. I managed to stop just short of the rocks but when I put my hand to my head it was covered with blood. As Barbara sailed by beautifully under control, I shouted that I had hit my head. At first she did not hear but then she saw the blood on the snow. It made a horrible mess but was actually only a scalp wound, and apart from a headache I felt nothing. Barbara produced a balaclava to soak up the blood and we went on down, trying to pretend that nothing had happened. The Sherpas wanted to carry me back into camp but when I declined and they realised it was not serious, they teased me unmercifully.

With two potentially serious accidents on the way down, we decided that perhaps after all it was as well that the climbing had come to an end and we need tempt Providence no longer. Munching delicious baked potatoes in the kitchen shelter, we put away all thoughts of the climbs we might have done and began to talk of the next phase, the 200-mile walk out to Pokhara.

23 OM MANI PADME HUM

From our valley of the Garpung Khola there were three possible exits, the high col south-east of Lha Shamma, the Kagmara La north of Kagmara I, or the track on which we had come up from Kaigaon. Both cols were still covered with too much soft snow to be practicable for laden porters but Dorothea was keen for a small party to cross one of the cols and explore the eastern side of the Kanjiroba Himal. Everyone felt that Dorothea should have the fun of this exploration, and I was chosen to accompany her in order to extend our survey over to the eastern side of Lha Shamma. Meanwhile the main party would return to Kaigaon to collect the food we had left there and organise porters or yaks to transport it up the Bheri valley to Rasi, where the two parties would rendezvous before setting off along the Barbung Khola around the north of Dhaulagiri to Pokhara. (See maps pp. 140 and 156.)

Remembering our aching shoulders on the previous survey trip, this time I packed the barest minimum - one sleeping bag, air bed, down jacket, one spare pair of socks, toothbrush, camera, film and survey equipment. Three Sherpas, Pemba Norbu 1, Katcheri, and Pasang Sonar, were coming with us to carry the two light tents and 60 pounds of food for the six days.

After some discussion we decided not to take a primus or paraffin but to rely on finding firewood every night; a bold assumption to make, but one that proved to be justified.

On the evening of 27th May we had a cheerful farewell party at Base Camp consuming large quantities of rum fudge toddy, then left at 9 a.m. next morning, arranging to meet in six days' time. Since no one knew how long our respective routes would take or how long would be needed to obtain porters in Kaigaon, this arrangement showed remarkable optimism.

We were not the first people to cross the Kagmara La that year, for a day or two earlier a Tibetan family had come over with a herd of yaks. They camped near our base and spent hours squatting round our camp examining such wonders as polythene bags, elastic bands and zip fasteners. Meanwhile from a safe distance we studied their yaks, the first yaks I had seen. They looked gloriously cuddly with long black hair and ridiculously dainty legs like shaggy bison, but their horns were long and sharply pointed, and at the slightest disturbance or the sight of a bright colour they would go wild, charging anyone in sight. The main party were using the yaks to carry the equipment back to Kaigaon, and as Dorothea and I climbed the hill opposite Base Camp towards the Kagmara La, we could see yaks hurtling round amongst the tents with boxes and Sherpas flying in all directions.

We reached the crest of the 16,000-foot col at 2 p.m. after a long pull up in very soft snow, at times waist deep. It was a grey misty day and on top of the pass a minor blizzard was raging. On the other side the snow was equally soft. We fell into snowdrifts or frequently broke through the icy crust into streams and were wet to the skin and almost exhausted when at last the snow gave way to bare earth and scree. The Sherpas found the way to a green flat area where there was dried yak dung for fuel. From 16,000 ft we had dropped to about 12,000 and were at the junction of the two gorges and the two tracks marked on the Survey of India map. Of these the Kagmara La was clearly the normal route and we saw no signs of a path leading over the other col, nor did we hear of anyone ever having crossed it.

The track continued to follow the river, leading through cool pine forests and grassy glades with a wonderful variety of wild flowers. In one clearing we came across two Tibetans and their herd of yaks. On the roof of their small stone shack they were drying the skin and carcase of a yak that they had recently killed. The rest of the herd were grazing on the hillside above and, as we watched, one of the Tibetans rounded them up by shouting and whistling to his dogs in the same way that a Welsh shepherd would round up sheep.

Farther on we came to the first village, marked Pudamigaon on the Survey of India map but called Pungmo by orientalist Snellgrove, who had visited it in 1956. Houses were very similar to those of Kaigaon, with the typical Tibetan flat roofs. All were stone built with horizontal wooden beams at intervals and two storeyed, the livestock being kept on the ground floor. Inside, a notched tree trunk formed a solid ladder through a stair-hole to reach the family living quarters on the upper floor and another ladder led out on to the roof.

We were to see these Tibetan-style houses all the way along the Barbung Khola north of Dhaulagiri, for we had now crossed into the Inner Himalayas whose inhabitants are almost exclusively Bhotiyas of Tibetan origin. This infiltration of Bhotiyas into the high valleys north of the main Himalayan chain has been going on since the Middle Ages and is still taking place. There has been virtually no mixing with the Nepalese population, since the valleys of the Inner Himalayas are so high that only those used to the high plateau of Tibet are acclimatised to living there. In the highest valleys of Central Nepal live the Thakalis and in East Nepal the Sherpas, who migrated together from Tibet as a single tribe in the Middle Ages. Both have preserved their Buddhist religion, customs, dress and general way of life intact, and the Sherpas have developed their own language which is closely related to Tibetan.

Between the Bhotiyas, Thakalis and Sherpas there are now some local differences such as the style of house building, but there is still a strong unity of culture, language and religion, which made our Sherpas very much at home as they talked to the villagers of Pungmo, over three hundred miles west of their own homes in Sola Khumbu.

At either end of the village was an entrance chorten surmounting the path, built as a porch with square base and round dome and painted inside on the ceiling and four walls. The paintings were not the usual Buddhist divinities, but contained elements of bon-po, the old indigenous religion of pre-Buddhist times. Excitedly the Sherpas told us that these round-domed chortens were exactly the same as those in Sola Khumbu.

'Om Mani Padme Hum' ('Hail to the Jewel in the Lotus Flower') the inscribed rocks proclaimed, and on every bridge and pass fluttered hundreds of prayer flags.

We camped for the night at the point where the river flowing down from Phoksumdo Lake joined the Suli Gad. Next morning we left at 6 a.m. for Phoksumdo Lake, planning to have breakfast later when the sun rose somewhere on the climb up. At first we followed the right bank of the river but then the path left it and toiled up and up without a sign of any more water. We were all very hot, thirsty and footsore when suddenly we crested a rise and saw before us a huge waterfall, a wide sheet of foaming water dropping two or three hundred feet in one slow bound. It was so stunningly beautiful that we just stood and stared.

Phoksumdo Lake was still out of sight but the river which tumbled so spectacularly into the gorge below was evidently the lake's outlet. Our precipitous little path led high above the waterfall and up over a ridge from where we had our first glimpse of the lake, a sparkle of blue water beyond the green meadows, houses and chortens of the village of Ringmo. Through cool beech woods we dropped down to the shore. It was a perfect spot, with the smooth, wide expanse of the lake stretching into the distance between rocky mountainsides. Not a ripple disturbed the surface and the water was that incredibly deep turquoise blue of the Italian mountain lakes.

On the map the Tibetan border was marked as lying forty miles north of Phoksumdo Lake, but in these remote parts the border is very indefinite and was neither marked nor patrolled. From the villagers our Sherpas learned that a few weeks earlier a party of eight armed Chinese had come over from Tibet and spent ten days around Ringmo, apparently surveying.

We found the villagers remarkably incurious, and although they were all well aware of the whereabouts of our camp only a few came near. As only three or four Westerners had ever visited Ringmo before, this lack of curiosity was very surprising after the crowds we had attracted on our way from Nepalganj to Kaigaon. We wondered at first if they were afraid of us. They were certainly afraid of our cameras and did not like us photographing even the yaks, houses or fields. Yet the few who did gather round our camp were charming people, smiling delightedly each time they saw some new miracle such as binoculars or air beds. The Sherpas were able to talk to them and soon Pemba Norbu initiated a great bargaining session, exchanging an empty tin for four pounds of potatoes, and another for three eggs.

Neither paper money nor coins seemed to be used but the surplus food from their fertile valley was bartered for salt and other products of Tibet. Their clothes were entirely homespun from yaks' wool or sheep skins and we saw no sign of anything imported from India. With their long dark hair and sheepskin clothes the men looked very fierce as they ploughed the terraced fields with primitive wooden ploughs drawn by yaks, but they could not have been more friendly or gentle.

Later we walked through the pine woods to the gompa, a monastery perched in splendid isolation on a high rocky promontory above the lake. It was a collection of two-storeyed flat-roofed houses, distinguished as a monastery by the huge prayer flags fluttering on poles at every corner. All the buildings were rather dilapidated and the inside was even more neglected with paint peeling off the walls, a damp musty smell and a thick layer of dust everywhere. We saw only one lama, a stooped old man in tattered purple robes, who silently showed us round. The inner sanctum of the gompa was a square room in the shape of a courtyard lit by a small central opening in the roof. We could see little in the gloom but at one end perceived a dust-covered image of Buddha. On the walls were faded paintings and from the wooden beams hung several old masks used by the lamas in devil dances, covered so thickly by white dust and cobwebs that they could not have been used for years.

Later, in Central Nepal, Dawa took us all to the gompa at Mukut, which was being reconstructed and repainted from funds contributed by the local people. There we saw local artists painting scenes from the life of Buddha onto the plaster walls, copying traditional designs from old tankas and books. Craftsmen too were cleaning and repairing the huge Tibetan books bound between long narrow wooden covers, the great temple drums, finely decorated libation cups and silver and brass prayer wheels.

Phoksumdo Lake was so idyllic that I could happily have never moved from its shores, had we not been anxious to obtain views of the Kanjiroba range from the east. We had no time for full-scale exploration, but were able to spend one day following the path north towards Sya Gompa around the western side of the lake. We gave the Sherpas the choice of coming with us or staying in camp, but were delighted when they all three elected to come with us. The local people were so trustworthy that we had no qualms about leaving our camp unattended. In holiday mood and unladen we set off along the tiny track which skirts round the cliffs. At times the rock face dropped straight into the water and the path was built across narrow gangways of logs precariously supported on wooden pegs driven into cracks in the rock. It looked a most unlikely route but was the only way round the lake; on the eastern side the cliffs were completely sheer. After an hour we came to an open wooded valley with a stream running down into the lake. The dense vegetation was reminiscent of the Maidan in the Jagdula Khola and here too we found clumps of wild rhubarb.

Reluctantly we left the shade of this cool green valley to climb up a bare hillside in the full glare of the midday sun. Above the cliffs a level path contoured round the mountain side, which was so steep that dislodged pebbles fell straight into the deep blue of the lake a thousand feet below. When we reached the crest of the spur I was surprised to see ahead not the gorge or bare rugged valley I had imagined, but a flat-bottomed expanse of green. We contoured some way up the south side of the valley to try to obtain a better view of the peaks at its head, and then scrambled up snow-filled gullies and rock ribs to the lowest summit on the spur descending to the lake. From here we were able to see the eastern side of the chain of peaks linking Lha Shamma and the 'Obergabelhorn' but cloud blocked any more distant views.

We spent another delightful evening at our camp by the lake, eating roast potatoes by a blazing campfire, and then headed down next day towards Rasi. This proved to be much farther from Phoksumdo Lake than the map indicated and it took two long hot days to reach it, climbing up and down through beech and spruce forests or high above the river traversing steep alpine pastures covered with primulas, anemones and purple flags.

Our last camp was in a grassy glade by the river Suli Gad. A bright moon gleamed on the river and the bushes of white syringa surrounding our camp, their intoxicating sweet smell mingling with the smoke of our wood fire. Dorothea relaxed in the tent reading whilst I sat out by the fire learning to play Sherpa tunes on my bamboo flute and listening to Pemba Norbu softly singing the songs of Sola Khumbu.

24 THROUGH THE LAND OF THE BHOTIYAS

It is a woman's prerogative to change her mind, and with six of us it was inevitable that there were changes of plan about the route out. Our original idea had been to return to Nepalganj, but when from the Mahabharat range we had our first view of the country around Dhaulagiri, it had looked so exciting that we immediately decided to try to walk out that way, a decision we never regretted, even when it seemed yaks would lose all our equipment in hazardous river crossings and that we would never reach Pokhara.

Few walks anywhere in the world can be so full of contrast as these two hundred miles from Kaigaon to Pokhara. We passed from pine forests in the Bheri valley to the barren desert and canyons of the high Tibetan plateau, across snow passes in the Mukut Himal and down into the tropical steaminess of the Kali Gandaki. Land formation, vegetation and architecture were constantly changing as we descended from the Tibetan-style villages of the Inner Himalaya to the Thakali and Gurung settlements of Central Nepal. It was fascinating country, with all the excitement of a new route both for us and for the Sherpas.

Dorothea and I found the main party encamped in dried-up paddy fields at Dunaihi, two miles up the Bheri valley from its junction with the Suli Gad at Rasi. They had arrived only a few hours earlier from Tibrikot but we were to spend the next two days in Dunaihi raising enough porters to continue eastwards. Nancy was busy as ever treating all manner of patients, including a sick water buffalo, but the rest of us became impatient to be off. Dunaihi was hot and dusty with unpleasant afternoon sandstorms, but higher up the valley were cool pine forests and bubbling streams where we bathed in clear rock pools. Pat used to lounge in these for hours, apparently impervious to the icy water. Ten miles above Dunaihi we came to Tarakot, a compact group of some twenty-five flat-roofed houses strategically situated on a hilltop commanding the deep-cut valley. An entrance chorten led into the village, for Tarakot is on the fringe of the Buddhist culture which dominates the whole of this Inner Himalayan region.

A few miles beyond Tarakot lies Chhandul (Sa-'dul) Gompa, up a remote side valley on the other side of the Bheri. It promised to be an interesting and beautiful place but eventually I set off to visit it on my own since Denise and Nancy were laid low with dysentery, Dorothea was busy organising our new porters, and Barbara and Pat were washing their clothes in an effort to get rid of sheep ticks acquired the previous night when they had bivouacked in a disused shepherds' hut.

We had breakfasted by a small stream high above the Bheri valley which had now narrowed into a rocky gorge. Looking back I could see the houses of Tarakot perched on a green hilltop above the river which we had crossed by a wooden bridge, but ahead the valley sides were so steep that I wondered how there could possibly be a way across to the monastery. After a mile or two of level walking through pine woods on the main track, a crazy little path descended in incredibly steep zigzags towards the river. Clutching on to tree roots I made my way down the sandy surface and flights of rock steps until I came to a large black hole. It was a sort of rock chimney with a notched pole leading down into a cave. Thence rock-slabs dropped down again on to a single plank bridge spanning the torrent below.

An equally steep path hairpinned up the other bank, flanked by huge rocks inscribed in Tibetan script with the invocation 'Om Mani Padme Hum'. As I climbed up I felt myself on the verge of a hidden paradise. There can be few places on earth so beautiful, remote and inaccessible as this lost valley where lamas came and built their monastery of Sa-'dul Gompa, 'Tranquillizer of the Land'. Cresting the lip I found myself in meadows and groves silent save for innumerable birds. There were chortens, prayer flags and the stone buildings of the gompa, overgrown and dilapidated. An old man was sitting outside spinning his prayer wheel. As I approached he looked up but showed no surprise although only one white man had ever been there before. I spoke to him in Nepali and English but he spoke only Tibetan, so after offering me some water from a copper flagon he returned to contemplation whilst I wandered round. It was an idyllic place with a magnificent view; I had thought Phoksundo Lake to be the apogee of peace and beauty but here was peace even more absolute.

The main track continued through forests of firs, larch and cedars and then crossed the turbulent river by a narrow log bridge. The grey glacial water of the Bheri was now our only water supply. It was so full of mud and mica that even after being thoroughly boiled and strained there was half an inch of sediment in each mug of tea.

We followed the Bheri across grassy flats where goats and yaks were grazing and Tibetan nomads were camping in low black tents. Then came an abrupt halt where a cliff dropped straight into the water. We thought we must have taken a wrong turning somewhere until we saw a notched pole leading out on to a small rock ledge from which more ledges dropped into the distance. It was the most sensational 'path' I have ever seen. A series of narrow birch logs linked one tiny ledge with the next and then there was a climb down smooth sloping rock slabs which would certainly have merited the grade of a Difficult to Very Difficult rock-climb in England. With a fifty-foot drop into the raging torrent below the price of a slip, we traversed very carefully diagonally downwards until we reached the last section where one had to wade along the bottom of the cliff, thigh-deep in the fast-flowing river.

It was no route for laden porters but they insisted on coming down. It seemed that the only alternative route was half a day's climb up the mountainside which they were not prepared to do. We compromised by rigging up safety ropes on the most dangerous section and splitting the seventy-pound loads into two wherever possible. The Sherpas as always were wonderful at helping and encouraging them along and in only two hours all were safely down.

Our expedition dog managed to fall into the river but he fought his way across on to a sand bank and emerged with wagging tail. No amount of coaxing would make him swim across again, and when Ang Pema and Pemba Norbu tried to wade across, the current almost swept them away. Denise and I tried from higher up and found it equally impossible. Finally we decided to set off up the bank in the hope that when he saw us all leaving he would be induced to take the plunge and, to our joy, this worked.

After this rock-climb we walked across the pebble flats of the wide river bed to Kakot, a small group of houses at the foot of the gorge where the Bheri becomes the Barbung Khola. Above Kakot the

210

country is arid and bare and we were to see no more trees until we dropped down to Sangda on the other side of the Mukut Himal, seven days walk away.

From Kakot we were employing yaks to transport our stores. Each family in Kakot owned one yak and as the great shaggy creatures shambled on to our campsite the entire population of Kakot arrived too. They were the least friendly people we met in the whole of Nepal and very soon trouble started as they stood in a menacing group demanding higher pay. They also maintained that the yaks would not carry our square expedition boxes and we would have to repack everything into sacks. As if to prove the point the first yak to be loaded with boxes immediately tossed them off. Yaks had carried boxes docilely from Base Camp to Kaigaon but under pressure from the crowd Dorothea diplomatically gave way and agreed to transfer all our stores into sacks.

As soon as the first box was empty the real reason for the fuss became apparent as a village-woman triumphantly carried it off to her house. Quickly others followed her example. It seemed that we had been very gullible but we were not going to be duped by this roguery since the boxes would be needed again when we had to return the sacks. The Sherpas chased off in pursuit and succeeded in prising them out of the women's hands. When the locals saw that they had been foiled they became really angry and a free fight developed. Dawa hurled a man into the bushes and another knocked Krishna to the ground, whilst the women stood on a bank overlooking the camp, shouting and gesticulating and throwing the occasional stone. Half-loaded yaks charging round added to the confusion, but eventually Dawa quelled the riot by threatening to employ other yaks belonging to Tibetans up the valley instead of the Kakot ones. This was a shot in the dark but it had the desired effect - the hubbub died down and they even helped the Sherpas load the last few beasts. Thankfully we left Kakot at midday, accompanied by two yakmen.

When we unpacked the loads that night we found that our equipment had suffered more damage in that one day than on the whole of the rest of the trip. The medical gear had fared the worst with hundreds of ampoules broken and screw-top tins so dented that they could not be opened. The survey tripod had been smashed and the food looked as though elephants had trampled on it, with tins grotesquely out of shape and crushed biscuits and chocolate covering everything. Barbara succeeded in making a sumptuous trifle out of the 'yakked' food, but it was infuriating that all this damage had been completely unnecessary since the yakmen now agreed that the yaks could carry the wooden boxes and we spent the evening repacking them.

The valley of the Barbung Khola was magnificently wild. To the north bare brown hills rolled towards Tibet. To the south lay the Dhaulagiri massif guarded by great rock walls and towers, the architecture of erosion. Slender pinnacles soared above the valley floor and dark chasms spilled bright waterfalls into the muddy river.

This is the high land of the Bhotiyas, the Buddhist inhabitants of the Inner Himalaya, and we passed many chortens and mani walls. These long stone walls bear slabs inscribed with prayers or pictures of Buddha and stand in the centre of the track with a path leading round them on either side. The devout always pass them on the left and even the yaks instinctively seemed to go that way. A few villages clung on to the northern slopes of the barren valley. Situated at over 13,000 ft, they must be some of the highest settlements in Asia. Below the village of Tarenggaon we crossed the Barbung Khola by an alarmingly springy single-plank bridge and then watched the dramatic spectacle of the yaks swimming across. From here it was only about three miles to the large village of Mukut where we were to change yaks again. One of the difficulties of yak transport is that yaks become very difficult and tired after only three or four days on the move and have to be rested for two days before going on again.

Mukut also lay at 13,000 ft but was a surprisingly prosperous place; its network of irrigated millet fields formed a vivid splash of green in the arid valley. With Dawa we went on a shopping expedition to the headman's house which stood inside a stone courtyard in the centre of the village. It had one large living room on the upper floor, the only light coming from a tiny window in one corner and the stair-well leading onto the roof. In the kitchen half of the room there were brass and copper ladles and cooking pots, large stones for grinding flour and the long wooden butter churns we had also seen in Tibetan tents in Kulu. On the wall was a sieve made out of hide and on the

212

floor a great pile of cured sheepskins. The other part of the room formed the living quarters with a hearth in the centre where cooking pots simmered on an iron tripod. Under the window was a long stone bench covered with rugs on which we were seated as guests of honour. There was no chimney and a thick black fuzz covered the rafters. Whilst Dawa purchased rice and atta (a wheat flour used to make chapattis) we were given brass cups filled with rakshi and then taken up on to the roof to see the mist-wreathed Dhaulagiri range towering to the south. In one corner of the roof was a small cubicle, the latrine. It was simply a chute into the ground floor and was joined by a similar one from the animals' winter quarters. Both fuel and manure are so scarce in these regions that no organic matter is allowed to go to waste.

We left Mukut again on 15th June with fourteen laden yaks and three spares. Bright purple saxifrage and white anemones clustered by the path and a brilliant rainbow arched over the rocky gorge below. We camped in mist at about 16,000 ft, far above supplies of firewood or even dry yak dung so that we had to cook on primus stoves. The next morning we woke to see the ethereal beauty of an ice peak floating above the clouds. It was one of the Dhaulagiri range on the other side of the Mukut Khola and over 25,000 ft high, but in the golden light of early morning it looked very close and almost climbable.

That day we crossed the Mukut Himal by an 18,000-foot pass which made us all puff and pant again. The yaks did not like the snow but scrambled up as agilely as mountain goats. From the back view they made a comic sight as they delicately picked their way, shaggy hair swishing like grass skirts above their dainty little legs.

On the other side we found snow peaks bounding a flat open valley. I have seldom seen a more desolate place, yet subtle tones of brown and grey gave it a wild beauty. We were now on the edge of the Tibetan plateau, the contours were more gentle and the landscape terraced by erosion. Next day we climbed to the last high pass of the journey. The top was just under 18,000 ft, but there was very little snow for the snow line here is much higher than in West Nepal. Alpine flowers edged the track, gentians peeped through the snow, and we caught a glimpse of Dhaulagiri. The 26,795 ft snow cone looked surprisingly unimpressive from our vantage point, but Mingma assured us that it was Dhaulagiri and, when he offered to wager a hundred rupees on it, we took his word. A long descent followed, dropping right down to the river Keha Lungpa which loops round the northern end of the Dhaulagiri massif to join the Kali Gandaki.

Whilst the yaks swam across the raging river we crossed a narrow bridge of slippery slates precariously balanced on two tree trunks, with no vestige of a handrail. This was one of the many 'no good bridges' we encountered. On the other side of the gorge the track was so narrow that the yaks had to be reloaded with the bulky items on the off-side. For a time they ambled docilely along head to tail, but then the leader baulked at a rocky slab and tried to turn round. They all turned and plunged to and fro on the edge of the drop but Ang Temba grasped the leader by the horns and got him moving forward again to avert disaster.

The yaks continued to give us trouble, often wandering away from our camp and some mornings the Sherpas had to spend several hours rounding them up. One particularly difficult beast had to be lassoed each day, a task reserved for Ang Temba who was a wizard with yaks. Below 10,000 ft it became too hot for yaks and we changed to dzos, crossbreeds between yaks and cows. The dzos were distinctly less temperamental but peculiar, ugly beasts, for whom we could not feel the same affection as for our shaggy yaks.

One night we were visited by two Tibetans who called themselves yak-men but were considerably better dressed than any other Tibetans we had seen. They wore Army-type boots and under their jackets carried pistols in leather holsters. At first the Sherpas thought they were Chinese and gave them a very cool reception but they proved to be Khampas, the warlike tribe of Tibetans who form the Tibetan army in exile. They were tall and good-looking with dazzling smiles, and very friendly, as were all the Khampas we met. Later we saw gaily-plumed caravans of ponies carrying their supplies up to the border area of Mustang.

At our camp at Dangarjong we woke to a superb view of Nilgiri and the Annapurna Range with their sparkling summits soaring out of a sea of cloud. Below us lay irrigated patches of green on the edge of the river, and to the north the brown hills and canyon-like valleys of the margin of Tibet.

A track bordered by vetch, purple thyme and wild roses led down into the wide alluvial valley of the Kali Gandaki. On these fertile flats were fields of golden barley. It was harvest time and the barley was being threshed by the laborious process of pulling the stalks through the teeth of a large 'comb'. We were now in Thakali country and found the houses built round courtyards and the mani walls surmounted by long rows of prayer wheels. The Thakalis are great traders and there was much traffic on the track between the north and their prosperous caravanserai, Tukucha.

Below Tukucha the valley narrowed and we entered the deepest gorge in the world. On one side lies 26,504-foot Annapurna, on the other, just twenty miles away, 26,795-foot Dhaulagiri, and in between flows the turbulent Kali Gandaki at only 8,000 ft above sea level. We traversed horrifyingly steep slopes above the thundering water and then crossed it on a precarious wooden suspension bridge. The bridge was swept away by monsoon floods two days later.

We had entered the monsoon zone and now our route led through bamboo thickets, sugar cane, and fields of rice and tall green sweetcorn. Apricot and banana trees bordered the track but they were not yet ripe and we had to wait till Kathmandu to satisfy our craving for fresh fruit. It rained almost continuously and the path was little more than a stream bed. We splashed through the puddles and mud and soon gave up trying to keep dry in the humid dampness.

Leeches were the worst trial of these last few days to Pokhara. The black worm-like creatures waved from every leaf and twig and however fast we moved somehow they managed to crawl into our boots to lodge between the toes. It was a painless but horrible sensation to feel them sucking one's blood, and Denise and I were so squeamish that we took to running through the woods to avoid them.

Fortunately we were not obliged to camp amongst the leeches, for on this main trading route between Pokhara, Mustang and Tibet there are many tea-houses where one can stop for a meal or spend the night. Most of them comprised just one large bare room with a hearth at one end, round which everyone bedded down. We paid nothing for the accommodation but only for the firewood used and the food and rakshi we consumed. It was a pleasant change from camping and we spent some congenial evenings trying out dishes of strange Nepalese vegetables, bamboo shoots, and makai (roasted sweetcorn).

We had now emerged into Gurung Country. Buddhist monuments gave way to Hindu, and instead of flat-roofed Tibetan-style houses we saw two-storeyed houses with roofs of sloping slate or conical thatch.

On 28th June, exactly four weeks after leaving Kaigaon, we reached Pokhara airport, our journey's end. Already farewells had begun for Denise and Nancy, who had to press on ahead to catch the earliest possible plane home. In a matter of hours they would be flying into London, whereas it would take us two months to cover the same distance by land. As Dawa, Mingma, Ang Pema and the others decked them with garlands and the white scarves of farewell, Denise and Nancy were not the only ones who were in tears. At least we could say "See you in September", whereas when would the Sherpas see them again?

We had looked forward to seeing Kathmandu all together so it was sad to have two of the party already gone. Major Charles Wylie and others of the British Embassy were most hospitable, and the Sherpas took great trouble to show us round the narrow streets, the Buddhist stupas and the huge wooden temples with their pagoda roofs and fantastic carvings. Our faded tartan shirts, jeans and dilapidated baseball boots were more suitable for this wandering round squares and bazaars and drinking with the Sherpas in their favourite chang (a local alcoholic drink) houses than for attending the official Embassy functions given for us. We felt most self-conscious in this garb but everyone else seemed delighted to see mountaineers in their ordinary expedition clothes.

At last we could delay our departure no longer. The Sherpas were leaving on the three-week walk back to their homes in Sola Khumbu, and Dorothea, Pat, Barbara and I were returning to Nepalganj and then Delhi. Ahead lay the 8,000-mile drive back to England, behind three enchanting months in West Nepal, surely one of the most beautiful countries in the world.

When would we go to the Himalayas again? I only know that we all wanted to go back to see the Sherpas and all our friends once more, to wander through the flower-filled valleys and climb to the heights of rock and snow.

It is now almost sixty years since the end of these Pinnacle Club expeditions and only two of us, Denise Evans and I, still survive. The Appendix gives a brief account of what happened next in our lives and the obituaries of those who sadly are no longer with us.

APPENDIX

JOSEPHINE PEACOCK (formerly FLOOD) (née SCARR)

After returning from the Himalayas in mid-1962 I spent the next eight months in a friend's holiday cottage in Kirkby Lonsdale in the Lake District, writing the first edition of *Four Miles High*, lecturing for Foyles and cross-country skiing, for this was the winter of the big snow. Meanwhile I had decided to go and climb in New Zealand but to make this financially possible, I emigrated in July 1963 as a 'Ten Pound Pom' to a job at the Australian National University in Canberra in Australia. There I knew a British CUMC climber, Dick Sykes, and he introduced me to Australian skiing at the resort of Perisher at 6,000 ft in the Snowy Mountains. To save money I slept in my Himalayan tent outside the Canberra Alpine Club hut and became known as 'the girl in the tent'. Both the downhill and cross-country skiing at Perisher and Guthega were superb, and on the Perisher chairlift I met my future husband, Philip Flood, an Australian diplomat. Then I began teaching Classical Archaeology at the Australian National University and in December 1963 flew to New Zealand for what turned out to be my final climbing holiday. In Christchurch I had an introduction to the Himalayan mountaineer, Norman Hardie. He and his wife, Enid, were most hospitable and arranged for me to join a New Zealand Alpine Club party going to an unsurveyed region of snow and ice north of Mount Cook, euphemistically called 'The Garden of Eden'.

We dug a snow cave and spent Christmas and New Year in it, icicles providing our water supply. We made the first detailed map of the area and then descended to the west coast by a three–day 'bush-bash' down the Perth River. There were innumerable turbulent creeks to cross, which we did by all linking arms in a line, hanging on to a large tree branch we had cut down. No one got swept away and when we at last reached the west coast highway, I was jubilantly told that we were the first party to descend that route without having someone drowned on the way.

Later, we drove south to Mt Aspiring, one of the most beautiful mountains in the world with its symmetrical, triangular, snow-covered peak soaring alone in the south of the South Island. This was to be my last serious climb of any sort, a fitting end to my mountaineering career.

Then it was back to Canberra, marriage in May 1964, and my move from Classical to Australian Aboriginal Archaeology and pioneering fieldwork. First I did an MA and my first son was born in October 1965. Then I accompanied my husband on a posting to Paris where my second son and a daughter were born. Back to Canberra where we were promised three years before the next posting. I immediately enrolled to do a PhD at the Australian National University. My professor, Jack Golson, was brave enough to take me on with three children under the age of four, but I think my mountaineering career helped him believe that I would rise to the challenge. My chosen subject was 'The Archaeology of the Snowy Mountains', involving much bush-walking. We had become a skiing family and I was even able to do some of my research on skis.

My PhD was finished by the three year deadline, quickly followed by Philip Flood's posting as High Commissioner to Bangladesh in 1974. There I became deeply involved in helping with various aid projects but also wrote up my PhD thesis as a book: *The Moth Hunters: Aboriginal Prehistory of the Australian Alps*. I also joined an Australian Himalayan expedition to Ladakh, catching the bus to Leh from Manali over the Rhotang Pass. Other excursions into the mountains were a family holiday in Kashmir and a trek from Kathmandu up to Everest Base Camp.

A posting to Washington DC followed but in 1978 it was back to Canberra, where I was appointed as Senior Conservation Officer and later Deputy Director of the Australian Heritage Commission. This was a dream job which I did for thirteen years until I took early retirement in 1991 to move back to the United Kingdom.

In 1989 Philip Flood and I divorced in an amicable parting of the ways; our children were all at University and Philip was resuming his diplomatic career with postings to Djakarta and later London. Then in 1990 my life changed again when I was over in Britain visiting my father in Yorkshire and then taking the train down to visit Barbara and her husband, Don Roscoe, in Anglesey. Barbara later denied match-making but cunningly invited my old flame, Nigel Peacock, for a walk and dinner. He was still recovering from the tragic loss to cancer of his wife, Kay Baker, in 1988 after a very happy marriage of twenty-seven years. Suffice it to say, the old flame rekindled. We spent the next year getting to know each other again and over a hundred letters passed each way between Canberra and Colwyn Bay, where Nigel was head of Penrhos College, an independent school for girls. We also climbed and trekked together in New Zealand and Nigel accompanied me on archaeological fieldwork in the Northern Territory. There were tough times as well as good ones but after becoming sure of each other, in 1991 I agreed to take early retirement from the Heritage Commission to move to Wales. We married in October 1991, with Barbara Roscoe as my bridesmaid and Pat Henry (previously Wood) attending.

Twenty-nine happy years have ensued. Together with the Roscoes we have enjoyed many days together out on the Welsh hills and, after Barbara sadly became ill with Parkinson's disease, on narrow boat holidays in UK and France. We also had occasional team reunions, including one at the Pinnacle Club hut in 2004 to celebrate the 40th anniversary of the Jagdula expedition.

Every year I have visited Australia once or twice to catch up with my three children and five grand-children and to continue some involvement in Australian aArchaeology. Nigel built me a study in the garden of our fifteenth century cottage within Snowdonia National Park, and there I have written three new archaeological books plus new editions of three earlier ones. Meanwhile Nigel keeps busy beekeeping and woodturning, but also hill-walking. (He has long been a member of both the Climbers' Club and the Alpine Club). He had to take early retirement from his exacting job after his first heart attack, but until his triple bypass operation, each year we took an active holiday walking or cycling in either Ireland, Yorkshire, the Lake District, Scotland or Crête. We also visited Colorado where Nigel taught in the Colorado Rocky Mountain School in the 1960s and 1970s, and climbed in the Grand Tetons and the Wind Rivers National Park. Then in October 1997 I went back to the Himalayas for a fabulous trek in Bhutan with Nigel and our friends John and Rowena Mellor. Buddhist Bhutan fondly reminded me of Nepal in 1962 and our flight past Everest and Kanchenjunga on our way back from Bhutan provided a wonderful last view of the high Himalayas.

DENISE EVANS (née MORIN) by Cathy Woodhead

Denise was born in Paris in 1931. Both of her parents, the Frenchman Jean Morin and Nea Barnard, were climbers. They lived in Paris but Nea, Denise and her brother Ian evacuated to Wales during the Second War. Jean joined the French Army before the war and at the fall of France he worked in London for the Free French Forces led by General de Gaulle. He was killed in 1943 when returning from a special mission and the plane he was travelling in was shot down.

After the war, the family moved to Kent. Later, Denise went to Oxford University studying languages and then worked with the BBC French service, at the same time translating Jean Franco's book *Makalu*. Denise often spent holidays abroad, skiing or climbing in the Alps with Nea and Ian. Nea describes some of these climbs in her book *A Woman's Reach*.

In 1949 Denise joined the Pinnacle Club, attending Club Meets and using the Club cottage in Cwm Dyli as a base for weekends and holidays. Often this involved hitchhiking from London, or travelling on the back of a climbing partner's motorbike. She and her friends were climbing hard routes, such as *Vember* on Clogwyn Du'r Arddu (Exceptionally Severe at that time, now E1). In 1956, she was invited by the glaciologist, Michael Holland, to join his expedition to the Sukkertoppen region of West Greenland, where the party made the first ascent of Mount Atter.

At about this time, she met Charles Evans whom she married in 1957. Charles had been Deputy Leader of the 1953 Everest expedition and then the Leader of the successful Kangchenjunga expedition in 1955. Professionally he was a surgeon and had served in Burma during the war. His book of these experiences, *Mandalay and Beyond*, is available as a digital file on the Alpine Club website.

After their marriage, Denise and Charles spent the autumn of 1957 climbing and trekking in Nepal, but soon after this Charles developed multiple sclerosis which put an end to his mountaineering and surgical career. He was appointed Principal of the University College of North Wales (now Bangor University) in 1958.

Their first son, Chuck, was born in 1959 and by 1961 Denise was once again climbing hard on routes such as *Spectre* (now HVS 5a) on Clogwyn y Grochan and *Curving Crack* (VS 4c) on Clogwyn Du'r Arddu. In 1962 Dorothea Gravina invited Denise to join the women's expedition to Jagdula, and Charles was asked to be the Patron. Denise's responsibilities were for organising the food and for filming the expedition. Nancy Smith wrote about the trip in the *Pinnacle Club Journal No.10 1961-1962* describing Denise as 'a bit of a devil, always disappearing round the next corner, whether with ciné in view or just pioneering, singing Bach fugues in the most improbable places and nearly always infectiously gay and happy'.

Following this expedition, Denise and Charles had two more sons, Robin and Peter, and Denise continued to climb with friends and, as they grew up, with her children. Her last significant Alpine climb was the *Traverse of the Meije* in 1986, which she had first climbed in 1956. She and Charles discovered sailing and developed a great passion for this. Denise continued with long-distance sailing until recently, taking her 33-foot yacht *Dunlin of Wessex* around South America (with her son Peter) and on numerous trips to Iceland, Spitzbergen and Greenland.

Charles Evans had been President of the Alpine Club in 1967-70, and in 1986 Denise became the first female President of the Alpine Club as she had been Vice-President to Anthony Rawlinson who died in office.

She still lives in the mountains, at Capel Curig.

Note: The film that Denise made on the Jagdula expedition in 1962 lay undisturbed in a cupboard in the house in Capel Curig for nearly sixty years, having only been shown once to a local audience. Denise had considered it to be too underexposed. In 2019 she passed the three reels of 16 mm colour film to Cathy Woodhead of the Pinnacle Club. Cathy had these digitised, which produced 50 minutes of silent film which is now being edited with commentary from Jo Scarr and Denise, with additional film and stills, to be a short and very presentable video.

OBITUARIES

DOROTHEA GRAVINA (née Briggs) 1905 - 1990

Dorothea Briggs was born in Yorkshire in 1905. After WWI her two brothers emigrated to South Africa and on one visit she climbed Mount Kilimanjaro and Mount Kibo. She started climbing in the Alps in the 1930s, working at the International Guiding Chalet in Adelboden in Switzerland, leading parties up the local mountains. In 1934 she met and married her husband, Count Gravina, a musician and a well known conductor. They lived in the South Tyrol, and two of their sons, Michael and Christopher, were born at this time.

When the Second World War began Dorothea and her sons moved back to Switzerland and by the end of the war Dorothea was living near Maidstone with their now three sons, but her husband who had joined the Italian Army lost his life in the conflict. It was when her family had grown up that Dorothea took to the mountains again, and from 1950 onwards she started climbing regularly in Britain and the Alps. In 1954 she joined the Ladies Alpine Club.

She attended her first Pinnacle Club meet at Cwm Dyli in November 1955, joining the club in 1956 at the age of fifty-one. To another new member, Margaret Darvall, she suggested a trip to the Himalayas and this was the genesis of the Cho Oyu Expedition in 1959. The two of them helped organise the Women's International Expedition there, a 26,750-foot peak about twenty miles NW of Everest. Claude Kogan was leader and Dorothea was her deputy. When Claude was killed Dorothea took charge.

After the shock and grief had subsided Dorothea decided there must be another women's expedition as soon as possible, and it needed to be successful in order to counter the inevitable ill-informed criticism. In due course this led to the Pinnacle Club Jagdula Expedition 1962 described in this book.

Dorothea and Pat drove back overland in the Hillman Husky and, undeterred, in 1963 Dorothea rode across France on a moped to lead the 1963 Pinnacle Club / Ladies Alpine Club Meet at Zinal. She was now the President of the Pinnacle Club.

The following years saw Dorothea hitchhiking, for example from South Africa to Egypt, mountain climbing, trekking but always travelling by the cheapest means possible. 1978/79 saw one of the last of Dorothea's famous trips when she travelled on local buses from Istanbul to Nepal, then trekked on to Annapurna. There was trouble during the journey in Tehran, Kabul and Delhi, but once again 'it was much more amusing than flying'.

In 1989 Dorothea attended her last Alpine meet, and in 1990 she bullied her doctor into giving her a certificate of fitness for an RGS Cruise to the Antarctic, but before she could make this trip she died at the age of 85. Her obituary in the Pinnacle Club Journal describes her as 'one of the Club's outstanding personalities immensely competent, energetic, cheerful and full of life.' 'She was endlessly interested in what everyone had been doing and on those rare occasions when she could be induced to talk about herself, endlessly interesting.'

PAT HENRY (née WOOD) 1933 - 2007

Pat grew up in Staffordshire and was first introduced to mountains and rock climbing by her two uncles, Ged and John Poole who were both quite well known climbers in North Wales in the 1950s. Her whole family enjoyed the countryside and nature and Pat herself was a knowledgeable bird watcher.

Pat was introduced to the Pinnacle Club by Annis Flew, whom she met while working as a dentist in Leek. After several trips to Wales she joined the club in 1957. Pat managed to combine her work as a dentist with weekends away and climbing trips to the Alps. She was able to take extended leave from her job not only to drive out to India with Dorothea but also to drive home again, all in a Hillman Husky.

In the years following the expedition Pat returned to her dentistry work in Leek and she made full use of her weekends for not only rock climbing but also canoeing. She made trips to Scotland including Skye and the Skye Ridge and again to the Alps, the Pyrenées, the Picos de Europa, the Taurus Mountains in South East Turkey, Arctic Norway and Morocco where, as a result of various 'adventures' in Marrakech, Pat and her climbing partner Barbara Spark ended up using a map traced onto stitched-together pieces of toilet paper to walk and climb in the area around the Neltner Hut.

In 1970 Pat married Laurie Henry and soon afterwards started a family with a son and daughter.

Although she continued to enjoy the countryside and walking and shared her interests in music and bird watching with Laurie, this was more or less the end of her climbing activities as she then devoted herself to the needs of her husband and young family.

Her last years were spent in the Lake District enjoying family life and her grandchildren. Pat died on April 28th 2007 at the age of 74 after a long struggle with cancer.

BARBARA MARY ROSCOE (née SPARK) 1936 - 2019

Barbara was born on the 11th April 1936, in Birkenhead. Soon after the war, the family settled in Bagillt, a small village between Flint and Holywell.

Both Barbara and her elder sister, Jean, went to Merllyn Junior School, and later to Holywell Grammar School. It was here that Barbara's sporting prowess became obvious and she made the first teams in both tennis and hockey at a much younger age than was normal. She represented Flintshire Schools at hockey.

Barbara trained as a PE teacher at I M Marsh College of Physical Education in Liverpool, and then taught at a secondary girls' school in Liverpool for four years. During this time she rock climbed while on courses at Plas y Brenin. It was here that she met Jo Scarr, who remained a lifelong friend. Jo was planning the trip described in this book and invited a restless Barbara to be her companion.

On returning to Wales in mid-1962, Barbara became an instructor at Plas y Brenin. In 1964, Barbara had a climbing accident on Pillar Rock in the Lake District when a belay gave way. The significant injuries she suffered plagued her for the rest of her life.

In 1965, Barbara was invited by Sir Charles Evans to start a PGCE, teacher training, course in Outdoor Activities at Bangor University, the first in the UK, where she continued her respected work in Outdoor Education until her retirement in 1983. Barbara met her future husband, Don Roscoe, initially at Plas y Brenin, and later worked with him at Bangor. They married in 1975 and remained together for over 40 years. Exploiting a creative talent which probably came from her mother, Barbara took up art after her retirement, completing a Foundation course, and the first year of a Fine Art degree. Art became a passion of Barbara's; she was a prolific painter and had a number of successful exhibitions.

Barbara remained physically active well into her retirement. She and Don cycled around the world in 1988/89, following the summer through Asia, Australia, New Zealand and America. Together they fished, walked, climbed, cycled and canoed regularly until a series of knee and ankle operations in the early 2000s restricted her adventurous activity. Barbara was diagnosed with Parkinson's disease in 2005. Despite the limitations and challenges of her final years, Barbara remained her positive and enthusiastic self, enjoying support from a host of friends, neighbours, family and ex~students. She was able to remain in their home on Anglesey throughout her illness and died there on 27th March 2019.

NANCY SMITH (née HERON) 1922 - 2007

Nancy Heron was born in Otley in the lee of Almscliff Crag. From the earliest age, she could be found climbing trees and as she grew bigger she began to explore the crag near her home and the local millstone grit on Ilkley Moor. During boarding school at Hunmanby Hall, she went to Canada with the school cricket team and saw her first real mountains, the Rockies in 1939. On returning to England that year, she enrolled at Leeds University to study medicine and started rock climbing with Leeds University Climbing Club. In December 1939 on her first meet (Langdale) she was already leading the lads. Over the next few years, she climbed in Wales and the Lake District whenever her studies allowed.

By 1945 when she became a house surgeon in Leeds Maternity Ward, she was climbing with many of the top climbers of her generation, and soon after that she met her future husband, Cym Smith (C M G Smith), a physicist and President of the Cambridge University Mountaineering Club and a great nephew of Owen Glynne Jones.

In 1947, when she was working as a psychiatrist in a Glasgow hospital, she became an honorary member of the (men only) Lomond Club and put up many good Scottish routes with Tommy McGinness, and it was with him that she had her first Alpine season, climbing the Matterhorn and the Breithorn, and then the rarely climbed Untergabelhorn Ridge with only an 1896 Baedeker to guide them!

In both 1950 and 1951 she went to the Alps with Cym and early in 1951 they got married. Among other climbs, they made the first British guideless traverse of the complete Aiguilles du Diable and the first ascent of the year of Piz Badile by the North Ridge. But tragedy struck shortly afterwards. Cym was returning home one night on his motorbike in a snowstorm when he ran into the back of a lorry parked without lights and was killed.

With typical courage, Nancy picked herself up and concentrated on her medical work. When she became a house surgeon in a hospital near Tunbridge Wells, she found hard climbing on Harrison's Rocks where she met Nea Morin, who introduced her to the Pinnacle Club.

Then, towards the end of the 1950s, Nancy turned north and became a trainee assistant to a general practice in Kirkby Lonsdale. Here she met Frances Tanner who was to become her receptionist and general factotum when she opened her own practice in Darwen. Frances was, of course, roped into Nancy's climbing life and eventually she too joined the Pinnacle Club in 1960.

During the Jagdula Expedition, while not only having the role of doctor to the team and to very many local people she tended to, Nancy was successful in summitting Lha Shamma. However her contact with the Buddhist Sherpas was to change her whole outlook on life.

On return to Britain she found herself drawn to the psychological work of Jung, realising that many of her patients at her practice needed psychological help as much as, if not more than, physical medicine. She decided to take time off and go to study at the Jung Institute. Accordingly, she gave up her practice and spent 2-3 years in Zurich. On her return, she moved to London and eventually general practice - typically in a very run-down area. Here she remained until she retired and, some years later, decided to spend the rest of her life in the Lake District.

Her last few years, dogged by ill health, were blessed by contact with old friends and younger family. Finally, in hospital in intensive care, when she was told that she had a ruptured aorta and there was nothing more that could be done, she turned to her cousin with the words 'so that's it then'. In the Westmorland Gazette she was described as 'doctor, climber, mountaineer'. She died on December 12th 2007 aged eighty-five. Her ashes were scattered on Gimmer Crag.

The Popular History of England: From the Civil War of the Reign of Charles I, 1642 to the Commencement of the Reign, of William and Mary, 1689

Charles Knight

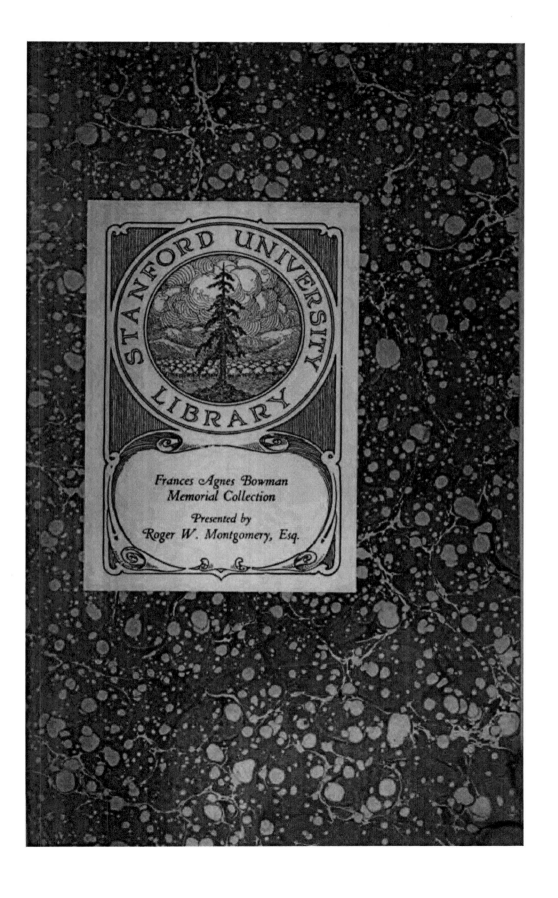

THE POPULAR

HISTORY OF ENGLAND:

An Illustrated History

OF SOCIETY AND GOVERNMENT FROM THE EARLIEST PERIOD TO OUR OWN TIMES.

BY CHARLES KNIGHT.

VOLUME IV.

FROM THE CIVIL WAR OF THE REIGN OF CHARLES I., 1642, TO THE
COMMENCEMENT OF THE REIGN OF WILLIAM AND MARY, 1689.

BOSTON:
ESTES AND LAURIAT, 143, WASHINGTON STREET.
1874.

CONTENTS.

———•———

CHAPTER XI.—A.D. 1653.

CHAPTER XII.—A.D. 1653 to A.D. 1655.

CHAPTER XIII.—A.D. 1655 to A.D. 1658.

CHAPTER XIV.—A.D. 1658 to A.D. 1660.

CHAPTER XXI.—A.D. 1678 to A.D. 1679.

CHAPTER XXII.—A.D. 1680 to A.D. 1682.

CHAPTER XXIII.—A.D. 1682 to A.D. 1683.

CHAPTER XXIV.—A.D. 1685.

CHAPTER XXV.—A.D. 1685 to A.D. 1686.

LIST OF ILLUSTRATIONS.

PORTRAITS ON STEEL.

LITHOGRAPHED PLAN.

WOOD ENGRAVINGS.

London. From the Print by Hollar.

POPULAR HISTORY OF ENGLAND.

CHAPTER I.

Beginnings of the Civil War—The king marches to Shrewsbury—Skirmish at Worcester—Battle of Edgehill—The night and day after the battle—Richard Baxter visits the battle-field—The king marches upon London—The fight at Brentford—The royalists retire—The Londoners march to Turnham Green—The war spreading through England—The queen lands with an army—The court at Oxford—Administration of justice—Reading surrendered to Essex.

THE flame of war is bursting forth in many places at once. Fortified towns are changing their military occupants. Portsmouth had capitulated to the parliament's army a fortnight before the king raised his standard at Nottingham. Lord Northampton, a royalist, had seized the stores at Banbury, and marched to the attack of Warwick castle. That ancient seat of feudal grandeur was successfully defended by the commander who had been left in charge, whilst lord Brook marched with some forces to the parliament's quarters. Every manor-house was put by its occupiers into a posture of defence. The heroic attitude of the English ladies who, in the absence of their husbands, held out against attacks whether of Cavaliers or Roundheads, was first exhibited at Caldecot manor-house, in the north of Warwickshire. Mrs. Purefoy, the wife of William Purefoy, a member of the House of Commons, defended her house against prince Rupert and four hundred Cavaliers. The little garrison consisted of the brave lady and her two daughters, her son-in-law, eight male servants, and a few female. They had twelve muskets, which the women loaded as the men discharged them from the windows. The out-buildings were set on fire, and the house would have been burnt, had not the lady gone forth, and claimed the protection of the Cavaliers. Rupert respected her courage, and would not suffer her property to be plundered. This young man, who occupies so prominent a part in the military operations of the Civil War, was only twenty-three when Charles made him his general of horse. He had served in the wars for the recovery of the Palatinate, and had exhibited the bravery for which he was ever afterwards distinguished. But in his early warfare he had seen life unsparingly sacrificed, women and children put to the sword, villages and towns burnt, the means of subsistence for a peaceful population recklessly destroyed. His career in England did much to make the king's cause unpopular, though his predatory havoc has probably been exaggerated. The confidence which the king placed in him as a commander was not justified by his possession of the high qualities of a general. The queen who, dangerous as she was as a counsellor of the king, had remarkable abilities, thus described the nephew of Charles when he was about to sail for England. "He should have some one to advise him, for, believe me, he is yet very young and self-willed. I have had experience of him. This is why I thought it fitting to warn you of it. He is a person that is capable of doing anything that he is ordered, but he is not to be trusted to take a single step out of his own head."*

About the middle of September, Charles marched with his small army from Nottingham to Derby. Essex, with the forces of the parliament, was at Northampton. The king's plans were very vague; but he at last determined to occupy Shrewsbury. He halted his army on the 19th at Wellington, where he published a "Protestation," in which, amongst other assurances, he said, "I do solemnly and faithfully promise, in the sight of God, to maintain the just privileges and freedom of parliament, and to govern by the known laws of the land to my utmost power; and, particularly, to observe inviolably the laws consented to by me this parliament." There is a remarkable letter of the queen to the king, dated the 3rd of November, in which she expresses her indignant surprise that he should have made any such engagement. "You promise to keep all that you have passed this parliament, which, I confess, had I been with you I should not have suffered it." She intimates that there are persons about him, "who, at the bottom of their hearts, are not well disposed for royalty. * * * As to believing that they wish you to be absolute, their counsels plainly show the contrary. They must be made use of, notwithstanding."† The only notion that the queen had of "royalty" was that it was to be "absolute." Who can believe that Charles ever resigned that fatal idea? Clarendon says the king's protestation "gave not more life and encouragement to the little army than it did to the gentry and inhabitants of these parts, into whom the parliament had infused, that if his majesty prevailed by force, he would, with the same power, abolish all those good laws which had been made this parliament."‡ Their comfort and satisfaction might have been less, if the queen's letter, now amongst the Harleian Manuscripts, and another of the same import, had been as public as the king's protestation. The discovery and publication of

* Green's "Letters of Henrietta Maria," p. 97.   † Ibid., p. 144.
‡ "Rebellion," vol. iii. p. 222.

other such letters produced unbounded evil to the royal cause, whilst the issue of the contest was doubtful. Time has revealed many more secrets of the same nature, which may somewhat qualify the enthusiasm of those who after the lapse of two centuries, read the history of the Civil War in a spirit more cavalier than that of the Cavaliers.

On the 22nd of September, Essex moved his army to Worcester. Here the first rencounter took place between the cavalry of Rupert and the parliamentary cuirassiers. The royalists had a decided advantage. Ludlow, who was in the skirmish, gives a ludicrous account of the inexperience, and something worse, of the parliament's raw troops. The lieutenant "commanded us to wheel about; but our gentlemen, not yet well understanding the difference between wheeling about and shifting for themselves, their backs being now towards the enemy whom they thought to be close in the rear, retired to the army in a very dishonourable manner; and the next morning rallied at head-quarters, where we received but cold welcome from our general, as we well deserved."*

Cuirassier. From a specimen
at Goodrich Court.

After remaining at Shrewsbury about twenty days, Charles resolved to march towards London. He expected that, as the armies approached each other, many soldiers would come over to the royal standard. He was almost without money, except a sum of six thousand pounds which he received by "making merchandise of honour," to use Clarendon's expression—being the price for which he created Sir Richard Newport a baron. His foot-soldiers were mostly armed with muskets; but three or four hundred had for their only weapon a cudgel. Few of the musketeers had swords, and the pikemen were without corslets. The royal army moved from Shrewsbury on the 12th of October, on to Wolverhampton, Birmingham, and Kenilworth. Two days after, the earl of Essex marched from Worcester in the direction which Charles had taken. They were only separated by twenty miles when the king first moved from Shrewsbury, but it was ten days before they came near each other. "Neither army," says Clarendon, "knew where the other was." On the night of the 22nd of October, the king was at Edgcot, a village near Banbury. The council broke up late. There was disunion in the camp. The earl of Lindsey by his commission was general of the whole army; but when Charles appointed prince Rupert his general of horse, he exempted him from receiving orders from any one but the king himself—to such extent did this king carry his over-weening pride of blood. Rupert insolently refused to take the royal directions through lord Falkland, the secretary of state.

* "Memoirs," p. 46.

In the same spirit, when a battle was expected, Charles took the advice of his nephew, rejecting the opinion of the veteran Lindsey. At twelve o'clock on the night of the 22nd Rupert sent the king word " that the body of the rebel army was within seven or eight miles, and that the head-quarters was at a village called Keinton, on the edge of Warwickshire." On Sunday morning, the 23rd, the banner of Charles was waving on the top of Edgehill, which commanded a prospect of the valley in which a part of the army of Essex was moving. The greater portion of the parliament's artillery, with two regiments of foot and one of horse, was a day's march behind. The king, having the advantage of numbers, determined to engage. He appeared amongst his ranks, with a black velvet mantle over his armour, and wearing his star and garter. He addressed his troops, declaring his love to his whole

Pikeman.   From a specimen at Goodrich Court.

kingdom, but asserting his royal authority " derived from God, whose substitute, and supreme governor under Christ, I am." * At two o'clock the royal army descended the hill. Clarendon, in noticing the dissensions created by Rupert's exclusive appointment, says, it " separated all the horse from any dependence upon the general." Lindsey went into the battle, pike in hand, at the head of the foot guards, in the centre of the first line. " Sir Jacob Astley," writes Warwick, " was major-general of the army under the earl of Lindsey ; who, before the charge of the battle at Edgehill, made a most excellent, pious, short, and soldierly prayer : for he lifted up his eyes and hands to Heaven, saying, ' O Lord, thou knowest how busy I must be this day ; if I forget thee, do not Thou forget me.' And with that rose up, crying ' March on, boys.' " †

Between the town of Keinton and Edgehill was " a fair campaign, save that near the town it was narrower, and on the right hand some hedges and inclosures." Ludlow, who was in the battle, confirms this description of the ground, given by Clarendon : " The great shot was exchanged on both sides, for the space of an hour or thereabouts. By this time the foot began to engage ; and a party of the enemy being sent to line some hedges on our right wing, thereby to beat us from our ground, were repulsed by our dragoons." The foot soldiers on each

* Colonel Weston's letter, quoted in Lord Nugent's "Hampden," vol. ii. p. 239.
† Warwick is the sole authority for this. It has been questioned, from the construction of the sentence, whether the "who" applies to Lindsey or Astley. See Warburton's "Rupert and the Cavaliers," vol. ii. p. 21.

side engaged with little result. But Rupert, at the head of his horse, threw the parliament's left wing into complete disorder. The disaster was mainly attributable to the desertion of Sir Faithful Fortescue, who went over with his troop to the royalists, when he was ordered to charge. The fiery prince pursued the flying squadrons for three miles; and in the town of Keinton he was engaged in plundering the parliamentary baggage-waggons, whilst the main body of the king's forces was sorely pressed by the foot and horse of Essex. The king's standard was taken. Sir Edmund Verney, the standard-bearer, was killed. The standard was afterwards recovered by a stratagem of two royalist officers, who put on the orange-scarf of Essex, and demanded the great prize from his secretary, to whom it had been entrusted. It was yielded by the unfortunate penman to those who bore the badge of his master. Brave old Lindsey was mortally wounded, and taken prisoner. Other royalists of distinction were killed. "When Prince Rupert returned from the charge," writes Clarendon, "he found this great alteration in the field, and his majesty himself with few noblemen and a small retinue about him, and the hope of so glorious a day quite banished." Many around the king counselled a retreat; but Charles, with equal courage and sagacity, resolved to keep his ground. "He spent the night in the field, by such a fire as could be made of the little wood and bushes which grew thereabouts." When the day appeared, the parliamentary army still lay beneath Edgehill. "The night after the battle," says Ludlow, "our army quartered upon the same ground that the enemy fought on the day before. No man nor horse got any meat that night, and I had touched none since the Saturday before, neither could I find my servant who had my cloak, so that having nothing to keep me warm but a suit of iron, I was obliged to walk about all night, which proved very cold by reason of a sharp frost. Towards morning, our army having received a reinforcement of Colonel Hampden's and several other regiments, to the number of about four thousand men, who had not been able to join us sooner, was drawn up; and about day-light we saw the enemy upon the top of the hill: so that we had time to bury our dead, and theirs too if we thought fit. That day was spent in sending trumpeters to inquire whether such as were missing on both sides were killed, or prisoners." * It was, in most respects, a drawn battle. Gradually each army moved off, one to attack London, the other to defend it. There is a little incident of this Edge-hill fight which has been told by the

Harvey. From a Portrait by Cornelius Jansen.

gossiping chronicler, Aubrey, of the famous Harvey, the physician. "When king Charles I., by reason of the tumults left London, he attended him, and

* "Memoirs," p. 50.

was at the fight of Edge-hill with him; and during the fight, the prince and duke of York were committed to his care. He told me that he withdrew with them under a hedge, and took out of his pocket a book and read; but he had not read very long before a bullet of a great gun grazed on the ground near him, which made him remove his station."

The number of the slain at Edgehill was variously estimated by the two parties. Ludlow very impartially says, "it was observed that the greatest slaughter on our side was of such as ran away, and on the enemy's side of those that stood." There was no general desire in either army to renew the struggle. In the royal camp there was so visible an averseness "to re-engage in most officers, as well as soldiers, that the king thought not fit to make the attempt." * In the parliamentary army, Hampden and others vainly urged that their reinforcement would enable Essex to attack with decided success. "We hoped," says Ludlow, "that we should have pursued the enemy, who were marching off as fast as they could, leaving only some troops to face us upon the top of the hill; but, instead of that, for what reason I know not, we marched to Warwick." †

The great events of the Civil War are to be traced in the proceedings of Parliament, the state-papers, the histories and memoirs of the politicians and soldiers who were engaged on either side, and the letters of the actors in the busy scenes. But we occasionally meet with the relations of some who were scarcely more than lookers-on, and were not committed to very strong opinions. Such a witness was Richard Baxter. He was, at one and the same time, a royalist and a puritan. It is most interesting to follow this remarkable observer in those details of his life which, in a few graphic touches, exhibit the general state of society far more distinctly than the laboured narratives of the contemporary historians. We see him, in his twenty-seventh year at the beginning of the war, driven from his ministry at Kidderminster by those he calls "the rabble;" who reviled all the religious of the place as Roundheads; where "every drunken sot that met them called out, 'We shall take an order with the puritans ere long.'" He says, "it was the undoing of the king and bishops that this party was encouraged by the leaders in the country against the civil religious party. . . . The fury of the rabble was so hot at home that I was fain to withdraw." He goes to Worcester, where a body of the parliamentary troops were lying in a meadow. "I had a great mind to go see them, having never seen any part of an army." He there looks upon the scattering of the parliamentary forces by Rupert's horse. "This sight quickly told me the vanity of armies, and how little confidence is to be placed in them." Essex marches into Worcester "with many lords and knights, and a flourishing army, gallantly clothed, but never tried in fight." The young divine had no safety in staying at home; but "the civility of the earl of Essex's army was such that among them was no danger, though none of them knew me: and there was such excellent preaching among them at Worcester that I stayed there among them a few days, till the marching of the king's army occasioned their remove." Baxter preached at Alcester on the Lord's day following. "As I was preaching, the people heard the cannon play, and perceived that the armies were engaged; when sermon was done, in

the afternoon, the report was more audible." At sun-setting many troops
fled through the town, and said that all was lost on the parliament's side.
The people sent a messenger to Stratford-upon-Avon to know the truth. At
four o'clock in the morning the messenger returned. He gave an account of
the battle which corresponds in a remarkable manner with the authentic
narratives. "The next morning, being willing to see the field where they
had fought, I went to Edgehill, and found the earl of Essex with the remaining
part of his army keeping the ground, and the king's army facing them upon a
hill a mile off, and about a thousand dead bodies in the field between them ; and
I suppose many were buried before." The armies drew off. The poor wanderer
says, "I knew not what course to take. I had neither money nor friends :
I knew not who would receive me in any place of safety." He went at last
to Coventry, to the minister there, an old acquaintance, "with a purpose to
stay there till one side or other had got the victory, and the war was ended,
and then to return home again. For so wise in matters of war was I, and all
the country besides, that we commonly supposed that a very few days or
weeks by one other battle would end the wars ; and I believe that no small
number of the parliament-men had no more wit than to think so too."*
    After the battle of Edgehill the king wasted a few days in occupying
Banbury and other small places, and on the 26th was with his army at
Oxford. Essex was slowly advancing with his army towards London, and at
the end of the month was at Northampton. The people of the metropolis
had been greatly agitated by the uncertain rumours of the great fight in
Warwickshire. On the night of the battle of Edgehill, the beacons had
been lighted — a pre-arranged signal of the parliament's success. But
the fugitives whom Rupert had chased from the field filled the roads,
and proclaimed a royalist victory. But at the beginning of November
the king's army was decidedly known to be marching upon London. Rupert
was quartered at Maidenhead with the advanced guard. Two days after
Essex arrived, and received the thanks of the two Houses. On the 11th
of November Charles was at Colnbrook. Thither went a deputation from
the Parliament, under a safe conduct, to propose that the king should appoint
some convenient place to reside, near London, "until committees of both
Houses of Parliament may attend your majesty with some propositions for
the removal of these bloody distempers and distractions." The king met the
deputation favourably, and proposed to receive such propositions at Windsor.
"Do you your duty," he said, "we will not be wanting in ours. God in his
mercy give a blessing." Ludlow records the duplicity which followed this
negotiation : "Upon which answer the parliament thought themselves secure,
at least against any sudden attempt : but the very next day the king, taking
the advantage of a very thick mist, marched his army within half a mile of
Brentford before he was discovered, designing to suprise our train of artillery
(which was then at Hammersmith), the parliament, and city." Clarendon
endeavours to throw the blame of this dishonour upon Rupert. The king,
he says, resolved to have gone to Windsor, if the parliament had removed
their garrison there, "or at least to have stayed at Colnbrook till he heard
again from the parliament. But prince Rupert, exalted with the terror

---

* "Reliquiæ Baxterianæ," 1696, part i. pp. 42 and 43.

he heard his name gave to the enemy, trusting too much to the vulgar intelligence every man received from his friends at London—who, according to
their own passions and the affections of those with whom they corresponded,
concluded that the king had so great a party in London, that, if his army
drew near, no resistance would be made—without any direction from the
king, the very next morning after the committee returned to London, advanced
with the horse and dragoons to Hounslow, and then sent to the king, to desire
him that the army might march after; which was, in that case, of absolute
necessity; for the earl of Essex had a part of his army at Brentford, and the
rest at Acton and Kingston."

From the time of the battle of Edgehill there was a general feeling in
London that the king's army, not materially discomfited, would advance to
strike a blow at the capital. The parliamentary earls, Pembroke, Holland,
and Say and Sele, made speeches at Guildhall, to stir up the ardour of the
citizens. They spoke eloquently, especially Say and Sele. "Let every man
shut up his shop; let him take his musket; let him offer himself readily and
willingly. Let him not think with himself who shall pay me? but rather
think this, I will come forth to save the kingdom, to serve my God, to maintain his true religion, to save the parliament, to save this noble city." An
ordinance of parliament declared that any apprentices who should enlist
should be secured from forfeiture of their bonds, and that their masters
should receive them back again. Milton heard the din of preparation in his
quiet house in Aldersgate-street; and had perhaps slight assurance of safety
from the trained bands of the neighbouring artillery ground, when he sat
within his "defenceless doors," and implored protection for "the Muses'
bower."* The "assault intended for the city" at last became a reality. On
the morning of the 12th of November, the sound of distant guns was heard
in London. Two traders who had been seized by the royalist pickets afterwards related that they saw the king and prince Rupert together on Hounslow-heath, marching towards Brentford, and that Rupert "took off his scarlet
coat, which was very rich, and gave it to his man, and buckled on his arms,
and put a grey coat over it." Before noon Rupert was charging in the
streets of Brentford. The regiment of Hollis was quartered there, and
they were not unprepared for the attack. The long and narrow street was
barricaded. The contest was obstinately maintained for three hours by
Hollis's regiment. Hampden was at Acton, and Brook in a neighbouring
cantonment. Again and again the parliamentary forces charged the Cavaliers.
But the main body of the royal army now invested Brentford. The fighting
went on till evening, when the royalists had a decided advantage, and compelled their enemy to retire from the town. They took many prisoners,
amongst whom was John Lilburne, who began his career, when an appren-
tice, by calling down stripes and imprisonment upon his contumacy, and was
now a captain of the trained bands. The old enemies of "sturdy John" did
not forget his offences. He was tried for his life, and was about to be
executed as a rebel, when Essex threatened that for every one of the Parliament's officers thus put to death, he would execute three royalist prisoners.
Lilburne was released, to be always foremost in opposition, whether to

* Sonnet viii.

Charles or to Cromwell. Many of the Parliament's men were drowned in the Thames; but the greater number made their way in boats down the stream. Essex had arrived at Turnham Green with some trained bands, who, whilst the fighting was going on, had been exercising in Chelsea fields. To understand this scene we must figure to ourselves a London with houses extending little beyond St. James's palace; the western roads from St. Giles's to Acton,

John Lilburne.

and from Hyde Park Corner to Brentford, dotted only with scattered houses or petty hamlets, standing amidst broad pasture lands and gardens. It was dark when the trained bands, with the parliamentary regiments then recruited advanced again to Brentford, and the royalists fell back to the king's quarters at Hounslow. That Saturday evening was one of confusion and alarm. " All that night the city of London poured out men towards Brentford, who every hour marched thither; and all the lords and gentlemen that belonged to the parliament army were there ready by Sunday morning, the 14th of

November."* Skippon, the general of the city trained bands, came out with his well-disciplined shopkeepers and apprentices; talking now with one company, now with another, and calling them about him to make that famous oration which is more telling than all the rhetoric of Livy's Romans. "Come, my boys, my brave boys, let us pray heartily and fight heartily. I will run the same fortunes and hazards with you. Remember the cause is for God, and for defence of yourselves, your wives, and children. Come, my honest brave boys, pray heartily and fight heartily, and God will bless us." Twenty-four thousand of the parliamentary army were marshalled on that Sunday on Turnham Green. They were subjected to no very serious privations in their short campaign. The good housewives of London sent out abundant provisions of meat and beer; and the wine-cups were filled and the tobacco smoked, as if those thousands were assembled for a fair, instead of a battle. "The soldiers were refreshed and made merry," says Whitelocke, "and the more, when they understood that the king and his army were retreated." Pacific councils again prevailed. Hampden was recalled, when, in pursuance of a settled plan of attack, he was about to march by Acton and Osterley Park to take the royal army in the rear. Essex remained inactive, instead of advancing to Hounslow as had been agreed. The war, according to some writers, might have been brought to a conclusion in one day of certain triumph if the irresolution of Essex had yielded to the counsels of bolder spirits. The men were not yet in the field who were resolved to make war in earnest, whatever might be the consequences. Essex was brave and skilful; but, like many other good men, he fought with reluctance against his countrymen and his familiar friends. Sir Philip Warwick has a passage, in which he has a gentle sneer at Essex for his indecision. At Hounslow, he says, "there was a large fair heath for the two armies to have tried once again their courage and their fortunes." The king "marched off towards a summer house of his own at Oatlands, betwixt Windsor and Hampton Court, where there were still fair heaths for the two armies to have engaged, if the parliament forces would have made the adventure."† Charles rested at this pleasant seat of royalty for two days; then went on to Reading, where he fixed a garrison; and on the 29th of November was in winter quarters at Oxford.

After the royal army had withdrawn from the neighbourhood of London, the citizens, who had seen war so close at their doors, began to talk more earnestly of peace. The peace party comprised many persons who could not be classed amongst the thorough royalists; for their petitions to the parliament expressed as strongly as ever their hatred of popery and arbitrary power. But the exertions of this moderate party produced a corresponding determination of "the pious and movement party" that the war should be carried on with renewed energy. The Guildhall was the scene of many an angry debate. At length, on the 2nd of January, a petition from the common council was carried to the king at Oxford, in which he was asked to return to the capital, when all disturbance should be suppressed. Charles replied, that they could not maintain tranquillity amongst themselves. He sent a gentleman to read his formal answer to the people in the Guildhall.

* May.   † "Memoirs," p. 234.

It was full of reproaches, and breathed any language but that of conciliation. Amidst an immense uproar, Pym and lord Manchester addressed the multitude, and the prospect of peace faded from the people's view. Some attempts were made in the northern and western counties to preserve a neutral attitude in the struggle; but these were regarded with equal disfavour by Cavalier and Roundhead. Yorkshire and Cheshire, Devon and Cornwall, counties that had tried this impossible policy, soon became foremost in the strife. The eastern counties adopted a much more efficient course of action. They formed themselves into an "Association," in the organisation of which Cromwell was the master-spirit. Under his vigorous direction, Norfolk, Suffolk, Essex, Cambridge, Herts, not only kept the war away from their own localities, but furnished the most efficient support to its vigorous conduct in other quarters. The counties of Lincoln and Huntingdon soon joined this Eastern Association, with the like results. In the Seven Associated Counties the Cavaliers were never of any importance. During the winter a partisan warfare was going on in many places. The most important incident of these minor contests was the death of lord Brook at Lichfield. A royalist party had obtained possession of the Close of the cathedral, which was walled and moated. Lord Brook was in the command of a body of horse and foot, with artillery, brought to Lichfield to dislodge the occupiers of the Close. Sitting in a house, with the window open, he was shot in the eye, and instantly died. Laud, in his Diary, describes this death of lord Brook as a special wonder, for his beaver was up, and as a judgment; "he having ever been fierce against bishops and cathedrals."

The war, as it proceeded, gradually assumed a fiercer character. It became, to some extent, a war of classes. Clarendon says, "The difference in the temper of the common people on both sides was so great, that they who inclined to the parliament left nothing unperformed that might advance the cause, and were incredibly vigilant and industrious to cross and hinder whatsoever might promote the king's; whereas they who wished well to him thought they had performed their duty in doing so, and that they had done enough for him, in that they had done nothing against him."[*] We may be perfectly sure that the "common people on both sides" had great reason to be dissatisfied with the temper of the Cavaliers and their followers. "Thousands," says Baxter, "had no mind to meddle with the wars, but greatly desired to live peaceably at home, when the rage of soldiers and drunkards would not suffer them; some stayed till they had been imprisoned; some till they had been plundered, perhaps twice or thrice over, and nothing left them; some were quite tired out with the abuse of all comers that quartered on them."[†] But if "the common people" were puritans, "noted for praying and hearing sermons," they, as Baxter's father experienced, "were plundered by the king's soldiers, so that some of them had almost nothing but lumber left in their houses." In the beginning of 1643, the national feeling was exasperated by the landing of the queen with a foreign army. During a year she had been indefatigable in making the most of the funds she had acquired by the sale of the crown jewels, to purchase arms and ammunition, and to raise men. On the 22nd of February she arrived with

---

* "Rebellion," vol. iii. p. 452.   † "Reliquiæ Baxterianæ," p. 44.

four ships, and landed at Burlington. The admiral of the parliament had failed in intercepting her convoy; but he adopted measures of greater vigour than generosity when he arrived two days after the queen and her men had disembarked. These proceedings are described in the following characteristic letter of Henrietta Maria to Charles :—

"As soon as I landed in England, I sent Progers to you; but having learned to day that he was taken by the enemy, I send you again this man to give you an account of my arrival, which has been very fortunate, thanks be to God; for just as stormy as the sea was the first time I set sail, just so calm was it this time till I was within some fifteen hours of Newcastle, and on the coast, when the wind changed to the north-west, which forced us to make for Burlington Bay, and after two hours waiting at sea, your cavalry arrived. I landed instantly, and the next day the rest of the army came to join me.

"God, who took care of me at sea, was pleased to continue his protection by land, for that night, four of the Parliament ships arrived at Burlington without our knowledge, and in the morning about four o'clock, the alarm was given that we should send down to the harbour to secure our ammunition boats, which had not yet been able to be unloaded; but, about an hour after, these four ships began to fire so briskly, that we were all obliged to rise in haste, and leave the village to them : at least the women, for the soldiers remained very resolutely to defend the ammunition. In case of a descent, I must act the captain, though a little low in stature, myself.

"One of these ships had done me the favour to flank my house, which fronted the pier, and before I could get out of bed, the balls were whistling upon me in such style that you may easily believe I loved not such music. Everybody came to force me to go out, the balls beating so on all the houses, that, dressed just as it happened, I went on foot to some distance from the village, to the shelter of a ditch, like those at Newmarket; but before we could reach it, the balls were singing round us in fine style, and a serjeant was killed twenty paces from me. We placed ourselves then under this shelter, during two hours that they were firing upon us, and the balls passing always over our heads, and sometimes covering us with dust. At last the Admiral of Holland sent to tell them, that if they did not cease, he would fire upon them as enemies; that was done a little late, but he excuses himself on account of a fog he says there was. On this they stopped, and the tide went down, so that there was not water enough for them to stay where they were."[*]

The admiral, Batten, was denounced as a traitor by the royalists. The earl of Newcastle, who came to escort the queen to York, had been authorised by the king to raise men for his service, "without examining their consciences;" and thus his army was styled by the parliament "the queen's army," and "the Catholic army." The prejudice against foreigners and Romanists thus came into renewed activity. Subsequent tamperings with the more violent papists in Ireland led to the belief that the king was not sincere in his professions of regard for the Protestant cause; and thus the two parties of Cavaliers and Roundheads came to be more widely separated by religious as well as political differences; and those who held the most extreme opinions became the most powerful—the general course of all great revolutions.

[*] Green's "Letters of Henrietta Maria," p. 166.

The spring of 1643 was passed by the court at Oxford.   The noble city of academical palaces must have presented the most singular contrasts of gown and cuirass crowding the streets ; of grave doctors and ardent students talking the most impassioned loyalty to throngs of ladies in those ancient halls ; of outward splendour amidst secret want, and of gay hearts struggling with anxious fears.   Lady Fanshawe, one of the most interesting of royalists,

Oxford. From a drawing by Hollar.

—at that time unmarried,—has given the following picture of the Oxford of 1643 :

" My father commanded my sister and myself to come to him to Oxford, where the Court then was, but we, that had till that hour lived in great plenty and great order, found ourselves like fishes out of the water, and the scene so changed, that we knew not at all how to act any part but obedience, for, from as good a house as any gentleman of England had, we came to a baker's house in an obscure street, and from rooms well furnished, to lie in a very bad bed in a garret, to one dish of meat, and that not the best ordered ; no money, for we were as poor as Job ; nor clothes more than a man or two brought in their cloak bags : we had the perpetual discourse of losing and gaining towns and men : at the windows the sad spectacle of war, sometimes plague, sometimes sicknesses of other kind, by reason of so many people being packed together, as, I believe, there never was before of that quality ; always in want, yet I must needs say that most bore it with a martyr-like cheerfulness.   For my own part, I began to think we should all, like Abraham, live in tents all the days of our lives."

To this Oxford came Commissioners from the parliament, towards the end of March, authorised to negotiate a suspension of arms, and a treaty of peace. The earl of Northumberland, the chief of the commission, made the somewhat miserable city brilliant with his feasts. He had a magnificent retinue. His table was covered with luxurious dishes and rich wines. His plate was sumptuous. The royalists accepted his feasts—and persuaded the king to reject his propositions. Charles displayed his usual vacillation. He made concessions one day, and revoked them another. The queen's especial friends were always about him. The queen wrote to him, " Why have you taken arms ? You are betrayed. I will let you see it. Never allow your army to be disbanded till it [the parliament] is ended, and never let there be a peace till that is put an end to." * The officers of the garrison, in a petition to the king, opposed a suspension of arms. Charles had instigated them to petition. The parliament peremptorily recalled its commissioners. The battle must be fought out.

We have mentioned that during the Civil War the judges went their usual circuits. In the spring of 1643 this local administration of justice was temporarily suspended. The two Houses of Parliament, embarrassed by the king's possession of the Great Seal, ordered that the Session of Oyer and Terminer should not be proceeded with "until it shall please God to end these distractions between the king and people." Charles issued a proclamation, commanding that the Easter term should be held at Oxford instead of Westminster. The judges were ordered there to attend the king. Had this state of things continued, a greater evil would have ensued than the bloodshed and plunder of the war. But, by what was a practical compromise for the remedy of an enormous social mischief—one that might have led to a general insecurity of life and property—the Parliament resolved to establish a Great Seal : and under this authority, and that of the king, judges executed their functions as usual, after a suspension of a few months. No doubt, according to their political prepossessions, they regarded the king either as deriving his power from divine right, or as a trustee for his people. At a later period, we find a judge of assize laying down as a principle, " that kings, rulers, and governors, and particularly the king of this realm, should be accountable to the people for their misgovernments ;" and, on the other hand, there were, we may conclude, judges who maintained the position which this judge controverts, " that the king had an original right to rule over men upon earth ; and that God had not given power to earthly men to call him to account." These were the two great theories with regard to " a pure monarchy," and " a political monarchy, or monarchy governed by laws." † But whatever was considered the original foundation of government, none of the administrators of justice relaxed the principle that the law should be rigidly maintained, as regarded all private transactions. During these unhappy times England was in a great degree exempt from crimes of violence, except those committed under the pretence of martial necessity. No bands of plunderers infested the country ; no lawless and ferocious spirits who, as many passages of the histories of other countries record, considering a time of public commotion as their opportunity, held the peaceful in terror. England was safe from those massacres and spoliations

* Green's " Letters of Henrietta Maria," p. 182.
* Serjeant Thorpe's Charge to the Grand Jury. Harleian Miscellany, vol. vi. p. 113.

which characterise a nation when the reins of just government are loosened. This immeasurable blessing she owed to her ancient civil organisation, and to that respect for law which has made the constable's staff the efficient representative of the sovereign's sceptre.

The repose of Oxford was soon broken up by new military enterprises. The suspension of arms contemplated in the negotiations which commenced at the end of March, were, on the 15th of April, declared by the parliament to be at an end. On that day Essex marched his army to the siege of Reading. The town had been fortified; and the garrison there, although wanting provisions and ammunition, was composed of resolute men. The approaches were regularly constructed, batteries erected, and trenches dug. The possession of Reading was considered of great importance. The king himself, on the 24th of April, set out from Oxford to head a force for the relief of the besieged. The army which he led was numerous and well appointed. At Caversham bridge the royalist forces were repulsed by those of the parliament, and fell back upon Wallingford. That day Reading was surrendered to Essex. The cavaliers were indignant that the commander of the garrison had not longer held out; and he was tried, and sentenced to death. The king reprieved him. Hampden, who had taken an active part in the siege of Reading, now urged Essex to follow up their success by an attack upon Oxford. The bold counsels were overruled. The parliamentary commander gradually became distrusted by his party. His honour and his capacity were unquestionable; but he was too inclined to forego present good in the contemplation of uncertain evils. He could not make war upon his king and his fellow-countrymen as if he were in a foreign land. Such a man should not have drawn the sword at all. Meanwhile, the war was proceeding with doubtful fortune in other quarters. Sir William Waller was successful against the royalists in the south and west. Fairfax was disputing with lord Newcastle the supremacy of the north. The Cornish men, in arms for the king, had gained a battle over lord Stamford. What could not be accomplished in the open field by the Cavaliers was sought to be effected by a secret plot. The lady Aubigny had received a permission from the parliament, with a pass, to proceed to Oxford to transact some business arising out of the death of her husband, who was killed at Edgehill. On her return to London she was commissioned by the king to convey a box thither, with great care and secrecy. His majesty told her "it much concerned his own service." This is Clarendon's account, who represents the box to have contained a commission of array to certain persons in the city, for the promotion of the king's service. Ludlow says, "The king, to encourage his friends in the city to rise for him, sent them a commission for that purpose by the lady Aubigny, which she brought, made up in the hair of her head." On the 31st of May, the members of the two Houses were listening to a sermon in St. Margaret's church, when a note was delivered to Pym. He hastily left. That night Edmund Waller, once famous as a poet, but whose "smooth" verse we now little regard, was arrested. His brother-in-law, Mr. Tomkins, Mr. Challoner (a citizen), and other persons, were also taken into custody. Waller was a member of parliament, and had been at Oxford, in March, with the commissioners. There was unquestionably a plot to arm the royalists in London, to seize the persons of the parliamentary leaders, and to bring the king's troops into the capital. Waller, in a base spirit which contrasts with the conduct of most of the eminent of either party, made very abject confessions, with exaggerated denunciations of others, to save his own life. The Parliament behaved with honourable moderation. Five persons were condemned by court-martial : two, Challoner and Tomkins, were executed. Waller was reserved, to exhibit in his literary character a subserviency to power which has fortunately ceased to be an attribute of poets—to eulogise the happy restoration of Charles II., as he had eulogised the sovereign attributes of the Protector Cromwell. " He had much ado to save his life," says Aubrey, " and in order to do it sold his estate in Bedford-shire, about 1300*l.* per annum, to Dr. Wright, for 10,000*l.* (much under value), which was procured in twenty-four hours' time, or else he had been hanged. With this money he bribed the House, which was the first time a House of Commons was ever bribed." *

Important events succeeded each other rapidly during this summer. Rupert's trumpet sounded to horse in Oxford streets on the 17th of June. After the occupation of Reading, the troops of Essex were distributed in cantonments about Thame and Wycombe. Rupert dashed in amongst the small towns and villages where these troops were quartered. Hampden had been visiting the scattered pickets, and urging upon Essex a greater concentration of his forces. Lord Nugent, with accurate local knowledge, has described the localities into which Rupert had made his irruption. " Hampden had obtained in early life, from the habits of the chase, a thorough knowledge of the passes of this country. It is intersected, in the upper parts, with woods and deep chalky hollows, and in the vales, with brooks and green lanes ; the only clear roads along the foot of the hills, from east to west, and those not very good, being the two ancient Roman highways, called the upper and lower Ickeneld way." Hampden had expected some attack, and immediately he heard of Rupert's movement, he was in the saddle. On the morning of the 19th the prince was with a large force in Chalgrove Field, near Thame. Hampden, with a small detachment, attacked the cavaliers ; expecting the main body of the parliamentary army soon to come up with reinforcements. The man who had triumphed in so many civil victories fell in this skirmish. On the first charge he was shot in the shoulder. The parliamentary troops were completely routed before Essex came up. Rupert retreated across the Thames to Oxford. The news of the great leader having received a serious wound soon reached Oxford : " One of the prisoners taken in the action said, ' that he was confident Mr. Hampden was hurt, for he saw him ride off the field before the action was done, which he never used to do, with his head hanging down, and resting his hands upon the neck of his horse.' "† He was alone. The troops of Rupert were in the plain between the battle field and Thame, where the wounded man desired to go for help. A brook crossed the grounds through which he must pass. By a sudden exercise of the old spirit of the sportsman he cleared the leap, and reached Thame ; there to die, after six days of agony. " O Lord, save my bleeding country," were his last words. Clarendon has done justice, though not full justice, to the character of the man with whom he was so intimately associated in the struggle against

* "Lives," vol iii. p. 564.   † Clarendon, vol. iv. p. 88.

despotism. " He was of that rare affability and temper in debate, and of that seeming humility and submission of judgment, as if he brought no opinion of his own with him, but a desire of information and instruction; yet he had so subtle a way of interrogating, and, under the notion of doubts, insinuating his objections, that he infused his own opinions into those from whom he pretended to learn and receive them. * * * * He was indeed a very wise man, and of great parts, and possessed with the most absolute spirit of popularity, and the most absolute faculties to govern the people, of any man I ever knew. For the first year of the parliament, he seemed rather to moderate and soften the violent and distempered humours, than to inflame them. * * * * After he was among those members accused by the king of high treason, he was much altered; his nature and carriage seeming much fiercer than it did before. * * * * He was very temperate in diet, and a supreme governor over all his passions and affections, and had thereby a great power over other men's. He was of an industry and vigilance not to be tired out or wearied by the most laborious; and of parts not to be imposed upon by the most subtle or sharp; and of a personal courage equal to his best parts; so that he was an enemy not to be wished wherever he might have been made a friend; and as much to be apprehended where he was so, as any man could deserve to be. And therefore his death was no less pleasing to the one party, than it was condoled in the other." *

* " Rebellion." vol. iv. p. 92.

Bristol in the Seventeenth Century.

CHAPTER II.

The queen joins her husband—Various incidents of the war—Bristol taken by assault—Proposals for peace rejected by a small majority of the Commons—Popular disturbances in London—The siege of Gloucester—Defence of Gloucester—Essex marches to its relief—The king and his army retire—The Parliamentary army march towards London—The battle of Newbury—Prowess of the Trained Bands—Death of lord Falkland—The Sortes Virgilianæ—The royal success becoming more doubtful—Negotiations for an alliance between the Scots and the Parliament—The solemn League and Covenant—Essex returns to London—Growing importance of Cromwell—Skirmish of Winceby—Death of Pym—The Covenant severely enforced—Ejected ministers.

Four months had elapsed between the landing of the queen in England and her return to her royal husband. However Charles might have been personally affected by her counsels, his best advisers, the moderate men who desired peace, were afraid of her influence, and she was suspicious of their fidelity. Her dominant idea was to restore the absolute power of the king. Her ruling passion was hatred of the Parliament. She writes to Charles, " to die of consumption of royalty is a death which I cannot endure, having found by experience the malady too insupportable." * Again, " I do not see the wisdom of these Messieurs rebels,. in being able to imagine that they will make you come by force to their object, and to an accommodation ; for as

* Green's "Letters," p. 117.

long as you are in the world, assuredly England can have no rest nor peace, unless you consent to it, and assuredly that cannot be unless you are restored to your just prerogatives." * She was a bold and determined woman, who aspired to direct councils and to lead armies. On the 27th of May she writes to the king from York, " I shall stay to besiege Leeds at once, although I am dying to join you; but I am so enraged to go away without having beaten these rascals, that, if you will permit me, I will do that, and then will go to join you; and if I go away I am afraid that they would not be beaten." † She had her favourites, especially Jermyn and Digby, whose advancement she was constantly urging. The scandalous chroniclers of the time did not hesitate in casting the most degrading suspicions upon the queen in connection with one of these. Jermyn was made a peer. He is pointed out as " somewhat too ugly for a lady's favourite, yet that is nothing to some; for the old lady [Mary de Medicis] that died in Flanders regarded not the feature." ‡ At length Henrietta Maria determined to leave the north, and join the king at Oxford. On the 11th of July she entered Stratford-upon-Avon, at the head of four thousand horse and foot soldiers. She slept at the house in which Shakspere lived and died,—then in the possession of his daughter, Mrs. Hall. On the 13th she met Charles where his first battle had been fought; and from Keinton they proceeded to Oxford. The tidings of a victory on the 15th over the parliamentary forces at Roundway Down, in Wiltshire, greeted their arrival. A previous victory over sir William Waller at Lansdown, in Somersetshire, filled the royalists with the most sanguine hopes. Such partial successes on the other side as the brave defence of Nottingham Castle by colonel Hutchinson had no material influence upon the state of affairs. The feelings of the adverse parties were growing more bitter. We see the proud Cavaliers and the stern Puritans hating and hated. Female tenderness and courage shine out as sunny gleams in a dark day. On each side there were women as noble as Lucy Hutchinson, who thus describes what she was doing in the spirit of Christian love, whilst the so-called teachers of religion were cruel and revengeful:—

"There was a large room, which was the chapel, in the castle; this they had filled full of prisoners, besides a very bad prison, which was no better than a dungeon, called the Lion's den; and the new captain Palmer, and another minister, having nothing else to do, walked up and down the castle-yard, insulting and beating the poor prisoners as they were brought up. In the encounter, one of the Derby captains was slain, and five of our men hurt, who for want of another surgeon, were brought to the governor's wife, and she having some excellent balsams and plaisters in her closet, with the assistance of a gentleman that had some skill, dressed all their wounds, whereof some were dangerous, being all shots, with such good success, that they were all well cured in convenient time. After our hurt men were dressed, as she stood at her chamber-door, seeing three of the prisoners sorely cut, and carried down bleeding into the Lion's den, she desired the marshal to bring them in to her, and bound up and dressed their wounds also: which while she was doing, captain Palmer came in and told her his soul abhorred to see

* Green's " Letters," p. 108.   † *Ibid.* p. 202.
‡ " Character of an Oxford Incendiary," Harleian Miscellany, vol. v. p. 346.

this favour to the enemies of God; she replied, she had done nothing but what she thought was her duty, in humanity to them, as fellow-creatures, not as enemies." *

In the summer of 1643 the power of the Parliament is visibly in danger. On the 27th of July, Bristol, a city only exceeded by London in population and wealth, is surrendered to Rupert, after an assault, with terrible slaughter on both sides. Nathaniel Fiennes, its governor, was described by Clarendon as "for root and branch" in 1640; but one whose courage being had "in disesteem," encouraged the plan of assaulting this important place. He was subsequently tried and condemned "for not having defended Bristol so well, and so long, as he ought to have done." He had interest enough to obtain a pardon; but he quitted the country. A design of sir John Hotham to surrender Hull to the king was detected. He and his son were committed to the Tower on a charge of betraying the cause of the Parliament. London was in a state of unusual agitation. The Lords came to resolutions, upon a proposal of peace, of a far more moderate character than had previously been determined on. There was a conference between the two Houses, in which the upper House urged that "these unnatural dissensions" would destroy all the former blessings of peace and abundance. The Commons, by a majority of nineteen, decided that the proposals of the Lords should be considered. The city was in an uproar. A petition from the common-council called for the rejection of the proposals. Multitudes surrounded the Houses to enforce the same demand. The proposals were now rejected by a majority of seven. An attempt was then made to enforce the demand for peace by popular clamour. Bands of women, with men in women's clothes, beset the doors of the House of Commons, crying out, "Give us up the traitors who are against peace. We'll tear them in pieces. Give us up that rascal Pym." The military forced them away; but they refused to disperse. They were at last fired upon, and two were killed, one of whom was an old ballad-singer of the London streets. Many peers now left Parliament and joined the king at Oxford, amongst whom was lord Holland. Those who remained, peers or commoners, saw that the greatest danger was in their own dissensions. The royalist army was growing stronger in every quarter. London was again in peril. There was one man of extraordinary vigour who felt the immediate danger of his own district. There is not a more characteristic letter of Cromwell than the following to the Commissioners at Cambridge, dated from Huntingdon on the 6th of August:—"You see by this enclosed how sadly your affairs stand. It's no longer disputing, but out instantly all you can. Raise all your bands; send them to Huntingdon;—get up what volunteers you can; hasten your horses. Send these letters to Norfolk, Suffolk, and Essex, without delay. I beseech you spare not, but be expeditious and industrious! Almost all our foot have quitted Stamford: there is nothing to interrupt an enemy, but our horse, that is considerable. You must act lively; do it without distraction. Neglect no means!" †

Had there been unanimity in the councils of the king at this period of dissensions in London amongst the people; with the two Houses divided.

* Hutchinson's "Memoirs," vol. i. p. 274.
† Carlyle's "Cromwell Letters," vol. i. p. 129.

amongst themselves; men of influence deserting the parliamentary cause; no man yet at the head of the parliamentary forces who appeared capable of striking a great blow,—it is probable that if he had marched upon the capital the war would have been at an end. There would have been peace,—and a military despotism. Charles sent sir Philip Warwick to the earl of Newcastle to propose a plan of co-operation between the armies of the south and north. " But I found him very averse to this," Warwick writes, " and perceived that he apprehended nothing more than to be joined to the king's army, or to serve under prince Rupert; for he designed himself to be the man that should turn the scale, and to be a self-subsisting and distinct army, wherever he was." * With this serious difficulty in concentrating his forces, Charles determined upon besieging Gloucester. The garrison consisted of fifteen

Gloucester.

hundred men, under Edward Massey, the parliamentary governor. The inhabitants were under five thousand. On the 10th of August the king's army was stationed " upon a fair hill, in the clear view of the city, and within less than two miles of it." Charles sent a summons for its surrender, by a trumpet to the town, offering pardon to the inhabitants, and requiring an answer within two hours. Clarendon has described, with more than his accustomed attention to details which regard the common people, how the answer was brought: " Within less than the time prescribed, together with the trumpeter returned two citizens from the town, with lean, pale, sharp,

* " Memoirs," p. 243.

and bad visages, indeed faces so strange and unusual, and in such a garb and posture, that at once made the most severe countenances merry, and the most cheerful hearts sad; for it was impossible such ambassadors could bring less than a defiance. The men, without any circumstances of duty, or good manners, in a pert, shrill, undismayed accent, said, 'they had brought an answer from the godly city of Gloucester to the king;' and were so ready to give insolent and seditious answers to any question, as if their business were chiefly to provoke the king to violate his own safe conduct." * The answer was in writing, to the effect that the inhabitants and soldiers kept the city for the use of his majesty, but conceived themselves " wholly bound to obey the commands of his majesty, signified by both Houses of Parliament." The people of Gloucester immediately set fire to all the houses outside the walls. From the 10th of August till the 6th of September these resolute people, in spite of their strange and unusual faces, and their uncourtly manners, defended their city with a resolution and bravery unsurpassed in this warfare. The king dreaded the loss of men in an assault; and it was therefore resolved to compel a surrender by cutting off all supplies. The continued possession of Gloucester was most important to the Parliament. All differences having been reconciled in London, the earl of Essex took the command of a force destined for the relief of " the godly city." At the head of fourteen thousand men he set out from London on the 24th of August. On the 5th of September he had arrived by forced marches within five miles of Gloucester. The king sent a messenger to him with pacific proposals. The answer was returned in a spirit of sturdy heroism: " The Parliament gave me no commission to treat, but to relieve Gloucester; I will do it, or leave my body beneath its walls." The soldiers shouted, " No propositions." Gloucester was relieved. From the Prestbury hills Essex saw the flames of burning huts rising from the king's quarter. The royal army had moved away. On the 8th the parliamentary general entered the beleaguered city, bearing provisions to the famished people, and bestowing the due meed of honour upon their courage and constancy. On the 10th he was on his march back to London.

Of the army of fourteen thousand men which marched to the relief of Gloucester, four regiments were of the London militia. These regiments were mainly composed of artisans and apprentices. They had been drilled and reviewed in Finsbury fields and Chelsea fields for twelve months, and they had looked upon the approach of real war when Rupert was at Brentford. But they had seen no actual service. Their forced march to Gloucester, though scarcely exceeding a rate of ten miles a day, was a remarkable feat. They had, in the latter days of their march by Bicester, Chipping-Norton, and Stow-in-the-Wold, to pass through an enemy's country, in which the people were hostile, and the royalist cavalry were hanging on their rear. At Prestbury they had to fight their way through Rupert's squadrons; and to try how pikemen could stand up against a charge of horse. In less than a fortnight their prowess was to be proved in a pitched battle field. Charles and his army were lying round Sudeley Castle, to the north-east of Gloucester. Essex marched to the south. In Cirencester, which he surprised, he found

* "Rebellion," vol. iv. p. 179.

valuable stores for his men. The king's army moved in the same direction.
Essex had passed Farringdon, and was rapidly advancing upon Newbury, on
his road to Reading, when his scattered horse were attacked by Rupert and
his Cavaliers. According to Clarendon, the prince, "with near five thousand
horse, marched day and night over the hills, to get between London and the
enemy, before they should be able to get out of those enclosed deep countries
in which they were engaged between narrow lanes, and to entertain them
with skirmishes till the whole army should come up." * Essex had marched
over Amborne Chase, intending to have quartered at Newbury that night.

Newbury; Donnington Castle in the distance. From an old Print.

There was a sharp conflict for several hours, and Essex was compelled to halt
at Hungerford. The king marched at the head of his foot soldiers; "though
his numbers, by his exceeding long and quick marches, and the licence which
many officers and soldiers took whilst the king lay at Evesham, were much
lessened." † When Essex came near to Newbury on the 19th of September,
he found the royal army in possession of the town. The king had come there
two hours before him. Essex was without shelter, without provisions.
Charles had "a good town to refresh his men in, whilst the enemy lodged in
the field." ‡ It was absolutely necessary that Essex should hazard a battle.
The road to London was barred against him. He. "must make his way
through or starve." In the king's quarters it was resolved not to fight,
except upon such grounds as should ensure victory. On the morning of the
20th, Essex being encamped upon Bigg's hill, about a mile from Newbury,
the outposts of each force became engaged, and the battle was soon general.
It was fought all day "with great fierceness and courage;" the Cavaliers

* "Rebellion," vol. iv. p. 232.   † *Ibid.* p. 234.   ‡ *Ibid.*

charging " with a kind of contempt of the enemy ; " and the Roundheads making the Cavaliers understand that a year of discipline had taught them some of the best lessons of warfare.   " The London Trained Bands and auxiliary regiments (of whose inexperience of danger, or any kind of service, beyond the easy practice of their postures in the Artillery Garden, men had till then too cheap an estimation), behaved themselves to wonder ; and were, in truth, the preservation of that army that day. For they stood as a bulwark and rampire to defend the rest ; and, when their wings of horse were scattered and dispersed, kept their ground so steadily, that, though prince Rupert himself led up the choice horse to charge them, and endured their storm of small shot, he could make no impression upon their stand of pikes, but was forced to wheel about." *   The men of London, taken from the loom and the anvil, from the shops of Ludgate or the wharfs of Billings- gate, stood like a wall, as such men have since stood in many a charge of foreign enemies. The contempt of the Cavaliers for the " base mechanicals " was one great cause of the triumph of the roundheads. The base mechanicals, in their turn, had an equal contempt for the Cavaliers. Of the two men who went out from Gloucester, and spoke to the king " in a pert, shrill, undis- mayed accent," one was a bookbinder. Such enthusiasts knew no fear, and had small respect for rank and power, as far as outward demeanour was concerned. " Their backs turned scarce thirty yards, on clap they their caps in the king's presence, with orange ribbons in them." † But they had an ever present belief that they were doing " the Lord's work ; " and whether starving in a fortress, or ridden down by men in steel, they would not be moved

> " With dread of death to flight or foul retreat. '

On the night of the battle of Newbury, each army remained in the position it had occupied before that day of carnage. The loss of royalists of rank was more than usually great. Three noblemen fell, for whom there was lamentation beyond the ranks of their party—lord Carnarvon, lord Sunder- land, and lord Falkland. Falkland, especially, still lives in our memories, as one of the noblest and purest,—the true English gentleman in heart and intellect. What is called his apostacy has been bitterly denounced, and not less intemperately justified, by historical partisans. One whose intellect was as clear as his feelings were ardent in the cause of just liberty, has thus written of Falkland :—" A man who leaves the popular cause when it is triumphant, and joins the party opposed to it, without really changing his principles and becoming a renegade, is one of the noblest characters in history. He may not have the clearest judgment or the firmest wisdom ; he may have been mistaken, but as far as he is concerned personally, we cannot but admire him. But such a man changes his party not to conquer but to die. He does not allow the caresses of his new friends to make him forget, that he is a sojourner with them and not a citizen : his old friends may have used him ill, they may be dealing unjustly and cruelly : still their faults, though they may have driven him into exile, cannot banish from his mind

* " Rebellion," vol. iv. p. 235.
† Journal of the Siege, quoted in Warburton's " Rupert and Cavaliers," vol. ii. p. 280.

the consciousness that with them is his true home: that their cause is habitually just and habitually the weaker, although now bewildered and led astray by an unwonted gleam of success. He protests so strongly against their evil that he chooses to die by their hands rather than in their company ; but die he must, for there is no place left on earth where his sympathies can breathe freely ; he is obliged to leave the country of his affections, and life elsewhere is intolerable. This man is no renegade, no apostate, but the purest of martyrs: for what testimony to truth can be so pure as that which is given uncheered by any sympathy; given not against enemies amidst applauding friends ; but against friends, amidst unpitying or half-rejoicing enemies. And such a martyr was Falkland ! " *

Aubrey says of this most interesting of the heroes of the Civil War: "At the fight of Newbury, my lord Falkland being there, and having nothing to do to charge, as the two armies were engaging rode in like a madman, as he was between them ; and was, as he needs must be, shot." Clarendon tells another and more consistent story: "In the morning before the battle, as always upon action, he was very cheerful, and put himself in the first ranks of lord Byron's regiment, then advancing upon the enemy, who had lined the hedges on both sides with musketeers ; from whence he was shot with a musket in the lower part of the belly, and in the instant falling from his horse, his body was not found till the next morning." It was not Falkland's duty to be in the battle. He was urged to stay away. "No," he said, "I am weary of the times ; I foresee much misery to my country, but I believe I shall be out of it before night." Clarendon tells us why his life had become a burthen to Falkland: "From the entrance into this unnatural war, his natural cheerfulness and vivacity grew clouded, and a kind of sadness and dejection of spirit stole upon him, which he had never been used to. But after the king's return from Brentford, and the furious resolution of the two Houses not to admit any treaty for peace, those indispositions which had before touched him, grew into a perfect habit of uncheerfulness ; and he, who had been so exactly easy and affable to all men, that his face and countenance was always present, and vacant to his company, and held any cloudiness and less pleasantness of the visage a kind of rudeness or incivility, became, on a sudden, less communicable; and thence, very sad, pale, and exceedingly affected with the spleen. In his clothes and habit, which he had minded before always with more neatness, and industry, and expense, than is usual to so great a soul, he was not now only incurious, but too negligent; and in his reception of suitors, and the necessary or casual addresses to his place, so quick, and sharp, and severe, that there wanted not some men (strangers to his nature and disposition), who believed him proud and imperious, from which no mortal man was ever more free. * * * * When there was any overture or hope of peace, he would be more erect and vigorous, and exceedingly solicitous to press any thing which he thought might promote it; and, sitting among his friends, often, after a deep silence and frequent sighs, would, with a shrill and sad accent, ingeminate the word *Peace, Peace;* and would passionately profess, 'that the very agony of the war, and the view of the calamities and desolation the kingdom did

* Arnold's "Lectures on Modern History," p. 238.

and must endure, took his sleep from him, and would shortly break his heart.' " *

The untimely death of lord Falkland must have been to some of the cavaliers, probably to the king himself, a presage of greater disaster; if we may credit the well-known anecdote which Dr. Welwood thinks not " below the majesty of history to mention." Agreeing with him, we repeat it in his own words:

"The king being at Oxford during the Civil Wars, went one day to see the public library, where he was shewn among other books a Virgil nobly

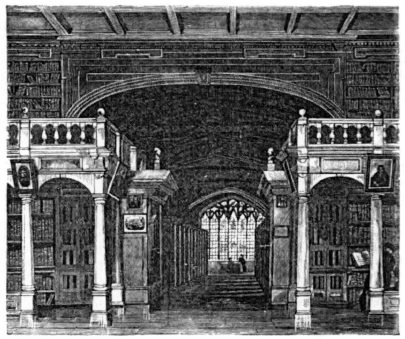

Interior of the Bodleian Library, Oxford.

printed and exquisitely bound. The lord Falkland, to divert the king, would have his majesty make a trial of his fortune by the *Sortes Virgilianæ*, which every body knows was an usual kind of augury some ages past. Whereupon the king opening the book, the period which happened to come up was that part of Dido's imprecation against Æneas; which Mr. Dryden translates thus:

' Yet let a race untam'd, and haughty foes,
His peaceful entrance with dire arms oppose;
Oppress'd with numbers in th' unequal field,
His men discourag'd, and himself expell'd,

---

* "Rebellion," vol. iv. p. 231.

> Let him for succour sue from place to place,
> Torn from his subjects, and his son's embrace,
> First let him see his friends in battle slain,
> And their untimely fate lament in vain;
> And when at length the cruel war shall cease,
> On hard conditions may he buy his peace.
> Nor let him then enjoy supreme command,
> But fall untimely by some hostile hand,
> And lie unbury'd on the barren sand.' *

It is said king Charles seemed concerned at this accident; and that the lord Falkland observing it, would likewise try his own fortune in the same manner; hoping he might fall upon some passage that could have no relation to his case, and thereby divert the king's thoughts from any impression the other might have upon him. But the place that Falkland stumbled upon, was yet more suited to his destiny than the other had been to the king's; being the following expressions of Evander, upon the untimely death of his son Pallas, as they are translated by the same hand.

> ' O Pallas! thou hast fail'd thy plighted word,
> To fight with caution, not to tempt the sword:
> I warn'd thee, but in vain; for well I knew
> What perils youthful ardour would pursue:
> That boiling blood would carry thee too far:
> Young as thou wert in danger, raw to war!
> O curst essay of arms, disast'rous doom,
> Prelude of bloody fields, and fights to come!' " †

The relief of Gloucester and the battle of Newbury were fatal to many of the sanguine hopes of a speedy victory over disunited rebels which the royalists up to this time had entertained. They had seen how the despised Trained Bands had been disciplined into good soldiers. They had seen how such men as held the " godly city of Gloucester " for a whole month against the best troops of the king would die rather than surrender. There was a fatal concurrence of events to render it certain that, although the queen was bestowing places upon her favourite courtiers, as if Oxford were Whitehall —offering the marquis of Newcastle to be chamberlain or lord of the bed-chamber, and intriguing to make the faithless lord Holland groom of the stole,—the real power of the monarchy was fading away. The royalists called the battle of Newbury " a very great victory." ‡ Before this issue had been tried the Parliament had appointed commissioners to negotiate a treaty of alliance with the Scots; for the Parliament felt weak and dispirited. Sir Henry Vane, the chief negotiator, had acceded to the imperative demand of the Scots parliament that the religious system of Scotland should be adopted as that of England. Vane, who was an Independent, and a supporter of toleration, contrived, after great debate, to satisfy the zealous Presbyterians, who proposed " a Covenant." Vane stipulated for " a solemn *league* and covenant." This obligation was to be taken by both nations. The Scots proposed a clause " for the preservation of the king's person." Vane added, " in preservation of the laws of the land and liberty of the subject." To the clause for " reducing the doctrine and discipline of both churches to the

---

* " Æneid," iv. l. 880.   † *Ibid.* xi. l. 230.   ‡ Letter of the queen to Newcastle.

pattern of the best reformed," Vane added "according to the word of God." *
This solemn League and Covenant was to bind those who subscribed it, "to
endeavour, without respect of persons, the extirpation of popery and prelacy."
A passage from Baxter shows how earnestly it was sought to reconcile the
moderate party to this declaration: "This Covenant was proposed by the
Parliament to the consideration of the Synod at Westminster; the Synod
stumbled at some things in it, and especially at the word prelacy. Dr. Burges
the prolocutor, Mr. Gataker, and abundance more, declared their judgments
to be for episcopacy, even for the ancient moderate episcopacy, in which one
stated president, with his presbytery, governed every church; though not for
the English Diocesan frame, in which one bishop, without his presbytery, did,
by a lay chancellor's court, govern all the presbyters and churches of a
diocese, being many hundreds; and that in a secular manner by abundance
of upstart secular officers, unknown to the primitive church. Hereupon grew
some debate in the assembly: some being against every degree of bishops
(especially the Scottish divines), and others being for a moderate episcopacy.
But these English divines would not subscribe the Covenant, till there were
an alteration suited to their judgments: and so a parenthesis was yielded to,
as describing that sort of prelacy which they opposed, viz., that is, Church
government by archbishops, bishops, deans and chapters, archdeacons, and
all other ecclesiastical officers depending on that hierarchy. All which conjoined are mentioned as the description of that form of church government
which they meant by Prelacy, as not extending to the ancient Episcopacy.
When the Covenant was agreed on, the Lords and Commons first took it
themselves, and Mr. Thomas Coleman preached to the House of Lords, and
gave it them with this public explication, That by Prelacy we mean not all
Episcopacy, but only the form which is here described." †   Mr. Hallam says,
"These controversial subtleties elude the ordinary reader of history." But
history cannot be understood unless some reference be made to them.
Without regarding these subtleties, we might conclude that the Parliament
and the people of London were unanimous for the unconditional adoption of
the same form of church government as that which was established in Scotland. The Scots no doubt expected that this would be the result. The
exultation of their commissioners in London must have been unbounded when,
on the 25th of September, all the members of Parliament, assembled in St.
Margaret's church, swore to maintain "the solemn League and Covenant."
The oath was signed by two hundred and twenty-eight members of the
Commons. It was adopted in the city with enthusiastic demonstrations of
religious fervour. On the next day Essex was received in London with a
warmth that may have consoled him for some previous complaints of his want
of energy, and for annoyances which he had received in his command. The
Lords and Commons gave him an assurance of their confidence: and he
remained the general-in-chief, without the divided powers which had created a
jealousy between himself and sir William Waller.

   Whilst the members of parliament in London are lifting up their hands
in reverent appeal to Heaven as they accept the Covenant, and the people are
shouting around the earl of Essex as the banners are displayed which he

* See Ludlow's "Memoirs." p. 65.   † "Reliquiæ Baxterianæ," p. 48.

won in Newbury fight, there is one man, fast growing into one of the most notable of men, who is raising troops, marching hither and thither, fighting whenever blows are needful—work which demands more instant attention than the ceremony of St. Margaret's church. In the early stages of his wonderful history nothing is more interesting than to trace the steps of this man, now *Colonel* Cromwell. Whatever he says or does has some mark of the vigour of his character,—so original, so essentially different in its manifestations from the customary displays of public men. In Cromwell's speeches and writings we must not look for the smooth and equable movement of common diplomatists and orators. His grand earnestness makes the artifices of rhetoric appear petty by comparison. The fluency of the scholarly writer is weak by the side of his homely phrases. He is urging some great friends in Suffolk to raise recruits, and choose captains of horse: "A few honest men are better than numbers. * * * * I had rather have a plain russet-coated captain, who knows what he fights for, and loves what he knows, than that which you call 'a Gentleman,' and is nothing else. I honour a Gentleman that is so indeed."* In this spirit Cromwell is forming his "Ironsides," and at this period is heading them in the earliest of those famous charges which determined so many battles. On the 10th of October, in the skirmish of Winceby, near Horncastle, his career is well nigh ended. His horse was killed at the first charge ; and as he rose, he was knocked down by sir Ingram Hopton, who led the royalists. He seized another horse, and the enemy was routed. Denzil Hollis, in his Memoirs, more than insinuates doubts of Cromwell's personal courage. He calls him "as errand a coward, as he is notoriously perfidious, ambitious, and hypocritical ;" and states, of his own knowledge, that he basely "kept out of the field at Keinton battle, where he, with his troop of horse, came not in, impudently and ridiculously affirming, the day after, that he had been all that day seeking the army and place of fight, though his quarters were but at a village near hand."† We must receive this testimony for what it is worth, as coming from one who had become a bitter enemy of Cromwell, as the leader of the Independents. For the ambition of such a man as Cromwell, whether as a soldier or a politician, there was now ample room. His religious party was fast rising into importance. The sectaries of all denominations eagerly gathered under the standard of a leader who insisted that his men should be religious, but left the particular form of religion to their own choice. The religious principle of the Civil War thus became more and more prominent, when enthusiasts of every denomination regarded it as a struggle for the right of private judgment in matters of faith, and despised every authority but that of the Bible. Such a leader as Cromwell had tougher materials to conquer with than Hampden, with his green-coated hunters of the Chilterns. He had themes to discourse upon in his oratory, so forcible, however regardless of proem and peroration, which, far more than Pym's eloquent declamation, stirred the hearts of a parliament that had come to consider "the power of godliness" to be a higher cause than "the liberties of the kingdoms." Cromwell's opportunity was come. The man who had destroyed arbitrary taxation, and the man who had sent the coun-

---

* Mr. Carlyle has done inestimable service for the historical student by his publication of "Oliver Cromwell's Speeches and Letters, with Elucidations." For the first time Cromwell is presented to us as a real man.　　　　　　† "Memoirs," p. 17.

sellor of a military despotism to the block, were no more. The year 1643 was memorable for the deaths of three of the greatest of the early patriots of the Long Parliament—Hampden, Falkland, and Pym. We have seen how two of the illustrious three died on the battle-field. Pym died on the 8th of December, having sunk under a lingering illness. He was buried in Westminster Abbey, his body being carried to its resting place on the shoulders of ten of the leading speakers and influential members of the House of Commons. The men who now came upon the scene as the chief actors were of a different stamp than these earlier tribunes of the people. Henceforward the war will assume a broader character and a fiercer aspect. The prospect of accommodation will grow more and more faint. The religious element will go forward into what all who look impartially upon those times must consider as relentless persecution by one dominant party, and wild fanaticism amongst sectaries not yet banded into a common purpose. The arbitrary imposition of the Covenant upon every minister of the Anglican Church was the first great result of the alliance with the Scots. The Presbyterian Parliament of England became more violent for conformity than the Court of High Commission which the Parliament had destroyed. The Canons of Laud had fallen lightly upon men who were indifferent about the position of the altar, or the precise amount of genuflexions; but the imposition of the Covenant upon all the beneficed clergy was the declaration of an intolerant tyranny against the most conscientious. The number of incumbents ejected from their livings, for their refusal to sign this obligation, has been variously reckoned. According to Neal, the historian of the Puritans, it was sixteen hundred; according to Walker, an extreme high churchman, it reached eight thousand. The statement of Walker is evidently a gross exaggeration. The sixteen hundred of Neal was about a fifth of the benefices of England. Whatever was the number of ejected ministers, and however some might have been, as was alleged, of evil lives, the tyranny of this measure is most odious, as coming from men who had themselves struggled against religious persecution. "The remorseless and indiscriminate bigotry of Presbyterianism might boast that it had heaped disgrace on Walton, and driven Lydiat to beggary; that it trampled on the old age of Hales, and embittered with insult the dying moments of Chillingworth."* Amongst the eminent public men who advocated the Covenant as a political measure, there were some who abhorred it as an instrument of persecution. The younger Vane, the chief promoter of it, declared upon the scaffold, that "the holy ends therein contained I fully assent to, and have been as desirous to observe; but the rigid way of prosecuting it, and the oppressing uniformity that hath been endeavoured by it, I never approved."

* Hallam, "Constitutional History,' vol. ii.

York. Micklebar Gate.

CHAPTER III.

The Scots enter England—The Irish army defeated at Nantwich—A Parliament summoned to meet at Oxford—Combined armies besiege York—Lathom House—Battle of Marston Moor—The queen leaves England—Essex defeated in the West—Second battle of Newbury—Differences between the Parliamentary Commanders—Laud condemned for treason by ordinance of parliament—Treaty of Uxbridge—Montrose's victories in the Western Highlands—Self-denying Ordinance—Fairfax lord-general of the re-modelled army—Cromwell lieutenant-general—The battle of Naseby—The king's Cabinet Opened—Surrender of Bristol by Rupert—Basing House taken.

THE year 1644 opened with great events. On the 19th of January the Scottish army entered England. They marched from Dunbar, "in a great frost and snow "—"up to the knees in snow," say the narratives. Lesley, now earl of Leven, commanded them. The marquis of Newcastle was not strong enough long to oppose them. He had given up his attempt to take Hull, and was in winter-quarters at York. Lesley's army marched on to Newcastle, which they summoned to surrender. The governor and garrison were faithful to their trust. The Scots were straitened for provisions ; and the royalist army of fourteen thousand men was intercepting their supplies. They determined to advance further into the heart of the country. At this juncture the English regiments that had been recalled by the king from Ireland, were besieging the parliamentary garrison at Nantwich. Sir Thomas Fairfax hurried to the relief of the place, and totally defeated this Anglo-Irish army, which was under the command of Sir John Byron. The recall by the king of those troops who had been sent to repress the rebellion in Ireland, was preceded by the conclusion of a truce with the rebels themselves. The Irish protestants were alarmed for their safety. The English protestants became more than ever suspicious of Charles, and especially of his queen, who had always maintained a correspondence with the Irish papists. Many of these had come over with the English troops. The cessation of arms in Ireland, says Clarendon, "was no sooner known in England, but the two Houses declared against it, with all the sharp glosses upon it to his majesty's dishonour that can be imagined." He goes on to say, with reference to Irish affairs, that "the calumnies and slanders raised to his majesty's disservice and dishonour made a more than ordinary impression upon the minds of men, and not only of vulgar-spirited people, but of those who resisted all other infusion and infection." * The historian of the rebellion seeks to acquit the king of all underhand proceedings with the Romanists of Ireland. But he must have had a difficult task for a conscientious man to perform, in slurring over in this and other instances of his master's willingness to adopt covert and dishonourable measures. The next year, when Charles was engaged in the most dangerous projects with Herbert, earl of Glamorgan, for raising a great army of Irish to invade England under the auspices of the pope and foreign princes, he kept these matters a profound secret from his council. Of these Irish transactions there is the conclusive evidence against the king of Clarendon himself, in a letter addressed by him to the secretary Nicholas. "I must tell you, I care not how little I say in that business of Ireland, since those strange powers and instructions given to your favourite Glamorgan, which appears to me so inexcusable to justice, piety, and prudence. And I fear there is very much in that transaction of Ireland, both before and since, that you and I were never thought wise enough to be advised with in. Oh, Mr. Secretary, those stratagems have given me more sad hours than all the misfortunes in war which have befallen the king, and look like the effects of God's anger towards us." †

Negotiation after negotiation between the king and the parliament having failed, and the appeal to the sword still remaining of doubtful issue, some strong measure was thought expedient to lower the character of the two Houses sitting at Westminster. The king's notion was to issue a proclamation declaring the parliament to be dissolved; forbidding them to meet; and requiring all persons to reject their authority. Hyde told the king his honest opinion upon this project: "I cannot imagine that your majesty's forbidding them to meet any more at Westminster will prevent one man the less going there. * * * It was the first powerful reproach they corrupted the people with against your majesty, that you intended to dissolve this parliament; and, in the same way, repeal all the other acts made by that

---

* "Rebellion," vol. iv. p. 364.   † "Clarendon Papers," quoted in Lingard.

parliament, whereof some are very precious to the people. As your majesty
has always disclaimed any such thought, such a proclamation now would confirm all the jealousies and fears so excited, and trouble many of your true
subjects."* Charles very unwillingly accepted Hyde's own counter-proposi-
tion. It was that of summoning the peers and commons that had adhered to
the royal cause to meet him in parliament at Oxford. On the 22nd of
December, 1643, the proclamation convoking this Parliament was issued. On
the 22nd of January, 1644, the parliament, or more truly convention, met at
Oxford. A letter written from this assembly to the earl of Essex, expressing
a desire for peace, was signed by forty-three peers, and one hundred and
eighteen commoners. Others were absent on the king's service. In the
same January, according to Whitelocke, two hundred and eighty members
appeared in the House of Commons, besides those absent on the parliamentary
services. A large majority of the Commons were with the Westminster
parliament; a large majority of Peers with that of Oxford. The measure
might have been productive of advantage to the royal cause, had it not soon
been manifest that the king and queen were impatient under any interference
with the authority of royalty. This was more fatal than the absolute refusal
of the parliament at Westminster to recognise " those persons now assembled
at Oxford, who, contrary to their duty, have deserted your parliament," as
they wrote to the king on the 9th of March. The parliament at Oxford continued to sit till the 16th of April, voting taxes and loans, passing resolutions of fidelity, but irritating the king in their refusal to be mere instruments for registering his edicts. But they produced no visible effect upon
public opinion; and Charles congratulated the queen upon their being " freed
from the place of all mutinous motions, his mongrel parliament," when he
had willed its adjournment.

Whilst at Oxford the king's "mongrel parliament" only proved a
hindrance to the vigorous prosecution of the war, the parliament at Westminster had adopted the rational course of strengthening their executive
authority. A council was formed under the title of "The Committee of the
Two Kingdoms," consisting of seven Lords, fourteen members of the Commons,
and four Scottish commissioners. The entire conduct of the war, the correspondence with foreign states, whatever belongs to the executive power as
distinguished from the legislative, devolved upon this Committee. In the
spring of 1644 the Parliament had five armies in the field, paid by general or
local taxation, and by voluntary contributions. Including the Scottish army
there were altogether 56,000 men under arms; the English forces being commanded, as separate armies, by Essex, Waller, Manchester, and Fairfax.
Essex and Waller advanced to blockade Oxford. The queen, who was in a
situation that made the thought of remaining in a city exposed to siege very
irksome, determined to go to a place of greater safety. She went to Exeter
in April, and never saw Charles again. He remained shut up in Oxford.
Its walls were surrounded by lines of defence; but the blockading forces had
become so strong that resistance appeared to be hopeless. On the night of
the 3rd of June the king secretly left the city, and passed safely between the
two hostile armies. There had been jealousies and disagreements between

* Clarendon's Life.

Essex and Waller. The Committee of the two kingdoms had assigned to Waller the command of the army of the west, in the event of the separation of the two armies. Essex, supported by the council of war, resolved to march to the west himself. He was directed by the Committee to retrace his steps, and go in pursuit of the king. Essex replied to the Committee that their orders were opposed to military discipline; and he marched on. Waller, meanwhile, had gone in pursuit of the king into Worcestershire. Charles suddenly returned to Oxford; and then defeated Waller, at Cropredy

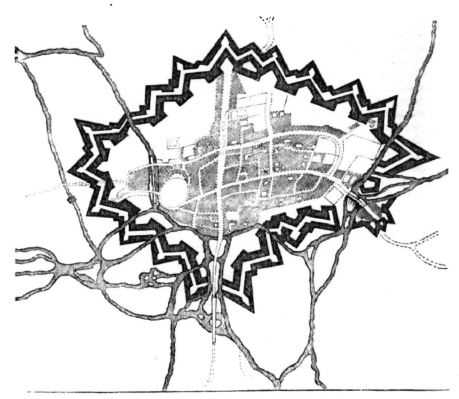

Oxford, with the Lines raised for its defence by Charles I.

Bridge, near Banbury, who had hastened back to encounter him. Essex was before the walls of Exeter, in which city the queen had given birth to a princess. The king hastened to the west. He was strong enough to meet either of the parliamentary armies, thus separated. Meanwhile the north of England became the scene of the most momentous conflict that distracted England had yet beheld. The dashing enterprise of Rupert in the relief of Lathom House, so bravely held by Charlotte de la Tremouille, countess of Derby, became of small importance amidst the greater event that was to follow in the north.

The moated house of the Stanleys had been defended by the heroic countess for eighteen weeks against a detachment of the army of Fairfax. Their artillery could produce little impression upon the thick walls and lofty towers; and the demand to submit herself, her children and followers to the mercy of Parliament, produced from the lady, immortalised by history and romance, the reply, that "the mercies of the wicked are cruel." Rupert hung the walls of Lathom House with the parliamentary banners which he had captured in a fierce battle at Bolton; and he went on towards York to a fiercer strife and a perilous defeat. The combined English and Scottish armies were besieging York. Rupert received a letter from the king, containing these words: " I command and conjure you, by the duty and affection which I know you bear me, that all new enterprises laid aside, you immediately march, according to your first intention, with all your force to the relief of York." He did march. Marston Moor saw the result.

As Rupert advanced towards York with twenty thousand men, the allied English and Scots retired. Their councils were not unanimous. Some were for fighting, some for retreating, and at length they moved from Hessey Moor, near York, to Tadcaster. Rupert entered York with two thousand cavalry. The earl of Newcastle was in command there. He counselled a prudent delay. The impetuous Rupert said he had the orders of the king for his guidance, and he was resolved to fight. Newcastle was a man of ceremony; jealous of interference, for he had ruled the north with vice-regal magnificence; raising large bodies of troops, and paying them with the coinage of the York mint. He was indignant with the prince; but he left

York Half-Crown.

him to his own course. On the 2nd of July, having rested two days, in and near York, and enabled the city to be newly provisioned, the royalist army went forth to fight. They met their enemy on Marston Moor. The two armies looked upon each other for two hours, with scarcely a cannon-shot fired. Newcastle asked Rupert what office he was to take. He replied that the earl might repose, for he did not intend to begin the action till the morrow. Newcastle went to his carriage, and left the prince to his supremacy. The sun was in the west on that July evening when the battle began. The sun had scarcely set when the battle was finished; and there were four thousand one hundred and fifty bodies lying dead on that plain. The issue would have been more than doubtful, but for Cromwell, who for the first time had headed his Ironsides in a great pitched battle. The right wing of the parliamentary army was scattered. Rupert was chasing and slaying the Scottish cavalry. The centre of each army, each centre composed of infantry, were fighting with the sturdy resolution of Englishmen, whatever be the quarrel. The charges of Fairfax and Cromwell decided the day. The flight of the Scottish horse proclaimed that the victory of the Cavaliers was complete; and a messenger who reached Oxford from Newark announced such news to the enraptured courtiers as made the gothic pinnacles red with bonfires. In another day or two the terrible truth was known. The victory of the parliamentary armies was so complete, that the earl of Newcastle had left York, and had embarked at Scarborough for the continent. Rupert marched away also, with the wreck of his army, to Chester. Each had announced his determination to the other, as they gloomily entered York on the night of the battle. Fifteen hundred prisoners, all the artillery, more than a hundred banners, remained with the victors. And the men who had achieved this success were the despised Puritans; those who had been a laughing-stock for half a century. "We had all the evidence," writes Cromwell to his brother-in-law, colonel Valentine Walton, "of an absolute victory obtained by the Lord's blessing upon the godly party principally. We never charged but we routed the enemy. The left wing, which I commanded, being our own horse, saving a few Scots in our rear, beat all the prince's horse. God made them as stubble to our swords." Cromwell had to tell his brother-in-law of a calamity that would most touch a father's heart. "Sir, God hath taken away your eldest son by a cannon-shot. It brake his leg. We were necessitated to have it cut off, whereof he died." He expatiates upon this sorrow with no vain attempts at ordinary condolence. "The Lord be your strength" is his emphatic conclusion. When Cromwell's character came to be judged, first in an age of profligacy, and then in an age of religious indifference, no one could comprehend that he had any higher sustaining principles than craft and selfishness.

The queen, sinking under a serious illness, unable to call back the high spirit which had made her so determined in her councils and her actions, now fled to France. Essex was approaching with his army towards Exeter. She asked a safe conduct from him to go to Bath or Bristol. He offered to wait upon her himself to London; but he could not obey her desire to go to any other place without directions from the Parliament. On the 9th of July she wrote a letter from Truro, to bid her husband adieu. "I am hazarding my life that I may not incommode your affairs." She embarked from Falmouth on the 14th, and landed at Brest. Henceforth her letters to Charles will continue to show how keen was the interest she took in his proceedings, and how strenuously she held to her original idea of never conceding anything to rebels. Soon after her departure the king's arms had a considerable success over lord Essex in Cornwall. The parliamentary party are in alarm. Cromwell writes, "we do with grief of heart resent the sad condition of our army in the west, and of affairs there. That business has our hearts with it; and truly had we wings we would fly thither."* The army was indeed in a "sad condition." Essex wrote in vain for assistance; in vain urged a diversion, to take off the pressure of the royalist army by which he was surrounded. A letter from the king was delivered to him, calling upon

* Carlyle, vol. i. p. 156.

him to give peace to his country. Essex replied to his nephew, lord Beauchamp, who brought the letter, that he should give no answer; his advice to the king was to return to his Parliament. Another attempt was made to win Essex to a treaty. He had no authority to treat, he said, and could not treat without a breach of trust. By the latter end of August he was encompassed by the royalists. The greater part of his army desired to capitulate, though his cavalry had succeeded in passing the enemy's posts. Essex hastily left the camp to avoid that humiliation, leaving Skippon in command. The old campaigner proposed to his officers to follow the example of the cavalry, at all risks. But Charles offered honourable terms of capitulation, only requiring the surrender of the artillery, arms, and ammunition. The army of Essex returned as fugitives to London, or dispersed through the country. He wrote from Plymouth an account of "the greatest blow that ever befel our party." His fidelity to the cause he had adopted not only saved him from reproach, but the Parliament hastened to give him a new mark of their confidence. The king was resolved to march to London from the west. Montrose was in arms in Scotland, and had gained two battles. The time for a great blow was thought to have arrived. Three armies under Essex, Manchester, and Waller were called out for the defence of the capital. Essex, though retaining his authority, did not join the troops which fought the second battle of Newbury on the 27th of October. Manchester was there in command. This battle was hotly contested without any decisive results. The king withdrew to Oxford, renewing his project of advancing to London. The serious differences between the Presbyterians and the Independents were brought to an issue by this second battle of Newbury. There were no rejoicings in the city that the king had been checked in his approach. There was gloom and dissatisfaction amongst the people, which was evidently encouraged by men of bolder resolves than those who had the conduct of military affairs. In November, Cromwell, in his place in parliament, brought forward a charge against the earl of Manchester, of having "always been indisposed and backward to engagements, and the ending of the war by the sword." He renewed his attack in December. "It is now a time to speak, or for ever hold the tongue * * * I do conceive if the army be not put into another method, and the war more vigorously prosecuted, the people can bear the war no longer, and will enforce you to a dishonourable peace." In a few months, the army was put "into another method."

The Presbyterian party, including the Scottish commissioners, were now at open hostility with the Independents. At a meeting at the house of the lord-general Essex, the Scottish chancellor proposed that Cromwell should be proceeded against as "an incendiary." Whitelocke and Maynard, two eminent lawyers, were consulted. Whitelocke advised that they should be prepared with specific proofs before they brought forward such a charge. Whilst the supporters of Essex and the other generals were seeking for proofs against their dangerous rival, it was moved in the Commons, by Zouch Tate, a man of no great mark, "that no member of either House shall, during the war, enjoy or execute any office or command, civil or military, and that an ordinance be brought in accordingly." Long and furious debates followed this proposition. It was passed by the Lower House on the 21st of December, and transmitted to the Lords. The Presbyterian party saw their strength

passing away from them.   They endeavoured to rekindle all the violence of
religious intolerance, by resuming proceedings against archbishop Laud.   In
the previous March his trial had commenced upon specific charges, founded
upon those which had first been brought forward on his impeachment.   He
defended himself with skill and courage.   The arbitrary power of the ecclesiastical courts which he had upheld was at an end.   There was meanness
and cruelty in his prosecution, after four years of imprisonment.   It was the
triumph of a bigotry far more odious than his own attempt to tyrannise in
matters of religious opinion.   His most active persecutor was William Prynne,
who never relaxed in his thirst for vengeance upon the intolerance which he
now repaid in tenfold measure.   By an ordinance of Parliament, voted by a
few Lords—some say seven only—he was condemned for high-treason.   There
might be the plea of state necessity for the execution of Strafford; but to
send this aged prelate to the block, whose power for good or evil was wholly
gone, was atrocious in a higher degree, for this shedding of blood was useless.
He was beheaded on the 10th of January, 1645.   On the 8rd the Liturgy of
the Church of England, which had been previously tolerated, was abolished
by ordinance.   Four others were sent to the scaffold at the same time for
political offences;—Sir John Hotham and his son; lord Macguire; and sir
Alexander Carew.   The Presbyterians were left to these courses of severity,
whilst their opponents were urging the adoption of "the Self-denying
Ordinance."   It was rejected on the 18th of January, by the Lords.   The
reason for the rejection was that they did not know "what shape the army
will now suddenly take."   But the agitation of this question had rendered a
great change necessary.   On the 21st of January, Fairfax was nominated
general; and, within a month, a new model for the army was arranged and
carried.   The Self-denying Ordinance, with modifications, was ultimately
passed.
    The most strenuous attempt at pacification between the king and the
Parliament was made at the beginning of 1645.   Ludlow has briefly recorded
the main facts : " It was agreed that Commissioners should be sent from the
Parliament to treat with others to be sent from the king, about conditions of
peace.   The place of their meeting was at Uxbridge. * * * The king had
owned the two Houses as a parliament, to which he was not without difficulty
persuaded, though he had by an act engaged that they should continue to be
a parliament till they had dissolved themselves, which they had not done." *
Charles wrote to his queen, " As for my calling those at London a parliament,
I shall refer thee to Digby for particular satisfaction; this in general : if
there had been but two, besides myself, of my opinion, I had not done it;
and the argument that prevailed with me was, that the calling did no ways
acknowledge them to be a parliament." †   This was his apology to Henrietta
Maria, when she bitterly reproached him, saying, " When you were resolved
to make a little council of four, you showed me a paper in which were many
things about which you would never relax, of which this was the first." ‡   A
negotiation entered upon in such a spirit was not likely to end in any agreement for the public good.   Clarendon, who was one of the king's commis-

* "Memoirs," p. 149.   † "King's Cabinet Opened," Harleian Miscellany, vol. v. p. 513.
‡ Green's "Letters." p, 276.

sioners at Uxbridge, has left the amplest details of the progress of this treaty. The commissioners sent by the Parliament were chiefly of the more moderate party. Men who had been united in the first days of the Long Parliament, but had since become political enemies, now met in a common hope that once more they might become friends. Sir Edward Hyde and lord Colepepper renewed their intercourse with Mr. Hollis and Mr. Saint John. The chancellor of Scotland, lord Loudon, and the parliamentary lords Pembroke and Denbigh, had private discussions with Hyde and others, in which they imparted their mutual hopes and fears. "There was a good house at the end of the town, which was provided for the treaty, where was a fair room in the middle of the house, handsomely dressed up for the commissioners to sit in."* Each party ate in its own inn, for there were "two great ones

Uxbridge, showing, to the right, the house (called the Treaty House) in which the commissioners held their sittings.

which served very well to that purpose." The duke of Richmond presided at the table of the king's commissioners. Their debates were at first grave and courteous; seldom disturbed by any acrimonious reflections upon the past; always difficult and protracted for many hours. The three great points which they had to discuss were, the Church, the state of Ireland, the Militia. They took each separately. The Presbyterians, with the Scottish divines, were as strenuous for the abolition of episcopacy, as the Episcopalians, with the learned doctors from Oxford, were resolute for its maintenance. Some trifling concessions were made on either side; and an approach to an agreement did not seem absolutely hopeless. The question of Ireland was

* That "fair room," with its black oak panels, quaintly carved, was, within the last twelve years, the principal room of the "Treaty-house Inn." We have often rested there, to indulge, over a traveller's meal, in reveries of that discussion of twenty days which made this room famous.

not so difficult. That of the Militia,—the question which of two parties should hold the great instrument of power—was at one period of the discussion resolving itself into a manageable shape. Lord Southampton was deputed to proceed to Oxford to see if he could obtain some concession from the king that would place the military authority under the joint control of the Crown and the Parliament, each naming half of the leaders, for a limited number of years. Dr. Welwood has a remarkable story connected with this mission : "Though the Parliament's demands were high, and the king showed a more than ordinary aversion to comply with them; yet the ill posture of the king's affairs at that time, and the fatal consequences they feared would follow upon the breaking off of the treaty, obliged a great many of the king's friends, and more particularly that noble person the earl of Southampton, who had gone post from Uxbridge to Oxford for that purpose, to press the king again and again upon their knees, to yield to the necessity of the times; and by giving his assent to some of the most material propositions that were sent him, to settle a lasting peace with his people. The king was at last prevailed with to follow their counsel; and the next morning was appointed for signing a warrant to his commissioners to that effect. And so sure were they of a happy end of all differences, that the king at supper complaining his wine was not good, one told him merrily, He hoped that his majesty would drink better before a week was over, at Guildhall with the lord mayor. But so it was, that when they came early the next morning to wait upon him with the warrant that had been agreed upon over night, they found his majesty had changed his resolution, and was become inflexible in these points." This sudden change in the king's resolves might have been ascribed to the capricious vacillation which he often displayed, whether from the changing moods of his own mind, or the influence of the queen and other secret advisers. In the instance before us, the altered temper is referred to a letter from Montrose, which had been received by Charles during the night. In the middle of December that daring chieftain had forced an entry into the country of the Campbells, wasting all before him. The mountains were covered with snow; the passes were imperfectly known; yet Montrose made his way, burning and slaughtering, till at length Argyle himself fled from his castle of Inverary, and left the unhappy clans to the vengeance of his deadly enemy. Montrose having sated his revenge till the end of January, marched towards Inverness. Argyle had returned with some forces from the Lowlands to the Western Highlands; and was in a position near the castle of Inverlochy, when Montrose suddenly came down upon him from the mountains. The battle was a decisive victory on the part of the royalist leader, who wrote an account of his exploits to Charles, which letter Dr. Welwood prints, having "seen a copy under the duke of Richmond's hand." Montrose says that after he had laid waste the whole country of Argyle, " my march was through inaccessible mountains, where I could have no guides but cowherds, and they scarce acquainted with a place but six miles from their own habitations. * * * * The difficultest march of all was over the Lochaber mountains, which we at last surmounted, and came upon the back of the enemy when they least suspected us." Having described his victory over "the rebels," he then proceeds to offer Charles his advice. His exultation at his triumph was so unbounded, that he concluded a few victories in Scotland would again place the king, with uncontrolled power, upon the thrones of both kingdoms. He has heard news, he says, " as if your majesty was entering into a treaty with your rebel Parliament in England. The success of your arms in Scotland does not more rejoice my heart, as that news from England is like to break it. * * * * The more your majesty grants, the more will be asked; and I have too much reason to know, that they will not rest satisfied with less than making your majesty a king of straw. * * * * Forgive me, sacred sovereign, to tell your majesty, that in my poor opinion, it is unworthy of a king to treat with rebel subjects while they have the sword in their hands. And though God forbid I should stint your majesty's mercy, yet I must declare the horror I am in, when I think of a treaty, while your majesty and they are in the field with two armies; unless they disband, and submit themselves entirely to your majesty's goodness and pardon. * * * Give me leave, with all humility, to assure your majesty, that through God's blessing, I am in the fairest hopes of reducing this kingdom to your majesty's obedience. And if the measures I have concerted with your other loyal subjects fail me not, which they hardly can, I doubt not but before the end of this summer, I shall be able to come to your majesty's assistance with a brave army; which, backed with the justice of your majesty's cause, will make the rebels in England, as well as in Scotland, feel the just rewards of rebellion." *

The treaty of Uxbridge was to last twenty days. The last day expired on a Saturday, and nothing was concluded. " They having on Sunday performed their usual visits to each other, parted with such coolness, as if they scarce hoped to meet again." † When the parliamentary commissioners returned to London, they found that Fairfax had received his commission as sole general. The new model for the army was being practically carried into effect. Argyle arrived from Scotland, stung by defeat and disgrace; and agreed with the extreme party in urging forward whatever measures would lead to the active prosecution of the war. The peers withdrew from their opposition to the self-denying ordinance, and it was finally passed on the 3rd of April. The military services of Cromwell were of such importance that Fairfax and his officers urged that, without regard to the ordinance, he might be temporarily appointed the lieutenant-general, chief commander of the horse. The earls of Essex, Manchester, and Denbigh, gave in their resignations. There was a great change in the operations of the Parliament. There was to be an equal change in the councils of the king. It was resolved that the prince of Wales should be sent into the western counties with the title of generalissimo, and that the most discreet advisers of Charles should accompany the prince, yet only fifteen years old, to direct all measures in his name. The more violent of the Cavaliers now formed the advisers of Charles. Oxford resounded with songs of mockery against the pestilent Roundheads. The royalist newspapers derided the folly which had dismissed the old parliamentary leaders, to place in their room untried and obscure men. The followers of such were fanatical mechanics, who would fly at the first sound of their cannon. As the summer approached the king's affairs were rapidly mending. He had taken Leicester by storm. Taunton was besieged by the

* Welwood's " Memoirs," p. 306, ed. 1736.   † Clarendon, vol. i. p. 81.

royalists. Fairfax was surrounding Oxford, but inactive. Cromwell was active in the counties of the Eastern Association. Those who had opposed the re-modelling of the army complained that the new organisation had produced no effective results. Fairfax, on the 5th of June, received commands to raise the siege of Oxford, and go to the midland counties after the king.

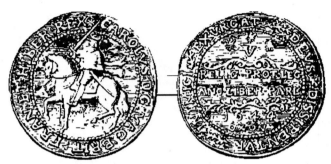

Crown from the Royal Mint at Oxford.

The general sent a requisition to the Parliament that Cromwell might be permitted to join him. He was indispensable, Fairfax and his colonels said, as commander of the cavalry. There is alarm in the eastern counties. Cromwell writes from Cambridge to the deputy lieutenants of Suffolk : "The cloud of the enemy's army hanging still upon the borders, and drawing towards Harborough, make some supposals that they aim at the Association." A postscript adds, "Since the writing hereof we received certain intelligence that the enemy's body, with sixty carriages, was on his march towards the Association, three miles on this side Harborough, last night at four of the clock." Cromwell calls for "horse and dragoons"—all your horse and dragoons to hasten to Newmarket. The foot are to rendezvous at Bury. On the 13th of June, Fairfax and Cromwell were marching after the king, who went before them from Daventry to Harborough. On the 14th of June was fought the battle of Naseby.

Cromwell wrote the despatch announcing the result of this battle to the Speaker of the House of Commons. This letter was written on the evening of that day which was fatal to the hopes of the royalists. "He [the king] drew out to meet us. Both armies engaged. We, after three hours' fight very doubtful, at last routed his army; killed and took about 5000—very many officers, but of what quality we yet know not. We took also about 200 carriages, all he had; and all his guns, being 12 in number, whereof two were demi-cannon, two demi-culverins, and I think the rest sackers. We pursued the enemy from three miles short of Harborough to nine beyond, even to the sight of Leicester, whither the king fled. Sir, this is none other but the hand of God; and to Him alone give the glory, wherein none are to share with Him."[*] Minuter chroniclers than the man who had the chief share of the work have given us ample details of this victory.[†] The Cavaliers were so confident of their strength that they were amusing

* Carlyle vol. i. p. 176.　　　　　† See Carlyle, vol. iii. Appendix, No. vii

themselves with hunting during the five days that their head-quarters were near Daventry. On the 12th the king was encamped on Burrough Hill, and had been hunting that day. Fairfax was near him, and saw from a place near Weedon, at four o'clock in the morning of the 13th, the huts of the royal camp on fire, for the army was moving off. At six o'clock that morning Cromwell arrived with his Ironsides from the Associated Counties; and he was received with shouts; "the horse gave a mighty shout for joy of his coming to them." The united parliamentary forces now marched forward towards Harborough. The king had taken up his quarters for the night at the "Hall House," at Lubenham, near Harborough, where his van was stationed. His rear was at Naseby. Late that evening, Ireton and his troopers suddenly dashed in amongst the royalists there. Some fled to the old Hall, where the king was gone to rest. He set off instantly to Rupert's quarters at Harborough; and in a midnight council of war it was determined not to retire to Leicester, as had been previously agreed, but to fight Fairfax. "They would not stay to expect his coming," says Clarendon, "but would go back to meet him." The parliamentary army was on its march at three in the morning of the 14th, and at five it was at Naseby. Of this old hamlet on a hill in the centre of England there is a rough sketch in a curious book by a chaplain of Fairfax.[*] Mr. Carlyle has given the present aspect of the place in a few words: "A peaceable old hamlet of some eight hundred souls; clay cottages for labourers, but neatly thatched and swept; smith's shop, saddler's shop, beer-shop, all in order; forming a kind of square which leads off southwards into two long streets: the old church, with its graves, stands in the centre. * * * The ground is upland, moorland, though now growing corn; was not enclosed till the last generation, and is still somewhat bare of wood." [†] According to Clarendon the king's army was drawn up early in the morning of the 14th in order of battle, about a mile from Harborough, there to wait for the enemy. The several commands were thus assigned: prince Rupert commanded the left wing; sir Marmaduke Langdale the right wing; lord Ashley the main body. The reserves were with the king. The scout-master came in and reported that he had been three or four miles, and could gain no intelligence of any enemy near. Rupert then went forward with his horse; and indistinctly seeing the van of the Parliament's troops, fancied they were retreating, and sent a messenger to desire that the royalist main body should immediately move up. When Fairfax saw the king's army advancing, he formed his troops in a large fallow field north-west of Naseby, the brow of the hill running east and west for about a mile. The centre was commanded by Fairfax himself and Skippon; the right wing by Cromwell; the left wing by Ireton. The reserves were commanded by Pride, Hammond, and Rainsborough. On Rupert hurried. "Thus," says Clarendon, "the army was engaged before the cannon was turned, or the ground made choice of upon which they were to fight." The hill on which the parliamentary army was drawn up bears the name of "Mill Hill." The king's army was on a hill opposite. A wide table-ground known as "Broad Moor" was between them. Here was the chief point of the deadly struggle. Rupert charged up the hill against the left wing of Fairfax. Cromwell charged from the extreme right,

---

[*] Sprigge, "Anglia Rediviva."   [†] Vol. i. p. 173.

down the hill upon Langdale's squadrons. Rupert is carrying all before him with his battle-cry of "Queen Mary." He has beaten Ireton's left wing back to Naseby; but there he has been tempted to lose time in taking a survey of his enemy's baggage. Cromwell has scattered the left wing of the royalists. Langdale's horse have fled through the furze-bushes and rabbit-warrens, before the battle-cry of "God is our strength." But Fairfax in the centre is hotly pressed. The king's foot have come over the hill, and poured in volley after volley upon the parliamentary ranks. They have closed. Fairfax is riding from division to division bare-headed. His helmet has been lost in the first charge. Old Skippon is wounded, but he "will not stir while a man will stand." But help is at hand. The Ironsides now turn

Obelisk on Naseby Field.   Erected to commemorate the Battle.

from their flying enemies on the right; and retrieve the day by their assaults on the king's main battle. When Rupert returns he sees the royal army in utter confusion. Fairfax has rallied his men; and the royalists yield. But the king's reserve of horse, consisting of his own guards, what are they doing? A panic fear seizes them, which Clarendon thus explains :—"The king was even upon the point of charging the enemy, in the head of his guards, when the earl of Carnewarth, who rode next to him, (a man never suspected for infidelity, nor yet one from whom the king would have received counsel in such a case,) on a sudden, laid his hand on the bridle of the king's horse, and swearing two or three full-mouthed Scottish oaths, (for of that nation he was,) said, 'Will you go upon your death in an instant?' and before his majesty understood what he would have, turned his horse round; upon which a word ran through the troops, 'that they should *march* to the right hand;' which led them both from charging the enemy, and assisting their own men.

Upon this they all turned their horses, and rode upon the spur, as if they were every man to shift for himself." * Rupert's men, says Clarendon, "having, as they thought, acted their parts, could never be brought to rally themselves again in order, or to charge the enemy. That difference was observed all along, in the discipline of the king's troops, and of those which marched under the command of Fairfax and Cromwell, (for it was only under them, and had never been remarkable under Essex or Waller,) that, though the king's troops prevailed in the charge, and routed those they charged, they seldom rallied themselves again in order, nor could be brought to make a second charge the same day." †

The battle was at an end. The most precious spoil of that day was "the king's cabinet," which, when "opened," disclosed secrets which more injured his cause than any victory of his enemies. When the banners taken at Naseby were hung up in Westminster Hall, there was joy and pride; but there was bitter indignation when the letters taken in the cabinet at Naseby were read aloud in Guildhall. There was no sincerity in the king's desire for peace; there was no abatement of his determination to govern by absolute power. Foreign princes were asked to send their soldiers to conquer rebel England. The dreaded Papists were to be freed from every restraint on the condition of such assistance. The best blood of the Cavaliers had been shed on the Broad Moor near Naseby.‡ Other defenders of the king's standard might arise; but these letters were the damning evidence of deceit; and those who saw that the word "loyalty" had ceased to charm, could only complain that domestic confidence was violated when the private correspondence of a king and queen was published to the whole world.

"Naseby being not far from Coventry where I was," writes Baxter, "and the noise of the victory being loud in our ears; and I having two or three that of old had been my intimate friends in Cromwell's army, whom I had not seen of above two years; I was desirous to go see whether they were dead or alive. And so to Naseby-field I went two days after the fight, and thence by the army's quarters before Leicester, to seek my acquaintance."§ The worthy man whose curiosity thus took him amongst scenes of horror, has left us no description of the traces of carnage here. But he has given a vivid picture of the men by whom the work was done. In his despatch of the 14th of June to the Speaker of the Commons, Cromwell did not neglect, even in his brief rest after the battle and the pursuit, to call attention to these men—the flower of the new-modelled army. "Honest men served you

* "Rebellion," vol. v. p. 184.   † Ibid., p. 185.
  ‡ The slaughter of the 14th of June was terrific, both on the battle-ground and in Cromwell's charge of the fugitives beyond Harborough. Mr. Thorne, in his charming "Rambles by Rivers," has well described the battle, and says, that "the field itself still retains evidence of the event. The bodies were collected and buried in several huge pits that were hastily dug; and the earth with which they were covered has sunk considerably, so that now they form large hollows—some of the deeper, from the water collecting in them, except in very dry weather, form ponds, and being left waste round the borders, have become fringed with brambles and weeds. The plough is not carried over any of the graves, and they have a solemn effect when it is known what they are. In cultivating the soil, bullets, cannon-balls, and fragments of arms, are frequently turned up. The man I had with me when examining the place had been a servant of Mr. Mastin's [the historian of Naseby], and had dug for him in several of the pits. The bodies, he said, were not more than eighteen inches or two feet from the surface. The arms are usually rusted to pieces, but not always; my man had dug up 'a swoard not very long ago, and polished her up as broight as bran-new.'"   § "Reliquiæ Baxterianæ," p. 56.

faithfully in this action. Sir, they are trusty; I beseech you, in the name of
God, not to discourage them. I wish this action may beget thankfulness
and humility in all that are concerned in it. He that ventures his life for
the liberty of his country, I wish he trust God for the liberty of his conscience, and you for the liberty he fights for." "The liberty of his conscience"
thus proclaimed in the hour of Cromwell's triumph, was a startling notion to
the majority of public men at that time. When Baxter found his old
acquaintance in the camp, he stayed with them a night. He had been
"unfeignedly for king and Parliament." He had thought "that the war
was only to save the Parliament and kingdom from papists and delinquents." He understood the Covenant to be "against papists and schis-
matics." He thought it a mere lie when "the court news-book told the
world of the swarms of anabaptists in our armies." He came amongst
Cromwell's soldiers, and "found a new face of things which I never dreamt
of." Sectaries in the highest places "were Cromwell's chief favourites,
and by their very heat and activity bore down the rest." He says, "they
were far from thinking of a moderate episcopacy, or of any healing way
between the Episcopal and the Presbyterians. They most honoured the
Separatists, Anabaptists, and Antinomians; but Cromwell and his Council
took on them to join themselves to no party, but to be for the liberty of all."
Shortly after, Baxter, whose reputation as a preacher was very high, was
invited by colonel Whalley to be chaplain to his regiment. Whalley was
"orthodox by religion, but engaged by kindred and interest to Cromwell."
Baxter went. "As soon as I came to the army, Oliver Cromwell coldly bid
me welcome, and never spake one word to me more while I was there."
The good man was ridiculed: "There was a reformer come to the army to
undeceive them, and to save Church and State." Thus discountenanced, the
zealous minister pursued what he thought his duty. "I set myself day by day
to find out the corruptions of the soldiers; and to discourse and dispute them
out of their mistakes, both religious and political. My life among them was
a daily contending against seducers, and gently arguing with the more
tractable." He was ever disputing with them about Civil government, or
Church order and government. "But their most frequent and vehement
disputes were for liberty of conscience, as they called it; that is, that the
civil magistrate had nothing to do to determine of any thing in matters of
religion, by constraint or restraint; but every man might not only hold, but
preach and do in matters of religion what he pleased: that the civil
magistrate hath nothing to do but with civil things; to keep the peace, and
protect the Church's liberties." Amidst all this vehemence—amidst the
ignorance, pride, and self-conceitedness which Baxter reprehends—it is
impossible not to be struck by the fact of a great army, after a mighty
victory, being occupied with discussions which appear more properly to belong
to parliaments and synods. But without a due perception of the zeal which,
whether rightly or wrongly directed, counted an earnest faith the one thing
needful, we cannot comprehend the events of these times, and more especially
those events which placed, ultimately, the monarchy and the Parliament under
the power of the army.

During the summer of 1645 singular confederacies had been formed in
some places, avowedly for protecting their property against both parties.

Those who belonged to them were known as "Clubmen." They were to some extent neutrals; but they were principally called into activity by royalist gentry. They were not "clubbable" men in Johnson's sense of the term. Their business was to use their clubs as valiantly as they might. They became annoying in the south-west to the parliamentary army; and Cromwell, in a march towards Shaftesbury, encountered about two thousand of them. They fired upon a party of his horse, but of course were soon routed. "We have taken about three hundred," Cromwell writes to Fairfax, "many of which are poor silly creatures, whom if you please to let me send home, they promise to be very dutiful for time to come, and will be hanged before they come out again." Fairfax had taken some of the Clubmen previously; and Cromwell told those who interceded for them that "they were to be tried judicially for raising a third party in the kingdom."*

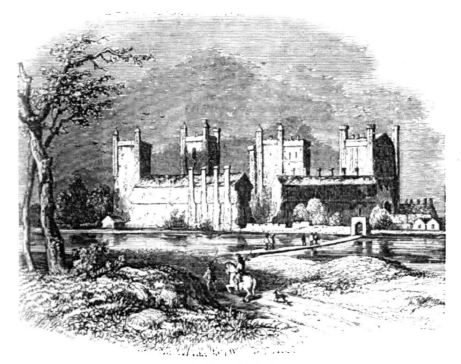

Basing House after the siege.

King Charles had fought his last battle at Naseby. The military career of prince Rupert in England was now fast coming to an end. Bristol, which Rupert was charged to defend, was invested by Fairfax and Cromwell on the 22nd of August. The positions taken by the several divisions of the parliamentary army are minutely described in a letter from Cromwell to the

* Carlyle, vol. ii. p. 184.

Speaker. On the 10th of September the city was stormed. The royalists caused the city to be set on fire at three places. Whilst the parliamentary commanders "were viewing so sad a spectacle," Rupert sent a trumpet to propose a surrender. The articles were agreed upon ; and the prince marched out with a convoy of two regiments of horse. He went to Oxford. Charles wrote him a bitter letter of reproach from Hereford : "My conclusion is, to desire you to seek your subsistence until it shall please God to determine of my condition, somewhere beyond seas." A royal proclamation was issued the same day, revoking and disannulling all commissions of military authority given to "our nephew prince Rupert." The surrender of Bristol was perhaps the wisest act of Rupert's life ; for he had no chance of holding it against the parliamentary forces, and the king was utterly unable to render him assistance. But Charles would not learn from the bitter lessons of adversity. It is justly said, "after his defeat at Naseby his affairs were, in a military sense, so irretrievable that, in prolonging the war with as much obstinacy as the broken state of his party would allow, he displayed a good deal of that indifference to the sufferings of the kingdom, and of his adherents, which has been sometimes imputed to him." *

At the beginning of October; Winchester surrendered to Cromwell; and he then went on to the siege of Basing House. Of the many memorable places of the Civil War there is none more interesting than this. It was amongst the strongest of those private houses of the nobility which offered such strenuous resistance to the progress of the parliamentary troops. It had endured siege after siege for four years. The traveller on the South Western railway looks down upon a great ruined pile, not far from Basing-stoke, lying on the other side of a little stream. The ruin will repay a closer inspection. This was the house called " Loyalty " which Cromwell battered from the higher ground till he had made a breach ; and then stormed with a resolution which made all resistance vain. Never was such a rich plunder offered to the Roundheads, as was found in the mansion "fit to make an emperor's court," of the magnificent Pawlet, marquis of Winchester.

* Hallam, vol. ii. p. 182.

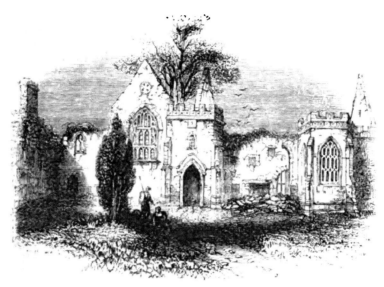

Remains of Winfield Manor House.

CHAPTER IV.

Destruction of Manor Houses—Miseries of Sieges—Montrose defeated at Philiphaugh—Defeat of Digby—His Cabinet taken—The King in Oxford—Overtures for Pacification—Termination of the War in the West—Prince of Wales leaves for Scilly—The King negotiates with the Scots—The King's Flight from Oxford—Adventures of the King on his way to the Scottish Army—The King with the Army before Newark—State of Parties—Negotiations—The King surrendered to English Commissioners—Capitulation of Oxford—End of the first Civil War.

THE traces of the Civil War in England are to be found in the existing ruins of several old mansions, besides those of Basing House. Amongst the most interesting and picturesque are the remains of the manor-house of South Winfield. This was one of the estates of the Shrewsbury family; and here Mary, Queen of Scots, resided for some time under the care of the earl, who is associated with her unhappy story. Sir John Gell, who was very active in the parliamentary interest in Derbyshire, here placed a garrison. In 1643 the place was taken by the Royalists. But it was retaken by Sir John Gell; and Colonel Dalby, the governor, was killed in the storming. In 1646 the Parliament ordered the place to be dismantled. Such was the course with regard to other great mansions of historical interest. Of the various conflicts for the possession of detached castles and manor-houses, that of Basing House is amongst the most memorable. The rapine and slaughter there were probably greater than at any other of such strongholds. It was a post of importance, which had held out against the Parliament so long that it was deemed almost impregnable. Its large garrison was amply supplied by the rich surrounding country. The roads between London and the " Western Parts " were entirely commanded by this fortified mansion, and by Donnington Castle, near Newbury. At the siege of Basing House was present Hugh Peters, a chaplain in the parliamentary army, and at that time secretary to Cromwell. After the storm he " took a view of the works, which were many, the circumvallation being above a mile in compass." He then looked about him to see the extent of the victualling department ; finding " provisions for some years rather than months ; four hundred quarters of wheat ; bacon, divers rooms-full, containing hundreds of flitches ; cheese proportionable ; with oatmeal, beef, pork ; beer, divers cellars full, and that very good." Seventy-four persons, according to Mr. Peters, were slain in the house ; amongst whom was one lady " who by her railing provoked our soldiers, then in heat, into a further passion." Amongst the slain was " Robinson the player, who a little before the storm was known to be mocking and scorning the Parliament and our army." * Some of the details of the plunder and destruction, as given by Peters, will furnish an idea of the havoc of this terrible Civil War : " The plunder of the soldiers continued till Tuesday night ; one soldier had a hundred and twenty pieces in gold for his share ; others plate, others jewels ; among the rest, one got three bags of silver, which (he being not able to keep his own counsel) grew to be common pillage amongst the rest, and the fellow had but one half-crown left for himself at last. The soldiers sold the wheat to country-people, which they held up at good rates awhile ; but afterwards the market fell, and there were some abatements for haste. After that, they sold the household stuff, whereof there was good store, and the country loaded away many carts ; and they continued a great while fetching out all manner of household stuff, till they had fetched out all the stools, chairs, and other lumber, all which they sold to the country-people by piecemeal. In all these great buildings there was not one iron bar left in all the windows (save only what were on fire) before night. And the last work of all was the lead ; and by Thursday morning they had hardly left one gutter about the house. And what the soldiers left, the fire took hold on, which made more than ordinary haste, leaving nothing but bare walls and chimneys in less than twenty hours ;—being occasioned by the neglect of the enemy in quenching a fire-ball of ours at first. We know not how to give a just account of the number of persons that were within. For we have not quite three hundred prisoners ; and, it may be, have found a hundred slain, whose bodies, some being covered with rubbish, came not at once to our view. Only, riding to the house on Tuesday night, we heard divers crying in vaults for quarter ; but our men could neither come to them, nor they to us."

The details of horror in sieges of large towns ; the misery of blockades ; the more sudden distress of assaults and bombardments ; are generally passed over slightingly in the official narratives of such scenes. But some notion of

* From the construction of a sentence in the report of Peters, it does not seem quite clear that Robinson was slain by Harrison, as Sir Walter Scott assumes in " Woodstock :" " There lay dead upon the ground Major Cuffle, a man of great account amongst them, and a notorious Papist, slain by the hands of Major Harrison, that godly and gallant gentleman ; and Robinson, the player, who," &c. (See Carlyle, vol. i. p. 194.)

the sufferings of the people, to whichever party they belonged, may be derived even from such a formal document as an Ordinance of Parliament. Taunton had been besieged three times by the Royalists. It was undergoing the horrors of a siege on the 3rd of July, when Fairfax, after the great victory of Naseby, came to its relief. But, a month before this, the Parliament, having regard to its calamities, had ordered " that a collection be made of all well-affected persons " for the relief of " the poor distressed inhabitants of the town of Taunton," and adjacent places. This Ordinance is written with remarkable unction : " It is notoriously known to all the kingdom, that the said town hath for these two years past, endured all the calamities almost that war (the sharpest of all outward judgments) can bring upon a people. . . . . . They endured three as sharp and cruel sieges from a bloody enemy as ever any place hath suffered since the wars began ; in which their houses were consumed by fire, their persons slain, the famine and the sword contendeth which should prey upon them first ; poor mothers looking when the time would come that they should hear the children cry for bread, and there would be none to give them ; when ' they should see them swoon in the top of every street,' as Lam. ii. 11. However, God upholds their spirits with unshaken resolution in the midst of fire and blood. . . . . But yet, by these calamities and troubles, the estates of those who have escaped the sword are utterly exhausted and consumed, five hundred of their houses burnt down to the ground (being one-half of the town), by which almost one thousand families are turned harbourless and helpless to the mercy of their neighbours, who can only melt upon them, and weep over them, but are not able to relieve them. And therefore, you that have escaped these miseries are earnestly besought to look upon this sad distressed town (sometimes the most eminent of those parts for building and situation, and, which is more, for Piety and true Religion), now by the just displeasure of the Lord against it raked in its own ashes, reduced almost to the extremity of misery and want, for the defence of that Cause which you profess, and take upon you to maintain : listen, and hear it crying to you in the Churches' Lamentations, ' See if there be any sorrow like to my sorrow, wherewith the Lord hath afflicted me in the day of his fierce anger ; ' and do not stop your ears against their cry for pity from you, lest the Lord deal accordingly with you, and stop His ears against your crys for mercy, when you have most need of it. In such a singular and extraordinary case as this, stir up yourselves to do some extraordinary thing ; do not draw out your purses only to your poor distressed brethren, but your very souls too, as the Prophet speaks. This is your duty, and this will be your policy, if you desire to save your persons, houses, and estates from that heavy misery which hath exposed them to your mercy." *

With the exception of a few conflicts for the possession of garrisoned towns and detached manor-houses, the war, during the autumn of 1645, was wholly in the west. The great royalist army was utterly broken and dispersed. After the surrender of Bristol all reasonable hope was gone of once more matching the Cavaliers of Rupert against the Ironsides of Cromwell. But in Scotland there was a royalist leader whose name had become a terror to the Covenanters. Wherever Montrose led his Highlanders he was

---

* Husband's "Ordinances in Parliament," 1642 to 1646, p. 651.

victorious. As he carried the war into the Lowlands he was joined by many who had formerly dreaded to declare themselves. It was no longer a war of clanship, but a great national contest. On the 15th of August the Covenanting army, commanded by Baillie, was utterly defeated. It was the seventh great victory of Montrose; and it laid Scotland, for a few weeks, at his feet. Edinburgh surrendered to him. In the king's name he summoned a parliament at Glasgow. Before the surrender of Bristol, Charles had conceived the possibility of joining Montrose. The hope returned even after Bristol was lost. He decided to attempt the relief of Chester, then besieged by the Parliament's forces; for at that port only could he receive succours from Ireland. He was at Hereford, anxious and undecided, when, after a week's delay, he marched, with five thousand men, over the Welsh mountains; and on the 24th of September was within view of Chester. Poyntz, the parliamentary commander, was watching the king's movements; and he suddenly came upon the rear-guard of the Royalists, at Rowton Heath. Sir Marmaduke Langdale,—he who had fought at Naseby,—vigorously charged the parliamentary forces; but a detachment of the besieging troops came upon his rear, and decided the day. The king retired again to the mountains. His chance of joining Montrose was gone. But at this juncture, if Charles had defeated Poyntz and relieved Chester, this last faint hope would have been destroyed. On the 24th of September, Montrose was himself a fugitive. He had advanced towards the English border, with diminished followers. His Highlanders had dispersed; his Lowland adherents had fallen off. Lesley had moved from England to encounter him. On the 13th of September, at Philiphaugh, on the left bank of the Ettrick, Montrose was surprised by the veteran Covenanter. There was a thick mist. No scout gave notice of Lesley's approach. The camp of Montrose was attacked on each flank. The great leader himself was in the town of Selkirk, on the right bank of the Ettrick. He hastened upon the first alarm to cross the river with his cavalry. But it was impossible to rally the main body of his followers. He retreated to the Highlands. Instead of being the commander of a victorious army, he was now only the leader of a few bands of mountaineers. Lesley re-established the Covenanting power in the Lowlands. His victory was disgraced by a cold-blooded slaughter of prisoners; and by the subsequent execution of many of the royalist leaders. One, who was a true Scotsman in his nationality, but whose genius was too high to make him blindly partial, has thus compared his countrymen with the English during this warfare: "Greatly to the honour of the English nation,—owing, perhaps, to the natural generosity and good-humour of the people, or to the superior influence of civilisation,—the civil war in that country, though contested with the utmost fury in the open field, was not marked by any thing approaching to the violent atrocities of the Irish, or the fierce and ruthless devastation exercised by the Scottish combatants. The days of deadly feud had been long past, if the English ever followed that savage custom, and the spirit of malice and hatred which it fostered had no existence in that country. The English parties contended manfully in battle, but, unless in the storming of towns, when all evil passions are afloat, they seem seldom to have been guilty of cruelty or wasteful ravage. They combated like men who have quarrelled on some special point, but, having had no ill-will against each other before, are resolved to fight it out fairly, without bearing malice. "*

When Charles reached Denbigh Castle after the defeat near Chester, he rested there three days. After much debate it was decided to go to Newark, which was held by a royalist garrison of about two thousand horse and foot. The excesses of these men, in a time of so general calamity, had excited the indignation of all the country.† News now came that Montrose had recovered his defeat, and that his army was again victorious. The king again set forward with the ill-conditioned Newark garrison to the aid of Montrose. On the way they learnt the truth of his final ruin. The king returned to Newark; but Digby, with the presumption that marked his character, went on to the north. At Sherborne, in Yorkshire, he was overtaken by the parliamentary troops, and utterly routed. Amongst Digby's baggage his private papers were taken; and these, being published by order of Parliament, "administered afterwards so much occasion of discourse." Thus Clarendon glances at their contents. But the Parliament, when publishing them in the spring of 1646, took care to set forth the policy that was to be collected from this secret correspondence between the queen's favorite, Jermyn, and the king's chief adviser, Digby: "The reader, comparing Cabinet with Cabinet, the king's with the lord Digby's, will easily observe how the unnatural enemies to this their native country (imitating their General, the grand enemy to mankind) have gone about seeking how they may devour it, by their restless endeavours to bring in foreign aid from Holland, Courland, Denmark, Portugal, Ireland, France, and from Rome itself, of shipping, arms, ammunition, men, money, horse and foot, and that in no small proportions; 4000 foot and 1000 horse expected from France, 10,000 men from Ireland, and 10,000 more from Lorraine; a strange conjuncture, to concur in the ends pretended! The king and pope to defend the Protestant religion, Denmark and Lorraine to maintain laws and liberties, bloody rebels in Ireland to uphold the privileges of Parliament in England! But blessed be God, who hath discovered the counsels of the enemies, and thereby hath in a great part opened the eyes, and undeceived not only multitudes of their principal adherents at home, but also foreign princes and states abroad, and hath withal defeated their forces and expectations both abroad and at home. This is God's work, and it is marvellous in our eyes." ‡

The stormy meeting between the king and prince Rupert at Newark; the half-mutinous conduct of the royal garrison there,—events minutely related by Clarendon—are indicative of the fallen fortunes of the unhappy king. "He must undergo a new kind of mortification from his friends, much sharper than any he had undergone from his enemies." Rupert and his brother Maurice left Charles for ever. He was alone; with no one to counsel him. His troops were reduced to a few hundreds. Poyntz and Rossiter, the parliamentary generals, were closing round Newark, which had so long been for him a place of security. To wait there was no longer safe. At eleven o'clock on the night of the 3rd of November, the king, with four or five hundred cavaliers, set out for Oxford. After a wearisome march, with hostile

---

* Scott's "Tales of a Grandfather."   † Clarendon, vol. v. p. 289.
‡ Husband, "Ordinances of Parliament," 1646, p. 869.

troops all around, they reached the loyal city in safety on the 6th. "So he finished the most tedious and grievous march that ever king was exercised in; having been almost in perpetual motion from the loss of the battle of Naseby to this hour, with such a variety of dismal accidents as must have broken the

Newark Shilling.

spirits of any man who had not been truly magnanimous." * There is another magnanimity besides endurance of fatigue and privation without loss of heart—the magnanimity of refusing to employ dishonourable means of averting danger and overcoming difficulty. On the day after his arrival at Oxford, the king wrote to prince Charles, desiring him to leave England: "I have resolved," he says, "to propose a personal treaty to the rebels at London; in order to which a trumpet is by this time there, to demand a pass for my messengers, who are to carry my propositions; which, if admitted, as I believe it will, then my real security will be your being in another country." † Beaten in open warfare, the king now resorted to the more dangerous weapons of craft and intrigue. His ultimate destruction may in a great degree be attributed to the fatal course of endeavouring to win by stratagem what he despaired of attaining by arms—a course which he pursued through so many winding paths after the decisive summer of 1645.

During the long vacation of this year, the Commons had resolved to fill up the vacancies in their House, caused by the absence of the royalist members, by issuing out writs for the election of representatives to supply their places. Denzil Hollis complains of the artifices that were employed to procure the return of members favourable to the policy of the Independents; but he adds, "that far the greater part of these new members deceived the expectations of these men." ‡ Many persons of eminence came into parliament through this election. The "certain mean sort of people in the House, whom to distinguish from the more honourable gentlemen they called Worsted-stocking men," § became of less importance, when Hutchinson, Ireton, Blake, Algernon Sidney, Fleetwood, Ludlow, Fairfax, and others of mark, were returned for counties and boroughs. But such men were not likely to yield the great points of difference for which they had so long

---

* Clarendon, vol. v. p. 302.   † Ibid. p. 277.   ‡ "Memoirs," p. 43.
§ Mrs. Hutchinson's "Memoirs," vol. ii. p. 71.

fought. The Independents were unquestionably strengthened. They were fast becoming a real power, as much opposed to the narrower views of the Presbyterians, as to the re-establishment of the sovereign without adequate securities. The controversy between the king and the Parliament was becoming more perplexed. The Scottish army in the north was discontented through the want of pay. The Parliament complained that an army which had entered England as allies should ravage the districts in which they were quartered. Charles meditated upon these distractions, and sought to take his advantage of them. But his overtures for peace were suspected to be hollow by the men who were now gradually assuming the lead in public affairs. The king on the 5th of December wrote to the Speaker of the House of Lords, offering to send a deputation to Westminster with propositions that should be "the foundation of a happy and well-grounded peace." He received no immediate answer; and he then proposed to proceed to Westminster, to treat in person. Meanwhile a reply had been returned to his first proposal, declining to receive his negotiators. He again wrote on the 29th of December, urging the plan of a personal treaty. This proposition was also rejected. To justify this rejection certain papers that had been found in the carriage of the Catholic archbishop of Tuam, who was killed in a skirmish in October, were laid before Parliament, and then published. They proved that the king had concluded a treaty of alliance with the Irish rebels, in which as the price of their landing in England with ten thousand men, under the earl of Glamorgan, popery was to be re-established in Ireland, and the Protestants brought under subjection. But Charles had gone further than these papers proved. The treaty was concluded with the Irish papists by Glamorgan, under a secret authority from the king himself to make any conditions Glamorgan pleased, which should be righteously observed. The marquis of Ormond, the lord-lieutenant, committed Glamorgan to prison; but he produced two royal commissions as his justification. Charles repudiated his agent in a letter to the Parliament, maintaining that he had given no power to make conditions in the matter of religion or church property, but merely to raise men for his service. The Parliament disbelieved the king; and documents, then undiscovered, prove that the Parliament was right.*

The overtures for pacification, so earnestly repeated by Charles, were probably held by the sagacious and incredulous men with whom he had to treat, as containing in themselves evidence of the want of that straightforwardness which could alone be successful. In the remarkable collection of letters brought to light in 1855,† we have one to the queen, dated Oxford, January 18th, 1646, in which Charles says, "Though I have stretched my wits to persuade them to accept of my personal treaty, yet examine my words well, and thou wilt find that I have not engaged myself in anything against my grounds. For, first, I am sure that there can be no scruple as concerning the Church. Then, for Ireland and the militia, it is true that it may be I give them leave to hope for more than I intended, but my words are only, to endeavour to give them satisfaction in either." It has been remarked by Mr. Hallam that, "Charles had unhappily long been in the habit of perverting

* See *ante*, p. 32.

† "Charles I. in 1646. Letters of King Charles I. to Queen Henrietta Maria, edited by John Bruce, Esq." Camden Society, 1856

his natural acuteness to the mean subterfuges of equivocal language." There was this folly about his cunning, that he fancied others would not examine his words well. In proposing to treat at Westminster he was clearly without any real expectation of there effecting a "happy and well-grounded peace." He was gratifying himself with the belief that he was able to triumph through the dangerous principle of "divide and govern." He writes to the queen: "Now, as to points which I expected by my treaty at London. Knowing assuredly the great animosity which is betwixt the Independents and Presbyterians, I had great reason to hope that one of the factions would so address themselves to me, that I might without great difficulty obtain my so just ends, and questionless it would have given me the fittest opportunity. For, considering the Scots treaty that would be besides, I might have found means to have put distractions amongst them though I had found none." *
In following out the remainder of this unhappy king's story for two years, we shall always trace this ruling principle of his actions; at every turn of his affairs having the same confident belief that the day would come when the monarchy "would spring up again as fair as ever." The root was left, he said; there were only "loppings." In seven years the very loppings "being to return as entirely to the crown as if I had entered London at a breach." †

The military events of the spring of 1646 brought the contest in the west to a termination. The remnant of the royalist army was completely demoralised. It was, says Clarendon, "terrible in plunder and resolute in running away." Lord Hopton very reluctantly accepted the command of this western army, at the express desire of the prince of Wales. A braver man could not have been chosen; a more high-minded friend of the royal cause; a leader who carried on war in the spirit most opposed to the rapacity of those he was expected to change from brigands into soldiers. As might have been foreseen, this honourable man utterly failed, when he brought these bands face to face with the orderly troops of Fairfax. Hopton had possession of Torrington, and his main body was placed on a common at its east end. When Fairfax forced the barricade, horse and foot took to flight, leaving their general and a few of his friends to shift for themselves. Shortly after, Hopton collected some of his runaways; and, with accessions of strength as he went on, marched to Truro, with Fairfax closely following. Hopton would have fought another battle; but his officers of horse declared that their men would never be brought to fight; and proposed to capitulate. Fairfax offered conditions that involved no dishonour; but the general would not yield; and at last a treaty was concluded without him, and the western army was dissolved. On the 22nd of March, lord Astley, marching from Worcester to join the king at Oxford, was defeated at Stow-in-the-Wold, and his three thousand cavaliers were killed, captured, or dispersed. The brave old general was himself taken prisoner. The soldiers brought him a drum to sit down upon. The Parliamentary captains respectfully surrounded the veteran: "Gentlemen," he said, "you have done your work, and may now go to play,—unless you will fall out among yourselves." These disasters at length determined the prince of Wales and his council to obey the king's injunctions to leave the country. The prince's governorship in the west was no longer a protection to his person.

* "Charles I. in 1646," p. 11.   † Ibid. p. 21.

He first sailed to Scilly. Two days after his landing he sent lord Colepepper to France to acquaint the queen " with the wants and incommodities of the place," and to desire "a supply of men and moneys."   Lady Fanshawe, whose husband acted as secretary to the Council, landed in miserable plight, having been pillaged by the seamen with whom they sailed from the Land's-end. The poor lady, sick, and far advanced in pregnancy, was set on shore almost dead; and from her narrative we may obtain some notion of "the incommodities of the place."   She says, " When we had got to our quarters near the castle, where the prince lay, I went immediately to bed, which was so vile, that my footman ever lay in a better, and we had but three in the whole house, which consisted of four rooms, or rather partitions, two low rooms and two little lofts, with a ladder to go up : in one of these they kept dried fish, which was his trade, and in this my husband's two clerks lay, one there was for my sister, and one for myself, and one amongst the rest of the servants.   But, when I waked in the morning, I was so cold I knew not what to do, but the daylight discovered that my bed was near swimming with the sea, which the owner told us afterwards it never did so but at spring tide.   With this, we were destitute of clothes; and meat and fuel, for half the Court to serve them a month, was not to be had in the whole island; and truly we begged our daily bread of God, for we thought every meal our last.   The Council sent for provisions to France, which served us, but they were bad, and a little of them." *   From Scilly, after three weeks of privation, the prince sailed for Jersey ; and in the summer proceeded to France, and afterwards to Holland.

Three months had elapsed since the proposals of the king had been rejected by the Parliament.   They were three months of repeated disaster. The royalist cause had never fallen so low.   Charles endeavoured to carry out his hope of dividing his enemies by propitiating the Independents through their leading statesman, the younger Vane.   Ashburnham, in the king's name, wrote to Vane to propose that the Independents and the Royalists should unite to put down " the tyrannical domination " of the Presbyterians.   It is not known whether Vane returned an answer.   The king then addressed a message to Parliament, offering to come to Whitehall, and proposing much the same terms as had been rejected by him during the treaty at Uxbridge. His great object was to produce such an effect by his presence in London as would cause a popular re-action in his favour.   Three days after he had sent this message to the Parliament, he wrote to Digby, " I am endeavouring to get to London, so that the conditions may be such as a gentleman may own, and that the rebels may acknowledge me king; being not without hope that I shall be able so to draw either the Presbyterians or Independents to side with me for exterminating the one or the other, that I shall be really king again." †   The leaders of both parties agreed to prevent this by a very strong ordinance, which gave the Committee of the Militia power to raise forces to prevent tumult in case of the king's coming; to apprehend any who should come with him or resort to him ; and which commanded all who had ever borne arms for the king immediately to depart from London, upon the penalty of being proceeded against as spies.   Meanwhile the army of Fairfax was advancing towards Oxford.   Montreuil, a special ambassador from France,

* "Memoirs," p. 74.   † Carte's " Ormond," quoted in Brodie and Hallam.

had been negotiating with the Scottish commissioners in London to induce the Scots to take up the cause of the king. His offers were received with civility, but with no distinct promises. He then proceeded to Edinburgh, and afterwards to the Scottish army. As might be expected, the question of establishing the Church in England according to the Scottish model was the great apparent difficulty. The real danger, which was perhaps most borne in mind, was the certainty of being involved in a serious quarrel with the English Parliament by a separate treaty. There were already sufficient causes of disunion; the principal being the sufferings of the people of the north, from the long presence of the Scottish troops amongst them. Hollis, who extenuates the conduct of these troops, says: "I must be very ignorant of the carriage of an unpaid army, if I did not believe that many disorders were committed; many a poor countryman exceedingly oppressed and abused by the unruly soldiers; and more by half taken and spoiled by them than would have sufficed for their pay and entertainment, if it had been orderly raised and provided by the authority and care of the state, which was to pay them."[*] The State did not pay them promptly, and the soldiers took their maintenance into their own hands. After two months of tedious negotiation, Montreuil at last saw that the first advice which he had given to the king to go to the Scottish army was not borne out by any definite promises, and he then dissuaded him from the attempt. On the 22nd of April Charles wrote to the queen from Oxford, complaining that his condition was much worse than ever "by the relapsed perfidiousness of the Scots." He so little suspected it from the previous advices from Montreuil, that, he says, "I did not care what hazard I undertook for the putting myself into their army. . . . . And that no time might be lost, I wrote a letter to Montrose to make him march up and join with them, in case he found by Montreuil, by whom I sent the letter, that they were really agreed with me. . . . . . . Thou wilt as plainly see, by what secretary Nicholas sends thee, their base unworthy dealing, in retracting of almost all which was promised Montreuil from London, even to the being ashamed of my company, desiring me to pretend that my coming to them was only in my way to Scotland."[†] Nearer and nearer Fairfax was drawing his troops round Oxford. In a few days the blockade would be complete. Whither was the unhappy king to fly? He would get privately to Lynn; he would go by sea to Scotland, if Montrose were in a condition to receive him; he would make for Ireland, France, or Denmark. He would go anywhere "to eschew all kind of captivity."[‡] If he who thus breathes out his sorrows to the only being in whom he has absolute confidence were a private man, who could refuse him pity? His very errors claim our pity. He has been trained to take the most dangerous view of his own position. "I am a king."—"They cannot do without me." He holds his sovereignty to be an inherent possession, and not a sacred trust. He sees only rebels; not a people that he has misgoverned. But there is a solemn pathos even in his egoism: "I conjure thee," he says to his wife in this his saddest hour; "I conjure thee by thy constant love to me, that if I should miscarry, whether by being taken by the rebels or otherwise, to continue the same active endeavour for prince Charles as thou hast done for me, and not

* "Memoirs," p. 49.   † "Charles I. in 1646," p. 37.   ‡ *Ibid.* p. 38.

whine for my misfortunes in a retired way, but, like thy father's daughter, vigorously assist prince Charles to regain his own."*

There were two persons in attendance upon the king at Oxford upon whom he bestowed his most secret confidences. One was his chaplain, Dr. Michael Hudson; the other, a groom of his bedchamber, Ashburnham, commonly called by Charles, Jack Ashburnham. Each of these have left relations of the manner of the king's escape from Oxford. After noticing some ineffectual attempts to induce Ireton to accept and protect the king's person, upon the conditions proposed to the Parliament of going to London, Ashburnham thus continues : "And now his majesty conceiving himself to be discharged from all obligation, which by any way could be fastened upon him by his Parliament, or by any authority derived from them, settled his thoughts upon his journey to the Scots army ; and in order thereunto did acquaint some of his Privy Council, as he was pleased to tell me, with his intentions to leave Oxford, if they should approve of that course to be best for his affairs, and their preservation ; but did not impart the truth of his design with the Scots, conceiving that most of them would have opposed with some unreasonable heat his conjunction with them, and therefore chose rather to put the design of London upon it."† In no situation of danger or difficulty could this unfortunate king give up his system of double-dealing and half-confidence. The groom of the bedchamber then very briefly relates how the journey from Oxford began and ended. Dr. Hudson, however, has amply filled up the details. He was arrested, and brought before the House of Commons, and his examinations present a very circumstantial account of nine days of wandering and peril."‡ On Sunday, the 26th of April, Hudson was desired by Ashburnham to come to his chamber at eleven o'clock at night. About twelve o'clock the king came, with the duke of Richmond. Ashburnham "cut off his lock, and some part of his beard," the lovelock, the well-known badge of the cavalier. Hudson was then sent to call the governor of Oxford, who arrived about two o'clock. To him the king confided his intention to leave the city ; the governor went for the keys ; and just as the clock struck three they passed over Magdalen-bridge. The king then commanded the governor that no gate of Oxford should be opened for five days. Onward rode the three—the king, Hudson, and Ashburnham—by Dorchester, Benson, Henley, Maidenhead, and Slough. They then turned out of the road towards Uxbridge, and rested not until they reached a tavern at Hillingdon, between ten and eleven o'clock. They encountered several parties of horse on the road ; but Hudson had obtained an old pass that had been granted to another person, and he was liberal of his money when he came to any guard. He was the master, the king and Ashburnham were his servants. "One of Colonel Ireton's men," says Hudson, "rid in our company from Nettlebed to Slough ; and seeing me give money always at the guards, asked him, the king, if his master were not one of the Lords of the Parliament ? He answered, No; his master was one of the Lower House." During their short rest at Hillingdon, "the king was much perplexed what course to resolve upon, London or northward." He at length determined "to go northward, and

---

* "Charles I. in 1646," p. 39.
† Ashburnham's "Narrative," vol. ii. p. 72.   ‡ See Peck's "Desiderata Curiosa."

through Norfolk, where he was least known," and there to stay whilst Hudson ascertained from Montreuil if he had effected any arrangement with the Scots. They slept that Monday night at St. Alban's. Such is Hudson's account in his examination before the parliamentary committee. But, in a previous examination before the deputy-mayor of Newcastle, he stated that he was commanded by the king not to reveal the place where they lodged on Monday night; he declined to answer whether the king was in London or no; and said, "that when they turned their face about for the north, his majesty lodged at Wheathamstead, near unto St. Alban's; but the time when, he is commanded by his majesty to conceal." This would indicate far greater indecision about the movements of the king than Hudson's other narrative. It is clear that no energetic course of action presented itself to him after he had ridden over Magdalen-bridge on that spring morning. Clarendon says that the king "had wasted time in several places, whereof some were gentlemen's houses (where he was not unknown, though untaken notice of), purposely to be informed of the condition of the marquis of Montrose, and to find some secure passage that he might get to him."[*] On the Tuesday, according to Hudson's circumstantial narrative, he separated from the king and Ashburnham, as they rode upon their way towards Baldock; he to go in search of Montreuil, they to stay at the White Swan at Downham till he returned to them. Here they remained till the Friday, when Hudson returned with a statement that the Scots would condescend to all the demands which the king had made for the security of his person and the satisfaction of his conscience; that they would declare for him if the English Parliament should refuse to restore him to his rights and prerogatives; but that they would give nothing under their hands. "I came to the king on Friday night," says Hudson, "and related all; and he resolved next morning to go to them." There is a relation from Miles Corbet and Valentine Walton, addressed to the Speaker of the House of Commons, which takes up the adventures of Charles at this point. Hudson, and a friend, Ralph Skipwith, on the Saturday morning, "did ride to Southrie ferry, a private way to go towards Ely; and went, by the way, to Crimplesham, and there were the other two; one in a parson's habit, which, by all descriptions, was the king. Hudson procured the said Skipwith to get a gray coat for the doctor, as he called the king, which he did. And there the king put off his black coat and long cassock, and put on Mr. Skipwith his gray coat. The king bought a new hat at Downham, and on Saturday went into the isle of Ely. Wherever they came they were very private, and always writing. Hudson tore some papers when they went out of the house. Hudson did enquire for a ship to go to the north, or Newcastle, but could get none." There was nothing left for Charles but to go to the Scots' army at all risks. On the Tuesday night, the 4th of May, they met Montreuil at Southwell. Commissioners from the Scottish army also met the king there. Their troops were spread about the district, surrounding the castle of Newark, which was held for the king. Ashburnham says that when Charles arrived at the Scots' army before Newark, "many lords came instantly to wait on his majesty with professions of joy, to find that he had so far honoured their army, as to

* "History," vol. v. p. 394

think it worthy his presence after so long an opposition." On the 6th of May, lord Leven, the Scots' general, and the Committee of Estates at Southwell, wrote to the Committee of both kingdoms, in the following

Newark Castle.

terms : "The earnest desire which we have to keep a right understanding between the two kingdoms, moves us to acquaint you with that strange Providence wherewith we are now surprised, together with our carriage and desires thereupon. The king came into our army yesterday in so private a way, that after we had carefully made search for him, upon the surmises of some persons who pretended to know his face, yet we could not find him out in sundry houses. And we believe your lordships will think it was matter of much astonishment to us, seeing we did not expect he would come into any place under our power. We conceived it not fit to inquire into the causes which persuaded·him to come hither ; but to endeavour that his being here might be improved to the best advantage, for promoting the work of uniformity, for settling of religion and righteousness, and attaining of peace according to the League and Covenant and Treaty, by the advice of the Parliaments of both kingdoms, or their commissioners authorised for that effect." Not a night passed before the king was made to understand his position. A guard, called a guard of honour, was placed at his door. He claimed to give out the watchword for the night. "Pardon me, sire," said Leven, "I am the oldest soldier here. Your majesty will permit me to undertake that duty." The king consented to sign an order that his governor of Newark should give up the place to the Scots, for the Committee of both kingdoms. They rendered it to Poyntz, the English parliamentary commander ; and very shortly after, the Scottish army, with the king, was on its march to Newcastle.

From the 6th of May, 1646, till the 30th of January, 1647, the king remained in the hands of the Scots. It was a time of unwearied political intrigue and agitation, more complicated than ever with the great question of religion. The Presbyterian party had a considerable majority in Parliament. They had carried ordinance upon ordinance for the exclusive establishment of their Church. In this great point they were completely in accord with the Scots, who held the king at their disposal. But a compact and firm minority is often more really powerful than a disjointed majority. The men of the greatest intellect and energy had the strongest hold upon public opinion. The liberty of conscience which they proclaimed had produced its effect upon many who chose to think for themselves, without being fanatics; and upon more who had reached the extremes of fanaticism. The eloquent reasoning of Milton had not been published in vain. The impassioned harangues of Vane had not fallen upon barren ground. The Presbyterian rule in spiritual affairs was slowly and imperfectly established. The great hold of that church was in London. It was also established in Lancashire. In other provinces the beneficed clergy were chiefly Presbyterian; but many pulpits were filled with sectaries of various denominations, agreeing in few things beyond the common claim of the right of men to toleration; Papists only were excepted from the operation of this principle. Whatever was their particular creed, the Independents maintained the claim of every separate congregation to be a church; held that the exercise of the ministry was warranted by a call of the congregation; and denied that any spiritual powers were conferred in ordination by those who asserted their apostolical succession. But the Independents were far more powerful than the talkers in Parliament, from a superiority that had grown naturally out of the struggles of four years. The army was composed of earnest men, who had fought for a cause in which all their religious enthusiasm had been called forth. They were as formidable in their opinions as citizens, as in their unequalled bravery and discipline as soldiers. The Independent leaders had the entire control of this army. Whilst the Scottish commissioners were urging the king to adopt the Presbyterian rule of church government, and the parliamentary majority was tending to the same conclusion; the army, at the slightest signal from their chiefs, would have been ready to oppose its power to any such settlement. It had only to abide its time. For eight months there was interminable discussion and negotiation between Westminster and Newcastle. · The Scots, who thought they possessed a preponderating influence in retaining the person of the king, were growing more and more unpopular in the sentiments of the English people. Petitions were sent to Parliament against their exactions. They came to be regarded as enemies rather than as allies. A vote was at length carried in the Commons, in June, that their presence was no longer required; and they were requested to return home, on receiving a payment of a hundred thousand pounds, on account of what might be due to them. They made no sign of removing. Their great object was to induce Charles to consent to the abolition of Episcopacy, and to the establishment of Presbyterianism in both kingdoms. They assailed him with reiterated solicitations, and even with menaces. On the 10th of June, he wrote to the queen: "I never knew what it was to be so barbarously treated before; and these five or six days last have much surpassed, in rude pressures against my conscience, all the rest since I came to the Scotch army."* They required the king to sign the Covenant himself, and command all his subjects to sign it. They sent for the learned and eloquent Henderson to convert the king. Charles maintained a theological controversy with the great preacher with equal temper and ability. But whilst he was asserting his devotion to the Anglican Church, and rejecting the Presbyterian form as zealously as the Scots pressed it upon him, he was writing to Glamorgan that he would place himself, if he could so by any means, in the hands of the pope's nuncio and his secret adviser in Ireland. His hatred of the Covenant was not altogether a religious conviction. He writes to the queen on the 26th of August: "Less will not serve them than the establishing of the Covenant in all my kingdoms, which, if it be, will ruin this monarchy."† Charles clung with a tenacity approaching to fanaticism to the Episcopal principle; but the maxim of his father, "no bishop, no king," was probably at the root of his inflexible resolution. The English Parliament, still governed by the Presbyterian party, sent him proposals in July. He was to adopt the Covenant; he was to abolish the Episcopal Church; he was to give up the command of the military arm for twenty years; he was to exclude seventy of his adherents from a general amnesty. The queen urged him to accept even these proposals. Without an absolute rejection of these hard terms, he prepared again to come to London. The Scottish commissioners told the king that unless he accepted the conditions, "though higher in some particulars than they could have wished, he must not be expected to be received in Scotland."‡ The money question between the Scots and the Parliament then occupied many weeks of controversy. Four hundred thousand pounds were at last voted; and a loan was raised for the immediate payment of half the amount. The terms were accepted. Another difficult question then presented itself. Which nation was to retain the king? It was at last voted "that to the Parliament alone belongs the right of disposing of the king's person." In November the Scottish Parliament had met, and evinced a disposition to advocate the re-establishment of Charles in both kingdoms, with honour and safety. But the General Assembly interfered. The obstinacy of the king upon the question of Episcopacy was quite sufficient to excite the most violent popular feeling, and the Scottish Parliament then took another tone. The treaty was completed for the retirement of the Scottish army. On the 16th of December there was a singular procession from London to the north. Thirty-six carts, laden with two hundred cases of silver, were guarded on the road to Newcastle by an escort of infantry, under the command of Skippon. The money and the men arrived at York on the 1st of January, 1647. In three weeks the payment was made. "I am sold and bought," said the king. Nine commissioners arrived from London. On the 30th of January the Scots marched from Newcastle, and Charles remained with the English commissioners. He was treated by them with marked respect. On the 9th of February he left Newcastle, escorted by a regiment of horse, and reached Holmby House, in Northamptonshire, his appointed residence, on the 16th.

The first Civil War was at an end. Oxford had been surrendered to

---

* "Charles I. in 1646," p. 45. † *Ibid.* p. 58.

‡ "Ludlow," p. 184.

Fairfax on the 22nd of June, under the terms of a treaty which allowed
the garrison to " march out of the city of Oxon with their horses and com-

Anderson s Place, Newcastle. The house in which Charles resided, when delivered to the Parliamentary
Commissioners. From a drawing made before its demolition in 1836.

plete arms that properly belong unto them, proportionable to their present
or past commands; flying colours, trumpets sounding, drums beating,
matches lighted at both ends, bullet in their mouths, and every soldier to
have twelve charges of powder, match and bullet proportionable." Those
who desired to go to their houses or friends were to lay down their arms
within fifteen miles of Oxford, and then to have passes, with the right of free
quarter; and a careful provision was made for those who wished to go
beyond sea to serve any foreign power. The Royalists and the parliamentary
troops had met as honourable enemies; and in this surrender of the loyal
city they each went their way as men whom happier times might make
willing friends. When Fairfax entered Oxford he secured the Bodleian
Library from spoliation, as Aubrey records : " When Oxford was surrendered
(24th of June, 1646), the first thing general Fairfax did was to set a good
guard of soldiers to preserve the Bodleian Library. 'Tis said there was more

hurt done by the Cavaliers (during their garrison) by way of embezzling and cutting off chains of books, than there was since. He was a lover of learning, and had he not taken this special care, that noble library had been utterly destroyed, for there were ignorant senators enough who would have been contented to have had it so. This I do assure you from an ocular witness." All the royalist garrisons had yielded before the end of 1646. Great changes had taken place since Charles fought his first battle of Edgehill. Essex, who there brought his undisciplined troops into conflict with the Cavaliers, died on the 16th of September. Other men and other influences were now to be paramount.

Medal struck in honour of the Earl of Essex. Engraved from the Parliamentary series executed by Simon.

Army Independent.

CHAPTER V.

HOLMBY HOUSE (or Holdenby), a mansion within six miles of Northampton, built by sir Christopher Hatton, no longer exists. We cannot judge
of its capacity for the accommodation of a fallen king; but we have ample
evidence that it was considered as a palace rather than a prison. There is an
order of "the Committee of the Revenue" for fitting Holdenby House with
hangings, beddings, and other wardrobe stuff and necessaries; and, with the
Puritan contempt of the externals of religious worship, for melting the
altar plate at Whitehall for the use of the king's table in his new abode.
Seventy-six officers of the household and domestic servants are to be chosen
by the earl of Northumberland, with Yeomen of the Guard. The king's
diet was to be supplied at the cost of 30l. a day; and the estimate for the

BAXTER   BUNYAN

WILLIAM PENN

whole cost of the household amounted to 3000*l.* for twenty days.* During this spring and early summer the king was not deprived of any of the trappings of royal state. Nor was his liberty much controlled. He rode to Althorp, and to more distant places, to enjoy his favourite game of bowls. He read, and he played at chess. He was attended by two gentlemen selected by the Parliament, Thomas Herbert and James Harrington, who became his fast friends. Of Harrington, Aubrey says, "The king loved his company, only he would not endure to hear of a Commonwealth; and Mr. Harrington passionately loved his Majesty. Mr. Harrington and the king often disputed about government." † To have "a genius which lay chiefly towards the politics and democratical government," as Aubrey describes the author of the "Oceana," was not then held a dangerous quality in a philosophical theorist. "Democratical government" in the abstract, was not regarded as incompatible with the order of a well-regulated State. Charles might contend for the security derived from absolute monarchy, such as he believed ought to exist in England; and Harrington might point to the republics of Holland and Switzerland, without offending royalty by the comparison. Had Charles seen how the safety of the crown would be best preserved by the largest enjoyment by the subject of civil liberty and the rights of conscience, Harrington and other republicans might have been more readily compelled to believe that freedom and toleration could be best secured under the free monarchy which was the basis of the English constitution. But Charles was impracticable with his convictions of divine right; and honest advocates of democratical government were equally impracticable in regard to a due balance of constitutional power. It is time only that has reconciled these apparent anomalies; and has rendered the hereditary crown of England the best type of republican freedom in the strictest alliance with monarchical solidity. But through what perils has this consummation been accomplished! Those who would properly value what we have attained, must steadily follow the difficult and uncertain steps of the people towards its attainment. Harrington at a later period is recorded to have found fault with "the constitution of our government, that it was by jumps." ‡ He said, "When no Parliament, then absolute Monarchy; when a Parliament, then it runs to Commonwealth." It was long before the "jumps" were converted into steady progress; and Monarchy and Commonwealth were reconciled into a Constitution whose practical excellence is best demonstrated by that slowness of its maturity which has rendered a successful imitation almost impossible.

If the Presbyterian party, with whom were the powers of the executive government, treated the king with the respect due to his great station, they had little regard to the rights of conscience which he properly asserted. He required to have chaplains of the Episcopal church. The Parliament sent two Presbyterian ministers to Holmby; but the king refused even to let them ask a blessing upon his meals. The controversy of the dominant party with the representatives of the various religious sects, was growing more and more fierce. "Liberty of conscience was now the common argument and quarrel,"

---

* These orders and estimates are in Peck's "Desiderata Curiosa."
† "Lives," vol. iii. p. 370.   ‡ *Ibid.* vol. iii. p. 374.

says Clarendon. The Presbyterians held the sectaries, as well as the prelatical party, " enemies to all godliness; " and they relied upon their parliamentary majority to effect another remodelling of the army. Cromwell, on the other hand, was bringing the army into a more general dislike of the narrow views of their Presbyterian rulers. Chaplains were in his camp who contended that all attempts to fetter men to the dogmas and ceremonies of any Church were " to restrain the Spirit." Cromwell preached and prayed with his officers and his men. The soldiers prayed and preached amongst themselves. The Ironsides, who had the Bible with them as constantly as their powder and bullet, and who in their night-watches meditated upon all the events of the Jewish history, and repeated every inspiriting verse that had reference to the fall of tyrants and the glory of the saints,—these gradually got banded together in a common enthusiasm which only required an influential head to obtain a victory more difficult even than Marston-Moor or Naseby. Cromwell gradually became that leader, although Fairfax was the commander of the army. The indignation of the Presbyterians against those " who were called by a new name, fanatics," * was therefore principally directed against him who was considered their military chief. Soon after the death of the earl of Essex, Cromwell, walking with Ludlow in sir Robert Cotton's garden, inveighed bitterly against the Presbyterian party; saying, " that it was a miserable thing to serve a Parliament, to whom let a man be never so faithful, if one pragmatical fellow amongst them rise up and asperse him, he shall never wipe it off." † Ludlow considers that Cromwell " had already conceived the design of destroying the civil authority and setting up for himself," when, in this conversation, he concluded by saying, " When one serves under a general he may do as much service, and yet be free from all blame and envy." This, we apprehend, is an opinion resulting from the republican convictions of Ludlow, which were firmly opposed to Cromwell's later career. Be that as it may, the rapid course of events threw a power into the hands of Cromwell which rendered the subsequent months of 1647 the most difficult and dangerous period of his life. That he should have come out of such a whirlwind of contending interests and passions with safety to himself, and without witnessing universal confusion if not anarchy, is one of the most striking proofs of the extraordinary sagacity of the man who saw, at every turn of affairs, a demand upon his common sense rather than upon any philosophical theory; and whose dominant will was sustained by the conviction that he was chosen to do the work appointed for him by a Power higher than that of man, whose aid he invoked on every occasion in which human doubts prevailed over habitual confidence. In the sense in which the new word of opprobrium was used then, and has continued in use, Cromwell was termed, from the religious bias of his character, the most fanatical of " the fanatics." But this remarkable man's principles and conduct are fast passing out of the narrow limits of historical partisanship; and we shall therefore be careful to speak of him without the flippant prejudice with which his name has been surrounded by the continued violence of the most opposite opinions. His revilers have disagreed on every point except that of calling this great Englishman, fanatic and regicide, hypocrite and tyrant.

* Clarendon.   † Ludlow, vol. i. p. 185.

At the period when the war had terminated, the leading men of the Independent party were in thorough agreement. As to civil rights, they held that an appeal having been made to the God of battles, and the issue having been decided against the king, he ought not to be restored except upon conditions which would render the public liberties no longer insecure. They held that such a restoration ought to be accompanied by the most complet. provision for liberty of conscience. Their conviction of the king's insincerit was fatal to any hasty re-acknowledgment of his authority. Their dislike of the Presbyterian exclusiveness prevented a cordial union with that party to rebuild the Constitution in its ancient harmony of king and parliament. The Presbyterian majority in the Houses wished to dissolve the army, from which they had to apprehend the only effectual resistance. The Independents, headed by Cromwell, Ireton, Vane, St. John, were equally determined that the army should remain intact. The City was in accord with the parliamentary majority; and in the subsequent events the two great parties seemed to resolve themselves into the City party and the Army party. There is one view of this conflict,—of which we have only the most obscure, prejudiced, and contradictory details,—which has been so justly and forcibly put, that we shall not attempt to add to its impressiveness: " Modern readers ought to believe that there was a real impulse of heavenly Faith at work in this Controversy; that on both sides, more especially on the Army's side, here lay the central element of all, modifying all other elements and passions;—that this Controversy was, in several respects, very different from the common wrestling of Greek with Greek for what are called ' political objects.' Modern readers, mindful of the French Revolution, will perhaps compare these Presbyterians and Independents to the Gironde and the Mountain. And there is an analogy; yet with differences. With a great difference in the situations; with the difference, too, between Englishmen and Frenchmen, which is always considerable; and then with the difference between believers in Jesus Christ and believers in Jean Jacques, which is still more considerable." *

Within three days after the king had arrived at Holmby House, the Commons voted that the army should be disbanded, with the exception of the troops required for the suppression of rebellion in Ireland, and for the service of the garrisons. This motion was adopted upon a division in which there was a majority of twelve. It was also voted that there should be no officers under Fairfax of higher rank than colonel; that every officer should take the Covenant, and conform to the Presbyterian church. There were large arrears of pay due to the army, and a loan was raised in the City to satisfy a portion of them. What was proposed to be paid was very insufficient. There were murmurings amongst men and officers. On the 25th of March, a petition, signed by fourteen officers, was presented to parliament on the subject of arrears; asking that auditors should report upon what was due to them for their service; and submitting some conditions with regard to their employment in Ireland. The anger of the parliamentary majority is expressed by a passage in the Memoirs of Hollis: " For an army, or any part of it, to join in a petition, though but for pay, when their superiors—that authority which they are to obey—require any duty to be performed, or service to be done by

---

* Carlyle; " Cromwell," vol. i. p. 222.

them, as the present relieving of Ireland was,—this, I think, by the rules of war, has in all armies been held a mutiny, and the authors at least punished with death." * The House, on the 30th of March, declared that whoever had a hand in promoting this petition, or other such petitions, was " an enemy to the State, and a disturber of the public peace." The declaration became in itself a cause of hostility between the army and the parliament. It was " a blot of ignominy." Deputations from the House went to the army. Officers were examined at the bar. On the 30th of April, Skippon produced in his place in parliament a letter which had been brought to him by some troopers, expressing the complaints and demands of eight regiments of horse. " They saw designs upon them, and upon many of the Godly Party in the kingdom." Three troopers who brought the letter were examined as to the meaning of certain words which it contained. They were only the agents of their regiments, they said. Did their officers approve of their proceedings? Very few knew anything about them. The more violent Presbyterian members were very indignant. Cromwell whispered to Ludlow, " These men will never leave till the army pull them out by the ears." † A new class of malcontents had arisen, more dangerous than the officers, who said to the parliamentary commissioners, " We hope, by being soldiers we have not lost the capacity of subjects, nor divested ourselves thereby of our interests in the Commonwealth." The army had organised itself into a Council of Officers, and a Council of Adjutators. The Adjutators, who came to be called Agitators, were delegates named by the common soldiers. The difficulties of reconcilement are now growing very formidable. The servants are fast advancing to become masters. Meanwhile the king has written to the Parliament, with reference to the proposals made to him at Newcastle. He still declared against Presbytery ; and his application was unheeded. The army Councils grow more and more resolved to have greater concessions than the Parliament is disposed to make. They are voted eight weeks' pay. A Committee goes to the army at Saffron Walden to see it disbanded. That is not so easy. We want eight times eight weeks' pay, say the Adjutators. There are disturbances in some of the military quarters. Will this contest end in something anarchical ? Fairfax is told, that if their officers refuse to take part with them in asserting their rights, they know how to meet and act without them. They petition again through their general. It is in vain that " when the House, wearied with long sitting, was grown thin, Mr. Denzil Hollis, taking that opportunity, drew up a resolution on his knee, declaring the petition to be seditious." It is in vain that there have been London petitions against the Army, and that the getters-up of counter-petitions in its favour have been imprisoned. There is a great gathering of Adjutators to confer with the general; and it is agreed that on the 4th of June there shall be a rendezvous of all the soldiers at Newmarket. Two days before that general assembly, an event has taken place which goes much farther to decide the question between Army and City, than resolutions at St. Stephen's, or petitions at Guildhall. A great crisis is impending. " It was privately resolved," says Clarendon, " by the principal persons of the House of Commons, that when Cromwell came the next day into the House, which he seldom omitted to do

* " Memoirs," p. 77   † Ludlow, vol. i. p. 189.

they would send him to the Tower; presuming, that if they had once severed his person from the Army, they should easily reduce it to its former temper and obedience. . . . . When the House expected every minute his presence, they were informed that he was met out of the town by break of day, with one servant only, on the way to the army." * That same morning that Cromwell left London, there was a memorable scene in Northamptonshire, also about "break of day" according to Clarendon.

On the afternoon of the 2nd of June the king is playing bowls on Althorp Down. The parliamentary commissioners and his accustomed attendants are looking on. There is a man standing amongst them, in the uniform of Fairfax's regiment. He is asked questions as to news from the army, which he answers civilly but somewhat proudly. A report spreads that a party of cavalry is in the neighbourhood. About midnight there is a tramping of horse around Holmby House; and entrance is demanded by the man who was looking at the game of bowls on Althorpe Down. He was a cornet, he said, in the general's guard; his name was Joyce; he desired to speak with the king. The commissioners had directed the garrison to hold themselves in readiness to repel the presumptuous soldiers; but the men on duty greeted their old comrades, and the gates were opened. The day wore on, amidst the alarm of the commissioners, who saw that armed resistance was impossible. At night Joyce requested to be taken to the king. He was in bed; but the inflexible cornet was conducted to the door of the royal apartments. By the king's desire he was at length admitted. Charles had a long conference with him, in the presence of the commissioners, who had been sent for; which ended in his cheerfully saying " Good night, Mr. Joyce," adding that he would readily go with him if the soldiers confirmed what the cornet had promised. The next day the king asked Joyce under what authority he acted. He was sent, he said, by authority of the army, to prevent the designs of its enemies, who would once more plunge the kingdom in blood. "Where is your commission?" said the king. "There, behind me," pointing to the soldiers. "Believe me," replied Charles, "your instructions are written in a very legible character." †

The king then said that force must be employed to remove him, unless he was promised that nothing should be required of him against his conscience or honour. "Nothing, nothing," exclaimed the men as one voice. The commissioners asked if they all agreed in what Mr. Joyce had said. "All, all." In a few hours, the king and the unwilling commissioners were on their way towards the army.

Whilst the king has been journeying towards the head-quarters of Fairfax, the appointed Rendezvous has taken place on Kentford Heath, near Newmarket. Another meeting of this military parliament is arranged for the 10th, at Triploe Heath, near Cambridge. The king arrives at Royston on the 7th. "Fairfax and Cromwell wait on him both together. He asks them whether they commissioned Joyce to remove him: they deny it. 'I'll not believe you,' says the king, 'unless you hang him.' " ‡ Colonel Whalley had been sent by Fairfax, when he learnt of the king's seizure at Holmby, to take him back; but Charles refused to go. When in presence of Fairfax

---

* "History." vol. v. p. 436.   † Warwick, p. 299.   ‡ Ibid.

and Cromwell he expressed the same desire to remain with the army. He preferred 'the air' of Newmarket to 'the air' of Holmby. Cromwell went to London; and took his place in the House. There is no very reliable account of what occurred when he who was held to be the chief manager of the great *coup-d'état*, appeared in his seat. Hollis represents Cromwell, as well as Ireton, Fleetwood, and Rainsborough, who were members of the House as well as officers of the army, " blaming the soldiers at that distance, as Cromwell did openly in the House, protesting, for his part, he would stick to the Parliament." * He then, continues the wrathful Presbyterian, " did steal away that evening, I may say run away post down to the Army, and presently join in the subscription of a rebellious letter."* The narrative of a more candid chronicler says, that Cromwell " got hastily and secretly out of town, and without stop or stay rid to Triploe Heath, his horse all on a foam, and there was welcomed with the shouts of the whole Army, to whom he declared the actions and designs of the Parliament." † Commissioners were again coming to the Army on the 10th; and Cromwell has arrived a little before them. Twenty-one thousand men are drawn up on Triploe Heath; not an ordinary body of soldiers, but men, as they described themselves in one of their petitions, " who had abandoned their estates, trades, callings, and the contentments of a quiet life, for the perils and fatigues of war in defence of the public liberty." Fairfax and the commissioners ride to each regiment. The votes of parliament are first read to the general's own regiment. An officer stands forth, saying that the regiment would determine upon an answer when the votes had been submitted to a Council of Officers and Adjutators. The men are asked if that is their answer? " All, all." This is not a tumultuous reply; they speak when leave is given. The question is also put, if any be of a contrary opinion to say " No." Not a voice is heard. The same formality is observed towards every regiment, with a similar result; and a cry goes up from each, as the commissioners pass on, of " Justice, Justice." In the afternoon, this Army is on its march towards London; and the " rebellious letter " of which Hollis speaks, is sent to the lord-mayor and aldermen. It is a remarkable letter, the composition, as Mr. Carlyle thinks, of Cromwell; signed by Fairfax, Cromwell, Ireton, and other chief officers— in number thirteen. " We desire," they say, " a settlement of the peace of the kingdom and of the liberties of the subject, according to the votes and declarations of Parliament, which, before we took arms, were, by the Parliament, used as arguments and inducements to invite us and divers of our dear friends out, some of whom have lost their lives in this war. . . . . For the obtaining of these things we are drawing near your city; professing sincerely from our hearts, that we intend not evil towards you; declaring, with all confidence and assurance, that if you appear not against us in these our just desires, to assist that wicked Party which would embroil us and the kingdom, neither we nor our soldiers shall give you the least offence. . . . . And although you may suppose that a rich city may seem an enticing bait to poor hungry soldiers to venture far to gain the wealth thereof,—yet, if not provoked by you, we do profess, rather than any such evil should fall out, the soldiers shall make their way through our blood to effect it." ‡ This is plain speaking.

* Hollis, p. 84.   † " Perfect Politician," p. 22, 1680.
‡ " Letters of Cromwell," vol. i. p. 230.

The Army has reached St. Alban's ; and a respectful answer is conveyed thither by a deputation from the City. On the 16th the Army demands the impeachment of eleven members of the Commons, Hollis, Stapleton, Massey, and eight others of the leading Presbyterians—the men of whom Cromwell spoke when he whispered about the army pulling them out by the ears. The City is in consternation. The Parliament is incapable of acting with any vigour. Messages are daily going between St. Alban's and Westminster with the interminable arguments of each of these great powers. But the one possesses a strength more immediately effective than the highest ability of the pen. If the parliamentary negotiators appear obstinate, the Army advances. On the 25th of June it is at Uxbridge. The shops in the City are shut. The Army has received a months' pay, as it demanded. But it has continued to advance. The effect is instantaneous. On the 26th the eleven obnoxious members retire from Parliament; the Commons vote for the adoption of all the proceedings of the Army; and commissioners are appointed on each side to regulate the affairs of the kingdom. There is no longer any talk of defending London ; and the Army falls back a few miles.

For more than three months have these serious differences between Parliament and Army gone on. There is a pause of nearly another month, in which the kingdom does seem approaching to a settlement. We have lost sight of the monarch during the busy two months in which London lies under the shadow of that eagle's wing. Is he a guest or a prisoner amidst that Army, so differently composed from his own roystering Cavaliers? He is certainly not an ill-used prisoner. "His majesty," says Clarendon, "sat still, or removed to such places as were most convenient for the march of the army ; being in all places as well provided for and accommodated, as he had used to be in any progress." All persons were allowed to resort to him—"the best gentlemen of the several counties through which he passed." His own chaplains had leave to attend upon him for his devotions, and "performed their function at the ordinary hours, in their accustomed formalities." Royalists of rank visited him without restraint; "and many good officers who had served his majesty faithfully were civilly received by the officers of the army, and lived quietly in their quarters." The king lodged at great houses in the neighbourhood of the army ;—at the earl of Salisbury's at Hatfield, when the troops were at St. Alban's ; at Caversham, the earl of Craven's, when the army had moved further from London. Sir Philip Warwick has a curious passage, implying that there was some general belief that the king's disgust at the harsher treatment he had received from the Presbyterians would moderate his own desire for episcopal uniformity, and lead him to look with approbation upon that liberty of conscience which the Independents professed and demanded : * "At Causham [Caversham] I had the honour to come into his presence, though I staid not there ; but, by all I could perceive either from himself or any other, he was very apprehensive in what hands he was, but was not to let it be discerned. Nor had he given that countenance to Dr. Taylor's 'Liberty of Prophesying' which some believed he had." † The prejudices of his education, and the principles of his govern-

* At p. 46 we gave an extract from the letter of Cromwell, in which, on the very day of the Battle of Naseby, he asserts this ruling principle of his mind. We insert here a fac-simile of that remarkable portion of the letter.   † "Memoirs," p. 301.

ment, were too exclusive to allow Charles to admit the doctrine of Toleration, although proclaimed by his own favourite chaplain.   When Jeremy Taylor

I wish this action may begett thankfullnesse and humilitye in all that are concerned in itt, Hee that venters his life for the libertye of his countrie, I wish hee trust God for the libertye of his conscience, and you for the libertye hee fights four, In this hee rests whoe is

your most humble servant

Oliver Cromwell

Junee. 14th. 1645.
Haurabroue.

Fac-simile of a portion of the letter written by Cromwell to the Speaker of the House of Commons, announcing the Victory of Naseby. (Harleian Collection of MSS. British Museum, No. 7502.)

from his lowly retreat in Wales sent forth this plea for religious liberty into an unquiet world, he said, " I thought it might not misbecome my duty and endeavours to plead for peace, and charity, and forgiveness, and permissions mutual; although I had reason to believe that such is the iniquity of men, and they so indisposed to receive such impresses, that I had as good plough the sands or till the air as persuade such doctrines."*   It was reserved for a

* " Epistle Dedicatory to Lord Hatton."

happier age to understand and act upon these principles. Taylor had been favoured by Laud; but he had broken away from Laud's narrow estimate of what was necessary for the security of an established Church. The problem that its power and dignity and usefulness might be upheld in connection with the most absolute spiritual freedom beyond its pale, required to be practically worked out for two centuries before it could be held to be solved. The reasoners in steel, who were as impatient of the domination of "New Presbyter" as of "Old Priest,"* were dealing more practically with this question of toleration than any previous set of men who had so advocated the rights of conscience. Few had advocated those rights, having strong religious convictions of their own. Cromwell was the great expositor of their principle; and he probably went as far as the spirit of Protestantism would then permit. Charles hated the Presbyterians, but he gave no confidence to the Independents. The king and his conqueror now sometimes met. The king had been allowed by Fairfax, with an instant attention to his request, to have an interview with his children, the dukes of York and Gloucester, and the princess Elizabeth. Sir John Berkeley, who came over from the queen when Charles had informed her of his reception by the army, had many conferences with Cromwell; who, although "wishing that the king was more frank, and would not tie himself so strictly to narrow maxims," told Berkeley "that he had lately seen the tenderest sight that ever his eyes beheld, which was the interview between the king and his children; and wept plentifully at the remembrance of it, saying, that never man was so abused as he in his sinister opinions of the king, who, he thought, was the uprightest and most conscientious man of his three kingdoms." And yet Berkeley, whilst he records this trait of Cromwell's character, which, after the accustomed fashion, we must call hypocrisy, writes, "I was of his majesty's sense, that men whose hands were yet hot with the blood of his most faithful subjects, ought not entirely to be trusted; but thought they ought absolutely to be well dissembled with, whilst his majesty was in their hands at least, that he might the better get out of them."†

It was towards the end of June that the king and the Independents,—Cromwell and Ireton, Vane and Henry Marten,—appeared to have come to such an understanding as promised a termination to the miseries of the kingdom; an understanding that would have restored the king to those just rights which were compatible with the existence of civil and religious liberty. Whether such an arrangement would have endured, had it been effected, may justly be questioned. But the proposals which were made by the leaders of the Army to Charles at this juncture, were far more moderate than any which had been previously tendered or suggested. They were to the effect that the Long Parliament should be dissolved within a year; that future Parliaments should be biennial, and not to be dissolved or adjourned except by their own consent, unless they had sat a hundred and twenty days; that the representation should be made more equal, by disfranchising decayed and inconsiderable towns, and giving a greater number of members to counties or other divisions of the kingdom; that the judicial power of both Houses

* "New Presbyter is but Old Priest writ large.'—*Milton.*
† "Memoirs of Sir John Berkeley," 1699.

should be limited ; that grand jurymen should be chosen in some equal way, and not at the discretion of the sheriff. These were national reforms, not materially affecting the royal prerogative; reforms which have been gradually established in the working of the constitution. The great question of the power of the sword was proposed to be settled, upon the principle that the royal authority over the militia should be subject to the advice of Parliament and a Council for ten years. The other great subject of difference, that of religion, was provided for by the proposition that an Act should be passed, taking away all ecclesiastical jurisdiction extending to civil penalties; that there be a repeal of all Statutes enjoining the use of the Common Prayer under penalties, as well as of those that imposed penalties for not attending the service of the Church; and, further, that the taking of the Covenant should not be enforced upon any, and all penalties taken away that had been imposed upon the refusers. These propositions being received as the basis for securing the rights, liberties, peace, and safety of the kingdom, it was to be provided that " his majesty's person, his queen and royal issue, may be restored to a condition of safety, honour, and freedom in the nation, without diminution of their personal rights, or further limitation to the exercise of the legal power." How the proposals were received by the king is minutely detailed by sir John Berkeley. Charles appears to have mainly objected to the minor condition which excepted seven of his adherents from a general amnesty, and from the privilege of compounding for their estates; and to that which stipulated that royalists should not sit in the next Parliament. " I procured his Majesty a sight of the Army's Proposals six or eight days before they were offered to him in public. His Majesty was much displeased with them in general, saying, That, if they had a mind to close with him, they would never impose so hard terms upon him. I replied, That, if they had demanded less than they had done, I should have suspected them more than I now did of intending not really to serve his Majesty, but only to abuse him; since it was not likely that men who had, through so great dangers and difficulties, acquired so great advantages, should ever sit down with less than was contained in the Proposals; and, on the other side, never was a crown (that had been so near lost) so cheaply recovered, as his Majesty's would be, if they agreed upon such terms. His Majesty was of another advice, and returned, That they could not subsist without him, and therefore he did not doubt but that he should see them very shortly be glad to condescend farther; and then objected to three particular points of the Proposals. The first was, The exception of seven, not named, from pardon. The second, The excluding his party from being eligible in the next ensuing Parliament. And the third, That though there was nothing done against the Church-government established, yet there was nothing done to assert it. To these, I replied, That after his Majesty and the Army were accorded, it would be no impossible work to make them remit in the first point; and, if he could not, when his Majesty was re-instated in his throne, he might easily supply seven persons beyond the seas, in such sort as to make their banishment supportable to them. To the second; That the next Parliament would be necessitated to lay great burdens upon the kingdom; and it would be a happiness to the king's Party, to have no voice in them. To the third, That the Law was security enough for the Church; and it was happy that men, who had fought against the Church, should be reduced (when they were superiors), not to speak against it. His Majesty broke from me with this expression, ' Well! I shall see them glad ere long to accept more equal terms.' " The king rejected the proposals; and he did so in a manner that sufficiently showed his resolution to persevere in his course of endeavouring to profit by the dissensions of the two great parties, but to concede nothing of importance to either. Berkeley attributes his dangerous resolve to the secret advice of Ashburnham, and to " the encouraging messages which his majesty had, by my lord Lauderdale and others, from the Presbyterian party and the City of London, who pretended to despise the Army, and to oppose them to death." He says, " his majesty seemed very much excited, insomuch that, when the proposals were solemnly sent to him, and his concurrence most humbly and heartily desired, his majesty, not only to the astonishment of Ireton and the rest, but even to mine, entertained them with very tart and bitter discourses." The king said, " You cannot be without me; you will fall to ruin if I do not sustain you." Those leaders of the Army who were present looked with wonder upon the scene. Berkeley at last went up to the king and whispered, " Sir, your majesty speaks as if you had some secret strength and power that I do not know of; and since your majesty hath concealed it from me, I wish you had concealed it from these men too." The king " soon recollected himself, and began to sweeten his former discourse with great power of language and behaviour. But it was now of the latest." This remarkable interview took place at Woburn. The cause of this deportment of the king—the " secret strength and power" which he believed himself to possess—was the expectation that the City would be too powerful for the Army. Bands of apprentices had surrounded Westminster Hall, clamorously demanding the return of the king. An engagement, signed by thousands, was entered into, pledging those who signed it to make all efforts to accomplish the king's return to London. This was at the exact period when Berkeley had shown Charles the proposals of the Army; but before the interview with Ireton and the other officers. Upon the news of these proceedings in London, Fairfax and his army had moved towards the capital. The tumults grew more serious. On the 26th of July, all the avenues of the Houses were beset with a violent multitude. They brought a Petition, which was received at the door of the Commons. No answer was returned, and shouts arose of " Let us go in." Members drew their swords, and drove back those who were crowding in the lobby. Some of the rioters climbed up to the windows of the House of Peers, and threw stones into the Chamber. The door of the House of Commons was at last forced open; and a body of men rushed in, calling out " Vote, Vote." They demanded that a resolution of the previous day, carried by the Independents, declaring those traitors who voted for the city " engagement," should be rescinded. The Speaker left the chair, and went into the lobby, after the House had voted as the rioters desired. Ludlow thus records the scene when the Speaker " was forced back into the chair by the violence of the insolent rabble." " It was thought convenient to give way to their rage; and the Speaker demanding what question they desired to be put, they answered, That the king should be desired to come to London forthwith: which question being put, they were asked again what further they would have. They said that he should be invited to come with honour, freedom, and safety: to both which I gave a loud negative, and some of the members as loud an affirmative, rather out of a prudential compliance than any affection to the design on foot." * This was on a Monday. The army lay at Windsor, Maidenhead, Colnbrook, and adjacent places. The Houses adjourned to Friday, the 30th of July. The Speakers of the Lords and Commons have withdrawn, and many members have withdrawn with them. The eleven members whose impeachment the Army had demanded, have now returned. The Presbyterian party appears to be triumphant. New Speakers are elected. The king has had his interview with Ireton and the Council of Officers, and has indiscreetly shown his reliance upon agitations which he is more than suspected of having excited. Suddenly the whole course of the political movement is changed. A train of carriages arrives from London with lord Manchester and Mr. Lenthall, the Speakers; and they are accompanied by fourteen of the Peers, and about one hundred members of the Commons.† Those who remain at Westminster have not been idle. Troops are to be enlisted. The army is commanded not to advance. But it does advance. On the 3rd of August, Hounslow Heath, then a vast unenclosed space, is appointed for a Rendez-vous of this formidable force. It is now something more than a power struggling against a parliamentary majority. The Speaker of the Lords, and the Speaker of the Commons,—the Sergeant-at-Arms with the mace—the most energetic of the Members—the visible authority and the real potency of Parliament are with the Army. "They appeared at the head of them," says Ludlow, "at which the Army expressed great joy, declaring themselves resolved to live and die with them." There is yet a hope that the king will still endeavour to retain the only power that can really help him. It was clear that London will succumb without a blow. Fairfax and his twenty thousand pause for a day or two, communicating with the authorities of the City. With the party at Westminster and their new Speakers, they have no intercourse. The army is quartered about Brentford, Hounslow, Twickenham, and adjacent villages; "without restraining any provisions, which, every day, according to custom, were carried to London; or doing the least action that might disoblige or displease the city: the army being, in truth, under so excellent discipline, that nobody could complain of any damage sustained by them, or any provocation by word or deed." ‡ Berkeley says that Cromwell, Ireton, and the rest of the superior officers of the army, knew that London would certainly be theirs; and "therefore sent an express to Mr. Ashburnham and to me, to express that, since his majesty would not yield to the proposals, yet he should, at least, send a kind letter to the army, before it were commonly known that London would submit." A meeting of the friends and advisers of the king was held at Windsor, and a letter of this nature was prepared. But Charles would not sign the letter till it was too late; and when he reluctantly sent it, "it had lost all its grace and efficacy." The City had yielded. There was no longer a present hope of profiting by dissensions between Parliament and Army. On the 6th of August Fairfax, surrounded

* "Memoirs," vol. i. p. 206.
† These numbers are given by Rushworth and Whitelock. Hollis says eight lords and fifty-eight commoners.
‡ Clarendon, vol. v. p. 466.

by four of his regiments, and conducting the Members of Parliament who had fled to the Army, proceeded to Westminster. At Hyde Park they were met by the Lord Mayor and Aldermen; at Charing Cross by the Common Council. The Independents, now supreme in parliament, took their seats. The mace was again laid on the table. Two days after, the whole army, horse, foot, and artillery, marched through Westminster and the City, and over London Bridge to their various quarters in Surrey. They marched, says Clarendon, "without the least disorder, or doing the least damage to any person, or giving any disrespective word to any man." Denzil Hollis, one of the eleven members whose little hour of supremacy had so quickly passed, describes with more than his usual bitterness, this march of the Ironsides: "Sir Thomas Fairfax and the whole Army marched in triumph, with laurel in their hats as conquerors, through the subdued city of London, to show it was at his mercy; which was an airy vanity I confess above my understanding, and might have raised a spirit of indignation, not so easily to have been laid. But a higher insolency of an Army composed of so mean people, and a more patient humble submission and bearing of a great and populous city, but a little before so full of honour and greatness, was, I think, never heard of." The king was lodged at Hampton Court. The head-quarters of the Army were at Putney.

The king remained at Hampton Court for three months. The spacious quadrangles of the old palace of Wolsey were well adapted for comfort. He had dwelt there with his young queen in the first year of their marriage; and ten years had scarcely passed since he was surrounded by his brilliant court at the Revels in the Great Hall, and had listened in freedom and security to the dramas of Shakspere and Fletcher, of Davenant and Cartwright. Some of the old familiar faces came about him in this autumn of 1647. His children were frequently with him. "Persons of all conditions repaired to his majesty of all who had served him; with whom he conferred without reservation; and the citizens flocked thither, as they had used to do at the end of a progress." * Evelyn has this entry in his Diary of October: "On the 10th to Hampton Court, where I had the honour to kiss his majesty's hand, and give him an account of several things I had in charge, he being now in the power of those execrable villains who not long after murdered him." They were very frequently with his majesty, "those execrable villains." They were really intent upon doing him as much service as lay in their power, if he could have trusted them, and they could have trusted him. Cromwell and Ireton endeavoured to serve the king, even with great danger to themselves. Charles was constantly sending messages to them at Putney by Ashburnham, as Berkeley states; Cromwell had many conferences with the king, according to Clarendon. "They had enough to do," says Berkeley, "both in the Parliament and Council of the Army, the one abounding with Presbyterians, the other with Levellers, and both really jealous [suspicious] that Cromwell and Ireton had made a private bargain with the king." † Lilburne, now in violent opposition to his old friends, was printing the most bitter denunciations against these betrayers of the people. The Presbyterians gave out that Berkeley had told lady Carlisle

* Clarendon.   † "Memoirs."

that Cromwell was to be earl of Essex; which statement Berkeley explicitly denied. Silly royalists about the king tried to persuade him that it would be for his interest "to divide Cromwell and the Army." These wheels within wheels required some chief motive power which Charles was incapable of furnishing. His natural want of decision of character was rendered more prominent by these complications. He had to deal with men who were the very opposite to himself in that simplicity of purpose which we recognise as the foundation of decision of character. Cromwell and Ireton had strong convictions of the value of democratic government; but they knew how infinite were the risques of democracy becoming universal licence, if the liberties of the people were attempted to be raised upon any other than the ancient foundations. They would therefore endeavour to save the king, if they could do so with security to the popular rights. None but the most prejudiced judges can trace in their actions, at this crisis, the slightest manifestation of a desire to betray the king. They were "faithful to their trust, and to the people's interest;" but they believed "that the king might have been managed to comply with the public good of his people after he could no longer uphold his own violent will." Mrs. Hutchinson, who expresses this confidence in Cromwell and Ireton, shows how the king destroyed these expectations. "Upon some discourses with him, the king uttering these words to him, 'I shall play my game as well as I can;' Ireton replied, 'If your majesty have a *game* to play, you must also give us the liberty to play ours.'" The foremost men of the Independent party still endeavoured to second the reasonable wishes of the king. The Presbyterians had again pressed upon him the terms of the treaty at Newcastle, slightly modified. Charles desired a personal treaty with the Parliament, and thought the proposals which had come from the Army appeared a better ground of settlement. Cromwell, Vane, Ireton, and their friends strenuously supported his desire for a personal treaty. "The suspicions were so strong in the House," says Berkeley, "that they lost almost all their friends there; and the Army that lay then about Putney, were no less ill-satisfied."

In the course of the autumn an incident occurred, which has so much of romance in it that historians have been somewhat doubtful of repeating a story so admirably calculated for stage effect. The scene is the Blue Boar inn in Holborn. There it still stands in the parish of St. Andrew, pretty much the same as it stood in the beginning of the seventeenth century—a well-preserved specimen of an ancient hostelry. The yard is dedicated to all the purposes of traffic. The buildings of the quadrangle form stables or common tap-rooms on the ground level. On the upper floors are the sitting-rooms and dormitories, with galleries carried all round, forming a corridor to the first floor. To this quaint old place come two men in trooper's clothes on an October evening. They enter by the wicket in the inn gate, leaving an attendant in the street. These jolly troopers go into "a drinking-stall:" and calling for the drawer, "sit drinking cans of beer till ten of the clock." They expect an arrival. Their watcher at the gate gives them notice that "the man with the saddle" is come. Their eyes are upon him from their drinking-stall. He goes into a stable; saddles his horse; and as he leads the steed forth, the troopers draw their swords, and tell him their duty is to search all those who go in or out. They say, however, that he looks like an honest fellow, and therefore they would only search his saddle. Into their drinking-stall they return; cut open "the skirts of the saddle;" take out a letter which they suspected to be therein concealed; and send the horseman on his way. The two troopers are Cromwell and Ireton. Cromwell told the story himself to lord Broghill, afterwards earl of Orrery, when they were serving together in Ireland. The two, with Ireton, were riding out of Youghal, when they fell into discourse about the king's death. Cromwell said that they had once "a mind to have closed with him;" but something happened, and they "fell off from that design." Broghill was curious to know the reason of this change. Cromwell told him that, finding the Scots and Presbyterians were growing more powerful, and were likely to agree with the king "and leave them in the lurch," they thought it best to offer first to come in upon reasonable conditions. "But," continued Cromwell, "whilst our thoughts were taken up with this subject, there came a letter to us from one of our spies, who was of the king's bedchamber, acquainting us that our final doom was decreed that very day; that he could not possibly learn what it was, but we might discover it if we could but intercept a letter sent from the king to the queen, wherein he informed her of his resolution: that this letter was sown up in the skirt of a saddle, and the bearer of it would come with the saddle upon his head about ten of the clock that night to the Blue Boar in Holborn, where he was to take horse for Dover. The messenger knew nothing of the letter in the saddle, though some in Dover did. We were at Windsor when we received this letter, and immediately upon the receipt of it, Ireton and I resolved to take one trusty fellow with us, and to go in troopers' habits to that inn. We did so." Cromwell then related the adventure; and further told what the discovery was that changed their purpose of closing with the king: "We found in the letter, that his majesty acquainted the queen that he was courted by both factions, the Scotch Presbyterians and the army; and that those which bade the fairest for him should have him: but yet he thought he should close with the Scots sooner than with the other. Upon this we returned to Windsor; and finding we were not like to have good terms from the king, we from that time vowed his destruction." This well-known story is told by the reverend Thomas Morrice, as related to him by the earl of Orrery, to whom he was chaplain. The contents of the letter thus described do not appear to us sufficiently important to have caused the resolution of Cromwell and Ireton for the king's destruction. They already knew that he was courted by both factions. They knew that "those who bade the fairest for him would have him." Orrery became a cabinet-counsellor of Charles II., and might have prudently generalised the contents of the letter which is said to have caused the final separation of Cromwell from the interests of Charles I. There is another story of a letter, which Hume thinks contradictory to the character of the king, and therefore rejects it as "totally unworthy of credit." It is thus related by Richardson, the painter: "Lord Bolingbroke told us, June 12, 1742 (Mr. Pope, lord Marchmont, and myself), that the second earl of Oxford had often told him that he had seen, and had in his hands, an original letter that Charles I. wrote to his queen. in answer to one of hers that had been intercepted, and then forwarded to him; wherein she had reproached him for having made those villains too great concessions, viz., that Cromwell should be lord-lieutenant of Ireland for life without account; that that kingdom should be in the hands of the party, with an army there kept which should know no head but the lieutenant; that Cromwell should have a garter, &c. That in this letter of the king's it was said that she should leave him to manage, who was better informed of all circumstances than she could be; but she might be entirely easy as to whatever concessions he should make them; for that he should know in due time how to deal with the rogues, who, instead of a silken garter, should be fitted with a hempen cord. So the letter ended; which answer as they waited for so they intercepted accordingly, and it determined his fate. This letter lord Oxford said he had offered 500*l.* for." *.

Those who carefully examine the intricate and discordant narratives of this exact period will probably come to the conclusion, that there were more imperative motives for Cromwell breaking off his intercourse with the king than his own personal mortification at being promised a hempen cord instead of a silken garter. He was fast losing his influence over the Army. The conqueror at Naseby was now held to be the traitor at Hampton Court. The Agitators had become unmanageable. They issued pamphlets, setting forth the most extreme principles. They became violent against monarchy in general, and especially furious against those who appeared to favour the cause of Charles in any degree. Cromwell has ceased his visits at Hampton Court. He is alarmed for the king's safety; or, as some hold, he pretends to be alarmed. His cousin, colonel Whalley, commands the guard about the king. Cromwell writes to him in November, "There are rumours abroad of some intended attempt on his majesty's person. Therefore, I pray, have a care of your guards. If any such thing should be done, it would be accounted a most horrid act." Charles yields to the fears natural enough in his helpless condition. He has unhappy dreams. His night-lamp going out is a presage of evil. About the 3rd of November Berkeley and Ashburnham, who had been removed from about the king's person, meet at Ditton at the desire of major Legg, who waited in the king's bed-chamber. They tell Berkeley "that his majesty was really afraid of his life by the tumultuous part of the army, and was resolved to make his escape." Berkeley afterwards saw the king, and was asked to assist in the project. Where to go was yet a question. It was no especial weakness in Charles, but a credulity belonging to the age, that William Lilly, the astrologer, was consulted by a female agent of the king, who paid a heavy sum to the "Sidrophel," who was ready to prophesy for all parties. Some plan was at last determined upon. On the evening of the 11th of November, the commissioners and Colonel Whalley, missing the king at supper, went into his chamber and found him gone. A newspaper of the time, "the Moderate Intelligencer," has a far more interesting notice of the event (as was the way of newspapers even then) than the official entries of Lords' Journals, and Commons' Journals: "November 11.—This day will be famous in after times because towards the end of it his majesty escaped a kind of restraint under which he was at Hampton Court: and according to

---

* "I have been informed that a memorandum nearly conformable to Richardson's anecdote is extant, in the handwriting of Lord Oxford."—HALLAM.

the best relation, thus :—He, as was usual, went to be private a little before evening prayer; staying somewhat longer than usual, it was taken notice of; yet at first without suspicion; but he not coming forth suddenly, there were fears, which increased by the crying of a greyhound again and again within : and upon search it was found the king was gone; and by the way of Paradise, a place so called in the garden; in probability suddenly after his going in, and about twilight.   He left a paper to the Parliament, another to the commissioners, and a third to colonel Whalley."   The faithful greyhound of Charles I. whining for the absence of his master, is a pretty contrast to Froissart's story of the unfaithful greyhound of Richard II.; "who always waited upon the king, and would know no man else : " but who, in the hour of his adversity, "left the king and came to the earl of Derby, duke of Lancaster, and made to him the same friendly countenance and cheer as he was wont to do to the king."

IRETON

Carisbrook.

CHAPTER VI.

Narratives of the king's Escape—He goes to the Isle of Wight—The Levellers in the Army—Their meeting suppressed—Berkeley's unsuccessful mission to Fairfax and Cromwell—Scotch and English Commissioners at Carisbrook—Parliament declares against any further treaty with the king—Royalist Re-action—Riots in London—Revolts in many districts—The king attempts to escape from Carisbrook—Insurrections quelled—Cromwell in Wales—Scottish Army in England—Cromwell's march from Wales—Battle of Preston—Cromwell in Edinburgh. Note on the Party-spirit during the Royalist reaction.

THERE are two minute relations of the circumstances that immediately succeeded the flight of the king from Hampton Court—the narratives of Berkeley and Ashburnham. Each of these was written with the intention of justifying its author from the charge of having betrayed the king, which the Royalists affirmed; and for this purpose they were circulated in manuscript after the Restoration.* Each tries to fix the unfortunate issue of the adventure upon the other adviser of the king. The interest of this controversy has long since passed; and we may therefore accept Clarendon's opinion "that neither of them were, in any degree, corrupted in their loyalty or affection to the king, or suborned to gratify any persons with a disservice to their master." † In the main points of the story both these companions of the flight of Charles do not materially differ.

* Berkeley's Narrative was printed in 1699; Ashburnham's not till 1830.
† "History," vol. v. p. 497.

The night of Thursday the 11th of November was dark and stormy. Berkeley and Ashburnham were waiting with horses by the Thames' side, and when Charles came out, accompanied by major Legg, they immediately rode towards Oatlands. Cromwell had been sent for, upon the escape being discovered; and at midnight he wrote a letter to the Speaker of the Commons, announcing the withdrawal of the king; who "had left his cloak behind him in the gallery of. the private way; and had passed by the back-stairs and vault, towards the water-side." The four rode "through the forest," * the king being their guide; but they lost their way, and were busied in discussions about the ultimate course they were to pursue. Ash-burnham says that previous to their departure the king had told him, "he had some thoughts of going out of the kingdom, but for the shortness of the time to prepare a vessel to transport him; and for the other reasons I had sent him by major Legg he was resolved to go to the Isle of Wight." At day-break of that dark November morning they were at Sutton in Hampshire, where they had sent a relay of horses; and they immediately continued their way towards Southampton. As they walked down a hill with their horses in their hands, they again discussed what to do; and then Berkeley says he heard for the first time anything of the Isle of Wight. It was arranged that the king and Legg should proceed to a house of lord Southampton at Titchfield; that Berkeley and Ashburnham should go into the Isle of Wight to colonel Hammond, the governor. Robert Hammond was connected with the royalist as well as with the parliamentary party. One of his uncles was chaplain to the king. Through the friendship of Cromwell he had himself married a daughter of Hampden. The two companions of the king slept at Lymington; and the next morning reached Carisbrook. They delivered to Hammond a message of the king, that he had been under the necessity of providing for his own safety, but would confide himself to the governor of the island, as one who had prosecuted the war against him without any animosity to his person; asking if he would promise protection to his majesty and his attend-ants to the best of his power. Berkeley says that Hammond grew so pale, and fell into such a trembling, that he expected him to fall from his horse, exclaiming, "O gentlemen, you have undone me by bringing the king into this island, if you have brought him." After much discussion, Hammond engaged "to perform whatever could be expected from a person of honour and honesty;" and, being then partly informed where the king was, proposed to go with them. They reached Cowes, and here took boat to Titchfield, Hammond having the captain of Cowes Castle with him. The scene which followed is related by Ashburnham, as if it were something very creditable to himself and to the king. The king was alarmed, and said that he was sure the governor would make him a prisoner; and then Ashburnham said, "I was happy that I had provided an expedient; so that if he would say what other course he would steer, I would take order that the governor should not interrupt him. His majesty asked me how that could possibly be, since the governor was come with us? I answered that his coming made any other way more practicable than if he had stayed behind. He then told me,

---

* The route from Oatlands into Hampshire would lead through Windsor Forest, then com-prising a vast circuit of many parishes.

that he had sent to Hampton for a vessel, to transport him into France, and was in good hope to be supplied, and that he expected news of it every moment, but very earnestly pressed to know how I would clear him of the governor. I answered that I was resolved and prepared to kill him and the captain with my own hands." The valiant Jack Ashburnham who, in his fever of loyalty, proposed to slay the man whom he believed worthy of all confidence, was not discarded by the king upon this proof that he had a treacherous nature. His relation thus continues: " His majesty walking some few turns in the room, and, as he was afterwards pleased to tell me, weighing what I had proposed to him, and considering that if the ship should not come, it would not be many hours before some, in pursuance of him, would seize him, the consequence whereof he very much apprehended, resolved he would not have execution done upon the governor, for he intended to accept of what he had proposed and to go with him, and therefore commanded he should be called up, sir John Berkeley being not yet come to the king." There was no news of the expected ship; orders had arrived at Southampton that the port should be closed; and in two hours the king was in a boat sailing to the Fair Isle. That night he slept at Carisbrook Castle.

The inevitable tendency of all revolutions to call into action violent bodies of men professing principles that strike at the foundation of secure and orderly government, was now clearly visible. The Levellers had become conspicuous in the army—those, according to Clarendon, who declared " that all degrees of men should be levelled, and an equality should be established, both in titles and estates, throughout the kingdom." * The historian of the Rebellion doubts " whether the raising of this spirit was a piece of Cromwell's ordinary witchcraft, in order to some of his designs, or whether it grew amongst the tares which had been sowed in that confusion." Had Clarendon lived through a period of sixty years of far more terrible revolutions in another kingdom, he would have known that it needs no " witchcraft" to evoke such a spirit out of the passions of the enthusiastic and the rapacity of the dishonest. Whatever the historian believes of Cromwell's witchcraft, he does full justice to his human powers of " dexterity and courage," by which " he totally subdued that spirit in the army," which would otherwise " have produced all imaginable mischief in the parliament, army, and kingdom." †
Four days after the king has quitted Hampton Court, Cromwell is dealing very summarily—in " a rough and brisk temper," as Clarendon has it—with some of those against whom he had warned colonel Whalley, in regard to the safety of Charles's person. A rendezvous is appointed at Corkbush field, between Ware and Hertford, for seven regiments. But there are nine regiments on the ground. Harrison's regiment of horse, and Lilburn's of foot, have come without orders. Lilburn himself has been sent to the Tower; but being permitted to ride out, for his health, has come to the rendezvous. His regiment is without its officers, for the Agitators have expelled all above the rank of lieutenant, with the exception of one captain. They have papers in their hats, of " Liberty for England, their rights for the soldiers." Fairfax and Cromwell read to the seven regiments a remonstrance against the proceedings of the Agitators, and they are received with acclamations. Fairfax

* " Rebellion," vol. v. p. 486.   † Ibid. p. 506.

addresses Harrison's cavalry, and the troopers exclaim that they will live and die with their general, and they tear the inscriptions from their hats. Lilburn's regiment reply to Fairfax with derisive shouts. Cromwell exclaims, "Take that paper from your hats." They refuse. He rushes into the ranks; orders fourteen of the mutineers to be seized; a drum-head court-martial is assembled, and three are condemned to death. The Council of Officers order that they shall draw lots which shall determine the fate of one. The immediate execution of that one restored the army to its wonted discipline. But such remedies cannot frequently be repeated. The most violent of the fanatics are preaching against the severity exercised towards their "saints." The Presbyterians look coldly upon the energy of the great military Independent; the republican politicians begin to fear and distrust him. Ludlow cries "No," when a vote of thanks to Cromwell is proposed in parliament. They do not see as clearly as he does the line which separates liberty from anarchy.

Colonel Hammond, according to Berkeley's relation, had many private conferences with the king; and was earnest that some authorised person should proceed from Charles to the generals who had put down the violence of the Agitators. Berkeley set out with letters from the king and also from the governor, and arrived at the head-quarters at Windsor. He delivered his letters to Fairfax, at a general meeting of officers. Being desired to withdraw, he was soon afterwards called in; and was sternly told by Fairfax that they were the Parliament's officers, and must refer the king's letters to the Parliament. Cromwell and Ireton looked coldly upon him, as well as other officers with whom he was acquainted. His servant went out to find some one to whom Berkeley could speak; and a general officer sent him a message to meet him in a close behind the Garter Inn, at twelve at night. They met; and his friend urged him to persuade the king to escape; for that it was resolved to seize his person and bring him to trial. The Agitators, he said, were not quelled; and had been repeatedly with Cromwell and Ireton to tell them that they would bring the whole army to the conviction that the king should be brought to trial. The general further said that he hazarded his own life in this interview; for it was agreed that no one should speak with Berkeley, under pain of death. Cromwell had despaired of bringing the army to his sense, and must make his peace with those who were most opposed to the king. "He was re-instated in the fellowship of the faithful." Berkeley the next day sent colonel Cook to Cromwell, to say that he had letters and papers for him from the king. "He sent me word, by the same messenger, that he durst not see me, it being very dangerous to us both; and bid me be assured that he would serve his majesty as long as he could do it without his own ruin; but desired that I would not expect that he should perish for his sake." Cromwell was on the edge of a precipice. There was a belief that he was privy to the escape of the king. Ludlow, the republican, says, "it was visible that the king made his escape by the advice of Cromwell." It is certainly not improbable that Cromwell, knowing the dangers of the king, might sincerely desire that he might escape out of the kingdom. The notion of Hollis, that he recommended the flight to the Isle of Wight "because he had there provided a gaoler," is irreconcileable with the facts. Charles during the first month might have escaped from Carisbrook without any difficulty, had proper means been supplied. A ship only was wanting. Berkeley went back to the king to recommend this course, which he had urged by letter; but the false hope of dealing with another party again prevailed over the natural fears of Charles for his own life. Berkeley's first words to the king were, "Why was he still in the island, where he could not long promise himself the liberty he now had?" Charles replied, "that he would have a care of that, time enough; and that he was to conclude with the Scots, because from their desire to have him out of the Army's hands they would listen to reason." The Scottish commissioners came to Carisbrook towards the end of December. It had been voted in the House of Lords at the end of November, that propositions should again be offered to the king in the shape of four bills, far more stringent as to the power of Parliament and the Militia than the offers at any previous time, but leaving the religious question untouched. The Scottish commissioners in London had secretly advised the king to reject these bills. Their own proposals were, that a Scottish army should come into England to restore him to his rights, provided that he confirmed the Presbyterian establishment in England for a period of three years, and then the constitution of the Church to be finally settled. "In that season of despair," says Clarendon, "they prevailed with him to sign the propositions he had formerly refused; and having great apprehensions, from the jealousies they knew the army had of them, that they should be seized upon and searched on their return to London, they made up their precious contract in lead, and buried it in a garden in the Isle of Wight, from whence they easily found means afterwards to receive it." * Having concluded this dangerous alliance, Charles delivered his answer to the English commissioners. He had in vain endeavoured to prevail upon lord Denbigh and the others to take back his determination in a sealed envelope. He rejected the propositions. That evening the gates of Carisbrook Castle were closed guards surrounded the fortress; and the greater number of the king's servants, including Berkeley and Ashburnham, were ordered to quit the island. An escape meditated for the next night was no longer practicable. The commissioners of the Parliament returned to Westminster, to proclaim what was, in truth, the complete triumph of the republicans. The last manœuvre of the unfortunate king rendered his difficult condition utterly desperate. Ludlow, speaking of the English and Scottish negotiations at Carisbrook, says, "Whilst these two sorts of commissioners were one day attending the king as he walked about the castle, they observed him to throw a bone before two spaniels that followed him, and to take great delight in seeing them contending for it; which some of them thought to be intended by him to represent that bone of contention he had cast between the two parties." † It was a delight that was to come to a fatal issue. Cromwell wrote to colonel Hammond on the 3rd of January, "The House of Commons is very sensible of the king's dealings, and of our brethren's [the Scots], in this late transaction." He tells his " dear Robin," that "now, blessed be God, I can write and thou receive freely." He alludes to some struggle of the governor in favour of his unhappy prisoner,—"thou in the midst of thy temptation, which, indeed, by what we understand of it, was a great one." The letter-writer exultingly communicates the result of the proceedings at Carisbrook : "The House of Commons has this day voted as follows :—1st. They will make no more Addresses to the king; 2nd. None shall apply to him without leave of the two Houses, upon pain of being guilty of high treason; 3rd, They will receive nothing from the king, nor shall any other bring anything to them from him, nor receive anything from the king." The Lords adopted the resolution, after some debate. Unless there be some speedy change, the end will be accomplished that the majority in Parliament contended for, "to settle the commonwealth without the king." That majority in the Commons was a very formidable one—141 to 91; and their resolution is justly described by Mr. Hallam as " a virtual renunciation of allegiance."

But, however the notion of a sovereign representative assembly as the government suited for England might please the political enthusiasts and the military fanatics, the great body of quiet people, who desired the protection of the law under a limited monarchy, were not prepared to endure that a democracy should be thrust upon them at the point of the sword. Discontent was very generally spread. Murmurings would shortly grow into revolts. Cromwell, who saw better than most men the inevitable result of political and religious discords, whilst the supreme authority was so unsettled, tried to effect some reconciliation between Presbyterians and Independents. The dinner at which Cromwell assembled them was given in vain. "One would endure no superior, the other no equal." Ludlow, who thus describes the result of this attempt, relates more minutely the proceedings of another meeting at which he was present. The Grandees of the House and Army, of whom he terms Cromwell the head, "would not declare their judgments either for a monarchical, aristocratical, or democratical government; maintaining that any of them might be good in themselves, or for us, according as Providence should direct us." The Commonwealth's men boldly declared against monarchy; that the king had broken his oath, and dissolved their allegiance; maintained that he had appealed to the sword, and should be called to account for the effusion of blood; after which an equal Commonwealth, founded upon the consent of the people. The discussion, solemn as it was, had a ludicrous termination. "Cromwell," says Ludlow, "professed himself unresolved; and having learned what he could of the principles and inclinations of those present at the conference, took up a cushion and flung it at my head, and then ran down the stairs ; but I overtook him with another, which made him hasten down faster than he desired." * Cromwell told Ludlow the next day that " he was convinced of the desirableness of · what was proposed, but not of the feasibleness of it." There was a meeting some time after, conducted in a very different mood by Cromwell—a meeting of officers of the Army at Windsor Castle, as reported by adjutant-general Allen. These zealous men spent one whole day in prayer. They were exhorted by Cromwell to a thorough consideration of their actions as an Army, and of their ways as private Christians. They became convinced that the Lord had departed from them, through " those carnal conferences which they held in the preceding year with the king and his party." They, with bitter weeping, took sense and shame of their iniquities. They came to a

* " Memoirs," p. 239.

clear agreement that it was their duty to go forth and fight the enemies that
had appeared against them. They finally came to a resolution, "That it
was our duty, that, if ever the Lord brought us back again in peace, to call
Charles Stuart, that man of blood, to an account for that blood he had shed,
and mischief he had done to his utmost, against the Lord's cause and people
in these poor nations." * These men, not hypocrites, not wholly fanatics, are
very terrible in their stern resolves. They will go forth to fight "the
enemies that had appeared against them"—and then! There is a re-action
in many quarters in England. The Scots are preparing to invade. A second
Civil War is fast approaching.

When the Parliament passed their resolution to receive no more commu-
nications from the king, and to forbid all correspondence with him, they published a declaration imputing all the misfortunes of his reign to himself personally, and not to evil counsellors, as had been the custom before monarchy
had lost its respect even in the eyes of those who were opposed to its evil
government. Clarendon ascribes the partial re-action of public opinion in a
great degree to what he calls "this monstrous declaration." But he wholly
misconceives or misrepresents the temper of the people, when he sets forth " a
universal discontent and murmuring of the three nations, and almost as general
a detestation both of parliament and army, and a most passionate desire that
all their follies and madness might be forgotten in restoring the king to all
they had taken from him, and in settling that blessed government they had
deprived themselves of." † Nations have sometimes unaccountable fits of
oblivion; but the memory of eleven years of the unmitigated despotism of
" that blessed government" was too deeply written upon the volume of the
people's brain, though Edward Hyde might choose to forget it. Nevertheless,
the nation was tired of its distractions. It wearied for some permanent settlement that might end the hoarse disputes and subtle intrigues of Parliament
and Army, of Presbyterian and Independent; that might free the possessors
of rank and property from the dread of wild men with notions of social
equality; that might restore industry to its healthful functions, and put an
end not only to the cost of a standing military force, but to its fearful
resistance to civil power. The desire of the peaceful portion of the nation
was feebly heard amidst the surrounding clamour. The attempt to express
their impatience of existing evils by riot and revolt was necessarily a vain
attempt. This spirit was displayed in the city of London, at the beginning
of April. Cromwell and some of the other leaders attend a Common-Council; but they find the Presbyterians indisposed to listen to what they call
" their subtleties." The next day there is a formidable riot. It is Sunday.
The puritan strictness in religious observances, and in minor matters, has
come to be less respected than before the close of the war. Royalists, amidst
their contempt for what they deem fanaticism, are now mixing again in the
ordinary intercourse with the despised Roundheads. The theatre is now not
wholly proscribed. Evelyn writes in his Diary, " 5th February, saw a tragi-
comedy acted in the Cockpit, after there had been none of these diversions
for many years during the war." On that Sunday, the 9th of April, there
are apprentices playing at bowls in Moorfields during church-time. They are

---

* Somers' Tracts, given in Carlyle's " Cromwell," vol. i.   † " Rebellion," vol. vi. p. 1.

ordered to disperse by the militia guard; but they fight with the guard, and hold their ground. Soon routed by cavalry, they raise the old cry of " Clubs;" are joined by the watermen, a numerous and formidable body; fight on through the night; and in the morning have possession of Ludgate and Newgate, and have stretched chains across all the great thoroughfares. There are forty hours of this tumult, in which the prevailing cry is "God and king Charles." At last a body of cavalry arrive from Westminster; there is an irresistible charge of the men who had rode down far more terrible assailants; and that movement is at an end. But in many towns there are similar riots. In Wales some Presbyterian officers of the parliamentary army, with colonel Poyer at their head, have raised a far more formidable insurrection. Pembroke Castle is in their hands. They soon have possession of Chepstow Castle. The gentry have proclaimed the king. It is a Presbyterian-royalist insurrection, allied in principle with the purposes of the moderate Presbyterians of Scotland, who are organising their army for the march into England. The Welsh outbreak is somewhat premature; but nevertheless it is very formidable. It is alarming enough to demand the personal care of lieutenant-general Cromwell. He leaves London on the 3rd of May, with five regiments. The Londoners are glad to be freed from his presence; for a rumour has been spread that the army at Whitehall are about to attack and plunder the city. Petitions were addressed to the Commons that the army should remove further; and that the militia should be placed under the command of Skippon. The re-action gave the Presbyterians again the command in Parliament; and it was voted on the 28th of April, that the fundamental government of the kingdom by King, Lords, and Commons, should not be changed; and that the resolutions forbidding all communication with the king should be rescinded. Popular demonstrations immediately followed the departure of Cromwell. Surrey gentlemen, freeholders, and yeomen, came to Westminster with a petition that the king should be restored with all the splendour of his ancestors. A broil ensued between the parliamentary guard and these petitioners, who asked the soldiers, " Why do you stand here to guard a company of rogues?" Several of the Surrey men, and one of the guard, were killed. The Royalists of Kent organised themselves in a far more formidable shape. They secured Sandwich and Dover; appointed as general, Goring, earl of Norwich; and assembled at Rochester to the number of seven thousand. Troops were raised for the royal service in the eastern and midland counties. More dangerous to the ruling powers than all these demonstrations, was the defection of the fleet. Clarendon has thus described the mariners of his time: " The seamen are in a manner a nation by themselves; a humorous, brave, and sturdy people; fierce and resolute in whatsoever they are inclined to; somewhat unsteady and inconstant in pursuing it; and jealous of those to-morrow by whom they are governed to-day." If Clarendon's description be correct, it must be taken solely with reference to a reign when the maritime power of England had been allowed to fall to the lowest condition. It could not apply to the sailors of Drake and Frobisher. Less could it apply to the sailors of Blake and Penn. The unsteadiness and the inconstancy, the jealousy of the government under which they served, belonged to a period when the government had long been indifferent to the national honour. These characteristics altogether passed away when the first thought

of the English fleet was how "not to be fooled by the foreigner." The
sailors of 1648 put their admiral on shore, and carried their ships to Holland,
to place them under the command of the prince of Wales, who appeared in
the Channel,—and did nothing. The Royalists were in the highest exultation.
They expected the king soon to be again at their head. The earl of Holland
had turned once more to what he thought would be the winning side; and
his mansion at Kensington was again the resort of Cavaliers. But the king
does not appear amongst them. An attempt at escape from Carisbrook has
a second time failed. On the 6th of April, Cromwell had written to
Hammond, "Intelligence came to the hands of a very considerable person,
that the king had attempted to get out of his window; and that he had a
cord of silk with him whereby to slip down, but his breast was so big that
the bar could not give him passage. This was done in one of the dark nights
about a fortnight ago. A gentleman with you led him the way and slipped
down. The guard, that night, had some quantity of wine with them. The
same party assures that there is aquafortis gone down from London, to
remove that obstacle which hindered; and that the same design is to be put
in execution on the next dark nights." He then points out that "Master
Firebrace" was the gentleman assisting the king; and mentions captain
Titus, and two others, who "are not to be trusted." It is probably to this
time that the statement of Clarendon must be referred, when he says that
the king "from thenceforth was no more suffered to go out of the castle

Carisbrook Castle; the window from which Charles I. attempted to escape.

beyond a little ill garden that belonged to it." His pleasant walks, upon the
beautiful green ramparts looking out upon the sea beyond the fertile valleys

about Carisbrook, were at an end. If the local traditions are to be trusted, the barred windows of his apartment had no prospect beyond the spacious court-yard. On the 31st of May, Hammond wrote to the Parliament that the king had again nearly effected his escape. Another dread now came over the Presbyterian party. They would negotiate with the king; but they would take strong measures against the Royalists. All papists and malignants were banished from London under more severe penalties than before. Fairfax was directed to proceed with all his forces against the insurgents in Kent and Essex and the other counties around London. They issued new ordinances against heresy, which affected the Independents; and against swearing, which touched the Cavaliers very nearly. The general and the army marched into Kent; dispersed the insurgents after an obstinate fight at Maidstone; and by rapid successes, wherever else there was resistance, put down the rising spirit. Lord Goring, after having led several thousand men to Blackheath, expecting assistance in London, was compelled to see the desertion of his followers, and he crossed the Thames into Essex. There the contest was more prolonged. Lord Capel and sir Charles Lucas had collected a large force, with which they intended to march from Colchester upon London. Fairfax invested the town; and for two months there was a renewal of the former work of blockade and siege, until the place was surrendered on the 27th of August. The triumph of Fairfax was tarnished by an exception to his usual humanity. Sir Charles Lucas and sir George Lisle were tried by court-martial, and were shot. The earl of Holland and the young duke of Buckingham broke out in revolt at Kingston-upon-Thames, when the main army of the Parliament was investing Colchester. There was an action near Kingston, in which they were defeated; and passing into Hertfordshire, the remnant was cut up at St. Neot's by a detachment from the army of Fairfax, and Holland was taken prisoner. In all these movements, we see the absence of any supreme organising power. They were isolated efforts, which were quickly suppressed. Whatever miseries England had still to endure, it was freed from the misery of a long partisan warfare. In Wales, where the resistance to the Parliament was more concentrated, the presence even of Cromwell was not at first successful. He is before Pembroke, but he has no artillery to make short work of the siege. It was not till the 10th of July that the town and castle of Pembroke were surrendered to him. Six days before the capitulation the Scottish army entered England, under the duke of Hamilton. He was joined by five thousand English, under sir Marmaduke Langdale. The English general, Lambert, was retreating before them, having been directed by Cromwell to avoid an engagement, and to fall back. Two days after the surrender of Pembroke, Cromwell was on his march from the west. He waited not for orders. He knew where he was wanted. At this juncture a charge of treason had been preferred against him by major Huntington, an officer of the army, which had been countenanced by some members of both Houses. He was accused of endeavouring, by betraying the king, parliament, and army, to advance himself. The occasion was not opportune for such an attempt. When he left London he was equally distasteful to the Presbyterians and the Commonwealth's men,—who, with some, went by the general name of Levellers. Mrs. Hutchinson says, " The chief of these Levellers following him out of the town, to take their leaves of him, received such professions from him, of a spirit bent to pursue the same just and honest things that they desired, as they went away with great satisfaction, till they heard that a coachful of Presbyterian priests coming after them, went away no less pleased: by which it was apparent he dissembled with one or the other, and by so doing lost his credit with both." * The Presbyterians suppressed their dislike to Cromwell in terror of the Scoto-royalist invasion. The Commonwealth's men were compelled to lay aside their jealousies. Ludlow speaks plainly about this:—"Some of us who had opposed the lieutenant-general's arbitrary proceedings, when we were convinced he acted to promote a selfish and unwarrantable design, now thinking ourselves obliged to strengthen his hands in that necessary work which he was appointed to undertake, writ a letter to him to encourage him, from the consideration of the justice of the cause wherein he was engaged, and the wickedness of those with whom he was to encounter, to proceed with cheerfulness, assuring him, that notwithstanding all our discouragements we would readily give him all the assistance we could."

The Scottish army that entered England could not be regarded as the army of the Scottish nation. The treaty which had been concluded with the king at Carisbrook gave satisfaction only to a portion of the Presbyterians. The Scottish Parliament, influenced by the duke of Hamilton and others, who professed moderate principles of ecclesiastical government, gave the engagements of that treaty their zealous support, especially that clause which provided that a military force should be sent to England to reinstate the king in his authority. They were in consequence called the "Engagers." But the clergy generally proclaimed that Charles had not conceded enough for the establishment of their form of worship in England to warrant a war for his assistance. The marquis of Argyle, and other powerful chiefs who had fought against Montrose, were burning with resentment against the Royalists of their own country, and were strenuously opposed to what was meant as an aid to the Royalists of England. An army was however raised; and the Engagers, with a raw and ill-disciplined force, crossed the Border.

The march of Cromwell, from the extremity of South Wales to the heart of Lancashire, was accomplished with a rapidity which belongs only to the movements of great commanders. He had to gather scattered forces on his way, and to unite himself with Lambert in Yorkshire. He was determined to engage with an enemy whose numbers were held to double his own. Through the whole breadth of South Wales, then a pastoral country, but now presenting all the unpicturesque combinations of mining industry, he advanced to Gloucester. This forced march of some hundred and fifty miles through Wales was an exhausting commencement. "Send me some shoes for my poor tired soldiers," wrote Cromwell to the Executive Committee in London. At Leicester he received three thousand pairs of shoes. At Nottingham he confers with colonel Hutchinson, and leaves his prisoners with him. His cavalry have pushed on, and have joined Lambert at Barnard Castle. All Cromwell's forces have joined the northern troops by the 12th

* "Memoirs," p. 129. Mrs. Hutchinson refers this to the time when "he was sent down, after his victory in Wales, to encounter Hamilton in the north." This is an evident mistake, for Cromwell marched from Pembroke by Gloucester and Warwick.

of August. The Scots, who, having passed Kendal, had debated whether they would march direct into Yorkshire, and so on towards London, have decided for the western road. The duke of Hamilton thinks he is sure of Manchester. Sir Marmaduke Langdale is their guide through the unknown ways into Lancashire, and leads the vanguard. There is very imperfect communication between the van and the rear of this army. On the 16th of August the duke is at Preston. The same night Cromwell is at Stonyhurst. Langdale, to the left of Hamilton's main body, has ascertained that the dangerous enemy is close at hand; and sends notice to the duke. "Impossible," exclaims Hamilton; "he has not had time to be here." The next morning Cromwell has fallen upon sir Marmaduke, and utterly routed him, "after a very sharp dispute." Hamilton's army is a disjointed one. His cavalry, in considerable numbers, are at Wigan, under the command of Middleton. When the affair was settled with Langdale, there was a skirmish close by Preston town between Hamilton himself and some of Cromwell's troopers. The duke was separated from his main force of infantry, under Baillie, but rejoined them only to see the bridge of the Ribble won by the enemy in a general battle. Cromwell describes the first four hours' fighting in a country all enclosure and miry ground, as "a hedge dispute." This being ended, the Scots were charged through Preston; and then not only was the bridge of the Ribble won, but the bridge of Darwen. Night was approaching, which put an end to any further fighting on the 17th. The Scottish generals in a council of war determined to march off, as soon as it was dark, without waiting for Middleton and his cavalry. The weather was rainy; the roads heavy; their men were wet, weary, and hungry. They left their ammunition behind; and the next morning were at Wigan Moor, with half their number. No general engagement took place that day; and the Scots held Wigan. Cromwell writes, "We lay that night in the field close by the enemy; being very dirty and weary, and having marched twelve miles of such ground as I never rode in all my life, the day being very wet." The next day the Scots moved towards Warrington; and after some hard fighting, general Baillie surrendered himself, officers, and soldiers, as prisoners of war. The duke, with three thousand horse, was gone towards Nantwich. His course was undetermined. The country people were hostile. His own men were mutinous. He surrenders to Lambert, and is sent prisoner to Nottingham. The Scottish army was now utterly broken and dispersed. The news of Hamilton's complete failure in the invasion of England was the signal for the great Presbyterian party that had opposed the policy of the Engagers to rise in arms. Argyle assembled his Highland clans. In the Western Lowlands large bodies of peasantry, headed by their preachers, marched to Edinburgh. The memory of this insurrection has endured to this hour in the name of *Whig*. It was called "the Whiggamore Raid," from the word used in the west of Scotland when the carter urges forward his horses with *Whig*, *whig* (get on); as the English carter says, *Gee*, *gee* (go). Argyle was restored to power. The most zealous Covenanters were again at the head of the executive authority. Cromwell entered Scotland on the 20th September, and was received at Edinburgh, not as the man to whose might their brave countrymen had been compelled to yield; but as the deliverer from a royalist faction that might again have put the national religion in peril.

NOTE ON THE PARTY-SPIRIT DURING THE ROYALIST RE-ACTION.

We have shown the temper of the Presbyterians and Commonwealth's men towards Cromwell when he was fighting in Wales and Lancashire. There was a general confusion of political principles in the dread of individual supremacy. May says that the chief citizens of London, and others called Presbyterians, wished good success to the Scots no less than the Malignants did. Mr. Hallam has observed that "the fugitive sheets of this year, such as the Mercurius Aulicus, bear witness to the exulting and insolent tone of the royalists. They chuckle over Fairfax and Cromwell, as if they had caught a couple of rats in a trap." As a curious specimen of the "fugitive sheets," we give an extract from "The Cuckow's Nest at Westminster; printed at Cuckow-time in a hollow tree, 1648." [*] The chief wit consists in a dialogue between Queen Fairfax and Lady Cromwell. Fairfax had been ill, and was reported to have died :—

"*Enter* QUEEN FAIRFAX *and* MADAM CROMWELL.

"*Mrs. Cromwell.* Cheer up, madam, he is not dead, he is reserved for another end ; these wicked malignants reported as much of my Noll, but I hope it is otherwise ; yet the profane writ an epitaph, as I think they call it, and abused him most abominably, as they will do me, or you, or any of the faithful saints, if we but thrive by our occupations in our husbands' absence ; if we but deck our bodies with the jewels gained from the wicked, they point at us, and say, those are plunder. But the righteous must undergo the scoffs of the wicked ; and let them scoff on. I thank my Maker, we lived, before these holy wars were thought on, in the thriving profession of brewing, and could, of my vails of grain and yeast, wear my silk gown, and gold and silver lace too, as well as the proudest minx of them all. I am not ashamed of my profession, madam.

"*Qu. Fair.* Pray, Mrs. Cromwell, tell not me of gowns or lace, nor no such toys ! Tell me of crowns, sceptres, kingdoms, royal robes ; and, if my Tom but recovers, and thrives in his enterprise, I will not say, pish, to be queen of England. I misdoubt nothing, if we can but keep the wicked from fetching Nebuchadnezzar's home from grass in the Isle of Wight. Well, well, my Tom is worth a thousand of him, and has a more kingly countenance ; he has such an innocent face, and a harmless look, as if he were born to be emperor over the saints.

"*Mrs. Cromwell.* And is not Noll Cromwell's wife as likely a woman to be queen of England as you ? yes, I warrant you, is she ; and that you shall know, if my husband were but once come out of Wales. It is he that has done the work, the conquest belongs to him. Besides, your husband is counted a fool, and wants wit to reign ; every boy scoffs at him : my Noll has a head-piece, a face of brass, full of majesty, and a nose will light the whole kingdom to walk after him. I say he will grace a crown, being naturally adorned with diamonds and rubies already ; and, for myself, though I say it, I have a person as fit for a queen as another."

The dialogue is broken off by a servant running in, and exclaiming, "O, madam, cease your contention, and provide for your safeties ; both your husbands are killed, and all their forces put to the sword ; all the people crying like mad, long live King Charles !"

[*] Reprinted in "Harleian Miscellany," 8vo, vol. vi.

St. James's Park.

CHAPTER VII.

WHEN the news of Cromwell's victory at Preston came to the Isle of Wight, "the king said to the governor that it was the worst news that ever came to England." Colonel Hammond replied, that if Hamilton had beaten the English he would have possessed himself of the thrones of England and Scotland. "You are mistaken," said the king; "I could have commanded him back with a wave of my hand." * It was evil news to the king that the last appeal to arms had failed. The Parliament now looked with as much alarm as the king might entertain at the approaching return of that victorious Army of the North. The Lords, especially, saw that their own power was imperilled by the dangers that beset the Crown; and they united with those who now constituted a majority in the Commons, to conclude a treaty with the king. There were violent debates; but it was at length agreed that commissioners should proceed to the Isle of Wight. The discussions were to take place in Newport. The commissioners for the treaty arrived there on the 15th of September. Clarendon says that those who wished ill to the treaty interposed every delay to prevent it being concluded during the

* Ludlow, vol. i. p. 261.

absence of Cromwell; and that those who wished well to it pressed it forward for the same reason. Yet there were men left behind who had formed as strong resolutions against the restoration of Charles to power as Cromwell himself. Ludlow had been to Fairfax at Colchester whilst the treaty was debated in Parliament, to urge upon him that it was not intended by those who pressed it on most vehemently, that the king should be bound to the performance of it; but that it was designed principally to use his authority to destroy the Army. Fairfax was irresolute. Ireton agreed with Ludlow that it was necessary for the Army to interpose; but did not think that the time was come for such a demonstration. With an Army ready to step in to break through the meshes of any agreement disapproved by them—with a king who in the midst of the negotiation was secretly writing, "my great concession this morning was made only to facilitate my approaching escape "— the Treaty of Newport can scarcely be regarded as more than "a piece of Dramaturgy which must be handsomely done." * For the opening of the last Act of this tragic history, the scene on the bank of the Medina is as impressive as any pageant, "full of state and woe," that the imagination could devise to precede a solemn catastrophe.

A house has been prepared in Newport for the king's reception; and its hall has been fitted up for this great negotiation, which might extend to forty days. The first day was the 18th of September. The king is seated under a canopy at the upper end of the hall. The parliamentary commissioners are placed round a table in advance of the royal chair. These are fifteen in number, five peers, and ten members of the Lower House. Behind the king are ranged many of his most confidential friends and advisers; of whom there are four peers, two bishops and other divines; five civilians; and four of his trusted attendants. Sir Philip Warwick, who was one of the privileged number, says :—" But if at any time the king found himself in need to ask a question, or any of his lords thought fit to advise him in his ear to hesitate before he answered, he himself would retire into his own chamber; or one of us penmen, who stood at his chair, prayed him from the lords to do so." The king was in a position favourable to the display of his talent for discussion ; and he left upon the assembly during these tedious debates, a deep impression of his abilities, his knowledge, and his presence of mind. Nor could the sympathies of even the most prejudiced of his auditors on this occasion be withheld from his general appearance and deportment. His hair had become gray; his face was care-worn; " he was not dejected," writes Clarendon, " but carried himself with the same majesty he had used to do." Certainly if it be held somewhat an unequal trial to place one man to contend alone against fifteen disputants, some of extraordinary ability, such as Vane; on the other hand the rank of him who was thus pleading for what he believed to be his inalienable rights—his misfortunes—his display of mental powers, for which few had given him credit—would produce impressions far deeper than if the advisers around his canopy had been allowed to argue and harangue, each after his own fashion. " One day," says Warwick, " whilst I turned the king's chair when he was about to rise, the earl of Salisbury came suddenly upon me, and said, 'The king is wonderfully improved :' to which I as sud-

* Carlyle.

denly replied, 'No, my lord, he was always so; but your lordship too late discerned it." Vane bore testimony to the talent of Charles; but he considered his "great parts and abilities" as a reason for very stringent terms. In this manner was the prolonged discussion of Newport conducted, from the 18th of September to the 29th of November, the original term of forty days for the duration of the treaty having been three times extended. All was in vain. Charles had conceded the questions of military command and of nomination to the great offices of state; he had even consented to acknowledge the legitimacy of the resistance to his power. But he had not conceded enough upon the question of religion to satisfy the more violent of the Presbyterians. There was unwise pertinacity on both sides, in the hour of a coming storm that would sweep away this paper-fabric of a Newport treaty like straws in a whirlwind. The commissioners had no absolute power to conclude a Treaty; the Parliament discussed every point with a scrupulosity that foreboded no good result. Warwick records a speech of the king to Mr. Buckley, one of the commissioners, which shows how impracticable was a speedy agreement: "Consider, Mr. Buckley, if you call this a Treaty, whether it be not like the fray in the comedy; where the man comes out, and says, there has been a fray, and no fray; and being asked how that could be, why, says he, there hath been three blows given, and I had them all. Look, therefore, whether this be not a parallel case. Observe, whether I have not granted absolutely most of your propositions, and with great moderation limited only some few of them: nay consider, whether you have made me any one concession, and whether at this present moment you have not confessed to me, that though upon any proposition you were all concurrently satisfied, yet till you had remitted them up to your superiors, you had not authority to concur with me in any one thing." * The conferences were broken up, after the most violent demonstrations had been made to Parliament of the temper of the Army. On the 28th of November the commissioners left Newport with the definitive propositions. In forty-eight hours it had become evident that two months had been wasted in vain contentions; that an inexorable fate was driving on to a dismal end of the long struggle between king and people.

Warwick has recorded that, during the progress of the Treaty, "every night, when the king was alone about eight of the clock, except when he was writing his own private letters, he commanded me to come to him; and he looked over the notes of that day's treaty, and the reasons upon which it moved; and so dictated the heads of a dispatch, which from time to time he made concerning the treaty, unto his present majesty, then prince." Clarendon drew up his minute account of the negotiation from these papers; and he gives a long and very interesting extract of a letter from the king to prince Charles, which he says, "deserves to be preserved in letters of gold." The sentiments which it breathes are certainly high-minded; but they also proclaim to what an extent the king was a self-deceiver. He writes, " by what hath been said, you see how long we have laboured in search of peace." He had solemnly promised during the negotiations that all hostilities in Ireland for his cause should be put an end to. At the very same time he wrote to the earl of Ormond, "Obey my wife's orders, not mine, until I

* "Memoirs," p. 323.

shall let you know I am free from all restraint; nor trouble yourself about my concessions as to Ireland; they will lead to nothing." Charles goes on to say to his son, " Censure us not for having parted with so much of our own right; the price was great, but the commodity was security to us, peace to our people." In his heart he felt that he had really not parted with anything. " We were confident," he says, " another parliament would remember how useful a king's power is to a people's liberty; of how much thereof we divested ourself, that we and they might meet once again in a due parliamentary way, to agree the bounds of prince and people." The unhappy monarch appears to have forgotten that " the bounds of prince and people " were agreed, " in a due parliamentary way," by the Petition of Right; and that from the day in 1629 when he declared that he would depart from that due way, making the free monarchy of England absolute, the terrible misfortunes that he had endured during seven years of Civil War were the price that he had to pay for eleven previous years of despotism. He draws a true lesson from the tyranny of others : " These men, who have forced laws which they were bound to preserve, will find their triumphs full of troubles." His prayer for his subjects " that the ancient laws, with the interpretation according to the known practice, might once more be a hedge about them," might have been more opportune when the ancient hedge was first broken down by the ministers of his own aggressions. But, with all this forgetfulness of the errors of the past, its sad lessons are not wholly forgotten, when he says, " Give belief to our experience, never to affect more greatness or prerogative than that which is intrinsically and really for the good of subjects, not the satisfaction of favorites." *

A week before the termination of the conferences at Newport, the Army from St. Alban's sends a " Remonstrance " to the Commons,—an unmistakeable document,—calling upon the Parliament to bring the king to trial; and to decree that the future king should be elected by the representatives of the people. It was distinctly intimated that if the Parliament neglected the interests of the nation, the Army would take the matter into their own hands. There was naturally a great commotion in the House; and the debate upon this " Remonstrance " was adjourned for a week. At about the end of that time the commissioners from Newport have made their report; and after twenty-four hours of debate it is voted that the king's concessions offered a ground for a future settlement. On the 25th of November the army of Fairfax is at Windsor. Cromwell had returned from Scotland, to the north of England, on the 11th of October. He is busily engaged in military affairs. The royalist governor of Pontefract refuses to surrender. A party from the garrison have sallied out on the 29th of October, and assassinated the parliamentary colonel Rainsborough, in his lodging at Doncaster. The Northern Army is badly off for shoes, stockings, and clothes, as Cromwell writes; but they are all full of zeal, and petition the General of the Army against the Treaty at Newport, which petition Cromwell forwards to Fairfax on the 20th of November, saying, " I find in the officers of the regiments a very great sense of the sufferings of this poor kingdom; and in them all a very great zeal to have impartial justice done upon offenders." There are nevertheless doubts

* Clarendon, vol. vi. p. 189—191.

and misgivings in the breasts of some Army men, as we may judge from a letter of Oliver to that "ingenuous young man," his friend colonel Hammond, at Carisbrook. who has expressed his dissatisfaction at the principle that "it is lawful for a lesser part, if in the right, to force a numerical majority." The king told sir Philip Warwick that the Governor was such a rogue that he could not be in worse hands. Though the Governor was faithful to his trust, he yet had a conscientious doubt whether the Army had a right to determine the great question at issue. The letter of Cromwell is dated from Pontefract on the 25th of November. It is altogether so characteristic of this extraordinary man, and moreover so strikingly illustrative of the nature of the principles by which he and many others were driving forward to perpetrate acts of violence and illegality, under a belief that they were moved by holy and just inspirations, that we may not unprofitably peruse one or two of its more striking passages :—

"You say: 'God hath appointed authorities among the nations, to which active or passive obedience is to be yielded. This resides, in England, in the Parliament. Therefore active or passive resistance,' &c. Authorities and powers are the ordinance of God. This or that species is of human institution, and limited, some with larger, others with stricter bands, each one according to its constitution. But I do not therefore think that the Authorities may do anything, and yet such obedience be due. All agree that there are cases in which it is lawful to resist. If so, your ground fails, and so likewise the inference. Indeed, dear Robin, not to multiply words, the query is, Whether ours be such a case? This ingenuously is the true question. To this I shall say nothing, though I could say very much : but only desire thee to see what thou findest in thy own heart to two or three plain considerations. *First*, Whether *Salus Populi* be a sound position? *Secondly*, Whether in the way in hand, really and before the Lord, before whom conscience has to stand, this be provided for ;—or if the whole fruit of the War is not like to be frustrated, and all most like to turn to what it was, and worse? And this, contrary to Engagements, explicit Covenants with those who ventured their lives upon those Covenants and Engagements, without whom perhaps, in equity, relaxation ought not to be? *Thirdly*, Whether this Army be not a lawful Power, called by God to oppose and fight against the king upon some stated grounds ; and being in power to such ends, may not oppose one Name of Authority, for those ends, as well as another Name, —since it was not the outward Authority summoning them that by *its* power made the quarrel lawful, but the quarrel was lawful in itself? If so, it may be, acting will be justified *in foro humano*. But truly this kind of reasonings may be but fleshly, either with or against : only it is good to try what truth may be in them. And the Lord teach us." . . . . "We in this Northern Army were in a waiting posture; desiring to see what the Lord would lead us to. And a Declaration [Remonstrance] is put out, at which many are shaken : —although we could perhaps have wished the stay of it till after the treaty, yet seeing it is come out, we trust to rejoice in the will of the Lord, waiting His further pleasure. Dear Robin, beware of men; look up to the Lord. Let Him be free to speak and command in thy heart. Take heed of the things I fear thou hast reasoned thyself into ; and thou shalt be able through Him, without consulting flesh and blood, to do valiantly for Him and His people." . . . . "Dost thou not think this fear of the Levellers (of whom there is no fear) 'that they would destroy Nobility,' &c., has caused some to take up corruption, and find it lawful to make this ruining hypocritical Agreement, on one part? Hath not this biassed even some good men? I will not say the thing they fear will come upon them; but if it do, they will themselves bring it upon themselves. Have not some of our friends, by their passive principle (which I judge not, only I think it liable to temptation as well as the active, and neither of them to be reasoned into, because the heart is deceitful),—been occasioned to overlook what is just and honest, and to think the people of God may have as much or more good the one way than the other? Good by this Man,—against whom the Lord hath witnessed: and whom thou knowest!"

On the 25th of November, the day on which Cromwell's letter is dated, colonel Hammond was directed to give up his post in the Isle of Wight to another officer, and return to the Army. The king had remained in the house at Newport in which the Treaty was conducted, when the commissioners quitted the town. On the evening of the 29th of November, the king was surrounded by several of the noblemen and others who had been with him during the conferences. A report came to them that troops had landed in the island; and the fact was ascertained by one of Charles' attendants, colonel Cook. He had ridden to Carisbrook and to the coast. When he returned about midnight the king's house was surrounded by soldiers; and its very passages were filled with armed men, their matches lighted. Cook entered the king's apartments, wet and wearied. The king's friends were persuading him to attempt to escape, at all risks; and Cook told him that horses were at hand and a vessel off the coast. Charles now hesitates to break his parole; yet he had given it to Hammond, and had attempted to break it on several occasions. The resignation of despair had now come over the unhappy king. He went to bed. At daybreak there was an alarm at his door. A colonel was there with a guard; and when the door was opened, the king was told by him that he had orders to remove him to Hurst Castle. They could not have named a worse place, said Charles. He apprehended assassination; and this castle at the mouth of the Solent,—which Warwick describes as " a place which stood on the sea, for at every tide the water surrounded it, and contained only a few dog-lodgings for soldiers,"—was more fitted for a deed of darkness than Berkeley or Pontefract, where deposed kings had perished. On that 30th of November, the Parliament had voted that they would not take the " Remonstrance " of the Army into consideration. The Army is at Windsor. On Saturday, the 2nd of December, it is on its march to London; and before night is quartered in Whitehall, St. James's, and the suburbs. That Sunday must have been a day of fear and anxious curiosity. Presbyterian preachers setting forth the atrocity of the seizure of the king. Zealous soldiers, gifted with the power of eloquence, haranguing crowds in the parks. " For Tophet is ordained of old; yea, for the king it is prepared," was the text of many a field-preaching of that Sabbath. On the Monday the Commons are debating all day—they are debating till five o'clock on Tuesday morning the 5th,—whether the king's concessions in the Treaty of Newport are a ground of settlement. The practised orators have been heard again and again on this great question. There is an old man amongst them—one who has only been a member three weeks—

who boldly stands up for the cause of fallen majesty. He is no royal favourite, he says. The favours he has received from the king and his party were, the loss of his two ears,—his pillorings, his imprisonments, his fines. It was Prynne, who spoke for hours ; with honest energy, but with no great prudence when he described the Army at their very doors as " inconstant, mutinous, and unreasonable servants." Yet, whatever might have been the effect of this learned man's courageous effort for reconciliation, the very recital of his ancient sufferings must have revived in some a bitter recollection of past tyrannies, and a corresponding dread of their return. The House decided, by one hundred and twenty-nine to eighty-three, that the king's concessions are a ground of settlement. There was another assembly on the same day whose resolutions at that moment were of more importance even than a vote of the Commons. " Some of the principal officers of the Army came to London with expectation that things would be brought to this issue, and consulting with some members of parliament and others, it was concluded, after a full and free debate, that the measures taken by the Parliament were contrary to the trust reposed in them, and tending to contract the guilt of the blood that had been shed, upon themselves and the nation : that it was therefore the duty of the Army to endeavour to put a stop to such proceedings." * They went about this work in a very business-like manner. " Three of the members of the House, and three of the officers of the Army, withdrew into a private room to attain the ends of our said Resolution ; when we agreed that the army should be drawn up the next morning, and guards placed in Westminster hall, the Court of Requests, and the Lobby; that none might be permitted to pass into the House but such as continued faithful to the public interests. To this end we went over the names of all the members, one by one.   .   .   .   Commissary general Ireton went to sir Thomas Fairfax, and acquainted him with the necessity of this extraordinary way of proceeding." † Lieutenant-general Cromwell is still in the North.

What was thus deliberately resolved on the 6th of December was as promptly effected on the 7th. An order is given that the trained bands of the city shall withdraw from their accustomed duty of guard at Westminster. Colonel Rich's regiment of horse take up a position on that morning in Palace Yard. Colonel Pride's regiment of foot throng Westminster Hall, and block up every entrance to the House of Commons. Colonel Pride has a written list of names in his hand,—the names of those against whom the sentence of exclusion has been passed. As the members of the House approach, lord Grey of Groby, who stands at the elbow of colonel Pride, gives a sign or word that such a one is to pass, or to be turned back. Forty-one were ordered that day to retire to " the Queen's Court." It is easier to imagine than to describe the indignation expressed by the ejected. They are kept under restraint all the day ; and in the evening are conducted to a tavern. There were two taverns abutting upon and partly under, the Hall, known as " Heaven " and " Hell,"—very ancient places of refreshment much used by the lawyers in term-time; mentioned by Ben Jonson; and which, with a third house called " Purgatory," are recited in a grant of the time of Henry VII.‡ To " Hell," perhaps without the intention of a bad joke, these

---

* Ludlow, "Memoirs," vol. i. p. 269.   † Ibid. p. 270.
‡ Gifford. Notes to " Alchemist,"—Jonson's Works, vol. iv. p. 174.

forty-one of the parliamentary majority were led, and lodged for the night. The process went on for several days; till some hundred members are disposed of. Before the minority have obtained an entire ascendancy, colonel Pride is questioned for his conduct; but no satisfaction is given. The House makes a show of disapprobation; but the Serjeant-at-arms has brought a message that the excluded members are detained by the Army; and business proceeds as if the event were of small consequence. Cromwell has arrived on the night after the sharp medicine known as "Pride's purge" has been administered; and "lay at Whitehall, where, and at other places, he declared that he had not been acquainted with this design; yet since it was done he was glad of it, and would endeavour to maintain it." * Vane, who had spoken vehemently in the great debate of the 4th, against accepting the king's concessions as a ground of settlement, even boldly proclaiming himself for a republic, appears to have taken no part in the illegal proceedings which laid the Parliament at the feet of the Army. He retired to his estate, and did not come again to Parliament till a month after the final blow against monarchy had been struck. "Young Vane" has had justice done to his lofty capacity in being classed with the "great men" who "have been among us"— "hands that penned and tongues that uttered wisdom."† Yet his conduct in this crisis can scarcely be attributed to his high-mindedness; and probably Mrs. Hutchinson points to him, in saying, "I know upon certain knowledge that many, yea the most part of them, retreated not for conscience, but for fear and worldly prudence, foreseeing that the insolence of the Army might grow to that height as to ruin the cause, and reduce the kingdom into the hands of the enemy; and then those who had been most courageous in their country's cause should be given up as victims. These poor men did privately animate those who appeared most publicly."‡ The parliamentary minority, being now almost unanimous in their resolve to overthrow the existing government, though perhaps not yet agreed as to the mode of accomplishing this as far as regarded the person of the king, voted to rescind all the votes which had recently passed as to the grounds of a settlement. Another act of military power soon marshalled the way to a resolution of such doubts.

The drawbridge of Hurst Castle is lowered during the night of the 17th of December, and the tramp of a troop of horse is heard by the wakeful prisoner. He calls for his attendant Herbert, who is sent to ascertain the cause of this midnight commotion. Major Harrison is arrived. The king is agitated. He has been warned that Harrison is a man chosen to assassinate him. He is re-assured in the morning, in being informed that the major and his troop are to conduct him to Windsor. Two days after, the king sets out, under the escort of lieutenant-colonel Cobbett. At Winchester he is received in state by the mayor and aldermen; but they retire alarmed on being told that the House has voted all to be traitors who should address the king. The troop commanded by Cobbett has been relieved on the route by another troop, of which Harrison has the command. They rest at Farnham. Charles expresses to Harrison, with whose soldierly appearance he is struck, the suspicions which had been hinted regarding him. The major, in his new buff coat and fringed scarf of crimson silk, told the king "that he needed not to entertain

* Ludlow, vol. i. p. 272.   † Wordsworth.   ‡ "Memoirs," vol. ii. p. 158.

any such imagination or apprehension; that the Parliament had too much honour and justice to cherish so foul an intention; and assured him, that whatever the Parliament resolved to do would be very public, and in a way of justice, to which the world should be witness; and would never endure a thought of secret violence." This, adds Clarendon, "his majesty could not persuade himself to believe; nor did imagine that they durst ever produce him in the sight of the people, under any form whatsoever of a public trial."* The next day the journey was pursued towards Windsor. The king urged his desire to stop at Bagshot, and dine in the Forest at the house of lord Newburgh. He had been apprised that his friend would have ready for him a horse of extraordinary fleetness, with which he might make one more effort to escape. The horse had been kicked by another horse the day before, and was useless. That last faint hope was gone. On the night of the 23rd of December the king slept, a prisoner surrounded with hostile guards, in the noble castle which in the days of his youth had rung with Jonson's lyrics and ribaldry; and the Gipsy of the Masque had prophesied that his "name in peace or wars, nought should bound."† But even here he continued to cherish some of the delusions which he had indulged in situations of far less danger. He was still surrounded with something of regal pomp. He dined, as the ancient sovereigns had dined, in public—as Elizabeth, and his father, and he himself had dined, seated under a canopy, the cup presented to him on the knee, the dishes solemnly tasted before he ate. These manifestations of respect he held to be indicative of an altered feeling. But he also had an undoubting confidence that he should be righted, by aid from Ireland, from Denmark, from other kingdoms: "I have three more cards to play, the worst of which will give me back everything." After three weeks of comparative comfort, the etiquette observed towards him was laid aside; and with a fearful sense of approaching calamity in the absence of "respect and honour, according to the ancient practice," he exclaimed, "is there anything more contemptible than a despised prince?"

During the month in which Charles had remained at Windsor, there had been proceedings in Parliament of which he was imperfectly informed. On the day he arrived there, it was resolved by the Commons that he should be brought to trial. On the 2nd of January, 1649, it was voted that, in making war against the Parliament, he had been guilty of treason; and a High Court was appointed to try him. One hundred and fifty commissioners were to compose the Court,—peers, members of the Commons, aldermen of London. The ordinance was sent to the Upper House, and was rejected. On the 6th, a fresh ordinance, declaring that the people being, after God, the source of all just power, the representatives of the people are the supreme power in the nation; and that whatsoever is enacted or declared for law by the Commons in Parliament hath the force of a law, and the people are concluded thereby, though the consent of King or Peers be not had thereto. Asserting this power, so utterly opposed either to the ancient constitution of the monarchy, or to the possible working of a republic, there was no hesitation in constituting the High Court of Justice in the name of the Commons alone. The number of members of the Court was now reduced to one hundred and

---

* "Rebellion," vol. vi. p. 223.   † "Gipsies Metamorphosed."

thirty-five. They had seven preparatory meetings, at which only fifty-eight members attended. "All men," says Mrs. Hutchinson, "were left to their free liberty of acting, neither persuaded nor compelled; and as there were some nominated in the commission who never sat, and others who sat at first but durst not hold on, so all the rest might have declined it if they would, when it is apparent they should have suffered nothing by so doing." * Algernon Sidney, although bent upon a republic, opposed the trial, apprehending that the project of a commonwealth would fail, if the king's life were touched. It is related that Cromwell, irritated by these scruples, exclaimed, "No one will stir. I tell you, we will cut his head off with the crown upon it." Such daring may appear the result of ambition, or fear, or revenge, or innate cruelty, in a few men who had obtained a temporary ascendancy. These men were, on the contrary, the organs of a wide-spread determination amongst thousands throughout the country, who had long preached and argued and prophesied about vengeance on "the great delinquent;" and who had ever in their mouths the text that "blood defileth the land, and the land cannot be cleansed of the blood that is shed therein, but by the blood of him that shed it." † They had visions of a theocracy, and were impatient of an earthly king.

Do we believe, as some, not without reasonable grounds, may believe, that the members of the High Court of Justice expressed such convictions upon a simulated religious confidence? Do we think that, in the clear line of action which Cromwell especially had laid down for his guidance, he cloaked his worldly ambition under the guise of being moved by some higher impulse than that of taking the lead in a political revolution? Certainly we do not. The infinite mischiefs of assuming that the finger of God directly points out the way to believers, when they are walking in dangerous and devious paths, may be perfectly clear to us, who calmly look back upon the instant events which followed upon Cromwell's confidence in his solemn call to a fearful duty. But we are not the more to believe, because the events have a character of guilt in the views of most persons, that such a declared conviction was altogether, or in any degree, a lie. Those were times in which, more for good than for evil, men believed in the immediate direction of a special Providence in great undertakings. The words, "God hath given us the victory," were not with them a mere form. If we trace amidst these solemn impulses the workings of a deep sagacity—the union of the fierce resolves of a terrible enthusiasm with the foresight and energy of an ever-present common sense—we are not the more to conclude that their spiritualism, or fanaticism, or whatever we please to call their ruling principle, was less sincere by being mixed up with the ordinary motives through which the affairs of the world are carried on. Indeed, when we look to the future course of English history, and see—as those who have no belief in a higher direction of the destiny of nations than that of human wisdom can alone turn away from seeing—that the inscrutable workings of a supreme Power led our country in the fullness of time to internal peace and security after these storms, and in a great degree in consequence of them, can we refuse our belief that the tragical events of those days were ordered for our good?

* "Memoirs," p. 158.
† Ludlow uses this text from "Numbers," c. xxxv., in explaining his convictions.

Acknowledging that the overthrow of a rotten throne was necessary for the building up of a throne that should have its sole stable foundation in the welfare of the people, can we affirm that the men who did the mightier portion of that work,—sternly, unflinchingly, illegally, yet ever professing to "seek to know the mind of God in all that chain of Providence,"—are quite correctly described in the Statute for their attainder, as "a party of wretched men, desperately wicked, and hardened in their impiety."

On the 19th of January, major Harrison appeared again at Windsor with his troop. There was a coach with six horses in the court-yard, in which the king took his seat; and, once more, he entered London, and was lodged at St. James's palace. The next day, the High Court of Justice was opened in Westminster-hall. An engraving, on which is inscribed "The pageant of this mock tribunal is thus represented to your view by an eye-and-ear witness of what he saw and heard there," furnishes a clearer notion of the arrangements than many words can convey. The king came from St. James's in a sedan; and after the names of the members of the court had been called, sixty-nine being present, Bradshaw, the president, ordered the serjeant to ·bring in the prisoner. Silently the king sat down in the chair prepared for him. He moved not his· hat, as he looked sternly and contemptuously around. The sixty-nine rose not from their seats, and remained covered. It is scarcely eight years since he was a spectator of the last solemn trial in this hall—that of Strafford. What mighty events have happened since that time! There are memorials hanging from the roof which tell such a history as his saddest fears in the hour of Strafford's death could scarcely have shaped out. The tattered banners taken from his Cavaliers at Marston-moor and Naseby are floating above his head. There, too, are the same memorials of Preston. But still he looks around him proudly and severely. Who are the men that are to judge him, the king, who "united in his person every possible claim by hereditary right to the English as well as the Scottish throne, being the heir both of Egbert and William the Conqueror?" * These men are, in his view, traitors and rebels, from Bradshaw, the lawyer, who sits in the foremost chair calling himself lord-president, to Cromwell and Marten in the back seat, over whose heads are the red-cross of England and the harp of Ireland, painted on an escutcheon, whilst the proud bearings of a line of kings are nowhere visible. Under what law does this insolent president address him as "Charles Stuart, king of England," and say, "The Commons of England being deeply sensible of the calamities that have been brought upon this nation, which are fixed upon you as the principal author of them, have resolved to make inquisition for blood?" He will defy their authority. The clerk reads the charge, and when he is accused therein of being tyrant and traitor, he laughs in the face of the Court. "Though his tongue usually hesitated, yet it was very free at this time, for he was never discomposed in mind," writes Warwick. "And yet," it is added, "as he confessed himself to the bishop of London that attended him, one action shocked him very much: for whilst he was leaning in the Court upon his staff, which had a head of gold, the head broke off on a sudden. He took it up, but seemed unconcerned, yet told the bishop it .really made a great

---

* Blackstone, book i. c. iii., p. 196, Kerr's edition.

impression upon him." It was the symbol of the treacherous hopes upon which he had rested,—golden dreams that vanished in this solemn hour

Trial of Charles I. (From a Print in Nalson's Report of the Trial, 1684.)

A, the King.   B, the Lord President Bradshaw.   C, John Lisle ;   D, William Say ;   Bradshaw's assistants. E, Andrew Broughton ;   F, John Phelps ;   clerks of the court.   G, Oliver Cromwell ;   H, Henry Marten ;   the Arms of the Commonwealth over them.   I, Coke ;   K, Dorislaus ;   L, Aske ;   Counsellors for the Commonwealth.   The description of the plate ends with these words :—" The pageant of this mock tribunal is thus represented to your view by an eye and ear-witness of what he heard and saw there."

Again and again contending against the authority of the Court, the king was removed, and the sitting was adjourned to the 22nd.   On that day the same scene was renewed ; and again on the 23rd.   A growing sympathy for the monarch became apparent.   The cries of " Justice, justice," which were heard at first, were now mingled with "God save the king." He had refused to plead; but the Court nevertheless employed the 24th and 25th of January in collecting evidence to prove the charge of his levying war against the Parliament. Coke, the solicitor-general, then demanded whether the Court would proceed to pronouncing sentence; and the members adjourned to the Painted Chamber. On the 27th the public sitting was resumed. When the name of Fairfax was called, a voice was heard from the gallery, "He has too much wit to be here." The king was brought in; and, when the president addressed the commissioners, and said that the prisoner was before the Court to answer a charge of high treason, and other crimes brought against him in the name of the people of England, the voice from the gallery was again heard, "It's a lie—not one half of them." The voice came from lady Fairfax. The Court, Bradshaw then stated, had agreed upon the sentence. Ludlow records that the king "desired to make one proposition before they proceeded to sentence; which he earnestly pressing, as that which he thought would lead to the reconciling of all parties, and to the peace of the three kingdoms, they permitted him to offer it: the effect of which was, that he might meet the two Houses in the Painted Chamber, to whom he doubted not to offer that which should satisfy and secure all interests." Ludlow goes on to say, "Designing, as I have been since informed, to propose his own resignation, and the admission of his son to the throne upon such terms as should have been agreed upon." * The commissioners retired to deliberate, "and being satisfied, upon debate, that nothing but loss of time would be the consequence of it, they returned into the Court with a negative to his demand." Bradshaw then delivered a solemn speech to the king, declaring how he had through his reign endeavoured to subvert the laws and introduce arbitrary government; how he had attempted, from the beginning, either to destroy Parliaments, or to render them subservient to his own designs; how he had levied war against the Parliament, by the terror of his power to discourage for ever such assemblies from doing their duty, and that in this war many thousands of the good people of England had lost their lives. The clerk was lastly commanded to read the sentence, that his head should be severed from his body; "and the commissioners," says Ludlow, "testified their unanimous assent by standing up." The king attempted to speak; "but being accounted dead in law, was not permitted."

On the 29th of January, the Court met to sign the sentence of execution; addressed to "colonel Francis Hacker, colonel Huncks, and lieutenant-colonel Phayr, and to every one of them." This is the memorable document:—

"Whereas Charles Stuart, king of England, is and standeth convicted, attainted and condemned of High Treason and other high Crimes: and Sentence upon Saturday last was pronounced against him by this Court, to be put to death by the severing of his head from his body; of which Sentence execution remaineth to be done:

"These are therefore to will and require you to see the said Sentence executed, in the open street before Whitehall, upon the morrow, being the

* "Memoirs," vol. i. p. 280.

thirtieth day of this instant month of January, between the hours of ten in the morning and five in the afternoon with full effect. And for so doing, this shall be your warrant.

"And these are to require all Officers and Soldiers, and others the good People of this Nation of England, to be assisting unto you in this service.

"Given under our hands and seals,

                                    " JOHN BRADSHAW.
                                    " THOMAS GREY.
                                    " OLIVER CROMWELL."
                                              And fifty-six others.

The statements of the heartless buffoonery, and the daring violence of Cromwell, at the time of signing the warrant, must be received with some suspicion. He smeared Henry Marten's face with the ink of his pen, and Marten in return smeared his, say the narratives. Probably so. With reference to this anecdote it has been wisely observed, " Such ' toys of desperation ' commonly bubble up from a deep flowing stream below." [*] Another anecdote is told by Clarendon; that colonel Ingoldsby, one who signed the warrant, was forced to do so with great violence, by Cromwell and others; " and Cromwell, with a loud laughter, taking his hand in his, and putting the pen between his fingers, with his own hand writ ' Richard Ingoldsby,' he making all the resistance he could." Ingoldsby gave this relation, in the desire to obtain a pardon after the Restoration; and to confirm his story he said, " if his name there were compared with what he had ever writ himself, it could never be looked upon as his own hand." Warburton, in a note upon this passage, says, " The original warrant is still extant, and Ingoldsby's name has no such mark of its being wrote in that manner."

The king knew his fate. He resigned himself to it with calmness and dignity; with one exceptional touch of natural human passion, when he said to bishop Juxon, although resigning himself to meet his God, " We will not talk of these rogues, in whose hands I am; they thirst for my blood, and they will have it, and God's will be done. I thank God, I heartily forgive them, and I will talk of them no more." He took an affectionate leave of his daughter, the princess Elizabeth, twelve years old; and of his son, the duke of Gloucester, of the age of eight. To him he said;—" Mark, child, what I say; they will cut off my head, and perhaps make thee king; but thou must not be king so long as thy brothers Charles and James live." And the child said, " I will be torn in pieces first." There were some attempts to save him. The Dutch ambassador made vigorous efforts to procure a reprieve, whilst the French and Spanish ambassadors were inert. The ambassadors from the States nevertheless persevered; and early in the day of the 30th obtained some glimmering of hope from Fairfax. " But we found," they say in their despatch, " in front of the house in which we had just spoken with the general, about two hundred horsemen; and we learned, as well as on our way as on reaching home, that all the streets, passages, and squares of London were occupied by troops, so that no one could pass, and that the approaches of the city were covered with cavalry, so as to prevent any one from coming in or going out. . . . The

* Forster. " Life of Marten," p. 314.

same day, between two and three o'clock, the king was taken to a scaffold coverered with black, erected before Whitehall." *

To that scaffold before Whitehall, Charles walked, surrounded by soldiers, through the leafless avenues of St. James's Park. It was a bitterly cold morning. Evelyn records that the Thames was frozen over. The season was so sharp that the king asked to have a shirt more than ordinary, when he carefully dressed himself. He left St. James's at ten o'clock. He remained in his chamber at Whitehall, for about three hours, in prayer, and then received the sacrament. He was pressed to dine, but refused, taking a piece of bread and a glass of wine. His purposed address to the people was delivered only to the hearing of those upon the scaffold, but its purport was that the people " mistook the nature of government; for people are free under a government, not by being sharers in it, but by due admininistration of the laws of it."† His theory of government was a consistent one. He had the misfortune not to understand that the time had been fast passing away for its assertion. The headsman did his office; and a deep groan went up from the surrounding multitude.

It is scarcely necessary that we should offer any opinion upon this tremendous event. The world had never before seen an act so daring conducted with such a calm determination; and the few moderate men of that time balanced the illegality, and also the impolicy of the execution of Charles, by the fact that " it was not done in a corner," and that those who directed or sanctioned the act offered no apology, but maintained its absolute necessity and justice. " That horrible sentence upon the most innocent person in the world; the execution of that sentence by the most execrable murder that was ever committed since that of our blessed Saviour ;" ‡ forms the text which Clarendon gave for the rhapsodies of party during two centuries. On the other hand, the eloquent address of Milton to the people of England has been in the hearts and mouths of many who have known that the establishment of the liberties of their country, duly subordinated by the laws of a free monarchy, may be dated from this event: " God has endued you with greatness of mind to be the first of mankind, who, after having conquered their own king, and having had him delivered into their hands, have not scrupled to condemn him judicially, and, pursuant to that sentence of condemnation, to put him to death."§ In these times in England, when the welfare of the throne and the people are identical, we can, on the one hand, afford to refuse our assent to the blasphemous comparison of Clarendon (blasphemy more offensively repeated in the Church Service for the 30th of January), and at the same time affirm that the judicial condemnation which Milton so admires was illegal, unconstitutional, and in its immediate results dangerous to liberty. But feeling that far greater dangers would have been incurred if " the caged tiger had been let loose," and knowing that out of the errors and anomalies of those times a wiser Revolution grew, for which the first more terrible Revolution was a preparation, we may cease to examine this great historical question in any bitterness of spirit, and even acknowledge that the

* Despatch from the Ambassador Extraordinary of the States General; in the Appendix to Guizot's " English Revolution."

† Warwick, p. 345.

‡ " Rebellion," vol. vii. p. 236.   § " Defensio pro populo Anglicano.

death of Charles, a bad king, though in some respects a good man, was necessary for the life of England, and for her "teaching other nations how to
live." We must accept as just and true Milton's admonition to his countrymen
in reference to this event, which he terms "so glorious an action," with many
reasonable qualifications as to its glory ; and yet apply even to ourselves his
majestic words :—"After the performing so glorious an action as this, you
ought to do nothing that is mean and little, not so much as to think of, much
less to do anything but what is great and sublime. Which to attain to,
this is your only way : as you have subdued your enemies in the field, so to
make appear, that unarmed, and in the highest outward peace and tranquillity,
you of all mankind are best able to subdue ambition, avarice, the love of
riches, and can best avoid the corruptions that prosperity is apt to introduce
(which generally subdue and triumph over other nations), to show as great
justice, temperance, and moderation in the maintaining your liberty, as you
have shown courage in freeing yourselves from slavery."

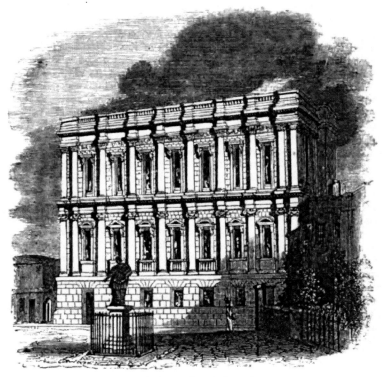

Banqueting house : from the Inner Court.

Oliver Cromwell. (From the Picture in the British Museum.)

CHAPTER VIII.

On the afternoon of Tuesday, the 30th of January, the Serjeant-at-Arms accompanied by poursuivants, and surrounded by cavalry, appears at Cheapside. Trumpets sound, and crowds gather about, to hear a proclamation, that whoever shall proclaim a new king, without authority of parliament, shall be deemed a traitor. An hour only has passed, since the last king, upon the scaffold at Whitehall,

"bowed his comely head
Down as upon a bed." *

What a night of curiosity and fear in the public haunts and private chambers of the great city! That afternoon the House of Commons order "that the

* Andrew Marvel.

Post be stayed until to-morrow morning, ten of the clock." That Post, which under the Parliament has become general, instead of being irregularly despatched upon a few roads, is now a weekly conveyance of letters into all parts of the nation. On that morning of the 31st it will go out of London with letters and little newspapers that will move terror and pity throughout the land. A few will rejoice in the great event; some will weep over it; others will vow a fearful revenge. "The more I ruminate upon it," writes Howell seven weeks afterwards, "the more it astonisheth my imagination, and shaketh all the cells of my brain; so that sometimes I struggle with my faith, and have much ado to believe it yet." * There was, at the time of the king's execution, a book being printed which was to surround his life with the attributes of a saint, and to invest him in death with the glory of a martyr. The "Icon Basiliké, or Portraiture of his Sacred Majesty in his Solitudes and Sufferings," purported to be written by Charles the first himself. Milton, who was directed by the Parliament to answer this Icon, or Image, treats it in his Iconoclastes, or Image-breaker, as if the king had "left behind him this book as the best advocate and interpreter of his own actions;" but at the same time Milton is careful to add, "as to the author of these soliloquies, whether it were the late king, as is vulgarly believed, or any secret coadjutor (and some stick not to name him), it can add nothing, nor shall take from the weight, if any be, of reason which he brings." The question of the authorship of this book has now passed out of the region of party violence; the controversy on that matter has almost merged, as a literary problem, into the belief that it was written by Dr. Gauden, afterwards bishop of Exeter. This divine probably submitted it to Charles during his long sojourn in the Isle of Wight; he published it as the work of the king; but he claimed the authorship after the Restoration. Mr. Hallam remarks upon the internal evidence of its authenticity that "it has all the air of a fictitious composition. Cold, stiff, elaborate, without a single allusion that bespeaks the superior knowledge of facts which the king must have possessed, it contains little but those rhetorical commonplaces which would suggest themselves to any forger." But these "rhetorical commonplaces" are the best evidence, not of the genuineness of the book, but of the skill of the author. They were precisely what was required to make "attachment to the memory of the king become passion, and respect, worship;"—so M. Guizot describes the effect of the Icon. It was an universal appeal to the feelings, in a style moving along with a monotonous dignity befitting royalty, though occasionally mingled with cold metaphors. It set forth the old blind claims to implicit obedience—or, as Milton has it, maintained "the common grounds of tyranny and popery, sugared a little over,"—amidst the manifestations of a sincere piety and a resigned sadness. In one year there were fifty editions of this book sold. "Had it appeared a week sooner it might have preserved the king," † thinks one writer. That may be doubted. But it produced the effect which those so-called histories produce which endeavour to fix the imagination solely upon the personal attributes and sorrows of kings and queens, instead of presenting a sober view of their relations to their subjects. Sentiment with the majority is always more powerful than reason; and thus Milton's 'Iconoclastes,' being

* "Letters," vol. iii. p. 36.   † Laing.

a partisan's view of Charles's public actions—a cold though severe view, in
the formal style of a state-paper,—produced little or no effect upon the
national opinions, and is now read only for the great name of the author.

On the 6th of February the Commons, now reduced to little more than a
hundred members, by their vote declared the House of Lords "useless and
dangerous." On the 7th another vote was recorded: "It hath been found by
experience, and this house doth declare, that the office of a king, in this
nation, and to have the power thereof in any single person, is unnecessary,
burthensome, and dangerous to the liberty, safety, and public interest of the
people of this nation, and therefore ought to be abolished." The body of
king Charles, on this day, when the abolition of the royal office had been thus
decreed, was removed to Windsor. On the 8th the duke of Richmond, the
marquis of Hertford, and the earls of Southampton and Lindsey, arrived at
the Castle, " to perform the last duty to their dead master, and to wait upon
him to his grave." Amidst a fall of snow the corpse was borne from the
great hall of the Castle to St. George's Chapel; and it was deposited " in a
vault, where two coffins were laid near one another, supposed to contain the
bodies of king Henry VIII. and queen Jane Seymour." * The governor of
the Castle forbad the Church Service to be performed, through his bigoted
resolve that, the Common Prayer having been put down, he would not suffer
it to be read in the garrison where he commanded.

A due provision for the Exercise of the Executive authority was speedily
made by the Parliament, in the appointment of a Council of State, consisting
of forty-one persons. This Council comprised the three chief judges; the
three commanders of the army; five peers, and thirty members of the House.
It was required of the individuals composing the Council that each should
sign a document expressing approbation of the proceedings by which the
monarchy had been overthrown. Twenty-two refused to enter into such an
engagement. There were violent debates; but moderation ultimately prevailed. The past was to remain unnoticed, in a pledge of fidelity for the
future. Sir Henry Vane has left his testimony to the course which he took
under these circumstances: " When required by the Parliament to take an
oath, to give my approbation, *ex post facto*, to what was done, I utterly
refused, and would not accept of sitting in the Council of State upon those
terms, but occasioned a new oath to be drawn, wherein that was omitted." †
Vane became an active member of the Council. He and others who had
refused to sanction the deeds of the regicides, did not shrink from labouring
with them in the public service. Bradshaw was chosen President of the
Council, and Milton was appointed its Latin secretary. The members chosen
saw the necessity of holding together in the great duty of saving the country
from intestine commotion and foreign assault. The Courts of Law were
re-opened; the command of the navy was put into able hands, who soon made
the flag of England respected in every sea. But although the vigilance of
the Council was sufficient for the repression of anarchy, with a powerful army

---

* "Herbert's Memoirs." Charles II. caused a search to be made for the vault, when the
parliament had voted a large sum for a public interment. The search was fruitless, and the
king put the money in his pocket. George IV. wished to gratify a reasonable curiosity, and the
vault with its coffins was readily found.

† Speech on his trial; given in Mr. Forster's Life.

at its command, it was not sufficient for establishing a willing obedience to
the Parliamentary Act, " That the People of England, and of all the dominions
and territories thereunto belonging, are and shall be, and are hereby constituted, made, established, and confirmed, to be a Commonwealth, or Free
State." It was the 30th of May before the Commonwealth was proclaimed
in the City, and the late king's statues thrown down at the Exchange, and at
the Portico of St. Paul's. The Lord Mayor had been deprived of his office,
and a new chief magistrate appointed, before the scruples of the municipal
body could be overcome. There was a like indisposition amongst the beneficed Clergy, the members of the Universities, and many civil functionaries, to
accept the oath of fidelity as the condition of retaining office or privilege.
But those who refused were exempt from any punishment, and thus the new
government gradually acquired consistency by its abstinence from any measures of general violence. There was one striking exception to its course of
moderation. Five state prisoners, royalists whom the fortune of war had
thrown into the hands of the Parliament, were to be sacrificed to what was
called justice upon delinquents. The duke of Hamilton, who had been in
confinement since his defeat at Preston; the earl of Holland, to whom an
opportunity of changing his side was not again to be permitted; the earl of
Norwich; lord Capel; and sir John Owen, were brought to trial before a
new High Court of Justice, in sittings which lasted from the 10th of February
to the 6th of March. Of these royalist leaders lord Capel was the most
eminent in courage and ability, and therefore the most dreaded by the
republicans. On the day after the House had resolved upon bringing these
adherents of the late king to trial, lord Capel made his escape from the
Tower, by dropping from his window into the ditch of the fortress; but he
was discovered the same evening, and conveyed back to his prison. The
High Court condemned all the five to be beheaded. The honest Welch
squire, sir John Owen, gave the Court thanks, saying " it was a very great
honour to a poor gentleman of Wales to lose his head with such noble lords,
and swore a great oath that he was afraid they would have hanged him." *
The Court, however, referred the execution of the sentence to the decision of
Parliament. For the duke of Hamilton's reprieve there were few votes.
The sentence of lord Holland was confirmed by a majority of one. The earl
of Norwich was saved by the casting vote of the speaker, Lenthall. Cromwell spoke upon the petition in favour of lord Capel. He bore testimony
to his high qualities; but his affection for the public, he said, weighed down
his private friendship—" the question now is, whether you will preserve the
most bitter and the most implacable enemy you have." When Cromwell
alluded to private friendship, he looked back upon the time when Capel was
the first in the Long Parliament to complain of grievances. He was reserved
for execution, with Hamilton and Holland. Owen escaped through the
intervention of Colonel Hutchinson. Mrs. Hutchinson relates the circumstance in a very interesting passage : " While there was such mighty labour
and endeavour for these lords, colonel Hutchinson observed that no man
spoke for this poor knight, and sitting next to colonel Ireton, he expressed
himself to him and told him, that it pitied him much to see that, while all

* Clarendon, vol. vi. p. 256.

were labouring to save the lords, a gentleman that stood in the same condemnation should not find one friend to ask his life; and so, said he, am I
moved with compassion that, if you will second me, I am resolved to speak
for him, who, I perceive, is a stranger and friendless. Ireton promised to
second him, and accordingly inquiring further of the man's condition, whether
he had not a petition in any member's hands, he found that his keepers had
brought one to the clerk of the house, but the man had not found any one
that would interest themselves for him, thinking the lords' lives of so much
more concernment than this gentleman's. This the more stirred up the
colonel's generous pity, and he took the petition, delivered it, spoke for him
so nobly, and was so effectually seconded by Ireton, that they carried his
pardon clear." * The three condemned noblemen were executed on the 9th
of March in Palace-yard. Capel, as Whitelocke records, carried himself
" much after the manner of a stout Roman." Public indignation was loudly
expressed against this severity. The time was not yet arrived when political
offences against the reigning power could be dealt with mercifully. But the
English republicans of 1649 abstained from any more such blood-shedding,
the case of colonel Poyer excepted. He was tried by court-martial, and shot
in Covent Garden. After these demonstrations of power the public excitement appears generally to have calmly settled down into a submission to the
new order of things; in spite of the violent demonstrations of the famous
John Lilburne. He published several pamphlets, one being entitled
" England's new chains discovered," and he was committed to the Tower, to
be tried in due time. Meanwhile, whilst the men of station and property,
the nobles and the gentry, the citizens and the yeomen, are settling into their
accustomed course of life, a spirit is getting loose which appears to be born
of all great revolutions; and which in modern times has rendered revolutions
very terrible to the apprehensions of all those who have anything to lose.
The "Levellers" of 1649 were, in a small way, the precursors of the
" Socialists" of 1849. At St. Margaret's Hill, and at St. George's Hill, in
Surrey,—a sandy district, now " a silent sea of pines,"—appeared a band of
thirty men, headed by one formerly in the army who called himself a Prophet.
They took possession of the ground, and began digging it, and dibbling beans,
in that sowing-time. They said they should shortly be four thousand in
number; that they should pull down park-pales and lay all open. The
residents near these Surrey hills were alarmed; and requested Fairfax to
send a troop of horse for their protection. The Diggers, as they called
themselves, were brought before the general; when the Prophet declared
that a vision had appeared to him and said, " Arise, and dig and plough the
earth, and receive the fruits thereof;" that their intent was to restore the
creation to its former condition; that they only meant to meddle with what
was common and untilled; but that the time was at hand, when all men shall
willingly come in and give up their lands and estates, and submit to this
community of goods.† These men, and many others who were adverse to
the existing republic, having various schemes of perfectibility, came to be
known by the general name of Levellers. They were only really formidable
when they had arms in their hands. But it required the utmost vigilance

* "Memoirs," vol. ii. p. 164.   † Whitelocke.

and decision to encounter the mutinous temper which was again breaking
forth amongst the military class.   The civil war had burst out again in
Ireland; and it was decided that twenty-eight regiments should be sent
thither, under the command of lieutenant-general Cromwell.   The regiments
to go are chosen by lot; but the common men have no inclination for the
service.   Lilburne's pamphlets are circulating amongst them.   They are
brooding over his wild declamations in their London and country-quarters.
A troop of Whalley's regiment lies at the Bull inn, at Bishopsgate; and
although not ordered for Ireland, they refuse to leave London; rise in open
mutiny.   Their conduct is sufficiently alarming to demand the instant presence of Fairfax and Cromwell.   The ringleaders are seized and tried by
court-martial.   Five are condemned; and one is the next day shot in St.
Paul's Churchyard—a strange place for a military execution; but not so
strange when compared with the uses to which the grand old Gothic cathedral
was now applied.   It had become a stable for cavalry.   "It was a bitter
taunt of the Italian who passing by Paul's Church, and seeing it full of horses,
'Now I perceive,' said he, 'that in England men and beasts serve God alike.'"*
The same amusing letter-writer says, "The air of this city is not sweet, spe-
cially in the heart of the city, in and about Paul's Church, where horse-dung
is a yard deep."   So amidst this filth was trooper Lockyer shot—and in a
week after this tragedy of the 27th of April, thousands of people are following
his corpse to the grave—a corpse "adorned with bunches of rosemary, one
half-stained in blood"—thousands of men and women, rank and file, with
sea-green and black ribbons on their hats and on their breasts.   Something
there is very serious in this, not only to the Commonwealth, but to any
stable order of society.   Lilburne, not under much restraint in the Tower,
sends out another pamphlet full of crude notions of what the people were to
do to establish a perfect government upon Bible principles, under which all
men were to gather unheard-of happiness.   A review takes place in Hyde
Park, where some of the men wear the sea-green ribbon, the symbol of disaffection; but Cromwell frightens or pacifies them.   Lilburne is now committed to close confinement.   But there are portions of the army in distant
quarters, and at Banbury two hundred men are in revolt; at Salisbury a
thousand.   Fairfax and Cromwell march with all haste to Salisbury.   The
mutineers have hurried away to join their companions in Oxfordshire.
Fairfax and Cromwell are rapidly on their track; having marched fifty miles
in one day.   The mutineers halt at Burford.   It is midnight when Cromwell
comes suddenly upon their quarters.   A few shots are fired; but there is no
escape for these men, who are without a head to guide them.   There is no
slaughter; but the principle of military obedience is sustained, now and
henceforward, by justice mingled with mercy.   A Court-Martial has been
held; and ten out of every hundred of the mutineers have been set aside
for death.   They are placed on the leads of the church, whilst a cornet and
two corporals are shot.   They are awaiting their own fate, when Cromwell
calls them before him in the church.   He speaks to them in one of his
peculiar harangues, apparently so involved, but always keeping the main point
in view.   The men weep.   They are pardoned.   In a few weeks they are on

* Howell, vol. iii. Letter xix.

their way to serve in Ireland. "Levelling, in the practical civil or military provinces of English things, is forbidden to be." * Cromwell had said to the Council of State, "You must make an end of this party or it will make an end of you." He accomplished the work with a moderation that shows that severity is not more powerful than mercy, in the generality of cases. The nation felt that it had escaped a great danger. There was a solemn thanksgiving-day; the House of Commons was invited to a civic feast; and Fairfax and Cromwell were presented with services of plate by the Corporation of London. The terror of anarchical disturbances had almost wholly passed away. The Council of State laboured to reconcile differences; to render the administration of the law more speedy and certain; to remove the impediments to a free exercise of religious observances amongst various denominations of Protestants. Evelyn heard the Common Prayer read in St. Peter's church at Paul's wharf, and listened to a sermon from archbishop Usher, in Lincoln's Inn chapel. But still there was danger to be apprehended in the intrigues of the more restless of the Cavaliers with the remnant of the Levellers; and unnatural as was such an alliance, one of these wrote to lord Cottington, who was with Charles in France, "his majesty's friends have no possibility of embodying, unless the Levellers lead the way." Their hopes rested upon Lilburne, who was again busy with his pamphlets. Conciliation was tried in vain with this man, who possessed none of the qualifications for a popular leader but those of reckless vanity and indomitable courage. The Parliament at length resolved to send him to trial. He was to be tried by a common Jury, though a Commission of members of parliament was appointed to determine his sentence. That office was spared them by his acquittal. Towards the close of the second day's proceedings at Guildhall, Lilburne, who had defended himself with great spirit, suddenly addressed the jury with these solemn words: "You are my sole judges, the keepers of my life, at whose hands the Lord will require my blood. And therefore I desire you to know your power, and consider your duty, both to God, to me, to your own selves, and to your country; and the gracious assisting spirit and presence of the Lord God Omnipotent, the governor of heaven and earth, and all things therein contained, go along with you, give counsel and direct you to do that which is just, and for his glory." And then all the spectators cried out "Amen! Amen!" The Chief Justice charged the Jury, amidst the dread of a popular disturbance. After three quarters of an hour the verdict was that John Lilburne was not guilty of all the treasons, or of any of the treasons charged upon him. A shout went up from all the people as the shout of one voice; bonfires were lighted throughout the City; and after a vain attempt to hold him in custody Freeborn John was set free. This event took place in October. It is satisfactory to contrast the independence of a jury at this revolutionary period, with the servile compliance to the behests of power by juries in the Tudor and Stuart times. Amidst the manifold evils of the Civil War, the people had learned to know the foundations of their liberties; and in the case of Lilburne and his Levellers, jurors were not carried away by a panic about property to yield to the desire of the government without a just sense of their own responsibility. Though in succeeding days of corrupt rulers juries were again the

* Carlyle, vol. ii. p. 29.

worst instruments of tyranny, the verdict of twelve men was to become the ultimate safeguard for an honest judgment in times of political excitement, when ministers have been as disposed to stretch the laws as subjects have been inclined to regard even their wholesome administration with jealousy and impatience.

Six months have elapsed since the death of Charles I. Charles II. is an exile at St. Germain's. He has Hyde and other experienced counsellors about him; and he has also more agreeable associates in adversity—frivolous and profligate courtiers who encourage his indolence and sensuality. English royalists resort to him, and to the queen dowager, who consoled herself in the society of lord Jermyn for the loss of her husband and her great station. The course of life of mother and son was regarded with complacency even by royalists of sober conduct. The staid Mr. Evelyn, on the 19th of August, "went to St. Germain's, to kiss his majesty's hand: in the coach, which was my lord Wilmot's, went Mrs. Barlow, the king's mistress and mother to the duke of Monmouth, a brown, beautiful, bold, but insipid creature." The next day he went to Paris, "to salute the French king and the queen dowager." The French king was Louis XIV., then a boy of about eleven years old; and at that time there was a brief suspension to the civil war of La Fronde. Though the Stuarts had an asylum at the French court there was no substantial aid to be expected in that quarter. Previous to his residence at St. Germain's Charles had been at the Hague, under the protection of his brother-in-law, the prince of Orange. He had been proclaimed king of Scotland, at Edinburgh, on the 5th of February, and Commissioners had come to him from the Scottish parliament to invite his return to his kingdom. They did not offer him an unconditional invitation. He was to proceed to Scotland, without Montrose and those other friends who were obnoxious to the Presbyterians; and he was to agree to the Covenant of 1638. He was urged by the sounder Scotsmen about him to accept the terms. He was counselled by Montrose to win his dominions by the sword. The great leader of the Scottish ultra-royalists was consistent. His one idea was to revenge the death of Charles I. :—

> "I'll sing thine obsequies with trumpet sounds,
> And write thine epitaph in blood and wounds."

So wrote Montrose when he heard of the execution of his master, and so he continued to believe was his own destiny in connexion with the son. The followers of Montrose carried out his feverish notions of loyalty by an act which can only find its defence in political fanaticism. On the 3d of May, whilst the Scottish commissioners were at the Hague, Dr. Isaac Dorislaus, a native of Holland, who had assisted as counsel at the trial of Charles I., and who had been sent by the Parliament as one of the embassy to the United Provinces, was murdered in his inn by six men in masks. They were Scotsmen, of the party of Montrose. This event was not calculated to smooth the difficulties of Charles's position with the Presbyterian Commissioners; and he dismissed them, with a negative upon their proposals. At this period, he was also especially urged by the marquis of Ormond to show himself in Ireland, where three-fourths of the nation were his faithful adherents. It is not easy to describe the state of parties in Ireland at this time. The majority of the people and their leaders were violent Papists—those with whom Charles I. had so often and so fatally intrigued to punish his rebellious subjects and establish the Anglican church. The Protestant portion of the population, English or Irish, lived in dread and hatred of those who had perpetrated the frightful massacre of 1641; and they, in common with some of the more moderate Catholics, had no disposition to welcome the king for whom the large body of Papists had declared. Ormond rallied under his banner any leader who was a royalist, and who would join this strange confederacy of Episcopalians, Presbyterians, Catholics of the Pale, Catholics of wild regions beyond the Pale—some for freedom of religion,—most for exterminating all creeds but their own. Ormond had concluded a special treaty with the Irish Catholics, on the part of Charles II., by which they agreed to maintain a large army to serve against the Commonwealth of England, on condition that the free exercise of the Catholic worship should be permitted. Ireland appeared thus on the point of being separated from English control; ready to take a prominent part in another English Civil War. The king had been proclaimed. Dublin, Belfast, and Londonderry were the only garrisons held by English commanders; and prince Rupert was in St. George's Channel with a formidable fleet. At this juncture it was determined that Cromwell should proceed to Ireland with full military and administrative powers—General-in-chief and Lord Lieutenant.

It was the 10th of July when Cromwell left London, "in that state and equipage as the like hath hardly been seen," said the newspapers. He proceeded to Bristol; and there he remained several weeks. Whether he lingered there to watch the course of events in London, or to make the requisite preparations for a difficult enterprise, is not very clear. Before he left London, one of the French ministers wrote to Cardinal Mazarin, "It can hardly be possible that Cromwell, who, according to the belief of many, carries his ideas beyond even the suggestions of the most undisciplined ambition, can resolve to abandon this kingdom to the mercy of the plots which may be formed in his absence, and which his presence can prevent from being so much as undertaken." * Cromwell by the end of July had gone towards Milford-Haven; and he embarked on the 13th of August. Meanwhile the news had reached him of a great victory obtained over the forces of the marquis of Ormond, who was besieging Dublin. Before the end of July a portion of Cromwell's army had landed; and thus re-inforced, Lieutenant-General Jones, the governor of Dublin, had sallied forth and utterly routed the besiegers at the village of Rathmines. Cromwell himself arrived in Dublin on the 15th of August. He was received, say the contemporary narratives, with the firing of guns and the acclamations of the people. The multitude that gathered about him was very great. They were anxious to see one "whom before they had heard so much of." He spoke to the crowd, "in an humble posture, having his hat in his hand," telling them "that as God had brought him thither in safety, so he doubted not but, by his divine Providence, to restore them all to their just liberties and properties;" promising the favour and gratitude of the Parliament of England to "all

* Letter of June 14th, 1649; "Archives des Affaires Étrangères de France," quoted by M. Guizot, in "History of Cromwell," vol. i. p. 88.

those whose hearts' affections were real for the carrying on of the great work against the barbarous and blood-thirsty Irish, and their adherents and confederates; for the propagating of the Gospel of Christ, the establishing of truth and peace, and restoring that bleeding nation to its former happiness and tranquillity." "Answer was returned by many hundreds that they would live and die with him." *

It is clear from this speech that Cromwell was preparing for some terrible work; and it is also manifest that the Protestant people of Dublin were well disposed to second his endeavours against "the barbarous and blood-thirsty Irish." It was in the minds of many that the time was come to avenge the massacre which had desolated so many homes. But the Lord Lieutenant contemplated no general waste and destruction; and he issued a proclamation requiring all officers and soldiers, at their utmost perils, "not to do any wrong or violence towards country people, or persons whatsoever, unless they be actually in arms or office with the enemy." The farmers and others were invited to come to the camp and sell their commodities for ready money. Nevertheless the Lord Lieutenant went forth to fight in a sterner mood than he ever showed in the English Civil Wars. He went to try his strength, not only against the hordes of half-savage men who, during the whole course of the war between the king and the parliament, had been burning and plundering and murdering, with slight regard to any common principle of action; but he went to do battle wherever, under the banner of the royalists, were gathered Catholics, English or Irish—Protestants, English, Scotch, or Irish,—captains who had fought at Naseby, or wild chieftains who came from their woods to exercise all the cruelties of partisan warfare. Ireland was in such a condition that the coming of this man in his wrath was eventually a real blessing. To follow this Irish war through its terrible details would be as wearisome as repulsive. But it has a strange interest, as recorded in the letters of the chief instrument in events which were decisive as to the future destiny of that kingdom, so long unhappy, so capable of happiness.

Tredah, now called Drogheda, in Leinster, was garrisoned by three thousand men under the command of sir Arthur Ashton, an old English royalist, who had lost a leg; and whose troops were chiefly English. Cromwell setting down before the place, summoned the governor to surrender. The governor refused. In a similar summons sent afterwards to the commander in Dundalk, Cromwell writes, "I offered mercy to the garrison at Tredah, in sending the governor a summons before I attempted the taking of it; which being refused brought their evil upon them. If you, being warned thereby, shall surrender your garrison to the use of the Parliament of England, which by this I summon you to do, you may prevent effusion of blood. If, upon refusing this offer, that which you like not befalls you, you will know whom to blame." † We give this brief threat before we recount "their evil" at Drogheda, to show that the horrible "effusion of blood" there was not the effect of any sudden impulse. On the 10th of September, then, surrender having been refused, the place was stormed, after bombardment. The first attacking party were driven back. The second, headed by

* "Perfect Politician," p. 53, ed. of 1680 (originally printed in 1660).
† Carlyle, (from an Autograph,) vol. ii. p. 48.

Cromwell himself, carried all the entrenchments. "Being thus entered," writes the General to the President of the Council of State, "we refused them quarter, having, the day before, summoned the town. I believe we put to the sword the whole number of the defendants. I do not think thirty of the whole number escaped with their lives. Those that did are in safe custody for the Barbadoes." He then relates that Trim and Dundalk have surrendered; and adds, with reference to the slaughter of Drogheda, where only one officer escaped, "The enemy upon this were filled with much terror. And truly I believe this bitterness will save much effusion of blood, through the goodness of God." We look with horror upon such wholesale butchery; and yet its perpetrator was in his nature the very opposite of cruel. He feels that some defence is necessary for such severities; and in a more detailed despatch to the Speaker, he repeats his belief "that it will tend to prevent the effusion of blood for the future; which are the satisfactory grounds to such actions, which otherwise cannot but work remorse and regret." We must follow this resolute man to Wexford. There again was a terrible slaughter; but it was not set about with a deliberate purpose. It was such a slaughter as has too often been the result of a storm by an infuriated soldiery. There had been negotiations for the surrender of the castle and town, upon merciful and honourable conditions, going on from the 3rd to the 11th of October. The castle was surrendered; but the town being supposed to hold out, and armed men advancing towards the castle, the troops of Cromwell stormed it; and "when they were come into the market-place, the enemy making a stiff resistance, our forces brake them; and then put all to the sword that came in their way." Cromwell then adds to this account, "it hath not, without cause, been deeply set upon our hearts, that, we intending better to this place than so great a ruin, hoping the town might be of more use to you and your army, yet God would not have it so; but by an unexpected providence, in his righteous justice, brought a just judgment upon them; causing *them* to become a prey to the soldier, who in their piracies had made prey of so many families, and now with their bloods to answer the cruelties which they had exercised upon the lives of divers poor Protestants." This confidence that an accidental and unnecessary slaughter was a divine judgment, is consistent with the whole character of Cromwell's mind. He did not express such opinions without a strong conviction. The slaughter at Drogheda, set about with a stern determination to make such a beginning of the war as should shortly bring it to an end, was perfectly comprehensible by Cromwell's contemporaries. Ludlow, no friend of Cromwell, remarks of this "extraordinary severity," that he presumes "it was used to discourage others from making opposition." * Another writer of the time says, "Yet cruelty could not be laid to his charge, for, like a politic state-physician, he here opens one vein, to preserve the whole body of the nation from a lingering war; and by this course likewise he wrought such a terror in the enemy, that ever after he made but short work of any siege, and in small time reduced the whole nation." † The Jacobite historian of the next age denounces "the execrable policy of that Regicide, which had the effect he proposed." An enlightened and truly pious minister of our own day writes of this Irish campaign, "For nine years a

* "Memoirs," vol. i. p. 308.   † "Perfect Politician," p. 56.

most insane war has been raging. Cromwell, by merciful severity, concludes it in nine months." * The view which dispassionate persons take of these events will always be a mixed one. They will regard them somewhat, but not altogether, in the spirit of M. Guizot, when he says, "It is the ordinary artifice of bad passions to impute the cruel satisfaction with which they glut themselves, either to some great idea whose accomplishment they are earnestly pursuing, or to the absolute necessity of success;" and they will feel with this writer, whose philosophy is so connected with a vast experience, that " human fanaticism also lies, or allows itself to be deluded by pride, when it pretends to be the executor of the high decrees of Divine justice." † But, whilst they remember many incidents of later times in which "bad passions " and "human fanaticism " have perpetrated cruelties and injustice, they will not, without due examination of the character of Cromwell, agree with M. Guizot, that "he was determined to succeed rapidly, and at any cost, from the necessities of his fortune, far more than for the advancement of his cause;" or admit that " he denied no outlet to the passions of those who served him." M. Guizot, well read as he is in English history, is pointing these remarks nearer home—a mode of expressing political opinions which may be safe in its immediate purposes, but not altogether consistent with historical impartiality.

Charles II. was at St. Germain's when he received the news of Ormond's defeat before Dublin. In the heroic vein, which little suited his nature, he exclaimed, "Then must I go there to die." He went as far as Jersey, where the news of the fall of Drogheda reached him. It produced the same effect upon his spirits as upon the courtiers he had left at St. Germain's. In Evelyn's Diary of the 15th of October we have this entry: " Came news of Drogheda being taken by the rebels, and all put to the sword; which made us very sad, fore-running the loss of all Ireland." Cromwell marched on, taking town after town, until he met with a stout resistance at Waterford; and the weather being very tempestuous he went into winter-quarters. But his rapid marches from fortress to fortress have changed the whole aspect of affairs. General Blake has interrupted the operations of prince Rupert in the Irish seas. Cork Harbour is now the victualling-place for the fleet, instead of Milford Haven. Rupert, with the ships which he has commanded since the revolt of the sailors in 1648, has taken refuge in Kinsale, instead of making rich prizes of English merchantmen. Lady Fanshawe, who at this time was at Cork, writes that Cromwell " so hotly marched over Ireland, that the fleet with prince Rupert was forced to set sail." This was an indirect consequence, in a little time after, of Cromwell's hot marches. A more immediate consequence was the submission of Youghal and of Cork to the authority of the Parliament. There is a passage in the Memoirs of Lady Fanshawe, which presents a vivid picture of the mode in which such warlike operations affect individuals; an interesting episode amidst graver matters of wars and bitter hatreds. The poor lady had been residing at Red Abbey, in Cork, for six months with her husband, who was waiting " his majesty's commands how to dispose himself." Sir Richard Fanshawe had gone for a day to Kinsale.

* "Lectures on Great Men," by the late Frederic Myers, M.A. p. 259, 1856.
† "History of Cromwell," vol. i. p. 98.

His wife, by the fall of a stumbling horse, had broken her left wrist; which was ill set, and put her to great pain. She was in bed on a night early in November: "At midnight I heard the great guns go off, and thereupon I called up my family to rise, which I did as well as I could in that condition. Hearing lamentable shrieks of men, women, and children, I asked at a window the cause; they told me they were all Irish, stripped and wounded, and turned out of the town, and that colonel Jefferies, with some others, had possessed themselves of the town for Cromwell. Upon this, I immediately wrote a letter to my husband, blessing God's providence that he was not there with me, persuading him to patience and hope that I should get safely out of the town, by God's assistance, and desired him to shift for himself, for fear of a surprise, with promise that I would secure his papers. So soon as I had finished my letter, I sent it by a faithful servant, who was let down the garden wall of Red Abbey, and, sheltered by the darkness of the night, he made his escape. I immediately packed up my husband's cabinet, with all his writings, and near 1000l. in gold and silver, and all other things both of clothes, linen, and household stuff that were portable, of value; and then, about three o'clock in the morning, by the light of a taper, and in that pain I was in, I went into the market-place, with only a man and maid, and passing through an unruly tumult with their swords in their hands, searched for their chief commander Jefferies, who, whilst he was loyal, had received many civilities from your father.* I told him it was necessary that upon that change I should remove, and I desired his pass that would be obeyed, or else I must remain there: I hoped he would not deny me that kindness. He instantly wrote me a pass, both for myself, family, and goods, and said he would never forget the respect he owed your father. With this I came through thousands of naked swords to Red Abbey, and hired the next neighbour's cart, which carried all that I could remove; and myself, sister, and little girl Nan, with three maids and two men, set forth at five o'clock in November, having but two horses amongst us all, which we rid on by turns. In this sad condition I left Red Abbey, with as many goods as were worth 100l. which could not be removed, and so were plundered. We went ten miles to Kinsale, in perpetual fear of being fetched back again; but, by little and little, I thank God, we got safe to the garrison, where I found your father the most disconsolate man in the world, for fear of his family, which he had no possibility to assist: but his joy exceeded to see me and his darling daughter, and to hear the wonderful escape we, through the assistance of God, had made. But when the rebels went to give an account to Cromwell of their meritorious act, he immediately asked them where Mr. Fanshawe was. They replied, he was that day gone to Kinsale. Then he demanded where his papers and his family were? At which they all stared at one another, but made no reply. Their General said, 'It was as much worth to have seized his papers as the town; for I did make account to have known by them what these parts of the country are worth.'"

The policy of Cromwell in Ireland was all throughout most intelligible and consistent; and we are not to conclude from the course of events during two centuries that it was not a wise policy. He wrote to the Parliament, "I

* Lady Fanshawe addressed her Memoir to her only son.

City of Worcester. From an old print.

CHAPTER IX.

Charles II. negotiates with the Scottish Parliament—His commission to Montrose—Montrose in Scotland—Execution of Montrose—Charles goes to Scotland—War with Scotland—Cromwell General—Cromwell's Advance—His Danger—Position of the two Armies at Dunbar—Battle of Dunbar—Charles crowned at Scone—Perth taken by Cromwell—Charles and the Scotch Army in England—The Battle of Worcester—Escape and Adventures of Charles—Charles returns to France—Note—Whitelocke's Description of Cromwell's Army, in a Conversation with Christina, queen of Sweden.

CHARLES II., essentially different in character from his father, had inherited that quality of his family which mainly led to the tragedies of Fotheringay and Whitehall. He was a double-dealer. When the affairs of Ireland became hopeless, he listened to the proposals of the Parliament of Scotland. He received an envoy from the Presbyterian authorities while at Jersey; and appointed them to meet him at Breda to conclude a treaty for his reception in Scotland. He was urged by his warmest friends to close with their offers, although there was no relaxation of the terms upon which the support of the great religious party, speaking the voice of the Scottish nation, was offered to him. Whilst he was thus negotiating with the Parliament, he gave Montrose a commission to levy troops in foreign countries, and wage war against the powers with whom he was bargaining. He wrote to the mortal enemy of the Covenanters, "I entreat you to go on vigorously, and with your wonted courage and care, in the prosecution of those trusts I

RAY.

SIR WILLIAM TEMPLE   SIR CHRISTOPHER WREN

have committed to you; and not to be startled with any reports you may hear, as if I were otherwise inclined to the Presbyterians than when I left you. I assure you I am upon the same principles I was, and depend as much as ever upon your undertaking and endeavours for my service." Urged thus, and by his own passionate loyalty, the exile of Philiphaugh was indefatigable in gathering followers, though with no great success. In the autumn of 1649 he had collected about twelve hundred men at Hamburg and Gottenburg, and he dispatched a portion of them, who perished at sea. A second body arrived safely at Kirkwall. With five hundred more, Montrose himself landed in the Orkneys early in March, 1650. He then crossed to the northern extremity of the main land; and, says Clarendon, "quickly possessed himself of an old castle; which, in respect of the situation in a country so impossible for an army to march in, he thought strong enough for his purpose: thither he conveyed the arms, ammunition, and troops which he had brought with him." Caithness, in which district he landed, has numerous ruins of old castles—grim monuments of days of cruel feuds and lawless rapine. Here Montrose was come with his threatening banners—one of the two royal ones exhibiting the bleeding head of Charles I., with the motto, "Judge and revenge my cause, O Lord;" and his own banner painted with a naked arm and a sword dripping with gore. Onward he marched into Sutherland. Few adherents joined him. The natives fled from him as from a public enemy, of whose military excesses the Scots had received terrible lessons. Some cavalry, under the command of colonel Strachan, were proceeding against Montrose, in advance of a main body of troops under David Lesley; and they came suddenly upon him near a pass in the parish of Kincardine. The place is now called Craigchonichen, or the Rock of Lamentation. Here Montrose's last battle was soon ended. His Orkney recruits quickly ran; his Germans and his Scottish companions fought valiantly, but without effect. The ill-compacted force was wholly broken; and he himself fled from the field, throwing away his ribbon and George, and changing clothes with a peasant. Wandering amongst the Highlands for many days, he was at last taken on the 3rd of May.

Clarendon's narrative of the last enterprise of Montrose and its fatal termination is regarded as one of the finest passages of his history. It should be read as a whole * to do justice to its merits as a composition. The facts which it relates, compared with other relations, lie in a short compass. After his capture, Montrose and the other Scottish prisoners were delivered to David Lesley; the foreigners were set at liberty. There was a ferocious exultation over the fall of the capital enemy of the Covenanters, which showed itself in such acts of meanness as carrying him from town to town in the unseemly garb with which he was disguised, and thus exposing him to the jeers of the populace. An Act of Attainder had been passed by the Parliament against Montrose in 1644; and upon that Act he was now sentenced to death, before he reached Edinburgh. When he arrived at the Watergate of the city he was delivered to the magistrates, and was conveyed to the Tolbooth, bound with cords, in an open cart, the common hangman riding before the cart, and wearing the livery of the fallen marquis. Thirty-

* "Rebellion," vol. vi. p. 408, to 422.

four of his officers, tied together, formed part of the cavalcade. The great object of popular curiosity sat serene amidst his indignities; and his proud composure moved pity in the beholders, instead of the demonstrations of hate which were anticipated. Argyle looked upon his illustrious enemy from a window in the house of the earl of Moray.* From the first scene of this tragedy to the last, Montrose acted his heroic part to perfection. His demeanour was somewhat more theatrical than the mode in which the highest species of heroism would care to exhibit itself; but it was well calculated to dazzle those who are most taken with the showy virtues. When he alighted from the cart, he gave the hangman a reward "for driving his triumphal chariot so well." When he was brought, two days after, before the Parliament, he was splendidly dressed; and looked around him with an air of studied haughtiness and contempt. The Chancellor Loudon spoke bitterly to him—" he had committed many horrible murders, treasons, and impieties, for all which he was now brought to suffer condign punishment." When permitted to speak, Montrose said that " since the king had honoured them so far as to treat with them, he had appeared before them with reverence, and bareheaded, which otherwise he would not willingly have done. He had done nothing of which he was ashamed or had cause to repent." He had withdrawn himself from the first Covenant, when he saw that it was intended to take away the king's just power and lawful authority. He had never taken the second Covenant. He defended himself from the charge of cruelty; and maintaining that having again entered the kingdom by his majesty's command, he advised them to consider well of the consequence before they proceeded against him. His sentence was then pronounced:—that on the morrow, the 21st of May, he should be hanged on a gallows thirty feet high; that his head should then be cut off and set on Edinburgh Tolbooth; and that his legs and arms should be hung up in other towns of the kingdom. After he was conveyed back to prison he was beset by ministers and magistrates; who only stirred his spirit to its loftiest mood. He told them that he had rather his head were stuck upon the Tolbooth than that his picture should be hung in the king's bed-chamber; that it troubled him not that his limbs should be exposed in other towns; " and that he heartily wished that he had flesh enough to be sent to every city in Christendom, as a testimony of the cause for which he suffered." In the same spirit he went to the scaffold. When the hangman, by way of adding to his indignities, hung about his neck the narrative of his military exploits, " the marquis smiled at this new instance of their malice, and thanked them for it, and said he was prouder of wearing it than ever he had been of the Garter." Clarendon's character of the great chieftain is not an unmixed eulogium: " He was a gentleman of a very ancient extraction, many of whose ancestors had exercised the highest charges under the king in that kingdom, and had been allied to the crown itself. He was of very good parts, which were improved by a good education: he had always a great emulation, or rather a great contempt, of the marquis of Argyle (as he was too apt to contemn those he did not love), who wanted nothing but honesty and courage to be a very extraordinary man, having all other good talents in a very great degree. Montrose was in his nature fearless of

* Guizot: upon the authority of a letter of the French Agent to Mazarin.

danger, and never declined any enterprise for the difficulty of going through with it, but exceedingly affected those which seemed desperate to other men, and did believe somewhat to be in himself above other men, which made him live more easily towards those who were, or were willing to be, inferior to him (towards whom he exercised wonderful civility and generosity), than with his superiors or equals. He was naturally jealous, and suspected those who did not concur with him, in any way, not to mean so well as he. He was not without vanity, but his virtues were much superior, and he well deserved to have his memory preserved, and celebrated amongst the most illustrious persons of the age in which he lived."

Charles came to a conclusion with the Scottish commissioners at Breda before the death of Montrose, although he was acquainted with the failure of his rash expedition. He consented to every proposition. He was to swear to be faithful to the Covenant; he was to submit himself to the advice of the Parliament and the Church; he was never to permit the exercise of the Catholic religion in any part of his dominions. He even denied that he had authorised the enterprise of Montrose. When he heard of his friend's execution, he manifested a disposition to draw back; but his courtiers " persuaded the king, who was enough afflicted with the news, and all the circumstances of it, that he might sooner take revenge upon that people by a temporary complying with them and going to them." Upon this righteous principle " his majesty pursued his former resolution of embarking for Scotland." This is Clarendon's account; who makes no remark in his History upon this miserable policy. But he says, in a private letter to secretary Nicolas, " If the king puts himself into the hands of the Scots, they cannot justly be accused of deceiving him; for, on my conscience, they will not use him worse than they promise, if he does all they require him to do in this last address. I wish, with all my heart, they who advise the king to comply, and join with them, would deal as clearly, and say that the king should now take the Covenant, and enjoin it to others, and all observe it; but to say he should put himself into their hands, and hope to be excused taking it, and be able to defend others from submitting to it,—or that he and we should take it and break it afterwards,—is such folly and atheism that we should be ashamed to avow or think it." Such was the political morality by which Charles was guided when he was twenty years old—a season of life in which deliberate untruth and purposed treachery are rarely the governing principles of actions. We have little sympathy for him in his humiliations and adversities among the Scots. We rejoice to know that, before he had landed in Scotland on the 16th of June, he was compelled to sign the Covenant; that few of his English friends were permitted to be about him; and that if : were still free to listen to the ribaldry of Buckingham and Wilmot, he had to do daily penance in being compelled to attend the long prayers and longer sermons of the clergy who were placed about him. Charles probably cared little for these restraints; for he had a good table, horses to ride, and the outward shows that belong to a king; but it has been sensibly conjectured that the gloomy austerity of these preachers " strengthened that indifference to religion and that proneness to dissipation by which his whole life was unhappily distinguished." *

* Cook, "History of the Church of Scotland, ' quoted by Sir Walter Scott.

Cromwell had arrived in London on the 31st of May. He was received with every honour that Parliament and City could bestow; and by the enthusiastic acclamations of the people. He did not despise popular applause; but he knew something of its intrinsic value. To the remark, "What a crowd come to see your lordship's triumph," he replied, "If it were to see me hanged how many more would there be!" He was soon called to other serious work. The Parliament has been preparing forces for a war with Scotland, having no great hope of repose in the presence there of a covenanted king. The Scots are also making some preparation for a war with England, the ministers of the Commonwealth not having taken in good part their remonstrance as to the course of civil and religious policy, and their negotiations with Charles. It is a question which shall strike the first blow. Fairfax was unwilling to invade the Scots; although, says Ludlow, "we laboured to persuade him of the reasonableness and justice of our resolution to march into Scotland, they having already declared themselves our enemies, and by public protestation bound themselves to impose that government upon us which we had found necessary to abolish."* Cromwell pressed that Fairfax, notwithstanding his resolution, should be continued as General of the Army, "professing for himself that he would rather choose to serve under him in his post than to command the greatest army in Europe." A Committee, upon Cromwell's motion, was appointed to confer with the General; and Ludlow adds that the Lieutenant-General "acted his part so to the life that I really thought he was in earnest." Ultimately Fairfax resigned his commission, receiving a large pension, and Cromwell was called to the great office. "I really thought he was in earnest," says Ludlow. There is another version from one who took a part in these events: "To speak the truth of Cromwell, whereas many said he undermined Fairfax, it was false; for in Colonel Hutchinson's presence, he most effectually importuned him to keep his commission, lest it should discourage the army and the people in that juncture of time, but could by no means prevail, although he laboured it almost all the night with most earnest endeavours. But this great man was then as unmoveable by his friends as pertinacious in obeying his wife; whereby he then died to all his former glory, and became the monument of his own name, which every day wore out."† And so Cromwell set forth to lead an army into Scotland; declaring in a private conversation with Ludlow, "that he looked upon the design of the Lord on this day to be the freeing of his people from every burden, and that he was now accomplishing what was prophesied in the 110th Psalm; from the consideration of which he was often encouraged to attend the effecting those ends." On the 26th of June, the Act was passed for constituting "Oliver Cromwell Captain General and Commander-in-Chief of all the forces raised and to be raised within the Commonwealth of England." On the 29th he left London. On the 22nd of July, with about sixteen thousand horse and foot, he marched through Berwick; and setting his foot on Scottish ground he addressed a "large discourse" to his troops, "as a Christian and a soldier:" "I exhort you," he said, "to be wary and worthy, for sure enough we have work before us. But have we not had God's blessing hitherto. Let us go on faithfully, and hope for the like

---

* "Memoirs," vol. ii. p. 314.   † Hutchinson's "Memoirs," vol. ii. p. 172.

still."   "The most dangerous of hypocrites," cries Hume.   "I have asked myself," says one who has studied Oliver somewhat more deeply than the popular sceptic, "if anywhere in modern European history, or even in ancient Asiatic, there was found a man practising this mean world's affairs with a heart more filled by the Idea of the Highest?"*

Charles, as a measure of policy, was taken to the Scottish camp.   It was composed of men of very different opinions, and of no opinions at all, in matters of religion; and the young king soon ingratiated himself with royalists of loose thoughts and irregular lives.   The Presbyterian leaders weeded the camp of those they called malignants; and compelled Charles to sign a declaration against Popery and Heresy, condemning the evil deeds of his father and the idolatry of his mother, and protesting and promising all that he had been required to subscribe for the Parliament and the Church. He winced, refused, consented; and then sent a message to Ormond that the declaration was extorted from him, and that he remained firm to his first principles as a true child of the Church of England, and a true Cavalier.

The advance of Cromwell into Scotland was met by a vigorous measure on the part of Lesley.   The population of the border districts were commanded to leave their villages; to drive their cattle from the fields, and to go with their goods towards Edinburgh.   From every Presbyterian pulpit the English army was denounced as composed of sectaries and blasphemers, who would put all the men to the sword, and abuse the women with frightful tortures.   The country was bare of all supplies; and Cromwell was compelled to march by the coast, to receive provisions from English vessels.   At Dunbar he got "some small pittance from our ships."   On the 29th he was encamped at Musselburgh.   Lesley's army was lying between Edinburgh and Leith, "entrenched by a line flankered from Edinburgh to Leith." There was a sharp skirmish on that day; but Cromwell writes, "I did not think it advisable to attempt upon the enemy, lying as he doth."   He conjectured that they desired to tempt him to attack them in their fastness; or else hoping that his army would famish for want of provisions—"which," he coolly adds, "is very likely to be, if we be not timely and fully supplied." The Scottish army has a very secure position, entrenched from Leith to the Calton Hill; well supplied, and the city protected.   For a month there is little done besides letters and declarations passing between the two armies. There was more skirmishing and manœuvring towards the end of August, when Cromwell had marched westward of Edinburgh towards Stirling; but on the 30th he fell back to Musselburgh, and on the 31st retired to Dunbar. Lesley followed him.   On the 1st of September the English army was lying round the old fortress, near their ships.   Cromwell is in a position of no common danger.   On the 2nd he writes to Sir Arthur Haselrig, at Newcastle or elsewhere, "The enemy hath blocked up our way at the pass at Copperspath, through which we cannot get without almost a miracle.   He lieth so upon the hills that we know not how to come that way without great difficulty; and our lying here daily consumeth our men, who fall sick beyond imagination. * * * Whatever becomes of us, it will be well for you to get what forces you can together. * * * The only wise God knows what is best."

* Carlyle, vol. ii. p. 157.

Oliver has written this letter of the 2nd; he has gone into the town of Dunbar about four o'clock to take some refreshment; and he comes back to his camp, which extends from Belhaven Bay to Brockmouth House—occupying the peninsula "about a mile and a half from sea to sea." On the Doon Hill, on the edge of Lammermoor, Lesley's army of twenty thousand men is strongly placed. At Brockmouth House, a rivulet which skirts the Doon Hill enters the sea. "It runs in a deep grassy glen, which the South country officers in the old pamphlets describe as 'a deep ditch, forty feet in depth, and about as many in width,'—ditch dug out by the little brook itself, and carpeted with greensward, in the course of long thousands of years. It runs pretty close by the foot of Doon Hill: forms, from this point to the sea, the boundary of Oliver's position: his force is arranged in battle order along the left bank of this Brockburn and its grassy glen." * Early on the morning of the 2nd. Lesley's horse had come down from the hill, and occupied the right bank of the rivulet. On that autumn afternoon Cromwell, walking in the garden of Brockmouth House, sees the whole Doon Hill alive with the movement of Lesley's main force,—coming down to the edge of the Brock, and occupying the confined ground which lies between it and the Hill. The right wing has

Dunbar.

moved out to the open space. The quick military eye sees that one false move has changed the whole aspect of affairs. He tells his plan to Lambert and Monk:—Attack the right wing with our whole force; drive it into the narrow space where the main force lies; let the men stand to their arms all night, and begin the attack before dawn. The night is wet. The Scots are

* Carlyle. The description of this battle-field, from which we derive our brief details, is a master-piece of that true picturesque which is derived from accurate observation.

lying in the harvest-fields amongst the corn-sheaves; they have no tents; they have put out their matches, all but two in a company. To the left, by the pass over the Brock, several regiments march quickly, by break of day. At six o'clock in the morning, Lambert, the major-general, had joined with his force to lead the attack. It was a fierce contest, in which the advanced guard was repulsed; but it was not long before the infantry had broken the Scottish lines "at push of pike." Cromwell writes, "The best of the enemies' horse being broken through and through, in less than an hour's dispute, their whole army being put into confusion, it became a total rout." There were three thousand slain on the field, and ten thousand taken prisoners. The prisoners were a serious trouble. Four or five thousand were dismissed. As many were sent to Newcastle. Cromwell on the 9th wrote to Haselrig, the governor of that town, "I hope your northern guests are come to you by this time. I pray you let humanity be exercised towards them; I am persuaded it will be comely." These poor creatures were not treated as the General desired. Many died from eating raw cabbages at Morpeth; many of pestilence in Durham. Others were sent to New England; and John Cotton, the minister of Boston there, writes to Oliver in 1651, describing that they were then kindly used, having been sold for a limited servitude in a country where their labour was welcome, and not ill-rewarded.

The dispatch of Cromwell on the 4th of September, in which he addresses to the Speaker of the Parliament a minute account of the victory of Dunbar, contains a remarkable paragraph, singularly illustrative of the character of the writer, and of his influence over the authority under which he is serving. He points out that this victory is " one of the most signal mercies God hath done to England and his people." He is writing with all the horrors of the recent battle around him; having just proclaimed that the inhabitants may come to the field with carts to carry away their wounded countrymen. But in the very thick of this turmoil he tasks his mind to tell the Parliament that success calls upon them to do their duty at home. " Disown yourselves, but own your Authority; and improve it to curb the proud and the insolent, such as would disturb the tranquillity of England, though under what specious pretence soever. Relieve the oppressed, hear the groans of poor prisoners in England. Be pleased to reform the abuses of all professions; and if there be any one that makes many poor to make a few rich, that suits not a Commonwealth." This is extraordinary language from a servant to his master, and he takes an extraordinary occasion to use it. Ludlow speaks of this advice as very seasonable; and the victory itself not more welcome than the General's letter to the Parliament, urging them " to do real things for the common good." Cromwell had left London, two months before, with these convictions full in his mind. He had told Ludlow during the short interval between his return from Ireland and his departure for Scotland, " That it was his intention to contribute the utmost of his endeavours to make a thorough reformation of the Clergy and the Law: but, said he, the sons of Zeruiah are yet too strong for us; and we cannot mention the reformation of the Law but they presently cry out, we design to destroy property: whereas the Law, as it is now constituted, serves only to maintain the lawyers, and to encourage the rich to oppress the poor." * We have here the first clear indication that

* " Memoirs," vol. ii. p. 319.

this remarkable man felt that he had other work before him than directing such attacks as those of the gray dawning of the 3rd of September. Before the days of Dunbar and Worcester, Milton's " chief of men " had decided that

> " peace hath her victories,
> No less renown'd than war ; "

and that upon him was laid the task of their achievement.

On the 5th of September, Cromwell marched away from the old fortress of Dunbar and the Burn of Brock. He had now the command of ample supplies, for Edinburgh and the country around were in his power, with the exception of Edinburgh castle. Charles, with the Scottish authorities, had retired to Perth. Lesley was gathering the wreck of his army about him at Stirling. The young king, utterly wearied with the Presbyterian statesmen and ministers, who had sent away all his Cavaliers except Buckingham, attempted to escape from them to join his more ardent friends in the Highlands. He got away fifty miles from Perth ; but was quickly brought back. The Presbyterian leaders then somewhat relaxed their intolerant demeanour towards Charles ; but this gave offence to the more violent. The Presbyterian party became divided ; and the royalists obtained a higher influence in the direction of the national policy. Charles, without further question of his real intentions, was crowned at Scone on the 1st of January, 1651. Cromwell was not warring upon the Scottish people, but was endeavouring to conciliate the religious party, by attending the sermons of their ministers, and expressing no resentment at their attacks upon himself. He has not been idle in his rougher work. After a three months' blockade, and then a bombardment, Edinburgh castle was surrendered to him on the 18th of December. Cromwell has little to do to make himself master of Scotland on the south of the Forth—some battery of detached castles, and some skirmishes with mosstroopers. On the 4th of February the army marched towards Stirling, but returned without any result, driven to the good quarters of Edinburgh by terrible storms of sleet and snow. The Lord-General became seriously ill through this exposure. On the day after Dunbar he wrote to his wife, " I assure thee I grow an old man, and feel infirmities of age marvellously stealing upon me." In March, in reply to the solicitude expressed by the Council of State, he says, " I thought I should have died of this fit of sickness ; but the Lord seemeth to dispose otherwise." In May his illness assumes a more dangerous appearance. The Parliament give him liberty to return home. But on the 5th of June he is out again ; and at the end of the month is vigorously prosecuting the campaign. The Scottish army was entrenched at Stirling. The king had been invited to take its command in person. Cromwell, on the 2nd of August, had succeeded in possessing himself of Perth. At that juncture the news reached him that the royal camp at Stirling was broken up, on the 31st of July ; and that Charles was on his march southward, at the head of eleven thousand men, his Lieutenant-General being David Lesley. Argyle was opposed to this bold resolution ; and had retired to Inverary. The letter which Cromwell wrote to the Parliament upon the receipt of this intelligence is frank and manly. He anticipated blame in leaving the road to England free for invasion, and he thus meets the certain imputation of neglect: " I do apprehend that if he goes for England, being some few days march before us, it will trouble some men's thoughts ; and may occasion some inconveniences ;—which I hope we are as deeply sensible of; and have been, and I trust shall be, as diligent to prevent as any. And indeed this is our comfort, that in simplicity of heart, as towards God, we have done to the best of our judgments; knowing that if some issue were not put to this business, it would occasion another winter's war : to the ruin of your soldiery, for whom the Scots are too hard in respect of enduring the winter difficulties of this country; and to the endless expense of the treasure of England in prosecuting this war. It may be supposed we might have kept the enemy from this, by interposing between him and England. Which truly I believe we might : but how to remove him out of this place, without doing what we have done, unless we had had a commanding army on both sides of the river of Forth, is not clear to us ; or how to answer the inconveniences afore mentioned, we understand not. We pray therefore that (seeing there is a possibility for the enemy to put you to some trouble) you would, with the same courage, grounded upon a confidence in God, wherein you have been supported to the great things God hath used you in hitherto,—improve, the best you can, such forces as you have in readiness, or as may on the sudden be gathered together, to give the enemy some check, until we shall be able to reach up to him ; which we trust in the Lord we shall do our utmost endeavour in."

Cromwell was not mistaken in supposing that the march of Charles towards England would " trouble some men's thoughts." There were " pale and unmanly fears " in some who directed the nation's councils. " Some raged and uttered discontents against Cromwell, and suspicions of his fidelity." Mrs. Hutchinson so describes this time of alarm. But bolder spirits went in earnest, upon Cromwell's advice, to gather forces together " to give the enemy some check, until we shall be able to reach up to him." Charles had the advantage of the start in this race for a kingdom. He took the western road by Carlisle ; and when on English ground issued a proclamation offering pardon to those who would return to their allegiance— excepting from his promised amnesty Bradshaw, Cromwell, and Cook. He was also proclaimed king of England, at the head of his army ; and similar proclamation was made at Penrith and other market-towns. Strict discipline was preserved ; and although the presence of Scots in arms was hateful to the people, they were not outraged by any attempts at plunder. " I dare say," writes lord Lauderdale, " we have not taken the worth of a sixpence." Charles, however, had few important accessions of strength. Lord Howard of Escrick came with a troop of horse, and was knighted. The earl of Derby, coming to join him, was defeated at Wigan, and taken prisoner ; but he then escaped. There was no general rising in his favour. There was no eager surrender of walled towns to the king. The gates of Shrewsbury were shut against him. At Warrington, his passage of the Mersey was opposed by Lambert and Harrison, who had got before him with their cavalry. Cromwell was coming on with his main force, having left six thousand men under Monk in Scotland. On the 22d of August Charles reached Worcester, the parliamentary garrison having evacuated the city. He there set up his standard. On that day nine years his father had set up his standard at

Nottingham. With the same solemnity attached to this act, a summons went forth for all male subjects of due age to gather round the banner of their Sovereign Lord, at the general muster of his forces on the 26th of August. An inconsiderable number of gentlemen came, with about two hundred followers. Meanwhile Cromwell had marched rapidly from Scotland with ten thousand men. As he advanced through Yorkshire, and onward by Nottingham, Coventry, Stratford, Evesham, the Militias of the Counties joined him with a zeal which showed their belief that another Civil War would not be a national blessing. On the 28th of August the General of the Commonwealth was close to Worcester, with thirty thousand men.

Clarendon has described, in general terms, the advantages which Worcester offered as a resting-place for the royalist army, and as a point at which a resolute stand might be made: " Worcester was a very good post, seated almost in the middle of the kingdom, and in as fruitful a country as any part of it; a good city served by the noble river of Severn from all the adjacent counties; Wales behind it, from whence levies might be made of great numbers of stout men. It was a place where the king's friends might repair, if they had the affections they pretended to have; and it was a place where he might defend himself, if the enemy would attack him, with many advantages, and could not be compelled to engage his army in a battle, till Cromwell had gotten men enough to encompass him on every side: and then the king might choose on which side to fight, since the enemy would be on both sides the river, and could not come suddenly to relieve each other."* No doubt these were very sagacious considerations; but Charles had to deal with a commander who thought that skill and daring might overcome disadvantages of position. Cromwell's despatch to the Parliament, written at ten o'clock of the night of the battle, tells the story of his strategy with sufficient precision to be intelligible: " Being so weary, and scarce able to write, yet I thought it my duty to let you know thus much. That upon this day, being the 3d of September (remarkable for a mercy vouchsafed to your forces on this day twelvemonth in Scotland), we built a bridge of boats over Severn, between it and Teme, about half a mile from Worcester; and another over Teme, within pistol-shot of our other bridge. Lieutenant-General Fleetwood and Major-General Dean marched from Upton on the southwest side of Severn up to Powick, a town which was a pass the enemy kept. We passed over some horse and foot, and were in conjunction with the Lieutenant-General's forces. We beat the enemy from hedge to hedge till we beat him into Worcester. The enemy then drew all his forces on the other side the town, all but what he had lost; and made a very considerable fight with us, for three hours' space; but in the end we beat him totally, and pursued him to his royal fort, which we took,—and indeed have beaten his whole army." We see from this rapid narrative that the Lord-General did not regard the risk of his forces being " on both sides the river." Clarendon says, " Cromwell had used none of the delay and circumspection which was imagined; but directed the troops to fall on in all places at once." About noon, according to the same authority, "everybody being upon the post they were appointed, and the enemy making such a stand that it was concluded he meant to make

* "Rebellion," vol. vi. p. 500.

no attempt then, and if he should he might be repelled with ease, his majesty, a little before noon, retired to his lodging to eat and to refresh himself, where he had. not been near an hour when the alarm came that both armies were engaged." Another account says that Charles, and his Council of War, from the top of the cathedral, had beheld the building of the bridge of boats over Teme, and the bridge of boats over Severn ; and then came down to attack Cromwell's men on the side from which he had crossed. But Cromwell was soon back again over his bridge of boats, and now the battle raged with desperate fury. "Indeed, it was a stiff business," writes pithy Oliver. .Clarendon briefly describes this fight ; and quickly comes to the catastrophe : " In no other part was there resistance made ; but such a general consternation possessed the whole army, that the rest of the horse fled, and all the foot threw down their arms before they were charged. When the king came back into the town, he found a good body of horse which had been persuaded to make a stand, though much the major part passed through upon the spur. The king desired those who stayed, that they would follow him, that they might look upon the enemy, who, he believed, did not pursue them. But when his majesty had gone a little way, he found most of the horse were gone the other way, and that he had none but a few servants of his own about him. Then he sent to have the gates of the town shut, that none might get in one way, nor out the other: but all was confusion ; there were few to command, and none to obey: so that the king stayed till very many of the enemy's horse were entered the town, and then he was persuaded to withdraw himself." The 3d of September was a night of terror in the district round Worcester—the Scottish horsemen flying in every direction—their foot-soldiers scattered amongst the harvest-fields, or hiding in woods from the fury of the country people. Baxter, who dwelt in Kidderminster, has described a scene at his own doors : " I was newly gone to bed when the noise of the flying horse acquainted us of the overthrow : and a piece of one of Cromwell's troops that guarded Bewdley bridge having tidings of it, came into our streets, and stood in the open market-place before my door, to surprise those that passed by : And so when many hundreds of the flying army came together, when the thirty troopers cried stand, and fired at them, they either hasted away, or cried quarter, not knowing in the dark what number it was that charged them : and so as many were taken there, as so few men could lay hold on: and till midnight the bullets flying towards my door and windows, and the sorrowful fugitives hasting by for their lives, did tell me the calamitousness of war." *

The prisoners taken at the battle of Worcester, and in the subsequent flight, exceeded seven thousand. They included some of the most distinguished leaders of the royalists in England and Scotland. Upon the entry of Charles into England, the Parliament had declared his adherents to be rebels and traitors to the Commonwealth. Upon this principle, courts-martial were held upon nine of the most distinguished of the prisoners ; and three, amongst whom was the earl of Derby, were executed. The duke of Hamilton, also a prisoner, died of his wounds. But there was one who escaped from the slaughter of Worcester, for whose apprehension a reward

* "Life," p. 69.

was proclaimed throughout the country—a reward of a thousand pounds to the person who should "bring in to the Parliament Charles Stuart, son of the late tyrant." The narrative of Charles Stuart's hidings and escapes during six weeks has been transmitted to us in many trustworthy accounts — one of which, in Magdalen College, Cambridge, purports to be "dictated to Mr. Pepys by the king himself." This escape is one of those episodes of history which relieves its weightier details; and which has a peculiar interest as exhibiting the faithfulness of high and humble to the sanctity of misfortune —a faithfulness as much to be ascribed to natural generosity under great temptation to selfishness, as to any passionate loyalty to the fallen prince. Not only was a large reward offered for his apprehension, but it was proclaimed that those who should knowingly conceal him or his adherents should be held "as partakers and abettors of their traitorous and wicked practices and designs."

Charles, on the night of the battle, when he had ridden in hot haste from Worcester, found himself suddenly in the midst of a party of horse. Buckingham was with him, with Derby, Lauderdale, Wilmot, and others. Charles says, "We had such a number of beaten men with us, of the horse, that I strove, as soon as it was dark, to get from them, and though I could not get them to stand by me against the enemy, I could not get rid of them, now I had a mind to it." At last, with about sixty gentlemen and officers, he slipt away by a bye-road, when it was dark; and by daybreak had got to a place called White Lady's. They then learnt that there were some three thousand of Scotch cavalry on an adjoining heath, all in disorder; and the king's friends urged him to join them, and endeavour to go into Scotland. Clarendon says that "scarce anything could worse befall the king." He resolved therefore to disguise himself "with a pair of ordinary gray cloth breeches, a leathern doublet, and a green jerkin." His notion was to walk to London, where Wilmot was to meet him. His other friends joined the Scots, who were soon routed by English horse; "which shows," says Charles, "that my opinion was not wrong, in not sticking to men who had run away." A "country fellow," Richard Penderell, a Catholic, was recommended to him as a guide. They rested a very short time at White Lady's; and spent all that day in a wood, without meat or drink. At night they got some bread and cheese; and Charles having changed his mind about London, they walked in the direction of the Severn. In the middle of the night they were in danger from a miller, who raised an outcry of "Rogues! rogues!" when they refused to stand at his bidding. At last Charles found a shelter in the house of Mr. Woolfe of Madeley, a gentleman "who had hiding-holes for priests." Mr. Woolfe being told that one who had escaped from Worcester asked his protection, said he would not venture his neck for any man unless it were the king himself. Penderell told the secret. Mr. Woolfe was faithful; and secreted them in his barn. But the locality was a dangerous one; for the ferry was guarded at Madeley, where they expected to cross the Severn. Charles therefore resolved to return to the neighbourhood of White Lady's, hoping to hear some news of Wilmot. He went to Boscobel, the house of Richard Penderell's brother William, a farmer; and there he found a royalist officer, Major Careless. They agreed to leave the house the next day; and instead of hiding in the wood near Boscobel, to get up into a great tree standing in an open plain, where they might see around them. The king thus continues: "Of which proposition of his, I approving, we (that is to say, Careless and I) went, and carried up with us some victuals for the whole day, viz.: bread, cheese, small beer, and nothing else; and got up into a great oak, that had been lopped three or four years before, and being grown out again, very bushy and thick, could not be seen through, and here we stayed all the day. * * * Memorandum: That while we were in this tree we see soldiers going up and down in the thickest of the wood, searching for persons escaped; we seeing them, now and then, peeping out of the wood." The Royal Oak, the glory of sign-painters and school-boys, thus had its origin in Charles's simple narrative. Clarendon gives the story a dramatic point, in saying they saw many from "that blessed tree," who came purposely to look after the king; and that Charles "heard all their discourse, how they would use the king himself if they could take him." The battle of Worcester was fought on Wednesday; the day of hiding in the oak was Friday. On the Saturday and Sunday Charles was concealed at Boscobel by William Penderell and his wife; but on that afternoon he received a message from Wilmot, that he was at the house of Mr. Whitgrave, a Catholic recusant, at Moseley; and desired the king to join him. There were six brothers of the Penderells; and they formed the royal body-guard, as Charles rode upon a jolting horse to this new place of refuge. Mr. Whitgrave left a MS. account of his participation in the king's escape,* minute and somewhat tedious, but containing one or two interesting passages. The arrival of Charles is thus related: "His lordship [Wilmot] said to me, this gentleman under disguise, whom I have hitherto concealed, is both your master, mine, and the master of us all, to whom we all owe our duty and allegiance; and so, kneeling down, he gave me his hand to kiss, and bid me arise, and said he had received from my lord such a character of my loyalty and readiness in those dangers to assist him and his friends, that he would never be unmindful of me or mine; and the next word after was, where is the private place my lord tells me of? which being already prepared and showed him, he went into it, and when come forth, said it was the best place he was ever in. Then he returning to his chamber, sitting down by the fire-side, we pulled off his shoes and stockings, and washed his feet, which were most sadly galled, and then pulled off likewise his apparel and shirt, which was of hurden cloth, and put him on one of Mr. Huddleston's [a priest], and other apparel of ours; then after he had refreshed himself a little by eating some biscuit, and drinking a glass of wine, he grew very cheerful, and said, if it would please Almighty God to send him once more an army of 10,000 good and loyal soldiers and subjects, he feared not to expel all those rogues forth of his kingdom." At Moseley, Charles was again in danger from the presence of the Commonwealth's soldiers; and it was determined that he should leave in a new character. The countryman in the leathern doublet was now transformed into a decent serving-man; who was to convey his mistress, the daughter of colonel Lane, of Bentley, to a relation near Bristol. The lady rode on a pillion behind him. It was fortunate for her reputation that a male cousin was of the party. Having a pass, they reached Bristol in three days

* First published in "Retrospective Review," vol. xiv. p. 62.

without interruption. On their way, the king's horse cast a shoe. "What news?" said the serving-man to the smith. "None, since the beating of those rogues, the Scots; he didn't hear that that rogue Charles Stuart had been taken yet." Charles thought that rogue ought to be hanged, and the smith applauded him as an honest man for his opinion. At Bristol, there was no vessel in which the fugitive could embark, and he had to seek another place of refuge. After a day's rest, he went to Trent House, the residence of colonel Wyndham, a devoted royalist; and his faithful Miss Lane and her cousin accompanied him. Here he remained till a vessel was engaged at Charmouth, near Lyme, to convey to St. Malo a nobleman and his servant. In other disguises Charles proceeded to the coast; but the master of the vessel was locked in his room by his wife, who declared that she and her children should not be ruined for the sake of any royalist. He now hurried, with Wyndham and Wilmot, to Bridport. The town was filled with soldiers, about to embark for Jersey. The king, in his old quality of servant, led the horses through a crowd of troopers, thrusting them out of the way with many a coarse word. There was now no immediate expedient but to return to Trent House. A second ship was engaged at Southampton; but was taken up for the transport of troops. His abode with colonel Wyndham now became unsafe. Another retreat was found in Wiltshire; and in a week a vessel was engaged to sail from Shoreham. The king and his friends again started on the 13th of October, with dogs, as a coursing party, proceeding to the Sussex Downs. They stopped that night at the house of a brother-in-law of one of Charles' friends; and the next day were at Brighthelmstone. This town of marine luxury was then a mean village; and there, at supper, the captain of the engaged vessel recognised the king; and said he would venture his life and all for him. The landlord also said to him—"God bless you. I shall be a lord, and my wife a lady, before I die." At five o'clock on the morning of the 15th the proscribed Charles Stuart went on board; and on the afternoon of the 16th he and Wilmot were landed at Fécamp. The secret of the royal fugitive had been entrusted to forty-five persons, whose names are recorded; and with no one of them was he ever in danger through treachery or want of caution.

Charles and Wilmot, in the travel-stained disguises which they had been compelled to adopt in the place of silks and love-locks, reached Rouen. Their miserable appearance made it difficult for them even to obtain the shelter of an inn. The king managed to obtain some money; and it soon became known that the fugitive of Worcester was safe. On the 29th of October he left Rouen; and, met by his mother and his brother James, he was once more safe in the Louvre. In a dispatch of the 1st of November, we have a glimpse of Charles and Henrietta Maria: "The queen keeps altogether at the Louvre since the king's coming hither. * * * * She is constantly wonderful merry, and seemeth to be overjoyed to see the king safe near her; but he is very sad, and sombre for the most part. That cheerfulness which, against his nature, he strove to show at his first coming hither, having lasted but a few days; and he is very silent always, whether he be with his mother, or in any other company." * Certainly his condition was not a pleasant one. It

* Sir Richard Brown's dispatch.—Green's "Letters," p. 373.

"was very deplorable," says Clarendon. "France was not at all pleased with his being come thither, nor did quickly take notice of his being there. The queen his mother was very glad of his escape, but in no degree able to contribute towards his support; they who had interest with her finding all she had, or could get, too little for their own unlimited expense." The queen's pension from the French court was irregularly paid; "nor had the king one shilling towards the support of himself and his family." *

* "Rebellion," vol. vi. p. 542.

Boscobel House.

WHITELOCKE'S DESCRIPTION OF CROMWELL'S ARMY, IN A CONVERSATION WITH CHRISTINA, QUEEN OF SWEDEN.

WE shall have occasion, in its due place in the text, to notice the embassy of Whitelocke to Sweden, at the end of 1653. His conversations with the famous queen, Christina, the daughter of Gustavus Adolphus, are singularly interesting; far more so than the ordinary records of diplomacy. We select one conversation, in which the Ambassador Extraordinary describes to the accomplished sovereign—who had an admiration of Cromwell very unusual amongst crowned heads—the composition of that Army with which the General won his great victories. At the first private interview between the queen of Sweden and the English minister, Whitelocke having presented her with his instructions which he saw she perfectly understood, her majesty went at once to matters in which she expressed her personal opinions, and sought for information beyond the ordinary range of state discussions :—

"*Queen.* Your General is one of the gallantest men in the world; never were such things done as by the English in your late war. Your General hath done the greatest things of any man in the world; the Prince of Condé is next to him, but short of him. I have as great a respect and honour for your General, as for any man alive; and I pray, let him know as much from me.

"*Whitelocke.* My General is indeed a very brave man; his actions shew it; and I shall not fail to signify to him the great honour of your majesty's respects to him; and I assure your majesty, he hath as high honour for you as for any prince in Christendom.

"*Queen.* I have been told that many officers of your army will themselves pray and preach to their soldiers; is that true?

"*Whitelocke.* Yes, madam, it is very true. When their enemies are swearing, or debauching, or pillaging, the officers and soldiers of the parliament's army used to be encouraging and exhorting one another out of the word of God, and praying together to the Lord of Hosts for his blessing to be with them; who hath shewed his approbation of this military preaching, by the successes he hath given them.

"*Queen.* That's well. Do you use to do so too?

"*Whitelocke.* Yes, upon some occasions, in my own family; and think it as proper for me, being the master of it, to admonish and speak to my people when there is cause, as to be beholden to another to do it for me, which sometimes brings the chaplain into more credit than his lord.

"*Queen.* Doth your General and other great officers do so?

"*Whitelocke.* Yes, madam, very often, and very well. Nevertheless, they maintain chaplains and ministers in their houses and regiments; and such as are godly and worthy ministers have as much respect, and as good provision in England, as in any place of Christendom. Yet 'tis the opinion of many good men with us, that a long cassock, with a silk girdle, and a great beard, do not make a learned or good preacher, without gifts of the Spirit of God and labouring in his vineyard; and whosoever studies the Holy Scripture, and is enabled to do good to the souls of others, and endeavours the same, is no where forbidden by that Word, nor is it blameable. The officers and soldiers of the parliament held it not unlawful, when they carried their lives in their hands, and were going to adventure them in the high places of the field, to encourage one another out of His

Word who commands over all ; and this had more weight and impression with it than any other word could have ; and was never denied to be made use of but by the popish prelates, who by no means would admit lay people (as they call them) to gather from thence that instruction and comfort which can no where else be found.

"*Queen.* Methinks you preach very well, and have now made a good sermon. I assure you I like it very well.

"*Whitelocke.* Madam, I shall account it a great happiness if any of my words please you.

"*Queen.* Indeed, sir, these words of yours do very much please me ; and I shall be glad to hear you oftener on that strain. But I pray tell me, where did your General, and you his officers, learn this way of praying and preaching yourselves ?

"*Whitelocke.* We learnt it from a near friend of your majesty, whose memory all the protestant interest hath cause to honour.

"*Queen.* My friend ! who was that ?

"*Whitelocke.* It was your father, the great king Gustavus Adolphus, who upon his first landing in Germany (as many then present have testified), did himself in person upon the shore, on his knees, give thanks to God for his blessing upon that undertaking ; and he would frequently exhort his people out of God's word ; and God testified his great liking thereof, by the wonderful successes he was pleased to vouchsafe to that gallant king." *

* "Journal of the Swedish Ambassy in 1653-4."

Arms of Oliver Cromwell.

Great Seal of the Commonwealth.

CHAPTER X.

Cromwell's return to London—Reforming policy of Cromwell—Conference on the Settlement of the Nation—Foreign Relations of the Commonwealth—Differences with the United Provinces —Dutch War—Commerce—The Navigation Act—The Navy of England—Blake—Battles of Blake and Van Tromp—Petition of the Army to the Parliament—Dialogue between Cromwell and Whitelocke—The question of future Representation—Dissolution of the Long Parliament—Public Opinion on the Dissolution—Summons for a Parliament.

THE Parliament and people of England felt that Cromwell had saved the Commonwealth. He had done more than maintain a form of government. He had stopped the triumphant return to unlimited power of a prince who, once seated at Whitehall by military superiority, would have swept away every vestige of the liberty and security that had been won since 1640. The greater part of Europe was fast passing into complete despotism; and the state vessel of England would have been borne along helplessly into that shoreless sea. The enemies of Cromwell—the enthusiastic royalists and the theoretic republicans—saw, with dread and hatred, that by the natural course of events, the victorious General would become the virtual head of the Commonwealth. He probably could not suppress the same conviction in his own breast. Ludlow thus writes of Cromwell's return to London after the battle of Worcester: "The General, after this action, which he called the crowning victory, took upon him a more stately behaviour, and chose new friends; neither must it be omitted, that instead of acknowledging the services of those who came from all parts to assist against the common enemy, though he knew they had deserved as much honour as himself and the standing army, he frowned upon them, and the very next day after the fight dismissed and sent them home, well knowing, that a useful and experienced militia was more likely to obstruct than to second him in his ambitious designs. Being on his way to London, many of the Members of Parliament, attended by the City, and great numbers of persons of all orders and conditions, went some miles out of the town to meet him, which tended not a little to heighten the spirit of this haughty gentleman.   * * *   In a word, so much was he elevated with that success, that Mr. Hugh Peters, as he since told me, took so much notice of it, as to say in confidence to a friend upon the road in his return from Worcester, that Cromwell would make himself king." * Again and again Ludlow dwells upon the expression used by Cromwell in his letter to the Parliament, as if it were a foreshadowing of his own " crowning." Later writers accept it in the same sense. Cromwell's real phrase is this : " The dimensions of this mercy are above my thoughts : it is, for aught I know, a *crowning mercy*." To one who was as familiar with Scripture phraseology as Ludlow was, it seems extraordinary that he should attach any more recondite sense to this epithet than that of a *perfecting* mercy or victory. " Thou *crownest* the year with thy goodness " is the same as " Thou *completest* the year with thy goodness."

The authority of the Commonwealth being supreme in every quarter— England tranquil ; Ireland subdued ; Scotland incapable of attempting any further enterprise of a royalist character ; the Channel Islands now garrisoned by a parliamentary force ;—the reduction of the army was a natural policy. The Militia had been disbanded ; but the great body of men in arms, who had so largely influenced the course of military and civil events, were still all-powerful. The regular army was reduced to twenty-five thousand men. The General made no opposition to a measure which in some degree arose from a jealous apprehension of his power. He was now most strenuous for the advancement of two great measures—an Act of Amnesty, and a Law for the Election of future Parliaments. These subjects had been often discussed, and as often laid aside. Upon Cromwell's return to London, he urged both measures forward with his wonted energy. They were just and salutary measures ; yet evil motives were ascribed to him by the republicans. " He grew," says Ludlow, " most familiar with those whom he used to show most aversion to ; endeavouring to oblige the royal party, by procuring for them more favourable conditions than consisted with the justice of the Parliament to grant, under colour of quieting the spirits of many people." † The Law for the Election of future Parliaments was passed, by the House voting that it would not continue its sittings beyond the 3rd of November, 1654. Even this half measure was only carried by a small majority. It became manifest that the Parliament did not rest on very secure foundations. The old question of a Settlement of the Nation was very forcibly revived in many minds. How difficult a question it was may be collected from Whitelocke's report of a Conference held at Speaker Lenthall's house, by request of Cromwell. We do not attempt to abridge this account,

* " Memoirs," vol. i. p. 365, and vol. ii. p. 447.   † *Ibid.* vol. ii. p. 447.

which has been termed "dramaturgic"—"of a date posterior the Restoration"
—but which, at any rate, shows us how these solid puritanical statesmen
conducted their business :—

"Upon the defeat at Worcester, Cromwell desired a meeting with divers
members of Parliament, and some chief officers of the army, at the Speaker's
house. And a great many being there, he proposed to them, That now the old
king being dead, and his son being defeated, he held it necessary to come to
a Settlement of the Nation. And in order thereunto, had requested this
meeting; that they together might consider and advise what was fit to be
done, and to be presented to the Parliament.

'SPEAKER. My Lord, this company were very ready to attend your Excellence, and the business you are pleased to propound to us is very necessary
to be considered. God hath given marvellous success to our forces under
your command; and if we do not improve these mercies to some settlement,
such as may be to God's honour, and the good of this Commonwealth, we
shall be very much blameworthy.

'HARRISON. I think that which my Lord General hath propounded is,
To advise as to a settlement both of our Civil and Spiritual Liberties; and
so, that the mercies which the Lord hath given unto us may not be cast away.
How this may be done is the great question.

'WHITELOCKE. It is a great question indeed, and not suddenly to be resolved! Yet it were pity that a meeting of so many able and worthy
persons as I see here, should be fruitless. I should humbly offer, in the first
place, Whether it be not requisite to be understood in what way this Settlement is desired? Whether of an absolute republic, or with any mixture of
monarchy.

'CROMWELL. My Lord Commissioner Whitelocke hath put us upon
the right point: and indeed it is my meaning, that we should consider,
Whether a Republic, or a mixed Monarchical Government, will be best to be
settled? And if anything Monarchical, then, In whom that power shall be
placed?

'SIR THOMAS WIDDRINGTON. I think a mixed Monarchical Government
will be most suitable to the Laws and People of this nation. And if any
Monarchical, I suppose we shall hold it most just to place that power in one
of the sons of the late king.

'COLONEL FLEETWOOD. I think that the question, Whether an absolute
Republic, or a mixed Monarchy, be best to be settled in this nation, will not
be very easy to be determined.

'LORD CHIEF-JUSTICE ST. JOHN. It will be found, that the Government
of this nation, without something of Monarchical power, will be very difficult
to be so settled as not to shake the foundations of our laws, and the liberties
of the people.

'SPEAKER. It will breed a strange confusion to settle a Government of
of this nation without something of Monarchy.

'COLONEL DESBOROW. I beseech you, my Lord, why may not this, as
well as other nations, be governed in the way of a Republic?

'WHITELOCKE. The laws of England are so interwoven with the power
and practice of Monarchy, that to settle a Government without something
of Monarchy in it, would make so great an alteration in the proceedings of

our Law, that you will scarce have time to rectify it, nor can we well foresee the inconveniences which will arise thereby.

'COLONEL WHALLEY. I do not well understand matters of Law: but it seems to me the best way, not to have anything of Monarchical power in the settlement of our Government. And if we should resolve upon any, whom have we to pitch upon? The king's eldest son hath been in arms against us, and his second son likewise is our enemy.

'SIR THOMAS WIDDRINGTON. But the late king's son, the duke of Gloucester, is still among us; and too young to have been in arms against us, or infected with the principles of our enemies.

'WHITELOCKE. There may be a day given for the king's eldest son, or for the duke of York, his brother, to come into the Parliament. And upon such terms as shall be thought fit and agreeable, both to our Civil and Spiritual Liberties, a Settlement may be made with them.

'CROMWELL. That will be a business of more than ordinary difficulty! But really I think, if it may be done with safety, and preservation of our rights, both as Englishmen and as Christians, That a Settlement with somewhat of Monarchical power in it would be very effectual.' "

Whether in this Conference the Grandees, as they were called, believed that when Cromwell expressed his thought "that a settlement with somewhat of monarchical power in it would be very effectual," he was consulting only his own ambition; or whether they felt that he was propounding a principle of which most men saw the practical wisdom, although "a business of more than ordinary difficulty "—this is not so clear as some have set forth. Whitelocke himself thought that Cromwell was "fishing for men's opinions "—a sort of angling in which he was generally successful.

The foreign relations of the English Commonwealth with the other European States here demand a brief notice; especially those which led to a great naval war with the Dutch.

The privateering hostilities of prince Rupert were necessary to be met by the Republican Parliament with no common energy. The navy was in the lowest condition of inefficiency in 1648; in three years it had become a most formidable force in every sea. The Packet-boat from Dover could now sail without being "pillaged," unless it had "a convoy," as in 1649, when Evelyn writes, "We had a good passage, though chased for some hours by a pirate; but he durst not attack our frigate, and we then chased him till he got under the protection of the castle at Calais; it was a small privateer belonging to the prince of Wales." Rupert had been driven by Blake from the Irish coast. The English Channel was well guarded by an adequate force. There was a Committee for the navy, of which Vane was President; and his zealous activity showed he was a man of action as well as of speech. English squadrons were cruising wherever there was a privateering enemy who could make commerce insecure; for as yet there was no actual war with a foreign nation. When Rupert had escaped from the blockade of Kinsale, he sailed to the coast of Portugal. Blake followed him to the mouth of the Tagus. The royal freebooter had obtained favour at the Court of Lisbon, as might have been expected from a Catholic king, incensed at republican audacity. The stout-hearted Captain who represented the honour of England demanded of king John IV. that he should expel from his ports the enemies of commerce between friendly nations; or that he, Robert Blake, should be allowed to enter the harbour and assert the demands of his government. The required admittance was refused. Blake, attempting to pass the bar, was fired on by the Portuguese forts; and he immediately made reprisals upon the ships of king John. Rupert escaped to the coast of Spain; and after similar demands and refusals from the Spanish government, Blake destroyed the greater number of the privateering fleet. France and Spain were each under very doubtful relations to England, although Spain had recognised the Commonwealth. The time had not arrived when it was necessary to make any strict alliance, or to come to a decided rupture, with either of these great powers—Spain essentially weak in the decay of national spirit; France embarrassed by intestine commotions. The relations of the Commonwealth with the United Provinces were changed by the death of the prince of Orange in 1650. Had he lived his influence would have probably excited a war with the republicans, who had put his father-in-law to death, and abolished monarchical government. There was large commercial intercourse between England and these Provinces. They were both Protestant. The Council of State of the Commonwealth conceived the ambitious project of " a more intrinsical and mutual interest of each other than has hitherto been, for the good of both." Two ambassadors, Oliver St. John and Walter Strickland, were sent to the Hague to accomplish this alliance; which really meant that the two republics should form one nation. This scheme was decidedly unpopular, as it deserved to be. At the Hague there were many English Cavaliers with the duke of York and his sister, the widow of the prince of Orange. The Dutch populace and the English royalists joined in insults to the suite of the ambassadors. Oliver St. John and the duke of York nearly came to crossing swords in the public park. These proceedings took place before the issue of affairs in Scotland. The ambassadors were at length recalled by the Parliament. It was manifest that the rival commercial states would not long remain at peace. A war was unavoidable, when the House carried the Navigation Act, under which no vessel could enter an English port with a cargo not produced or manufactured in the country to which the vessel belonged. This Act went to destroy the Dutch carrying trade. When the royalist cause was finally overthrown by the victory of Worcester, all the smaller states of Europe manifested the greatest eagerness for the alliance of the triumphant Commonwealth. The States-General now sent ambassadors to London. They were received with all outward manifestations of respect; but the English statesmen were resolved to restore the flag of their country to that supremacy which Elizabeth had asserted, but which her successors had suffered to pass away. The Great Seal of the Commonwealth ostentatiously exhibited the defences of " The British Sea." The salute of the English flag, the right of search, the limits of the fisheries, became the subjects of ardent contention between England and the States-General. Whilst these differences continued to be agitated in state papers; whilst the Dutch statesmen were demanding the repeal of the Navigation Act, and the English Council as strenuously refusing even a temporary suspension of that measure, so long considered the great foundation of our commercial prosperity; the fleets of Blake and the Dutch admiral, Van Tromp, came to a conflict on the 19th of May, 1652. The Dutchman had come into the Downs, with a fleet of forty-two vessels. Blake thought it right to look after them, and appeared with twenty-three ships. He fired three signal guns, to summon Van Tromp to lower his flag. Tromp paid no regard to the summons, and sailed on. He suddenly turned round, and sent a broadside into Blake's flag-ship. An

Great Seal of the Commonwealth.

engagement immediately took place which lasted four hours. Van Tromp lost one ship; and when morning dawned, the gazers from the heights of Dover saw no trace of a hostile fleet. There were conflicting statements from each nation. It was a premeditated attack, said the English; he came to insult us on our own seas. Stress of weather drove our admiral to your coasts, said the Dutch; he could have destroyed your fleet if he had meant war. The United Provinces appear to have been anxious to remain at peace; although there were party-divisions amongst their rulers. The English Council was probably not indisposed for a naval war. There was an end of land victories; and the popular excitement might find in maritime successes some occupation more safe than agitations for new reforms. War was declared against the States-General on the 8th of July.

The great naval power of the Dutch was founded, as naval power must necessarily be founded, upon the extent of their commerce. The industrial spirit of the reign of Elizabeth, the maritime discoveries, the bold but imperfect attempts at colonisation, created the material force and called out the national spirit, that swept the Spanish galleons from the seas over which they asserted a haughty dominion. A year or two before the Long Parliament, the commerce of England appears to have been in a languid condition. The East India Company, the Turkey Company, the Merchant Adventurers, had been long contending, with doubtful success, against the inevitable encroachments of private enterprise. The interlopers, as they were called, were sometimes permitted or connived at; and sometimes repressed by stringent proclamations. Individual energy during the palmy days of the Star-

Chamber was sufficiently retarded by small monopolies, in the shape of licenses and patents. Nevertheless the trade of the country went on increasing; and the plantations of America and the West Indies furnished new commodities in exchange for English produce. King James's " Counterblast to Tobacco" was forgotten; and many a good ship was now laden with the weed once sold for its weight in silver. The Civil War necessarily interfered with some mercantile operations; but if we look to the sums which were contributed by London and other commercial cities for the exigencies of the Parliament, we may be assured that in spite of fears and animosities, of civil and religious dissensions, the aggregate exchange of the country suffered no ruinous interruption. Under the Commonwealth there was undoubtedly a revival of commercial enterprise. A writer after the Restoration, complaining of the low condition of trade at that time (1668), attributes it to the mistaken foreign policy of Cromwell: " When this late tyrant, or Protector as some call him, turned out the Long Parliament, the kingdom was arrived at the highest pitch of trade, wealth, and honour that it, in any age, ever yet knew. The trade appeared by the great sums offered then for the customs and excise, nine hundred thousand pounds a year being refused." * There can be no doubt that upon the termination of the Civil War all industry recovered the check that it must have necessarily received. It was felt that property was secure; that a political revolution had been accomplished without any uprooting of the great principles of social order. The nation was prosperous; its rulers were proud of their triumphs and the peaceable results of their arduous contests. The Navigation Act, which was as real a manifestation of hostility to the Dutch as a declaration of war, originated in that increasing commerce which was grown powerful enough to contend with a long-established rivalry. The Dutch trade was founded upon many monopolies offensive to the English spirit of free adventure. A bold struggle was to be made for disputing their rival's possession of the carrying-trade of the world. The Navigation Act was a rude invention suited to the infancy of commerce; and it long held its influence over us, like many other political superstitions. Whether its immediate results were beneficial to the country may be doubted. The statesmen of that period and long after did not understand that buying and selling, freighting and unloading vessels, bringing home useful or luxurious products of foreign countries to exchange with our own growth or manufacture—that these complex operations were not of national benefit merely as conducing to the enrichment of merchants, but chiefly beneficial as they supplied the necessities, or increased the enjoyments, of the great mass of the people. And yet they had glimpses of this truth. In 1649 France prohibited all trade with England. On the 23rd of August, as Whitelocke reports, the House voted, that no wines, wool, or silk, of the growth of France, should be imported into England. But upon the question whether *linen* should be prohibited, " it was resolved in the negative, in regard of the general and necessary use thereof." But the Council of State could dispense with luxuries. The French minister in London wrote to Mazarin that when he told the Council " that they could not do without our wines, they answered jocosely that men soon got accustomed to anything;

* " The World's Mistake in Oliver Cromwell;" reprinted in Harl. Mis. vol. vii.

and that as they had without inconvenience dispensed with a king, contrary to the general belief, so they could also dispense with our French wines." *

In the spirit of commercial rivalry,—with sailors in both fleets that were sometimes serving in the mercantile marine, but always trained to fight, for there were sea-robbers hovering about every rich cargo,—Van Tromp and Blake were to try the mettle of their crews. In every material of naval warfare the Dutch were superior to the English. Their ships were far more numerous; their commanders were more experienced; their men better disciplined. Blake, and Deane, and Popham, and other sea-captains, were land-officers. When Cromwell writes from Ireland to the Council of State, he mentions "Colonel Blake" in one letter, and "General Blake" in another. The Dutch had a more practised body of naval tacticians, who had been educated for a special service connected with the rich commerce of their Indian and American settlements. But in the English fleet there was a devoted zeal which feared no encounter however unequal, and was indifferent to the grounds of a quarrel in the determination to uphold the national honour. In 1652, in anticipation of the Dutch war, Blake was appointed sole admiral and general of the fleet. The character which Clarendon gives of this great commander is candid and discriminating; and it shows how a resolute will, seconding natural talents, may triumph over the impediments of traditionary habits and imbecile routine : "Having done eminent service to the Parliament, especially at Taunton, at land, he then betook himself wholly to the sea ; and quickly made himself signal there. He was the first man that declined the old track, and made it manifest that the science might be attained in less time than was imagined, and despised those rules which had been long in practice, to keep his ship and his men out of danger; which had been held in former times a point of great ability and circumspection; as if the principal art requisite in the captain of a ship had been to be sure to come home safe again. He was the first man who brought the ships to contemn castles on shore, which had been thought ever very formidable, and were discovered by him to make a noise only, and to fright those who could rarely be hurt by them. He was the first that infused that proportion of courage into the seamen, by making them see by experience what mighty things they could do, if they were resolved; and taught them to fight in fire as well as upon water : and though he hath been very well imitated and followed, he was the first that gave the example of that kind of naval courage, and bold and resolute achievements." † The great men of the Civil War and of the Commonwealth were called out by the circumstances of the times. The genius of Blake, in the chases and battles of the sea, was the same creation of a strong necessity as the genius of Cromwell in his land-fights. The great admiral was made out of an idle country gentleman ; the great general was made out of a plain follower of rural industries. The statesmen of the time were fashioned by the same rough teaching. Howell, who was a sagacious observer of men's actions, and whose judgment was not much obscured by his political feelings, writes thus of the men of this period : "The world stands in admiration of the capacity and docibleness of the English, that persons of ordinary breeding,

* Guizot's "Cromwell," vol. i. p. 221 ; quoted from the despatch in Archives des Affaires Etrangères de France.
† "Rebellion," vol. vii. p. 216.

extraction, and callings, should become statesmen and soldiers, commanders and counsellors, both in the art of war and mysteries of state, and know the use of the compass in so short a tract of time." *

The sea-fights between the English and the Dutch in that war of two years have no great historical interest, for they originated in no higher principle than commercial rivalry. Nevertheless they abound in traits of individual heroism; and certainly, whatever have been her subsequent naval glories, England may still be proud of the fame of Blake. Never were her great admirals opposed to one more worthy than Van Tromp. Costly as this war was to the nation,—impolitic in the leaders of the republic—it revived that popular spirit of reliance on the navy which even the base humiliations of the next reign could not extinguish. The maritime glories of the Commonwealth could be referred to with honest pride when Englishmen blushed for the disgraces of the Restoration. We must tell the story very briefly. In June, 1652, Blake had a fleet of a hundred and five ships; carrying nearly four thousand guns. Van Tromp had a hundred and twenty ships. Blake's first business was to assert the bounds of the English fishery. In the seas of the north of Scotland he dispersed six hundred herring busses; capturing or sinking twelve ships of war that were protecting the fishermen's operations. Sir George Ayscough was defending the Channel. Van Tromp came out of the Texel with seventy-nine men of war and ten fire-ships, to engage with Ayscough's inferior squadron. He was becalmed, and unable to engage. He turned to the North Seas; and Blake met him between the Orkneys and Shetland. A tempest came on; the Dutch vessels were scattered and much damaged; and Van Tromp returned to Holland, pursued by Blake. The Dutch admiral was unjustly blamed for his misfortunes as if they had been faults. He resigned his command, and was succeeded by De Ruyter. This bold sailor came into the Channel with thirty vessels; and drove Ayscough into Plymouth. De Ruyter was joined by Cornelius De Witt; and, with a fleet of sixty-four sail, encountered Blake in the Downs. After a severe engagement on the 28th of September, the Dutch were driven back to their own coasts. Van Tromp was again re-instated in command; and he took the sea as winter was approaching, with a fleet of seventy-three sail. The possibility of a hostile navy appearing off the English coast at the end of November was little calculated upon. Blake had only thirty-seven ships to meet the Dutch admiral. But he resolved not to shrink from battle. The issue was a conflict off the Naze, which ended in the necessity of a retreat, with great loss, to the Thames. Van Tromp sailed up and down the Channel with a broom at his mast head, to manifest that he would sweep the seas of the proud islanders; and the States-General proclaimed England under a blockade. The Parliament was not disheartened; and they were just to the merits of their admiral. They sent him again to sea in February, 1653, with a fleet of eighty sail, having Penn and Lawson under his command. He met the Dutch fleet, on the 18th of February, between Portland Bill and Cape La Hogue. It consisted of seventy-five men of war, convoying two hundred and fifty merchantmen. The battle lasted all day, without any decided success. It was renewed on the following noon. Van Tromp made all sail for his own

* "Letters." vol. iv. 1655, p. 111.

coasts, with Blake following him. The same running fight was maintained for two more days, with equal courage and obstinacy on both sides. It was not a decisive victory, though the Dutch lost many ships. Each government bestowed rewards upon its brave captains; and the English parliament appointed a General Thanksgiving. The broom was not again set up at the Dutch mast-head during the war between the two republics.

The large expenses of this Dutch war drove the Parliament and their Council of State to resort to very arbitrary and oppressive measures. The Act of Amnesty afforded some security to the persons of royalists, but that indemnity was not extended to their property. Search for "delinquents" was to be strictly made. Those who had been spared were now called upon to compound for the possession of their estates. Of many Cavaliers all their real and personal property was confiscated. Hundreds of others were required to pay one-third of their property's value within very limited time. Cromwell was opposed to these proceedings. He might, as some may imagine, have desired to embarrass the government of which he was contemplating the overthrow; but we must do him the justice to believe, that, speaking in the face of his contemporaries, he was not making a pretence of moderation, when he thus declared his opinion in 1654: "Poor men, under this arbitrary power, were driven like flocks of sheep, by forty in a morning, to the confiscation of goods and estates, without any man being able to give a reason why two of them had deserved to forfeit a shilling. I tell you the truth. And my soul, and many persons' whom I see in this place, were exceedingly grieved at these things; and knew not which way to help them, except by our mournings, and giving our negatives when occasion served."[*] The victorious General of the armies of the Commonwealth had put himself into the position of the leading reformer of the tyrannies and neglects of the rulers of the Commonwealth. He necessarily had a large body of supporters in the people generally; but his strength was in that body of men whom he had led to conquest—whom he had moulded into a conviction that he was yet to be their instrument in completing the national deliverance from the evils which were still to be striven against. Whilst the English and Dutch were fighting in the Channel in the autumn of 1652, a Petition was presented to the Parliament by "the Officers of my Lord-General's Army." They craved Reform of the Law; they asked for a Gospel ministry; they most especially urged a swifter progress to the Bill for a new Representation in Parliament. Upon this very expressive intimation that there was something going on which was not to be despised, the lawyers applied themselves to settle some very intricate questions as to the possession of estates, so disturbed by the late intestine commotions; and the House voted that "the Committee for regulating the Law be revived." Subsequently they appointed a Commission "to take into consideration what inconveniences there are in the Law; and how the mischiefs that grow from the delays, the changeableness, and the irregularities in law proceedings may be prevented, and the speediest way to reform the same." The demand for a Gospel ministry—a vague demand— was only met by strong laws against "atheistical, blasphemous, and execrable opinions," and by continuing severities against Catholics and Episcopalians.

* Speech to the First Parliament of the Protectorate. Carlyle, vol. iii. p. 44.

The question of a new Representation went on very slowly to a solution. The undisguised hostility of Cromwell to the existing order of things seemed to make the prediction of Hugh Peters not unlikely to be realised. The nation began to feel the embarrassments occasioned by the union of the legislative and executive powers in an Assembly, not numerous enough to be the interpreters of opinion, and too numerous for salutary and consistent action. There is a well-known dialogue between Cromwell and Whitelocke which, although recorded with a little more elaboration than seems natural to the relation of an evening's talk in St. James's Park, may be received as a trustworthy notion of the state of affairs, and of the temper of the man who was destined to change the mode of government. Cromwell complains of "jarrings and animosities one against another;" he points out "the dangerous condition we are in." Whitelocke agrees with him : " My lord, I look upon our present danger as greater than ever it was in the field ; and, as your Excellency truly observes, our proneness is to destroy ourselves, when our enemies could not do it." It is " the factions and ambitious designs " of the army to which he is pointing. Cromwell admits that " their insolency is very great;" but, he continues, " as for the members of Parliament, the army begins to have a strange distaste against them, and I wish there were not too much cause for it. And really their pride and ambition, and self-seeking, engrossing all places of honour and profit to themselves ; and their daily breaking forth into new and violent parties and factions ; their delays of business, and designs to perpetuate themselves, and to continue the power in their own hands ; their meddling in private matters between party and party, contrary to the institution of Parliaments, and their injustice and partiality in those matters ; and the scandalous lives of some of the chief of them ;—these things, my lord, do give too much grounds for people to open their mouths against them, and to dislike them. Nor can they be kept within the bounds of justice, and law or reason ; they themselves being the supreme power of the nation, liable to no account to any, nor to be controlled or regulated by any other power ; there being none superior, or co-ordinate with them. So that, unless there be some authority and power so full and so high as to restrain and keep things in better order, and that may be a check to these exorbitances, it will be impossible in human reason to prevent our ruin." Whitelocke somewhat defends the members of Parliament : " Too many of them are much to blame in those things you have mentioned, and many unfit things have passed among them ; but I hope well of the major part of them, when great matters come to a decision." Cromwell does not quite agree : " Some course must be thought on, to curb and restrain them, or we shall be ruined by them." There is a difficulty in this, as Whitelocke judges : " We ourselves have acknowledged them the supreme power, and taken our commissions and authority in the highest concernments from them ; and how to restrain and rule them after this, it will be hard to find out a way for it." The reply is startling : " What if a man should take upon him to be King ?" Whitelocke replies, as if there could be no doubt that the Lord-General meant himself : " As to your own person, the title of king would be of no advantage, because you have the full kingly power in you already, concerning the militia, as you are General. As to the nomination of civil officers, those whom you think fittest are seldom refused ; and, although you have no negative vote in the passing of laws, yet what you dislike will not easily be carried; and the taxes are already settled, and in your power to dispose the money raised. And as to foreign affairs, though the ceremonial application be made to the Parliament, yet the expectation of good or bad success in it is from your Excellency, and particular solicitations of foreign ministers are made to you only. So that I apprehend indeed less envy, and danger, and pomp, but not less power and real opportunities of doing good, in your being General, than would be if you had assumed the title of King." This bold declaration of Cromwell was met by what appears a singular mode in Whitelocke to propitiate a man who had such power to carry his day-dreams into realities. "What if a man should take upon him to be King," was answered by him with an expedient which he propounds with very considerable alarm. He is re-assured when the Lord-General says, "There shall be no prejudice come to you by any private discourse between us. I shall never betray my friend." The expedient is this: "I propound for your Excellency to send to the king of Scots, and to have a private treaty with him." Cromwell postponed the consideration of this expedient to a further time; and Whitelocke adds, "My Lord-General did not in words express any anger, but only by looks and carriage; and turned aside from me to other company."

During the winter and spring the great question at issue between the Parliament and the man described by Whitelocke as having kingly authority in all but the name, was the long debated question of future representation. In February it was determined that the existing Parliament should dissolve on the 3rd of November of that year. The future number of Representatives was to be four hundred, to be elected by freeholders in counties, and owners or tenants in boroughs. But this was not to be wholly a new Parliament. The members then sitting were to remain as the Representatives of the counties or boroughs for which they then sat; and it was resolved that a general Committee should pronounce upon the validity of the new returns. Against the proposal " for the perpetuating the same men in Parliament," as Cromwell afterwards described this Bill, he gave his most strenuous opposition. On the 19th of April, 1653, there was a great conference of members of the House, and of officers of the Army, at Cromwell's residence of Whitehall. One party pressed the necessity of the Bill; the other desired that " they would devolve the trust over to some well-affected men, such as had an interest in the nation, and were known to be of good affection to the Commonwealth."* " At parting," continues the same narrator of these proceedings,— Cromwell himself—"one of the chief" of the members, and "two or three more, did tell us, that they would endeavour to suspend farther proceedings about their Bill for a new Representation until they had another conference with us. And upon this we had great satisfaction." † What the morrow brought forth is one of the strangest events in English history.

It was late at night when the conference on the 19th of April, at Cromwell's house, the Cockpit at Whitehall, was come to an end. It was understood that the discussion was to be renewed on Wednesday, the 20th. The Lord General is ready to receive the members of Parliament, he and his officers. Some few members are come; but the leaders have not made their

---

* Cromwell's Speech to the "Little Parliament," Carlyle, vol. ii. p. 317.   † Ibid.

appearance. Reports arrived that the Parliament was sitting; then, that Vane, and Algernon Sidney, and Henry Martyn, were urging the immediate passing of the Bill for their dissolution and a new Representation. Colonel Ingoldsby now came in haste, and said that there was not a moment to lose. The obnoxious Bill was about to become Law. Cromwell instantly went forth, followed by Lambert and several other officers. A detachment of soldiers was ordered to march to the House of Commons. The Lord General placed his men in the lobby, and then entered the House alone. "The Parliament sitting as usual, and being in debate upon the Bill with the amendments, which it was thought would have been passed that day, the Lord General Cromwell came into the house, clad in plain black clothes and gray worsted stockings, and sat down as he used to do, in an ordinary place." The scene which ensued has been described by Algernon Sidney, by Whitelocke, and by Ludlow. Sidney and Whitelocke were present. Ludlow was in Ireland; but he was in a position to obtain information, and he has put his details together in a very coherent narrative, little coloured by the wrath which he ever afterwards felt towards the formidable man "in plain black clothes and gray worsted stockings." "He sat down and heard the debate for some time. Then calling to Major-General Harrison, who was on the other side of the House, to come to him, he told him, that he judged the Parliament ripe for a dissolution, and this to be the time of doing it. The Major-General answered, as he since told me; 'Sir, the work is very great and dangerous, therefore I desire you seriously to consider of it before you engage in it.' 'You say well,' replied the General, and thereupon sat still for about a quarter of an hour; and then the question for passing the Bill being to be put, he said again to Major-General Harrison, 'This is the time—I must do it;' and suddenly standing up, made a speech, wherein he loaded the Parliament with the vilest reproaches, charging them not to have a heart to do anything for the public good, to have espoused the corrupt interests of Presbytery, and the lawyers, who were the supporters of tyranny and oppression, accusing them of an intention to perpetuate themselves in power, had they not been forced to the passing of this act, which he affirmed they designed never to observe, and therefore told them, that the Lord had done with them, and had chosen other instruments for the carrying on his work that were more worthy. This he spoke with so much passion and discomposure of mind, as if he had been distracted. Sir Peter Wentworth stood up to answer him, and said, That this was the first time that ever he had heard such unbecoming language given to the Parliament, and that it was the more horrid in that it came from their servant, and their servant whom they had so highly trusted and obliged: but as he was going on, the General stepped into the midst of the House, where continuing his distracted language, he said, 'Come, come, I will put an end to your prating;' then walking up and down the House like a madman, and kicking the ground with his feet, he cried out, 'You are no Parliament, I say you are no Parliament; I will put an end to your sitting; call them in, call them in.' Whereupon the serjeant attending the Parliament opened the doors, and Lieutenant-Colonel Worsley with two files of musketeers entered the House; which Sir Henry Vane observing from his place, said aloud, 'This is not honest; yea, it is against morality and common honesty.' Then Cromwell fell a railing at him, crying out with a loud voice, 'O Sir Henry Vane, Sir

Henry Vane ; the Lord deliver me from Sir Henry Vane.'   Then looking upon
one of the members, he said, 'There sits a drunkard;' and giving much
reviling language to others, he commanded the mace to be taken away,
saying, 'What shall we do with this bauble? here, take it away.'   Having
brought all into this disorder, Major-General Harrison went to the Speaker as
he sat in the chair, and told him, that seeing things were reduced to this pass,
it would not be convenient for him to remain there. The Speaker answered, that
he would not come down unless he were forced. 'Sir,' said Harrison, 'I will lend
you my hand;' and thereupon putting his hand within his, the Speaker came
down.   Then Cromwell applied himself to the members of the House, who
were in number between eighty and a hundred, and said to them, 'It's you
that have forced me to this, for I have sought the Lord night and day, that
he would rather slay me than put me upon the doing of this work.'   Hereupon
Alderman Allen, a member of parliament, told him, that it was not yet gone
so far, but all things might be restored again; and that if the soldiers were
commanded out of the House, and the mace returned, the public affairs might
go on in their former course ; but Cromwell having now passed the Rubicon,
not only rejected his advice, but charged him with an account of some
hundred thousand pounds, for which he threatened to question him, he having
been long treasurer for the Army, and in a rage committed him to the custody
of one of the musketeers.   Alderman Allen told him, that it was well known
that it had not been his fault that his account was not made up long since ;
that he had often tendered it to the House, and that he asked no favour from
any man in that matter.   Cromwell having acted this treacherous and
impious part, ordered the guard to see the House cleared of all the members,
and then seized upon the records that were there, and at Mr. Scobell's house.
After which he went to the clerk, and snatching the Act of Dissolution, which
was ready to pass, out of his hand, he put it under his cloak, and having
commanded the doors to be locked up, went away to Whitehall." *

The Council of State, in spite of the remonstrance of Bradshaw, its
President, was dismissed the same afternoon by the same strong hand.   In a
newspaper of the following day, *Mercurius Politicus*, appeared this semi-
official paragraph : " The Lord General delivered yesterday in Parliament
divers reasons wherefore a present period should be put to the sitting of this
Parliament, and it was accordingly done, the Speaker and the members all
departing ; the ground of which proceedings will, it is probable, be shortly
made public."   The French minister in London, writing to his government
on the 3d of May, describes this humiliating end of the famous Long Parliament.   " The people," he writes, " universally rejoice, and the higher ranks
(la noblesse) equally so, in the *generous* action of General Cromwell, and the
fall of the Parliament, which is reviled by every mouth.   There is written on
the House of Parliament—

'This house is now to be let, unfurnished.' " †

The forcible expulsion of that Parliament which had become supreme
through a similar unconstitutional violence, that of Colonel Pride's Purge,
appears to have produced very little public excitement.   Cromwell exclaimed,

* "Memoirs," vol. ii. p. 455.
† M. de Bordeaux to M. Servien, in Guizot, Appendix xxiii.

"We do not hear even a dog bark at their going." The republican leaders were indignant; but they were powerless. This great change had been effected without a single drop of blood being shed. It was followed by no severities against those who were known to be most hostile to the one man

Cromwell Dissolving Long Parliament—Central Group of West's picture.

who was regarded in many things as the real ruler of England. Many knew and avowed, as he himself knew, "that a settlement with somewhat of monarchical power in it would be very effectual" Speaker Lenthall, who was handed down from his chair, on the 20th of April, had expressed his opinion that "something of monarchy" was wanting for the government of this nation.* Many rejoiced at this approach to an authority more direct, less vacillating and less contentious, than the supreme government by a Parliament. Even the republicans, who had a natural dread of Cromwell's ambition, acquiesced in the instant change

which had been produced by his commanding will. Mrs. Hutchinson writes of her husband, who for nearly a year had been absent from his place in the House: "He was going up to attend the business of his country alone, when news met him upon the road, near London, that Cromwell had broken the Parliament. Notwithstanding, he went on, and found divers of the members there, resolved to submit to the providence of God; and to wait till He should clear their integrity, and to disprove these people who had taxed them of ambition; by sitting still, when they had friends enough in the Army, City, and Country, to have disputed the matter, and probably vanquished these accusers. They thought that if they should vex the land by war among themselves, the late subdued enemies, royalists and presbyterians, would have an opportunity to prevail on their dissensions, to the ruin of both. If these should govern well, and righteously, and moderately, they should enjoy the benefit of their good government; and not envy them the honourable toil."† The republican Colonel and Independent submitted, as the majority submitted, to an usurpation which seemed not wholly unlikely to increase "good government." Suspected as Cromwell was of aspiring to monarchical power, there was nothing in his character to make the people dread that he would rule cruelly and tyrannously instead of "righteously and moderately." The government went on without the slightest interruption. "The Lord-General and his Council of Officers" issued two

* See *ante*, p. 148.   † "Memoirs," vol. ii. p. 205.

declarations, in which it was promised that a certain number of persons should be summoned from all parts of the kingdom—God-fearing men, and of approved integrity,—who should have the direction of affairs. Meanwhile, a Council of State, consisting of thirteen, was appointed,—nine military men and four civilians, with Cromwell as their president. The country remained in perfect tranquillity. The four Commissioners to whom the government of Ireland had been entrusted since the death of Ireton in November, 1651, "continued to act in their places and stations as before," Ludlow, one of them, recording their hope that all would be for the best. Blake called together the puritan captains of his fleet to consider their change of masters. He was urged by some to take part against Cromwell. "No," was his reply, "it is not for us to mind affairs of state, but to keep foreigners from fooling us." Amidst this general submission to what was regarded as a probable blessing, or an inevitable evil, there was sent out, on the 6th of June, a summons to serve as a Member of Parliament, addressed to each of one hundred and thirty-nine persons. These had been selected, some after consultations of ministers with their congregations, others by their known public qualifications, and all by the approval of Cromwell and his Council. Very different was this from a Representation; but it was such an Assembly as had been proposed by Cromwell and his officers at the conferences which preceded the dissolution of April 20th. "That the government of the nation being in such condition as we saw, and things being under so much ill-sense abroad, and likely to end in confusion, we desired they would devolve the trust over to some well-affected men, such as had an interest in the nation, and were known to be of good affection to the Commonwealth. Which, we told them, was no new thing when this land was under the like hurlyburlies. And we had been labouring to get precedents to convince them of it; and it was confessed by them it was no new thing." * The following is the Summons by which the members of "the Little Parliament" were called together:—

"Forasmuch as, upon the dissolution of the late Parliament, it became necessary, that the peace, safety, and good government of this Commonwealth should be provided for: And in order thereunto, divers persons, fearing God, and of approved fidelity and honesty, are, by myself with the advice of my council of officers, nominated; to whom the great charge and trust of so weighty affairs is to be committed: And having good assurance of your love to, and courage for, God and the interest of His cause, and 'that' of the good people of this Commonwealth: I, Oliver Cromwell, Captain General and Commander in Chief of all the Armies and Forces raised and to be raised within this Commonwealth, do hereby summon and require you, —— ——, being one of the persons nominated, —— personally to be and appear at the Council-Chamber, commonly known or called by the name of the Council-Chamber at Whitehall, within the city of Westminster, upon the fourth day of July next ensuing the date hereof; Then and there to take upon you the said trust; unto which you are hereby called, and appointed to serve as a member for the county of ——. And hereof you are not to fail.

"Given under my hand and seal the 6th day of June, 1653,

"OLIVER CROMWELL."

* Cromwell's Speech, July 4. Carlyle, vol. ii. p. 346.

Defeat of the Dutch Fleet.

CHAPTER XI.

Defeat of Van Tromp—Character of the Little Parliament—Cromwell's Address to this Assembly
—Its Provisional Constitution—Their proceedings and tendencies—Resignation of the
Little Parliament—Oliver inaugurated as Protector—Social Condition of the Kingdom.

THE summons which Cromwell sent throughout the country for the
assembling of a body of men that should, in some degree, though not wholly
as a parliament, represent the interest of England, Scotland, and Ireland,
was made public at a propitious season of national triumph. On the 4th of
June, Blake and Monk had sent a despatch to Cromwell, announcing a great
victory over the Dutch fleet. Monk and Dean were cruising, with a portion
of the English fleet, between the North Foreland and Nieuport; Blake was
on our northern coasts. Van Tromp decided to encounter the fleet thus
separated from their great admiral. The engagement continued all through
the day of the 2nd of June. Dean had been killed by a cannon-shot at the

first broadside. Each of the fleets had been sorely crippled when night separated them. The action re-commenced on the 3rd. On that morning the sound of cannon from the north told the welcome news to Monk that the Sea-king was at hand. Blake's ships broke through the Dutch line. Van Tromp fought with desperation. His ship, the Brederode, was boarded by the crew of Penn's flag-ship, the James, after having repulsed Van Tromp's boarders. The Dutch admiral, resolved not to be a prisoner, threw a lighted match into his own powder-magazine. The explosion blew up the deck, but he himself escaped, to renew the battle in a frigate. He at last felt that he was beaten; retreated to his own coasts; and left with the triumphant English eleven vessels and thirteen hundred and fifty prisoners. The Council of State ordered a thanksgiving for the victory. Cromwell's Little Parliament met, on the 4th of July, under prosperous auspices.

The character of this Little Parliament has been studiously misrepresented. We are taught to believe, especially in histories addressed to the youthful understanding, that "the persons pitched upon for exercising this seemingly important trust were the lowest, meanest, and most ignorant among the citizens, and the very dregs of the fanatics." * Clarendon's statement, "there were among them divers of the quality and degree of gentlemen," is wholly suppressed in the usual narratives. Hume's chief objection to them is a characteristic one—"They began with seeking God by prayer." The great scandal of this Assembly was that amongst them "was Praise-God Barebones, a leather-seller of Fleet Street;" as Clarendon mentions, to enable men to form a judgment of the rest. It has no great historical interest to discuss, as some have done, whether the leather-merchant was named Barebones, or Barbone. There he is, sitting by the side of Robert Blake, when Robert has no fighting on his hands; and with Francis Rouse, Provost of Eton, and sundry men, not altogether the lowest, meanest, and most ignorant, bearing the aristocratic names of Montagu, Howard, and Anthony Ashley Cooper. To Cromwell's Summons only two answered by non-attendance. Whitelocke, not at that exact time in good humour with Cromwell, expresses his surprise that "many of this Assembly being persons of fortune and knowledge" they would accept the supreme authority of the nation from such hands. The "persons of fortune and knowledge"—even the leather-seller of Fleet Street—might justly think that it became them, at a crisis when most men perceived that it would have been dangerous to summon a regular Parliament, to accept a trust which might avert the two extreme evils of military despotism or popular outrage. And so, on the 4th of July, they came to the Council-Chamber at Whitehall; and sitting in chairs round a table, the Lord-General, surrounded by his officers, made a speech to the Assembly—"full of the same obscurity, confusion, embarrassment, and absurdity, which appear in almost all Oliver's productions," says Hume: "All glowing with intelligibility, with credibility; with the splendour of genuine veracity, and heroic depth and manfulness," says one who is not scandalised, as Hume is, at Cromwell's words of rejoicing that a body of men was there come to supreme authority upon the principle of "owning God and being owned by Him." That this principle was to involve the exercise

* Goldsmith.

of justice and mercy to the people, according to Oliver's notion, may be collected from a passage or two in his speech, which is characteristic enough of his style of oratory. "He was an entire stranger to oratorical art, to harmony of composition, and to elegance of language," says a great writer and orator; but he adds, "he impelled his auditors with resistless force towards the object which he wished to attain, by exciting in their minds, at every step, the impression which it was his object to produce." * What, we ask, can the highest oratorical art effect beyond this?

After going through a narrative of the circumstances which preceded the dissolution of the Long Parliament, and accounted for his participation in that act, Cromwell says, "Having done that we have done upon such ground of necessity as we have declared, which was not a feigned necessity but a real,—it did behove us, to the end we might manifest to the world the singleness of our hearts and our integrity who did these things, not to grasp at the power ourselves, or keep it in military hands, no, not for a day; but, as far as God enabled us with strength and ability, to put it into the hands of proper persons that might be called from the several parts of the nation. This necessity, and I hope we may say for ourselves, this integrity of concluding to divest the Sword of all power in the Civil Administration,—hath been that that hath moved us to put you to the trouble of coming hither; and having done that, truly we think we cannot, with the discharge of our own consciences, but offer somewhat to you on the devolving of the burden on your shoulders. * * *

"I think, coming through our hands, though such as we are, it may not be ill taken if we do offer somewhat as to the discharge of the trust which is now incumbent upon you. And although I seem to speak of that which may have the face and interpretation of a charge, it's a very humble one; and if he that means to be a servant to you, who hath now called you to the exercise of the supreme authority, discharge what he conceives to be a duty to you, we hope you will take it in good part. And truly I shall not hold you long in it; because I hope it's written in your hearts to approve yourselves to God. * * *

"It's better to pray for you than to counsel you in that matter, that you may exercise the judgment of mercy and truth. It's better, I say, to pray for you than counsel you; to ask wisdom from Heaven for you; which I am confident many thousands of Saints do this day, and have done, and will do, through the permission of God and His assistance. I say it's better to pray than advise: yet truly I think of another Scripture, which is very useful, though it seems to be for a common application to every man as a Christian,—wherein he is counselled to ask wisdom; and he is told what that is. That's 'from above,' we are told; it's 'pure, peaceable, gentle, and easy to be entreated, full of mercy and good fruits;' it's 'without partiality and without hypocrisy.' Truly my thoughts run much upon this place, that to the execution of judgment (the judgment of truth, for that's the judgment) you must have wisdom 'from above,' and that's 'pure.' That will teach you to exercise the judgment of truth; it's 'without partiality.' Purity, impartiality, sincerity: these are the effects of 'wisdom,' and these will help

* Guizot, vol ii. p. 16.

you to execute the judgment of truth. And then if God give you hearts to be 'easy to be entreated,' to be 'peaceably spirited,' to be 'full of good fruits,' bearing good fruits to the nation, to men as men, to the people of God, to all in their several stations,—*this* will teach you to execute the judgment of mercy and truth. And I have little more to say to this. I shall rather bend my prayers for you in that behalf, as I said; and many others will.

"Truly, the 'judgment of truth,' it will teach you to be as just towards an Unbeliever as towards a Believer; and it's our duty to do so. I confess I have said sometimes, foolishly it may be: I had rather miscarry to a Believer than an Unbeliever. This may seem a paradox; but let's take heed of doing that which is evil to either! Oh, if God fill your hearts with such a spirit as Moses had, and as Paul had,—which was not a spirit for Believers only, but for the whole people! Moses, he could die for them; wish himself 'blotted out of God's Book:' Paul could wish himself 'accursed for his countrymen after the flesh:' so full of affection were their spirits unto all. And truly this would help you to execute the judgment of truth, and of mercy also. * * * In my pilgrimage, and some exercises I have had abroad, I did read that Scripture often, forty-first of Isaiah; where God gave me, and some of my fellows, encouragement 'as to' what He would do there and elsewhere; which He hath performed for us. He said, 'He would plant in the wilderness the cedar, the shittah-tree, and the myrtle and the oil-tree; and He would set in the desert the fir-tree, and the pine-tree, and the box-tree together.' For what end will the Lord do all this? That they may see, and know, and consider, and understand together, that the hand of the Lord hath done this;—that it is He who hath wrought all the salvations and deliverances we have received. For what end? To see, and know, and understand together, that he hath done and wrought all this for the good of the Whole Flock. Therefore, I beseech you,—but I think I need not,—have a care of the Whole Flock! Love the sheep, love the lambs; love all, tender all, cherish and countenance all, in all things that are good. And if the poorest Christian, the most mistaken Christian, shall desire to live peaceably and quietly under you,—I say, if any shall desire but to lead a life of godliness and honesty, let him be protected."

We shall not often have occasion to introduce passages of this serious character into our text. It is necessary in this place to exhibit the sort of exhortations addressed by Cromwell to those described by Hume as "low mechanics, fifth monarchy men, anabaptists, antinomians, independents,— the very dregs of fanatics;" and although the style of oratory may differ from modern usage when parliaments are addressed, it may not be regarded as wholly inappropriate and ineffectual.

The constitution of Cromwell's Assembly was provisional. The supreme authority was devolved upon them by an instrument signed by the Lord-General and his officers, but they were to engage not to retain it beyond the 3rd of November, 1654; three months before that time they were to choose their successors; and these were not to sit longer than a year, and then to determine upon a future constitution of government. This was an arrangement not altogether consistent with the theory that Cromwell aimed at an arbitrary government in his own person; and is only explained by the assertion that he adopted a temporary expedient which he knew could not stand in the way of his own ambitious designs. Upon this principle it is held that it was "the deep policy of Cromwell to render himself the sole refuge of those who valued the laws, or the regular ecclesiastical ministry, or their own estates, all in peril from the mad enthusiasts who were in hopes to prevail "*—that he therefore chose the mad enthusiasts, "mingling them with a sufficient proportion of a superior class whom he could direct." A deep policy, no doubt, but also a policy of very uncertain result. When we look back upon the earnestness with which Cromwell had advocated the reform of the law; his zeal for amending the condition of the poor; his eager pleadings against the oppressions of prisoners for debt; his desires for the promotion of education,—it appears somewhat unlikely that if he meant these men to do nothing, and thus ultimately to throw the popularity of remedial measures into his hands, they should at once have applied themselves to these objects with a vigour that contrasted with the comparative torpor of the last days of the Long Parliament. They formed Committees to examine these questions, and others of political importance, such as Union with Scotland, the division of lands in Ireland, and the financial condition of the kingdom. They did, however, some things which gave offence to two powerful classes— the clergy and the lawyers. They abolished the Court of Chancery, and they decreed by a majority of two, that tithes should be abolished. The abolition of tithes, before a maintenance by law should have been otherwise provided, was against a report of their own Committee. The more enthusiastic of the religious party had gained the ascendancy over those who despised this world's wisdom. Cromwell did not despise it; and he saw the real evils that had developed themselves in an authority of which the majority, led by Major-General Harrison, held that "the Saints shall take possession of the kingdom and keep it." † These extreme doctrines were preached in the meetings of sectaries. Two anabaptists, Feake and Powell, were most violent in urging great social changes, at which the more moderate became alarmed. The men of station and property began to regard Cromwell as the only power interposed between order and anarchy. In the next year, when he called a general Parliament, he spoke very clearly upon these dangers of the Commonwealth. He pointed to "the ranks and orders of men, whereby England hath been known for hundreds of years;—a nobleman, a gentleman, a yeoman—that is a good interest of the nation, and a great one. For the orders of men and ranks of men, did not that Levelling principle tend to the reducing of all to an equality? What was the purport of it but to make the tenant as liberal a fortune as the landlord—which, I think, if obtained, would not have lasted long. The men of that principle, after they had served their own turns, would then have cried up property and interest fast enough." With reference to the most fanatical of the sectaries, those who believed in the approach of the Fifth Monarchy, when the Saints of Christ should alone reign in the earth, Cromwell says, "When more fulness of the Spirit is poured forth to subdue iniquity, and bring in everlasting righteousness, then will the approach of that glory be. The carnal divisions and contentions among Christians, so common, are not the symptoms of that kingdom. But for men, on this principle, to betitle themselves, that they are the only men

---

* Hallam, "Constitutional History," Chap. x.   † See Ludlow, "Memoirs," p. 565.

to rule kingdoms, govern nations, and give laws to the people, and determine of property and liberty and everything else, upon such a pretension as this is, —truly they had need to give clear manifestations of God's presence among them, before wise men will receive or submit to their conclusions." Cromwell, the hypocrite, or Cromwell, the fanatic, or Cromwell, the statesman and natural ruler of men—whatever we please to call him—saw that the Fifth Monarchy men, with Major-General Harrison at their head, were too strong in their enthusiasm, to make a stable government of the people a practicable thing. There were many of his adherents of the same opinion. On the 12th of December, colonel Sydenham rose in his place, and forthwith accused the majority of desiring to take away the laws of the land, and substitute a Mosaic code; of seeking to remove a regularly appointed Christian ministry; of opposing all learning and education. He proposed that they should repair in a body to the Lord-General, and resign the trust which had been committed to them. The motion was seconded by sir Charles Wolseley. The accusations were earnestly pronounced to be unjust; and the meritorious labours of the Assembly were dwelt upon. The Speaker suddenly left the Chair, followed by about forty members. Leaving a number of members behind, not sufficient to constitute a House, they repaired to Whitehall, and there hastily wrote a paper resigning their authority into the hands of Cromwell. In the course of the next four days it was signed by eighty members, constituting a majority of the whole House.

The resignation of the Little Parliament is quickly followed by the event to which it was, without doubt, a pre-arranged prelude. "The perfidious Cromwell," writes Ludlow, "having forgot his most solemn professions and former vows, as well as the blood and treasure that had been spent in this contest, thought it high time to take off the mask, and resolved to sacrifice all our victories and deliverances to his pride and ambition, under colour of taking upon him the office as it were of a High Constable, in order to keep the peace of the nation, and to restrain men from cutting one another's throats." * This honest republican does not, however, inform us that such an office was altogether unnecessary. Looking calmly back upon this great issue of a Civil War, we can scarcely doubt that a High Constable was absolutely wanted, and that if the man of due vigour had not been at hand, worse evils might have ensued, than this—that on the 16th of December,

* "Memoirs," vol. ii. p. 471.

1653, Oliver Cromwell was inaugurated "Lord Protector of the Commonwealth of England, Scotland, and Ireland."   On that day Oliver Cromwell,
then fifty-four years of age, dressed in a plain suit of black velvet, sat down
on a Chair of State in the Court of Chancery, when Major-General Lambert
prayed him to accept the office of Protector; and Cromwell consented "to
take upon him the protection and government of these nations, in the manner
expressed in the form of government."   That form was an instrument of
forty-two articles.   It was anything but an instrument constituting the
Protector a Dictator.   The sovereignty was to reside in the Parliament.   He
was not to have the power of a negative on their laws.   He had a power of
making temporary ordinances until the meeting of a Parliament.   A Council
of State was to assist the Protector in the government.   And so, "having
taken the oath as directed in the close of the said instrument," writes Ludlow,
"Major-General Lambert kneeling, presented him with a Sword in the
scabbard, representing the Civil Sword; which Cromwell accepting, put off
his own, intimating thereby that he would no longer rule by the military
sword." *   The indignant Ludlow adds, "though like a false hypocrite, he
designed nothing more."

Before this great change in the government of England, Whitelocke had
set forth on an embassy for the conclusion of a treaty with Sweden.   Cromwell had especially urged this mission upon the reluctant Commissioner, but at
last he had prevailed.† We here notice this embassy, to point to two remarkable
passages in the conversations between queen Christina and the ambassador
of the English Commonwealth, which have reference to Cromwell.   In an
interview, before the news of the event of the 16th of December had reached
Sweden, the following dialogue took place :—

"*Queen.* Much of the story of your general hath some parallel with that
of my ancestor, Gustavus the First, who, from a private gentleman of a noble
family, was advanced to the title of marshal of Sweden, because he had risen
up and rescued his country from the bondage and oppression which the king
of Denmark had put upon them, and expelled that king; and for his reward,
he was at last elected king of Sweden; and I believe that your general will
be king of England in conclusion.

"*Whitelocke.* Pardon me, madam, that cannot be, because England is
resolved into a Commonwealth; and my general hath already sufficient power
and greatness, as general of all their forces both by sea and land, which may
content him.

"*Queen.* Resolve what you will, I believe he resolves to be king: and hardly
can any power or greatness be called sufficient, when the nature of man is so
prone (as in these days) to all ambition."

But very shortly the news reached the Swedish Court of the altered
relations of the English government with foreign states; and then Christina
asks these pertinent questions :—

"*Queen.* Is your new government by a protector different from what it
was before as to monarchy, or is the alteration in all points?

"*Whitelocke.* The government is to be the same as formerly, by successive

---

* Ludlow, "Memoirs." vol. ii. p. 480.   † See note to Chapter ix.

representatives of the people in parliament; only the protector is the head
or chief magistrate of the commonwealth."

The queen is still curious upon several difficult points which arise out of
her meditations upon this novel form of chief magistracy:—

" *Queen.* Why is the title protector, when the power is kingly ?

" *Whitelocke.* I cannot satisfy your majesty of the reasons of this title,
being at so great a distance from the inventors of it.

" *Queen.* New titles, with sovereign power, proved prejudicial to the state
of Rome.

" *Whitelocke.* One of your majesty's ancestors was not permitted to keep
the title of marshal of Sweden.

" *Queen.* He was afterwards king, and that will be next for your protector.

" *Whitelocke.* That will not be so consonant to our Commonwealth as it
was to your crown.   *   *   *

" *Queen.* Is your protector sacred as other kings are ?

" *Whitelocke.* He is not anointed and crowned; those ceremonies were
not used to him.

" *Queen.* His power is the same with that of king, and why should not his
title have been the same ?

" *Whitelocke.* It is the power which makes the title, and not the title
which makes the power; our protector thinks he hath enough of both.

" *Queen.* He is hardly a mortal man then; but he hath brought his
business notably to pass, and hath done great things. I give you my hand
for it, that I have a great value for him."

Before we enter upon a narrative of the public events of the Protectorate,
let us endeavour, out of very imperfect materials, to present a brief view of
the social condition of the kingdom, in continuation of those " glimpses of the
life of the people " which we gave at the commencement of the Civil War.*
The changes of a decade are not very marked in ordinary times. But those
who had lived through the fierce struggles of this decade,—had seen the fall
of the Monarchy, and of the Anglican Church; the almost utter subjection of
the Cavaliers; the growing power of the Army; the triumphs of the Independents over the Presbyterians; the dissolution of the Long Parliament;
and the approach once again to a monarchical form of government—these
must have looked upon great vicissitudes. More than this, those who were
boys when the Puritan William Prynne stood in the pillory in 1633 must have
beheld an entire revolution in the domestic framework of society when the
Puritan Oliver Cromwell sat in the Chair of State in 1653. Such phases of
common life are rarely observed in the whirl of public events. A casual notice
here and there of a letter-writer or a diarist enables us to piece together
a few fragments. Such mosaic work could not be elaborated into a picture
with any pretension to verisimilitude. It can scarcely aspire to any symmetrical proportion.

The rapidity with which some nations, after they have been harassed
and devastated by foreign invasion or intestine wars, recover and become

* Vol. iii. p. 483.

prosperous, mainly depends upon the fact of nations being constituted of an industrious or slothful race. But it also in no small degree depends upon their political institutions,—the amount of individual liberty, the security of property. From a comparison of all accounts we may judge that England recovered with wonderful ease from the destruction of capital, from the taxes, the confiscations of the Civil War. Mrs. Hutchinson's account may be received with little qualification, that the Parliament before its dissolution "had restored the Commonwealth to such a happy, rich, and plentiful condition, as it was not so flourishing before the war; and although the taxes that were paid were great, yet the people were rich, and were able to pay them." The forfeitures of property, so calamitous to individuals, had thrown extensive estates into the hands of the middle classes, who cultivated them to greater profit than their hereditary proprietors. The war itself, calling forth a remarkable union of religious enthusiasm with sober industry, gave an elevation to the pursuits of the trading classes, which made the dignity of work more appreciated by themselves and by others. There was a general desire for religious knowledge which created an aspiration for higher things than money even in the humblest mechanical pursuits. It was not a period of very unequal distribution of wealth amongst those who lived by their industry, except in the larger operations of commerce. Baxter, speaking of his parishioners at Kidderminster, says, "my people were not rich. There were among them very few beggars, because their common trade of stuff-weaving would find work for all, men, women, and children, that were able. * * * * The generality of the master-workmen lived but a little better than their journeymen, from hand to mouth, but only that they laboured not altogether so hard." Yet amongst this humble community, according to this good man, "it was a great advantage to me that my neighbours were of such a trade as allowed them time enough to read or talk of holy things. * * * * As they stand in their loom they can set a book before them." *

Whatever might be the contrarieties of doctrine and discipline amongst the great body of Puritans, the time of scoffing and reviling them was entirely passed. There might be secret mutterings against fanatics amongst the old Cavaliers, but the great religious body was too powerful, their influence was too universal, to meet with violent resistance or open contempt. The more extreme sectaries necessarily provoked much suppressed ridicule; but the great body of the Puritan Clergy were too orderly in their lives, too active in their zeal for godliness and sobriety, and in many cases had established so great a reputation for sound learning, that the most devoted Episcopalians and staunchest Royalists could not pretend to despise them, as in the times of Laud. The toleration which was imperfectly carried out by the republican Independents, but which Cromwell made the ruling principle of his ecclesiastical policy, had a tendency to mitigate some of the old feuds of the surplice and the Geneva gown. Evelyn, the most devoted of men to the past system of government, spiritual and temporal, is naturally disgusted when, on the 4th of December, 1653, "going this day to our church, I was surprised to see a tradesman, a mechanic, step up; I was resolved yet to stay and see what he would make of it." The mechanic inferred from his text that "now

* "Life," p. 89 and 94.

the Saints were called to destroy temporal governments;" and Evelyn remarks
that "with such feculent stuff, so dangerous a crisis were things grown to."
Cromwell rather averted the danger of the crisis, as we have seen.   Evelyn
is severe upon "the usurper" being feasted at the Lord Mayor's, on Ash
Wednesday; though he expresses no grateful sense of the change which
permitted him "to hear the famous Dr. Jeremy Taylor, at St. Gregory's."
This true English gentleman has unconsciously given his testimony that the
kingdom was not in a very wretched condition when "the usurper" began
openly to take the regulation of affairs.   He saw indeed, at Caversham, in
1654, lord Craven's woods being felled " by the rebels,"—the confiscation of
this property having been an expiring act of the despotism of the Rump
Parliament of which Oliver complained.   But in this summer tour, he enjoys
"the idle diversions" of Bath; "trifling and bathing with the company who
frequent the place for health."   He goes to Bristol, "a city emulating
London, not for its large extent, but manner of building—shops, bridge,
traffic, exchange, market-place"—standing "commodiously for Ireland and
the Western world."   He was welcomed with old hospitality at Oxford; and
heard the famous Independent, Dr. Owen, preach, "perstringing [glancing
upon] Episcopacy."   Cromwell was Chancellor of Oxford, and Dr. Owen
Vice-Chancellor; yet Evelyn heard excellent orations; and was delighted at
All Souls, with "music, voices and theorbos, performed by some ingenious
scholars."   Some of the roaring habits of the Cavaliers were not yet banished
by Puritanism; for his party's coachmen, at Spie Park, the seat of sir Edward
Baynton, were made "exceeding drunk" by that "humourous old knight,"
who ordered all gentlemen's servants to be so treated.   At Wilton House,
the earl of Pembroke's, he beholds the mansion and gardens in the most
beautiful order.   He finds at Coventry "the streets full of great shops, clean
and well-paved."   In Rutlandshire he meets an exception to the general
neatness of English villages: "Most of the rural parishes are built of mud,
and the people living as wretchedly as in the most impoverished parts of
France, which they much resemble, being idle and sluttish."   In Leicester-
shire the gentry are "free drinkers."   With these exceptions, wherever he
travels he finds stately houses, fair gardens, ample parks, orderly and contented people.   He sees very few evidences of the ravages of war.   The
country seems quiet and prosperous—not altogether a bad country to live
in, though "an usurper" does rule it.   And so Mr. Evelyn completes his
purchase of Sayes Court; and sets out his oval garden; and trims his holly
hedge, afterwards so famous; and is not wanting for amusements even in
this strict age; for "my lady Gerrard treated us at Mulberry Garden, now
the only place of refreshment about town for persons of the best quality to
be exceedingly cheated at."   There are indications that some of the levities
are creeping in that preceded the coming age of licentiousness: "I now
observed how the women began to paint themselves."

The healthful influence upon the morals of the rural population, through
the exertions and examples of the religious gentry, is well illustrated by the
course of life which colonel Hutchinson pursued: "He had for about a year's
time applied himself, when the parliament could dispense with his absence, to the
administration of justice in the country, and to the putting in execution those
wholesome laws and statutes of the land provided for the orderly regulation of

the people. And it was wonderful how, in a short space, he reformed several abuses and customary neglects in that part of the country where he lived, which, being a rich fruitful vale, drew abundance of vagrant people to come and exercise the idle trade of wandering and begging. But he took such courses that there was very suddenly not a beggar left in the country; and all the poor in every town so maintained and provided for, as they never were so liberally maintained and relieved before nor since. He procured unnecessary alehouses to be put down in all the towns: and if any one that he heard of suffered any disorder or debauchery in his house, he would not suffer him to brew any more. He was a little severe against drunkenness, for which the drunkards would sometimes rail at him; but so were all the children of darkness convinced by his light, that they were in awe more of his virtue than his authority." In the instance of colonel Hutchinson, an accomplished gentleman of the Independent party, Puritanism is thus exhibited in its mildest mood It is suppressing vagrancy and assisting honest poverty. It is putting down unnecessary alehouses, and is a little severe against drunkenness. But Puritanism as exhibited in such a man is not playing the fantastic tricks which made it odious to the great body of the people, and drove the nation into the disgusting sensuality and base self-seeking of the Restoration. Puritanism naturally offended the large remaining body who were attached to the ceremonial of the Anglican Church, when it fasted on Christmas Day, and feasted on Ash Wednesday. It took this course upon the old principle, that the greater was the remove from Roman Catholicism the nearer was the approach to true religion. The people generally did not take these sour protestations against old customs very much to heart. Salt-fish and mince-pie were not banished from their boards, although the orthodox seasons for their consumption had a little varied. They had no great reverence for those who opposed Christmas carols and mummeries; to whom the Yule-log and the Boar's head were abominations. But in spite of them they had their dances and their health-drinkings; and wished their neighbours a merry Christmas after the good old fashion. But when Puritanism put itself into a rampant attitude, as it did in many districts, the people began to loath a power which was so intermeddling and so morose. The neglect of public worship in a few was not likely to be remedied by fines and the stocks. " Katherine Bartlett, widow, upon her own confession, did absent herself from Church the last Lord's day, contrary to the law, in the morning; was ordered to pay 2s. 6d., and in default of paying was ordered to be set in the stocks," says a record of the Dorchester justices. * From the same authority, we learn that John Samwages, not having been to Church for five weeks, and having not money to satisfy the law, was ordered to be stocked for his said offence. Nor was the just observance of Sunday likely to be greatly promoted by informations against husbands and wives, and also,—cruel Puritans,—against " sweethearts," for walking abroad in sermon time. One unhappy victim is stocked three hours for the heinous offence of going to Charminster immediately after dinner on Easter day, and eating milk and cream with some lads and lasses, upon which entertainment they spent

* Hearn's MS. Book of Proceedings, quoted in " Roberts's Southern Counties," p. 244.

twopence each.* Even the plea that the moving about on the Sabbath-day was to hear a preacher in another parish was no mitigation of the offence of taking a longer walk than to the Church at the offender's own door. Working on Sunday was punished by the rigid in the most exemplary manner. A tailor is brought up for labouring at two o'clock on a January morning, to have a piece of his manufacture completed in due time for some orthodox church-goer. Children were punished for playing at nine-stones. Hanging out clothes to dry on the Sabbath was an especial offence. Swearing had been a statutable crime since the time of James I.; but the extreme Puritans not only visited profane cursing with fine and the stocks, but punished even such as followed lady Percy's example of " good sooth," and " God shall mend me." To swear " like a comfit-maker's wife " † was a grievous sin. " Plague take you " was finable. The magisterial interference with private affairs was unceasing. Alice Hill " is found to keep company with Philip Bartlett, in unseasonable time ; " and William Steevens is sent to gaol for frequenting the company of Christian, the wife of Edward Coles, " in a very suspicious manner."

That the extreme severity of some Puritans not only made them hateful but ridiculous when their doctrines were in the ascendant, we may readily believe. But at the same time we cannot fail to discover that many of the imputations against them generally were gross exaggerations. They did not give their children such names as " Fight the good fight of Faith," and " Stand fast on high." When Hume solemnly records that the brother of Praise-God Barebone had for name, " If-Christ-had-not-died-for-you,-you-had-then-been-damned,-Barebone," Hume is hoaxed by a joke invented half-a-century after Barebone had terminated his career of politics and leather-selling. Neither were the Puritans, after the rantings of Stubbes and Prynne against every species of recreation were forgotten, distinguished for any capricious dislike of music, or any contempt of secular knowledge. No man was more eager than Cromwell himself to protect learning and learned men. He sought out scholars for public employments. But, what is more to our present purpose, his house, during the Protectorate, was as remarkable for its refined amusements as for its decorous piety. The love of music was with him almost a passion, as it was with Milton. But we can nowhere find a more complete refutation of the idle belief that all the Puritans were opposed to every harmless pleasure, than in Lucy Hutchinson's description of her own household. Her husband, after his retirement from public affairs, was occupied with the improvement of his estate in the vale of Belvoir. He was a sportsman, and recreated himself, for a little time, with his hawks; " but when a very sober fellow, that never was guilty of the usual vices of that generation of men, rage and swearing, died, he gave over his hawks, and pleased himself with music, and again fell to the practice of his viol, on which he played excellently well; and, entertaining tutors for the diversion and education of his children in all sorts of music, he pleased himself in these innocent recreations during Oliver's mutable reign. As he had great delight, so he had great judgment, in music, and advanced his children's practice more than their tutors: he also was a great supervisor of their learning, and indeed himself a tutor to them all, besides all those tutors which he liberally entertained in his house

---

* Hearn's MS. Book of Proceedings.   † Henry IV., Part 1, Act iii. sc. 1.

for them. He spared not any cost for the education of both his sons and daughters in languages, sciences, music, dancing, and all other qualities befitting their father's house. He was himself their instructor in humility, sobriety, and all godliness and virtue, which he rather strove to make them exercise with love and delight than by constraint. As other things were his delight, this only he made his business, to attend the education of his children, and the government of his own house and town. This he performed so well that never was any man more feared and loved than he by all his domestics, tenants, and hired workmen. He was loved with such a fear and reverence as restrained all rude familiarity and insolent presumptions in those who were under him, and he was feared with so much love that they all delighted to do his pleasure. As he maintained his authority in all relations, so he endeavoured to make their subjection pleasant to them, and rather to convince them by reason than to compel them to obedience, and would decline even to the lowest of his family to make them enjoy their lives in sober cheerfulness, and not find their duties burdensome. * * * * As he was very hospitable, and his conversation no less desirable and pleasant than instructive and advantageous, his house was much resorted to, and as kindly open to those who had in public contests been his enemies, as to his continued friends; for there never lived a man that had less malice and revenge, nor more reconcileableness and kindness and generosity in his nature than he."

Aubrey records that Hollar told him that when the Civil Wars broke out he went to the Low Countries, where he stayed till 1649: "When he first came to England, which was a serene time of peace, the people, both poor and rich, did look cheerfully; but at his return he found the countenances of the people all changed, melancholy, spiteful, as if bewitched." * It is not an unfavourable attribute of the English character that the people did take to heart their strife and bloodshed, their uncertainty as to the present and their dread of the future. Aubrey has no direct record that the old cheerful looks had returned; but we may well conceive, that in spite of the Puritan rigour occasionally breaking out, the nation was gradually resuming the habits, if not wholly of merry England, of stirring and well-employed England. Prosperous industry always brings its own cheerfulness, if it is moderate in its desires, and not inordinate in its cravings for wealth and luxury. We see the stir of inventive genius at this period. We trace the beginnings of that experimental philosophy which was to put England at the head of all industrious nations. "Honest and learned Mr. Hartlib," the friend of Milton, has made "an ink that would give a dozen copies, moist sheets of paper being pressed on it." Robert Boyle, "that excellent person and great virtuoso," is improving the air-pump, and prosecuting his studies in chemistry. Colonel Blount invites philosophers to inspect his new-invented ploughs. Sir P. Neale is famous for his optic-glasses. Greatorex, the mathematical-instrument maker, has an invention to quench fire. The no less important principles of commerce are come to the aid of all science and industry. The City Goldsmiths have opened Banking establishments. Superfluous money has ceased to be buried or locked in chests. Agriculture feels

* "Lives," vol. iii. p. 402.

the influence of the general stir of the national mind. The turnip-husbandry is teaching the farmer that the earth can bear as useful produce as corn; and the cultivation of clover is making a valuable addition to the " meadows trim with daisies pied," upon which the flocks of England have been hitherto sustained.

Amidst the many evidences that we occasionally meet with of the intellectual and industrial activity of the people, we also encounter many proofs of their subjection to superstitious fears. Even the learned and the scientific are not free from singular fancies, engendered in the atmosphere of fanaticism. Mr. Oughtred, " that renowned mathematician," says Evelyn in 1655, " had strong apprehensions of some extraordinary event to happen the following year, from the calculation of coincidence with the diluvian period; and added that it might possibly be to convert the Jews by our Saviour's visible appearance, and to judge the world." The Almanac makers of that time were deluding the people with those prophecies, which they continued to swallow for two centuries. Lilly was still in vogue; and Francis Moore had joined the ranks of imposture. The most remarkable of their exploits was to frighten the isle from its propriety, on the 29th of April, 1652, by the terrors of an eclipse of the sun. This fatal day was called Mirk Monday; and the dread of it " so exceedingly alarmed the whole nation that hardly any one would work, or stir out of their houses."

As regards the material prosperity of the country, we may conclude this sketch with the testimony of Howell, a devoted royalist, to the fact that the restorative powers that were possessed by an energetic people in their insular security and their ancient and renewed freedom, were the providential compensations for long years, first of tyranny and then of universal disturbance. " The calamities and confusions, which the late wars did bring upon us, were many and manifold, yet England may be said to have gained one advantage by it; for whereas before she was like an animal that knew not his own strength, she is now better acquainted with herself, for her power and wealth did never appear more both by land and sea." *

If the immediate effect of the Civil Wars was such that England " became better acquainted with herself," so that she increased in power and wealth, the more lasting consequence was that the whole nation became more earnest in its regard for the higher obligations of religion—that the great body of the people, amidst all the extravagances of sectaries, came to have a more elevated sense of the responsibilities that belonged to a condition approaching to religious liberty. The indifference and profaneness that came in with the return of the Stuarts were chiefly manifest amongst the upper classes,—the sycophants of a debauched Court, and the herd of writers who thought that wit and immorality were necessary companions. The fanaticism and intolerance died out; but the best portions of the Puritan spirit were never extinguished. When the Anglican Church again became oppressive and worldly, the principle of religious liberty asserted itself in strenuous non-conformity, and kept alive the zeal which ultimately placed the Church itself upon the only safe foundation for a wealthy establishment, that of emulation in the duty of diligently teaching, and kindly watching over, the congregations entrusted to

* " Letters," vol. iv. p. 110.

its charge.   Baxter, the Puritan, who was persecuted when the Episcopalians returned to power, is now regarded by English churchmen as the model of a parish priest ; and we may well conclude this view of the period of his ministry immediately following the establishment of the Commonwealth, by his just account of the advantage to religion, through " the change that was made in public affairs by the success of the war : "

" For before, the riotous rabble had boldness enough to make serious godliness a common scorn, and call them all Puritans and Precisians that did not care as little for God and Heaven and their souls as they did ; especially if a man were not fully satisfied with their undisciplined, disorderly churches, or Lay Chancellor's excommunications, &c., then no name was bad enough for him.   And the Bishop's Articles enquiring after such, and their courts and the High Commission grievously afflicting those that did but fast and pray together, or go from an ignorant drunken reader, to hear a godly able preacher at the next parish, &c.   This kept religion among the vulgar under either continual reproach or terror, encouraging the rabble to despise it and revile it, and discouraging those that else would own it.   And experience telleth us, that it is a lamentable impediment to men's conversion, when it is a way everywhere spoken against, and prosecuted by superiors, which they must embrace ; and when at their first approaches they must go through such dangers and obloquy as is fitter for confirmed Christians to be exercised with, than unconverted sinners or young beginners : Therefore, though Cromwell gave liberty to all sects among us, and did not set up any party alone by force, yet this much gave abundant advantage to the Gospel, removing the prejudices and the terrors which hindered it ; especially considering that godliness had countenance and reputation also, as well as liberty ; whereas before, if it did not appear in all the fetters and formalities of the times, it was the way to common shame and ruin." *

* " Life," p. 96.

NEWTON

DRYDEN   LOCKE

Silver Crown.

CHAPTER XII.

The Protectorate—Incentives to assassinate the Protector—Royalist Plot concocted in France—Cromwell's deportment to the French Government—His Foreign Policy generally—First Parliament of the Protectorate—Cromwell's Speech on opening the Session—Parliament questions the Protector's authority—The Parliament House closed—Cromwell requires a Pledge from Members—Recusant Members excluded—Subsequent Temper of the Parliament—Cromwell dissolves the Parliament—Royalist Risings organised—Failure of Risings in the West and North—Resistance to Taxation—The Major-Generals—Severities against Papists and Episcopalians—Tolerance to Sects.

THE Lord Protector of the Commonwealth, who had been inaugurated on the 16th of December, 1653, had, some four months afterwards, entered upon the occupation of the royal palaces of Whitehall and of Hampton Court. Warwick, the Cavalier, who, in 1640, had looked upon a gentleman speaking in Parliament "very ordinarily apparelled," yet lived, as he records, to see this very gentleman, "having had a better tailor, and more. converse among good company," appear at Whitehall "of a great and majestic deportment and comely presence." * The same courtier says, speaking of a period when the dignity of Oliver was further confirmed, "And now he models his house, that it might have some resemblance unto a Court; and his liveries, and lacqueys, and yeomen of the guard are known whom they belong to by their habit." † There was something more went to the making of the Protector Oliver than "a better tailor;" or than "liveries and lacqueys and yeomen of the guard;" something higher even than "more converse among good company." There had been fourteen years of such experience as belonged to no other man in his time. "I was by birth a gentleman; living neither in any considerable height, nor yet in obscurity. I have been called to several employments in the nation." More than this: "My manner of life, which was to run up and down the nation, had given me to see and know the temper and spirits of all men." Thus he spoke to his first Parliament, with a dignified modesty. Out of his own courage, sagacity, and abiding sense

* 'Memoirs,' p. 248.   † *Ibid.* p. 382.

that his destiny was in the hands of a supreme directing power, had a great ruler been made—one who " alone remained to conduct the government and to save the country." Such is the panegyric of Milton. When our most eloquent historian described Cromwell as " the greatest prince that has ever ruled England," * we had reached that state of historical counter-balance, that we could stop to inquire whether the familiar words of usurper, traitor, hypocrite, fanatic, dissembler, as applied to this prince, were not the merest echoes of the united hatred of cavalier and republican, of libertine and sceptic, which it would be well to lay aside after two centuries of abuse and misrepresentation. We shall endeavour to relate the events of the Protectorate, without being wholly carried away by our sense of the unquestionable superiority of this man over the most eminent of his contemporaries. We shall seek to regard him as the man best qualified to stand between the restoration of the monarchy and unmitigated despotism; as one who in his own manifestations of arbitrary power was ever striving to establish a system of constitutional liberty; as one who upheld the supremacy of the laws at a time when in the absence of such a ruler the State might have been plunged into the depths of anarchy and bloodshed. Oliver did many things that are repugnant to the principles of just freedom under an established government; but it may be honestly asked whether his example can justify that species of revolutionary despotism which seeks only to govern by the sword, without a persistent struggle to make the civil authority ultimately supreme. The Protectorate of Oliver was a constant attempt to unite the executive authority of one with the legislative control of many. He laboured to accomplish in his own day what time only could perfect, after many reverses. Had he lived long enough to have founded a dynasty, the problem might have been · more quickly solved. The partial and temporary despotism of the Protectorate is gone; the liberty and toleration which it proposed as its final objects remain. We may apply to the history of this crisis the words of Cromwell's own earnest conviction:—" What are all our Histories, and other traditions of actions in former times, but God manifesting Himself, that He hath shaken, and tumbled down, and trampled upon, everything that He hath not planted?" † We may especially apply these memorable words, so characteristic of their utterer, and yet so universal in their truth, to the whole history of the English Revolution of the seventeenth century. After the first great contest was over, the Divine Right of Kings came back upon England with unforgotten insolence in its pretensions, although with somewhat diminished power of working immediate evil. But it perished: for the Divine Right had to stand a test which its most powerful enemy had proposed as a test of all political action: " If it be of God, He will bear it up: If it be of man it will tumble." ‡

In the remarkable conversation between Cromwell and Whitelocke, which preceded the dissolution of the Long Parliament,§ Whitelocke, with great sagacity, had pointed out that in the assumption by Cromwell of monarchical power, " that question, wherein before so great parties of the nation were engaged, and which was universal, will by this means become in effect a private controversy only. Before it was national, what head of

* Macaulay, " History," vol. i. c. ii.
† Cromwell—Speech iv " Carlyle," vol. iii. p. 89.   ‡ Ibid.   § See ante, p. 156.

government we should have; now it will become particular, who shall be our governor, whether of the family of the Stuarts, or of the family of the Cromwells." Cromwell replied, "I confess you speak reason in this." The acceptance by Cromwell of the office of Protector immediately gave this character to the controversy. The great object of all the discontented Republicans or Cavaliers; the supporters of prerogative, or the enemies of all government but that of the reign of the Saints; those who would have re-entered into possession of the property which had changed hands, or those who sought a division of all property whatsoever; intolerant Episcopalians, equally intolerant Presbyterians, frantic Anabaptists;—all these classes now saw an enemy in the one man in whom the ruling power was concentrated. That power had become more vigilant, more far-seeing, more difficult to shake, than the distracted authority of the Long Parliament, or of the Little Parliament. Foreign governments recognised and dreaded this commanding power, well described by the great minister of the next century: "Oliver Cromwell, who astonished mankind by his intelligence, did not derive it from spies in the cabinet of every prince in Europe: he drew it from the cabinet of his own sagacious mind. He observed facts, and traced them forward to their consequences. From what was, he concluded what must be, and he never was deceived." * Foreign governments might therefore have rejoiced to see the downfall of this man, whose soul was bent upon sustaining the glory of his country, as well as consolidating its internal peace. But he was as prudent as he was watchful. He was surrounded with conspirators of every degree. The doctrine of assassination was openly preached by the Royalists abroad. From Paris, on the 23rd of April, 1654, came out a Proclamation in the name of Charles the Second, setting forth that "a certain base mechanic fellow, by name Oliver Cromwell—after he had most inhumanly and barbarously butchered our dear father, of sacred memory, his just and lawful sovereign—hath most tyrannically and traitorously usurped the supreme power over our said kingdoms." It thus proceeds: "These are therefore, in our name, to give free leave and liberty to any man whomsoever, within any of our three kingdoms, by pistol, sword, or poison, or by any other way or means whatsoever, to destroy the life of the said Oliver Cromwell; wherein they will do an act acceptable to God and good men, by cutting so detestable a villain from the face of the earth." It further promises all sorts of rewards to "whosoever, whether soldier or other, who shall be instrumental in so signal a piece of service." This proclamation has been attributed to Hyde—perhaps unjustly. It is not clear that this incentive to assassination "on the word and faith of a Christian king" really came from Charles Stuart, though undoubtedly it came from his "Court at Paris." But it was extensively circulated, openly abroad, secretly in England; and it produced its natural effects. On the 20th of May, being Saturday—a day on which the Protector usually went to Hampton Court—his guards were to be attacked by thirty stout men, and then and there was the deed to be done, of which the perpetrator was to be honoured with knighthood, and five hundred pounds a year in land, and honourable employment. But the Protector escaped the ambuscade; for

* Chatham's Speech on Spain, November 2, 1770.

five of the royalist projectors of the plot were arrested in their beds a few hours before its intended accomplishment. Forty persons were subjected to examination as confederates with colonel John Gerard, Peter Vowell, a schoolmaster, and Somerset Fox. These three were tried before a High Court of Justice. Fox pleaded guilty, and was pardoned. The other two were executed. Of their guilt the evidence is sufficiently clear; and it is equally manifest that the plan had been communicated to Prince Rupert at Paris. Hyde protested, in a letter to the Secretary Nicholas, that of the " whole matter the king knows no more than you do." There is one point connected with this plot which we give in the words of M. Guizot, who has published the documents upon which it is established: " Whatever may have been the amount of his participation in the plan for the assassination of the Protector, and whether Charles was aware of it or not, the fact itself was incontestable, and probably even more serious than Cromwell allowed it to appear; for there is reason to believe that M. de Baas,—at that time an envoy extraordinary of Mazarin to London, and temporarily connected with the embassy of M. de Bordeaux,—was not unacquainted either with the conspirators or their design. Cromwell was so convinced of this that he summoned M. de Baas before his council, and sharply interrogated him on the subject. But he had too much good sense to magnify the affair beyond what was required by a due regard for his own safety, or by laying too much stress on this incident, to interrupt, for any length of time, his friendly relations with Mazarin and the Court of France, which manifested the greatest anxiety to remain on good terms with him. He merely sent M. de Baas back to France, openly stating to Louis XIV. and Mazarin his reasons for so doing, and showing in this the same moderation which had induced him to bring to trial only three of the conspirators. He had escaped the danger; made known to England and Europe the active vigilance of his police; and proved to the royalists that he would not spare them. He attempted nothing further. He possessed that difficult secret of the art of governing which consists in a just appreciation of what will be sufficient in any given circumstance, and in resting satisfied with it." * Cromwell had made known to Europe, and especially to France, out of whose bosom the assassins came, the vigilance of his own police. He did not complain that France did not go before him to restrain and punish assassination, and to set a mark of reprobation upon such an incentive to the crime as the Proclamation issued in the name of Charles the Second. When it was indisputable, even, that an envoy of the French king had employed the name of Mazarin to encourage this scheme of murder, Cromwell was not diverted from what he regarded as the true national policy, an alliance with France, by his own personal resentment. He sent M. de Baas back to his own Court. He imputed blame to him alone. He writes to Louis XIV. with the true magnanimity of one who could lay aside all meaner considerations in a strong sense of public duty, " It has seemed advisable to us to assure your majesty that, in dismissing de Baas, we had no thought or wish to interrupt in any way the negotiations now pending; desiring, on the contrary, in all candour and simplicity of soul, that false interpretations and subjects of evil suspicions may be cast aside."†

* " Cromwell," vol. ii. p. 51.   † *Ibid.* Appendix ii. p. 420.

Whilst France and Spain were each employing all the resources of their diplomacy to secure the alliance of England, Cromwell, after tedious negotiations, had concluded a peace with the United Provinces. The naval power of the Dutch had been finally broken by the victory of Blake, in July, 1653, when Van Tromp was himself killed by a musket-ball. The conditions of peace which Cromwell exacted were moderate; and he was reproached by his enemies with having sacrificed the advantages gained in the war for the greater popularity of his rule at home. The nation wanted peace, and rejoiced at the termination of hostilities so injurious to its commerce. The Protector, moreover, accomplished his great desire of promoting the union of the Protestant States of Europe. In the treaty with Holland, which was signed on the 5th of April, 1654, were comprehended Denmark, the Hanseatic Towns, and the Swiss Protestant Cantons. A treaty of friendship and alliance with Sweden was concluded in the same month as that with Holland. In the foreign relations of England there was no comparison between the delays of a Parliament and the decision of the Protector. When the responsibility of determining great questions involving peace or war was in the hands of a supreme ruler and his council, the policy of the country was settled upon fixed principles, which, whether or not they were safe and profitable, were at any rate not timid or vacillating. Cromwell decided that the alliance of France was preferable to that of Spain. His opinions were opposed by many of his own officers. He had taken his own view of the question; but for a short time held himself aloof from any final measure, whilst he was assiduously courted by the ambassadors of these rival powers. Of Spain he demanded that the navigation of the West Indies should be free; and that Englishmen in Spain should be protected in the exercise of their religion against the interference of the Inquisition. The Spanish ambassador said that such a demand was to ask for the two eyes of his master. From France he required the expulsion of the Stuarts; and, in a nobler spirit, liberty and security for the French Protestants. No treaty with France was concluded in the first year of the Protectorate, and no hostilities were offered to Spain; but it became manifest that the disposition of Cromwell was to reject the alliance of the power that was the most devoted adherent to Rome. With Portugal he concluded a commercial treaty. But on the very day this treaty was signed, he caused the law to be unflinchingly executed upon the brother of the Portuguese ambassador, who had killed two Englishmen, and raised a tumult with the armed servants of the embassy, at the Exchange in London. No plea of diplomatic privileges could prevent Don Pantaleon de Sa from being tried, convicted, and executed for the offence. The foreigner beheld with dread and wonder the stern and fearless justice of the Commonwealth.

Under the Instrument of Government by which Cromwell was appointed Protector, it was provided that a Parliament should be elected to meet on the 3rd of September, 1654: but that in the interim the Protector, assisted by his Council of twenty-one members, should be entitled to issue Ordinances having the force of Laws, as well as to do all acts necessary for the public service. We have seen how vigorously Cromwell applied himself, during these nine months, to establish the foreign relations of the country upon a satisfactory foundation. But he devoted himself no less energetically to accomplish a series of domestic reforms, some of which have presented models to succeeding reformers; others have been pronounced crude and impracticable; but all have the merit of seeking the public good, though by courses which have that tincture of despotism which essentially belongs to a revolutionary period. When the first Parliament of the Protectorate met on the 4th of September, the Lord Protector went into an elaborate explanation of his measures, domestic and foreign. The one measure of his government that was all important was this: "It hath been instrumental to call a free Parliament; which, blessed be God, we see here this day. I say, a free Parliament." There had been no election to a Parliament in England for fourteen years. This Parliament was to include Representatives of the three kingdoms: "You are met here on the greatest occasion that, I believe, England ever saw; having upon your shoulders the interests of three great nations, with the territory belonging to them." The Parliament was composed of four hundred and sixty members. Of four hundred for England and Wales, two hundred and fifty-one were to be returned by counties, and a hundred and forty-nine by cities and boroughs. Scotland, which had been declared united to England by an Ordinance of the 12th of April, was to send thirty members; Ireland was to send also thirty members. The right of voting for representatives was in those who possessed real or personal property to the value of two hundred pounds. Roman Catholics, and those who had been in arms against the Parliament during the Civil Wars, were excluded from voting, or from being returned as members. But by the instrument of government, and in the terms of the writ for election, it was a condition "That the persons elected shall not have power to alter the government as it is settled in one single person and a parliament."

The 3rd of September, the day appointed for the assembling of Parliament, falling on a Sunday, the House adjourned to the next day, after meeting the Protector in the Painted Chamber. On that Monday the Parliament was opened with almost regal pomp. "The Protector rode in state from Whitehall to the Abbey Church in Westminster. . . . His highness was seated over against the pulpit, the members of the Parliament on both sides. . . . After the sermon, which was preached by Mr. Thomas Goodwin, his highness went in the same equipage to the Painted Chamber, where he took seat in a chair of state set upon steps, and the members upon benches round about." The long speech which Cromwell addressed to this Parliament was reported "by one who stood very near;" and was published "to prevent mistakes." Studied no doubt it was; for its sentences, however involved, are full of meaning,—but it was not delivered from a written paper. In its wide range, and careful explanations, it has a considerable resemblance to the speeches of the American Presidents. The Protector had a very difficult assembly to address. His own Council had been elected, with one exception. Some of the republican leaders, who were indignant at the whole course of government since the dissolution of the Long Parliament, were again returned. A large body of the Presbyterians were also members, with the ever-prevailing desire to maintain their own form of Church government. There was a peculiar significance in the Protector's words when he said that the great end of their meeting was "Healing and Settling. . . . . I trust it is in the minds of you all, and much more in the mind of God, to cause Healing." He would not touch upon past transactions too particularly, for the remembrance of

such, instead of healing, " might set the wound fresh a-bleeding." The oblivion of past animosities was scarcely yet to be accomplished. The social
improvements which were to grow out of a happy concord were nevertheless
to be earnestly striven for. Briefly the Protector referred to what had been
done in the way of Ordinances—" for the interest of the people alone, and
for their good, without respect had to any other interest." The administration of finance had been regulated; the hardships of prisoners for debt, an
old grievance, had been lessened; prison-discipline had been reformed; highways had been improved. These were matters at which the Protector only
glanced. But upon more important reforms he delivered himself without
reserve. And first of Law Reform : " The government hath had some things
to desire; and it hath done some things actually. It hath desired to reform
the Laws. I say to reform them :—and for that end it hath called together
persons, without offence be it spoken, of as great ability and as great interest
as are in these nations, to consider how the laws might be made plain and
short, and less chargeable to the people; how to lessen expense for the good
of the nation. And those things are in preparation, and bills prepared;
which in due time, I make no question, will be tendered to you. In the
meanwhile there hath been care taken to put the administration of the Laws
into the hands of just men; men of the most known integrity and ability.
The Chancery hath been reformed, I hope, to the satisfaction of all good men ;
such as for the things depending there, which made the burden and work of
the honourable persons intrusted in those services too heavy for their ability,
it hath referred many of them to those places where Englishmen love to have
their rights tried, the Courts of Law at Westminster." The Ordinance " for
reforming the Court of Chancery " consisted of sixty-seven articles. That
Court before its reform was in full possession of the character which it long
strove to preserve, in spite of law or ordinance, of public contempt and sena-
torial reprobation. It had twenty-three thousand causes before it, which had
been depending for long years ; it was in the pleasing exercise of its power
" of undoing many families." Cromwell's desire that " the Laws might be
made plain and short, and less chargeable to the people," has been the desire
of all honest rulers and legislators from that time to our own.

But there was a task still more difficult than the reform of the Law, which
the Protector had endeavoured to accomplish by Ordinances : " This Government hath endeavoured to put a stop to that heady way of every man making
himself a Minister and Preacher. It hath endeavoured to settle a method
for the approving and sanctioning of men of piety and ability to discharge
that work. And I think I may say, it hath committed the business to the
trust of persons, both of the Presbyterian and Independent judgments, of as
known ability, piety, and integrity, as any, I believe, this nation hath." . .
" The Government hath also taken care, we hope, for the expulsion of all
those who may be judged any way unfit for this work ; who are scandalous,
and the common scorn and contempt of that function."

In thus describing his measures for securing " men of piety and ability "
to discharge the duties of ministers and preachers, the Protector referred to
the Commissions which he had instituted—the Commission of Triers, and the
Commission of Expurgation. Such measures were the necessary results of
an endeavour to remedy the evils which had been produced by the total

suspension of an authorised ecclesiastical jurisdiction. The episcopal authority
had long ceased. The presbyterian authority was not established. Church
government was wholly at an end. With all his love of toleration, his strong
sense perceived the necessity of something better than what he described as
" the heady way of every man making himself a minister and a preacher."
His Commission for the trial of public preachers comprised nine laymen and
twenty-nine of the clergy. His other Commission consisted of gentry and
clergy in every county, to inquire into the conduct, and eject from their livings,
if necessary, " scandalous, ignorant, and insufficient" ministers. It is impossible
that such Commissions should not have been in many cases arbitrary, perhaps
prejudiced and unjust. But even Baxter has given his testimony to the general
benefit of these irregular attempts to remedy the absence of a competent ecclesiastical authority for providing religious instruction for the people. " Because
this Assembly of Triers is most heavily accused and reproached by some men,
I shall speak the truth of them, and suppose my word will be the rather
taken, because most of them took me for one of their boldest adversaries, as
to their opinion, and because I was known to disown their power. . . The
truth is, that though their authority was null, and though some few over-busy
and over-rigid Independents among them were too severe against all that were
Arminians, and too particular in inquiring after sanctification in those whom
they examined, and somewhat too lax in their admission of unlearned and
erroneous men, that favoured Antinomianism or Anabaptism; yet to give
them their due, they did abundance of good to the Church : They saved many
a congregation from ignorant, ungodly, drunken teachers. . . . All those
that used the Ministry but as a common trade to live by, and were never
likely to convert a soul; all these they usually rejected; and in their stead
admitted of any that were able serious preachers, and lived a godly life, of
what tolerable opinion soever they were." *

The exhortations of Cromwell to labour for " settling and healing " were
addressed to unwilling listeners. There was one sore that, in the thoughts
of a large number, would admit of no healing. In their view the great ulcer
of the State was the supremacy of one man. They would not recognise the
co-ordinate power of legislative and executive. Their idea of a Commonwealth was that of a permanent Assembly, in which all the elementary
principles of government should be perpetually discussed; all the relations of
the State to foreign powers debated and re-debated; all the religious animosities of unnumbered sects continually inflamed by alternations of intolerance and
liberality, according to the vote of the hour. Their complaint was, not that
Cromwell and his Council had ruled unwisely; but that he should be exalted
above his fellows to rule at all. The royalist lampooners said that the
Protector's escutcheon should exhibit

"The Brewers', with the King's arms, quartered." †

Those who had been saved from the annihilation of all their hopes of civil
and religious liberty by the Colonel from Huntingdon, now joined with the
most infuriate of the Cavaliers in abuse of the " base mechanic fellow "—the
" Cæsar in a Clown " before whom they were prostrate when he returned in

* " Life," p. 72.   † " Cleveland's Poems."

triumph from Dunbar and Worcester. Roundhead and Cavalier had now found a common principle of action. The Parliament had ample powers under the Instrument of Government. The authority of the Protector was great, but with very stringent limitations. The conjoined authority was, as described by the Protector himself, "likely to avoid the extremes of monarchy on the one hand, and of democracy on the other." * Nevertheless, the very first occupation of the representatives assembled on the 3rd of September, 1654, was to proceed to the discussion of the question whether the House shall approve of the system of government by a Parliament and a single Person. For three days this elementary question had been debated; and by a majority of a hundred and forty-six votes against a hundred and forty-one, the House resolved to go into Committee to deliberate still further upon this fundamental proposition. On the morning when the Committee was to meet, the doors of the Parliament were found closed. The member for Lynn, Mr. Goddard, has given some details of the incidents of this Tuesday morning : "Going by water to Westminster, I was told that the Parliament doors were locked up, and guarded with soldiers, and that the barges were to attend the Protector to the Painted Chamber." He attempted to pass up the Parliament Stair, but was repulsed by soldiers ; and was required, if he was a Member, to go into the Painted Chamber. "The Speaker and all the Members were walking up and down the Hall, the Court of Requests, and the Painted Chamber, expecting the Protector's coming." The Protector

Westminster.

did come, with his guards ; and took his seat in a chair of state ; and he then spoke for an hour and a half to the bare-headed assembly, with an

* Speech of 22nd January, 1655.

earnestness to which a feeling of wounded pride gave unwonted emphasis.
He had told them, not long before, that they were a free Parliament—" And
so you are, whilst you own the government and authority which called you
hither. . . . .   There was a reciprocity implied and expressed. I
called myself not to this place.   I say again, I called myself not to this place.
. . . . If my calling be from God, and my testimony from the People, God
and the People shall take it from me, else I will not part with it." He then
went over many passages of the past. " Having had some occasions to see,
together with my brethren and countrymen, a happy period put to our sharp
wars and contests with the then common enemy, I hoped, in a private
capacity, to have reaped the fruit and benefit of our hard labours and hazards.
. . . . I hoped to have had leave to retire to a private life. I begged to be
dismissed of my charge. I begged it again and again; and God be judge
between me and all men if I lie in this matter." His dissolution of the
Long Parliament is referred to as a measure of inevitable necessity. His
summoning of the Little Parliament was " to see if a few might have been
called together, for some short time, who might put the nation in some way
of certain settlement." He adds, with the same solemn appeal to Heaven,
" a chief end to myself was to lay down the power which was in my hands."
In the unlimited condition of General of all the forces—that " boundless
authority" conferred by Act of Parliament,—he " did not desire to live a single
day." The Little Parliament resigned the power and authority which had
been committed to them. " All things being again subject to arbitrariness,"
he was himself " a person having power over the three nations without
bound or limit." At the request of that Assembly he accepted the office of
Protector; he took the oath to the government. In obedience to that trust,
he and his Council had been " faithful in calling this Parliament." He
maintained that the people, in the expression of their voices by Grand
Juries, by addresses from Counties and Cities, were his witnesses of approbation to the place he filled. But the climax of his speech was that *they*, the
members of Parliament, were his last witnesses. They came there by his
writs directed to the sheriffs. To these writs the people gave obedience,
having had the Act of Government communicated to them, by printed copies, it
being also read at the places of election. The writ of return was signed with
proviso " that the person so chosen should not have power to alter the
government as now settled in one single Person and a Parliament." Certainly
Oliver Protector has very conclusively settled the question which the Parliament had been three days debating; and he can scarcely be called
tyrannous, when he required " some owning of your call and of the authority which brought you hither. . . . . I must deal plainly with you: What
I forbore upon a just confidence at first, you necessitate me unto now." This
thing (he produces a parchment) when assented to and subscribed is "the means
that will you let in"—(through those doors which are now locked) " to act those
things as a Parliament which are for the good of the People." The parchment
to be signed at the lobby-door bore these words: " I do hereby freely
promise, and engage myself, to be true and faithful to the Lord Protector and
the Commonweath of England, Scotland, and Ireland; and shall not (according to the tenor of the Indenture whereby I am returned to serve in this
present Parliament) propose, or give my consent, to alter the government

as it is settled in a Single Person and a Parliament." Many Members signed at once. Three hundred had signed before the end of the month. But the republican leaders refused to give any pledge; and the Parliament was thus reduced to little more than two-thirds of the members returned. Ludlow, who was then absent in Ireland, deeply sympathises with his brother republicans : " So soon as this visible hand of violence appeared to be upon them, most of the eminent assertors of the liberty of their country withdrew themselves ; being persuaded they should better discharge their duty to the nation by this way of expressing their abhorrence of his tyrannical proceedings, than by surrendering their liberties under their own hands, and then treating with him who was possessed of the sword, to recover some part of them again." The Parliament, thus mutilated, resumed its duties. Its first act was an assertion of some independence in resolving that the pledge not to make any change in the government did not apply beyond the first article under which the Protectorate had been constituted—that which referred to a Single Person and a Parliament; and it adopted that article in a resolution of its own. Cromwell had conquered the Parliament into a show of effecting by its own act what was the result of his strong will. He had said to them, " The wilful throwing away of this government,—I can sooner be willing to be rolled into my grave and buried with infamy, than I can give my consent unto."

When the destinies of a nation hang upon the life of a single man, the importance that is attached to the slightest accidents befalling him extend from his contemporaries to history. Cromwell soon after this great trial of

Elm, Hyde Park, London.

his strength was taking a little relaxation after his own simple fashion. He had been dining under the trees in Hyde Park—he might have sat under the ancient elm which still tells of a time long past.   A new set of six horses had been given him by the duke of Oldenburg ; and with his old country habits, he took the reins to drive home.   The horses plunged, and my Lord Protector was thrown from the box.   Marvellous to relate, a pistol went off in his pocket,—he carried a pistol, at a time when most men went armed ; and grave historians duly notice how apprehensive he must have been of his life to bear about with him such a weapon.   His life was certainly unsafe.   His aged mother, who died in the following November, " at the sound of a musket would often be afraid her son was shot, and could not be satisfied unless she saw him once a day at least."   The good old lady died at the age of ninety-four, blessing that son, and saying " The Lord cause his face to shine upon you, and comfort you in all your Adversities."   Yes, Adversities.   The height of his power was truly an adversity ; and we may well believe him to have been sincere, when in a burst of disappointment amidst the contentions around him, he said of the task of governing, " I had rather keep a flock of sheep." But his genius was fitted for governing, however Ludlow underrated it, in pointing the moral of the runaway horses : " He would needs take the place of his coachman, not doubting but the three pair of horses he was about to drive would prove as tame as the three nations which were ridden by him ; and therefore not contented with their ordinary pace he lashed them very furiously."   By his fall, says the republican philosopher, " he might have been instructed how dangerous it was to intermeddle with those things in which he had no experience."   Oliver's system of government was really founded upon his experience, and not upon refined theories aiming at impracticable perfection.   He drove the state carriage for some years without tumbling from the box ; and though he knew the use of the bit and the whip, he rarely " lashed very furiously."   Only when the state-carriage stood still, was he moved out of his wonted calmness.   For three months the first free Parliament, although the recusant Members had retired to their homes, made small progress in " settling."   From the 21st of September till the 20th of January, the Instrument of Government was in a constant course of amendments and additions.   It was natural enough that attempts should be made to apply every check to arbitrary authority in the Protector ; but the mistrust was too marked ; and the disposition to nullify the existing constitution of the Protectorate too apparent, not to produce a corresponding restlessness in the nation.   Very large questions were depending with foreign powers ; but the function of the executive was stultified by the perpetual discussion as to the authority in which should be confided the right of declaring war or making peace.   The legislative power of the Parliament was absolute ; for if the Protector did not give his consent to any Bill within twenty days of its passing, it became Law without his consent.   And yet the Assembly could not see the necessity of its legislative sanction to the necessary reforms which had been proposed, and partly effected, by Cromwell and his Council.   These measures were suspended, and referred to Committees for revision.   Other propositions of public importance, such as the celebration of marriage ; the treatment of lunatics ; the relief of prisoners for debt ; the equalisation of taxes ; were introduced as Bills, but none were adopted.   They triumphed over Cromwell's supposed ambition in deciding that the Protectorate should be elective, and not hereditary.   They outraged his principles of toleration, which had been recognised in the Instrument of Government, by appointing a Committee to define what was "faith in God by Jesus Christ;" and to settle what were "damnable heresies." They went farther, and ordered that several heretics, amongst whom was John Biddle, a Socinian school-master, should be imprisoned. The supplies were voted as tardily, and with as impolitic an economy, as if the foreign affairs of the country had been conducted with dishonour instead of a dignity which all nations bowed before. The government under a Parliament and a Single Person was becoming impossible. The crisis arrived. The Parliament was to sit five months. Five calendar months would have expired on the 3rd of February. Five lunar months expired on the 22nd of January. On that day the Protector summoned the House to attend him in the Painted Chamber. Another long speech—and the Parliament is dissolved. The Protector could be angry, and speak harsh truths. "Dissettlement and division, discontent and dissatisfaction, together with real dangers to the whole, have been more multiplied within these five months of your sitting than in some years before. Foundations have also been laid for the future renewing of the troubles of these nations by all the enemies of them abroad and at home." And so, concluded Oliver Protector, "I think it my duty to tell you that it is not for the profit of these nations, nor for common and public good, for you to continue here any longer." He has a difficult task before him. His army is unpaid: the people are wretched with soldiers at free quarter; royalists are encouraged to undertake new plots; the old Commonwealth men are ready to join with them. But Oliver keeps up his heart, though he must find his only resource in the same species of despotism against which he fought. "If the Lord take pleasure in England, and if He will do us good, He is very able to bear us up. Let the difficulties be whatsoever they will, we shall in His strength be able to encounter with them. And I bless God I have been inured to difficulties; and I never found God failing when I trusted to Him. I can laugh and sing, in my heart, when I speak of these things to you or elsewhere. And though some may think it a hard thing to raise money without parliamentary authority upon this nation; yet I have another argument to the good people of this nation, if they would be safe, and yet have no better principle: Whether they prefer the having of their will, though it be their destruction rather than comply with things of necessity?" Necessity, the tyrant's plea in all ages, cannot be avoided even by this man who had so few of the qualities of a tyrant besides the energetic will. It is manifest that if the Parliament had not blindly set itself to obstruct the honest exercise of that will in its labours to keep "the good people of this nation safe," any systematic display of arbitrary power would have been as impossible as it would have been impolitic on his part, even if not alien to his nature. He is conscious of his own strength; and he will front alone the storms that are gathering around him. But he had faithful public servants, whose devotion to their country was not weakened by the quarrels of factions. Blake, one of the noblest of these, thus answered Thurloe, Cromwell's secretary, when informed of the dissolution of the Parliament: "I was not much surprised with the intelligence; the slow proceedings and awkward motions of that assembly giving great cause to suspect it would come to some such period. And I cannot but exceedingly wonder that there should yet remain so strong a spirit of preju-

VOL. IV.—108.

dice and animosity in the minds of men who profess themselves most affectionate patriots, as to postpone the necessary ways and means for preservation of the Commonwealth, especially in such a time of concurrence of the mischievous plots and designs both of old and new enemies, tending all to the destruction of the same. But, blessed be God, who hath hitherto delivered, and doth still deliver us ; and I trust will continue so to do, although He be very much tempted by us."

Blake writes this letter from the Mediterranean, where he is doing some memorable things which we shall presently have to notice. Meanwhile "the mischievous plots and designs" to which the admiral refers, are making England very unquiet in this spring of 1655. Charles the Second, who, after some wandering, has settled himself at Cologne; has gone with the Marquis of Ormond to Middleburg, that he may be ready for a landing in England. Wilmot, now earl of Rochester, is in London, organising a general insurrection. " There cannot be," says Clarendon, " a greater manifestation of the universal prejudice and aversion in the whole kingdom towards Cromwell and his government, than that there could be so many designs and conspiracies against him, which were communicated to so many men; and that such signal and notable persons could resort to London, and remain there, without any such information or discovery as might cause them to be apprehended." * It was the policy of Cromwell, as it is of all really sagacious rulers, not to be too prompt with measures of repression—not to alarm and irritate the peaceful portion of the community by fears and suspicions, which are generally the sparks to explode combustible materials instead of being the safety lamps for their discovery. Cromwell left the "signal and notable persons" to pursue the course of their own rashness—even to the organisation of a conspiracy which Rochester represented as so sure of success, that the king's hopes "were so improved, that he thought of nothing more than how he might with the greatest secresy transport himself into England ; for which he did expect a sudden occasion." † The narrative which Clarendon gives of the result of the enterprise which was to place Charles at the head of an English army, sufficiently shows how justly the Protector measured his own strength and that of these sanguine Cavaliers. The assizes were being held at Salisbury. The city was full of grand jurymen and petty jurymen, of magistrates and witnesses, all sleeping quietly in their beds, before the dawning of another day on which the law should assert its wonted majesty in the judgment seat, whatever might be the political differences of republican or royalist. At five o'clock on the morning of the 11th of March, a party of two hundred horsemen rode into the streets of Salisbury, headed by sir Joseph Wagstaff, "a stout man, who looked not far before him,"—a jolly Cavalier, much beloved by the roaring set that Puritanism had not been able to tread out. Their first operation was to seize the sheriff and the two judges, and to break open the gaols. Clarendon recounts the proceedings of these loyal adherents of king Charles, with a solemn unconsciousness that he is showing how necessary was the government of a Cromwell to save England from utter lawlessness and bloodshed : " When the judges were brought out in their robes, and humbly produced their commissions, and the sheriff

* "Rebellion," vol. vii. p. 137.   † *Ibid.* p. 138.

likewise, Wagstaff resolved, after he had caused the king to be proclaimed, to cause them all three to be hanged." There was a country gentleman amongst these insane royalists, John Penruddock, who had some sense of decency, although Clarendon rather blames his scrupulousness: "Poor Penruddock was so passionate to preserve their lives, as if works of this nature could be done by halves, that the major-general durst not persist in it." The judges were dismissed, their commissions being taken from them; but the sheriff was to be hanged, because he refused to proclaim the king. This likewise was resisted; though very many of the gentlemen were much scandalised at the tender-heartedness. To have hanged the sheriff "would have been a seasonable act of severity to have cemented them to perseverance who were engaged in it." No one stirred to help these valiant supporters of the true monarchy and its attributes. In a few hours they left Salisbury, and carrying the sheriff with them, went forwards into Hampshire and Devonshire. There were none to join them. They were hungry and wearied; and a single troop of Cromwell's horse, being by chance in the country, dispersed them almost without a blow, three days afterwards. Some of the leaders, and about fifty of their followers, were taken prisoners. Wagstaff escaped to France. Penruddock, Grove, and others, were tried at Exeter. The two gallant Cavaliers, brave men who deserved much commiseration, were beheaded; a few others were hanged; the larger number were transported to Barbadoes. In the north, Wilmot had gone to take the command of the insurrectionary army. That army never extended beyond a few rash partisans. Wilmot got back to his master, out of heart; and Charles and his court sat down again at Cologne, to wait for times when the existing government might not be quite so strong or so popular as was manifested by the town-crier of a Dorsetshire town refusing, at the peril of his life, to utter the words " Charles the Second, king of England," when Penruddock dictated a royal proclamation.

The complex machine for governing England by a Single Person and a Parliament being again out of working condition, the simpler and ruder machine of the Single Person must work as it best may to prevent all government from coming to an end. This is despotism. But despotism, however odious as a principle, has many degrees of evil, and is only rendered tolerable by the desire of a despot to perform a bad office in the least mischievous way. Burke has truly described the government of Cromwell as " somewhat rigid, but for a new power no savage tyranny." * The period at which his despotism put on its most rigid form was in the year that followed the dismissal of the Parliament at the beginning of 1655. He was left without a legal revenue, for the maintenance of the civil and military powers of the government. A merchant named Cony had refused to pay custom duties, as illegally levied by ordinance. Cromwell tried to soothe the sturdy citizen, who reminded him that he himself had said in the Long Parliament, that the subject who yields to an illegal impost is more the enemy of his country than the tyrant who imposes it. The Protector sent the merchant to prison; and then more arbitrarily imprisoned the Counsel, who had, in pleading for his writ of Habeas Corpus, used arguments which went to deny altogether the legality of the

* " Policy of the Allies."

authority of the existing government. There was a compromise in which Cony at length withdrew his opposition to the impost, and his legal defenders were released. Sir Peter Wentworth refused to pay the taxes levied upon him, and was brought before Cromwell and his Council. He was required to withdraw an action which he had commenced against the tax-collector. "If you command it I must submit," said Wentworth to the Protector. He did command it, and the resistance was at an end. Clarendon, who records these acts of oppression, and especially Cromwell's lecture of the judges "that they should not suffer the lawyers to prate what it would not become them to hear," yet says, " in all other matters, which did not concern the loss of his jurisdiction, he seemed to have great reverence for the law, rarely interposing between party and party." In his fiscal measures the most invidious was the imposition of an especial tax upon a limited number of royalists—a property-tax, under which all those of the king's party who were considered disaffected, and who either possessed an income of a hundred a year from land, or a personal estate of fifteen hundred pounds in value, were called upon for a contribution of one-tenth. To assess and collect this tax it was necessary to call forth some new instruments. The Protector divided the country into ten districts, each under the authority of a Major-General, who had various large powers, and who had especially under his command the Militia of the Counties. The Militia was a force essentially different from the regular army ; a force not without strong popular instincts, and not so manageable in carrying through acts of oppression. It was a military police, especially appointed to enforce a system of partial repression. There was no resistance to the acts of the Major-Generals and their Commissioners, and there was no large amount of murmuring. The decimation of the richer royalists, who had already been so harassed by sequestrations, and for whose relief Cromwell had himself laboured to carry through the Act of Oblivion, was truly described by Ludlow as calculated to render its victims " desperate and irreconcileable, they being not able to call anything their own, whilst by the same rule that he seized one-tenth, he might also take away the other nine parts at his pleasure." * There is a worse evil in despotic courses than that of making men " desperate and irreconcileable "—that of making them time-serving, slavish, and apathetic. A passage in Baxter's life is illustrative of this : " James Berry was made Major-General of Worcestershire, Shropshire, Herefordshire, and North Wales,—the counties in which he had formerly lived as a servant, a clerk of iron-works. His reign was modest and short ; but hated and scorned by the gentry that had known his inferiority, so that it had been better for him to have chosen a stranger place. And yet many of them attended him as submissively as if they had honoured him ; so significant a thing is power and prosperity with worldly minds." † That these Major-Generals meddled with other royalists than those of good property is shown by the arrest of John Cleveland, " that incomparable son of Apollo " according to the creed of the Cavaliers, for whose cause he has been writing bitter satires since the first days of the Long Parliament. Colonel Haynes has arrested him at Norwich, and sent him to prison at Yarmouth. Cleveland addressed a petition to the Protector, though he had ridiculed his

* "Memoirs," vol. ii. p. 519.   † "Life," p. 97.

" copper-nose," in which the unfortunate poet says, " I am inclined to believe that next to the adherence to the royal party, the cause of my confinement is the narrowness of my estate, for none stand committed whose estate can bail them. I only am the prisoner who have no acres to be my hostage. Now if my poverty be criminal, with reverence be it spoken, I must implead your highness, whose victorious arms have reduced me to it, as accessory to my guilt." The Petition, an elaborate composition far more laudatory than insulting, procured the poet's release. *

At this period the government of the Protector was more than usually harsh towards the Catholics and the Clergy of the Anglican Church. The plots against the Commonwealth were generally mixed up with the intrigues of Papists, and the harshness towards them was the practical continuance of the spirit of the severe penal laws. The Episcopalians were harassed at the instance of the Presbyterians, in spite of Cromwell's own ardent desire for toleration. One of the most odious measures against them was an ordinance prohibiting them to be received in private families as preceptors. Archbishop Usher, for whom the Protector had a deep respect, remonstrated with him against this injustice. He did not withdraw the ordinance, but it remained inoperative. Prejudices were too strong to allow him to act up to his own principles. But with the great Puritan body, and the various sectaries that sprang from them, he was determined to keep their animosities under the control of an equal justice. "If a man of one form," he declared to the Parliament in 1656, "will be trampling upon the heels of another form; if an Independent, for example, will despise him who is under Baptism, and will revile him, and will reproach and provoke him, I will not suffer it in him." Neither should the Independent censure the Presbyterian, nor the Presbyterian the Independent. This toleration made him many enemies: "I have borne my reproach; but I have, through God's mercy, not been unhappy in hindering any one religion to impose upon another." The Quakers, who were hunted and persecuted by every other sect, found a friend in Cromwell. George Fox, who had been seized in his preachings, and carried to London, managed to see the Protector, and exhorted him to keep in the fear of God; and Cromwell, having patiently listened to his lecture, parted with him, saying " Come again to my house. If thou and I were but an hour of the day together, we should be nearer one to the other. I wish no more harm to thee than I do to my own soul." † George and some of his brethren had been dispersing "base books against the Lord Protector," as major-general Goffe informed Thurloe. Cromwell sent the Quaker unharmed away, having received from him a written promise that he would do nothing against his government.

* Printed with the Poems, edit. 1657.
† Fox's "Journal," quoted in Carlyle's "Cromwell," vol. ii. p. 121.

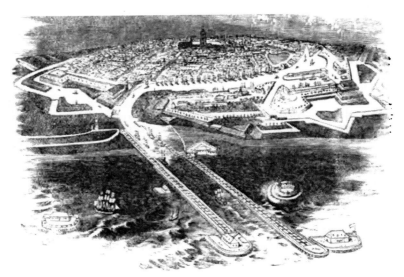

Dunkirk. From an old Print.

CHAPTER XIII.

Greatness of Cromwell in his Foreign Policy—Naval armaments—Blake's exploits—Jamaica taken—Cromwell's interference for the Vaudois—He attempts to procure the re-admission of the Jews to settle in England—Hostility of the Republicans to the Protector—Cromwell requires a pledge from Republican leaders—Meeting of the Protector's Second Parliament—Cromwell's opening Speech—Members excluded from the Parliament—Case of James Nayler—Sindercomb's plot—The Parliament votes that Cromwell shall be offered the Crown—Conferences on the subject of Kingship—Cromwell declines to accept the title—Blake's victory at Santa Cruz—Cromwell inaugurated as Protector under a new Instrument of Government—Second Session of Parliament—The Upper House—The old secluded Members admitted to sit—Cromwell's Speech—Violent dissensions—The Parliament dissolved—Projected rising of Royalists—Allied war in the Netherlands—Dunkirk—Cromwell's family afflictions—His illness and death.

"His greatness at home was but a shadow of the glory he had abroad." So writes Clarendon of him who, he says, "will be looked upon by posterity as a brave bad man." The mere courtiers of Charles II. used to talk of the Protector as "that wretch, Cromwell." [*] It is something for Clarendon to acknowledge that "he had some good qualities." He had the highest of all qualities in a prince—a sense of public duty. He was an Englishman, bent upon sustaining the honour of his country amongst the nations. In this great design his genius luxuriated. He was not beset with difficulties, as at home, when he sent forth his fleets to sweep the Barbary pirates from the Mediter-

[*] Letter of Henrietta Maria; Green, p. 380

ranean, or employed his diplomatists to express in distinct terms, that the Protestants of the Piedmontese valleys should not be massacred by a duke of Savoy, although supported by a king of France. He went straight to his object, when he concluded the French alliance, and rejected that of Spain, because "there is not liberty of conscience to be had from the Spaniard, neither is there satisfaction for injuries nor for blood." [*] "Elizabeth, of famous memory, that lady, that great queen," as Cromwell term‹ her, was the load-star of his foreign policy ; "nothing being more usual than his saying ' that his ships in the Mediterranean should visit Civita Vecchia, and that the sound of his cannon should be heard at Rome.' " [†] He raised his country out of the pitiful subjection to which the Stuarts had reduced it, to be again amongst the most respected of Christian powers. "It was hard to discover which feared him most, France, Spain, or the Low Countries, where his friendship was current at the value he put upon it." [‡] The price which he demanded for his friendship was, that the liberties of Englishmen, their personal security, and their rights of conscience, should be respected throughout the world; that no sea should be closed against English commerce; that no combination of crowned heads should attempt to control the domestic government of these kingdoms. He made no pretensions to national supremacy inconsistent with the rights of other countries ; but not a tittle would he abate of that respect which was due to his own country and his own government. He was raised to supreme power by a revolution upon which all monarchical rulers must have looked with dread and suspicion and secret hatred ; but he made no efforts to imbue other kingdoms with a revolutionary spirit. His moderation commanded a far higher respect than if he had formed schemes of European conquest ; or had attempted to conciliate discontented colonels and murmuring troopers, by leading them in person against Condé or Don John of Austria. Truly has it been said, "He was a soldier; he had risen by war. Had his ambition been of an impure or selfish kind, it would have been easy for him to plunge his country into continental hostilities on a large scale, and to dazzle the restless factions which he ruled, by the splendour of his victories." [§] He left to Blake the glory of making the flag of England triumphant on the seas, satisfied to counsel and encourage him. His practical spirit of doing everything for utility, and nothing for vain glory, was so infused into his officers, that when Turenne sent to Lockhart, Cromwell's general in the Netherlands, an explanation of the plan of the battle they were to fight with their allied forces, the Englishman, with a noble common sense that could lay aside the morbid vanity which too often mars the success of joint enterprises, exclaimed, "Very good : I shall obey M. de Turenne's orders, and he may explain his reasons after the battle, if he pleases." [||]

The maintenance and increase of the naval arm of our strength was the especial care of the Protector. "I went," writes Evelyn in his Diary of the 9th of April, 1655, "to see the great ship newly built by the usurper, Oliver, carrying ninety-six brass guns and 1000 tons burthen." Some months before, two armaments were being fitted out at Portsmouth. Their destination was unknown. Cromwell was one day surrounded in the streets by a large

---

[*] Speech, 17th September, 1656.
[†] "Clarendon," vol. vii. p. 297. [‡] Ibid.
[§] Macaulay, "Essays," vol. i. [||] Guizot, "Cromwell," vol. ii. p. 383.

all his dominions." The instant that Cromwell heard of the preliminary harsh measures of the duke of Savoy towards the Vaudois, he wrote to the English resident in Switzerland to advise the persecuted people to appeal to England. The news of the massacre arrived before any request was made for succour. The Protector immediately sent an envoy extraordinary to Louis XIV. and to the duke of Savoy, with letters of remonstrance. Upon all the Protestant princes he called for assistance in demanding justice for the Vaudois. A collection throughout England was made for these poor people, and Cromwell himself gave two thousand pounds. His language was as moderate as it was firm. But his meaning could not be mistaken. France was most anxious to conclude a treaty of peace and commerce with England; but Cromwell declared that he would not sign it till the French Court had procured from the Piedmontese government the Restoration of the Vaudois to their ancient liberties. The French minister at Turin now insisted on an immediate pacification, which should restore the Vaudois to their civil and religious liberties, as of old. The business was hastily concluded by the French agents, and some harsh conditions were connected with this settlement, which again caused the interference of the Protector in 1658. The earnest thought of Cromwell went through Europe clothed in the eloquent Latin of Milton; and even those who hated the Commonwealth acknowledged that England never stood higher than when she demanded justice for a few poor cultivators of the Alps—those who had kept the truth

" When all our fathers worshipped stocks and stones."

The efforts of the Protector to procure safety and liberty of conscience for a race of Christians dwelling in three small valleys of the Alps, were more successful than his endeavours to give a legal home in England to a persecuted race, scattered through every land. The Jews were banished, and their immoveable· goods were confiscated, in 1290. In 1655 Cromwell assembled his Council, and " divers eminent ministers," to consider the petition of Rabbi Manasseh-Ben-Israel of Amsterdam, that the Jews might have liberty to settle again in England. Three hundred and sixty-five years of obstinate prejudice might probably have sufficed to exhaust the bigotry of a Christian community. Cromwell thought the term quite long enough; and so the matter of allowing the Jews to reside again amongst us, and trade, and have public synagogues, and a cemetery out of the town to bury their dead, was discussed in four conferences; and the Protector advocated the measure; and one present says, "I never heard a man speak so well." But there were then, as there always will be, grave divines and learned lawyers who patch a rag of ancient intolerance into their modern garments, to show the colour and substance of the old material that all men once proudly wore. Of this species was William Prynne, who headed the cry of Christianity in danger, by publishing a manifesto against the Jews, in which "their ill-deportment, misdemeanours, condition, sufferings, oppressions, slaughters, plunders by popular insurrections, royal exactions, and final banishment," were brought forward in connection with Laws and Scriptures, " to plead and conclude against their re-admission into England." The old clamour against the Jewerie was revived, especially in the city, where the merchants were jealous of the wealth of the Hebrews; and the Protector, seeing it was in vain to expect any agreement upon this question, sought for no legal sanction to their settling here, but raised no objection to a Portuguese synagogue being opened in 1656.

The government of the Protectorate had ample public business to engage its attention, during the twenty months in which a Single Person, without a Parliament, was the supreme director of the affairs of three kingdoms. The alliance with France, and the war with Spain, gave occasion to new movements of royalists, and new combinations of republicans. Charles the Second was living in dissolute poverty at Cologne, caring little for state concerns, and laying no burden upon his conscience when he had to make some contrary pledge to Protestant or Papist, openly to the one, or in secret to the other. He was a little roused from his exclusive attention to his mistresses, when the war with Spain induced him to believe that he might obtain some assistance from that power against their common enemy. Colonel Sexby, a furious republican, prepared with schemes of conspiracy and assassination, joined the councils of Charles and the Spanish ministers. In April, 1656, a treaty of alliance was concluded between Philip IV. and the exiled king of England, by which the Spanish monarch promised Charles a pension and an army, and Charles engaged that with the aid of the Irish serving in France he would make a landing in England. The government of the Protector was more effectually endangered by the attitude of the great republican leaders at home, than by preparations for war and assassination. Sir Harry Vane had come forth with a pamphlet, which Thurloe described in a letter to Henry Cromwell, as "a new form of government, plainly laying aside thereby that which now is. At the first coming out of it, it was applauded; but now, upon second thoughts, it is rejected as being impracticable, and aiming in truth at the setting up of the Long Parliament again." Cromwell, in July, had issued writs for a new Parliament. A second pamphlet, more exciting than the first, was also published, and extensively circulated. The influence of such appeals to the people, setting forth "infringed rights "—" invaded properties "—" imprisoned friends "—would be full of danger in the result of the elections; and Cromwell was placed in an attitude of more determined hostility against the republican party. The elections were fiercely contested, amidst many popular tumults. The government had secured a majority, but many of its declared opponents were elected. Cromwell and his Council tried to persuade Vane, Harrison, and other opponents, to pledge themselves not to commit any act to the prejudice of the government. They refused; and were imprisoned. The nature of the pledge required may be judged from a remarkable conference between Cromwell and Ludlow, recorded by the sturdy republican, who had been dismissed from his employment in Ireland. When Ludlow drew near to the Council Table, Cromwell charged him with dispersing treasonable books in Ireland. He denied that they were treasonable. Cromwell said that he was not ignorant of many plots to disturb the present power, and that he thought it his duty to secure such as he suspected. Ludlow replied that whether his actions were good or bad he was ready to submit to a legal trial. Cromwell then required him to give assurance not to act against the government. " I desired," says Ludlow, " to be excused in that particular, reminding him of the reasons I had formerly given him for my refusal." The reasons were thus given at the previous interview referred to: "If Providence open a way, and give an opportunity of appearing in behalf of the people, I cannot consent to tie my own hands beforehand, and oblige myself not to lay hold on it. * * * My dissatisfactions were not grounded upon any animosity against his person; and that if my own father were alive, and in his place, they would, I doubted not, be altogether as great." * At this second conference Ludlow maintains the same resolute mind, and Cromwell exhibits the same desire to conciliate him: "Pray then, said he, what is it that you would have? May not every man be as good as he will? What can you desire more than you have? It were easy, said I, to tell what we would have. What is that, I pray, said he? That which we fought for, said I, that the nation might be governed by its own consent. I am, said he, as much for a government by consent as any man; but where shall we find that consent? Amongst the Prelatical, Presbyterian, Independent, Anabaptist, or Levelling Parties? I answered, amongst those of all sorts who had acted with fidelity and affection to the public. Then he fell into the commendation of his own government, boasting of the protection and quiet which the People enjoyed under it, saying, that he was resolved to keep the nation from being imbrued in blood. I said, that I was of opinion too much blood had been already shed, unless there were a better account of it. You do well, said he, to charge us with the guilt of blood; but we think there is a good return for what hath been shed; and we understand what clandestine correspondences are carrying on at this time between the Spaniard and those of your party, who make use of your name, and affirm that you will own them and assist them. I know not, said I, what you mean by my party, and can truly say, that if any men have entered into an engagement with Spain, they have had no advice from me so to do, and that if they will use my name I cannot help it. Then in a softer way he told me, that he desired not to put any more hardships on me than on himself; that he had been always ready to do me all the good offices that lay in his power, and that he aimed at nothing by this proceeding but the public quiet and security. Truly Sir, said I, I know not why you should be an enemy to me who have been faithful to you in all your difficulties. I understand not, said he, what you mean by my difficulties. I am sure they were not so properly mine as those of the public; for in respect to my outward condition I have not much improved it, as these gentlemen, pointing to his Council, well know. To which they seemed to assent, by rising from their chairs; and therefore I thought not fit to insist farther on that point, contenting myself to say, that it was from that duty which I owed to the public, whereof he expressed such a peculiar regard, that I durst not give the security he desired, because I considered it to be against the liberty of the People, and contrary to the known law of England." † After this bold manifestation Ludlow went quietly away; to maintain that Cromwell was a usurper, and that the only legitimate authority was the Long Parliament. "In general there is as much difference between a usurper and an hereditary king, as there is between a wild boar and a tame one: but Cromwell had nothing in him ferocious." ‡

The Parliament assembled on the 17th of September—a crowded meeting

* "Memoirs," vol. ii. p. 554-5.   † Ibid, p. 570.
‡ Landor, "Imaginary Conversations."—Works, vol. i. p. 554.

in the Painted Chamber on a hot day—so hot, that the Protector seems to imply that he will not detain them by a long speech, seeing " that condition and heat that you are now in." But he does speak at great length, with abundant words, although he says " Truly our business is to speak things " . . . "things that concern the glory of God, and his peculiar interest in the world." A large subject,—but one which Oliver mainly associates with " the being and subsistence of these nations with all their dependencies." Of their present dangers he chiefly speaks ;—of "your great enemy, the Spaniard ; " of the circumstances which "justify the war which has been entered upon with the Spaniard ; " of the danger of " any peace with any State that is Popish, and subject to the determination of Rome and the Pope himself," for then " you are bound and they are loose." France was not " under such a tie to the pope." Spain, he says, " hath espoused that interest which you all along hitherto have been conflicting with—Charles Stuart's interest." He adds, " as there is a complication of these interests abroad, so there is a complication of them here. Can we think that Papists and Cavaliers shake not hands in England. . . . Your danger is so great, if you will be sensible of it, by reason of persons who pretend other things." He points to past dangers—to assassination plots, and insurrections in the preceding year. The present great danger was from " a generation of men in this nation who cry up nothing but righteousness, and justice, and liberty ; and these are divided into several sects and sorts of men. They are known to shake hands with,—I should be loath to say with Cavaliers—but with all the scum and dirt of this nation." To meet such dangers " we did find but a little poor invention, which I hear has been much regretted—the erecting of your Major-Generals. . . . Truly I think if ever anything were justifiable as to necessity, this was." He then proceeds to Remedies :—First to consider all that ought to be done in order to Security ; next doing all things that ought to be done in order to Reformation. For outward security join heartily in the prosecution of the war. " If you can come to prosecute it, prosecute it vigorously, or not at all." As to the distempers of people that pretend religion, " our practice since the last Parliament hath been, to let all this nation see that whatever pretensions to religion would continue quiet, peaceable, they should enjoy conscience and liberty to themselves, and not to make religion a pretence for arms and blood." He points to the means which have been adopted " for the ejecting of scandalous ministers, and for the bringing in of them that have passed an approbation." He calls for Reformation of Manners. " In my conscience, it was a shame to be a Christian, within these fifteen, sixteen, or seventeen years in this nation—whether in Cæsar's house, or elsewhere. It was a shame, it was a reproach to a man, and the badge of Puritan was put upon it. We would keep up Nobility and Gentry ; and the way to keep them up is, not to suffer them to be patronisers or countenancers of debauchery and disorders." These are wise words ; and there were other words altogether as wise, which statesmen heeded not for more than a century and a half ; holding, with learned Blackstone, the necessity of entirely disregarding as unworthy of notice " the crude and abortive schemes for amending the laws in the times of confusion which followed " the times of Charles I.* Let us conclude our brief notice of this remarkable speech

* Book iv. Chap. 33.

of 1656, with a passage which contains, according to a high authority, " stronger indications of a legislative mind than are to be found in the whole range of orations delivered on such occasions, before or since." * " There are some things which respect the estates of men ; and there is one general grievance in the Nation. It is the Law. Not that the laws are a grievance, but there are laws that are ; and the great grievance lies in the execution and administration. I think I may say it, I have as eminent judges in this land, as have been had, as the Nation has had, for these many years. Truly I could be particular, as to the executive part of it, as to the administration of the Law ; but that would trouble you. The truth of it is, there are wicked and abominable laws, which it will be in your power to alter. To hang a man for six-and-eightpence, and I know not what ; to hang for a trifle, and acquit murder,—is in the ministration of the Law, through the ill-framing of it. I have known in my experience abominable murders acquitted. And to see men lose their lives for petty matters ; this is a thing God will reckon for. And I wish it may not lie upon this nation a day longer than you have an opportunity to give a remedy ; and I hope I shall cheerfully join with you in it. This hath been a great grief to many honest hearts and con-scientious people ; and I hope it is in all your hearts to rectify it."

The legislative mind of Cromwell could rarely find adequate encourage-ment in his legislators. We have seen how earnestly he was always calling, even from the battle-field, for reform of the laws. Surely Mr. Hallam must have been strangely prejudiced against the man and his principles, when, in his " Parallel between Cromwell and Napoleon," he says, " In civil govern-ment there can be no adequate parallel between one who had sucked only the dregs of a besotted fanaticism, and one to whom the stores of reason and philosophy were open. But it must here be added that Cromwell, far unlike his antitype, never showed any signs of a legislative mind, or any desire to fix his renown on that noblest basis, the amelioration of social institutions." Such a passage is unworthy of the usual calm and impartial tone of the " Constitutional History." It might have been better suited to the historian who designates Cromwell as " a barbarian." It would have been better suited to that historian, David Hume, to speak of " the dregs of a besotted fanaticism," as opposed to " the stores of reason and philosophy," who had little sympathy with, if not positive hatred to, the man or the race of men, who sought to live in the " great Task-master's eye." Cromwell, the bar-barian, did not aspire to go down to posterity with a Code in his hand. He had not to build up new laws out of chaos, but to clear away the rubbish which encumbered the old laws. " If he erected little that was new, it was because there had been no general devastation to clear a space for him." †

The strong declamation of the Protector against men who cry up nothing but righteousness and justice and liberty—the men of several sects—the levelling party—the Commonwealth's men—seemed to point at some extra-ordinary course with this Parliament. About three hundred members had received a certificate in the following form : " These are to certify that ⸺ is returned by indenture one of the Knights [or Burgesses] to serve in this present Parliament for the county [city or borough] of ⸺, and approved

* Macaulay, " Essays," vol. i.   † Ibid.

by his Highness's Council," which certificate was signed by the " Clerk of
the Commonwealth in Chancery." This was a manifest violation of the
ancient parliamentary privileges,—a violation upon the broadest scale. A
hundred and two members, who had received no certificate, were prevented
entering the House. Sixty-five sent a letter of remonstrance to the Speaker.
The Clerk of the Commonwealth produced his instructions from the Council ;
and the House having then demanded of the Council why certain duly elected
had not been admitted to sit, Nathaniel Fiennes, one of the Commissioners
of the Great Seal, attended, and showed that according to the Instrument of
Government " no persons could be elected to serve in Parliament but such as
were of known integrity, fearing God, and of good conversation ; " and that,
by the same Instrument, the Council was authorised and directed " to
examine whether the persons elected were agreeable to the above-mentioned
qualifications." The formal letter of the Constitution had been adhered to ;
its application was a bold exercise of arbitrary power. The excluded members
protested against this total infraction of the conditions of a free Parliament ;
and denounced all the members who should continue to sit as "betrayers
of the liberties of England, and adherents to the capital enemies of the Commonwealth." The public indignation was great and general ; but a national
success came opportunely to qualify it. A squadron of Blake's fleet off
Cadiz had captured two Spanish galleons returning home with the treasures
of the Indies ; and the people crowded the roads and streets from Portsmouth
to the Tower to look upon a procession of thirty-eight waggons laden with
ingots and piastres. The treasury was replenished. The Parliament became
tranquillised. The power of the Protector seemed established on a firm
basis. He felt that he could relax in some measures of repression ; and the
Major-Generals were abolished. There was a mutilated Parliament ; but the
government of a Single Person was again coming within the bounds of
constitutional liberty. The powers of the Parliament and the Protector
now worked harmoniously together. Acts were passed for the security of
his person ; and for disannulling the title to the Crown of Charles Stuart
and his descendants. The war with Spain was declared to be just and
necessary ; and four hundred thousand pounds were voted for the expenses
of the war. The ordinances which the Protector had issued were for the
most part confirmed. His appointments to judicial offices were approved.
The revolution was thought by many to have passed its period of disturbance
and experiment. It was even popularly considered to be probable and
desirable that the Protector should assume a higher title, and with the powers
of a king should receive the name. Poetical flattery talked of the Spanish
gold being made into a crown and a royal sceptre. Amidst all sorts of
speculations upon such an event, an incident which appeared to have little
connexion with a matter of such importance brought into view the necessary
antagonism between the executive authority of the Protector, and the ill-
defined and ill-understood executive power of the Parliament. Amongst the
new sect of Quakers was James Nayler, who, in his frantic enthusiasm, had
proclaimed that the Redeemer was incarnate in his person ; and he had
moreover given a great public scandal in going about in a state of nudity.*

* There is a curious passage in the very interesting autobiography of Thomas Ellwood which

The quaker was arrested at Bristol; and brought up to the bar of the House of Commons. There were ten days of wearisome debate, in which it was maintained that the House possessed the right of life and death. The madman narrowly escaped hanging; for eighty-two voted for his execution. He was finally condemned to be put in the pillory, to have his tongue bored through with a hot iron, and to be whipped through the streets. Cromwell saw, as the more fanatical members had not seen, that the whole course of legal government was threatened by this procedure of the House—that this assumption of judicial power was incompatible with the due course of justice. He addressed this letter to the Speaker: "Right trusty and well-beloved, we greet you well. Having taken notice of a judgment lately given by yourselves against one James Nayler: although we detest and abhor the giving or occasioning the least countenance to persons of such opinions and practices, or who are under the guilt of the crimes commonly imputed to the said person; yet we, being intrusted in the present government, on behalf of the people of these nations; and not knowing how far such proceeding, entered into wholly without us, may extend in the consequence of it,—Do desire that the House will let us know the grounds and reasons whereupon they have proceeded." Part of Nayler's sentence had been inflicted when this letter was received. The House immediately rejected a proposition for deferring the completion of the punishment. The people became more and more convinced that in a due balance of the executive and legislative functions they must look for safety. The obstinacy of the Parliament was Cromwell's triumph with the sober part of the nation. But his very pertinent desire to know "the grounds and reasons" for a "proceeding entered into wholly without Us," led to inquiries about the due apportionment of power, which had very remarkable results. Meanwhile a new assassination plot excited a general interest in the life of the Protector; and, like all such abortive schemes, made the authority stronger which it was intended to overthrow.

Charles the Second was residing at Bruges at the beginning of 1657. He had obtained money from Spain, with which he was making some show of preparation for an expedition to England. But Cromwell—there is the difficulty. Colonel Sexby has been in England, and is again with the king. He has left a trusty agent behind him, and a certain service is to be well rewarded. Miles Sindercomb was one of the Levellers of the army, who was sentenced to be shot at Burford in 1650. But he escaped then; was received as quartermaster into Monk's army in Scotland; got involved in new plots; and was cashiered. Sexby has left this man a large sum for the conduct of his operations. He hired a house at Hammersmith, and provided deadly combustibles of a sort to blow the Protector and his carriage into atoms as he took his Saturday ride to Hampton Court. Sindercomb

somewhat explains this. Ellwood's father violently opposed, even by blows and horsewhippings, his son's determination to be a Quaker. The old squire said, "they held many dangerous principles; that they were an immodest, shameless people; and that one of them stripped himself stark naked, and went in that unseemly manner about the streets, at fairs, and on market-day at great towns." The young man replied to his father by citing "the example of Isaiah, who went naked among the people for a long time." Isaiah was a prophet, said the father. "How know we but this Quaker may be a prophet too," rejoined the son.

arranged, moreover, to fire Whitehall, and have a safe blow at the Protector
in the confusion.   On the night of the 8th of January, the sentinel at the
Palace finds a basket of wildfire, and a slow match gradually burning onwards
to explode it.   A life-guardsman comes before the Council, and proclaims
that Miles Sindercomb is the man who has made these midnight arrangements.
Sindercomb is taken; is tried; and convicted by a jury in the King's Bench:
the day of execution is fixed; but he is found dead in his bed.   His sister
has conveyed poison to him.   The author of "Killing no Murder"—whether
Colonel Titus or Colonel Sexby—says that Sindercomb was smothered and
not poisoned.   With the wonted rant of political fanatics, he exclaims, "The
brave Sindercomb hath shown as great a mind as any old Rome could boast
of; and, had he lived there, his name had been registered with Brutus and
Cato, and he had had his statues as well as they."   This assassination plot
was extinguished as quickly as the lighted match at Whitehall.   The
Parliament went in a body to congratulate the Protector on his escape; and
his Highness made an appropriate reply.   A Thanksgiving day followed;
and two sermons at "Margaret's Church;" and a princely entertainment to
the House by the Protector, and after dinner, "rare music, both of voices
and instruments till the evening."

When Secretary Thurloe, on the 19th of January, related the discovery
of Sindercomb's plot to the Commons, and the House resolved to congratulate
the Protector on his escape, Mr. Ashe, a member of no great mark, moved
that it be added to the congratulatory address, that his Highness would be
pleased to take upon him the government according to the ancient constitution.   Great was the clamour.   The ancient constitution was Charles Stuart's
interest.   Was a kingly government now to be set up, against which the
Lord had borne testimony.   The matter was dropped.   On the 23rd of
February, alderman Pack requested leave to read a paper "tending to the
settlement of the nation."   The House was again in most disorderly condition.
But the alderman did read his paper, in accordance with the desire of a large
majority.   Thurloe described the occurrence in a letter to Monk: "Yesterday
we fell into a great debate in Parliament.   One of the aldermen who serve
for the city of London, brought in a paper called a Remonstrance, desiring
my Lord Protector to assume kingly power, and to call future Parliaments,
consisting of two Houses. * * * I do assure you it ariseth from the
Parliament only; his Highness knew nothing of the preambles until they
were brought into the House."   Four days after Pack's Remonstrance had
been read, a hundred officers, with several of the Major-Generals, amongst
whom was Cromwell's son-in-law, Fleetwood, waited upon the Protector, to
say that they had heard with great dismay that there was a project in hand
to make his Highness King—a hazardous project—a scandal to the people of
God.   Cromwell somewhat resented this interference.   He had not been
caballing about this project, either for or against it.   They need not, however,
start at this title King, a feather in a hat, for they had themselves pressed it
upon him when this government was undertaken.   He thought the Instrument of Government did need mending.   That a House of Lords, or some
other check upon the arbitrary tendencies of a single House might be useful.
Look at the case of James Nayler.   May it not be any one's case some other
day?   The deputation went their way; and the debate upon the great

question proceeded in the House with little interruption. Through the whole of March it was debated; and it was at last voted, by a majority of sixty-one, to address the Protector in these words: "That your Highness will be pleased to assume the name, style, title, dignity, and office, of King of England, Scotland, and Ireland, and the respective dominions and territories thereunto belonging; and to exercise the same according to the laws of these nations." On the 31st of March, the House proceeded to Whitehall, to present the document which they now called "Petition and Advice." It was an Instrument of eighteen articles,—touching Kingship, second House of Parliament, mode of electing members, permanent public revenue, exclusive Protestant religion, provision for tender consciences,—with lesser matters. The Speaker presented these articles for the Protector's acceptance, saying that they requested that all should be adopted—the rejection of one article might make all the rest impracticable. Cromwell's reply was to the effect that he asked time for consideration: "That seeing you have made progress in this business, and completed the work on your part, I may have some short time to ask counsel of God and of my own heart."

Three days after this interview Cromwell requested that a Committee might be appointed to receive his answer to the Petition and Advice. He spoke briefly, and with a tone somewhat different from his usual decision. "You do necessitate my answer to be categorical; and you have left me without a liberty of choice save as to all "—all of the articles. "It is a duty not to question the reason of anything you have done, * * * But I must needs say, that that may be fit for you to offer which may not be fit for me to undertake. * * * I must say I have been able to attain no farther than this, that seeing the way is hedged up so as it is to me, and I cannot accept the things offered unless I accept all, I have not been able to find it my duty to God and you to undertake the charge under that Title." The deputation returns to the House; reports the reluctant negative of his Highness— perhaps not exactly in the words of Casca, "There was a crown offered him, and being offered him, he put it by with the back of his hand, thus." * The House will prepare reasons for adhering to its Petition and Advice, and will go again to Whitehall. On the 8th of April they declare, in a body, to his Highness, that they do so adhere as "the Great Council and Representative of the three nations," and again desire his assent thereto. He still hesitates. "I had, and I have, my hesitations as to that individual thing. If I undertake anything not in faith, I shall serve you in my own unbelief; and I shall then be the most unprofitable servant that People or Nation ever had." He wishes for more particular information upon certain points. Casca again comes in to interpret this "coy, reluctant, amorous delay:"—"He put it by again; but, to my thinking, he was very loth to lay his fingers off it." The next day, London is in a tumult upon other questions of monarchy—not the poor temporary question of protector or king, but whether the Fifth Monarchy—the Assyrian Monarchy, the Persian, the Greek, and the Roman, being all four extinct—the greatest monarchy of all—the reign of the Saints on earth for a thousand years,—be not visibly at hand. It is to be proclaimed this day the 9th of April, on Mile-end Green, by its great herald, Thomas Venner

---

* Shakspere, "Julius Cæsar," Act i. sc. 2.

the wine-cooper; with its standard of the Lion of the Tribe of Judah. A troop of horse settles the Fifth Monarchy with small difficulty; and, without bloodshed, its lieges are lodged in the Tower. This attempt to put down all carnal Sovereignties passes quietly away, without trial or punishment. The Parliament has to debate the question of real Kingship with his Highness, which it does, for many days, by the voices of a Committee of ninety-nine, talking, and listening to my Lord Protector at Whitehall. Lord Whitelocke, and Chief Justice Glynn, and Lord Commissioner Fiennes, and lord Broghill, all have their say; and Cromwell has his comment. He still wants a little more time to consider. He takes counsel about this business of the kingship, with Broghill, Pierpoint, Whitelocke, Wolseley, and Thurloe—as Whitelocke records—and " would sometimes be very cheerful with them; and, laying aside his greatness, he would be exceedingly familiar; and by way of diversion would make verses with them, and every one must try his fancy. He commonly called for tobacco, pipes, and a candle, and would now and then take tobacco himself. Then he would fall again to his serious and great business." On the 13th of April, he speaks at much length; but he still hesitates: " I have nothing to answer to any arguments that were used for preferring Kingship to Protectorship. . . I am ready to serve, not as a King, but as a Constable. For truly I have, as before God, often thought that I could not tell what my business was in the place I stood in, save comparing myself to a good Constable set to keep the peace of the Parish. And truly this hath been my consent and satisfaction in the troubles I have undergone that you yet have peace." The real objection which Cromwell has to a higher dignity than that of Protector-Constable is very manifest: " If I know, as indeed I do, that very generally good men do not swallow this Title,— though really it is no part of their goodness to be unwilling to submit to what a Parliament shall settle over them,—yet I must say, it is my duty and my conscience to beg of you that there may be no hard things put upon me,— things, I mean, hard to them, which they cannot swallow." Another conference in another week. The same reluctance to accept; the same unwillingness to offend by a refusal. It is a tedious farce, say some;—and yet a farce with something serious about it;—quite enough of pressing solicitation to make a vain ambitious man put the precious diadem in his pocket;—not enough to make Cromwell peril many interests, including his own, by a rash consent. His Highness and the Committee now go into discussion of the other articles of the Petition and Advice, to which the Protector has offered a paper of amendments. Long are the discussions; though full of real meaning amidst a maze of words. The Parliament adopts most of the Amendments; and, at last, again attends my Lord Protector in a body, to receive his final answer upon the great question. There was no mistaking his meaning now : " I think the Act of Government doth consist of very excellent parts, in all but that one thing of the Title to me. . . . I am persuaded to return this answer to you, that I cannot undertake this Government with the Title of King." The other parts of the Instrument of Government were adopted, the term Protector being substituted for that of King. " The Protector," says Whitelocke, " was satisfied in his private judgment that it was fit for him to accept the Title of King, and matters were prepared in order thereunto. But afterwards, by solicitation of the Commonwealth's men, and many officers of the army, he decided to attend some better season and opportunity in the business, and refused at this time." Ludlow tells a little anecdote of this interference of " officers of the army," which may conclude this somewhat tedious relation of the discussions about Kingship, which had gone on from the 23rd of February to the 8th of May :—Cromwell, says Ludlow, whilst " he scrupled to take upon him the Title of King, as a thing scandalous, and of great hazard "— yet, " in the meantime he endeavoured by all possible means to prevail with the officers of the army to approve his design, and knowing that lieutenant-general Fleetwood and colonel Desborough were particularly averse to it, he invited himself to dine personally with the colonel, and carried the lieutenant-general with him, where he began to droll with them about Monarchy, and speaking slightly of it, said it was but a feather in a man's cap, and therefore wondered that men would not please the children, and permit them to enjoy their rattle. But he received from them, as colonel Desborough since told me, such an answer as was not at all suitable to his expectations or desires. For they assured him, that there was more in this matter than he perceived ; that those who put him upon it were no enemies to Charles Stuart ; and that if he accepted of it, he would infallibly draw ruin on himself and friends. Having thus sounded their inclinations, that he might conclude in the manner he had begun, he told them, they were a couple of scrupulous fellows, and so departed. The next day he sent a message to the House, to require their attendance in the Painted Chamber the next morning, designing, as all men believed, there to declare his acceptation of the crown. But in the meantime meeting with colonel Desborough in the great walk of the Park, and acquainting him with his resolution, the colonel made answer, that he then gave the cause and Cromwell's family also for lost ; adding, that though he was resolved never to act against him, yet he would not act for him after that time."

The public mind of England is kept sufficiently alive during the early summer of 1657. First, the long deliberations about Kingship, and the unexpected refusal of the Title—unexpected by most men, for the story went that the crown was made, and was ready at Whitehall for the coronation. Then came out the daring pamphlet of " Killing no Murder," recommending the duty of putting the tyrant to death, and threatening that, in imitation of Sindercomb, " there is a great roll behind, even of those that are in his own muster-rolls, and are ambitious of the name of the deliverers of their country ; and they know what the action is that will purchase it. His bed, his table, is not secure ; and he stands in need of other guards to defend him against his own." Such words made men anxious and alarmed. But the bitterest enemies of Cromwell felt that his rule was not an indolent one. The news came of a great victory by Blake over the Spanish navy at Santa Cruz—one of those daring exploits in which there is the greatest safety in what the timid call rashness. Under the fire of tremendous batteries the great admiral attacked the Spaniards in their own harbour, and burnt their entire fleet. Oliver sent Blake a jewel in the name of the Parliament and the Protector, with instructions to return home. The noble sailor,—the true successor of Elizabeth's heroes,—the honoured predecessor of a long file of England's bravest sons—died on board his ship within sight of Plymouth. Then, six thousand English troops land in May near Boulogne, and a fleet is cruising off that coast—an army and a fleet to co-operate with the French in an attack upon the Spanish power in the Netherlands. Meanwhile, the Session of Parliament is coming to a close; but first is to be performed a great national ceremony—the inauguration, under the new Instrument of Government, of him who, without the Title of king, is to be clothed with regal honours and powers. In Westminster Hall there is a gorgeous assembly on the 26th of June. The coronation chair, with the famous stone of Scotland, is placed beneath a canopy of state. The Protector stands up under his canopy; surrounded by his Council and foreign ambassadors; the Speaker is seated beneath him; the members of Parliament in seats built like an amphitheatre; the Judges on his right hand; the Corporation of London on his left; the great hall crowded with spectators. The Speaker invests the Protector with the Robe of Purple, "emblem of Magistracy;" presents him first with a Bible, the book of books, which "doth contain both precepts and examples for good government;" then with the Sceptre, "not unlike a staff, for you are to be a staff to the weak and poor;" lastly, with the sword, "not a military, but civil sword." Then Cromwell takes this oath: "I do in the presence and by the name of Almighty God, promise and swear, that to the uttermost of my power I will uphold and maintain the true Reformed Protestant Christian Religion, in the purity thereof, as it is contained in the Holy Scriptures of the Old and New Testament, to the uttermost of my power and understanding; and encourage the profession and professors of the same; and that to the utmost of my power I will endeavour, as Chief Magistrate of these three nations, the maintenance and preservation of the peace and safety, and just rights and privileges, of the people thereof; and shall in all things according to my best knowledge and power, govern the people of these three nations according to law." A prayer was then made; the heralds proclaimed Oliver Cromwell, Protector of England, Scotland, and Ireland; and the people shouted "God save the Lord Protector." In all but the name these three nations were now a kingdom.

The second Session of Parliament is to assemble in January. It is to be of a different composition from that of the first Session. The excluded members are to be now admitted. There is to be a "Second House." England appears approaching very nearly to its old form of government—one supreme man, by whatever name called—Lords, Commons. Still there is one something wanting—that something which lord Broghill especially pointed out in the conference about Kingship: "By your Highness bearing the title of King, all those that obey and serve you are secured by a law made long before any of our differences had a being—in the 11th of Henry VII.—where a full provision is made for the safety of those that shall serve whoever is king." It was this want of the ancient title in the head of the government of which the lawyers availed themselves at the Restoration of Charles II., when they held that his regnal years must be computed from the death of his father, because no one had in the interval between the 30th of January, 1649, and the 29th of May, 1660, assumed the title of king. The same absence of the ancient designation of the supreme governor unquestionably influenced the aristocracy during the life of the Protector, and compelled him to form a "Second House" of a very anomalous character. He had, however, strengthened his interest with the old nobility to some extent. In November, 1657, lord Falconbridge married his daughter Mary; and Robert Rich, grandson of the earl of

Warwick, married his daughter Frances. But of the members of the old House of Lords only seven accepted the Protector's writ of summons. He filled up its number of sixty-three with great civil officers, generals, and some eminent country gentlemen and citizens. Ludlow tells us of the neglect which sir Arthur Haslerig paid to the summons to be a member of the Upper House, and of the anxiety of the old Speaker, Lenthall, to be a lord. Only one of those Peers who had accepted the writ took their seats. "The earl of Warwick himself," says Ludlow, "though he ventured to marry his grandson to one of Cromwell's daughters, could not be persuaded to sit with colonel Hewson and colonel Pride, whereof the one had been a shoemaker, and the other a drayman : and had they driven no worse trade, I know not why any good man should refuse to act with them. Divers of the gentry did not appear ; yet others, and particularly such as were related to those in power, were prevailed with to be of this assembly."

The scheme of A Second House was not favourable to the disposition of the Commons to uphold the Protector's government. Forty members took their seats as quasi-lords, who would otherwise most probably have been in the Commons, and have given their support to the existing authority. The members who had been excluded in the first Session were competent to sit in this second Session, if they took the oaths. They did take them; and were ready for a vigorous opposition. On the 20th of January the Parliament met. His Highness is now in the House of Lords, and the Commons are duly summoned thither by Black Rod, as of old; and the Protector begins his speech, as of old, with "My Lords, and Gentlemen of the House of Commons." He made a short speech. "I have some infirmities upon me. I have not liberty to speak more unto you; but I have desired an honourable person here by me to discourse a little more particularly what may be more proper for this occasion and this meeting." Nathaniel Fiennes, one of the Commissioners of the Great Seal, made a figurative speech, recommending unanimity. The Commons, upon their return, went at once upon heady debate—day by day—as to what the new House should be called. Haslerig will not be a member of "the other House." He will obey no writ of summons. He will sit as an elected Representative. Clearly the new Constitution is going very fast to pieces. Cromwell summons the Parliament to the Banqueting House, five days after the opening of the Session. He addresses the members in a manly speech. He speaks firmly and boldly, and says some truths that are universal : " Misrule is better than no rule ; and an ill-government, a bad government, is better than none . . . . I know you are rational, prudent men. Have you any frame or model of things that would satisfy the minds of men, if this be not the frame, which you are now called together upon, and engaged in,—I mean the two Houses of Parliament and myself ? What hinders this nation from being an Aceldama, if this doth not ? . . . . I never look to see the people of England come into a just Liberty, if another Civil War overtake us. I think, at least, that the thing likely to bring us into our liberty, is a consistency and agreement at this meeting. . . . . I shall be ready to stand or fall with you, in this seemingly promising Union, which God hath wrought among you, which I hope neither the pride nor envy of men shall be able to make void. . . . I trust, by the grace of God, as I have taken my oath to serve this Commonwealth on such an account, I shall—I must—see it done, according to the articles of government. That every just interest may be preserved; that a godly Ministry may be upheld, and not affronted by seducing and seduced spirits; that all men may be preserved in their just rights, whether civil or spiritual,—upon this account did I take oaths and swear to this Government." This appeal—" the words as of a strong great captain addressed in the hour of imminent shipwreck " *—was in vain. The discontented are powerful in the Commons. No real business can proceed, whilst the question of " the other House " is daily debated. Oliver Protector will bring the matter to an end. The Commons are again summoned by the Black Rod. " What care I for the Black Rod ?" cries Haslerig. But they obey the summons. And then the Protector speaks with an angrier voice than was his wont, even in former disquietudes : " You have not only disjointed yourselves but the whole nation, which is in likelihood of running into more confusion in these fifteen or sixteen days that you have sat, than it hath been from the rising of the last Session to this day—through the intention of devising a Commonwealth again—that some people might be the men that rule all. . . . It hath not only been your endeavour to pervert the army while you have been sitting, and to draw them to state the question about a Commonwealth; but some of you have been listing of persons, by commission of Charles Stuart, to join with any insurrection that may be made. . . . If this be the end of your sitting, and this be your carriage, I think it high time that an end be put to your sitting. And I do dissolve this Parliament. And let God be judge between you and me."

The Parliament is gone; but the Protector is not left to repose. There are dangers around him of no common magnitude. He meets them bravely. The Parliament is dismissed in the morning of the 14th of February. In the afternoon Oliver is writing to his captains of militia in the country, to " be most vigilant for the suppressing of any disturbance which may arise from any party whatsoever." He summons his officers to Whitehall, and asks if they are willing, with him, to maintain the Instrument of Government ? Most answer, they will live and die with him. A few look gloomy, and are silent. In a day or two he removes suspected officers from the army. " The cavaliers," says Mrs. Hutchinson, " had not patience to stay till things ripened of themselves; but were every day forming designs, and plotting for the murder of Cromwell, and other insurrections; which, being contrived in drink, and managed by false and cowardly fellows, were still revealed to Cromwell, who had most excellent intelligence of all things that passed, even in the king's closet. And by these unsuccessful plots they were the only obstructors of what they sought to advance, while, to speak truth, Cromwell's personal courage and magnanimity upheld him against all enemies and malcontents." † Lambert encouraged the disaffected officers, who desired to set him up in Cromwell's place : " His ambition had this difference from the Protector's ; the one was gallant and great; the other had nothing but an unworthy pride, most insolent in prosperity, and as abject and base in adversity." ‡ Mrs. Hutchinson says that the disaffected officers—" some of the Lambertonians "—proposed to gain admission to Cromwell with a petition, and then, whilst he was reading

* Carlyle, vol. iii. p. 247.

† " Memoirs," vol. ii. p. 214.   ‡ Ibid.

it, to throw him out of a window at Whitehall into the Thames. Colonel Hutchinson became acquainted with the plot by chance; and revealed it to the Protector, "judging that Lambert would be the worse tyrant of the two." Hutchinson warned Cromwell against petitioners; but could not be prevailed upon to give any more information than was necessary to prevent the design. Royalists and fanatics, republicans and levellers, were all ready to assail the man who would not suffer them "to imbrue their hands in blood." On the 12th of March Cromwell received the Corporation of London at Whitehall, and explained the reasons which had induced him to dissolve the Parliament, in order to avert the dangers with which the government was threatened— invasions and insurrections—the Spaniard and the exiled being in league,— Royalists and Anabaptists plotting together. The marquis of Ormond only left London on Tuesday last, he told them;—the marquis of Ormond, who had come disguised to London on a mission from Charles Stuart. Ormond had gone away "on Tuesday last," upon a very intelligible hint. "There is an old friend of yours in town," said Cromwell to lord Broghill. "The marquis of Ormond lodges in Drury Lane, at the Papist surgeon's. It would be well for him if he were gone." Ormond was very soon at Bruges, and reported to Charles that Cromwell had better be left alone for the present. Nevertheless, London is ready for trying insurrection upon a limited scale. There was to have been a great outbreak on the 15th of May. The royalist leaders have lost heart now Ormond is gone; but there are malcontents ready for a rising— wild apprentices and other rash persons, who propose to fire houses, and do a considerable amount of slaughter. The Lieutenant of the Tower comes out with five pieces of artillery, and the apprentices get within their masters' houses as fast as possible. The ringleaders of this intended insurrection are seized at "the Mermaid in Cheapside." Others are arrested in the country. A High Court of Justice, appointed by Act of the last Parliament, is summoned for trial of the conspirators. Fifteen were arraigned; amongst whom were sir Henry Slingsby, and Dr. Hewit, an episcopal divine. These two were condemned and executed; although the highest interest was made to save their lives. Six of the insurrectionists were also condemned, of which number three suffered. There were no more insurrections during the life of Cromwell.

That life, like a brilliant sun-set in a stormy sky, has its parting glories. The foreign policy of the Protectorate was triumphant. The alliance with France was not a mere pretext for combined action rendered impossible by national jealousies on our part. When the English troops landed at Boulogne, the young king Lewis XIV. came to review them. Lockhart Cromwell's ambassador, said: "Sire, the Protector has enjoined both officers and soldiers to display the same zeal in the service of your majesty, as in his own." The French government construed this too literally, and thought that England was to have an equal share of danger and expense but a very disproportionate amount of advantage. The English were employed by France in securing fortresses in the interior, instead of in combined operations against Gravelines, and Mardike, and Dunkirk, on the coast, as stipulated by treaty. Cromwell was not a man to be duped. He ordered his ambassador to see that the treaty was carried out, or send the English troops home. Mazarin was not inclined to quarrel with the Protector, and so

Mardike was besieged, and delivered provisionally to the English general. The next spring, amidst all his home distractions, Cromwell renewed the treaty of offensive alliance with France, and sent more troops. On the 25th of May Dunkirk was invested by the allied French and English army. Turenne was the commander. The town was defended by the marquis of Leyden. Don John of Austria marched from Brussels with a Spanish force to drive back the besiegers. Condé was with this army, and also the dukes of York and Gloucester. The Spaniard persisted in giving battle, against the advice of Condé. "Did you ever see a battle fought?" said Condé to the young duke of Gloucester. He had not. "Well: you will soon see a battle lost." The English, commanded by Lockhart, fought for four hours, and carried the most difficult posts. They were often opposed to their own countrymen,

French Cavalier.

headed by the duke of York. This battle on the Dunes was a complete victory. On the 25th of June, Dunkirk surrendered; and the town was placed in the hands of the English. It was a compensation for the loss of Calais, as the nation thought. To have a footing on foreign ground was a proud thing for England—a mistaken pride, but not an impolitic one in those days. Dunkirk was an English garrison, till—but it is unnecessary to anticipate the coming time of national degradation.

Triumphant abroad; freed from insurgents at home; Cromwell again looked towards a Parliament. Were the popular desires for monarchy to be gratified by a change of name? Was the nation to accept the subtle argument of lord Broghill, "There is at present but a divorce between the pretending king and the imperial crown of these nations, and we know that persons divorced may marry again; but if the person be married to another, it cuts off all hope." Such might have been the Protector's thoughts, until something more absorbing than worldly power or dignity obtruded itself to make him as anxious and wretched as the lowliest of those he ruled. His daughter, lady Claypole, was dying. In every domestic relation, son, husband, father, we see the tenderness of this man's nature. In 1648 his eldest son was killed in battle. There is not a trace of the father's sorrow in any letter or memorandum of the time; till the new affliction calls up bitter remembrances out of their sacred depths. Lady Claypole died on the 6th of August, her father having been fourteen days watching by her bedside at Hampton Court, "unable to attend to any public business whatever." A few days after, says Harvey, groom of his bedchamber, "he called for his Bible, and desired an honourable and godly person there, with others present, to read unto him that passage in Philippians fourth: ' Not that I speak in respect of want: for I have learned, in whatsoever state I am, therewith to be content. I know how to be abased, and I know how to abound: everywhere and in all things I am instructed both to be full and to be hungry, both to abound and to suffer need. I can do all things through Christ which strengtheneth me.' Which read, said he, to use his own words as near as I can remember them: 'This Scripture did once save my life, when my eldest son died; which went as a dagger to my heart, indeed it did.' " A few months before, Cromwell had lost his son-in-law, Rich; and then Rich's grandfather, the earl of Warwick, the Protector's one constant friend amongst the nobility, also died. Oliver's stout heart was sorely bowed down by public cares and private griefs. He roused himself, however, and was out again at his duties. George Fox tells us something about the Protector's looks, at this season, soon after the time when London was gay with ambassadors extraordinary from France; and Mazarin's nephew was there to assure the Protector of the profound veneration his uncle had for him—"the greatest man that ever was." The day was past for pomps and flatteries. " Taking boat I went to Kingston," says Fox, " and from thence to Hampton Court, to speak with the Protector about the sufferings of Friends. I met him riding into Hampton Court Park; and before I came to him, as he rode at the head of his Lifeguards, I saw and felt a waft of death go forth against him; and when I came to him, he looked like a dead man. After I had laid the sufferings of Friends before him, and had warned him according as I was moved to speak to him, he bade me come to his house. So I returned to Kingston; and the next day went up to Hampton Court, to speak further with him. But when I came, Harvey, who was one that waited on him, told me the doctors were not willing that I should speak with him. So I passed away, and never saw him more." On the 24th of August, Cromwell left Hampton Court for Whitehall. Ten days of acute suffering, and then the end.

On the 30th of August, a mighty storm of wind filled the land with dismay. There is deeper cause for alarm to most men, for the Protector is dying. What is to come next? By the Instrument of Government he is to name his successor. His eldest son, Richard, is an idle country-gentleman, harmless, but somewhat incapable. Thurloe puts the question of Succession to the dying man. There is a sealed-up paper in a certain place at Hampton Court. The paper is not to be found. On the night of the 2nd of September, the question is put again. The answer, faintly breathed out, was said to be " Richard." That night, again one of terrible storm, was to usher in Cromwell's " Fortunate Day," the 3rd of September, the anniversary of Dunbar and Worcester. The prince and soldier passed away, in a state of insensibility, in the afternoon of that 3rd of September. The prayer which he addressed to Heaven a night or two before his death has a consistent reference to his public life; in connexion with his religious belief: " Lord, though I am a miserable and wretched creature, I am in covenant with Thee through grace. And I may, I will, come to Thee, for Thy people. Thou hast made me, though very unworthy, a mean instrument to do them some good, and Thee service; and many of them have set too high a value upon me, though others wish and would be glad of my death. Lord, however Thou do dispose of me, continue and go on to do good for them. Give them consistency of judgment, one heart, and mutual love; and go on to deliver them, and with the work of reformation; and make the name of Christ glorious in the world. Teach those who look too much on Thy instruments, to depend more upon Thyself. Pardon such as desire to trample upon the dust of a poor worm, for they are Thy people too. And pardon the folly of this short prayer :—Even for Jesus Christ's sake. And give us a good night, if it be Thy pleasure. Amen." At this time, " wherein his heart was so carried out for God and His people," says Harvey, " he seems to forget his own family and nearest relations." His last notion,—a wrong or right notion as men may differently conclude,—was that he had been an instrument of good to England. The night before his death he said, " I would be willing to live to be further serviceable to God and His People : but my work is done. Yet God will be with His People."

Richard Cromwell.

CHAPTER XIV.

Richard Cromwell proclaimed Protector—General calm upon his succession to power—Funeral of Oliver Cromwell—A Parliament called—Different Constitution of Parliament—Conflicts between the Republican leaders and the majority—Demands of the Army—Richard Cromwell yields to their pretensions—He is compelled by the Officers to dissolve the Parliament—End of the Protectorate—Assembly of the Long Parliament—Resolutions that the Military power should be under the Civil—Discussions as to the form of Government—The Rota Club—Disunion of Parties—Royalist insurrection—Sir George Booth defeated by Lambert—Petitions of the Officers—The Parliament, subjected to the Army, ceases to sit—Committee of Safety—Monk in Scotland—Resolves to restore the Parliament—Lambert sent against Monk—The Parliament restored by the Council of Officers—Monk marches to London—Movements of the Royalists—Disaffection in the City, which Monk is ordered to suppress—His demand that a Parliament shall be called—Popular exultation—Monk restores the secluded Members—The measures of the Parliamentary majority—Charles's Court—The Long Parliament finally dissolved—Monk agrees to act for Charles—Lambert's insurrection—Meeting of the New Parliament—The King's Letter—Debates on the Bill of Indemnity—Charles the Second proclaimed—He lands at Dover—His entry into London.

THE death of Oliver Cromwell was followed by no popular agitation—scarcely by any immediate demonstration of party dissensions. The Council was summoned. Evidence was given of the verbal declaration of the Protector that his son Richard should be his successor. Fleetwood, the lieutenant-general of the army, was thought by some to have been nominated to the succession in the paper which could not be discovered; but he gave his pledge to respect the appointment of Richard.   On the 4th of September the new Protector was solemnly proclaimed; and he took the oath contained in the Instrument of Government.   The ready acceptance by the nation of the son of the late ruler offers a proof that, during the contests of the Protectorate, its power had been gradually consolidating; and that the great name of the Protector remained as a shield for the weakness of his son. Richard was weak in all the essential qualities necessary for preserving an authority as legitimate not recognised by many.   Mrs. Hutchinson describes him as " a peasant in his nature, yet gentle and virtuous, but became not greatness."   If, yielding to the flattering idea of hereditary succession, his father had really nominated him, that nomination must have been against his own previous convictions of his eldest son's unfitness for government.   On the contrary, his son Henry had displayed very high qualities as Lord-Lieutenant of Ireland.   He had shown firmness with conciliation; he had kept the land at peace and in subjection to the laws.   Yet the accession of Richard Cromwell, if it excited no confidence in the people, produced no distrust. They saw a quiet and unambitious young man quietly take his father's seat, they scarcely thought that the mild indifference of authority may be more dangerous than its severe watchfulness.   Abroad, the royalists were vexed and surprised at the calm in England.   Hyde thought there would be great changes: " I cannot believe," he writes, " that all will submit to the government of this young coxcomb."   Henrietta Maria, however, doubted whether any great advantages could accrue from " the death of that wretch," as she writes to Madame de Motteville.   Three months after that important event, Hyde almost lost heart: " We have not yet found that advantage by Cromwell's death as we reasonably hoped; nay, rather, we are the worse for it, and the less esteemed, people imagining by the great calm that has followed that the nation is united, and that the king has very few friends." Foreign governments readily gave their adherence to the Commonwealth. The Court of France put on mourning to do honour to Oliver's memory. Nevertheless, " the great calm " was gradually becoming disturbed.   Within six weeks of his accession, a body of officers, headed by Fleetwood, presented a petition to Richard for such organic changes in the military constitution as would have placed all control of the army out of his hand.   He mildly but firmly refused his assent, as contrary to the " Petition and Advice " on which the Protectorate was founded.   Henry Cromwell saw the coming danger; and wrote to his brother, " I thought those whom my father had raised from nothing would not so soon have forgot him, and endeavour to destroy his family before he is in his grave."   Richard was not only harassed by the ambition of the officers, but had to encounter the greatest peril of governments, financial difficulties.   His father had left no wealth—contrary to the belief of most persons.   He had higher thoughts than those of making his family rich.   Richard was soon embarrassed, the more so as the pompous funeral of the late Protector absorbed all his immediate resources, and left him greatly in debt.   That funeral was deferred till the 23rd of November.   The preparations for this public solemnity were upon an extravagant scale, utterly unsuited to the simple grandeur which the Protector had affected in his life-time.   Evelyn has briefly described this ceremonial: "Saw the superb funeral of the Protector. He was carried from Somerset House on a velvet bed of state, drawn by six horses, housed with the same; the pall held by his new Lords; Oliver lying in effigy, in royal robes, and crowned with a crown, sceptre, and globe, like a king. The pendants and guidons were carried by the officers of the army; the imperial banners, achievements, &c., by the heralds in their coats; a rich caparisoned horse, embroidered all over with gold; a knight of honour armed cap-a-pied; and, after all, his guards, soldiers, and innumerable mourners." Evelyn adds, "in this equipage they proceeded to Westminster: but it was the joyfullest funeral I ever saw; for there were none that cried but dogs, which the soldiers hooted away with a barbarous noise, drinking and taking tobacco in the streets as they went." Ludlow, speaking with similar contempt of this pageantry, says, of the lying in state, "This folly and profusion so far provoked the people, that they threw dirt in the night on his escutcheon that was placed over the great gate of Somerset House."

In the middle of November, Thurloe wrote to Henry Cromwell that when the funeral was over the Council would begin business, "if troubles do not begin before." The Council met on the 29th and resolved on calling a Parliament. It was not to be such a Parliament as Oliver had called. The old Representative system was to be restored. Small and decayed Boroughs, which had been disfranchised, were again to elect burgesses. Commercial towns, such as Manchester, which had grown into importance, were again to cease to have members. The loss of ancient privileges by petty communities had given more offence than the gain of new franchises by large sections of the people had afforded satisfaction. The government strove as much as possible to exclude the Republicans from Parliament; but it was not successful to a great extent. Many in the service of the government obtained seats. The Royalists influenced many of the elections, but few declared Royalists offered themselves as candidates. The Parliament, which met on the 29th of January, appeared to contain more moderate men than violent partisans. There was nothing in its composition to indicate that the Protectorate would become insecure through legislative action. The Lords, or Upper House, were summoned by the Protector's writ, as the Lords of Oliver had been summoned. The members of both Houses were required to take the oath to the government. Some few

Richard, Protector.   From a Patent in Landsdowne MS.

republicans refused, and did not take their seats. Ludlow, and probably others, evaded the oath; and, after some dispute, were permitted to sit. The passions of various factions soon manifested themselves. A bill having been proposed "for a recognition of the Protector," no dislike was exhibited towards Richard Cromwell. On the contrary, even the strong Republicans spoke kindly of him: "If you think of a Single Person, I would have him sooner than any man alive," said Scott,—one of the most violent against the late Protector. But the Republicans came back to their old assertion of the right of Parliament alone to exercise the government, as it had been exercised before the dissolution of the Long Parliament. By that action, said Vane, they lost their possession, not their right. "The chief magistrate's place was assumed without a law." It was dangerous to confess a title in being that was not of their own giving, maintained Vane. After long and violent debates, the Bill for the recognition of the Protector was passed. The Royalists looked on rejoicingly at these conflicts; believing that they would end in confusion. There was still greater disagreement when the question came to be debated, whether there should be two Houses. The Commons voted that the Parliament should consist of two Houses; but then proceeded to discuss the bounds and powers of the other House. After weeks of debate, it was resolved, by a considerable majority, that the House would treat with the persons now sitting in the other House, as a House of Parliament; and that such Peers as had been faithful to the Parliament might be summoned to serve as Members of that House. The Republicans and the Royalists were beaten.

But, however triumphant at Westminster, as to these material points, there was a power yet unpropitiated, which Oliver could control, but which was wholly unmanageable by the gentle hand of Richard. Soon after his accession he said to the officers who came to him with a petition, "It is my disadvantage that I have been so little amongst you, and am no better known to you." He now began to feel how great was this disadvantage. There were some regiments, commanded by his friends, of whose fidelity the young Protector had no doubt. The armies of Scotland and Ireland were equally faithful. But the violent sectarian soldiers disliked his moderation. He was threatened by Desborough that the army would desert him if he attempted to conciliate the Royalists. It was objected against him that he preferred others beside "the godly." The Parliament and the Army were secret antagonists. Their mutual hostility soon became manifest. Looking merely at their legislative influence, it was no serious evil that the most signal strokes of the policy of the late Protector had been condemned by the few Republican members; that they reprobated the peace with the Dutch; the alliance with France; the war with Spain. They were insensible to the real triumphs of Oliver; they were indifferent to the high position in which he had placed his country amongst the nations. They made no allowance for the difficulties he had experienced in restraining contending factions at the least expenditure of blood. They hated the participation of one Single Person in the power of a Parliament; and that hatred made them little careful to avoid the old strifes. But there was serious danger when the Army fell in with this humour; and saw, with jealousy, a majority of the Parliament inclined to peace and moderation. Richard indiscreetly consented to the appointment of a general Council of Officers. Five hundred assembled at Wallingford House. A violent test was proposed, which was indeed laid aside, but they came to resolutions which aimed at separating the command of the Army from the Civil Power. The Parliament soon saw its danger. A member, lord Falkland, said, "You have been a long time talking of three Estates; there is a fourth which, if not well looked-to, will turn us all out of doors." The House of Commons then voted that no general Council of Officers should be held without permission of the Protector and the Parliament; and that every officer should sign an engagement that he would not disturb the free meetings or proceedings of Parliament. Richard was urged to be firm. He went amongst the officers at Wallingford House; and told them that he would see their complaints righted in Parliament, but that he dissolved their Council. The Council obstinately continued to sit. Those officers who were devoted to the Protector urged him to adopt some strong measure. Richard shrank from the responsibility: "I have never done anybody any harm," he exclaimed, "and I never will: I will not have a drop of blood spilt for the preservation of my greatness, which is a burden to me." Broghill, and Howard, and other faithful friends, saw that one course alone was possible to avert military despotism or anarchy—to restore the legitimate king. Richard himself was solicited to assist in this object; but he refused to forsake the cause to which he was committed. It was soon manifest that the power of the Protector was coming to an end. His brother-in-law Fleetwood, his relative Desborough, deserted him. The few officers who were faithful were abandoned by their men. Desborough came from St. James's to Whitehall —from St. James's, where the whole army was ordered to rendezvous, to Whitehall, where Richard had been deserted by his own guards—and demanded that the Parliament should be dissolved. Richard at length

Great Seal of Richard Cromwell.

yielded, making it a condition that he should not be required to dissolve the House in person. An ordinance was issued, which Fiennes, as Commissioner of the Great Seal, was ordered to communicate to Parliament. On the 22nd of April the Commons were summoned to the Upper House. Very few went.

Those who remained behind passed various resolutions, violent in proportion to their impotence. In the evening a Proclamation for dissolving the Parliament was issued, and upon the doors of the House of Commons padlocks were fastened. The Army was supreme, with no master-mind to direct its supremacy.

With the fall of the Parliament fell Richard Cromwell. " His Highness," wrote Thurloe to Lockhart, " is now excluded from having any share in the government, and must retire as a private gentleman." He still continued to reside at Whitehall. But all real government was at an end. The army became insubordinate. All power of directing the affairs of the nation seemed lost. In this emergency, the officers and the republican leaders of the Commons coalesced; and it was determined to restore the Long Parliament. After much difficulty forty-two of the old Members were gathered together; and that anomalous authority commenced, which was destined ignominiously to expire under the name of " The Rump." Richard Cromwell soon after left Whitehall. Henry Cromwell took no part in public

Cromwell's Wife.

affairs. The wife of Cromwell—the " domestic drudge " as she was called in the lampoons of the time—had made little provision for a transition from Whitehall to a plain country-house. The whole family passed into obscurity —humbled. but not disgraced.

English Commissioners at the Hague. (From an old Print.)

A sufficient number of members of the Long Parliament having been
assembled to form a House, "We went," says Ludlow, "to take our places,
Mr. Lenthall, our Speaker, leading the way; and the officers of the Army
lining the rooms for us, as we passed through the Painted Chamber, the
Court of Requests, and the Lobby itself; the principal officers having placed
themselves nearest to the door of the Parliament House, every one seeming
to rejoice at our restitution, and promising to live and die with us." Such
promises are easily made and easily broken in revolutionary periods. The
first step of the Parliament was to appoint a Committee of Safety; and,
subsequently, a Council of State. The Council was composed of soldiers and
civilians, in nearly equal proportion. They were sincere and zealous men,
faithful to their great idea of a Republic, of which all the authority should
abide in a Parliament. But the theory of parliamentary supremacy soon
reduced itself to the more practical question—which power should be
supreme, the civil or the military? The Parliament asserted its claims with
resolute independence. Fleetwood was to be appointed Commander-in-Chief;
"but instead of authorising the Lieutenant-General to grant commissions to
such officers as should be appointed by the Parliament, it was ordered that
the said commissions should be subscribed by the Speaker, and received from
his hands; by which it was endeavoured to bring the military sword under
the power of the civil authority, as it ought to be in a free nation." Ludlow,
who relates this, adds: "But observing that these things were greatly
disliked by the officers, and knowing how much it imported the very being
of our cause to maintain a good correspondence between the Parliament and

the Army, I earnestly pressed the House not to insist upon the restrictions." * The Parliament, however, was firm, and the officers submitted, though with an ill grace. The government was in the hands of men of decision and energy. Its foreign policy was conciliatory. It professed its desire for peace ; and though abandoning somewhat of the high tone of Cromwell, it averted some immediate dangers by its moderation. But the people of England had no confidence in the stability of the dominion of this remnant of the Parliament, which was a necessity during the Civil War, but was unsuited to the monarchical traditions of the country, revived, to a certain extent, in the " something approaching to monarchy " of Oliver. The ultimate form of government was a constant matter of debate within the House. Beyond its walls every theory of the perfection of a Commonwealth was anxiously discussed. Harrington, who had twelve years before been " disputing about government " with Charles I., was now disputing " daily at coffee-houses." In 1659, writes Aubrey, " at the beginning of Michaelmas time, he had every night a meeting at the Turk's Head, in the New Palace Yard, where they take water—the next house to the stairs, at one Miles's—where was made purposely a large oval table, with a passage in the middle for Miles to deliver his coffee. About it sate his disciples and the virtuosi." The arguments in the Parliament House were, to Aubrey, " flat " by comparison with this talk of the " virtuosi;" who had a balloting-box, and balloted " how things should be carried,"—how " the third part of the House should vote out by ballot every year, so that every ninth year the House would be wholly altered ;—no magistrate to continue above three years, and all to be chosen by ballot." Pepys went to Harrington's Club in January, 1660, " and heard very good discourse." The Parliament continued debating ; with real dangers all around. The greatest danger was in its own divisions. " Parties are like so many floating islands, sometimes joining and appearing like a continent ; when the next flood or ebb separates them ; so that it can hardly be known where they will be next." †

As the natural result of this disunion, a royalist insurrection was organised. The old Cavalier party in England had been wholly inactive since the death of Oliver. The probability is, that if the hand of Richard had been sufficiently strong to have held the Army in due subordination to the civil authority, and the Parliament could thus have proceeded in its duties without molestation, the country would have gradually settled down under a government which afforded security for property, and continued stability for the various interests that had acquired a firm footing during ten years. But under the disunited republicans who had obtained possession of power, the restoration of Charles the Second became a fixed idea that gradually took possession of many minds besides those of the more devoted Royalists. The impatience of the king's adherents was the most likely source of injury to the king's cause. This impatience was for some time kept down by the prudence of Hyde. But a general plan of insurrection was at length completed in July. The Parliament obtained a knowledge of the project, and took the most active measures of precaution. Charles and

* " Memoirs," p. 660.
Letter of 3rd June, quoted in Guizot's " Richard Cromwell," vol. i. p. 183.

his brother James met at Calais, with the intention of proceeding to England. But the chief leaders of the proposed insurrection were intimidated; and the Royalists saw that the time for united action was not yet come. Sir George Booth had, however, appeared in arms in Cheshire, on the 1st of August. In a few days he was at the head of several thousand men, and had obtained possession of the citadel of Chester. Large additional forces were immediately raised by the Parliament; and their command was entrusted to Lambert. He left London at the head of an adequate force, and marched rapidly to Chester. The defeat of sir George Booth and his party was complete. The Royalist cause appeared again to be hopeless. Lambert returned to London at a very slow pace. The Parliament had voted him a thousand pounds to buy a jewel; but he came not to receive their thanks in person. He was preparing, in concert with officers in London, to dispute their authority. A Petition had been presented to the House from the officers under his command. It was to repeat certain demands for the appointment of General Officers, which had been proposed before the Parliament had been restored. The House now voted against the prayer of the Petition. Other meetings of officers were held, and another Petition was resolved upon. These movements were evidently preparations for a rupture between the two powers of the State. The quarrel became serious. ·Lambert, Desborough, and other officers were dismissed from their posts; and Fleetwood was removed from his command of the Army. On the 13th of October, Westminster was surrounded by troops upon whose fidelity the Parliament relied. Lambert boldly marched thither at the head of his regiment. A conflict appeared likely to take place; but Lambert addressed the troops, and they quickly went over to him. Lenthall, the Speaker, was stopped by the soldiers, who laughed at him when he said that he was their chief general. There was a conference between the civil and military members of the Council of State, which ended in a resolution that the Parliament should cease to sit; and that the maintenance of the public tranquillity should rest with the Council of Officers.

The Committee of Safety appointed by the Army began to exercise the functions of administration on the 23d of October. On the 30th the French ambassador writes to Mazarin, "There is as yet no government established in England, notwithstanding the attempts which have been made for some days by the leaders of the Army, and some ministers of the Council of State, to agree to one. . . . The conjuncture seems favourable for all sorts of enterprises." * There was one, far distant from the scene of confusion, who was watching what this conjuncture would bring forth. George Monk, "the sly fellow" as Cromwell termed him, was courted by the republican leaders, civil and military; but he gave no signs of adhesion to any faction. His army in Scotland was entirely devoted to him. Like its commander, that army had no great sympathy with the movements of the soldiers in London. The Royalists had long been making efforts to engage Monk in their cause. But Monk would not stir at the invitation of any party. Charles himself wrote to Monk, and the letter was placed in the hands of Monk's brother, a humble clergyman. He was afraid to be the bearer of it; but he committed

* Guizot, Appendix 1, vol. ii.

it to memory, and proceeded to his brother's head-quarters at Dalkeith. Booth's insurrection was known; and Monk was about to take some decided resolve. The news of Booth's defeat by Lambert arrived, and Monk was saved from a premature declaration against the Parliament. His soldiers had thought that their general was the man to fill the void occasioned by the death of Cromwell; but he was too cautious to risk this perilous advancement. When he believed the opportunity had passed for taking any steps to restore the Stuarts, he sent a letter to the Speaker, Lenthall, asking to retire from public life. The letter was suppressed by Lenthall; and soon afterwards, the Parliament was ejected. Monk immediately took his resolution. He addressed the troops at Edinburgh; told them that the army in England had broken up the Parliament, to hinder the settlement of the nation; that they would next attempt to impose their insolent extravagances upon the army in Scotland; and that he was resolved to keep the military power in obedience to the civil; they had received their pay and commission from the Parliament, and it was their duty to defend it. He wrote letters to declare his intentions to Lambert and Fleetwood, and to the Speaker, Lenthall. He cashiered those officers who opposed his views, which were expresely limited to a resistance to military tyranny in England. To every approach of the Royalists he was inflexibly cold and distant. In London, the determination of Monk produced the greatest alarm amongst the factions. Their views were vacillating and discordant. At one time, they thought of recalling Richard Cromwell to the Protectorship. They finally resolved to send a deputation to Monk to effect a reconciliation; and if that failed to proceed to a trial of strength in battle. Lambert was appointed commander of the troops in the north. More soldiers were raised in London; and a loan from the City was asked of the Common Council. It was refused. The commissioners sent to Monk executed their commission, and represented to him the dangers which surrounded his course. He called a Council of his officers; and it was agreed that three commissioners should proceed to London to negotiate with the army there. Monk had given them instructions to endeavour to gain time; but contrary to his instructions they had, in three days, concluded a treaty with the Committee of Safety, by which the government was left in the administration of a Council of Officers, no provision was made for the recall of the Parliament, and Monk's own appointment of officers was to be revised. Great indignation was excited in Monk's army, and it was resolved that the treaty should not be ratified. Nine members of the old Council of State that had been thrust from office by the army now resolved to make common cause with Monk. He had marched to Berwick, with six thousand infantry, and four regiments of cavalry. He now fixed his head-quarters at Coldstream, where he could easily cross the Tweed. He had written to the Common Council of London, to declare his intentions; and he was proclaimed as a deliverer by some members of the old Council of State. The people were universally discontented, refusing to pay taxes, and shouting for a free Parliament. The fleet, under the command of admiral Lawson, declared that they would obey no authority but that of a Parliament. The various leaders, civil and military, were fiercely quarrelling. Some even of the republicans talked of the restoration of the king. At last it was resolved to call a new Parliament. On the 15th of December a proclamation was issued, summoning a Parliament to meet on the 24th of January. The country was under no law but that of the tyranny of detached bands of soldiers, roving about at free quarters. Mrs. Hutchinson has described a scene to which there were probably many parallels;—outrages that went on, "till the law was again in force:"—

"Six of Lambert's troopers came to gather money, laid upon the country by an assessment of Parliament, whom the colonel telling that in regard it was levied by that authority, he had paid it, but otherwise would not; two of them, who only were in the room with the colonel, the rest being on horseback in the court, gave him such insolent terms with such insufferable reproaches of the Parliament, that the colonel drew a sword which was in the room to have chastised them. While a minister that was by held the colonel's arm, his wife, not willing to have them killed in her presence, opened the door and let them out, who presently ran and fetched in their companions in the yard with cocked pistols. Upon the bustle, while the colonel having disengaged himself from those that held him, was run after them with the sword drawn, his brother came out of another room, upon whom, the soldiers pressing against a door that went into the great hall, the door flew open, and about fifty or sixty men appeared in the hall who were there upon another business. For Owthorpe, Knolton, and Hitchin, had a contest about a cripple that was sent from one to the other; but at last, out of some respect they had for the colonel, the chief men of the several towns were come to him, to make some accommodation, till the law should be again in force. When the colonel heard the soldiers were come, he left them shut up in his great hall; who by accident thus appearing, put the soldiers into a dreadful fright. When the colonel saw how pale they looked, he encouraged them to take heart, and calmly admonished them of their insolence; and they being changed and very humble through their fear, he called for wine for them, and sent them away. To the most insolent of them he said, 'These carriages would bring back the Stuarts.' The man, laying his hand upon his sword, said, 'Never while he wore that.' Among other things, they said to the colonel, when he demanded by what authority they came, they showed their swords, and said, 'That was their authority.'"

The necessity for some immediate authority beyond that of the Council of Officers at length became manifest to the Army in London. It was resolved to restore the expelled Parliament. The Generals saw that their power was gone. Fleetwood sent the keys of the House of Commons to Lenthall; and on the 26th of December, forty members, with the Speaker at their head, again entered this House, the scene of so many strange transactions, whilst groups of soldiers shouted their approval, in the torch-light which glared upon anxious faces of men who had more natural fears than reasonable hopes. A contest took place the instant Lenthall had taken the chair. Twenty-three of the members who had been excluded in 1648, demanded admittance, as they had previously demanded on the 7th of May. The House resolved to take the business of the absent members into consideration on the 5th of January. They withdrew to abide their time. Lambert was at Newcastle, and Monk at Coldstream. But Fairfax, who had been in correspondence with Monk, assembled his friends and dependents; and some of Lambert's officers joined him with their men. He entered York and was welcomed by

the Cavaliers of that city. Lambert marched to attack Fairfax, and Monk
crossed the Tweed to support him. At Wooler, Monk received a cold letter
from the Parliament that had re-commenced its sittings; and he learnt that
Lambert's troops had been ordered to return to their several quarters. When
he reached Newcastle he found Lambert's army disbanded. He went on to
York, and saw Fairfax. But he maintained a strict reserve as to his future
plans; and he struck an officer with his cane who said that Monk would bring
in Charles Stuart. The Royalists abroad were perplexed. The Republicans
in London were suspicious. Monk sent forward his chaplain, Gumble, to
express his opinions to the Parliament on certain important points of administration. Gumble wrote to Monk some truths as to the character of the
parliamentary leaders : " The prevailing and governing influence of the Parliament is reduced into the hands of a few and inconsiderable persons,—either
harebrained and hot-headed fools, or obscure and disregarded knaves." They
talked of sending the prudent and trimming Whitelocke to the Tower, and
voted that the enthusiastic and honest Vane should cease to be a member of
the House. Their chief thought was to propitiate Monk. He had taken his
determination to march to London—with what ultimate purpose beyond that
of asserting the power of civil government was uncertain. He left many
of his troops in York and others he sent to Scotland. With four regiments
of foot and three of horse, he went on, amidst popular acclamations. But
he would enter into no promises or make any special demonstration. He was
but a servant, he said, of the Parliament, and all great questions must be left
to the Parliament. He was suspected by one two Commissioners that the
House had sent to him; but his wariness eluded all their curiosity, even
while he was receiving agents from the Royalists abroad. On the 28th of
January he sent from St. Albans a letter to the Speaker, pointing out the
necessity that the troops in and near London should be removed—it was not
for their service that the soldiers who had been so lately in rebellion against
the Parliament should mingle with his faithful troops. His proposals were
agreed to, " partly from some sparks of hope that Monk could not be such a
devil as to betray a trust so freely reposed in him." *

The Royalists, meanwhile, were far from inactive. Some who had lived
quietly under the rule of Oliver, and had not stirred whilst the government
which had succeeded him was confined within some limits of legal order, now
moved, however cautiously, to bring about the restoration of the ancient
monarchy. Such was Evelyn. On the 22nd of January he writes in his
Diary, " I went this afternoon to visit colonel Morley." Morley was one of
the Commissioners appointed by the Long Parliament to the command of the
army; and he was faithful to his trust, when Lambert, on the 13th of
October, was proceeding to Westminster to dissolve the Parliament, for
Morley met him, pistol in hand, and said he would shoot him if he did not go
back, upon which threat Lambert went another way. Evelyn first approached
Morley by sending him a tract he had written, entitled " An Apology for
the Royal Party ; " and he afterwards addressed a letter to him, exhorting
him, by the remembrance of their ancient friendship, to aid " in restoring us
to our ancient known laws, native and most happy liberties." † Morley, in

---

* Ludlow, " Memoirs," p. 816   † Appendix to Evelyn's " Diary," No. II.

January, 1660, was Lieutenant of the Tower of London: "I went this afternoon to visit colonel Morley. After dinner, I discoursed with him; but he was very jealous, and would not believe that Monk came in to do the king any service. I told him he might do it without him, and have all the honour. He was still doubtful, and would resolve on nothing yet, so I took leave." Evelyn, four months after, writes: "O, the sottish omission of this gentleman! What did I not undergo of danger in this negotiation, to have brought him over to his majesty's interest, when it was entirely in his hands." On the 3rd of February Monk entered London. For two days the capital had been in uproar. The regiments that had been ordered to march, had refused to obey. The apprentices were parading the city in formidable bands, crying out for "a free Parliament." Pepys, the most amusing of diarists, presents us many glimpses of events through the "blanket of the dark" which the graver historians pass over. On the 25th of January, a gibbet is set up in Cheapside, and "the picture of Hewson hung upon it in the middle of the street,"—Hewson, the shoemaker-Lord, that Warwick would not sit with. People, in the midst of their alarms, eat and drink as usual; and Pepys' wife, on the 26th, "had got ready a very fine dinner." On the 30th, he records: "This morning, before I was up, I fell a singing of my song, 'Great, good and just,' and put myself thereby in mind that this was the fatal day, now ten years since, his majesty died." Montrose's lines were probably in the minds of other Royalists on that anniversary. On the 2nd of February he saw the Strand full of soldiers; and "saw the foot face the horse and beat them back, and stood bawling and calling in the street for a free Parliament and money." The next morning the soldiers were all quiet. Pepys saw Monk march in: "In his passing through the town he had many calls to him for a free Parliament, but little other welcome." He was lodged in Whitehall. The troops who came to preserve order were not very orderly. On the 7th, Pepys writes, "In the palace I saw Monk's soldiers abuse Billing and all the Quakers, that were at a meeting-place there, and indeed the soldiers did use them very roughly, and were to blame." On the 9th, Monk is gone to the City. There is arbitrary work there; but the calm progress of the law is uninterrupted, for Pepys hears "an action very finely pleaded· in Westminster Hall." Monk went to the City by command of the Parliament. It was believed in the House that the powerful general was wholly with them. The more obscure Republicans were the leading spirits in the House. There was no commanding genius to call up a new and vigorous Commonwealth out of the expiring embers of "the good old cause." The destinies of the nation were in the hands of the cold, sullen, impenetrable George Monk, who chewed his tobacco in ominous silence, opening his heart to no man. The Lord Mayor, Aldermen, and Common Council of London, had voted that they would pay no taxes, but such as were imposed by a free Parliament. The Council of State sent for Monk, and proposed that the Common Council should be forbidden to sit, the gates of the City broken down, the portcullises wedged up, and the chains across the streets removed. All the material means of resistance were to be destroyed. Monk said that he would do these things if they would give the order. "He added," says Ludlow, "that the disaffection of the City was so great, that they would never be quiet, till some of them were hanged." This ready consent of Monk to an unpopular act of violence may be doubted. However, on the morning of the 9th, before the citizens were awake, and the great shutters of the shops had been dropped down, Monk and his men were marching to the neighbourhood of Guildhall. He explained his orders to his officers. Some remonstrated. "Will you not obey the orders of the Parliament?" was his answer. The posts and chains were then attacked, amidst the indignation of the people. A deputation of leading citizens came to him, to complain of the force thus used by those whom they thought their friends. He told them that his orders were to take down the gates as well as the chains; but that he would request the Parliament to suspend the further execution of their commands. The Parliament was indignant; sent an order to Monk to execute his instructions to the letter; ordered that the Common Council should be dissolved, and a new Council elected, with such qualifications as Parliament should dictate. The next morning Monk and his soldiers went to the completion of the work prescribed to them. In the evening of the 10th he returned to Whitehall. The slow man now came to a decisive resolution. He had seen the temper of the people, and he was prepared to defy those who claimed to be his masters. He called a Council of his officers; and they agreed upon a letter to Parliament, expressing the public grievances, and requiring them to satisfy the nation's just demands before a certain day. Early in the morning he and his army were on their way to the City; and the troops were halted in Finsbury Fields. Monk waited on the Lord Mayor; requested him to summon a meeting of the Common Council at four o'clock; and the civic dignitaries and the general and his officers sate down to dinner. Two members deputed by the House arrived to confer with Monk. His letter, which was of the boldest character, had thrown the Parliament into consternation. He was urged to return to Whitehall. Monk's only reply was, "All will be well if you attend to the letter, and issue out your writs on Friday for filling up your House." Monk went to the Common Council and told them what he had done. Guildhall resounded with cries of "God bless your Excellency!" The soldiers were feasted. The cry went forth throughout London of "Down with the Rump." Pepys has described, as none but an eye-witness could describe, the scene of that night: "In Cheapside there was a great many bonfires, and Bow bells and all the bells in all the churches as we went home were a-ringing. Hence we went homewards, it being about ten at night. But the common joy that was everywhere to be seen! The number of bonfires, there being fourteen between St. Dunstan's and Temple Bar, and at Strand Bridge I could at one time tell thirty-one fires. In King-street seven or eight; and all along burning and roasting, and drinking for rumps. There being rumps tied upon sticks and carried up and down. The butchers at the May Pole in the Strand rang a peal with their knives when they were going to sacrifice their rump. On Ludgate Hill there was one turning of the spit that had a rump tied upon it, and another basting of it. Indeed it was past imagination, both the greatness and the suddenness of it. At one end of the street you would think there was a whole lane of fire, and so hot that we were fain to keep on the further side."

Charles and his Court were at Brussels when the news reached them of these events in London. "They thought all their sufferings over," says Clarendon. And yet the best informed men in London, whether republican or royalist, could not penetrate the thick veil of Monk's real intentions. Aubrey, who lived a gossiping life in places of public resort, and had access to persons of influence, says of certain friends, "they were satisfied that he [Monk] no more intended or designed the king's restoration, when he came into England, or first came to London, than his horse did." Sir Henry Vane, after the menacing letter had been written to the Parliament, said to Ludlow, that "unless he were much mistaken, Monk had yet several masks to put off." Ludlow went to see him in the City, and after much discourse Monk exclaimed, " Yea, we must live and die together for a Commonwealth." Whatever were his real intentions, he maintained his ascendancy by the most earnest professions of fidelity to the republican party and their opinions. Yet his actions were more than doubtful. The House had twice resolved that the secluded Members should not be admitted. Monk had determined the contrary. The infusion of so many of these who had been originally thrust out of Parliament for the moderation of their opinions, was the surest way to neutralise the power of the republican faction, who clung to authority with a tenacity that indicated their real weakness. Monk, on the 21st of February, sent an escort of his soldiers to accompany a body of the secluded Members to the House of Commons, he having previously read them a speech, in which he formally declared for a Commonwealth. When they took their seats the greatest heats were exhibited; and some of the Republicans withdrew from the House. Seventeen of them went in a body to Monk, to demand his reasons for these proceedings. He protested his zeal to a Commonwealth Government; "and they then pressed him more home by demanding, if he would join with them against Charles Stuart and his party?" He took off his glove, and putting his hand within sir Arthur Haslerig's hand, he said, "I do here protest to you, in the presence of all these gentlemen, that I will oppose to the utmost the setting-up of Charles Stuart, a Single Person, or a House of Peers." Ludlow, who records this, says that Monk then expostulated with them touching their suspicions, saying, " What is it that I have done in bringing these Members into the House? Are they not the same that brought the king to the block? though others cut off his head, and that justly." The Members thus restored by Monk were chiefly of that great Presbyterian body who had been ejected by the Independents; and who now expected that they should be strong enough, in the event of the restoration of the monarchy, to make terms for the establishment of their form of Church government. They immediately became a majority in Parliament; appointed Monk general-in-chief; formed a new Council of State; and superseded sheriffs, justices of the peace, and militia officers, who were supporters of republican institutions. The Covenant was again to be promulgated; the Confession of Faith of the Assembly of Divines to be adopted; the penal laws against Catholics, which Cromwell rarely put in force, were to be called into full vigour. The tendencies of some of the members towards monarchy were still very feebly indicated. Uncertainty everywhere prevailed, whilst the man who had the power of the sword was well known to have no fixed principles of politics or religion—was more greedy of wealth than excited by any daring ambition—and would only declare himself by some irrevocable action when he had made up his mind as to the probable success and permanency of King or Commonwealth.

On the 2nd of March, Pepys writes: "Great is the talk of a Single Person, and that it would now be Charles, George, or Richard. For the last of which, my lord St. John is said to speak high. Great also is the dispute now in the House, in whose name the writs shall run for the next Parliament; and it is said that Mr. Prynne, in open House, said, 'In king Charles's!'" Admiral Montague had been appointed "general at sea," the republican admiral Lawson being put aside. He was the patron of Pepys, and told him, on the 6th of March, that there were great endeavours to bring in the Protector again, but that he did not think it would last long if he were brought in. Montague added, "No, nor the king neither—though he seems to think he will come in—unless he carry himself very soberly and well." How Charles carried himself was perfectly well known to his most zealous friends—even to those who themselves lived "soberly and well." When a proposal was made to Oliver Cromwell that Charles should marry his daughter, the Protector objected his "debauched life" as an insuperable difficulty. The Royalists, Presbyterian or Episcopalian, saw no such objection in the marriage of Charles with the State of England. Very curious combinations of men long separated were now forming. Old faithful friends of his house were flocking to the king at Breda. Amongst them now and then appeared some country gentleman, whose clothes were of a soberer hue and a more English cut, than

Court Costume. Charles II.

those of Charles's habitual courtiers. These had discarded the love-locks of the Cavaliers, their slashed doublets and flowing mantles, for the hideous periwigs and embroidered surtouts of the Parisian fashion. The staid royalist, who for some twenty years had seen no court costume, wondered at the metamorphosis; and might fancy that there was more sympathy between himself and the Puritan in neat and decorous habit of plain black,—neat from the band to the shoe-tie,—than the men in the ugliest of laced liveries, who bent double when they approached their exiled prince, and then turned to Wilmot or Buckingham to laugh at the stalest jest or the newest scandal. Very tarnished were the gold and silver embroideries of the courtiers at Brussels, or Breda, or the Hague, in the early spring of 1660, when Englishmen from home gathered about them. " Their clothes were not worth forty shillings, the best of them," says Pepys. London soon sent money to the exiles, and Paris was ready to provide fineries of which the Louvre might have been proud. For there was a growing confidence that the Commonwealth was fast coming to an end. Men, by a sort of instinctive feeling, were setting up the King's arms; and drinking the King's health, though Monk and his bands were still dominating in the City and at Whitehall. The Long Parliament was to terminate its sittings on the 16th of March. On the 13th, that once formidable republican assembly voted that the oath of a Member of Parliament —to be " true and faithful to the Commonwealth of England, as the same is now established, without a King or House of Lords,"—should be abolished. On the 15th of March the popular sentiment was manifested at the Royal Exchange. A statue of Charles I. had been removed after the tragedy of the 30th January; and in the niche where it stood was written, " Exit tyrannus, regum ultimus, anno libertatis Angliæ restitutæ primo, annoque Domini 1648." For twelve years few had ventured to affirm that " tyrant and the last of kings " were words of offence; or had asserted that the year 1648 was not the first year of the restored liberty of England. On the evening of the 15th of March, a ladder was placed against this niche; soldiers stood around; a house painter mounted the ladder, painted out the inscription, and waving his cap, shouted " God bless King Charles the

Oliverian or Puritan.

Second!" Again bonfires blazed in the streets. On the 16th of March, the Parliament met to vote their own dissolution, and England hoped that a long term of rest and security had been earned by the sufferings and changes of twenty years. Some few uplifted their voices against the inevitable event; and still clung to their faith in a Commonwealth; to their assured belief that liberty and peace would be best maintained by the absolute authority of a " Grand or General Council of the Nation." This was Vane's opinion, having no misgivings for his past actions and no dread of his future lot, even though it were the hardest: " He had all possible satisfaction of mind as to those actions God had enabled him to do for the Commonwealth, and hoped the same God would fortify him in his sufferings, how sharp soever, to bear a faithful and constant testimony thereto." * This was also his friend Milton's opinion: " What I have spoken is the language of that which is not called amiss, the good old cause: if it seem strange to any, it will not

* Ludlow, p. 828.

seem more strange, I hope, than convincing to backsliders : thus much I should, perhaps, have said, though I were sure I should have spoken only to trees and stones, and had none to cry to but with the prophet, ' O earth, earth, earth!' to tell the very soil itself what her perverse inhabitants are deaf to. Nay, though what I have spoke should happen (which Thou suffer not who didst create mankind free! nor Thou next who didst redeem us from being servants of men!) to be the last words of our expiring liberty." *

The clouded determinations of Monk were very soon becoming more transparent. He had secretly received his cousin, sir John Grenville, who had long sought an interview in vain, to deliver a letter from the king. He would write no letter in answer; but he entrusted Grenville to promise to Charles that he would be his devoted servant. Monk made no conditions, but he tendered some advice—that there should be a general amnesty, with only four exceptions ; that the possessors of confiscated property should not be disturbed; that there should be liberty of conscience. Grenville repaired to the king at Brussels, where they met in secret. A more formal body of envoys from England now presented themselves to the king—a deputation of Presbyterians, who came to offer the same terms which had been proposed to his father in the Isle of Wight. The Parliament was to have the control of the army; the Civil War was to be declared lawful; new patents of nobility were to be annulled. Charles laughed in his sleeve. "Little do they think," he said, "that general Monk and I are upon so good terms." The Presbyterians believed that they alone had any chance of success. "Leave the game in our hands," they said to the Cavaliers. They probably thought correctly that Charles was indifferent as to the form of worship under which England should be when he came to be king. But they knew that Hyde was devoted to the restoration of the Anglican Church, as a necessary consequence of the restoration of the monarchy. They wished that Hyde should be expelled from power or influence, and used the strongest arguments to induce the belief that the Restoration could not be accomplished whilst he was a royal counsellor. In spite of their conviction of Monk's adhesion to their cause, the few to whom Charles had entrusted the secret of his correspondence with him, still sometimes doubted. The French ambassador tried to obtain Monk's confidence. He would give no opinion as to the future Government of England. That must be settled by the next Parliament. Monk's real opinions were the less necessary to be disclosed; for all England was becoming impatient for the Restoration. Old servants of the Commonwealth —Broghill, and Thurloe, and Lenthall—

Clarendon.

offered to Charles their submission and their advice. The king, from mixed motives of indolence and prudence, suffered matters to proceed without committing himself to any party, or making any engagements for his future

* "Ready and Easy Way to establish a Free Commonwealth."

conduct. He yielded to Monk's advice in one particular. He left the Spanish Netherlands, and established himself at Breda.

In the midst of the apparent certainty of the Restoration being at hand, a new cause of alarm suddenly arose. Lambert had been committed to the Tower, when Monk's interest became predominant. He escaped on the 9th of April, and was speedily at the head of some soldiers, who had revolted; and, marching through the midland counties, he called upon all to join him who would preserve the Commonwealth. Monk sent Ingoldsby to encounter Lambert; and declared to Grenville that, if Lambert met with any success, he would no longer have any reservation, but act in the king's name and under his commission, to summon the Royalists to arms. On the 22nd of April, Lambert and his men were met at Daventry by Ingoldsby's troops. A parley was proposed; but Ingoldsby refused any accommodation. The two armies had advanced close to each other, and the conflict seemed imminent, when Lambert's cavalry threw away their pistols; and their leader was quickly a prisoner. The last battle of the Commonwealth had now to be fought at the hustings. The elections took place. A few of the old republicans were returned. Some members were elected who believed that the restoration of the monarchy could be effected, without losing any of the liberties which had been won since the days of Laud and Strafford. The greater number were men who were either led away by a fever of loyalty, or were indifferent to any re-action which would end the struggles and uncertainties of twenty years. It was impossible that a king thus restored amidst a conflict of passions and prejudices—of old hatreds and new ambitions—should be forward to make any professions of public duty, or cherish any deep affection for the people he was to govern. It was fortunate that Charles was only a heartless voluptuary, and was too selfish in his craving for ease and pleasure, to add the personal energy of the tyrant to the almost inevitable tyranny of those who believed that the king and the people could return to the same condition in which they were before Hampden refused to pay ship-money. The king's position with regard to the Church was, in a similar degree, under the control of the same spirit of indifference. Secretly a Papist, openly a scoffer, Episcopalian, Presbyterian, or Independent might harass each other, so that Charles was quiet. He fancied himself most safe with those who professed to believe that his authority was divine; and that "Render unto Cæsar" meant, if rightly interpreted, Let Cæsar's will be the one law.

Five hundred and fifty-six members had been elected to the House of Commons, the greater number of whom took their seats on the 26th of April. Ten Peers only met in the House of Lords on that day. Presbyterians and Cavaliers looked suspiciously at each other; but the Presbyterians, more accustomed to act in union, manœuvred that one of their party should be elected Speaker. The first business of both Houses was to return thanks to Monk for his services, and the Lords voted that a statue should be erected in his honour. Colonel Ingoldsby also received the thanks of the Commons for his prompt action against Lambert. The House was not yet in the humour to forget the sound advice of Monk to the Lords when he returned them his thanks—"to look forward and not backward in transacting affairs." The Cavaliers soon made the House and the nation understand that the day of a triumphant re-action was fast approaching. Their spirit spread amongst the moderate and independent : "Every one hoped in this change to change their condition, and disowned all things they had before advised. Every ballad singer sang up and down the streets ribald rhymes, made in reproach of the late Commonwealth." * The day after Parliament met, sir John Grenville went to the sitting of the Council of State, and asked to speak with the Lord General. To his hands he delivered a packet sealed with the royal arms. Monk affected surprise and alarm, and it was decided that Grenville should be called in. He said that the packet had been entrusted to him by the king, his master, at Breda. The Council resolved that the letters which Grenville brought should be delivered to the Parliament. On the first of May, Grenville appeared at the door of the Lower House, and being called to the bar presented a letter addressed " To our trusty and well beloved the Speaker of the House of Commons." He then went through the same formality at the House of Lords. With each letter was enclosed a document addressed to the whole nation—the Declaration from Breda.† Grenville then proceeded to the City, and presented a letter from the king addressed to the Lord Mayor, Aldermen, and Common Council, which also contained the Declaration. In all these papers, the composition of Hyde, there was little to alarm, and much to propitiate, the prudent and peaceful. The Commons were assured " upon our royal word,—that none of our predecessors have had a greater esteem for Parliaments than we have ; "—Parliaments were " so vital a part of the constitution of the kingdom, and so necessary for the government of it, that, we well know, neither prince nor people can be, in any tolerable degree, happy without them." The Declaration professed the king's desire " that all our subjects may enjoy what by law is theirs, by a full and entire administration of justice throughout the land." It declared " a free and general Pardon to all our subjects,"—excepting only such persons " as shall hereafter be excepted by Act of Parliament." All are invited to a perfect union amongst themselves. Deploring the existence of religious animosities, " we do declare a liberty to tender consciences ; and that no man shall be disquieted, or called in question, for differences of opinion in matters of religion, which do not disturb the peace of the kingdom." All matters relating to the possession of estates " shall be determined in Parliament." Both Houses immediately applied themselves to prepare answers to the royal letters ; declared that, " according to the ancient and fundamental laws of this kingdom, the government is, and ought to be, by King, Lords, and Commons ; "—voted fifty thousand pounds to the king as a gift ; ‡ and presented Grenville with five hundred pounds to buy a jewel. Commissioners from both Houses were chosen to convey their

---

* Mrs. Hutchinson's "Memoirs," vol. ii. p. 261.

† See Note at the end of this Chapter.

‡ "Of a tall stature, and of sable hue,
    Much like the son of Kish, that lofty Jew ;
    Twelve years complete he suffered in exile,
    And kept his father's asses all the while.
    At length, by wonderful impulse of fate,
    The people call him home to help the State :
    And, what is more, they send him money too,
    And clothe him all, from head to foot, anew."
                    ANDREW MARVELL.

answers to the king.   Grenville preceded them with the best proof of loyalty
and affection—four thousand five hundred pounds in gold, and a bill of
exchange for twenty-five thousand pounds.   Pepys tells us that Charles, when
Grenville brought him the money, was " so joyful, that he called the Princess
Royal and Duke of York, to look upon it, as it lay in the portmanteau before
it was taken out."

On the 8th of May the two Houses of Parliament proclaimed Charles
the Second, King of England, Scotland, and Ireland, at Westminster, at
Whitehall, and in the City.   Although the king had not arrived, the
Restoration of the Monarchy was completed.   In a delirium of loyalty the
Convention Parliament never thought of making conditions for the liberties
of the country.   Hale, the great judge, and Prynne, the learned lawyer, had
ventured to propose a Committee for considering what propositions should
be made to Charles, before the destinies of the country were irrevocably
committed to his guidance.   Monk opposed this : " I cannot answer for the
peace either of the nation or of the army, if any delay is put to the sending
for the king.   What need is there of sending propositions to him ?   Might
we not as well prepare them, and offer them to him when he shall come
over ?   He will bring neither army nor treasure with him, either to fright
or corrupt us."   The House assented by acclamation.   It rested the con-
servancy of all that the nation had won since the opening of the Long
Parliament upon the flimsy foundation of the Declaration from Breda.   Bills
were prepared, which were to be presented for the acceptance of the king,
" when he shall come over."   Magna Charta and the Petition of Right ;
Privilege of Parliament ; Pardon, Indemnity, and Oblivion,—were words
glibly used as if they were things of course.   Bills were prepared for
confirming purchases of property during the times of trouble ; and for the
abolition of Knight Service, the feudal tenure which was most obnoxious.
But the real temper of this Parliament was to be subjected to a severer test—
the question of Amnesty had yet to be settled.   Monk had just protested
that if he were to suffer any one to be excluded from such Amnesty, he
would be the arrantest rogue that ever lived.   Ashley Cooper had said to
Hutchinson, " If the violence of the people should bring the king upon us,
let me be damned, body and soul, if ever I see a hair of any man's head
touched, or a penny of any man's estate, upon this quarrel."   Ingoldsby had
received the thanks of the Commons for recent services.   He, and others
who had signed the warrant for the king's execution, were members of the
Commons.   On the 9th of May, the debate on the Amnesty Bill came on in
both Houses.   The earl of Northumberland said, that though he had no part
in the death of the king, he was against questioning those concerned ; " that
the example may be more useful to posterity, and profitable to future kings,
by deterring them from the like exorbitances."   Fairfax, in a noble spirit of
generosity, exclaimed, " If any man must be excepted, I know no man that
deserves it more than myself ; for I was General of the army at that time,
and had power sufficient to prevent the proceedings against the king ; but I
did not think fit to make use of it to that end."   Lenthall, the son of the
famous Speaker, provoked the House to tumult by boldly saying, " He that
first drew his sword against the king committed as high an offence as he that
cut off the king's head."   The House at last voted as to the number of

regicides to be excluded from the Amnesty, and decided that seven should be excepted. But it also resolved that every one should be arrested who had sat upon the king's trial, and their property seized. Other arrests took place. Some who had laboured best with Cromwell to uphold the honour of England, such as Thurloe, were impeached. The titles bestowed by the two Protectors were annulled. Upon all great questions, political or religious, which affected the future safety and liberties of these nations, postponement was the ruling policy of the Cavaliers. The Presbyterians, who were the first to aim at religious supremacy, began clearly to see that the day was fast approaching, when they would regret the tranquillity they had enjoyed under the toleration of that ruler whom they had now agreed to declare a traitor.

The fortunes of Charles had so decidedly changed in the course of a little month, that the foreign Courts who had looked adversely or coldly upon him, now embarrassed him with their rival professions of friendship. He was wisely advised not to be too forward to receive such civilities from France or from Spain as might compromise him in the future policy of England. The States of Holland invited him to take his departure from the Hague; and he arrived there from Breda on the 15th of May. Thither came the commissioners of the Parliament; the town-clerk of London, with aldermen and lesser dignitaries; deputations of the Presbyterian clergy; and a swarm of Englishmen of every variety of opinion, who wanted to prostrate themselves at the feet of power. Hollis, who had been one of the earliest leaders in the battle of the Long Parliament, was the orator on the part of the House of Commons. Their hearts, he said, were filled with veneration and confidence; their longings for their king, their desires to serve him, expressed the opinions of the whole nation—"lettings out of the soul, expressions of transported minds." Other lords had had dominion over them; but their hearts and souls did abhor such rulers, and ever continued faithful to their king. Anthony Ashley Cooper had civil words from Charles. Fairfax was received with kindness. The king made smooth speeches to the Presbyterians; but they obtained no satisfaction as to the future of England in the great question of religious union. No one, however, pressed hardly upon him. There were no strong words spoken, as the earlier race of Puritans would have spoken. Burnet, describing the general character of Charles, says, " He was affable and easy, and loved to be made so by all about him. The great art of keeping him long, was the being easy, and the making everything easy to him." The modern phrase is " to make things pleasant; " and both phrases mean that there should be a large ingredient of falsehood in human affairs. Admiral Montague, who was to have the honour of receiving the king on board his ship, had long been in communication with him. The ship which carried the admiral's flag had an ugly name, " The Naseby." On the 23rd, the king, with the dukes of York and Gloucester, and a large train, came on board. " After dinner," says Pepys, who was now Montague's secretary, " the king and duke altered the name of some of the ships, viz., the Naseby into Charles; the Richard, James; the Speaker, Mary; the Dunbar (which was not in company with us), the Henry." Lady Fanshawe, who was on board, is in ecstacies: " Who can express the joy and gallantry of that voyage; to see so many great ships, the best in the world; to hear the trumpets and all other music; to see near a hundred brave

ships sail before the wind with vast cloths and streamers; the neatness
and cleanness of the ships, the gallantry of the commanders, the vast plenty.
of all sorts of provisions; but, above all, the glorious majesties of the king
and his two brothers, were so beyond man's expectation and expression." *
The sky was cloudless, the sea was calm, the moon was at the full. Charles
walked up and down the quarter-deck, telling all the wonders of his escape
from Worcester—his green coat and his country breeches—the miller
stopping his night walk—the inn-keeper bidding God bless him. "He was
an everlasting talker," writes Burnet; and his gossip amongst his new
friends in this moonlight voyage gave some better promise than the cold
dignity of his father, which many must have remembered. It was a merry
trip,—and Pepys chuckles over "the brave discourse," and especially the
stories of "Thomas Killigrew, a merry droll, but a gentleman of great
esteem with the king." On the morning of the 25th they were close to
land at Dover, and every one was preparing to go ashore. "The king and
the two dukes did eat their breakfast before they went, and there being set
some ship's diet, they ate of nothing else but pease and pork, and boiled
beef"—a politic appetite, which no doubt won the favour of Blake's old
sailors.

When Charles landed at Dover, Monk was at hand to kneel before him—
"to receive his majesty as a malefactor would his pardon,"—says a biographer
of the wary general. With a feeling that belonged to another time the
mayor of Dover presented the king with a Bible. "It is the thing that I
love above all things in the world," said the ready actor, who knew his part
without much study. The royal train went on to Canterbury. There Monk
ventured beyond his usual caution, by presenting the king a list of seventy
persons that he recommended for employments—men whose names stank in
the nostrils of all Cavaliers. Hyde, through Monk's confidential adviser,
Morrice, made the general understand that such interference was unpleasant,
and Monk quickly apologised after a very awkward attempt at explanation.
Hyde was at Charles's side, and prevented him being too easy. Monk
received a lesson; but he was consoled by the Order of the Garter being
bestowed upon him.

On the 28th of May king Charles set out from Canterbury, and slept
that night at Rochester. At Blackheath the royal cavalcade had to pass the
Army of the Commonwealth. Thirty thousand men were there marshalled.
Many of these veterans had fought against the family and the cause which
was now triumphant. The name of Charles Stuart had been with them a
name of hatred and contempt. They had assisted in building up and pulling
down governments, which had no unity but in their determination to resist him
who was now called to command them, with no sympathy for their courage,
no respect for their stern enthusiasm. The great soldier and prince who
had led them to so many victories had now his memory profaned, by being
proclaimed a traitor by a Parliament that when he was living would have
been humbled at his slightest frown. The procession passed on in safety;
for the old discipline, that no enemy was ever able to prevail against in the
battle-field, was still supreme in this pageant,—this last harmless exhibition

* "Memoirs," p. 131.

of that might through which the liberties of England had been won; through whose misdirection they were now imperilled.

Charles went on in the sight of all London to Whitehall,—a wearisome procession, which lasted till nine at night, amidst streets strewed with flowers, past tapestried houses and wine-spouting fountains; with civic authorities wearing chains of gold, and nobles covered with embroidered velvets; trumpets braying, mobs huzzaing. In this delirium of joy there was something beyond the idle shouts of popular intoxication. It was the expression of the nation's opinion that the government of England had at length a solid foundation upon which peace and security, liberty and religion, might be established.

Medal in Commemoration of the Restoration.

NOTE. HIS MAJESTY'S DECLARATION FROM BREDA, TO ALL HIS LOVING SUBJECTS.

C. R.

CHARLES, by the Grace of God, King of England, Scotland, France, and Ireland, Defender of the Faith, &c. To all our loving subjects, of what degree or quality soever, greeting: If the general distraction and confusion which is spread over the whole kingdom, doth not awaken all men to a desire and longing that those wounds, which have so many years together been kept bleeding, may be bound up, all we can say will be to no purpose; however, after this long silence, we have thought it our duty to declare how much we desire to contribute thereunto; and that as we can never give over the hope, in good time, to obtain the possession of that right which God and nature hath made our due; so we do make it our daily suit to the Divine Providence, that he will, in compassion to us and our subjects, after so long misery and sufferings, remit, and put us into a quiet and peaceable possession of that our right, with as little blood and damage to our people as is possible; nor do we desire more to enjoy what is ours, than that all our subjects may enjoy what by law is theirs, by a full and entire administration of justice throughout the land, and by extending our mercy where it is wanted and deserved. And to the end that the fear of punishment may not engage any, conscious to themselves of what is past, to a perseverance in guilt for the future, by opposing the quiet and happiness of their country, in the Restoration both of king, peers, and people, to their just, ancient, and fundamental rights, we do, by these presents, declare, That we do grant a free and general Pardon, which we are ready, upon demand, to pass under our Great Seal of England, to all our subjects, of what degree or quality soever, who, within forty days after the publishing hereof, shall lay hold upon this our grace and favour, and shall, by any public act, declare their doing so, and that they return to the loyalty and obedience of good subjects; excepting only such persons as shall hereafter be excepted by parliament, those only to be excepted. Let all our subjects, how faulty soever, rely upon the word of a king, solemnly given by this present Declaration, That no crime whatsoever, committed against us or our royal father before the publication of this, shall ever rise in judgment, or be brought in question, against any of them, to the least endamagement of them, either in their lives, liberties, or estates, or (as far forth as lies in our power) so much as to the prejudice of their reputations, by any reproach or term of distinction from the rest of our best subjects; we desiring and ordaining, that henceforth all notes of discord, separation, and difference of parties be utterly abolished among all our subjects, whom we invite and conjure to a perfect union among themselves, under our protection, for the Re-settlement of our just Rights and theirs, in a Free Parliament, by which, upon the word of a king, we will be advised. And because the passion and uncharitableness of the times have produced several opinions in Religion, by which men are engaged in parties and animosities against each other, (which, when they shall hereafter unite in a freedom of conversation, will be composed, or better understood) we do declare a Liberty to tender Consciences, and that no man shall be disquieted, or called in question, for differences of opinion in matters of Religion, which do not disturb the peace of the Kingdom; and that we shall be ready to consent to such an act of parliament as, upon mature deliberation, shall be offered to us, for the full granting that indulgence. —And because, in the continued distractions of so many years, and so many and great revolutions, many grants and purchases of estates have been made to, and by, many officers, soldiers, and others, who are now possessed of the same, and who may be liable to actions at law upon several titles, we are likewise willing that all such differences, and all things relating to such grants, sales, and purchases, shall be determined in parliament; which can best provide for the just satisfaction of all men who are concerned.—And we do further declare, That we will be ready to consent to any act or acts of parliament to the purposes aforesaid, and for the full satisfaction of all arrears due to the officers and soldiers of the army under the command of general Monk, and that they shall be received into our service upon as good pay and conditions as they now enjoy. Given under Our Sign Manual and Privy-Signet, at our Court at Breda, this 14th day of April, 1660, in the 12th year of our reign.

Great Seal of Charles II.

CHAPTER XV.

WE can once more open the ponderous "Statutes of the Realm," and therein find the most important materials for the history of the State and the history of the People. The last Statute of Charles I. bears the date of 1640. The first Statute of Charles II. bears the date of 1660. During these twenty years of Civil War, and of the Commonwealth, there were Ordinances and Acts of Parliament which had the force of Laws—many directed to temporary objects, but many, also, of permanent utility. Some of the Statutes of the Restored Monarchy were founded upon these,—often without the slightest reference to them. But occasionally, when a wise law of the Long Parliament, or of the Protectorate, had become an established principle, it was recognised in a new Statute, in which it was called "a pretended Act." The royalist theory of the Constitution was, that there was no vitality in any legislative body not called into being by the Crown—that all laws were a dead letter that had not received the assent of the Crown. The royalists maintained that from the 30th of January, 1649, Charles the Second had been king *de facto* as well as king *de jure*; that although kept out of the exercise of his authority by traitors and rebels, he had been for twelve years the sole governor of England; that 1660 was the twelfth year of his reign, as the dates of Acts of Parliament, and of other instruments, set forth.* The Parliament of the Restoration, which was begun to be holden on the 25th of April, 1660—the Convention Parliament, as it is called—in their first Statute declared the Long Parliament to be dissolved, and enacted that the Lords and Commons then sitting at Westminster were the two Houses of Parliament "notwithstanding any want of the King's Majesty's Writ or Writs of Summons."† They had recalled the legitimate heir of the Crown; but this their first Act virtually acknowledged that they had no constitutional power to do so. The next Parliament, which was duly summoned by the King's writ, always termed this Convention Parliament "the last Assembly;"‡ for the second Parliament was far more servile in its royalist fervour than the first; and many of its members regarded Charles Stuart simply as the heir who had come to take possession of his estate of England, together with five millions of people, his lawful chattels. In a few years this so-called loyalty put on more offensive shapes; and the people began to see that the old battle against arbitrary power had to be renewed, with the full benefit of a bitter experience.

The Parliament of 1660, in the exuberance of its devotion, but not altogether unwisely, resolved to make such an ample provision for the executive power as should place it beyond the pretended necessity of raising money by unlawful means. They settled the yearly revenue of the Crown at an amount considerably beyond the supplies voted to Charles I., and they voted the subsidy of tonnage and poundage, for the term of the king's life.§ One stipulation, of great importance to the owners of landed property, was associated with this liberality of the Commons. When the king and the Parliament came to the fatal issue of Civil War in 1641, the feudal revenues of the Crown were necessarily set aside. There was an end to the ancient claims of the Crown upon tenures by Knight-Service, with all their oppressive conditions of fines for alienation, of forfeitures, and of wardship. There was an end, also, of the more generally obnoxious demands of purveyance. These relics of prerogative would have revived with the re-establishment of the monarchy. The Parliament made a bargain to relieve the landed proprietors; but this bargain was completed at the expense of the Commonalty. Charles surrendered the Court of Wards, and Purveyance, and

* "This had not been the usage of former times. Edward IV., Richard III., Henry VII., had dated their instruments either from their proclamation, or at least from some act of possession."—HALLAM.   † 12 Car. II. c. i.

‡ The reader is requested to correct an absurd typographical error in p. 236, where the *Convention* Parliament is printed *Convocation* Parliament.

§ 12 Car. II. c. 4. The duties of Tonnage and Poundage, or, as we now term them, Customs, as settled by the Schedule of Rates of Merchandise in this Statute, continued, with little variation, through the reigns of Charles II., James II., William III., and part of the reign of Anne. Reduced to one-half, they continued till George III. had reigned twenty-seven years. This Statute of the Convention Parliament was thus the foundation of that system of taxing at a separate rate the smallest as well as the largest article of merchandise—a system which embarrassed all commercial operations almost up to the present day. In the Table of Rates of 1660, there are about fourteen hundred articles of import upon which there is a varying duty. Looking at the value of money at that time, the duties were enormous, and their effect in retarding all manufacturing and commercial progress for half a century cannot be over-estimated.

the Commons granted him and his successors the Excise of beer and other liquors,* a tax first introduced during the Civil War. It was originally a temporary tax. The two great sources of modern revenue were thus placed absolutely in the king's hands. Charles was rendered more independent of Parliament for the ordinary expenditure of the Crown than his father, or grandfather, or Elizabeth, had been. No one seems to have dreaded that the money destined in great part for the proper dignity of the sovereign, and

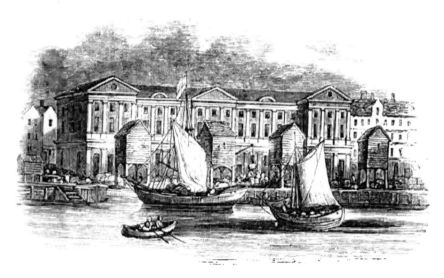

The Custom-House, London, as it appeared before the Great Fire.   (From a Print by Hollar.)

the due administration of all executive authority, was likely to be wasted in the most unblushing profligacy. The character of the king, and the habits of his associates, were not unknown; but men deceived themselves into the belief that long years of exile and poverty would have taught their lessons of prudence and moderation; that Adversity, "stern, rugged nurse," would have inspired some thoughts of honour and justice. But with Charles "self-pleasing Folly's idle brood" had not been scared at Adversity's frown. The House had voted an especial sum, to be raised by an especial mode of taxation, for disbanding the army. In his speech at the close of the Session the king said, "I do promise you, which is the best way I can take to gratify you, I will not apply one penny of that money to my own particular occasions, what shift soever I make, till it is evident to me that the public will not stand in need of it."† He seems to think that there is something magnanimous in this declaration;—that he might do what he liked with the sum which was considered as entrusted

* 12 Car. II. c. 24.   † "Parl. Hist." vol. iv. p. 122.

to him for a specific purpose, but that he would abstain from exercising his right of doing what he pleased with his own as a gracious condescension to "the public." In six years more the Parliament discovered the value of his majesty's self-denial; and in the bill for a poll-tax introduced a clause that a commission should be appointed to inspect all the accounts of the money supplied, and the expenses incurred, during the war. Pepys records that in the lord treasurer's accounts there was a sum unaccounted for of more than two millions; and that it was thought that £400,000 of the money voted for the war had gone into the Privy Purse. He then says that the notion of a commission to inspect the accounts "makes the king and court mad; the king having given order to my lord chamberlain to send to the playhouses and brothels, to bid all the parliament-men that were there to go to the parliament presently."* To the playhouses and brothels to search for the parliament-men! The times were altered since they were to be sought for in the churches and conventicles.

At the period of the Restoration, the Army, which had been the instrument of effecting that great change, as it had effected so many other great changes, consisted of fifteen regiments of horse, and twenty-two regiments of foot, besides garrisons. That army was supported by monthly assessments of seventy-thousand pounds. An Act was passed "for the speedy provision of money for disbanding and paying off the forces of this kingdom both by land and sea."† A contribution was to be raised from all ranks and degrees, under a commission in every county; and large sums were voted for the complete disbanding, in subsequent Acts.‡ The Act for the speedy disbanding of the Army and garrisons, and also for paying off twenty-five ships,§ was followed by "an Act for enabling the soldiers of the Army now to be disbanded, to exercise Trades." This salutary Statute provides that the disbanded men, who would willingly employ themselves in the trades they had formerly been accustomed to, or those who were apt and fit for trades, might exercise their employments in corporate cities and towns, without being restrained by any bye-laws; and that those who had been apprenticed to trades, but had not served the seven years required by the Statute of the 5th of Elizabeth, should be qualified to labour in their vocation as freely as if they had completed their legal term. The industry of the country absorbed this formidable Army. It was composed of a higher order of men than were usually found in military service; and they became the most industrious of citizens as they had been the best disciplined of soldiers. The revenue assigned to the crown did not contemplate the continuance of any standing army; but Charles retained two regiments of horse in his pay, who were called his guards. Upon this narrow foundation was the present regular army of the United Kingdom established. In 1662, the king had five thousand troops in his service. A few years afterwards he began to talk of making the Commons "a courageous speech," for that he was "master of an army." ‖

The great question of the Church Establishment was not brought forward in the Convention Parliament. The Presbyterian members were too strong

---

* "Diary," December 8, 1666.   † 12 Car. II. c. 9.   ‡ 12 Car. II. c. 20, and c. 21.
        § 12 Car. II. c. 15.   ‖ Pepys, October 4, 1666.

in that Assembly to render it safe to propose such a sweeping change as
would again make the Anglican Church supreme in endowments and political
power. Amidst all the sectarian violence of the Civil War and of the Commonwealth, the legal provision for the Clergy had never been disturbed, and
the private rights of presentation to benefices had been uninterruptedly
exercised. The pulpits were, indeed, for the most part filled with ministers
of Puritan principles, Presbyterian or Independent; and the Liturgy, with
the ceremonial observances connected with it, had been abolished. These
ministers, although they were not encouraged to believe that the Presbyterian
form, which had never been universal, would be adopted, hoped for some
compromise that would ensure them the quiet possession of their livings, and
free them from any obligations repugnant to their consciences. "Because,"
said the king's Declaration from Breda, "the passion and uncharitableness of
the times have produced several opinions in Religion, by which men are
engaged in parties and animosities against each other (which, when they shall
hereafter unite in freedom of conversation will be composed, or better understood), we do declare a liberty to tender consciences, and that no man shall
be disquieted, or called in question, for differences of opinion in matters of
Religion, which do not disturb the peace of the kingdom." In the Convention Parliament no attempt was made to contravene the spirit of this
Declaration. The imposition of the Covenant upon all the beneficed Clergy
had ejected large numbers of conscientious men from their livings.* Seventeen years had intervened; and another large body of conscientious men,
differing as to Church government, had succeeded to the duties and emoluments of the Episcopal Clergy. The Parliament of 1660 enacted that all the
ejected ministers who survived should be restored to their benefices, but
without the right of claiming any past emoluments. By the same Statute
those who were in actual possession of those livings for which there was no
claimant as previous possessor, were confirmed in their titles. This measure,
apparently so just, was in reality a delusion. Clarendon, the ruling minister
of the first years of the Restoration, although infinitely superior in honesty
and ability to the profligate courtiers and unprincipled politicians with whom
he was associated, seldom scrupled to "palter" with "the word of promise,"
when he had a long-cherished hope to realise, or a deliberate revenge to gratify.

The settlement of the Church establishment was only one amongst the
complicated questions that arose, of necessity, out of the Restoration. Many
of the Crown lands and the Church lands had been sold under the authority
of the Long Parliament. The title seemed so safe that in many cases they
had been sold at fifteen, and even eighteen years' purchase. A Bill was
brought in to determine this matter, which involved so many adverse interests.
It was strenuously debated by the Commons, in 1660; and the only agreement that the House came to was, that the Crown lands should be left out
of the proposal for sales to be confirmed or indemnity to be given. One member declared himself against the purchasers of the Crown lands by quoting a
proverb that "he that eats the king's goose should be choked by its feathers."
The House was disinclined to such an unconditional restoration of Church
property. But the discussion was at length cut short by the dissolution of

* See *Ante*, p. 30.

the Parliament; and the purchasers had no protection against the due course of law, under which their titles were defective. Unconditional restitution was the necessary result. The Declaration of Breda had said, "because, in the continued distractions of so many years, and so many and great revolutions, many grants and purchases of estates have been made to, and by, many officers, soldiers, and others, who are now possessed of the same, and who may be liable to actions at law upon several titles, we are likewise willing that all such differences, and all things relating to such grants, sales, and possessions, shall be determined in Parliament." By the adroit management of Clarendon, Parliament was relieved from the responsibility of the determination. Loud complaints, no doubt, were made by many who had been honest purchasers; but their complaints were neutralised by the louder murmurings of the Cavaliers, who, although some had returned to the possession of their estates, were deprived of any compensation for their sequestrations, and compositions for delinquency, during the authority of the Long Parliament. They were shut out from any legal process for relief by the Act of Indemnity. Bitter were their murmurings against the ingratitude of the king, from whom they expected the magician's power of annihilating all the natural and moral consequences of twenty years of vicissitude. Such are the mortifications and miseries to be endured by all parties when revolutions have run their course. During the conflicts of great principles men are elevated above their merely selfish interests; but when the sword is sheathed there arise the bitterer animosities of changed fortunes and disappointed hopes. Then come the odious thoughts of revenge for the part,— schemes of insulting triumph or dangerous machination. The calm after a great revolution is more to be dreaded than its storms. Clarendon saw this danger, though, when his own passions and prejudices were concerned he yielded to the baser influences. At the adjournment of the Parliament, in September, after the Act of Oblivion and Indemnity had been passed, he thus spoke, as Chancellor:—"Shall we fold our arms towards one another, and contract our hearts with envy and malice to each other, by any sharp memory of what hath been unneighbourly or unkindly done heretofore? What is this but to rebel against the person of the king, against the excellent example and virtue of the king, against the known law of the land, this blessed Act of Oblivion? My Lords and Gentlemen, the king is a suitor to you, makes it his suit very heartily, that you will join with him in restoring the whole nation to its primitive temper and integrity, to its old good manners, its old good humour, and its old good nature;—Good nature, a virtue so peculiar to you, so appropriated by God Almighty to this nation, that it can be translated into no other language, hardly practised by any other people: And that you will, by your example, by the candour of your conversation, by your precepts, and by your practice, and by all your interest, teach your neighbours and your friends how to pay a full obedience to this clause of the Statute, how to learn this excellent art of forgetfulness." "This excellent art of forgetfulness" was not easy to be learnt. Certainly the government did not encourage its acquirement by the example of its own magnanimity; but, eager as the Court was for the exercise of some vengeance for the past, it was but a faint expositor of the passions of many of the Lords and Commons, who cried "havoc" with their loudest voices.

Three weeks before the return of Charles II., the House of Commons had decided that seven persons should be excepted from a proposed Amnesty; and that all who had sate upon the king's trial should be arrested, as well as some others who had been ministers of the Protectorate.* After the Restoration it became evident that the Court was by no means satisfied with so limited an exception from a general pardon as that of seven who had been engaged in the transactions of twelve years of revolution. The debates in both Houses on the Bill of Indemnity and Oblivion are very imperfectly recorded; but there is enough to show how the spirit of the country had been abased and demoralised—how completely the feeling of national pride had departed from the public men of England—how insensible the majority had become to those principles of honour, by which the evils of the Civil War had been mitigated on both sides. For three months this Bill of Indemnity was debated in both Houses. The Commons went on adding name after name to those of the seven who were originally excepted. The Lords voted that all who had signed the death-warrant of Charles I., as well as five others, should be excepted, either as regarded life or estate. They carried the principle of private revenge so far, that they declared that the surviving relations of four peers who had been executed under the Long Parliament, should nominate four to be put to death of the surviving members of the High Court of Justice by which those peers had been condemned. There was a difficulty, however, in the way of the sweeping proscription which the Lords desired, which became a touchstone of honourable feeling in both Houses. The king, shortly after his landing, had issued a proclamation, in which he commanded those who had sat as judges of his father to render themselves up within fourteen days, "on pain of being excepted from any pardon or indemnity as to their lives or estates." The Parliament had suggested this proclamation. Was it a trap to induce these men to surrender, or was it an indirect pledge that, so surrendering, they should partake of the benefits of a general pardon? The honour of the king was unquestionably committed to the most favourable construction of the proclamation. Some, such as Ludlow, had the prudence not to place confidence in ambiguous words; and they fled abroad. "Other poor gentlemen were trepanned that were brought in by proclamation."† Clarendon, the chancellor, shuffled odiously about a document whose ambiguity was doubtless well studied by him. Southampton, the treasurer, with the high spirit of the old Cavaliers, maintained "that since it was not thought fit to secure the lives of those who had been ordered to surrender their persons upon the faith of the proclamation, they ought at least to give them the like number of days for saving themselves as were appointed by that paper for their coming in."‡ The Commons debated this point of the proclamation with a more moderate and honester feeling than the majority of the Lords. Although one rabid member had the baseness to say "that these people's lives were but as a bucket of water in the ocean, in regard of so many more as were to receive benefit by the Act of Pardon;" and another had the effrontery to maintain that "their coming in upon the proclamation was, that God had infatuated them to bring them to justice,—" yet the general temper of the Commons was better represented by Hale, who

* *Ante*, p. 236.

† Hutchinson, vol. ii. p. 279.   ‡ Ludlow, iii. p. 43.

pleaded "for the honour of the king and the two Houses;" and by Colonel Birch, who said "if he should give articles to a garrison, he should think himself very unworthy to break them." This matter was at last compromised between the Lords and Commons by a proviso in the Bill, that if the nineteen persons therein named should be legally attainted, then nevertheless the execution of the persons so attainted should be suspended until execution should be ordered by Act of Parliament.* The most remarkable exceptions to the Statute of Indemnity, in addition to all the regicides with few omissions, were Sir Henry Vane and General Lambert; but the Houses concurred in an address to the king that if these two leading men of the revolution were tried and attainted, their lives should be spared. The king assented.

The trials of the regicides and others in custody, who were excepted from pardon as to life and estate, took place in October. Twenty-five of those who had sat in judgment upon Charles I. were dead: nineteen had fled to foreign countries. Twenty-nine persons were brought to trial as traitors, before a Court of thirty-four commissioners; and they were all convicted. Of these, the nineteen who had surrendered under the proclamation were imprisoned for life. Ten were executed. These were Harrison, and five others, who had subscribed the death-warrant of Charles; Cook, who acted as leading counsel upon the trial; Axtell and Hacker, two officers who commanded the guard over the royal prisoner; and the famous Hugh Peters. These men died in the belief that they unjustly suffered for the discharge of a great public duty. In their strong religious principles, which approached to the enthusiasm of martyrs, in Harrison especially, they found support under the cruelties of the old law of treason, which was executed to the minutest point of its brutality. It is not creditable to Charles that he was a spectator of these scenes. Evelyn writes, on the 17th of October, "Scott, Scroop, Cook, and Jones, suffered for reward of their iniquities at Charing Cross, in sight of the place where they put to death their natural prince, and in the presence of the king his son, whom they also sought to kill. I saw not their execution, but met their quarters, mangled, and cut, and reeking, as they were brought from the gallows in baskets on the hurdle." A more disgusting spectacle took place on the 30th of January 1661, which Evelyn also records: "This day (O the stupendous and inscrutable judgments of God!) were the carcases of those archrebels, Cromwell, Bradshaw (the judge who condemned his Majesty), and Ireton (son-in-law to the Usurper), dragged out of their superb tombs in Westminster among the kings, to Tyburn, and hanged on the gallows there from nine in the morning till six at night, and then buried under that fatal and ignominious monument in a deep pit; thousands of people who had seen them in all their pride being spectators." On the 4th of December, the Parliament, upon the motion of colonel Titus—the colonel Titus who now claimed the honour of having written "Killing no Murder"—had voted unanimously that this revolting exhibition should take place. One Englishman has recorded his sentiment upon this vote as regarded Cromwell— "which, methinks, do trouble me that a man of so great courage as he was should have that dishonour."† On the 12th of September, by a special order of the king to the dean of Westminster, these bodies had been taken out of

* 12 Car. II. c. 11.   † Pepys' "Diary," December 4, 1660.

their vaults, and thrown into a pit. On the same day, the body of Blake was removed from its honoured resting-place and re-interred in St. Margaret's churchyard. To our minds there is nothing in the whole course of this evil reign so prophetic of the coming national degradation, as the indignities offered to the remains of the greatest soldier and the greatest sailor that England had produced. Cromwell and Blake by their genius and their patriotism made their country the most honoured and dreaded of the nations. They bequeathed to the heir of the ancient kings, a national dignity which was more solid than the glories of the Edwards and Henries, and as dearly prized by the people as the triumphs of Elizabeth. This miserable heir of the grand English monarchy was utterly destitute of that nationality without which a sovereign is more degraded than the meanest of his subjects. The future pensioner of France was incapable of comprehending what England owed to the man whose corpse he hung up on the gallows at Tyburn.

The restoration of surviving bishops to their sees, with the consecration of new bishops, was a policy which the Presbyterian party must have considered inevitable. That party had to a great extent become powerless; and was in no condition to renew the struggles against Episcopacy which had so materially interfered with any pacific arrangement with Charles I. For twenty years there had been no display of copes and surplices in the service of cathedrals. The young had never heard organs and choral voices in parish churches. Now, the bishops assembled in Westminster Abbey "all in their habits," as Pepys records; "But, Lord! at their going out, how people did most of them look upon them as strange creatures, and few with any kind of love or respect." * The passion for the restoration of the monarchy did not extend to this necessary consequence of that restoration. The serious citizens of London and other towns had been accustomed to the ministration of the Puritan clergy, whether Presbyterian or Independent; and they looked with apprehension and dislike to any change that would interfere with their old habits. Their spiritual welfare had not been neglected; nor had they been committed to the guidance of ignorant or unlearned men, looking at the majority of the Puritan ministers. The serious portion of the community were sufficiently represented in the Convention Parliament to render some caution necessary in the measures of the Court. On the 25th of October the king published a Declaration, in which he avowed his own attachment to Episcopacy, but expressed his opinion that it might be so modified as to remove all reasonable objections; and he declared that the reading of the Liturgy, certain ceremonial observances, subscription to all the articles, and the oath of canonical obedience, should not be pressed upon those who had conscientious scruples. Calamy, Baxter, and other Presbyterian ministers, had been appointed Chaplains in ordinary to the king, in the month after his restoration. The Puritans appear to have deceived themselves into the belief that a happy concord would be established; and the Court, whether from duplicity or weakness, appears to have fostered the delusion. Some of the leading Puritan ministers, amongst whom were Calamy, Baxter, Ash, and Reynolds, were introduced to the king; and declared "their large hope of a happy

* "Diary," October 4, 1660.

union among all dissenters by his means." Baxter records that the king gave them a gracious answer; professed his gladness to hear their inclinations for agreement; suggested that both sides should abate somewhat of their pretensions; nay, that he was resolved to see this agreement brought to pass;—with much more to the same effect; "insomuch that old Mr. Ash burst out into tears with joy, and could not forbear expressing what gladness this promise of his majesty had put into his heart." * In less than a year the value of his majesty's promise was to be better understood, when the Act of Uniformity was passed. In two years non-conformity was made penal. We shall have briefly to notice these healing measures. Their general effect is set forth with all the bitterness of disappointed hope by the most eminent interpreter of the feelings of the Puritan divines—those who, "in times of usurpation had mercy and happy freedom," but who, "under the lawful governors which they desired, and in the days when order is said to be restored, do some of us sit in obscurity and unprofitable silence, and some lie in prisons, and all of us are accounted as the scum and sweepings and off-scourings of the earth." †

The king's Declaration, and his promises to the Presbyterian ministers, were looked upon with satisfaction by honest men of both parties. There was a possibility of such an agreement upon points of discipline as would have made the Protestant Church of England a real barrier against the revival of Popery, which was not altogether a frivolous apprehension; and, through the concord of earnest men who had long exercised an important spiritual influence, would have opposed a sober religious spirit equally removed from indifference or fanaticism, to the profligacy which was fast becoming fashionable. To render the king's Declaration effectual a Bill was brought into Parliament by Sir Matthew Hale. It was opposed by the united power of the courtiers in Parliament, and was rejected. This was the test by which the royal professions were to be tried. "Such as were nearest the king's councils well knew that nothing else was intended by the Declaration than to scatter dust in men's eyes, and to prevent the interference of Parliament." ‡ Whilst the Convention Parliament lasted, all such awkward questions were tided over. It was dissolved on the 29th of December.

Amongst the non-political Acts passed in this Parliament was the Navigation Act, which was in substance a re-enactment of the famous measure of the Long Parliament in 1651. § An Act for the establishment of a General Post Office in London was also framed upon the model of the Postal establishments of the Protectorate. The complex arrangements which prevailed till our own time were prescribed by this Act—one rate for a single sheet, another rate for two sheets;—one rate for a distance not exceeding eighty miles, another rate for a greater distance. The rates for foreign letters were not exorbitant. No private persons were to carry letters; and all ship letters brought from foreign ports were to be delivered to the Postmaster General or his deputies.

The Parliament had not risen longer than a week when an extraordinary

---

* Baxter, "Life," Part II. p. 231; folio.   † Ibid. Part I. p. 84.
‡ Hallam, Chap. xii.   § Ante, p. 152.

insurrection broke out in London. It was a renewal of that fanatical outbreak which Cromwell put down with a troop of horse on the 9th of April, 1657. The Fifth-Monarchy men again rose on the 6th of January, 1661, under their old leader, Thomas Venner, the wine-cooper. These men had a meeting-house in the city; and some fifty or sixty of them, after an encounter with the feeble municipal police, marched to Caen-wood, near Highgate, and having been there concealed for two days, returned to encounter the trained bands, and even a regular body of guards, in the confidence that their cause, the establishment of the reign of Christ on earth, and the suppression of all other authority, would be miraculously upheld. The capital was in fearful alarm; the shops were shut; the city gates barricaded. But these wild men drove all before them; till a rally was made, and they were for the most part slaughtered, refusing quarter. Venner, and sixteen of his followers who were secured, were tried and executed. This mad tumult was made the excuse for a proclamation for closing the conventicles of Quakers, Anabaptists, and other sectaries. The members of various sects throughout the country, who were proscribed as dangerous, were very numerous; but the severity exercised towards them was really more favourable to their extension than the toleration of Cromwell. The Quakers especially held their ground against every severity—even against an Act of Parliament of 1662, by which they were to be fined for assembling for public worship, and for a third offence to be banished.

The Coronation of the king took place on the 23rd of April. Every ceremony in Westminster Abbey, and in Westminster Hall, was of the most gorgeous nature. In the streets there were bonfires out of number; and "many great gallants, men and women" drinking the king's health upon their knees.* The people of London had not recovered from their delirium. Throughout the land men were equally intoxicated by the return to the ancient order of things. The May-poles had been again set up; the Christmas ale was again flowing in the squire's hall; the peasantry were again wrestling and cudgel-playing on the village-green; the stocks were no longer a terror to the drunkard; the play-houses were open in London, and itinerant actors again gathered their gaping audiences in booth or barn. The old asceticism of the Puritans was bitterly remembered. Their zeal for liberty, their pure lives, their earnest religion, were regarded as disloyalty and hypocrisy. The great share which the larger number of them had taken in the restoration of the monarchy was also forgotten; and amidst an exaggerated contempt for their formal manners, and a real dislike of the restraint which they imposed upon audacious profligacy, the Cavaliers carried the elections for a new Parliament by immense majorities. The first Session lasted from the 8th of May to the 30th of July; and in that short time reflecting persons began to see "how basely things have been carried in that Parliament by the young men, that did labour to oppose all things that were moved by serious men."† But "to oppose all things that were moved by serious men" was a very small part of the zeal of the Parliament of 1661. Far more eagerly than Charles himself, or his minister Clarendon, the royalists laboured as much as possible to prepare the way for the return of

* Pepys.   † Ibid. "Diary," August 4.

the glorious days of the Star-Chamber and the High Commission. The king and the chancellor carried on a little farther the artifice of a desire for agreement in ecclesiastical affairs. Before the meeting of Parliament, Conferences were held at the Savoy between the bishops and twelve of the leading Puritan divines, for the revision of the Liturgy. These discussions, which were protracted for more than three months, could only conclude in one way. The objections of those who called themselves "primitive Episcopalians" were put with a due acknowledgment that the Book of Common Prayer is "an excellent and worthy work;" but they desired that "such further emendations may be now made therein, as may be judged necessary for satisfying the scruples of a multitude of sober persons who cannot at all, or very hardly, comply with the use of it as now it is."* The emendations which they desired were very numerous, both in the prayers and in the rubric. Whilst the churchmen were discussing these objections, sometimes not in the most Christian spirit, the Parliament was settling the question of conformity in a very summary manner; and when the Liturgy, a few months after, came to be reviewed in Convocation, the points which gave offence to "tender consciences" were left untouched. The Anglican Church felt its power; and the notion of conciliation, if ever seriously entertained, was soon supplanted by the readier and simpler principle of coercion.

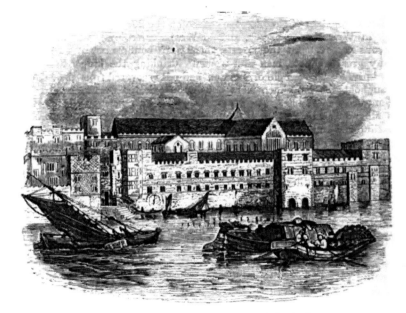

The Savoy Palace, in 1661. (From Visscher's London.)

The altered character of the House of Commons was very soon indicated

* Baxter, "Life," Part II. p. 316.

by its proceedings. The Parliament met on the 8th of May. On the 17th it was voted that every member should receive the sacrament according to the forms of the Anglican Church. It was also resolved that the Solemn League and Covenant should be burned by the hands of the common hangman. There was no hesitation now in proclaiming that the Presbyterians were a crushed and degraded party. In the common hatred of all Puritans, the Independents were necessarily included. The one great principle of the policy of Clarendon was to re-establish the Church of England in its ancient splendour; and this desire would have been as commendable as it was natural, could it have been accomplished without a violation of those principles of religious freedom to which the royal word was pledged. But Clarendon, who in exile had been surrounded by suffering dignitaries of the Established Church, had contracted a violent hatred of the entire body of the Puritan Clergy; and he constantly speaks of them in terms of contempt, which only indicate his real ignorance of the condition of the people during the long period in which he was shut out from any intercourse with the great majority of his countrymen. With him the whole body of the non-conforming ministers were "fellows." He bitterly opposed the inclination of the king to mitigate some of the evils which the temper of the Cavaliers was ready to inflict upon them. This temper is thus accounted for by our constitutional historian: "The gentry, connected for the most part by birth or education with the episcopal clergy, could not for an instant hesitate between the ancient establishment and one composed of men whose eloquence in preaching was chiefly directed towards the common people." The gentry did "not for an instant hesitate" to deprive "the common people" of the spiritual instructors to whom they looked up with reverence; and to thrust upon them a new set of ministers who had little sympathy with their religious or political convictions. The inevitable consequence was that the indifference of "the higher classes" to all earnest principles gradually spread through the whole community; that the clergy were more intent upon preaching the doctrine of passive obedience, so as to produce a nation of slaves and sycophants, than desirous of setting forth the great truths of Christian doctrine and Christian morals, so as to separate "the common people" from the contagion of the horrible profligacy of the Court. Lauderdale related to Burnet that the king told him to let presbytery go, "for it was not a religion for gentlemen." The religion which the king and his courtiers desired, was something that would be as kind to their merits as blind to their faults; and their wishes were gratified to an extent which makes the most sincere friend of the Church of England look back with loathing at the servility, the intolerance, and the cowardice with which its hierarchy so long grovelled at the feet of tyranny and sensuality. But if Clarendon went beyond all the bounds of honest and wise statesmanship in his zeal to replace the Church in the position which it had occupied before the days of the Long Parliament, he manifested both wisdom and integrity in firmly clinging to the Act of Indemnity and Oblivion. At the opening of this Second Parliament he put the king forward to desire the confirmation of that Act, in stronger terms of entreaty than were usually placed in the mouth of the sovereign. Clarendon himself says, "This warmth of his majesty upon this subject was not then more than needful; for the armies being now disbanded, there were great combinations entered into, not to confirm the Act of Oblivion, which they knew without confirmation would signify nothing. Men were well enough contented that the king should grant indemnity to all men that had rebelled against him; that he should grant their lives and fortunes to them who had forfeited them to him: but they thought it unreasonable and unjust that the king should release those debts which were immediately due to them, and forgive those trespasses which had been committed to their particular damage." * One example of the extent to which the passions of the Cavaliers carried them away from the high feeling which was their general characteristic is very striking. The pen of the novelist has made us familiar with the real or fancied wrongs of the house of Stanley; and there is another record not quite so enduring as the laments of Scott's Charlotte de la Tremouille: "At the earl of Derby's seat of Knowsley in Lancashire, a tablet is placed to commemorate the ingratitude of Charles II., in having refused the royal assent to a bill which had passed both Houses for restoring the son of the earl of Derby, who had lost his life in the royal cause, to his family estate. This has been so often reprinted by tourists and novelists that it passes current for a great reproach on the king's memory. It was however, in fact, one of his most honourable actions. The truth is, that the Cavalier faction carried through Parliament a Bill to make void the conveyances of some manors which lord Derby had voluntarily sold before the Restoration, in the very face of the Act of Indemnity, and against all law and justice. Clarendon, who, together with some very respectable peers, had protested against this measure in the Upper House, thought it his duty to recommend the king to refuse his assent." †

The firmness of the great minister of the Restoration in maintaining the Act of Indemnity made him as unpopular with the extreme Royalists, now all-powerful, as his somewhat extravagant zeal for the Church of England rendered him odious to the Puritans, now all-humiliated. His position was one of extreme difficulty. He was an object of dislike and ridicule to Charles and his courtiers because, from his age and his character, he looked disapprovingly upon their excesses. He had become connected in a remarkable way with the royal family, by the marriage of his daughter with the duke of York. Unless he conducted himself with the most extreme duplicity, the possible injurious consequences to himself of this unequal union appear to have terrified him beyond the bounds of sanity. The mother of two future reigning queens of England had indulged the passions of the king's brother under an alleged betrothal. Six months after the king was placed on the throne, a private marriage was avowed, and, soon after, the lady gave birth to a son. Clarendon has himself recorded that he proposed to send his daughter to the Tower; and he maintained that an Act of Parliament should be passed for cutting off her head, which he was ready himself to propose. The passion, real or feigned of the chancellor, received no encouragement from the king; and the licentious courtiers, after an attempt had been made to blacken the character of Miss Hyde, in the relation of circumstances which only the basest natures could have detailed, accepted the lawyer's daughter as a properly qualified duchess of York. The story is told in the "Memoirs of Grammont"

* "Continuation of Life." † Hallam, chap. xi.

with a dramatic force worthy of the imitation of "the dignity of history." Hamilton, the author of these Memoirs, which so completely exhibit the character of the courtiers of Charles II., in their perfect unconsciousness of their degradation, tells how the earl of Arran, Talbot, Jermyn, and Killigrew, at the desire of James himself, each related "the particulars of what he knew, and more than he knew, of poor Miss Hyde." The duke then went into his brother's cabinet, and continued there a long while in secret conversation. The scandal-mongers remained without, in eager expectation; and when the duke came forth with marks of agitation on his countenance, they had no doubt of the result of the conference. "Lord Falmouth began to be affected for her disgrace, and to relent that he had been concerned in it, when the duke of York told him and the earl of Ossory to meet him in about an hour's time at the chancellor's. They were rather surprised that he should have the cruelty himself to announce such a melancholy piece of news: they found his royal highness at the appointed hour in Miss Hyde's chamber: a few tears trickled down her cheeks, which she endeavoured to restrain. The chancellor, leaning against the wall, appeared to them to be puffed up with something, which they did not doubt was rage and despair. The duke of York said to them, with that serene and pleasant countenance with which men generally announce good news: 'As you are the two men of the court whom I most esteem, I am desirous you should first have the honour of paying your compliments to the duchess of York: there she is.'"*

Clarendon, really strengthened in power and influence by the high marriage of his daughter, met with little opposition in leading a willing Parliament to trample upon all dissent from the Episcopal Church; to restore those prerogatives of the Crown which had been set aside by the Long Parliament; and to keep alive the spirit of revenge against the republican party. The Act for the preservation of the king and government increased the strictness of the law of treason; and declared that no legislative power existed in the Parliament, except in conjunction with the king.† The Act for the command of the militia went rather beyond the constitutional principle of recognising the sole power of the Crown to command the forces by land or sea. It declared not only that neither House of Parliament could pretend to such power, but could not lawfully levy any war, offensive or defensive, against the king.‡ "These last words," says Mr. Hallam, "appeared to go to a dangerous length, and to sanction the suicidal doctrine of absolute non-resistance." Tumultuous petitioning was provided against by limiting the number to ten who should present a petition to the king or the Parliament; with some stringent regulations as to the mode of signing petitions.§ The Corporation Act went much farther than justly attempting to restore the executive power to its due authority in the state. Mingling the political and religious principles of coercion, it required that all persons elected to corporate offices should have received the sacrament, according to the rites of the English Church, within one year before their election; and it required an oath from such officers that they believed it unlawful, on any pretence whatever, to take arms against the king; and required them to abjure the traitorous

---

* "Memoirs of Grammont," Sir Walter Scott's Edition.

† 13 Car. II. c. 1.   ‡ 13 Car. II. 2, c. 6.   § 13 Car. II. c. 5.

position of taking arms by the king's authority against himself or his officers.*
In the municipal boroughs the supporters of the contest against Charles I.
had been principally found — men equally resolved in their love of civil
liberty and their hatred of prelacy. The Corporation Act put as strong a
restraint upon them as an oath could effect. The restoration of the bishops
to the House of Lords was accomplished without any opposition by this
Parliament, in which the Presbyterians had lost all influence. The crowning
measure of ecclesiastical polity was the Act of Uniformity.† By this Statute
it was required that all the beneficed clergy, all fellows of colleges, and all
schoolmasters, should declare their unfeigned assent and consent to all and
everything contained in the Book of Common Prayer, as amended in Convocation and approved by the king. By another clause in this Act, episcopal
ordination was required of all persons holding ecclesiastical preferments.
Those of the clergy who, previous to the Feast of St. Bartholomew, 1662,
had not declared their acceptance of the Book of Common Prayer, in the
terms of the Statute, were to be absolutely ejected from their livings. On
that day more than two thousand ministers of religion went forth into the
world without any provision for their future support. They had received a
striking example of conscientious integrity in the refusal of the episcopal
clergy to take the Covenant in 1648.‡ In that revolutionary crisis the
ejected incumbents had not been wholly unprovided for; one-fifth of the
income of the new incumbents having been allotted to them. Such a merciful
consideration for men of piety and learning—and most of the Puritan clergy
were zealous in their callings and pure in their lives—was not granted by
this revengeful Parliament. Measures of absolute persecution against the
ejected ministers were subsequently enacted—measures which, in their
application to all non-conformity, it required a long and arduous struggle to
obliterate from the Statute-book.

* 13 Car. II. Session 2, c. 1.   † 14 Car. II. c. 4.   ‡ Ante, p. 30.

Autograph of Charles II. (From the original in Harleian Library.)

Execution of Argyle, 1661.   (From a Drawing of the time.)

CHAPTER XVI.

THE real spirit of the Restoration is more clearly illustrated by the proceedings of the government in Scotland than by its actions at corresponding
periods in England.   Practically, since the victory of Dunbar, Scotland had
ceased to be an independent kingdom.   For the true prosperity of both
countries it was desirable that this union should have been continued.   To
give the Stuart a fair field for carrying matters with a high hand in his
ancient kingdom, it was expedient again to isolate the smaller and poorer
portion of the island from the larger and wealthier.   Of course, when the
survivors of the Committee of Estates, that had been nominated by Charles
in 1651, were again called to resume the government of Scotland; when a
Lord Commissioner and other high officers were appointed; when a parliament was summoned to meet at Edinburgh,—the national pride was abun-

dantly gratified, and Charles the Second was the best of kings. The people soon found that they had to pay a heavy price for this nationality, which was to involve the loss of the civil and religious rights which were dearest to the nation.

The Parliament which met at Edinburgh on the 1st of January, 1661, has been honoured with the name of "the drunken Parliament." Burnet says, "It was a mad roaring time, full of extravagance; and no wonder it was so, when the men of affairs were almost perpetually drunk." In England, the passions of the Cavaliers were less fierce, and were held more in subjection by the obvious danger of provoking another Civil War. In Scotland, the dominant party had no thought beyond that of keeping its opponents under its feet. Argyle, as the great leader of the Covenanters, was now to offer the satisfaction of his head for the fall of his rival Montrose. Upon the restoration of Charles, Argyle had hastened to London to offer his homage to the king. He was arrested; and then sent to Scotland, to be brought to trial for his alleged offences. When questioned before the Parliament he pleaded the amnesty of 1651, and the English government determined to admit the plea. He was then accused of having received a grant from Cromwell; of having aided the English invaders; and of having sat in Richard Cromwell's parliament, and voted for a bill which abjured the rights of the Stuarts to the Crown. The fate of Argyle was sealed when a packet arrived from England, containing letters from him to Monk, inimical to the king and favourable to Cromwell. To produce such private letters against an old associate in the same cause, was as base in Monk as it was infamous in the Parliament to be moved by such treachery to Argyle's condemnation. He was sentenced to be beheaded within forty-eight hours. He accepted his fate with courage and resignation. At the same time Guthrie, a Presbyterian minister, violent and uncompromising in his opinions, was put to death as an example to the clergy. He was personally obnoxious to Middleton, who in this, and in every other instance, went headlong to the gratification of his revenge. He procured the condemnation by the Scottish parliament of the son of the Marquis of Argyle, for writing a letter reflecting upon the acts of the government; and he would have put this nobleman to death, under the barbarous law of "leasing-making"—sowing dissensions by falsehood—had not Clarendon interfered to stop the iniquity. Amidst these excesses against individuals, the more extensive tyranny of forcing Episcopacy upon a people so devoted to Presbytery was resolutely pushed forward. James Sharpe, who had been sent to London on a mission from his Presbyterian brethren, returned Bishop of St. Andrew's and Primate of Scotland. Other prelates were appointed, of whom four were consecrated in London. In the parliament of 1662, by the first Act of the session, "the whole government and jurisdiction of the church in the several dioceses was declared to be lodged in the bishops, which they were to exercise with the advice and assistance of such of their clergy as were of known loyalty and prudence: all men that held any benefice in the church were required to own and submit to the government of the church, as now by law established." * The violence of the drunken Parliament was finally shown in the wanton absurdity of what

* Burnet, "Own Times," Book ii.

was called the "Act Rescissory," by which every law that had been passed
in the Scottish parliament during twenty-eight years was wholly annulled.
The legal foundations of Presbytery were thus swept away. "The bill was
put to the vote, and carried by a great majority; and the earl of Middleton
immediately passed it without staying for an instruction from the king. The
excuse he made for it was, that since the king had by his letter to the Presbyterians confirmed their government as it was established by law, there was
no way left to get out of that, but the annulling all those laws." *

The Parliament of England, as if to furnish a little excitement to the
dull debates that had reference to non-conformity, in the beginning of 1662
turned its attention to the duty of shedding a little more blood, to expiate
that of the royal martyr. The Parliament was hounded on to this work from
the high places of the restored Church. The 15th of January was a general
fast-day, "to avert God's heavy judgments on this land," the season being
unusually rainy. Dr. Ryves, or Reeves, dean of Windsor, preached before
the House of Commons, "showing how the neglect of exerting justice on
offenders (by which he insinuated such of the old king's murderers as were
yet reprieved and in the Tower) was a main cause of God's punishing a land."†
His text was from Joshua, c. vii. v. 13, "There is an accursed thing in the
midst of thee, O Israel: thou canst not stand before thine enemies until
ye take away the accursed thing from among you." In the week in which
Evelyn coolly records this Christian exhortation to avert the judgments of
God, he has looked upon "an accursed thing," against which the pulpit of
Westminster has no denunciations—the passion of gaming "in a Court which
ought to be an example of virtue to the rest of the kingdom." Mr. Pepys
says of this roaring time,—"At Court things are in very ill condition, there
being so much emulation, poverty, and the vices of drinking, swearing, and
loose amours, that I know not what will be the end of it, but confusion."
Rumours of conspiracies were rife at this period; and the virtuous Cavaliers
of the Lower House thought, with Dr. Ryves, that it would be a salutary
measure to execute all the regicides whose fate, after conviction, had been
suspended for the decision of parliament. The Commons passed a Bill for
their immediate execution, in direct opposition to the feeling of the Convention
Parliament that their lives should be spared. The Lords read this Bill a first
time, and then let it drop. Charles, to his honour, said to Clarendon, "I am
weary of hanging, except for new offences;" and he trusted that the Bill
against the regicides would not come to him; "for," said he, "you know that
I cannot pardon them." Some of the minor offenders who had been excepted
from the penalty of death, were now degraded from honours, and deprived
of their estates. Lord Monson, Sir Henry Mildmay, and Robert Wallop,
who were sentenced by Act of Parliament,‡ to be drawn upon sledges, with
ropes about their necks from the Tower to Tyburn, and back again, suffered
this indignity. The nineteen condemned regicides were confined in various
prisons, and wore out their lives in such hopeless captivity as Henry Marten
endured at Chepstow. Three regicides, Okey, Corbet, and Barkstead, who
had not surrendered upon the king's proclamation, were captured in Holland,

---

* Burnet, "Own Times," Book ii.
Evelyn's "Diary."   ‡ 13 Car. II. c. 15.

in March, 1662, by the agency of Downing, who had been Cromwell's ambassador at the Hague. " The Dutch were a good while before they could be persuaded to let them go, they being taken prisoners in their land. But Sir G. Downing would not be answered so: though all the world takes notice of him for a most ungrateful villain for his pains." * They were executed on the 19th of April, and died defending the justice of their actions. The compliance of the Dutch government in the surrender of political offenders, contrasted unfavourably with the sturdy independence of the little states of Vevay and Berne. Ludlow, and others, received ample protection and liberal hospitality in Switzerland; and the royalists thus failing to secure them, had resort to base attempts at assassination. One of these only was successful. John Lisle was shot at Lausanne, in 1664, as he was going to a church near the town-gate.

For some time after the promise of the king to the Convention Parliament that Vane and Lambert, in their exception from the Act of Indemnity, should not suffer death if found guilty of treason, they had remained prisoners in the Tower. On the 30th of October, 1661, Pepys enters in his Diary, " Sir Henry Vane, Lambert, and others, are lately sent suddenly away from the Tower, prisoners to Scilly; but I do not think there is any plot, as is said, but only a pretence." Vane solaced his captivity by compositions which show how earnestly he sought the one true and abiding comfort in misfortune. His enthusiastic religion, his ardent aspirations for civil liberty, his unselfish life, his eminent ability, render him the most interesting of the republican party. Clarendon sought his exemption from the Act of Indemnity because he was " a man of mischievous activity." On the 7th of March, 1662, in a letter to his wife, Vane writes, " They that press so earnestly to carry on my trial do little know what presence of God may be afforded me in it, and issue out of it, to the magnifying of Christ in my body, by life or by death. Nor can they, I am sure, imagine how much I desire to be dissolved and to be with Christ, which of all things that can befall me I account best of all." † Thus fortified against the worst, he was arraigned before the Court of King's Bench on the 2nd of June, 1662, as " a false traitor." The overt acts of treason alleged against Vane and Lambert were, their exercise of civil and military functions under the Commonwealth. When we consider the number of men who had filled high offices during the suspension of the monarchy, and yet had been active instruments in its restoration, we marvel at the effrontery which should wrest the law to the conviction of two men who had been faithful servants of their country. The condemnation of Vane and Lambert was wholly against the spirit, if not the letter, of the statute of Henry VIII., which declared indemnity for all persons rendering obedience to a king for the time being, although his title might be defective. By parity of reasoning, obedience to the Parliament, which stood in the place of a king, could not be deemed a crime against the king *de jure*. But the judges maintained that Charles the Second was a king *de facto*, and had never been out of possession. Vane, who defended himself throughout with marvellous ability, replied that if the king was never out of possession the indictment against him must fall to the ground; for it alleged that he

* Pepys, "Diary," March 17.   † Quoted in Mr. Forster's "Life of Vane." p. 210.

endeavoured to keep out the king. The courage, the proud consciousness of right, the lofty principles of Vane, were the reasons which would have induced a high-minded sovereign to adhere gladly to his promise that his life should be spared in the event of his condemnation. Charles was not a high-minded sovereign—he was selfish, corrupt, faithless, shameless. The letter which he wrote to Clarendon the day after Vane's trial is as characteristic of the man as any other of the acts of his unworthy life :

"The relation that has been made to me of Sir Henry Vane's carriage yesterday in the hall is the occasion of this letter, which, if I am rightly informed, was so insolent as to justify all he had done, acknowledging no supreme power in England but a Parliament, and many things to that purpose. You have had a true account of all; and if he has given new occasion to be hanged, certainly he is too dangerous a man to let live, if we can honestly put him out of the way. Think of this, and give me some account of it to-morrow, till when I have no more to say to you.—C. R."

The deportment of a prisoner on his trial could not " give new occasion to

Catherine of Braganza. (From an Original Painting in the Pepysian Library.)

be hanged," even if it had been most violent. Vane in his justification avoided every topic of offence to the king personally, as none of Vane's public acts had been marked by any personal hostility to him. The " if we can honestly

put him out of the way," was not a scruple which Charles would long entertain. He was put out of the way on the 14th of June, dying with a courage
which, says Pepys, "is talked on everywhere as a miracle." The life of
Lambert was spared, according to that promise which the king did not
scruple to violate when his victim was "too dangerous a man to let live."
Vane was the last of the sacrifices on the scaffold to the revenges of the
monarchy.

On the opening of the Parliament of 1661, the king announced that he
was about to marry "a daughter of Portugal." This marriage had been
advised by Louis XIV., who, although he had engaged to Spain to give no
support to Portugal in its struggles to maintain its independence, saw in
this English alliance a mode of strengthening Portugal against the power
which entered into rivalry with him. The Spanish ambassador in London
opposed the match, declaring that Spain would never cease to maintain her
claims against the House of Braganza. Vatteville, the ambassador from
Spain, and Bastide, the ambassador from France, each pressed their opinions
upon the Council of Charles. When the Portuguese alliance was settled,
they entered into a personal contest, which is an amusing variety of the dull
battles of protocols. They resolved to fight out, in the streets of London,
the claims of the two Crowns for precedency. Charles issued a proclamation
forbidding his subjects to take part in the conflict which was to take place

Coaches of the time of Charles II.

on the expected entry of the Swedish ambassador. On the Tower Wharf
was drawn up, on one side of the stairs, the carriage of the Spanish ambassador; on the other side the carriage of the French ambassador. They were
each surrounded by many liveried servants, on foot and horseback, fully

armed. The Swede landed; and, occupying a royal carriage, went on his way. Then began the mighty strife of the representatives of the two greatest sovereigns in Europe, as to which should next follow. Their attendants fought till fifty were killed or wounded; but the Spaniard won the race, by cutting the traces of the Frenchman's carriage. Why should not the quarrels of *courts* always be fought out in this fashion, which might give ambassadors some real business that would allow them less leisure to embroil *nations ?*

In spite of the triumphant Vatteville, Charles married Catherine of Braganza. She was not remarkable for beauty, but she was sensible and amiable; and the king professed himself fortunate, and avowed his resolution to seek his future happiness in conjugal affection. His first act of devotion to his queen was to present lady Castlemaine to her in the midst of the Court. It was known to all, and to the queen herself, that "the lady" was his avowed mistress. Catherine suppressed her indignation; but the effort caused the blood to gush from her nose, and she was carried in a fit from the royal presence. The gracious king was indignant at the squeamishness of the queen; and insisted that Castlemaine should be one of the ladies of her bed-chamber. Clarendon remonstrated with his master, and ventured to compare royal harlots with other lewd women; but the remonstrances ended by the Chancellor undertaking to persuade the queen "to a full compliance with what the king desired." Catherine threatened to return to Portugal. Charles

Charles II. and his Queen, 1662.

did more than threaten—he sent away her old servants, with the exception of a few, who were allowed to remain when the queen's spirit was humbled to ask a favour. Clarendon, in his 'Life,' tells the issue of this characteristic scoundrelism of "our most religious and gracious king"—the title which the discriminating bishops now gave Charles in the Liturgy: "The king pursued his point: the lady came to the court,—was lodged there,—was every day in the queen's presence,—and the king in continual conference with her, whilst the queen sat untaken notice of; and if her majesty rose at the indignity and retired into her chamber, it may be one or two attended her; but all the company remained in the room she left, and too often said those things aloud which nobody ought to have whispered . . . . All these mortifications were too heavy to be borne; so that at last, when it was least expected or suspected, the queen on a sudden let herself fall first to conversation and then to familiarity, and, even in the same instant, to a confidence with the lady; was merry with her in public, talked kindly of her, and in private used nobody more friendly."

The Infanta of Portugal brought to Charles three hundred and fifty thousand pounds as her dowry. The English Crown also acquired Tangier, a fort on the coast of Africa. The possession of Tangier, which the nation regarded as worthless, was to compensate for the sale of Dunkirk, which the nation regarded as one of the chief triumphs of the foreign policy of the great Protector. Charles was more eager to put money into his purse, than to gratify the national pride; and Louis the Fourteenth was as desirous to obtain Dunkirk as Charles to convert the Gibraltar of that day into jewels for new mistresses. Louis made a cunning bargain. He gave four millions of livres in bills; and then employed his own ready money to discount his own bills, at a saving of half a million. According to Louis's own account of the transaction, his rival in the treaty was the city of London, the lord mayor having been

Clarendon House.

deputed to offer any sum, that Dunkirk might not be alienated. Clarendon had advised the sale, although he had a little before, in a speech in Parliament, dwelt on the value of the place. The people, naturally enough, however unjustly, held that the Chancellor had been bribed. The magnificent palace that he was building near St. James's was popularly called "Dunkirk House;" and the national dislike of the sale of Dunkirk was one of the first symptoms that his power was on the wane. His participation in that sale subsequently formed an article of his impeachment. The popular opinion that the sale of Dunkirk was to supply new funds for the profligacy of the Court, was confirmed by the public demonstrations of that profligacy. Lord Buckhurst and Sir Charles Sedley had outraged all decency by an exhibition which Pepys recorded in cypher, but which his editor says is "too gross to print." Baxter gives us some notion of "the horrid wickedness" of these titled blackguards, "acting the part of preachers, in their shirts, in a balcony" in Covent Garden.* With such companions was Charles now generally surrounded. All thoughts of business were abhorrent to him. To lady Castlemaine's lodgings he was followed by his "counsellors of pleasure," who laughed at the "old dotards" who presumed to talk in a serious vein. Rivals to "the lady" now sprung up, with the usual incidents of jealousies and poutings, to be averted by lavish presents to the old favourite, or heavier bribes to the new. The English Court became the ridicule of foreigners. The Dutch caricatured the king in various of his characteristic positions. In one print he was shown with "pockets turned the wrong side outward, hanging out empty;" in another, with two courtiers picking his pockets; in a third, leading two ladies, whilst other ladies were abusing him.† The heart-

Pall Mall, St. James's Park.

less swindler had appropriated great part of his queen's jointure to his rapa-

* "Life," Part iii. p. 13.   † Pepys, November 28, 1663.

cious mistresses. The people, who groaned under the tax of "chimney-money," and declared they would not pay it without force, were yet pleased with the gossiping familiarity of the king, as he sauntered among them, feed·ing his ducks in the new Canal in St. James's Park, or joining his nobles in a game at "Pell-Mell." The Chevalier de Grammont saw Cromwell, "feared at home, yet more dreaded abroad, at his highest pitch of glory." He then saw "an affectation of purity of manners instead of the luxury which the pomp of Courts displays." He came to the Court of Charles II., and "accustomed as he was to the grandeur of the Court of France, he was surprised at the politeness and splendour of the Court of England." What that "politeness and splendour" really covered is disgusting to look back upon, when we know that we are beholding the manners of our own countrymen. There were other men than the republican John Milton, who felt that they had "fallen on evil days." There were others than Puritans who listened not to

> "the barbarous dissonance
> Of Bacchus and his revellers."

But, taken as a whole, the nation was degraded. Its old spirit was gone. There was a feeble attempt at insurrection in the north in 1663. This outbreak was partly of a religious character, and partly of a political. The insurrection, which was put down by a few of the king's guards, was an excuse for persecuting some of the surviving republicans,—amongst others, colonel Hutchinson, whose quiet and decorous life was an offence which was to be expiated by his death in the damp vaults of Sandown castle. The day of retribution was not yet come: but the handwriting was on the wall. "We are much indebted," says Mr. Hallam, "to the memory of Barbara, duchess of Cleveland, Louisa, duchess of Portsmouth, and Mrs. Eleanor Gwyn. We owe a tribute of gratitude to the Mays, the Killigrews, the Chiffinches, and the Grammonts. They played a serviceable part in ridding the kingdom of its besotted loyalty. They saved our forefathers from the Star-chamber and the High-commission court; they laboured in their vocation against standing armies and corruption; they pressed forward the great ultimate security of English freedom, the expulsion of the House of Stuart."

The abortive insurrection of the autumn of 1663 was made the pretext for a new measure against non-conformists in the session of 1664; and for an important change in the constitution of Parliament. The king, in his speech on the opening of this session, said, "You may judge by the late treason in the north, for which so many men have been executed, how active the spirits of many of our old enemies still are. . . . It is evident they have correspondence with desperate persons in most counties, and a standing council in this town. . . . Some would insist upon the authority of the Long Parliament, of which, they say, they have members enough, willing to meet; others have fancied to themselves, by some computation of their own upon some clause in the Triennial Bill, that this present parliament was at an end some months since." The alleged connection of some Fifth Monarchy men with this trifling insurrection of Farnley Wood, near Leeds, — of which Bennet, one of Charles's ministers, said that the country was too ready to prevent the disorders—was made the pretext for " An Act to prevent and suppress seditious Conventicles." * The preamble states that the Act is " for providing further and more speedy remedies against the growing and dangerous practices of seditious sectaries, and other disloyal persons, who under pretence of tender consciencies do at their meetings contrive insurrections, as late experience hath showed." But, insolently assuming that all religious assemblies of non-conformists were seditious, it enacted that if five or more persons besides the household were present at " any assembly, conventicle, or meeting, under colour or pretence of any exercise of religion in other manner than is allowed by the Liturgy or practice of the Church of England," then every person so present should, upon record before two justices of the peace, or the chief magistrate of a corporate town, be liable to certain fines, imprisonment, or transportation, for a first, second, or third offence. Under this abominable statute, puritan ministers who had been ejected from their benefices, and their admiring followers, were thrown into prison. Baxter has related in his plain and forcible manner how this law interfered with the ordinary affairs of life amongst serious people: " It was a great strait that people were in, especially that dwell near any busy officer, or malicious enemy (as who doth not?). Many durst not pray in their families, if above four persons came in to dine with them. In a gentleman's house it is ordinary for more than four, of visitors, neighbours, messengers, or one sort or other, to be most or many days at dinner with them: and then many durst not go to prayer, and some durst scarce crave a blessing on their meat, or give God thanks for it: Some thought they might venture if they withdrew into another room, and left the strangers by themselves. But others said, ' It is all one if they be but in the same house, though out of hearing, when it cometh to the judgment of the justices.' In London, where the houses are contiguous, some thought if they were in several houses, and heard one another through the wall or a window, it would avoid the law. But others said, ' It is all in vain whilst the justice is judge whether it was a Meeting or no.' Great lawyers said, ' If you come on a visit or business, though you be present at prayer or sermon, it is no breach of the law, because you meet not on pretence of a religious exercise.' But those that tried them said, ' Such words are but wind when the justices come to judge you.' And here the fanatics called Quakers did greatly relieve the sober people for a time: for they were so resolute, and gloried in their constancy and sufferings, that they assembled openly (at the Bull and Mouth, near Aldersgate) and were dragged away daily to the common jail; and yet desisted not, but the rest came the next day nevertheless; so that the jail at Newgate was filled with them. Abundance of them died in prison, and yet they continued their assemblies still."† For years were the persecutions under this Statute continued with all the severity that the government could call forth. Clarendon intimates that the Act was not rigorously executed, otherwise it would have produced a thorough reformation. Dr. Creighton, preaching before the king, said that " the greatest part of the lay magistrates in England were Puritans, and would not do justice; and the bishops' powers were so taken away and lessened, that they could not exercise the power they ought."‡ With accommodating magistrates, and a persecuting

* 16 Car. II. c. 4. † " Life," p. 436. ‡ Pepys, " Diary," March 26, 1664.

hierarchy, the times of the Star Chamber would soon have come back.   But some magistrates were honest, and some church-dignitaries merciful and tolerant.   The Parliament was still compliant enough.   They were yet far from manifesting any serious doubts of the value of passive obedience.   But their very intolerance towards Protestant dissenters was, in some degree, a result of their suspicion of the king's desire to show favour to the Papists. He claimed a dispensing power as to the relaxation of penal laws in eccle-siastical matters.   The Parliament gently denied the king's right to this dispensing power, and a Bill to confirm that power was dropped, to Charles's great displeasure.   In the constitutional point of the duration of Parliaments, the Crown was more successful in carrying out its own desires.   By the Triennial Act of 1641, in default of the king summoning a new parliament within three years after a dissolution, the peers might issue writs; or the sheriffs in default of the peers; or in default of constituted authorities the people might elect their representatives without any summons whatever. These provisions against such violations of the constitution as had been seen in the time of Charles I., could not affect a sovereign who desired to govern in connection with Parliaments.   Charles, in his opening speech in the session of 1664, said, " I need not tell you how much I love Parliaments.   Never king was so much beholden to Parliaments as I have been; nor do I think the Crown can ever be happy without frequent Parliaments.   But, assure yourselves, if I should think otherwise, I would never suffer a Parliament to come together by the means prescribed by that Bill." *   The first Charles, in the pride of his triumphant despotism, could not have made a more insolent avowal.   The famous Triennial Act was repealed; all its provisions for holding Parliaments in defiance of an arbitrary power of the Crown were set aside; and yet it was declared that Parliaments should not be suspended for more than three years.   Charles II. lived to violate this law.

The first war in which the government of the restored monarchy was engaged originated in the commercial rivalry of the English and the Dutch. The African Company of England and the African Company of Holland quarrelled about the profits derived from slaves and gold-dust.   They had fought for some miserable forts on the African coast; and gradually the contests of the traders assumed the character of national warfare.   The merchants petitioned Parliament to redress their injuries; the House of Commons listened with ready ear; the king saw plentiful supplies about to be granted him, some of which might be diverted from their destined use; the duke of York was desirous of showing his prowess as Lord High Admiral. War was declared; and on the 3rd of June, 1665, the fleets of the two great commercial nations were engaged off Lowestoffe.   The victory was complete on the side of England.   The old sailors of the Commonwealth had still some animating remembrances of Blake, with which they inspired the emulation of their new comrades.   The duke of York was not deficient in animal courage ; and the courtiers who served as volunteers had not lost the national daring in their self-indulgence.   But the victory raised no shouts of exultation in the marts and thoroughfares of London.   The great City was lying under the dread of the most terrible infliction, which was approaching to sweep away a

* "Parliament Hist." vol. iv. col. 291.

third of its crowded population.   The destroying angel was abroad: his
avenging weapon was The Plague!

The June of 1665 comes in with extraordinary heat.   The previous
winter and spring had been the driest that ever man knew.   The summer was
coming with the same cloudless sky.   There was no grass in the meadows
around London.   "Strange comets, which filled the thoughts and writings of
astronomers, did in the winter and spring a long time appear."   The "great
comet," says Burnet, "raised the apprehensions of those who did not enter
into just speculations concerning those matters."   The boom of guns from
the Norfolk coast is heard upon the Thames; and the merchants upon
Change are anxiously waiting for letters from the fleet.   In the coffee-houses,
two subjects of news keep the gossipers in agitation—the Dutch fleet is off
our coast, the Plague is in the City.   The 7th of June, writes Pepys, was
"the hottest day that ever I felt in my life.   This day, much against my will,
I did in Drury Lane see two or three houses marked with a red cross upon
the doors, and 'Lord have mercy upon us' writ there; which was a sad

Conduit at Leadenhall, erected 1665.

sight to me, being the first of the kind that to my remembrance I ever saw."

The red cross upon the doors was too familiar to the elder population of London.   In 1636, of twenty-three thousand deaths ten thousand were ascribed to the Plague.   The terrible visitor came to London, according to the ordinary belief, once in every twenty years, and then swept away a fifth of the inhabitants.   From 1636 to 1647 there had been no cessation of the malady, which commonly carried off two or three thousand people annually.   But after 1648 there had been no record of deaths from the Plague amounting to more than twenty, in any one year.   In 1664 the Bills of Mortality only registered six deaths from this cause.   The disease seemed almost to belong to another generation than that which had witnessed the triumph and the fall of Puritanism—which had passed from extreme formalism to extreme licentiousness.   How far the drunken revelries of the five years of the Restoration might have predisposed the population to receive the disease, is as uncertain as any belief that the sobriety of the preceding time had warded it off.   One condition of London was, however, unaltered.   It was a city of narrow streets and of bad drainage.   The greater number of houses were deficient in many of the accommodations upon which health, in a great degree, depends.   The supply of water was far from sufficient for the wants of the poorer population ; and with the richer classes the cost of water, supplied either by hand-labour or machinery, prevented its liberal use.   The conduits, old or new, could only afford to fill a few watercans daily for household uses.   There was much finery in the wealthy citizens' houses, but little cleanliness.   It is to be remarked, however, that the Plague of 1665 was as fatal in the less crowded parts of Westminster and its suburbs, as in the City within the walls.   Building had been going forward from the time of Elizabeth in St. Giles's-in-the-Fields, and in St. Martin's-in-the-Fields ; and we might conclude that the streets would be wider and the houses more commodious in these new parts than in the close thoroughfares, over which the projecting eaves had hung for many a year, shutting out air and light.   But in these suburban liberties the Plague of 1665 first raged, and then gradually extended eastward.   On the 10th of June the disease broke out in the City, in the house of Dr. Burnett, a physician, in Fenchurch Street.   "I saw poor Dr. Burnett's door shut ; but he hath, I hear, gained great good will among his neighbours ; for he discovered it himself first, and caused himself to be shut up of his own accord—which was very handsome."   This is a quaint comment upon the good doctor's voluntary subjection to misery worse than death—to be shut up—with the red-cross on the door ; no one coming with help or consolation ; all stricken with the selfishness of terror.*

* There is a remarkable picture of a solitary man abiding in a house whilst the plague was around him, written by one who has many of the qualities of the true poet. George Wither, during the Plague of 1625, resolved to remain in his lodging in London, and thus he describes a night of "darkness and loneliness :"—

"My chamber entertain'd me all alone,
And in the rooms adjoining lodged none.
Yet, through the darksome silent night, did fly
Sometime an uncouth noise ; sometime a cry ;
And sometime mournful callings pierc'd my room,
Which came, I neither knew from whence, nor whom.

Defoe's famous "Journal of the Plague Year" has made this terrible season familiar to most readers. The spirit of accuracy is now more required than when the editor of a popular work informed his readers that Defoe continued in London during the whole time of the plague, and was one of the Examiners appointed to shut up infected houses.[*] Defoe, in 1665, was four years old. Yet the imaginary saddler of Whitechapel, who embodies the stories which this wonderful writer had treasured up from his childhood, relates nothing that is not supported by what we call authentic history. The "Citizen who continued all the while in London," as the title of Defoe's Journal informs us, and whose dwelling was "without Aldgate, about midway between Aldgate church and Whitechapel bars," relates how, through May and June, the nobility and rich people from the west part of the city filled the broad street of Whitechapel with coaches and waggons and

Broadstone, East Retford.

carts, all hurrying away with goods, women, servants, and children; how horsemen, with servants bearing their baggage, followed in this mournful cavalcade, from morning to night; how the lord mayor's doors were crowded with applicants for passes and certificates of health, for without these none

And oft, betwixt awaking and asleep,
Their voices, who did talk, or pray, or weep,
Unto my list'ning ears a passage found,
And troubled me, by their uncertain sound."

[*] "Beauties of England and Wales."

would be allowed to enter the towns, or rest in any way-side inn. The citizen of Whitechapel thought "of the misery that was coming upon the city, and the unhappy condition of those who would be left in it." On the 21st of June, Pepys writes, "I find all the town almost going out of town; the coaches and waggons being all full of people going into the country." In the country, the population dreaded to see the Londoners. Baxter remarks, "How fearful people were thirty, or forty, if not an hundred miles from London, of anything that they bought from any mercer's or draper's shop; or of any goods that were brought to them; or of any persons that came to their houses. How they would shut their doors against their friends; and if a man passed over the fields, how one would avoid another, as we did in the time of wars; and how every man was a terror to another." The Broadstone of East Redford, on which an exchange was made of money for goods, without personal communication, is an illustration of these rural terrors. A panic very soon took possession of the population of London. They talked of the comet, "of a faint, dull, languid colour, and its motion very heavy, solemn, and slow." They read 'Lilly's Almanac,' and 'Gadbury's Astrological Predictions,' and 'Poor Robin's Almanac,' and these books "frightened them terribly." A man walked the streets day and night, at a swift pace, speaking to no one, but uttering only the words "O the great and the dreadful God!" These prognostications and threatenings came before the pestilence had become very serious; and they smote down the hearts of the people, and thus unfitted them for the duty of self-preservation, and the greater duty of affording help to others. Other impostors than the astrologers abounded. The mountebank was in the streets with his "in-

Mountebank.

fallible preventive pills," and "the only true plague-water." Pepys records that "my lady Carteret did this day give me a bottle of plague-water home with me." But gradually the astrologers and the quacks were left without customers, for London was almost wholly abandoned to the very poorest. Touchingly does Baxter say, " the calamities and cries of the diseased and impoverished are not to be conceived by those who are absent from them. . . . . The richer sort remaining out of the city, the greatest blow fell on the poor." The Court fled on the first appearance of the disease. Some few of the great remained, amongst others the stout old duke of Albemarle, who fearlessly chewed his tobacco at his mansion of the Cockpit. Marriages of the rich still went on. Pepys is diffuse about a splendid marriage at Dagenham's, which narrative reads like the contrasts of a chapter of romance. " Thus I ended this month (July) with the greatest joy that ever I did any in my life, because I have spent the greatest part of it with abundance of joy, and honour, and pleasant journeys, and brave entertainments, and without cost of money." A week after, he writes, " Home, to draw over anew my will, which I had bound myself by oath to dispatch tomorrow night, the town growing so unhealthy that a man cannot depend upon living two days."

The narrative of Defoe, and other relations, have familiarised most of us from our boyhood with the ordinary facts of this terrible calamity. We see the searchers, and nurses, and watchmen, and buryers marching in ominous silence through the empty streets, each bearing the red wand of office. We see them enter a suspected house, and upon coming out marking the door with the fatal red cross, a foot in length. If the sick within can pay, a nurse is left. We see the dead-cart going its rounds in the night, and hear the bell tinkling, and the buryers crying " Bring out your dead." Some of the infected were carried to the established pest-houses, where the dead-cart duly received its ghastly load. The saddler of White-chapel describes what he beheld at " the great pit of the churchyard of our parish at Aldgate:"—" I saw two links come over from the end of the Minories, and heard the bellman, and then appeared a dead-cart, as they called it, coming over the streets, so I could no longer resist my desire of seeing it, and went in. . . . . It had in it sixteen or seventeen bodies; some were wrapt up in linen sheets, some in rugs, some little other than naked, or so loose that what covering they had fell from them in the shooting out of the cart, and they fell quite naked amongst the rest; but the matter was not much to them, nor the indecency to any one else, seeing they were all dead, and were to be huddled together into the common grave of mankind, as we may call it, for here is no difference made, but poor and rich went together; there was no other way of burials, neither was it possible there should, for coffins were not be had for the prodigious numbers that fell in such a calamity as this." Soon, as Pepys tells us on the 12th of August, " the people die so, that now it seems they are fain to carry the dead to be buried by day light, the night not sufficing to do it in." The terrors which the sleek Secretary of the Navy feels when he thus encounters a dead body are almost ludicrous. The Reverend Thomas Vincent, one of the non-conforming clergy who remained in the city, has thus described the scenes of August : " Now people fall as thick as the leaves in autumn when they are shaken by a mighty wind. Now there is a dismal solitude in London streets; every day looks with the face of a Sabbath-day, observed with a greater solemnity than it used to be in the city. Now shops are shut in, people rare and very few that walk about, insomuch that the grass begins to spring up in some places, and a deep silence in every place, especially within the walls. No prancing horses, no rattling coaches, no calling in customers nor offering wares, no London cries sounding in the ears. If any voice be heard it is the groans of dying persons breathing forth their last, and the funeral knells of

Post House, Tothill Fields.   (From Hollar.)

them that are ready to be carried to their graves. Now shutting up of visited houses (there being so many) is at an end, and most of the well are mingled among the sick, which otherwise would have got no help. Now, in some places, where the people did generally stay, not one house in a hundred but what is affected; and in many houses half the family is swept away; in some, from the eldest to the youngest: few escape but with the death of one or two. Never did so many husbands and wives die together; never did so many parents carry their children with them to the grave, and go together into the same house under earth who had lived together in the same house upon it. Now the nights are too short to bury the dead: the whole day, though at so great a length, is hardly sufficient to light the dead that fall thereon into their graves." At the beginning of September the empty streets put on another aspect, equally fearful. The bonfire, which was the exhibition of gladness, was now the token of desolation. Every six houses on each side of the way were to be assessed towards the expense of maintaining one great fire in the middle of the street for the purification of the air,—fires which were not to be extinguished by night or by day. A heavy rain put out these death-fires, and perhaps did far more good than this expedient. As winter approached, the disease began rapidly to decrease. Confidence a little revived. A few shops were again opened. The York waggon again ventured to go to London with passengers. At the beginning of 1666 "the town fills again." "Pray God," says Pepys, "continue the Plague's decrease; for that keeps the Court away from the place of business, and so all goes to rack as to public matters." He rides in Lord Brouncker's coach to Covent Garden: "What staring to see a nobleman's coach come to town. And porters everywhere bow to us: and such begging of beggars." The sordid and self-indulgent now began to come back: "January 22nd. The first meeting of Gresham College since the plague. Dr. Goddard did fill us with talk, in defence of his and his fellow-physicians' going out of town in the plague-time; saying that their particular patients were most gone out of town, and they left at liberty, and a great deal more." This is Pepys' entry of the 4th of February: "Lord's day: and my wife and I the first time together at church since the plague, and now only because of Mr. Mills his coming home to preach his first sermon; expecting a great excuse for his leaving the parish before anybody went, and now staying till all are come home: but he made but a very poor and short excuse, and a bad sermon." Mr. Mills, and his doings, and the doings of such as Mr. Mills, were not without important consequences, which bring us back to the political history of this time of suffering, in which the few manifested a noble devotion to their duty, and the many exhibited the more general characteristic of their generation — intense selfishness. Defoe tells, with the strictest accuracy, the mode in which the spiritual condition of the plague-struck city was attended to: "Though it is true that a great many of the clergy did shut up their churches, and fled, as other people did, for the safety of their lives, yet all did not do so; some ventured to officiate, and to keep up the assemblies of the people by constant prayers, and sometimes sermons, or brief exhortations to repentance and reformation, and this as long as they would hear them. And dissenters did the like also, and even in the very churches where the parish ministers were either dead or fled; nor was there any room for making any difference at such a time as this was." Baxter also relates that, when "most of the conformable ministers fled, and left their flocks in the time of their extremity," the non-conforming ministers, who, since 1662, had done their work very privately, "resolved to stay with the people; and to go into the forsaken pulpits, though prohibited; and to preach to the poor people before they died; and also to visit the sick, and get what relief they could for the poor, especially those that were shut up." The reward which the non-conforming ministers received for their good work was "The Five Mile Act."

The Statute which popularly bore this name is entitled "An Act for restraining Non-conformists from inhabiting in Corporations." * In consequence of the plague raging in London, the Parliament met at Oxford on the 9th of October. Their first Act was for a supply of 1,250,000l. Their second was this "new and more inevitable blow aimed at the fallen Church of Calvin." † All persons in holy orders who had not subscribed the Act of Uniformity were required to take the following oath: "I, A. B., do swear, that it is not lawful, under any pretence whatsoever, to take arms against the king; and that I do abhor the traitorous position of taking arms by his authority against his person, or against those that are commissionated by him, in pursuance of such commissions; and that I will not at any time

---

* 17 Car. II. c. 2.   † Hallam.

endeavour any alteration of government either in Church or State." In default of taking this oath they were forbidden to dwell, or come, unless upon the road, within five miles of any corporate town, or any other place where they had been ministers, or had preached, under a penalty of Forty Pounds and six months' imprisonment. They were also declared incapable of teaching in schools, or of receiving boarders. This Act had for its object wholly to deprive the conscientious Puritans of any means of subsistence connected with their former vocation of Christian ministers or instructors of youth Mr. Hallam truly says, "The Church of England had doubtless her provocations; but she made the retaliation much more than commensurate to the injury. No severity comparable to this cold-blooded persecution had been inflicted by the late powers, even in the ferment and fury of a civil war." An attempt was made to impose the non-resisting oath upon the whole nation; but it was defeated by a small majority.

The extent of the miseries inflicted by the Plague in London was probably diminished by "The Settlement Act" of 1662.* This was entitled "An Act for the better relief of the Poor." The preamble of the Statute declares the continual increase of the Poor, not only within the cities of London and Westminster, but also through the whole kingdom; but there is little reason to doubt that the main object of the Bill was to thrust out from the parishes of the metropolis, all chargeable persons occupying tenements under the yearly value of ten pounds. By this Act the power of removal was first established—a measure which, however modified, has done as much evil to the labouring population in destroying their habits of self-dependence, as a legal provision for their support, prudently administered, has been a national blessing. The Settlement Act was carried by the metropolitan members, with little resistance from the country members. "The habitual congregating of the vagrant classes in London, and the dread of pestilence likely to be thereby engendered, appear to have overborne or neutralised all other considerations at the time, and hastened the passing of the Act." † The united efforts made by the Londoners to carry this Bill, leave little room to doubt that they acted upon it very promptly and vigilantly; and thus some considerable portion of the indigent population must have been driven forth from London and Westminster, to seek their parishes under the old laws which determined their lawful place of abode. The ten pound rental, either in London or the country, could protect none of the really indigent. It gave a privilege only to the well-to-do artisan or tradesman who had no legal settlement by birth, apprenticeship, or other legal claim. In 1675, in a debate on a Bill for restraint of building near London, one member said that "by the late Act the poor are hunted like foxes out of parishes, and whither must they go but where there are houses?" Another declared that "the Act for the settlement of the poor does, indeed, thrust all people out of the country to London."‡ The intent of the framers of the Act had probably been defeated by the reprisals of the rural magistrates and overseers. The system of hunting the poor went on amidst the perpetual litigation of nearly two centuries; and it is not yet come to an end.

* 14 Car. II. c. 12.   † Sir G. Nicholls: "History of the English Poor Law," vol. i. p. 297.
‡ "Parl. Hist." vol. iv. col. 679.

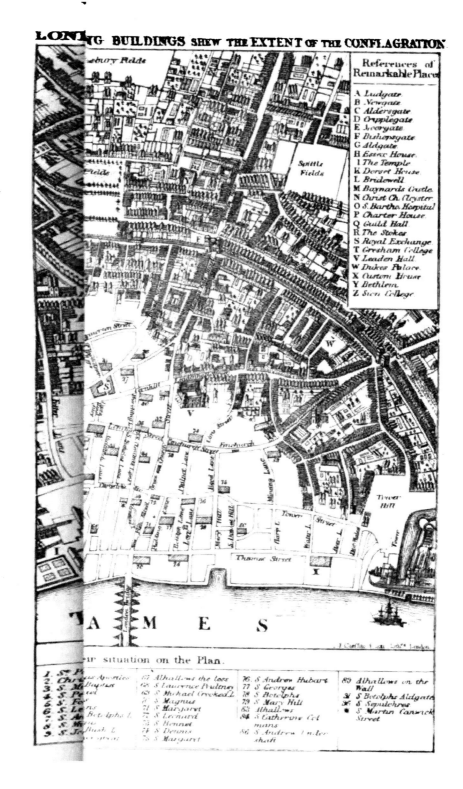

ebury Fielde

Fields

Spittle Fields

References of Remarkable Places

A *Ludgate*
B *Newgate*
C *Aldersgate*
D *Cripplegate*
E *Mooregate*
F *Bishopsgate*
G *Aldgate*
H *Essex House*
I *The Temple*
K *Dorset House*
L *Bridewell*
M *Baynards Castle*
N *Christ Ch. Cloyster*
O *S. Bartho. Hospital*
P *Charter House*
Q *Guild Hall*
R *The Stokes*
S *Royal Exchange*
T *Gresham College*
V *Leaden Hall*
W *Dukes Palace*
X *Custom House*
Y *Bethlem*
Z *Sion College*

Tower Hill

Thames Street

T A M E S

ir situation on the Plan.

1. *So Pe*...	67 *Alhallows the less*	76. *S Andrew Hubart*	89 *Alhallows on the Wall*
2. *Chr*...	68 *S Laurence Pultney*	77 *S Georges*	
3. *S. M*...	69 *S Michael Crooked L.*	78 *S Botolphs*	90 *S Botolphs Aldgate*
4. *S. Pe*...	70 *S Magnus*	79 *S Mary Hill*	91 *S Sepulchres*
5. *S. Fe*...	71 *S Margaret*	83 *Alhallows*	* *S Martin Canwick*
6. *S. Le*...	72 *S Leonard*	84 *S Catherine Col mans*	*Street*
7. *S. An*... *S Botolph. L.*	73 *S Bennet*		
8. *S. M*...	74 *S Denius*	86 *S Andrew Under shaft*	
9. *S. Jo*...	75 *S Margaret*		

Medal exhibiting a First-rate Ship of War: Struck to commemorate the appointment of James, Duke of York, Lord High Admiral.

CHAPTER XVII.

Naval affairs—Annus Mirabilis—France joins the Dutch against England—The sea-fight of four days—The London Gazette—Restraints upon the Press—Ravages of the English fleet on the Dutch Coast—The Great Fire of London. Note, on Wren's Plan for rebuilding the City.

THE naval victory of the 3rd of June, 1665, was a fruitless triumph, won at a lavish expenditure of blood. The most loyal of the subordinate administrators of public affairs considered that a great success had been thrown away. Evelyn writes, (June 8th) " Came news of his highness' victory, which indeed might have been a complete one, and at once ended the war, had it been pursued ; but the cowardice of some, or treachery, or both, frustrated that." When the Dutch fled from off Lowestoffe to their own shores, the English fleet commenced a pursuit ; but in the night the King Charles, the duke of York's ship, slackened sail, and brought to. In a Council of War, as Burnet relates upon the authority of the earl of Montague, Admiral Penn affirmed that they must prepare for hotter work in the next engagement ; for he well knew the courage of the Dutch was never so high as when they were desperate. The courtiers said that the duke had got honour enough, and why should he venture a second time. His royal highness went to sleep ; and in the night Brunkhard, one of his servants, delivered an order to the master of the King Charles to slacken sail, which order purported to be written by the duke. The House of Commons instituted an inquiry; and it was alleged that Brunkhard forged the order. Burnet says, "Lord Montague did believe that the duke was *struck*, seeing the earl of Falmouth, the king's favourite, and two other persons of quality, killed very near him; and that he had no mind to engage again." Some members of the House of Commons thought it a very desirable thing for the nation that the king's brother should incur no more such dangers. The duke remained at home, to contribute his share to the scandals which the Court habitually provoked, whether at Whitehall or at Oxford.

The Plague-year has passed; the "Year of Wonders" is come. Dryden called his *Annus Mirabilis* "an historical poem." In his preface he says, "I

Prince Rupert's House, Beech Lane, Barbican. As it appeared before its demolition. (Drury House.)

have taken upon me to describe the motives, the beginning, progress, and successes, of a most just and necessary War; in it, the care, management, and prudence of our king; the conduct and valour of a royal admiral, and of two incomparable generals; the invincible courage of our captains and seamen; and three glorious victories, the result of all. After this, I have, in the Fire, the most deplorable, but withal the greatest, argument that can be imagined: the destruction being so swift, so sudden, so vast and miserable, as nothing can parallel in story." The year 1666 is, indeed, an eventful year; and the relation of its miseries, so closely following upon the calamity of the Plague, carries with it the consolation that the spirit of the English people, founded upon their industrious habits and their passion for liberty, has always been able to surmount the greatest political evils, and to acquire, even under the severest dispensations of Providence, the courage and perseverance which convert chastisements into blessings.

At the beginning of 1666, Louis XIV., for objects purely personal, joined the Dutch against England, and declared war. This policy of the French Court had a tendency to make the war with the Hollanders more popular in England. Prince Rupert, who was now a resident in London, and who had a command in the engagement off Lowestoffe, was not regarded with any public confidence; and the king felt it necessary to associate the duke of Albemarle with him in the command of the fleet. On the 8th of May the two Generals were at the Nore with their squadrons. " I sailed to the buoy of the Nore to my Lord-General and Prince Rupert, where was the rendez-vous of the most glorious fleet in the world, now preparing to meet the Hollander." *   The people of London, dispirited by the ravages of the plague, many outraged by the persecutions against the non-conformists, unable or indisposed to pay the taxes for the war, had little enthusiasm as to its results. The 29th of May came, and Pepys is heavily afflicted at beholding few bonfires on the east-side of Temple-bar. Clarendon says " Monies could neither be collected nor borrowed where the Plague had pre-vailed, which was over all the City, and over a great part of the country; the collectors durst not go to require it or receive it."†   On the 31st a public Fast-day was appointed to pray for the success of the fleet; "but," says Pepys, " it is a pretty thing to consider how little a matter they make of this keeping a Fast, that it was not declared time enough to be read in the churches, the last Sunday; but ordered by proclamation since: I suppose upon some sudden news of the Dutch having come out." The Dutch fleet had come out; and on the 1st of June it was in the Downs, with Monk in sight of their formidable line of fighting vessels. On the 2nd there is a curious spectacle at Greenwich. The king and the duke of York have come down the river in their barge; and they walk to the Park to hear the loud firing of the ships in the Channel. The group of lordly attendants on Green-wich hill, whispering and pointing as the sullen boom of the guns comes up the Thames;—Charles and James standing apart in puzzled conference, or laughing at some ill-timed jest;—a bowing courtier approaching the royal presence to bring news just arrived at Whitehall,—this is a scene which painting might properly make its own. That distant roar of cannon was not imaginary. Monk and Rupert had separated. It had been believed that the Dutch fleet was not ready for sea; and Monk, with fifty-four sail, had floated calmly from the Nore; when behold, there are eighty Dutch men-at-war at anchor off the North Foreland. The surprise was unaccountable; but it is a proof how rashly naval warfare was conducted when landsmen were the chief com-manders. The English courage was too much relied upon; the science and experience which can alone make courage truly efficient were thought subor-dinate requisites. Monk was a hardy soldier, but a very imperfect naval

* Evelyn, " Diary," May 8.　　　　　† "Life."

tactician ;—moreover he was now elated and presumptuous. He dashed at the Dutch ; fought all day ; and at night looked round upon disabled ships. De Witt was in the fleet of Holland ; and chain-shot, of which he was held to be the inventor, cut the English rigging to pieces. They fired at our towering sails ; we at their high-raised decks. The battle was resumed at the early

Charles II. and Courtier. From a Print by Faithorne.

dawn of the 2nd of June. De Ruyter had received a re-inforcement of sixteen ships during the night. Monk was looking in vain for Rupert to come to his aid. Another day of terrible fight, with losses severe enough on the English side, to have driven to despair a commander less resolute than Monk. Dryden has pictured him at nightfall, standing upon deck, while "the moon shone clear on the becalmed flood," musing on the probable issue of another day, and mournfully preparing for an ocean grave. On the 3rd he burnt some of his disabled ships, and retreated, fighting De Ruyter's rear-guard. The noblest ship of the English navy ran on the Galloper sand, and was lost. Late on the 3rd, Rupert arrived from St. Helen's ; and the battle was renewed with more equality. The poet describes how the anxious prince had heard the cannon long, and drew dire omens of English overmatched.* The historian says, "he had received orders to return from St. Helen's on the first day of the battle ; nor was it ever explained why he did not join Albemarle till the evening of the third."† The Diarist divides the blame between the government at home, and the proud prince, whose obstinate self-reliance had produced so many of the royalist disasters in the Civil War : " I to sir G. Carteret, who told me there hath been great bad management in all this ; that the king's orders that went on Friday for calling back the prince were sent but by the ordinary post on Wednesday ; and come to the prince his hands but on Friday ; and then, instead of sailing presently, he stays till four in the evening. And that which is worst of all, the Hampshire, laden with merchants' money, come from the Straits, set out with or but just before the fleet,

* "Annus Mirabilis," stanza cvi.   † Lingard.

and was in the Downs by five of the clock yesterday morning ; and the prince with his fleet come to Dover but at ten of the clock at night. This is hard to answer, if it be true. This puts great astonishment into the king, and duke, and court, everybody being out of countenance. Home by the 'Change, which is full of people still, and all talk highly of the failure of the prince in not making more haste after his instructions did come, and of our managements here in not giving it sooner and with more care and oftener." The first desire of the court, and the more natural one, was to set forth that there had been a great victory. Newspapers, then, had no peculiar sources of information, to check the tendency of all governments to deceive the people as to the results of their warlike enterprises—a tendency which only makes disappointment more severe when truth comes out, and thus exhibits falsehood not only as a crime but as a fault. The court had now got its " Gazette," which was first published at Oxford on the 7th of November, 1665 ; and soon after became "The London Gazette." Roger L'Estrange, Esquire, had commenced his " Intelligence published for the satisfaction and information of the People," and his " Newes," in 1663 ; the one issued on a Monday, the other on a Thursday. What real satisfaction and information the public could derive from these productions may be gathered from the address of their conductor. He was " Surveyor of the Imprimery and Printing-Presses ;" and he tells his readers that his sacred majesty has been graciously pleased " to grant and commit the privilege of publishing all intelligence, together with the survey and inspection of the Press, to one and the same person." He candidly informs his subscribers that, " supposing the press in order, the people in their right wits, and news or no news to be the question, a public Mercury should never have my vote." He is of opinion that it makes the multitude " too familiar with the actions and councils of their superiors, too pragmatical and censorious ; and gives them, not only an itch, but a colourable right and licence to be meddling with the government." To keep the multitude in the right course, he thinks " the prudent management of a Gazette may contribute to a very high degree." * This worthy Licenser was preceded in his high endeavours for the reformation of the pragmatical and censorious multitude by the Licensing Act of 1662, by which all books, according to their subjects, were to be licensed by the chancellor, the secretary of state, the bishops, and other great personages. All these authorities, practically, became merged in Roger L'Estrange, Esquire. The number of master printers in London was limited to twenty ; no books were allowed to be printed out of London, except at the two Universities and at York ; and all unlicensed books were to be seized, and the publisher punished by heavy penalties. The Stationers' Company was made a principal agency for carrying through these despotic regulations. We may well judge, therefore, that the real issue of the four days' fight in the Downs would be explained to the multitude after a fashion which the " prudent management " of the virtuous licenser of the Press, and candid monopolist of all intelligence, would prescribe. When Mr. Pepys entered in cipher in his Diary, " Lord, to see how melancholy the Court is, under the thoughts of this last overthrow, for so it is, instead of a victory, so much and so unreasonably

* See Nicholls' " Literary Anecdotes," 1812. vol. iv. p. 36.

expected," it was the duty of Roger L'Estrange to make the ignorant multitude very joyful. Still there were material evidences of the truth. There were no Dutch prizes in the Thames; and when Mr. Evelyn, with all his royalist devotion, went to Sheerness on the 15th of June, he made this record: "Here I beheld the sad spectacle—more than half that gallant bulwark of the kingdom miserably shattered; hardly a vessel entire, but appearing so many wrecks and hulls, so cruelly had the Dutch mangled us." The "sad sight" makes him acknowledge that none knew "for what reason we first engaged in this ungrateful war." There was a partial success when a portion of the two fleets met again on the 25th of July, each being refitted. The Dutch were chased to their ports; and Monk and Rupert kept their coasts in alarm. A squadron of boats and fire-ships entered the channel at Schelling; burnt two men-of-war and a hundred and fifty merchantmen; and, to the disgrace of civilised warfare, reduced to ashes the thousand houses of the unfortified town of Brandaris. For this success, a day of Thanksgiving was appointed. It was kept; "though many muttered that it was not wisely done, to provoke the Dutch, by burning their houses, when it was easy for them to do the like by us, on our sea-coasts." * De Witt saw the havoc of Brandaris; and he swore a solemn oath, that till he had obtained revenge, he would never sheathe the sword. He kept his oath. The 'Annus Mirabilis' was at an end before the great Dutch statesman inflicted a terrible retribution. At the close of the year came Dryden, intent upon earning the laureate wreath, and proclaimed the glories of 1666, in magnificent quatrains :—

> " Already we have conquered half the war,
> And the less dangerous part is left behind :
> Our trouble now is but to make them dare,
> And not so great to vanquish as to find." †

The story of the Great Fire of London has been related with minuteness by many trustworthy observers. We can place ourselves in the midst of this extraordinary scene, and make ourselves as familiar with its details as if the age of newspapers had arrived, and a host of reporters had been engaged in collecting every striking incident. But it is not in the then published narratives that we find those graphic touches which constitute the chief interest of this event at the present time. Half a century ago the materials for a faithful record of the Great Fire were to be sought in the report of a Committee of the House of Commons, in the State Trials, and in various tracts issued at the period. There are also several striking passages of Baxter's ' Life,' which relate to the fire. But such notices are meagre compared with the personal records in the two remarkable Diaries which have been rescued from obscurity during our own day. We are with Mr. Pepys in his nightgown at three o'clock in the morning of Sunday, the 2nd of September, looking out of his window in Seething Lane, at the east end of the City, and, thinking the fire far enough off, going to sleep again. We accompany him later in the morning to a high place in the Tower, and see the houses near London Bridge on fire. The weather is hot and dry, and a furious east wind is blowing. The active Mr. Pepys takes a boat from the Tower Stairs; and

---

* Baxter, "Life," part iii. p. 16.   † "Annus Mirabilis," ccciii.

slowly sculling up stream, looks upon the burning houses in the streets near the Thames; distracted people getting their goods on board lighters; and the inhabitants of the houses at the water's edge not leaving till the fire actually reached them. He has time to look at the pigeons—of which the Londoners generally were then as fond as the Spitalfields weavers of our time —hovering about the windows and balconies till they burned their wings and fell down. There is nobody attempting to quench the fire in that high wind. Everything is combustible after the long drought. Human strength seems in vain, and the people give themselves up to despair. The busy Secretary of the Navy reaches Whitehall, and tells his story to the king; and he entreats his majesty to order houses to be pulled down, for nothing less would stop the fire. The king desires Pepys to go to the lord mayor, and give him this command. In Cannon-street he encounters the lord mayor, who cries, like a fainting woman, " Lord! what can I do? I am spent. People will not obey me." He had been pulling down houses. He did not want any soldiers. He had been up all night, and must go home and refresh himself. There is no service in the churches, for the people are crowding them with their goods. The worthy Pepys had invited a dinner-party on this Sunday; and so he goes home; and " we had an extraordinary good dinner, and as merry as at that time we could be." But he and his guests sit not long over their feast. He walks through the streets; and again he takes boat at Paul's Wharf. He now meets the king and the duke of York in their barge. They ordered that houses should be pulled down apace; but the fire came on so fast that little could be done. We get glimpses in this confusion of the domestic habits of the citizens. " The river full of lighters and boats taking in goods; and good goods swimming about in the water; and I observed that hardly one lighter or boat in three that had the goods of a house in, but there was a pair of virginals in it." The severer Puritans had not driven out the old English love of music; the citizens' wives and daughters still had the imperfect spinet upon which Elizabeth and her maids of honour played. That hot September evening is spent by our observer upon the water. Showers of fire-drops are driving in his face. He sees the fiery flakes shooting up from one burning house, and then dropping upon another five or six houses off, and setting that on flame. The roofs were in many streets only thatched : the walls were mostly timber. Warehouses in Thames-street were stored with pitch, and tar, and oil, and brandy. The night came on; and then Pepys, from a little alehouse on the Bankside, saw the fire grow, and shoot out between churches and houses, " in a most horrid, malicious, bloody flame, not like the fire flame of an ordinary fire." And then, as it grew darker, he saw the fire up the hill in an arch of above a mile long. Then rose the moon shedding a soft light over the doomed city; and amidst the terrible glare and the gentle radiance the whole world of London was awake, gazing upon the conflagration, or labouring to save something from its fury.

We turn to the Diary of Mr. Evelyn—a more elegant writer than Pepys, but scarcely so curious an observer of those minute points that give life to a picture. He has seen the fire from the Bankside on Sunday afternoon; and on Monday he returns to see the whole south part of the city burning. It was now taking hold of the great cathedral, which was surrounded by scaffolds for its repair. "The noise and cracking and thunder of the impetuous flames, the shrieking of women and children, the hurry of people, the fall of towers, houses, and churches, was like a hideous storm; and the air all about so hot and inflamed, that at the last one was not able to approach it, so that they were forced to stand still, and let the flames burn on,

Burning of Newgate; Old St. Paul's in the background.

which they did, for near two miles in length and one in breadth. The clouds, also, of smoke were dismal, and reached, upon computation, near fifty miles in length. Thus I left it this afternoon burning, a resemblance of Sodom, or the last day."

On Tuesday, the 4th, Evelyn saw that the fire had reached as far as the Inner Temple. "All Fleet-street, the Old Bailey, Ludgate-hill, Warwick-lane, Newgate, Paul's-chain, Watling-street, now flaming, and most of it reduced to ashes; the stones of Paul's flew like grenados, the melting lead running down the streets in a stream, and the very pavements glowing with fiery redness, so as no horse, nor man, was able to tread on them, and the demolition had stopped all the passages, so that no help could be applied; the eastern wind still more impetuously driving the flames forward." On that day the houses near the Tower were blown up; and the same judicious plan was pursued in other places. On the 5th the Court at Whitehall was in unwonted bustle. The king and his brother had set an excellent example of personal activity; and gentlemen now took charge of particular streets, and directed the means of extinguishing the flames. The people now began to bestir themselves. The civic authorities no longer rejected the advice, which some seamen had given at first, to blow up the houses before the flames reached them, instead of attempting to pull them down. The wind abated. Large gaps were made in the streets. The desolation did not reach beyond the Temple westward, nor beyond Smithfield on the north. On Wednesday, the 5th, the mighty devourer was arrested in his course. Three days and three nights of agony had been passed; but not more than eight lives had been lost. Mr. Pepys at last lies down and sleeps soundly. He has one natural remark: "It is a strange thing to see how long this time did look since Sunday, having been always full of variety of actions, and little sleep, that it looked like a week or more, and I had forgot almost the day of the week."

The contemporary accounts of the Fire, such as we find in a sensible pamphlet entitled 'Observations on the Burning of London,'* have little pretension to be picturesque in their details. The more elaborate passages of Evelyn's ' Diary ' have been quoted again and again; and, grouped together, they form the best connected narrative of an eye-witness. There is one passage in Baxter's ' Life ' which is not so familiar; but which, in its rapid eloquence, is as impressive as Evelyn, and more truly poetical than Dryden's vague sublimities: "It was a sight that might have given any man a lively sense of the vanity of this world, and all the wealth and glory of it, and of the future conflagration of all the world. To see the flames mount up towards heaven, and proceed so furiously without restraint: To see the streets filled with people astonished, that had scarce sense left them to lament their own calamity: To see the fields filled with heaps of goods; and sumptuous buildings, curious rooms, costly furniture, and household stuff, yea, warehouses and furnished shops and libraries, all on a flame, and none durst come near to receive anything: To see the king and nobles ride about the streets, beholding all these desolations, and none could afford the least relief: To see the air, as far as could be beheld, so filled with the smoke, that the sun shone through it with a colour like blood; yea, even when it was setting in the west, it so appeared to them that dwelt on the west side of the city. But the dolefullest sight of all was afterwards, to see what a ruinous confused place the city was, by chimnies and steeples only standing in the midst of cellars and heaps of rubbish; so that it was hard to know where the streets had been, and dangerous, of a long time, to pass through the ruins, because of vaults, and fire in them. No man that seeth not such a thing can have a right apprehension of the dreadfulness of it."

Whilst indifferent spectators were gazing on the fire from Bankside, and the high grounds on the south of the Thames, the fields on the north were filled with houseless men, women, and children. "I went," says Evelyn, "towards Islington and Highgate, where one might have seen two hundred thousand people, of all ranks and degrees, dispersed and lying along by their heaps of what they could save from the fire, deploring their loss; and, though ready to perish for hunger and destitution, yet not asking one penny for relief." There were liberal contributions from the king, and the nobility, and the clergy. Collections were made and distributed in alms to the most needy. But the real difficulty must have been to ensure a supply of food, when all the usual channels of interchange were choked up. Proclamations were made for the country people to bring in provisions. Facilities were offered to the people to leave the ruins, by a command that they should be received in all cities and towns to pursue their occupations: and that such

---

* Reprinted in "Harleian Miscellany."

reception should entail no eventual burthen on parishes. No doubt it was necessary to strive against the selfishness that vast calamities too often produce in the sufferers and the lookers-on. The country-people for miles around had gazed upon the flames.* There was an immense destruction of books; and their half-burnt leaves were carried by the wind even as far as

London during the Great Fire, from the Bankside, Southwark.

Windsor. The dense cloud of smoke shut out the bright autumn sun from the harvest-fields, and upon distant roads men travelled in the shade. The extent of the calamity was apparent. Yet it may be doubted if many of the great ones received the visitation in a right spirit. Pepys says, "none of the nobility came out of the country at all, to help the king, or comfort him, or prevent commotions at this fire." Some of the insolent courtiers exulted in the destruction : "Now the rebellious city is ruined, the king is absolute, and was never king indeed till now." † One profligate "young commander" of the fleet "made mighty sport of it ;" and rejoiced that the corruption of the citizen's wives might be effected at a very reduced cost.‡

The Monument erected in commemoration of the Fire has an elaborate Latin inscription, in which it is set forth that the destruction comprised eighty-nine churches, the city-gates, Guildhall, many public structures, hospitals, schools, libraries; a vast number of stately edifices; thirteen thousand two hundred dwelling-houses, four hundred streets. The extent of the destruction is

* The author of this History, talking of the fire of London with a friend, in his 88th year, whose intellect is as bright as his knowledge is extensive, was much impressed by the fact that an event happening two centuries ago may have come to the ear of one now living, with only a single person intervening between himself and an eye-witness. Such a fact ought to lead us not to reject traditional information as unworthy of historical record. · Our friend was born in 1769. His aunt, who died at 84 years of age, was accustomed to talk with him about his great-grand-father, who died in 1739, at 93 years of age. That great-grandfather used to describe his impressions of the Fire of London, which he saw from a hill at Bishop's Stortford.

       † Baxter.   ‡ Pepys.

shown in the plan we have engraved, founded upon an official survey. An account, which estimates the houses burnt at twelve thousand, values them at an average rent of 25*l.* a year, and their value, at twelve years' purchase, at £3,600,000. The public buildings destroyed are valued at £1,800,000 : the private goods at the same rate. With other items, the total amount of the loss is estimated at £7,335,000.*

Monument in the beginning of the 18th century.

But the interruption to industry must have involved even a more serious loss of the national capital. We have stated, on the authority of Clarendon, how the Plague had rendered it difficult to collect the revenue. He says of the necessities of the Crown in 1666, " Now this deluge by fire had dissipated the persons, and destroyed the houses, which were liable to the re-imburse-ment of all arrears; and the very stocks were consumed which should carry on and revive the trade." †

The Monument, which was erected on the spot where the fire first broke out, recorded that the burning of this protestant city was begun and carried on by the treachery and malice of a popish faction. The " tall bully " lifted his head and lied in choice Latin for a century and three-quarters; and

* " Harleian Miscellany," vol. vii. p. 331.   † " Life."

when the majority of men had grown more truly religious, and did not hold it the duty of one Christian to hate another who differed from him in doctrines and ceremonies, the Corporation of London wisely obliterated the offensive record.   In the examinations before the Committee of the House of Commons, there was nothing beyond the most vague babble of the frightened and credulous, except the self-accusation of one Hubert, a French working-silversmith, who maintained that he was the incendiary.   He was hanged, much to the disgrace of the administration of justice.   "Neither the judges," says Clarendon, "nor any present at the trial, did believe him guilty ; but that he was a poor distracted wretch, weary of his life, and chose to part with it this way."

Dryden's stanzas on the Fire thus conclude, with reference to the popular superstition, which had its influence even upon the well-informed :

> "The utmost malice of the stars is past,
>   And two dire comets, which have scourg'd the town,
> In their own Plague and Fire have breathed their last,
>   Or dimly in their sinking sockets frown."

A medal was struck in commemoration of the Plague and Fire.   The eye of God is in the centre ; one comet is showering down pestilence and another flame.   The east wind is driving on the flames.   Death in the foreground is encountering an armed horseman.   The legend is " *Sic punit* "—So He punishes.

NOTE ON WREN'S PLAN FOR REBUILDING THE CITY.

—◦—

Our noble Cathedral of St. Paul's, and many Churches which exhibit the genius of sir Christopher Wren in many graceful and original forms of towers and spires, grew out of the Great Fire. But the occasion was lost for a nobler city to arise,

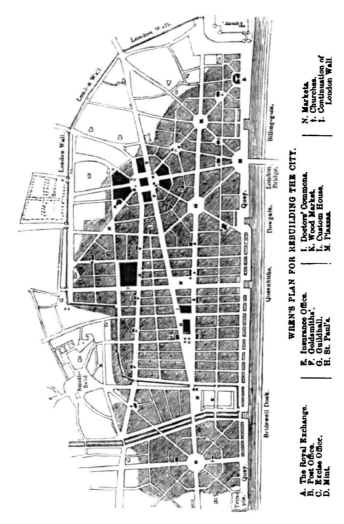

WREN'S PLAN FOR REBUILDING THE CITY.

A. The Royal Exchange.
B. Post Office.
C. Excise Office.
D. Mint.

E. Insurance Office.
F. Goldsmiths'.
G. Guildhall.
H. St. Paul's.

I. Doctors' Commons.
K. Wood Market.
L. Custom House.
M. Piazzas.

N. Markets.
†. Churches.
‡. Continuation of London Wall.

of wide streets, and handsome quays. The old wooden fabrics were replaced by those of brick ; but the same narrow thoroughfares were preserved as of old. The owners of property could not be brought to unite in any common plan ; and each built his house up again, upon his own spot of ground. The constant labour of succeeding times, and of our own especially, has been to clear away, at enormous cost, what the fire had cleared away in three days and nights. This want of co-operative action was not the result of any ignorance of what required to be done. Wren's labours and wishes are thus recorded : " In order to a proper reformation, Wren, pursuant to the royal command, immediately after the fire, took an exact survey of the whole area and confines of the burning, having traced over with great trouble and hazard the great plain of ashes and ruins ; and designed a plan or model of a new city, in which the deformity and inconveniences of the old town were remedied, by the enlarging the streets and lanes, and carrying them as near parallel to one another as might be ; avoiding, if compatible with greater conveniences, all acute angles ; by seating all the parochial churches conspicuous and insular ; by forming the most public places into large piazzas, the centre of six or eight ways ; by uniting the halls of the twelve chief companies into one regular square annexed to Guildhall ; by making a quay on the whole bank of the river, from Blackfriars to the Tower. . . . . The streets to be of three magnitudes ; the three principal leading straight through the City, and one or two cross streets, to be at least ninety feet wide ; others sixty feet ; and lanes about thirty feet, excluding all narrow dark alleys without thoroughfares, and courts. . . . . The practicability of this scheme, without loss to any man or infringement of any property, was at that time demonstrated, and all material objections fully weighed and answered. The only, and as it happened insurmountable, difficulty remaining, was the obstinate averseness of great part of the citizens to alter their old properties, and to recede from building their houses again on the old ground and foundations ; as also the distrust in many and unwillingness to give up their properties, though for a time only, into the hands of public trustees or commissioners, till they might be dispensed to them again, with more advantage to themselves than otherwise was possible to be effected. . . . . The opportunity in a great degree was lost of making the new City the most magnificent, as well as commodious for health and trade, of any upon earth." *

* Wren's "Parentalia," p. 269.

Dutch Fleet in the Medway; Burning of Sheerness. (From a Drawing of the time of Charles II.)

CHAPTER XVIII.

Meeting of Parliament—Discontents—Public Accounts—Insurrection of Covenanters in Scotland —State of the Navy—Dutch Fleet at the Nore—Ships burnt in the Medway—Blockade of London—Peace with the Dutch—Clarendon deprived of Office—He is impeached—He leaves England—The Cabal Ministry—Treaty of Triple Alliance—Secret Negotiations of the king with Louis the Fourteenth.

THE flames of London were still smouldering when the Parliament met at Westminster on the 21st of September. The king said, " Little time hath passed, since we were almost in despair of having this place left us to meet in ; you see the dismal ruins the fire hath made." There had been a prorogation for ten months. But money was wanting. " I desire," said Charles, " to put you to as little trouble as I can ; and I can tell you truly, I desire to put you to as little cost as is possible. I wish with all my heart that I could have the whole charge of this war myself, and that my subjects should reap the benefit of it to themselves." No doubt it was very disagreeable that the king's subjects, being to be called upon to pay largely, should by any possibility take the liberty of asking what they were to pay for. Clarendon tells us of the somewhat dangerous temper which was spreading after the experience of six years and a half of the happy Restoration. " Though they made the same professions of affection and duty to the king they had ever done, they did not conceal the very ill opinion they had of the Court and the continual riotings there."* They were tending to the accomplishment of Harrington's prophecy: "Well! The king will come in. Let him come in, and call a Parliament of the greatest Cavaliers in England, so they be men of estates, and let them sit but for seven years, and they will all turn Commonwealth's men."† A bill was brought in for the appointment of Commissioners "to examine all accounts of those who had received or issued out any moneys for this war; and where they found any persons faulty, and who had broken their trust, they should be liable to such punishment as the Parliament should think fit." Sir George Carteret, and lord Ashley, who were chiefly aimed at, "both applied themselves to the king for his protection in this point. His majesty was no less troubled, knowing that both had issued out many sums upon his warrant, which he would not suffer to be produced." To such a bill the king was resolved never to give the royal assent. This is Clarendon's relation of the matter; and yet he is not ashamed to say that he urged the king "to prevent the excesses in Parliament, and not to suffer them to extend their jurisdiction to cases they have nothing to do with." Mr. Hallam says, "Such a slave was Clarendon to his narrow prepossessions, that he would rather see the dissolute excesses which he abhorred suck nourishment from that revenue which had been allotted to maintain the national honour and interests, and which, by its deficiencies thus aggravated, had caused even in this very year the navy to be laid up, and the coasts to be left defenceless, than suffer them to be restrained by the only power to which thoughtless luxury would submit."‡ Every effort was made to oppose the bill; § and the Parliament was prorogued in 1667 without its being passed. Next year, 1668, the Parliament carried its salutary measure of control. A supply of £1,800,000 was granted; and at the prorogation the king said, "I assure you the money shall be laid out for the ends it is given."

The calamities which London had endured of Pestilence and Conflagration were not wholly unacceptable to the corrupt court. Clarendon informs us that there were those about the king, who assured him that the Fire "was the greatest blessing that God had ever conferred on him, his restoration only excepted; for the walls and gates being now burned and thrown down of that rebellious city, which was always an enemy to the Crown, his majesty would never suffer them to repair and build them up again, to be a bit in his mouth, and a bridle upon his neck; but would keep all open, that his troops might enter upon them whenever he thought it necessary for his service, there being no other way to govern that rude multitude but by force." Charles was not pleased with these suggestions, adds Clarendon. Desirable as it might be to have the Londoners under his feet at this time of their desolation, there was still the old spirit abroad in England. "Mr. Williamson stood, in a little place, to have come into the House of Commons, and they would not choose him; they said 'No courtier.' And, which is worse, Bab May went down in great state to Winchelsea with

* "Life."   † Aubrey's "Lives," vol. ii. p. 373.
‡ "Constitutional History," c. 12.   § Ante, p. 244.

the duke of York's letters, not doubting to be chosen; and there the people chose a private gentleman in spite of him, and cried out they would have no court pimp to be their burgess; which are things that bode very ill." * The indiscretion of the king, to apply the least offensive term to his conduct, was sufficient to alienate the affection which had been so lavishly bestowed upon him, even if the people, with their bitter experience, stopped short of rebellion. There were large numbers of the humbler retainers of the royal household who, when Lady Castlemaine ordered of her tradesmen every jewel and service of plate that she fancied, and told her servant to send a note of their cost to the Privy Purse, were themselves absolutely starving. It sounds very like exaggeration when we read that one of the king's musicians, "Evans, the famous man upon the harp, having not his equal in the world, did the other day die for mere want, and was fain to be buried by the alms of the parish." But this is not idle gossip of Mr. Pepys. There is an account in existence of " The state of the Treasurer of the Chamber, his office, at Midsummer, 1665," which shows the yearly payments due to officers of the king's household, and of the sums " behind unpaid." † There were forty-two musicians, to whom their salaries had been due for three years and one quarter. High and low, the Bishop Almoner and the rat-killer, the Justice in Oyer beyond Trent and the bird-keeper, footmen, falconers, huntsmen, bear-warders, wardrobe officers, watermen, messengers, yeomen of the guard, and many others, useful or useless, had been " behind unpaid," some for five years, some for four years, some for three or two years, very few only for one year. To three apothecaries, more than 5000l. was due. That these persons, frequenting the coffee-houses or alehouses of London, did not spread abroad their griefs, cannot reasonably be imagined. A sullen discontent, a silent indignation, settled deep into the hearts of the whole community. If a sword had been drawn against the English people, there would have been another Civil War, with one certain result. Men were satisfied for twenty years longer to endure and murmur. " It is strange how everybody do now-a-days reflect upon Oliver, and commend him, what brave things he did, and made all the neighbour princes fear him; while here a prince, come in with all the love and prayers and good-liking of his people, who have given greater signs of loyalty and willingness to serve him with their estates than ever was done by any people, hath lost all so soon, that it is a miracle what way a man could devise to lose so much in so little time." Not at all strange, Mr. Pepys, that the people looked back upon Oliver, and what brave things he did. But the vicissitudes of nearly twenty years—the dread of property becoming insecure—the religious divisions—the respect for the monarchical principle, however degraded in the immediate wearer of the Crown—the love for the ancient Church, amidst all its pride and intolerance—these considerations kept Englishmen quiet. The government, moreover, was corrupt, but in England it was not cruel, beyond the cruelty of preventing men's religious opinions by statute. On this side the Tweed the government provoked little more than the contempt of those whom it fined and imprisoned for non-conformity. In Scotland, it drove them to desperation; and when they rebelled

* Pepys, " Diary," October 21, 1666.
† Preface to "Secret Services of Charles II. and James II." Camden Society.

the thumbikin and the boot were ready to be administered to the victims, under the forms of justice by the apostate Lauderdale, or they were shot down and hanged by the brute Dalziel. The archbishops of St. Andrews and Glasgow hounded on the persecutors.

The restoration of the monarchy was, to Scotland the establishment of a policy of unmitigated despotism. The orders of the king and council in matters ecclesiastical were to have the force of laws. A large army was raised to hold the people in subjection, whilst episcopacy, which they abominated, was established, without any modification by general assemblies. The churches were deserted; and the non-conforming preachers had immense congregations in barns and fields; on wild heaths, and in the gorges of the mountains. The assemblies were dispersed by the soldiers; but no violence could put them down. Those who were most zealous had soldiers quartered in their houses, to grind out of them the fines which they were unwilling or unable to pay. In the West of Scotland, where the Non-conformists were most numerous and most determined, sir James Turner, a fitting instrument of tyranny, was sent to enforce obedience by mulcts and severer penalties, levied at his bidding by his rapacious dragoons. To a resolute and hardy population, maddened by injuries, and defiant of danger, resistance in arms seemed not only a worldly policy but a sacred duty. A body of Covenanters of the West marched to Dumfries, and seized sir James Turner. They were for the most part peasants, with a few Presbyterian ministers amongst them. But they were not ignorant of military discipline, and soon became alarming in their numbers and their subordination. About three thousand set off to march from Lanark to Edinburgh, but these bands gradually dwindled to eight or nine hundred. When they had reached within four miles of the city, they learnt that it was fortified, and its gates shut against them. They retreated to the Pentland Hills. On the evening of the 28th of November, Dalziel came upon them with a body of horse. Twice the insurgents drove back the cavalry; but their ranks were at last broken, and they were utterly dispersed. The slaughter was inconsiderable; but many were executed, and some tortured. "One Maccail, that was only a probationer preacher, and who had been chaplain in sir James Steward's house, had gone from Edinburgh to them; it was believed he was sent by the party in town, and that he knew their correspondents; so he was put to the torture, which in Scotland they call the boots; for they put a pair of iron boots close on the leg, and drive wedges between these and the leg. The common torture was only to drive these in the calf of the leg; but I have been told they were sometimes driven upon the shin-bone. He bore the torture with great constancy; and either he could say nothing, or he had the firmness not to discover those who trusted him. Every man of them could have saved his own life, if he would accuse any other; but they were all true to their friends. Maccail, for all the pains of the torture, died in a rapture of joy: his last words were, farewell sun, moon, and stars—farewell kindred and friends—farewell world and time—farewell weak and frail body—welcome eternity—welcome angels and saints—welcome Saviour of the world, and welcome God the judge of all; which he spoke with a voice and manner that struck all that heard it." *

* Burnet's "History of his own Time."

On the 31st of December, 1666, the official person who had the most intimate knowledge of the affairs of the navy thus writes in his Diary: "Thus ends this year of public wonder and mischief to this nation. Public matters in a most sad condition; seamen discouraged for want of pay, and are become not to be governed: nor, as matters are now, can any fleet go out next year. . . . A sad, vicious, negligent court, and all sober men there fearful of the ruin of the whole kingdom this next year; from which, good God deliver us." * Such ships as were in commission were commanded by haughty young nobles, wholly ignorant of naval affairs. One of these fair-weather captains, a son of lord Bristol, was heard to say that he hoped not to see " a tarpawlin " in command of a ship for a twelvemonth. The honest tarpawlins confessed that " the true English valour we talk of is almost spent and worn out." † Direful calamities at the hands of the All-seeing had not broken the national spirit; but the infamous corruption of the higher classes was eating into the foundation of England's greatness. Her people were losing that masculine simplicity, that healthy devotion to public and private duties, that religious earnestness—intolerant, no doubt, but rarely simulated by the followers of Calvin or the followers of Arminius in the greatest heat of their conflicts—the English were losing that nationality, whose excess may be ludicrous, but whose utter want is despicable. Their high intellect was being emasculated by a corrupt literature. Science was groping in the dark under the auspices of the Royal Society; and Divinity was holding forth from orthodox pulpits on the excesses of the early Reformers, and the duty of non-resistance to kings deriving their power direct from Heaven. These follies probably did little harm; and men gradually shook off their delusions, and went forward to seek for experimental Science that had useful ends, and for practical Theology that would make them wiser and happier. But the corruptions of the Court soon worked upon the principles of the people,

D'Avenant.

tnrough a debasing popular Literature. The Drama had come back after an exile of twenty years. When the Drama was banished, Tragedy was still a queen wearing her purple and her pall; and the " wood-notes wild " of

* Pepys.   † Ibid. October 29, 1666.

Comedy were as fresh and joyous as those of the lark in spring. The Drama came back in the shameless garb, and with the brazen look, and the drunken voice, of the lowest strumpet. The people were to be taught that Shakspere was a barbarian, and not to be tolerated in his own simplicity. He was, if heard at all, to furnish the *libretto* of an opera, to be got up with dresses and decorations by sir William D'Avenant. "I saw," says Evelyn in 1662, "Hamlet, Prince of Denmark, played; but now the old plays began to disgust this refined age, since his majesty being so long abroad." This refined age, when it brought women to personate female characters, heard from the lips of Eleanor Gwynn and Mary Davis, the foulest verses, which they were selected to speak to furnish additional relish to the licentiousness of the poet. The theatre was at the very height of fashion when it was most shameless. The actresses were removed from "The King's House," to become the mistresses of the king, by their gradual promotion from being the mistresses of the king's servants. Nelly threw up her parts, and would act no more when lord Buckhurst gave her a hundred a year, in 1667. In 1671, when Mr. Evelyn walked with the the king through St. James's Park, Mrs. Nelly looked out of her garden on a terrace at the top of the wall, and there was "familiar discourse" between his majesty and the "impudent comedian," at which scene Mr. Evelyn was "heartily sorry." It was well for England that her salt had not wholly lost its savour; that the middle-class of London, though they rushed to the savage Bull-baitings

Costume of the Richer Commonalty, temp. Charles II.

of the Bear-garden, which had been shut up during the time of the Long Parliament, were too indignant at the costliness of the court to be enamoured of its gilded profligacy. It was better still for England that some little of the old Puritan spirit was left amongst the humblest classes—that the Bible was read by the poor, and Rochester and Shadwell were to them unknown.*

* We recommend to the *genre* painters subjects for a Picture of two compartments, re-

Amidst the abandonment of the Court to its pleasures,—the rapacity of the royal favourites, who received gratuities and pensions not to be counted by hundreds but by thousands of pounds—the jealousy of the Parliament in granting money which they knew would be wasted—the spring of 1667 arrived, without any preparations for carrying on the naval war. When the king's treasurer had got some of the money which the House of Commons tardily voted, there were more pressing necessities to be supplied than the pay of sailors, or the fitting out of ships. The satirical verse of Andrew Marvell has represented this crisis with historic accuracy :

> " Each day they bring the tale, and that too true,
> How strong the Dutch their equipage renew.
> Meantime through all the yards their orders run
> To lay the ships up, cease the keels begun.
> The timber rots, the useless axe doth rust ;
> Th' unpractised saw lies buried in its dust ;
> The busy hammer sleeps, the ropes untwine,
> The store and wages all are mine and thine ;
> Along the coasts and harbours they take care
> That money lacks, nor forts be in repair." *

On the 23rd of January, the sailors were in mutiny at Wapping, and the Horse Guards were going to quell them. They were in insurrection for the want of pay. When the money was obtained from Parliament they still mutinied, for they were still unpaid. On the 5th of June the Portuguese ambassador had gone on board 'The Happy Return,' in the Hope, ordered to sail for Holland ; but the crew refused to go until they were paid. Other ships were in mutiny the same day. On the 8th of June the Dutch fleet of eighty sail was off Harwich. It was time to stir. The king sent lord Oxford to raise the militia of the eastern counties ; and " my lord Barkeley is going down to Harwich also to look after the militia there ; and there is also the duke of Monmouth, and with him a great many young Hectors, the lord Chesterfield, my lord Mandeville, and others ;" but, adds Mr. Pepys, " to little purpose, I fear, but to debauch the country women thereabouts." On the 10th of June the Dutch were at the Nore. Then, indeed, the matter was past the skill of the " young Hectors." The enemy had advanced almost as high as the Hope. Monk has rushed down to Gravesend— "in his shirt," writes Marvell. Money is now forthcoming to pay the revolted seamen ; but, sighs Pepys, " people that have been used to be deceived by us as to money won't believe us ; and we know not, though we have it, how almost to promise it." The Dutch fleet has dropped down to Sheerness. " The alarm was so great," writes Evelyn, " that it put both country and city into fear—a panic and consternation, such as I hope I shall never see more ; everybody was flying, none knew why or whither." Monk was at

presenting High Life and Low Life, after Sketches by Mr. Pepys, at Epsom, on Sunday, the 14th of July, 1667 :—

" By eight o'clock to the Well, where much company. And to the town to the King's Head ; and hear that my Lord Buckhurst and Nelly are lodged at the next house, and Sir Charles Sedley with them ; and keep a merry house. Poor girl ! I pity her."

" I walked upon the Downs, where a flock of sheep was ; and the most pleasant and innocent sight that ever I saw in my life. We found a shepherd, and his little boy reading, far from any houses or sight of people, the Bible to him."

* " Instructions to a Painter about the Dutch Wars,"—Works, vol. ii. p. 101 ; 1726.

Gravesend, "with a great many idle lords and gentlemen." Opposite them was Tilbury. Did any of these "idle lords and gentlemen, with their pistols and fooleries," think of the time when the great queen stood like a rock upon that shore; and her people gathered round her with invincible confidence; and the greatest armament that ever threatened England was scattered by her true gentlemen—the Raleighs and Carews, who loved their country with a filial love, and hurled foul scorn at the invader? Charles, if not belied by the Dutch, was deliberating in Council on the propriety of a flight to Windsor, by way of example to his terrified people.* On the 11th, news came to London that Sheerness was taken. The drums were beating all night for the trained bands to be in arms in the morning, with bullets and powder, and a fortnight's victuals. The Londoners were momentarily relieved of their panic; for the Dutch fleet had sailed up the Medway. Chatham was safe, the courtiers said. Monk had stopped the river with chains and booms; and Upnor Castle was fortified. Chains and booms, and Upnor Castle, availed not long against the resolution of Ruyter and De Witt, who were about to exact the penalty for the wanton desolation of the coasts of the Texel. They went about their work in a manly way—not burning Gravesend, which was really defenceless, but breaking through the defences of the Medway, behind which our ships lay unrigged. They were quickly set on fire. In Upnor Castle and the forts at Chatham, there was little ammunition; and the Dutch "made no more of Upnor Castle's shooting, than of a fly." The proud ship which bore the king to England, "the Royal Charles," was secured by the invaders as a trophy; and when they had made their strength sufficiently manifest to the panic-stricken sycophants of the depraved court, they quietly sailed back to the Thames, and enforced a real blockade of London for many weeks. The spirit of patriotism was trodden out of the sailors by neglect and oppression. There were many of them on board the Dutch ships, who called out to their countrymen on the river, "We did heretofore fight for tickets; now we fight for dollars." The sailors' wives went up and down the streets of Wapping, crying "This comes of your not paying our husbands." Mobs assembled at Westminster, shouting for "a Parliament, a Parliament." They broke the Lord Chancellor's windows, and set up a gibbet before his gate. Had the Dutch gone up the Thames beyond Deptford, it is not impossible that the iniquities of the Stuarts might have more quickly come to an end. Such a consummation was not to be desired. The English people had to endure two more decades of misrule, that they might gather strength to fit themselves for constitutional government. Besides the disgrace and humiliation, England suffered little from the Dutch in the Thames and the Medway. The Londoners were cut off from their supply of sea-borne coal—no irremediable evil in summer, but one that probably hastened a peace. On the 24th of June, Mr. Evelyn writes, "The Dutch fleet still continuing to stop up the river, so as nothing could stir or come out, I was before the Council, and commanded by his majesty to go with some others and search about the environs of the city, now exceedingly distressed for want of fuel, whether there could be any peat or turf fit for use." The report was, that there was abundance. On the 28th the Dutch fleet was lying triumphantly at the Nore,—"a dreadful spectacle," says Evelyn, "as

* "Correspondence of Evelyn." vol. iii. p. 213; 1852.

ever Englishmen saw, and a dishonour never to be wiped off." It was a spectacle of dishonour which has never been seen since, and will never be seen again, unless there should again be such a combination of anti-national elements as in the days of Charles the Second—a profligate and corrupt Court, avaricious and selfish ministers, a bribed Parliament, an intolerant Church, a slavish Bench of Justice. If such instruments of evil should again unite their forces, then the ordinary supineness of office may become a heartless indifference to every duty; then the pretensions of the high-born to engross all the functions of administration may become the most shameless avidity for the exorbitant pay of useless posts; then the people may be gradually brought to lick the dust like oriental slaves; then our soldiers and sailors may be marshalled in our enemy's ranks, and pilot our enemy's ships, and exult that they fight for dollars. The disgrace of 1667 will not have been in vain, if it teach the great lesson that the corruption of the high is the corruption of the national honour at its fountain head.

On the 29th of July a treaty of peace between England, Holland, and France, was concluded at Breda.

The fall of lord Clarendon from power, in 1667, is one of those events whose causes can only be adequately developed, if they can ever be fully and satisfactorily set forth, through an intimate acquaintance with the public documents and private memorials of the period. To attempt such an exposition here, even if the materials for it were at our hand, would manifestly be beyond the scope of a History so general as this. The intrigues of rival statesmen, the vacillations of the sovereign, the passions of parliamentary factions, require to be fully examined, if we would thoroughly comprehend the concurring influences which hurled the most eminent statesman of the Restoration from his high position. A faint outline of these combinations, in connection with an estimate of the character of the fallen man, is all that we can pretend to offer.

Sir Edward Hyde, of all the companions of the adversity of Charles, was by far the fittest minister to guide him through the extreme difficulties of his altered position. He was hated by the queen-mother. His habits of thought and action were diametrically opposed to the levities and vices of the king and the younger courtiers. He had many early associations with the struggle for civil rights, which made him a stumbling-block in the way of any broad attempts to emulate the despotisms of other European monarchies. He was by principle and education devotedly attached to the Protestantism of the Church of England. He was thus no object of affection amongst many whose poverty he had shared, but from whose habits he was altogether alien. But his great abilities were indispensable to Charles; and thus sir Edward Hyde became the earl of Clarendon, Lord Chancellor, and the real minister of England, all other administrative functionaries being subordinate to him. It was necessary to govern through Parliaments; and Clarendon, by his experience, his dignified carriage, his rhetorical and literary powers, was eminently fitted for the duties of a parliamentary minister. He was for a while all-successful. The rooted dislike of the queen-mother was neutralised, even to the point of her graciously receiving the plebeian duchess of York. The king and his associates were compelled to manifest respect to the decorous Chancellor, and to compensate their submission to his wisdom by their ridicule of his manners.

Clarendon's notions of the prerogative, and of the rights of parliaments, were not in accordance with the vague schemes of being "every inch a king," that silly nobles and slavish churchmen whispered to Charles; but then Clarendon had imbibed none of the broader doctrines of civil liberty which had entered into the popular mind since 1640, and was heartily disposed to re-model the monarchy upon the precedents of the days of Elizabeth and the first Stuart. Charles was indifferent to the Church of England, for which Clarendon was strenuous; and Charles was for such a toleration of Protestant Dissenters as would include the Catholic; but when Clarendon equally persecuted Puritans and Papists, Charles let him have his way, for, a Papist at heart himself, if anything, he thought that a general persecution would hasten on a general toleration. There was thus, with the court, a perpetual compromise between the dislike of Clarendon's personal character and the desire to snatch from his policy such advantages as a less scrupulous minister could not have obtained from Parliament. He was hated by the king and the favourites because he had not, when the Parliament was lavish and the nation mad, extracted from the temper of the hour a far greater fixed revenue, such as would have made Parliaments less necessary for the king. But when Parliament had the presumption to ask for an account of the disposal of the sums that had been voted, then Clarendon's opposition to any interference with the old power of the Crown made his conscientious scruples about the limits of prerogative less obnoxious. The principles of the man were not fitted for the retrogressive objects of the Crown, or the progressive movement of the Nation. He was a Conservative, to use the party name of our own day, clinging to the non-essentials of old institutions and laws, with the obstinate tenacity which makes Conservatism a mere negation. The triumphs of statesmanship are not to be accomplished like the victory of the deliverers of Gibeon, whilst the sun remains in the same place of the heavens.

As early as 1663, the earl of Bristol, a Catholic peer, in his seat in Parliament, attributing to the Lord Chancellor all the evils under which the country laboured, impeached him of high-treason. The opinion of the judges was required; and they answered, that by the laws of the realm no articles of high-treason could be originally exhibited in the House of Peers, by any one peer against another; and that the matters alleged in the charge against the Lord Chancellor did not amount to treason. Personal hostility appears to have provoked this ill-judged attack. Four years afterwards it was pretty well known that the king was alienated from his grave adviser. Clarendon had made enemies all around him by his faults as well as by his virtues. He was haughty and passionate. He was grasping and ostentatious. He had returned from exile in the deepest poverty. In seven years he had acquired a sufficient fortune to build a mansion superior to ducal palaces, and to furnish it with the most costly objects of taste and luxury. He was envied by the nobility. He was hated by the people; for in the grandeur of what they called "Dunkirk House" they saw what they believed to be the evidence of foreign bribery. The duke of Buckingham had been banished from court through a quarrel with lady Castlemaine; and revenge threw him into the ranks of those to whom the government was obnoxious. He became the advocate of the sectaries; he became the avowed and especial enemy of the Chancellor. For a short time he was sent to the Tower, upon the supposed discovery of some treasonable intrigues; but he soon regained his liberty, and his royal master was propitiated when the duke had made his peace with "the lady." She interceded for Buckingham; but at first was unsuccessful. The court tattle said that the king had called Castlemaine a jade that meddled with things she had nothing to do with; and that Castlemaine called the king a fool, who suffered his businesses to be carried on by those who did not understand them.* But very soon "the lady" carried her point; Buckingham was restored to favour; Clarendon was sacrificed. Charges of the most serious nature were got up against him. The imputation of having sold Dunkirk for his private advantage was confidently maintained. It became known that whilst the Dutch were in the Thames, and the Treasury was without a guinea, he had resisted the advice of the Council that Parliament should be called together, upon the plea that it had been prorogued to a more distant day; but had recommended that money should be levied to pay the troops in the places where they were quartered, and that the sums so raised from individuals should be deducted out of their future taxes. That he had some scheme for forced contributions as a temporary expedient was admitted by himself. Other accusations, all of a very vague nature, were poured into the king's ear; who, no doubt, was not indisposed to get rid of one who was a severe monitor, and, though pliant in some things, was not an unscrupulous tool. Charles, through the duke of York, asked Clarendon to resign. He indignantly refused, saying, that his resignation would amount to a confession of guilt. After a conference of two hours the great minister saw that his disgrace was resolved upon—disgrace which "had been certainly designed in my lady Castlemaine's chamber." Her aviary looked into Whitehall garden; and when he went from the king, she rushed from her bed at twelve o'clock at noon—"and thither her woman brought her her night-gown; and she stood blessing herself at the old man's going away; and several of the gallants of Whitehall,—of which there were many staying to see the Chancellor's return—did talk to her in her bird-cage." † The king sent for the seals. Evelyn went to see Clarendon, and says, "I found him in his bed-chamber, very sad. . . . He had enemies at Court, especially the buffoons and ladies of pleasure, because he thwarted some of them, and stood in their way." The Parliament had assembled. On the 15th of October, the two Houses voted an address of thanks to the throne for the removal of the Chancellor, and the king in his reply pledged himself never to employ lord Clarendon again in any capacity. This was not enough. Seventeen charges were prepared against him by a Committee of the Commons; and on the 12th of November, the House impeached him of high-treason at the bar of the Peers. There were animated debates in that House, in which Clarendon had many supporters. The two Houses got angry. The court became alarmed. Clarendon was advised to leave the kingdom clandestinely, but he refused. Then the king sent him an express command to retire to the Continent. He obeyed; addressing a letter, vindicating himself, to the House of Peers. An Act was passed on the 29th of December, banishing him for life, unless he should return by the following 1st of February.

* Pepys, July 12.   † Pepys, August 27.

The close of the political careeer of Clarendon, under circumstances of punishment and disgrace so disproportioned to his public or private demerits, has left no stain upon his memory. Whatever were his faults as a statesman, he stands upon a far higher elevation than the men who accomplished his ruin. As to the king, his parasites and his mistresses, who were in raptures to be freed from his observation and censure, their dislike was Clarendon's high praise. In the encouragement which Charles indirectly gave to attacks upon the minister who had saved him from many of the worst consequences of the rashness of the royalists, and had laboured in the service of his father and himself for twenty-seven years, either in war, or in exile, or in triumph, with a zeal and ability which no other possessed, we see only the heartless ingratitude of the king, and his utterly selfish notions of the duties of a sovereign. Clarendon had become disagreeable to him, through the very qualities which made the government endurable to high-minded and sober men. Nor was it from any desire to carry out more tolerant principles of ecclesiastical rule, nor from any conviction that his Chancellor's notions of civil policy were antiquated and in many respects unsuited to the times, that the king sought other advisers. The men who succeeded the great minister made one attempt to remove some of the oppressions under which the Non-conformists laboured. They failed; and their failure was followed by a more indiscriminate persecution. They made one bold endeavour at a course of foreign policy which might have again placed England at the head of a union of Protestant free states. For a very brief period the influence of France was shaken off; and then England's king was the pensioner of Louis. Clarendon went into exile. He was some time before he was permitted to find a resting place; but he found it at last at Montpelier. He was probably never sincerely reconciled to the loss of power and grandeur; but he believed that he was reconciled; and in dedicating himself to a renewal of that literary employment which has given him the best title to the respectful remembrance of mankind, he found that consolation which industry never failed to bestow upon a robust understanding, that was also open to religious impressions. He says of himself:—"It pleased God, in a short time, after some recollections, and upon his entire confidence in Him, to restore him to that serenity of mind and resignation of himself to the disposal and good pleasure of God, that they who conversed most with him could not discover the least murmur or impatience in him, or any unevenness in his conversations."

When the seals were taken away from Clarendon they were given to sir Orlando Bridgman. The conduct of affairs fell into new hands. Southampton, the most respectable of Charles's first advisers was dead. Monk was worn out. Buckingham first came into power with Arlington as secretary of state, and sir William Coventry. But soon the ministry comprised the five persons known as "The Cabal"—a name which signified what we now call The Cabinet; but which name was supposed incorrectly to have been formed out of the initial letters of the names of the members,—Clifford, Arlington, Buckingham, Ashley, Lauderdale. The word Cabal had been used long before, to indicate a secret council. Of the new advisers of Charles, Buckingham was the most influential at Court, and he made great efforts to be at the same time the most popular. When Buckingham was taken to the Tower, Clarendon was depressed by the acclamations of the people, who shouted round the prisoner. As Clarendon had supported the Church, Buckingham was the champion of the sectaries. Baxter says, " As the Chancellor had made himself the head of the prelatical party, who were all for setting up themselves by force, and suffering none that were against them, so Buckingham would now be the head of all those parties that were for

York House.

liberty of conscience." The candid Non-conformist adds, " For the man was of no religion, but notoriously and professedly lustful;" but he qualifies his censure with this somewhat high praise,—" and yet of greater wit and parts, and sounder principles as to the interests of humanity and the common good, than most lords in the court." * The duke lived in York House, the temporary palace which his father had built, of which nothing now remains but the Water Gate. Here he dwelt during the four or five years of the Cabal administration, affording, as he always continued to afford, abundant materials for the immortal character of Zimri :—

> " A man so various, that he seem'd to be
> Not one, but all mankind's epitome :
> Stiff in opinion, always in the wrong,
> Was every thing by starts and nothing long ;
> But, in the course of one revolving moon,
> Was chemist, fiddler, statesman, and buffoon :
> Then all for women, painting, rhyming, drinking,
> Besides ten thousand freaks that died in thinking." †

* "Life," Part iii. p. 21.　　　　　† Dryden, " Absalom and Achitophel."

Ashley, afterwards earl of Shaftesbury—the Antony Ashley Cooper of the Protectorate, who clung to the Rump Parliament till he saw that Monk had sealed its fate, and then made his peace with Charles with surprising readiness —the ablest, and in some respects the most incomprehensible of the statesmen of his time,—has had the double immortality of the satire of Butler as well as of Dryden.   In Thanet House, in Aldersgate-street, Ashley was at

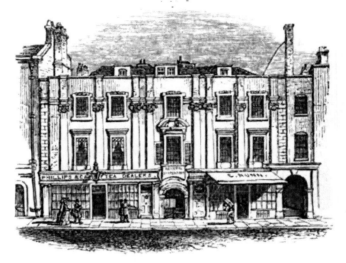

Shaftesbury House, Aldersgate Street.

hand to influence the politics of the city.   When the mob were roasting rumps in the streets, and were about to handle him roughly as he passed in his carriage, he turned their anger into mirth by his jokes.   When the king frowned upon him, he went straight from office to opposition, and made the court disfavour as serviceable to his ambition as the court's honours and rewards :—

> " For by the witchcraft of rebellion
> Transform'd to a feeble state-cameleon,
> By giving aim from side to side
> He never fail'd to save his tide ;
> But got the start of every state,
> And at a change ne'er came too late." *

In a few years more Shaftesbury had earned the praise, or dispraise, of Dryden,

> " A daring pilot in extremity,
> Pleas'd with the danger when the waves run high."

---

* "Hudibras," Part iii.

The history of the Cabal ministry, which extends over a period of six years, is not the history of a Cabinet united by a common principle of agreement upon great questions of domestic and foreign policy. Nor is it the history of a Sovereign asserting his own opinions, and watching over the administration of affairs, under the advice of a Council, and through the agency of the great officers of State. The monarchs of England, from the Norman times, had been, for the most part, men of remarkable energy of character; and in default of their capacity for warlike action and public business, some representative of adequate qualifications wielded the executive power. The great kings of the Plantagenet race were essentially their own ministers. Henry VII., Henry VIII., Elizabeth, were remarkable for their laborious attention to the duties of their great office. Charles I., whether aiming to be despotic, or struggling for his crown and his life, was zealous, active, and self-confident. Charles II. was absolutely indifferent to any higher objects than personal gratification; and to this circumstance we must refer some of the extraordinary anomalies of the government after the fall of Clarendon. Abraham Cowley heard Tom Killigrew say to the king, "There is a good, honest, able man that I could name, that if your majesty would employ, and command to see all things well executed, all things would soon be mended; and this is one Charles Stuart, who now spends his time in employing his lips about the Court, and hath no other employment; but if you would give him this employment, he were the fittest man in the world to perform it." * Killigrew's estimate of the character of his royal master was altogether false. He was neither honest nor able, with reference to any aptitude for the condition of life to which he was called. He did not desire, he said, to sit like a Turkish sultan, and sentence men to the bowstring; but he could not endure that a set of fellows should inquire into his conduct. Always professing his love of Parliaments, he was always impatient of their interference. There is something irresistibly comic in the way in which he tried to manage the House of Lords, in 1669, by being present at their debates. He first sat decently upon the throne, thinking to prevent unpleasant reflections by this restraint upon the freedom of speech. But what he commenced out of policy, under the advice of the crafty Lauderdale, he continued for mere amusement. "The king," writes Burnet, "who was often weary of time, and did not know how to get round the day, liked the going to the House as a pleasant diversion: so he went constantly. And he quickly left the throne, and stood by the fire, which drew a crowd about him, that broke all the decency of that House; for, before that time every lord sat regularly in his place; but the king's coming broke the order of their sitting as became senators. The king's coming thither had a much worse effect; for he became a common solicitor, not only in public affairs, but even in matters of justice. He would in a very little time have gone the round of the House, and spoke to every one that he thought worth speaking to. And he was apt to do that upon the solicitation of any of the ladies in favour, or of any that had credit with them." With such a sovereign, as utterly indifferent to the proprieties of his public station as to the decencies of his private life, we can scarcely expect that there should have been any consistent

* Pepys, December 2, 1666.

principle of administration. The terrible experience of thirty years imposed upon Charles some caution in the manifestation of his secret desire to be as absolute as his brother Louis of France. The great Bourbon was encumbered with no Parliament; he had not to humble himself to beg for supplies of insolent Commons; he was not troubled with any set of fellows to inquire into his conduct, and ask for accounts of expenditure; he had the gabelle and other imposts which fell upon the prostrate poor, without exciting the animosity of the dangerous rich; he was indeed a king, whose shoe-latchet nobles were proud to unloose, and whose transcendant genius and virtue prelates rejoiced to compare with the divine attributes. Such a blissful destiny as that of the Bourbon could not befall the Stuart by ordinary means. Charles would become as great as Louis, as far as his notion of greatness went, by becoming the tributary of Louis. He would sell his country's honour,—he would renounce the religion he had sworn to uphold,— for an adequate price. But this bargain should be a secret one. It should be secret, even from a majority of his own ministers. Upon this point hinges the disgraceful history of the Cabal.

But though Charles and two of his ministers, Arlington and Clifford, were ready to go any length to make the policy of Whitehall utterly subservient to the policy of the Louvre, and to bring the creed of Lambeth into very near if not exact conformity with the creed of the Vatican—though Buckingham and Shaftesbury had some complicity in these iniquitous purposes—yet there was a power in the State which had become too formidable for king and ministers utterly to despise. The Parliament, servile and corrupt in many compliances, was yet a power that might be roused into sudden indignation by any outrageous exercise of prerogative, and, above all, by any daring attack upon the Protestant tendencies of the nation. The shiftings of politicians, of whom Shaftesbury was the type, from courtiers one day to demagogues the next, were the natural result of the want, during the first ten years of the Restoration, of any great principle of action which would raise politicians on either side above the mere influences of personal ambition. The Monarchy was an accomplished fact: to fight again for a Commonwealth was no longer possible. The Church was re-established, in triumphant intolerance: Presbyterians and Independents had no standing place for a new struggle. The Crown and the Parliament were both open to corruption; and their venality tainted, though not in an equal degree, the advocates of non-resistance and the enemies of that debasing principle. Placemen and patriots each held out the "itching palm" to France. There was no manifest struggle of opinion against power, till the design to bring back England to the communion of Rome became evident. The resistance to this attempt roused the nation out of its apparent apathy. The intolerant passion of the multitude—blind, cruel, frantic in its fears—was quickly absorbed into the general determination that England should be Protestant, which identified itself with civil liberty. Religious liberty grew slowly out of the contest, when the reign of the great enemies of all freedom was terminated by their own folly and bigotry.

The story of the next twenty years, which brings us to the great era of our modern history, would be incomprehensible, if we did not constantly bear in mind, that public opinion had become a real element in national progress. The Crown was constantly dreaming of the revival of despotism, to be accomplished by force and by corruption. Yet the Crown, almost without a struggle, was bereft of the power of imprisoning without trial, by the passing of the Habeas Corpus Act; and it lost its control over the freedom of the Press by the expiration of the Licensing system. The Church thought it possible to destroy non-conformity by fines and fetters. In its earlier Liturgy it prayed to be delivered from "false doctrine and heresy;" it now prayed for deliverance from "false doctrine, heresy, and schism." Yet when it had ejected the Puritans from the Churches, and had shut up the Conventicles, it laid the foundation of schisms which, in a few years, made dissent a principle which churchmen could not hope to crush and statesmen could not dare to despise. How can we account for the striking anomaly, that with a profligate Court, a corrupt Administration, a venal House of Commons, a tyrannous Church, the nation during the reign of Charles II. was manifestly progressing in the essentials of freedom, unless we keep in view that from the beginning of the century there had been an incessant struggle of the national mind against every form of despotic power? The desire for liberty, civil and spiritual, had become almost an instinct. The great leaders in this battle had passed away. The men who by fits aspired to be tribunes of the people were treacherous or inconstant. But the spirit of the nation was not dead. It made itself heard in Parliament, with a voice that grew louder and louder, till the torrent was once again dammed up. A few more years of tyranny without disguise——and then the end.

The first movements of the Cabal ministry were towards a high and liberal policy—toleration for non-conformists, and an alliance with free Protestant States. A greater liberty to dissenters from the Church followed the fall of Clarendon. We see transient and accidental motives for this passing toleration, rather than the assertion of a fixed principle. The bishops had supported Clarendon, and the king and his new ministers and favorites were therefore out of humour with the bishops. The fire of London had rendered it impossible to carry on the spiritual instruction of the people by the established Clergy; and therefore assemblies to hear the sermons of Presbyterians and Independents were not visited with the penalties of the Conventicle Act. It was, says Baxter, "at the first a thing too gross to forbid an undone people all public worshipping of God, with too great rigour; and if they had been so forbidden, poverty had left them so little to lose as would have made them desperately go on." * Sir Orlando Bridgman, now Lord Keeper, desired a conference with Baxter, "about a comprehension and toleration," in January 1668. The Lord Chief Baron Hale, and Bishop Wilkins, were agreed with the Lord Keeper in promoting this salutary work. The king, says Burnet, "seemed now to go into moderation and comprehension with so much heartiness, that both Bridgman and Wilkins believed he was in earnest in it; though there was nothing that the popish councils were more fixed in, than to oppose all motions of that kind. But the king saw it was necessary to recover the affections of his people." The opportunity of recovering the affections of the great Puritan body, scattered, depressed, but still influential, was thrown away. There were propositions on the part of the non-confor-

* "Life," Part iii. p. 22.

mists; and amendments were suggested and accepted. Baxter says that fourteen hundred non-conformable ministers would have yielded to these "hard terms;" but that when the Parliament met, the active prelates and prelatists prevailed to prevent any bill of comprehension or indulgence to be brought in; "and the Lord Keeper that had called us, and set us on work, himself turned that way, and talked after as if he understood us not." In the king's speech, February 10, 1668, he recommended that they would seriously think of some course to beget a better union and composure in the minds of his Protestant subjects in matters of religion. On the 8th of April, a motion in the House of Commons that his majesty should send for such persons as he should think fit, to make proposals to him in order to the uniting of his Protestant subjects, was negatived by 176 votes against 70.

At the opening of the Session of Parliament in 1668, the king announced that he had made a league defensive with the States-General of the United Provinces, to which Sweden had become a party. This was the Triple Alliance. The nation saw with reasonable apprehension the development of the vast schemes of ambition of Louis XIV. He was at war with Spain; but the great empire upon which the sun never set was fast falling to pieces—not perishing like a grand old house, overthrown by a hurricane's fury, but mouldering away with the dry-rot in every timber. France, on the contrary, was rising into the position of the greatest power in Europe. Her able but vain-glorious king already looked upon the Spanish Netherlands as his certain prey. The United Provinces were hateful to him as the seat of religious and civil liberty. The crisis was come when England, by a return to the policy of Cromwell, might have taken her place again at the head of the free Protestant states of Europe. Was there any real intention in the king or in his ministry to raise up England as a barrier against the designs of France? Or was the mission of Temple to the Hague, by which a defensive alliance was concluded with De Witt in five days, a mere blind to conceal the dark and dangerous schemes for a secret alliance with France? When Charles announced to Parliament this league with the United Provinces and Sweden, it was thought to be "the only good public thing that hath been done since the king came into England."* It was a marvel of diplomacy. De Witt and Temple met as two honest men, without any finesse; and they quickly concluded a treaty which they believed to be for the honour and safety of both their countries. "Their candour, their freedom, and the most confidential disclosures, were the result of true policy."† This treaty, says Burnet, "was certainly the masterpiece of king Charles's life; and if he had stuck to it, it would have been both the strength and glory of his reign. This disposed the people to forgive all that was past, and to renew their confidence in him, which was shaken by the whole conduct of the Dutch war."

At the very time when the ambassador of England was negociating the treaty which promised to be "the strength and glory of his reign," the king was making proposals to Louis for a clandestine treaty, by which England was to be "leased out" to France,

"Like to a tenement or pelting farm."

---

* Pepys   † Burke, "Regicide Peace."

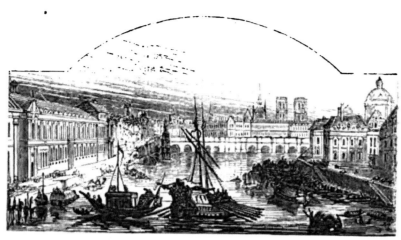

Paris in the time of Louis XIV

CHAPTER XIX.

Visit to England of the Duchess of Orleans—Secret Negotiations of the king with Louis XIV.
—Renewed persecutions of Non-conformists—Trial of William Penn—The Coventry Act
—Assault on the Duke of Ormond—Blood attempts to steal the Regalia—The mystery of
his pardon—Shutting-up of the Exchequer—Alliance with France—War with Holland—
Naval War—Invasion of the United Provinces—Murder of the De Witts—The Prince of
Orange—Shaftesbury Lord Chancellor—Declaration of Indulgence—The Test Act.

THERE is a brief record, in the Memoirs of Sir John Reresby, of
an event, seemingly unimportant, which led to very serious consequences:
"In the summer of 1670 the duchess of Orleans, the king's sister, came over
to Dover, where she was met by the king, the duke of York, and the whole
Court. Here it was that she confirmed his highness the duke in the Popish
superstition, of which he had as yet been barely suspected." * The duke of
York required no confirmation in his belief. He had long been in secret a
Roman Catholic, and attended the private rites of that religion; but at the
same time he was in communion with the Church of England. A Jesuit
missionary remonstrated with him against this double dealing. James communicated to the king his determination publicly to embrace the Roman
Catholic faith. Charles professed the same desire. He, also, though known
to be indifferent as to religious matters, had been suspected. Cosmo, the duke
of Tuscany, came to England in 1669; and the author of the duke's travels
says of Charles, that though he " observes with exact attention the religious
rites of the Church of England, there is reason to believe that he does not
exactly acquiesce, and that he may perhaps cherish other inclinations." Of

* "Travels and Memoirs of Sir John Reresby," 1831; p. 171.

the Cabal ministry Clifford and Arlington were attached to the Church of Rome. Charles and James took these ministers into their confidence at the beginning of 1669. The result was, a negociation with France, which went on for many months; and of which the duchess of Orleans came over, in 1670, to urge the points which the French king was anxious to accomplish by irresistible temptations. The secret treaty between Louis XIV. and Charles II. was concluded at Dover, on the 22nd of May, 1670.[*] Its principal stipulations were, that the king of England should publicly profess himself a Catholic, when he should consider it expedient to make such declaration; that he should join with the king of France in a war against the United Provinces; that to enable Charles to suppress any insurrection of his own subjects, he should receive two millions of livres, and be aided with an armed force of six thousand men; that of the conquests arising out of the joint war Charles should be satisfied with a part of Zealand. The secret treaty having been accomplished, another treaty was prepared, in which the article concerning the king's change of religion was omitted; and to this Shaftesbury, Buckingham, and Lauderdale were privy. Charles and his ministers went back to London, to carry on a system of falsehood towards the nation, almost unmatchable amongst the frauds of Courts and Cabinets. The beautiful duchess of Orleans returned to France, to die a victim, as many believed, to the jealousy of her husband. At the meeting of Parliament in October, 1670, the Lord Keeper Bridgman—who we may conclude to have been ignorant of the atrocious confederacy of the king and his more confidential servants—set forth the advantages of the Triple Alliance, and the necessity of being prepared against the ambition of France, by an augmentation of the fleet. The Commons voted that " his majesty should be supplied proportionably to his present occasions; " and when a grant of eight hundred thousand pounds was obtained, the Parliament was prorogued.

The manifestation of a tolerant principle at home, at the beginning of 1668, was as short lived as the inclination to a high and honourable foreign policy. The Act of 1664 against Conventicles, which was about to expire in 1670, was renewed in a more stringent shape. The 12th Clause of this Statute threw down the barriers against the most illegal exercise of its severities: " That this Act, and all clauses therein contained, should be construed most largely and beneficially for the suppressing of Conventicles, and for the justification and encouragement of all persons to be employed in the execution thereof; and that no record, warrant, or mittimus to be made by virtue of this Act, or any proceedings thereupon, shall be reversed, avoided, or any way impeached, by reason of any default in form." [†] Waller, who, at his advanced age, was still the wit of the House of Commons, said of the dissenters, " these people are like children's tops; whip them, and they stand up; let them alone, and they fall." [‡] Calamy attributes the saying to bishop Wilkins, who, with one other bishop, opposed this Statute. Sheldon, the primate, urged the most vigorous execution of the penal clauses, which were to drive

---

* It was published for the first time by Dr. Lingard, from the original in the possession of Lord Clifford. But the most important of the articles had long previously appeared in sir John Dalrymple's History.

† Statutes of the Realm, 22 Car. II. c. i. vol. v. p. 656.

‡ "Parliamentary History," vol. iv. col. 445.

the non-conforming preachers from the boarded hovels, which they called tabernacles, fitted up by their congregations when the parish churches of London were in ruins. This Act, according to Burnet, " put things in such disorder, that many of the trading men of the city began to talk of removing with their stocks over to Holland." The spirit of too many of the higher clergy was in decided opposition to the temper of bishop Wilkins. Parker, chaplain to Sheldon, and afterwards bishop of Oxford, laid himself open to the lash of Andrew Marvell, when he proclaimed that " tender consciences, instead of being complied with, must be restrained with more peremptory and unyielding rigour than naked and unsanctified villainy." * Burnet says of this Statute against Conventicles, " the king was much for having it pass, not that he intended to execute it, but he was glad to have that body of men at mercy, and to force them to concur in the design for a general toleration." This was a part of the scheme, upon which the Secret Treaty with France was built. Severity at one time against non-conformists, indulgence at another time, had one sole object in view,—to prepare the nation for such an exercise of the pre-rogative as would dispense with the laws against Papists, and make the people indifferent to a Roman Catholic king, and a Roman Catholic heir-apparent. It was not that Charles cared for any form of religion ; but he had an earnest longing for the wages of proselytism which Louis was to bestow.

The fines and imprisonments under the Conventicle Act fell, for the most part, upon obscure persons. But there was one young man, whose father was of historical celebrity, and of an elevated station, who came under the penalties for non-conformity, and fought the battle of dissent in a manner very embarrassing to intolerant churchmen and arbitrary lawyers. William Penn, the only son of the famous admiral, much to the annoyance of his family, had embraced the principles of George Fox, the founder of the sect of Quakers. He had manifested his spiritual tendencies when a student at Oxford. He had been imprisoned in Ireland, in 1667, for attending the meet-ings of Friends ; he had begun to preach and to publish in 1668. On the 14th of August, 1670, William Penn, who, in common with others of his fraternity, wholly disregarded the Conventicle Act, going to the Meeting-house in Gracechurch-street, found the door closed and guarded ; and having addressed the people outside, was arrested. On the 1st of September, he, with William Mead, a linen-draper, was indicted at the Old Bailey for preaching and speaking, to the great disturbance of the king's peace. On the 3rd of September they were brought to trial. It was altogether a remarkable scene ; in which the prisoners conducted themselves with unusual boldness ; the lord-mayor and recorder manifested more than the common insolence of authority in bad times ; and the jury could not be compelled to give a dishonest verdict. In the first instance the jury acquitted Mead, and found Penn guilty of speaking to an assembly in Gracechurch-street. They refused to find that it was an unlawful assembly, as the recorder insisted. They were locked up without fire or food through Saturday night. On Sunday, they again and again refused to amend their verdict. The recorder, Howel, a fitting predecessor of George Jefferies, who afterwards carried judicial infamy to its extreme height, in a paroxysm of fury declared it would be never well with England, till something like the

* See Marvell's " Rehearsal Transprosed," vol. ii. p. 290, ed. 1673.

inquisition was introduced. For another night the jury were locked up, to endure hunger and thirst. When they were brought into court on Monday morning, they still clung to their first verdict. But the recorder maintaining it was no verdict, they jointly and separately pronounced William Penn not guilty. The jury were each fined forty marks; Penn was fined for contempt of Court. All refused to pay the fines, and were imprisoned. The jury appealed to the Court of Common Pleas, and were released by a decision of the judges. Penn's fine was paid without his knowledge.[*]

Doctor Parker, in his zeal for arbitrary power, had ventured to say " 'Tis better to submit to the unreasonable impositions of Nero and Caligula, than to hazard the dissolution of the State." Marvell, with a terrible bitterness, pointed the moral of the crimes and the fates of Nero and Caligula.[†] The profligacy of the Court had begun to show itself in more daring outrages than the indecencies and riots which rivalled the orgies of the lowest of mankind. "The jolly blades, racing, dancing, feasting, and revelling, more resembling a luxurious and abandoned rout than a Christian Court," might scandalise decent loyal gentlemen such as Evelyn.[‡] The new concubine, Mademoiselle Querouaille, that Louis had sent over to confirm Charles in his proposed apostasy to his religion and his treason to his country, might suggest some fears to honest statesmen such as Temple. But the great

Costume of the Nobility and Gentry, temp. Charles II.

majority of the Parliament, and especially of the House of Commons, chosen

* A full account of this trial is given in "William Penn, an Historical Biography," by W. H. Dixon.   † "Rehearsal Transprosed," vol. ii. p. 155.   ‡ "Diary," October 21, 1671.

in the royalist excitement of the Restoration, had long looked upon such matters with indifference. Another feeling was now growing up. Suspicions attached to the foreign policy of the Court. The nation felt disgraced in its extravagant profligacy. Murmurs were heard even amongst the habitual supporters of the government. In a Committee of Ways and Means it was proposed in the Commons that a tax should be paid " by every one that resorts to any playhouses," of a shilling for a box-seat, sixpence for the pit, and threepence for other places. It was argued that the Players were the king's servants, " and a part of his pleasure." Sir John Coventry, member for Weymouth, asked " If the king's pleasure lay amongst the men or the women players ? " * The offence was visited with a very summary punishment, perpetrated under the orders of the duke of Monmouth, the king's son, and, as was universally believed, with the king's connivance. As sir John Coventry was passing through the Haymarket, he was set upon by Sandys, the lieutenant of Monmouth's troop, and a number of his men, and by these ruffians his nose was nearly cut off. The House had adjourned for the Christmas holidays, and upon its re-assembly the first business was to inquire into this breach of privilege. Some members wished the matter to be left to the course of law; but the great body were resolved to have reparation for this outrage. Strong words were spoken, such as indicated that the spirit of 1640 was not dead. Are we to be under proscriptions, as in the times of Sylla and Marius, asked sir John Hotham. Sir Robert Holt exclaimed that Prætorian guards had been the betrayers of the empire. He alluded to a recent assault upon the duke of Ormond, saying, " Lords' noses be as ours are, unless they be of steel." * A Bill was passed " to prevent malicious maiming and wounding." It recited the outrage upon sir John Coventry on the 21st of December; and, setting forth that sir John Sandys and three others, who had been indicted for felony, had fled from justice, enacted that they should be banished for ever unless they surrendered by a given day. Other clauses of this Bill constitute what is known as the Coventry Act, by which malicious maiming is made a capital felony. † The king, as if to show his resentment of the humiliation to which he was subjected in giving his assent to this Bill, had the indecency to grant a pardon to all the persons who, on the 28th of February, had assaulted the watch, and deliberately killed the beadle of the ward. His son, Monmouth, was the leader of that riot, as he was the contriver of the assault on sir John Coventry.

The outrage upon the duke of Ormond, to which allusion was made in the House of Commons, took place on the 6th of December, 1670. He was returning in his carriage from a city dinner. Two footmen at the side of the carriage were suddenly stopped; and the duke being dragged out, was placed on horseback behind a man to whom he was fastened by a belt. Onward they sped towards Tyburn; but the duke contrived to hoist his companion out of the saddle, and both coming to the ground together, the ruffian unloosed the belt, and fled upon the approach of some passengers. At Tyburn preparations were made for hanging the duke upon the common gallows. An inscrutable mystery surrounded this crime. Large rewards were offered,

---

* " Parliamentary History," vol. iv. col. 461.　　　　† 22 & 23 Car. II. c. 1.

with pardon to accomplices.   On the 9th of May, 1671, five months after the
assault upon the duke, the famous attempt was made to steal the regalia in
the Tower.   It was not till after the Restoration that the crown jewels were
exhibited to strangers.   In April a man in a clergyman's cassock, with his

Regalia in the Tower.

wife, came to see the regalia.   The lady being taken ill, was kindly accommodated in the house of Talbot Edwards, the keeper of the jewel-office.   An
acquaintance commenced.   The pious clergyman said the grace at dinner
with the extremest unction; proposed that his wealthy nephew should marry
the keeper's daughter; altogether a most fascinating man.   The nephew was
to come on a certain day.   The clergyman was duly there, with three friends.
One remained in the house, whilst the three others went with the keeper to
behold the crown, and orb, and sceptre, and other regal splendours.   They
gagged the old man; beat him till he was senseless; began to file the sceptre
into two pieces: but being disturbed by the unexpected arrival of Edwards'
son, made off with the crown and orb.   The alarm was given; and they were
finally seized on the Tower Wharf.   The matter being reported to the king,
they were sent for to Whitehall; and Charles was himself present at their
examination.   The chief in the robbery of the regalia was found to be a man
known as colonel Blood.   He boldly avowed that he was the leader of the
assault upon the duke of Ormond, and that he meant to have hanged him at
Tyburn.   He once, he said, had been prepared to shoot the king himself, but

awed by the presence of majesty, the pistol dropped from his hand. He might be put to death; but there were three hundred ready to avenge his blood; who, if he were spared, would become the king's faithful followers. Charles pardoned him; asked the duke of Ormond to pardon him; and gave him a pension. The king told Ormond that he had certain reasons for asking him to pardon Blood. There were mysteries about that Court of which the good nature of "the merry monarch"—to use the dainty words of glib historians—was the convenient veil. It is difficult to believe in such a state of society as we find recorded by Evelyn: "Dined at Mr. Treasurer's, in company with Monsieur de Grammont and several French noblemen, and one Blood, that impudent bold fellow who had not long before attempted to steal the imperial crown itself out of the Tower." How he came to be pardoned, and received rewards, Evelyn says he could never come to understand. "This man," he adds, "had not only a daring but a villainous unmerciful look, a false countenance, but very well spoken, and dangerously insinuating."

A supply having been obtained, the Parliament was prorogued on the 22nd of April. The king candidly said it was not his intention that they should meet again for almost a year. The prorogation was hastened by the desire to put an end to a controversy between the two Houses, as to the right of the Lords to make alterations in Money-bills sent up from the Commons. The Lords had reduced the amount of an imposition on sugar. The Commons had established the right of originating money-bills, but the Peers contended that the power of alteration, as well as of rejection, remained with them.* With the Parliament got rid of, at least for a year, the government had now a clear field for carrying out their foreign policy. France was now to receive the fullest support in its designs upon the United Provinces. The Triple Alliance was to be flung to the winds. Temple had come home in the autumn of 1670; had been coldly received by the ministers and the king; and had been told by Clifford that he might declare publicly how the ministers of the States "were a company of rogues and rascals, and not fit for his majesty or any other prince to have anything to do with." † Temple retired from public life to his garden and his books. Clifford was prepared to find resources for a war with Holland—a treacherous, wanton, and anti-national war—in an act compared with which Blood's stealing the crown was a small villainy. Bankers and other possessors of capital had been accustomed to make advancements to the Exchequer, upon receiving assignments of some portion of the revenue, to be set aside for paying the principal and interest of the money borrowed. One million three hundred thousand pounds, were at this time pledged for immediate payment. A proclamation was issued, suspending all payments for one year; but promising interest at the rate of six per cent. This interest was not paid for many years. The bankers made the advances to the government chiefly upon sums intrusted to them. Daniel Defoe, in 1671, was a boy of ten years' old; but he became early associated with trade, and he describes how the shutting the Exchequer came like a clap of thunder upon the city. The panic was universal. There was a run

* The arguments of the Conferences are given fully in the Parliamentary History, and there is a very able summary of the historical question as to this right in Mr. Hallam's "Constitutional History," Chap. xiii.
† Letters of Temple in "Courtenay's Life," vol. i. p. 344.

upon all the goldsmiths, whether their cash was in the Exchequer or in their own strong boxes. The most reputable traders were compelled to break. Private families were exposed to extreme distress. Widows and orphans were ruined, says Evelyn. The promise of payment in a year was, of course, not kept. There was not only the war to provide for; but a new mistress, exceeding in prodigality all who had gone before her. Mademoiselle de Querouaille, the agent and spy of the French king, became duchess of Portsmouth. The lady had been installed as chief "Miss," with ceremonies, short of those of the altar, "after the manner of a married bride." * "Rob me the Exchequer, Hal," said the king to Clifford; and then "all went merry as a marriage-bell." Clifford hinted the scheme to Evelyn; "but, says he, it will soon be open again, and everybody satisfied." A scheme was concerted, as iniquitous as the shutting the Exchequer. At a time when the confidence of the government of the States in the faith of England was not wholly destroyed, it was decided to capture a fleet of Dutch merchantmen from the Levant as it passed up the Channel. The scheme, worthy of a band of pirates rather than of a great nation, signally failed. The Hollanders, though not prepared for any act of hostility, appointed a convoy to the vessels which bore the rich Smyrna merchandise. Sir Robert Holmes and lord Ossory had been appointed to the command of the fleet that was to make prize of the Dutch merchantmen. Holmes had no desire to share the prize with any other admiral, and therefore in his cruise asked no assistance from sir Edward Sprague's fleet from the Mediterranean, that he met at the back of the Isle of Wight. The English admiral was unprepared for the Dutch convoy of seven men of war. He was gallantly met; and was repulsed, having captured only four sail out of sixty. The government of king Charles was not able to repay the subjects whom it had robbed, by the robbery of its neighbours, as it had proposed. The agents of this inglorious enterprise were ashamed of it. Lord Ossory deplored to Evelyn that he had been ever persuaded to engage in an expedition which revolted against his sense of honour and justice.

The declaration of war from England against Holland appeared on the 17th of March, 1672. That of France was issued at the same time. Some show was made in the English declaration of causes of offence—commercial injuries; refusal to strike to the English flag in the narrow seas; insults to the king by defamatory publications. Supporters of the government in England, as well as its opponents, felt that it was a war of wrong and tyranny Evelyn writes that the pretended occasion was that, "some time before, the Merlin yacht chancing to sail through the Dutch fleet, their admiral did not strike to that trifling vessel. . . . . . Surely this was a quarrel slenderly grounded, and not becoming Christian neighbours." It was a corrupt attempt to aid the powerful in oppressing the weak. At first successful, it ultimately failed. At the beginning of May, the duke of York took the command of the English fleet. Having united with a French squadron, they found the Dutch fleet lying near Ostend. But the skill of De Ruyter avoided an engagement, and the English fleet returned to the coast to take in further supplies of men and provisions. De Ruyter came out, and a

* Evelyn, 10th October, 1671.

stubborn battle took place on the 28th of May, in Southwold bay. The French had little share in the engagement. The fight lasted the whole day, with little advantage on either side. The earl of Sandwich and most of his crew were lost in the Royal James, which was blown up by a fire-ship. Evelyn insinuates that the earl was left to perish, fighting like a lion, though hating the war, " to gratify the pride and envy " of some that were not his friends.*

Whilst England was battling at sea with little real advantage, the French armies were pouring into Holland. The fortresses on the Rhine were quickly in their possession; town after town of the United Provinces yielded without a struggle; the outposts of the French were seen from Amsterdam. Then was the great commercial republic on the point of becoming an easy prey to the ambition of that power that had already visions of universal dominion. The government of the United Provinces was torn by factions. Petty oligarchies presided over the separate States. The dignity of Stadtholder had expired with Prince William II. in 1650. His widow, the daughter of Charles I., gave birth to a son, a few days after her husband's death. That son was now twenty-two years of age—the head of the illustrious house of Orange-

Murder of De Witt.

Nassau, but without power in his own country. The highest duties of the first magistrate of the republic had been honourably discharged by John de Witt, the Grand Pensionary of the Province of Holland. When the French invasion filled the people of the Seven Provinces with terror, their rage was

* Evelyn, "Diary," May 31.

not directed against their enemies, but against their government. The popular feeling in favour of the prince of Orange broke forth in the blind hatred of an infuriated multitude against the statesmen who desired the permanent suppression of the office of Stadtholder, a dignity almost monarchical. The young prince William was called to the command of the forces when the French troops entered the States. Cornelius de Witt was arrested, upon an accusation of having plotted against the life of prince William. The accusation could not be established; and his brother John went to his prison at the Hague to convey him away. Both the brothers were murdered by an infuriated mob. Suspicious as was the commencement of his great career, the young prince of Orange proved the deliverer of his country. He roused the fainting courage of the Deputies in the States General. He rejected all the overtures of Charles and Louis. No terms of advantage to himself would induce him to compromise the honour of his nation. Relationship with the Crown of England was to him nothing in comparison with saving the Seven Provinces from the yoke of France. The dykes were opened. The land was subjected to the dominion of the water, an enemy less to be dreaded than a foreign foe. There was no subsistence for the invading army in that desert of sand and sea. The French retreated. The guilty league of England and France was powerless. Louis returned to Paris, leaving some troops in the garrisons he had won. The Dutch admiral avoided another engagement with the English fleet. The war went on languidly for two years, amidst the dissatisfaction of the English people. The treasury of Charles was exhausted. The promised payment to the public creditors was postponed by proclamation. The Parliament had been prorogued from the 22nd of April, 1671. It was called together on the 5th of February, 1673. For twenty-one months the government had pursued an unmolested career. It had now to meet an opposition, jealous and indignant, but more factious than high principled.

In November, 1672, Anthony Ashley Cooper, who had been created earl of Shaftesbury in the previous April, was raised to the dignity of Lord Chancellor, upon the retirement, or dismissal, of Sir Orlando Bridgman from the office of Lord Keeper. The dislike which the lawyers of his time naturally felt at the elevation to the highest judicial office of a man not of the legal profession, may be found in the "Examen" of Roger North. His great offence was that he declaimed "against the tribe of the Court of Chancery, officers and counsel, and their methods of ordering the business of the Court. . . . For the Chancery, he would teach the Bar that a man of sense was above all their forms." *   Shaftesbury possibly saw that a servile adherence to forms was a real impediment to the course of equity; and by a vigorous demonstration against forms which ruined the suitors by delay, was enabled to earn the high praise as a judge of the poet who was employed to blacken his character as a statesman. " Discerning eyes ; " " clean hands ; " " swift of despatch ; " " easy of access ; "

" Unbrib'd, unbought, the wretched to redress ; "

are qualities which have some weight with us, although "the great poet probably never was in the Court of Chancery in his life, and, though the first of Eng-

* " Examen," p. 46.

lish critics in polite literature, he could not have formed a very correct opinion as to the propriety of an order or decree in Equity." * Dryden, as is reported, displeased the king by this tribute to the judicial virtues of Shaftesbury. Abhorring the statesman, he ought not to have praised the judge. Another contemporary writer is to be disbelieved, according to lord Campbell, because his estimate of Shaftesbury was unmixed panegyric. The enemy, and the friend, are equally untrustworthy. "Except being free from gross corruption, he was the worst judge that ever sat in the Court." † How is this to be proved? "There are a few of his decisions to be found in the books, but none of them are of the slightest importance." ‡ We still hold ourselves free to believe Dryden, and the other contemporary, who says that, under Shaftesbury, "justice ran in an equal channel, so that the cause of the rich was not suffered to swallow up the right of the poor;" that "the mischievous consequences which commonly arise from the delays, and other practices, of that Court were, by his ingenious and judicious management, very much abated." § Nor do we consider that as Chancellor he "played fantastic tricks which could be expected only from a fool and a coxcomb,"‖ because he revived the ancient form of the Chancellor and the Judges riding to Westminster Hall, on the first day of Hilary term, on which occasion Judge Twisden "was laid along in the dirt;" and because he sat upon the bench "in an ash-coloured gown, silver laced." These amusing characteristics of one who, not wholly different from subsequent Chancellors, possessed some of the eccentricities with the more sterling qualities of genius, are set forth with much vivacity by Roger North, who hated Shaftesbury with an intensity that the opposite opinions of factions alone can engender. Whenever we encounter this remarkable man in his future political career, we must judge him not uncharitably if we would judge him rightly. He was long made the scape-goat for the political offences whether of the Court party or the Country party. It is very difficult to understand his principles or his policy; but it is sufficient to make us cautious in his condemnation, to know that he was maligned by the supporters of arbitrary power, and looked up to by the advocates of freedom and toleration. Mr. Fox probably came to the safest conclusion upon his character when he said, "As to making him a real patriot, or friend to our ideas of liberty, it is impossible, at least in my opinion. On the other hand, he is very far from being the devil he is described." ¶

The Parliament met on the 4th of February, 1673. In March, 1672, two days before the war was declared against the United Provinces, Charles had issued a Declaration of Indulgence in religion, in which he declared his "will and pleasure to be, that the execution of all and all manner of penal laws in matters ecclesiastical, against whatsoever sort of non-conformists or recusants be immediately suspended, and they are hereby suspended." The relief to Protestant dissenters may be estimated from the fact that John Bunyan, who for twelve years had been confined in Bedford gaol, during which long period he had written "The Pilgrim's Progress," was almost immediately released.

* Lord Campbell; "Lives of Chancellors," p. 310.
† Ibid., p. 311.   ‡ Ibid., p. 313.   § "Rawleigh Redivivus."
‖ "Lives of Chancellors," p. 307.   ¶ Introduction to "History of James II."

It would be difficult to understand how such a measure of justice and humanity should not have been universally acceptable to all but the most bigoted, unless we take into account that through its general operation the laws against Papists were relaxed, as well as those against Protestant non-conformists.   But the Declaration of Indulgence produced a ferment in the nation which rendered it unpopular even amongst the numerous class who had been harassed by the Act of Uniformity, the Five Mile Act, and the Conventicle Acts.   They were more favoured than the Roman Catholics, who were expressly refused public places for their worship, though its private exercise was indirectly sanctioned.   In a tract, written by John Locke, the intimate friend of Shaftesbury, the arguments in favour of the Declaration of Indulgence are fully set forth.   The writer of this " Letter from a Person of Quality to his friend in the country," says that he asked Lord Shaftesbury what he meant by supporting the Declaration, which seemed to assume a power to repeal and suspend all our laws, to destroy the Church, to overthrow the Protestant religion, and to tolerate Popery.   He represents the earl to have contended that a government ought to be enabled to suspend any penal law, in the interval of the legislative power, but that the two Houses of Parliament ought to determine such indulgence, and restore the law to its full execution ; that he had joined in the Declaration for preserving the Protestant religion, by opening a way for the English Church to live peaceably with the dissenters ; that Papists ought to have no pressure laid upon them except to be made incapable of office ; and he asked whether, in this age of the world, articles and matters of religion should become the only accessible ways to our civil rights ? *   There was a passage in the Declaration which was sufficient to fill the people with alarm : " We think ourselves obliged to make use of that supreme power in ecclesiastical matters which is not only inherent in us, but hath been declared and recognised to be so by several statutes and acts of parliament."   Upon their meeting, the Commons voted, upon a division of 168 to 116, " that penal statutes, in matters ecclesiastical, cannot be suspended but by Act of Parliament."   Mr. Love, one of the members for the city of London, strenuously supported the address to the king to withdraw the Declaration.   A member said to him, " Why, Mr. Love, you are a Dissenter yourself ; it is very ungrateful that you who receive the benefit should object against the manner."   Defoe, who calls Mr. Alderman Love " that truly English Roman," records his answer to the objection : " I am a Dissenter, and thereby unhappily obnoxious to the law ; and if you catch me in the corn you may put me in the pound.   The law against the Dissenters I should be glad to see repealed by the same authority that made it ; but while it is a law, the king cannot repeal it by proclamation : And I had much rather see the Dissenters suffer by the rigour of the law, though I suffer with them, than see all the laws of England trampled under the foot of the prerogative, as in this example." †
The Parliament and the nation were not sufficiently advanced to repeal all penal laws that affected the exercise of religion.   To prevent the dangers

---

* The letter is printed in Locke's Works ; also in " Parliamentary History," Vol. IV., Appendix V.
† See Wilson's " Life of Defoe," vol. i. p. 58.

which were almost universally dreaded of the growth of Romanism, the principle of intolerance was still upheld. The Court, not indeed from any sense of justice, but for the advancement of its covert objects, for some time resisted this vote of the Commons. But the spirit of opposition was too strong to be rashly braved. The king withdrew the Declaration of Indulgence, after Shaftesbury, in the House of Lords, had turned to the popular side, and declared it illegal. But the Country party, as opposed to the Court party, were resolved to manifest their hostility to Popery by a practical measure which should reach the highest places. The duke of York's opinions were no secret; the king was suspected; the articles on religion in the treaty with France could not be shrouded in impenetrable mystery; the first duchess of York had died in the profession of Catholicism; another alliance was about to be formed with a young Catholic princess, Mary of Modena. The barrier to be raised against the great dangers to repel which the nation was rousing itself, was the Test Act. The House of Commons resolved on the 28th of February, 1673, "that all persons who shall refuse to take the oaths of allegiance and supremacy, and receive the sacrament according to the rites of the Church of England, shall be incapable of all public employments, military and civil." On the 12th of March, the Test Act, entitled a "Bill to prevent the Growth of Popery," was read a third time. It required, in addition to the oaths, that a declaration renouncing the doctrine of transubstantiation should be made before admission to office. The proposed law affected the Puritans as much as the Papists, in the point of communion with the Church; but they made little opposition. They partook of the common dread that Romanism might come back in some bold or insidious form, and with it the arbitrary power which had so generally been its companion. An attempt to give them a special measure of relief was defeated by the prorogation of Parliament. The effect of the Test Act was decisive. The duke of York resigned his post of Lord High Admiral, and prince Rupert was appointed to the command of the fleet. Lord Clifford refused to take the test, and retired from his great office of Lord High Treasurer. The Commons voted the supplies with little reluctance, without going into the questions of the Dutch war or the shutting the Exchequer. There were six months of prorogation, during which the war was continued at sea with alternate success and defeat. At home the signs of an approaching storm were becoming manifest.

Crown. Charles II.

CHAPTER XX.

THE Parliament had been prorogued to the 20th of October. The instant the Commons met they voted an address to the king, desiring that the intended marriage of the duke of York with the princess of Modena should not take place. The Parliament was immediately prorogued for a week. On the 27th the king opened the Session in person; and his Chancellor, Shaftesbury, addressed the members in the usual terms of eulogy and hope. The address against the marriage of the duke of York was presented; and Charles returned for answer that the alliance " was completed, according to the forms used amongst princes, and by his royal consent and authority." A spirit of decided hostility against the government was now evident in the Commons. They refused a supply until "this kingdom be effectually secured from the dangers of Popery, and Popish counsels and councillors." They voted that a Standing Army was a grievance. They resolved upon a second Address on the subject of the duke's marriage. It was to have been presented on the 4th of November, but the king came suddenly to the House of Lords, and ordered that the Commons should be summoned. A singular scene took place. The Speaker and the Usher of the Black Rod met at the door of the House of Commons; and the Speaker having entered, the door was shut, and he was hurried to the chair. It was immediately moved that the alliance with France was a grievance; that the evil counsellors about the king were a grievance; that the duke of Lauderdale was a grievance. The Black Rod was knocking at the door with impatient loudness; the House resounded with cries of 'question'; the Speaker leapt out of the chair, and in a wild tumult the members followed him to the House of Lords. The king then prorogued the Parliament to the 7th of January. During the interval Shaftesbury was dismissed from the custody of the Great Seal; Buckingham retired; the Cabal ministry was broken up. Sir Thomas Osborne, soon after created earl of Danby, became the chief minister, and retained power till 1678; Shaftesbury became the great leader of the party opposed to the Court. The history of England for the next seven years is the history of a continual struggle between the Crown and the Commons, during which time we trace, amidst some honesty of purpose, an equal degradation of the principles of loyalty and of independence. Monarchical government was never more profligate and anti-national, and representative government was never more factious and corrupt, than in the years from 1673 to 1681. The House of Commons elected after the Restoration first met on the 8th of May, 1661. It continued to sit till the 25th of January, 1679. Vacancies had been filled up from time to time by new elections; and in these what was called the Country Party gradually preponderated. But the general composition of the House was a curious admixture of by-gone and current opinions. There is "A Letter from a Parliament Man to his Friend," published in 1675, and attributed to Shaftesbury, which describes with admirable humour, and probably with equal truth, the composition of the House of Commons: *—" Sir, I see you are greatly scandalized at our slow and confused proceedings. I confess you have cause enough; but were you but within these walls for one half day, and saw the strange make and complexion that this house is of, you would wonder as much that ever you wondered at it; for we are such a pied Parliament, that none can say of what colour we are; for we consist of Old Cavaliers, Old Round-heads, Indigent Courtiers, and true Country-Gentlemen: the two latter are most numerous, and would in probability bring things to some issue were they not clogged with the humourous uncertainties of the former. For the Old Cavalier, grown aged, and almost past his vice, is damnable godly, and makes his doting piety more a plague to the world, than his youthful debauchery was: he forces his Loyalty to strike sail to his Religion, and could be content to pare the nails a little of the Civil Government, so you would but let him sharpen the Ecclesiastical talons: which behaviour of his so exasperates the Round-head, that he, on the other hand, cares not what increase the interest of the Crown receives, so he can but diminish that of the Mitre: so that the Round-head had rather enslave the man than the conscience; the Cavalier, rather the conscience than the man; there being a sufficient stock of animosity as proper matter to work upon. Upon these, therefore, the Courtier usually plays: for if any Anti-Court motion be made, he gains the Round-heads either to oppose or assent, by telling them, If they will join him now, he will join with them for Liberty of Conscience. And when any affair is started on behalf of the country, he assures the Cavaliers, if they will then stand by him, he will then join with them in promoting a Bill against the Fanatics. Thus play they on both hands, that no motion of a public nature is made but they win upon the one or other of them: and by this art gain a majority against the country gentlemen, which otherwise they would never have: wherefore it were happy that we had neither Round-head nor Cavalier in the House; for they are each of them so prejudicate against

* Printed in "Parliamentary History," vol. iv., Appendix IV.

the other, that their sitting here signifies nothing but their fostering their old venom, and lying at catch to snap every advantage to bear down each other, though it be in the destruction of their country." The same letter does not spare the corruption of that very considerable body of members that it terms "Indigent;" a corruption which king Charles and king Louis each found availing with patriots as well as with placemen: "You now see all our shapes, save only the Indigents, concerning whom I need say but little, for their votes are publicly saleable for a guinea and a dinner every day in the week, unless the House be upon Money, or a Minister of State: for that is their harvest; and then they make their earnings suit the work they are about, which inclines them most constantly as sure clients to the Court. For what with gaining the one, and saving the other, they now and then adventure a vote on the Country side; but the dread of Dissolution makes them straight tack about. The only thing we are obliged to them for is, that they do nothing gratis, but make every tax as well chargeable to the Court as burdensome to the country, and save no man's neck but they break his purse."

At the opening of the Session of Parliament in 1674, the king uttered these words with his own lips: "I know you have heard much of my alliance with France, and I believe it hath been very strangely misrepresented to you, as if there were certain secret articles of dangerous consequence; but I will make no difficulty of letting the treaties, and all the articles of them, without any the least reserve, to be seen by a small committee of both Houses, who may report to you the true scope of them." Charles I. did not hesitate to employ indirect falsehood; but he never uttered such an audacious lie as his son now used, to stem the discontents which were gathering around him. Supplies were wanted to carry on the Dutch war; but the nation hated the war, and the Commons would not grant the supplies. To avert greater dangers a separate peace was made with Holland. The war went on between France and the United Provinces, who were now fully supported by Spain and the German powers. The noble resistance of the prince of Orange to the ambition of Louis had saved his country; but had England taken a more honest course, future wars arising out of the same lust of dominion might have been effectually prevented. The Parliament was in some degree propitiated by the separate peace with Holland; but it was in a dangerous temper, and was quickly prorogued. It met again on the 13th of April, 1675. English troops under Monmouth had been left to assist the French, notwithstanding the English peace with Holland. The House of Commons demanded their recall. The violent scenes between furious partisans were suddenly mitigated, as if a god had descended to separate the combatants in a cloud. The god of money had effected this peacefulness. The English troops remained as auxiliaries of the French. After a protracted struggle to extend the oath required to be taken by officers of corporations to privy counsellors and members of parliament, which attempt was defeated by Shaftesbury, the Parliament was prorogued. There was another short Session. It was again prorogued for fifteen months on the 22nd of November.

The alternations of indulgence towards non-conformists and their persecution was one of the most striking symptoms of the utter want of principle in the conduct of public affairs. The sufferings of a large body of people were never taken into account when the Court and the Parliament were each striving to rule by factions. Defoe, who well knew the system which had been in operation from his boyhood, said, "the persecution of Dissenters has been all along the effect of state policy, more than error of zeal or a mistake of religion." Persecution "has very seldom been carried on any where from mere zeal, but with a complication of private ends, intrigues, and all kinds of abstracted villainy." * Under Danby's administration, in 1675, the king issued proclamations enforcing the laws against nonconformists. How these measures worked may be seen in Baxter's simple relation: "I was so long wearied with keeping my doors shut against them that came to distrain on my goods for preaching, that I was fain to go from my house, and sell all my goods, and to hide my library first, and afterwards to sell it." He shifted his abode. "When I had ceased preaching I was, being newly risen from extremity of pain, suddenly surprised in my house by a poor violent informer, and many constables and officers, who rushed in and apprehended me, and served on me one warrant to seize on my person for coming within five miles of a Corporation, and five more warrants to distrain for an hundred and ninety pounds, for five sermons." † Though the king was straitened in his means of extravagance by the jealousy of Parliament, the prodigality of the Court was as manifest as ever. On the 10th of September, 1675, Evelyn writes in his Diary: "I was casually showed the duchess of Portsmouth's splendid apartment at Whitehall, luxuriously furnished, and with ten times the richness and glory beyond the queen's; such massy pieces of plate, whole tables, and stands of incredible value." The lady looked down with contempt upon her sister-strumpets. She affected a decency that was not characteristic of some other ladies. When the wit of Nell Gwynn was praised, "yes," exclaimed La Querouaille, "but any one may know she has been an orange-wench by her swearing." The great duchess was the arbitress of the destiny of statesmen. She quarrelled with Buckingham, and he was driven into opposition. She corresponded with the French monarch, who settled an estate upon her for her valuable aid in the degradation of England. Time did not diminish her influence over the besotted king. Incredible as it may appear, there is a record of particular payments to her out of the Secret Service Money in the one year of 1681, of 136,668*l.* 10*s.*‡ The most hidden crimes cannot wholly be concealed, especially when subordinate agents are connected with them. The long prorogation of the Parliament in November, 1675, was a specific arrangement between Charles and Louis, for which the unworthy king of England received five hundred thousand crowns. The two sovereigns, with the connivance of Danby and Lauderdale, concluded a formal agreement not to enter upon any treaties but with mutual consent; and Charles accepted a pension, upon his pledge to prorogue or dissolve any Parliament that attempted to force such treaties upon him. The money was regularly paid by the French minister to Chiffinch, the notorious pander to the vices of his master; and the degraded king regularly signed a receipt for the wages of his iniquity.

* "Review," vol. ii. quoted in Wilson's "Life," vol. i. p. 60.
† "Life of Baxter," Part iii. pp. 172, 191.
‡ "Moneys received and paid for Secret Services;" Camden Society.

Such things could not go on without exciting some suspicion. How could the extravagance of the Court be maintained? Where did the money come from? The annual revenue was large, but all knew that it was insufficient to meet the riots and follies of Whitehall. Serious thinkers began to murmur. Gossiping loungers about the coffee-houses began to sneer and whisper. Coffee-houses were in those days what clubs are in our day—the great marts for the interchange of town talk, political, or literary, or fashionable, or scandalous, or simply stupid. A Coffee-house, says a tract of 1673, " is an exchange where haberdashers of political small-wares meet, and mutually abuse each other, and the public, with bottomless stories."* Roger North takes a more serious view of Coffee-house gossip, in 1675: " There was such licentiousness of seditious and really treasonable discourse, in coffee-houses, of which there were accounts daily brought to the king, that it was considered if coffee-houses ought not to be put down."† Clarendon, in 1666, had proposed either to put down coffee-houses, or to employ spies to frequent them and report the conversation. If in 1675 the king had daily reports of " treasonable discourse," we may presume that the spy-system had been tried, although it was not quite efficient. On the 29th of December, a proclamation appeared, recalling all the licences issued for the sale of coffee, and ordering all coffee-houses to be shut up, " because in such houses, and by the meeting of disaffected persons in them, divers false, malicious, and scandalous reports were devised and spread abroad, to the defamation of his majesty's government, and the disturbance of the quiet and peace of the realm." The licences were withdrawn, through a legal quibble upon the same Statute under which they had been issued. By the Act granting the king certain excise duties in perpetuity,‡ a duty of fourpence was imposed " for every gallon of coffee made and sold, to be paid by the maker." The licence to sell was under a subsequent Act, by which the Justices in Sessions, or the Chief Magistrate of a Corporation, were to grant Licences for the selling of Coffee, Chocolate, Sherbet, or Tea, no Licence being to be granted unless the retailer had first given security for the payment of the dues to the king.§ There was no complaint that the securities had not been given, or that the dues were unpaid. The pretence under which the licences were recalled was, that as the Statute made no mention of a time for which the licences were granted, they might be recalled at any time by a higher authority than that of the magistrates who issued them. There never was a more flagrant violation of law under a show of some submission to law. The Coffee-houses were closed. " The great Coffee-house in Covent Garden "— Will's Coffee-house—where Mr. Pepys saw in 1664, " Dryden the poet, and all the wits of the town, and Harris the player, and Mr. Hoole of our college," was suddenly shut up at the merry Christmas time. Mr. Dryden had no longer there " his armed chair, which in the winter had a settled and prescriptive place by the fire." ‖ His opera of " The State of Innocence and Fall of Man " was his last previous dramatic production; and he could no longer tell to the groups around him, how when he went to the old blind

---

* " Harleian Miscellany," vol. viii. p. 7.
† " Lives of the Norths," vol. i. p. 316.   ‡ 12 Car. II. c. 21.   § 15 Car. II. c. 11.
‖ " Johnson's Lives of the Poets;" Cunningham's edit. vol. i. p. 338.

schoolmaster in Bunhill-fields, and "asked leave to put his Paradise Lost into a drama in rhyme, Mr. Milton received him very civilly, and told him he would give him leave to tag his verses." * Milton about a year before, had been carried to his last resting-place in Cripplegate-church ; and amongst the "treasonable discourse" of the frequenters of coffee-houses some might have uttered the thought that Milton was not far wrong when, in his last political treatise, he raised his warning voice against the way his countrymen were marching, "to those calamities which attend always and unavoidably on luxury, all national judgments under foreign and domestic slavery." † Pro-

Interior of Cripplegate Church.

bably no political measure was more indicative of a disposition in the government to attack the liberties of the people in their social habits than this shutting-up of the coffee-houses. The popular indignation soon compelled the government to retract its proclamation. "The faction was much incensed," writes North. "They said that Mr. Attorney [sir William Jones] should answer it in Parliament." Mr. Attorney was frightened ; and possibly some higher authorities were not at their ease. Permission was given to re-open the houses for a certain time ; under a severe admonition to the keepers, that they should stop the reading of all scandalous books and papers, and hinder every scandalous report against the government. Despotism would be more dangerous though not more odious than it is, amongst nations with preten-

* Aubrey. "Lives," vol. iii. p. 444.   † "Way to establish a free Commonwealth."

sions to civilisation, if it had something less of the weakness and folly which always accompanies its measures for the repression of opinion.

At the opening of the Session of Parliament on the 15th of February, 1677, the Lord Chancellor, Finch, made an elaborate speech which, says Mr. Southey, "contains passages which are as worthy of attention now as they were when they were delivered." * Such a passage as the following would be more worthy of attention, had it not been repeated, with very slight variation, by every parliamentary orator from that day to this, with whom the dead calm of national apathy is the perfection of national happiness—the highest glory of a sovereign to " be rowed in state over the ocean of public tranquillity by the public slavery." † The words of Lord Chancellor Nottingham are these: " It is a great and a dangerous mistake in those who think that peace at home is well enough preserved, so long as the sword is not drawn; whereas, in truth, nothing deserves the name of peace but unity; such an unity as flows from an unshaken trust and confidence between the king and his people; from a due reverence and obedience to his law and his government; from a religious and an awful care not to disturb the ancient landmarks." ‡ These are the common-places which have been entered in many a book besides Mr. Southey's. " Trust and confidence between the king and his people " had been manifested by a prorogation of Parliament for fifteen months. A fierce debate took place on this question. The duke of Buckingham maintained that the prorogation for so long a time amounted to a dissolution, being contrary to the statutes of Edward III., which require the annual calling of a Parliament. Lords Shaftesbury, Salisbury, and Wharton supported this opinion; and by way of silencing them were ordered to be sent to the Tower, unless they begged pardon of the king and the House. They refused, and were imprisoned. Such committals by either House terminate with the Session; but the government contrived to keep these dangerous rivals out of the way for more than a year, by adjournments instead of prorogations. In the Commons, the Country party were in a minority upon this question. The bribery of the Lord Treasurer had been more effectual than the eloquence of the Lord Chancellor. The instalment of the king's pension from France, paid in February, was applied to get votes for a large grant. But the greater part of the supply was devoted to the support of the navy; and with this sum the Commons would not trust the Treasurer, but appointed their own receivers to superintend its disbursement. The French were now carrying all resistance before them, in the Spanish Netherlands. The prince of Orange was defeated at Cassel. Valenciennes and Cambray were surrendered. The Commons voted an address praying the king to oppose the French monarch, and save the Netherlands from his grasp. Charles required an immediate grant as a preliminary to a declaration of war. The House refused it. Then was resorted to that disgusting system of foreign bribery, by Spain to obtain the grant, by France to prevent it, which has brought such great disgrace upon many of the public men of this period, and which in some degree qualifies the same baseness in the king. The grant being refused, Charles adjourned the

* " Southey's Common-place Book," vol. i. p. 106.
† Marvell. " Rehearsal Transprosed," vol. ii. p. 195
‡ " Parl. History," vol. iv. col. 809.

Parliament; obtained an increase of his pension from Louis; and gave his promise accordingly that he would keep off the meeting of the troublesome representatives who urged him into war, and yet were afraid to give him the means of carrying it on.

When sir William Temple, in 1668, having concluded the Triple Alliance, returned to the Hague as Ambassador, he described the prince of Orange as "a young man of more parts than ordinary, and of the better sort; that is, not lying in that kind of wit which is neither of use to one's self nor to any body else, but in good plain sense." Temple adds, "never any body raved so much after England, as well the language, as all else that belonged to it." * William was then in his nineteenth year. When Temple went back to the Hague in 1674 the young man had applied his plain sense and his higher qualities—if most high qualities be not included in plain sense—to take the position of the deliverer of his country. He had measured his strength with the great Condé; and in the battle of Seneffe, disastrous as it was, had earned from the French veteran the praise that he had acted in everything like an old captain, except in venturing his person too much like a young soldier. Temple in his second embassy had hinted at the possibility of an union with the daughter of the duke of York. The proposal was renewed more formally, but the prince of Orange did not then respond. He suspected the disposition of the English government to favour the designs of Louis XIV. He was himself resolved to struggle, "as he had seen a poor old man tugging alone in a little boat upon a canal, against the eddy of a sluice. This old man's business, and mine, are too like one another." † But the desire for an English alliance overcame this repugnance to the union. Probably he looked far into the future. William came to England in 1677. On the 19th of October the marriage between him and Mary, the eldest daughter of the duke of York, was agreed upon. On the 4th of November it was solemnised—"to the great joy of the nation," says Reresby; "for his highness being a protestant prince, this match in a great measure expelled the fears that the majority had conceived concerning popery." ‡ Dr. Edward Lake, who was chaplain and tutor to the princesses Mary and Anne, in his diary of the 16th of November writes: "The wind being easterly, their highnesses were still detained at St. James's. This day the court began to whisper the prince's sullenness or clownishness, that he took no notice of his princess at the play and ball, nor came to see her at St. James's the day preceding this designed for their departure." § With the usual earnestness of his character, William was labouring to induce the king his uncle to take a bold and honourable part in the negociations for peace with France; and it is very likely that he neglected to pay to his bride those attentions which policy, if not love, would have demanded. In after life Mary showed the depth of her affection for her husband, so cold in his demeanour, so high-minded in real deeds. The sweetness of her nature was eminently fitted for his support and consolation in the great trials, and the arduous duties, of his life. The chaplain records that Mary wept incessantly all the morning of their departure. "The queen observing her highness to weep as she took leave of her majesty,

* Letter quoted in Courtenay's "Life of Temple," vol. i. p. 286.
† Conversation with Temple, *Ibid.* p. 488.   ‡ "Memoirs," p. 199.
§ "Camden Miscellany," vol. i.

would have comforted her with the consideration of her own condition when she came into England, and had never till then seen the king; to whom her highness presently replied, ' But, madam, you came into England; but I am going out of England.' " *

The marriage of the prince of Orange with the princess Mary gave offence to the king of France. He regarded it as a breach of faith on the part of his pensioner, the king of England, and he stopped the payment of the sum for which Charles had agreed to prevent any meeting of Parliament till April, 1678. Before that time Louis expected to have been in a condition to dictate terms to the Allies. When the pensioner saw his pay stopped, he called the Parliament together, on the 28th of January. To attempt to unravel the knot of the complicated intrigues of this period would be as wearisome to our readers as unsatisfactory to ourselves. The king announced to the Parliament that he had made such alliances with Holland as were for the preservation of Flanders, and had withdrawn the auxiliary English troops from the French service. The king further asked for money to carry on the war against France, so as to support a fleet of ninety sail, and an army of forty thousand men. The fast-and-loose game which was played throughout this Session has left a stain upon parliamentary government. It was impossible for the Dutch and their allies, and equally impossible for the English people, to understand the movements of the Court party and the Country party as exhibited in the votes of Parliament. Well might the prince of Orange say, " Was ever anything so hot and so cold as this Court of yours ? Will the king never learn a word that I shall never forget since my last passage to England, when, in a great storm, the captain was all night crying out to the men at the helm, ' Steady ! Steady ! Steady ! ' ? " The independent members of the House of Commons knew that a prompt assistance to the Allies was absolutely necessary to control the ambitious designs of France. They urged the war, but they hesitated to vote the supplies, or clogged the vote by vexatious conditions. " Great debates," says Reresby, " had arisen upon this affair, and the reason of the violent opposition it met with was the desire in some to oppose the Crown, though in the very thing they themselves wished for, the nation being ever desirous of a war with France ; and a jealousy in others that the king indeed intended to raise an army, but never designed to go on with the war; and, to say the truth, some of the king's own party were not very sure of the contrary." † There was a violent debate on the 14th of March, very imperfectly reported. Reresby says of this debate, " Several speeches were made in the House, full fraught of jealousies and fears, and particularly with regard to the army at this time levying; as if it rather intended to erect absolute monarchy at home, than infest the enemy abroad." ‡ The Commons on the 29th of April received a message from the king, desiring that the House would immediately enter into a consideration of a supply for him, for his majesty must either disband the men, or pay them. The king and the representatives of the people now came to violent issues. A supply was refused unless a war was declared against France; if not the army must be disbanded. The army had beeen raised, and was encamped on Hounslow Heath. Evelyn there looked upon these forces on the 29th of June:

---

* " Camden Miscellany," vol. i.

† " Memoirs," p. 200.   ‡ *Ibid.* p. 303.

" We saw the new-raised army encamped, designed against France, in pretence at least; but which gave umbrage to the Parliament. His majesty and a world of company were in the field, and the whole army in battalia, a very glorious sight. Now were brought into service a new sort of soldiers called grenadiers, who were dexterous in flinging hand grenades, every one having a pouch full." What Evelyn, a steady loyalist, thought a pretence, is the only justification for the undoubted fact that some of the opposition to the Court was the result of a secret connexion formed with the Ambassadors of Louis by some of the parliamentary leaders. Money was bestowed upon the more unscrupulous. We cannot think, even if the designs of Charles upon the liberties of his country had been manifest to Hollis, and Russell, and Sidney, instead of being merely suspected, that they were justified in their intrigues with any foreign prince, and especially with a monarch so opposed to freedom and national independence as Louis XIV. Undoubtedly their conduct was some apology for Charles in that policy of evasion and delay which allowed France to conclude a peace upon far more advantageous terms than Louis could have obtained if William of Orange had been adequately supported. The peace of Nimeguen, concluded on the 4th of August, left Louis a large portion of his gains in this war of aggression. England had the disgrace of the most complicated faithlessness to all honourable principle. She lost her national position in Europe, and became a by-word for despotic states, and a scandal to the few nations that were free. She stood alone in possessing a government in which the opinions of the people were supposed to have a voice through their representatives. These manifestations of weakness and dishonour were held to be inherent in a mixed constitution of king and parliament, and men were taught to think that arbitrary power was a safer and more glorious thing than regulated freedom. Despotism is always ready to rejoice when the due balance of representative government is disturbed by the violence or the corruption of selfish factions.

On the 8th of July an Act was passed for granting a supply to the king of upwards of £600,000, " for disbanding the army, and for other uses." On the 15th the Parliament was prorogued. Amidst the conflicts of party one Statute of this period marks the great fact that religious intolerance had assumed a milder form. "It is enacted "That the Writ commonly called Breve de Heretico comburendo, with all process and proceedings thereupon, in order to the executing such Writ, or following or depending thereupon, and all punishment by death in pursuance of any Ecclesiastical Censures, be from henceforth utterly taken away and abolished." * But if the progress of opinion had wiped out of the Statute Book the horrible law that heretics should be burnt, the recollection of the days when that law was no dead letter was still strong and vivid as ever in the popular mind. The dread of Popery was the one inextinguishable spark in the temper of the people which the slightest breath might raise into a flame. The great bulk of the nation knew little of the vices of the Court; and even those who dwelt in and around Westminster looked with complacency upon the tall swarthy gentleman who walked up and down the Mall in St. James' Park at his "wonted large pace;" and who, when very humble strangers were presented to him

* 29 Car. II. c. 9.

in the Long Gallery at Whitehall, would give them his hand to kiss, and say "God bless you." *   They were accustomed to hear of the duke of York's irregular life, and little heeded his private indiscretions; but when he became a declared Romanist and had married a Catholic princess, there were no bounds to their dislike and their suspicion.   Dissenters from the Church, who practically knew all the hardships of exclusion from civil offices, and from the privilege of worship according to their own consciences, would hear of no scheme of toleration for Papists.   Rousing themselves out of the apathy which had succeeded to their delirium of loyalty, the people had again begun to take a strong interest in public affairs.   They felt that the nation had lost character in its foreign transactions.   They saw the old principles of servile obedience, which had been struck down in 1640, again proclaimed as the duties of subjects.   They believed, with lord Shaftesbury, that "popery and slavery, like two sisters, go hand in hand; and sometimes one goes first, and sometimes the other, but wheresoever the one enters the other is following close behind."   In the temper that prevailed amongst the people in the summer of 1678, the excesses connected with what is known as the Popish Plot were, like Shakspere's characteristic of murder, "most foul;" they were also "strange;" but they were not "unnatural."   The nation was under a panic which manifested itself in a temporary insanity.   But we are not therefore to conclude that the panic was wholly unreasonable; that the plot was a pure invention got up by witnesses altogether false, at the instigation of Shaftesbury and other unprincipled politicians; that there was no design on the part of Romish intriguers to restore their religion in England, to which the near prospect of a Popish successor to the throne gave abundant encouragement.   It is unquestionable that the Jesuits did believe, as was expressed in the letter of Coleman, the secretary of the duke of York, that for "the subduing of a pestilent heresy"—the "mighty work" on their hands—"there were never such hopes of success since the death of queen Mary, as now in our days, when God has given us a prince who is become zealous of being the author and instrument of so glorious a work."   The zeal of James was neutralised by the indifference of Charles; and therefore it was maintained that the destruction of the king was the first object of the Plot.   Charles himself ridiculed the notion; but that is no proof that he wholly disbelieved the existence of some wild scheme for his removal.

The rumours of a Popish plot burst upon the nation at the beginning of October.   Evelyn records, under date of the first of this month, that he went to Dr. Tonge, the rector of St. Michael's, Wood Street, to see and converse with him at Whitehall, and "with Mr. Oates, one that was lately an apostate to the Church of Rome, and now returned again with this discovery" of the Popish plot.   "Oates was encouraged," continues Evelyn, "and everything he affirmed taken for gospel.   The truth is, the Roman Catholics were exceedingly bold and busy everywhere."   Reresby says that the first news of the plot, "a design of the Papists to kill the king," came to him in the country, on the 10th of October.   "Nobody can conceive that was not a witness thereof, what a ferment this raised amongst all ranks and

* See "Diary of Henry Teonge," p. 232.

degrees." Burnet, who says that he was so well instructed in all the steps of
the plot, that he is more capable to give a full account of it than any man he
knows, records that three days before Michaelmas Dr. Tonge came to him—
"a very mean divine, and seemed credulous and simple, but I had always
looked on him as a sincere man. At this time he told me of strange designs
against the king's person." Burnet communicated the information to the
Secretary's office; but learnt that Tonge had been already "making discoveries
there, of which they made no other account, but that he intended to get himself to be made a dean." Burnet told Tonge's story "to Littleton and
Powel, and they looked on it as a design of lord Danby's, to be laid before
the next Session, thereby to dispose them to keep up a greater force, since
the papists were plotting against the king's life." Roger North, on the contrary, suggests that Shaftesbury "was behind the curtain, and in the depths
of the contrivance." * The generally received account is that one Kirby, on
the 13th of August, warned the king, who knew him, not to walk alone in the
Park; that the same evening he brought Tonge to Charles, with a narrative
of the plot; that the king referred it to the Lord Treasurer; that Charles was
incredulous, and laughed at the simplicity of Danby in his wish to lay the
narrative before the Privy Council. But it may occur to some, bearing in mind
the time that elapsed between the first information to the king and the official
notification to the Council, that there was some ground for the conjecture of
Littleton and Powel that the Court had its own objects in raising the alleged
Plot into importance, by encouraging the witnesses in their extravagant relations. The objection of lord Halifax to this theory was reasonable enough.
He told Burnet that "considering the suspicions all people had of the duke's
religion, he believed every discovery of that sort would raise a flame which
it would not be easy to manage." But the objection assumed that the con-
trivers of such state-engines were duly sensible of the effects they might
produce—that "the ingener" might contemplate the possibility of being
"hoist with his own petar." If Danby stimulated the revelations of the plot
to alarm the Commons into granting supplies, it did not follow that he would
foresee such a storm as would give a violent impulse to all the political movements of the next ten years. Shaftesbury, says Roger North, "was the dry-
nurse, and took the charge of leading the monstrous birth till it could crawl
alone." It is quite within the range of probability that the Court got up the
Plot for its own purposes; and that "the discontented party" took it out of
the Court's hands for its own purposes also.

Burnet, who relates conversations that he had with the king, represents
Charles as saying that after Tonge's audience he did not know but some of
the particulars related to him might be true, and sent him to lord Danby.
"The matter lay in a secret and remiss management for six weeks," till, on
Michaelmas eve, Oates was brought before the Council. He related many
discourses he had heard among the Jesuits at St. Omer's of their design to
kill the king; he named persons, places, and times almost without number
he accused Coleman, the duke's secretary. Many Jesuits were seized.
Coleman removed the bulk of his letters previous to his apprehension; but
two were accidentally left, addressed to the confessor of Louis XIV., which

* "Examer," p. 35

in some degree confirmed the belief of a design to overthrow the government. Burnet went to Whitehall, and there found Oates and Tonge under a guard. Previous to Oates being examined a second time by the Privy Council, he went before sir Edmondbury Godfrey, a zealous Protestant justice of peace, and made oath to the narrative which he afterwards published. A fortnight after, Godfrey was missing, having left his home on a Saturday morning. On the following Wednesday his corpse was found in a ditch at some distance out of the town, near Primrose-hill. His own sword was thrust through his body, but no blood was on his clothes: on his neck were the marks of strangulation. The Papists were, of course, suspected of his murder; although the motive was altogether a mystery. On the other hand it was maintained that he had committed suicide. A medal was struck ridiculing this notion, in showing the unfortunate Justice walking with a halter about his neck after he is dead, and St. Denis on the obverse, with his own head in his hand. There was another medal with a portrait of Godfrey, and a representation of the

murderers carrying his body on a horse. Roger North, who labours in every way to fasten the invention of the Plot upon the party opposed to the Court, describes the fury of the people on the discovery of this supposed murder; and says that their leaders would have hounded them on to any massacre and destruction, had the military not been in good order. The popular notion was that the murder of Godfrey was to deter all men from any further inquiry into the Plot. There was great excitement at the funeral of the Protestant magistrate, which North has described with some humour. "The crowd was prodigious, both at the procession, and in and about the church; and so heated that anything called Popish, were it cat or dog, had probably gone to pieces in a moment. The Catholics all kept close in their houses and lodgings, thinking it a good composition to be safe there; so far were they from acting violently at that time. But there was all this while upheld among the common people an artificial fright, so as almost every man fancied a Popish knife just at his throat. And, at the sermon, besides the preacher, two other thumping divines stood upright in the pulpit, one on each side of him, to guard him from being killed, while he was preaching, by the Papists." * In this feverish state of the popular mind, the Parliament met on the 21st of October. Charles alluded to information

* " Examen," p. 204.

received by him of a design against his person by the Jesuits, but said he would leave the matter to the law. The Parliament immediately determined to take the subject into their own hands. They appointed a Committee to inquire into Godfrey's murder and into the Plot; they addressed the king to appoint a solemn fast; they further desired the removal of all Popish recusants from the metropolis and ten miles round; before a week had elapsed, a bill was passed by the Commons to exclude Catholics from both Houses. Oates was examined. Coleman's letters were read. On the 1st of November, the Commons came to a resolution, "That, upon the evidence that has already appeared to the House, this House is of opinion, that there hath been, and still is, a damnable and hellish Plot, contrived and carried on by Popish recusants, for the assassinating and murdering the king, and for subverting the government, and rooting out and destroying the Protestant religion." The Lords unanimously agreed in the Resolution of the Commons.

There are two descriptions by impartial witnesses which present striking pictures of the state of the popular mind at this season. On the 17th of November, queen Elizabeth's birth-day, there was a mock procession which Calamy, the son of the famous non-conformist, saw in his boyhood, and thus relates: "In the midst of vast crowds of spectators, who made great acclamations and showed abundance of satisfaction, there were carried in pageants upon men's shoulders through the chief streets of the city, the effigies of the Pope, with the representation of the devil behind him, whispering in his ear, and wonderfully soothing and caressing him (though he afterwards deserted him, and left him to shift for himself, before he was committed to the flames), together with the likeness of the dead body of sir Edmondbury Godfrey, carried before him by one that rode on horseback, designed to remind the people of his execrable murder. And a great number of dignitaries in their copes, with crosses; monks, friars, and Jesuits; Popish bishops in their mitres, with all their trinkets and appurtenances. Such things as these very discernibly heightened and inflamed the general aversion of the nation from Popery; but it is to be feared, on the other hand, they put some people, by way of revulsion, upon such desperate expedients as brought us even within an ace of ruin." Daniel Defoe, then also a youth, was greatly excited by the Popish plot, some of the credulities accompanying which he described in his maturer years: "I did firmly believe the reality of the plot; yet, when we ran up that plot to general massacres, fleets of pilgrims, bits and bridles, knives, handcuffs, and a thousand such things, which people generally talk of, I confess, though a boy, I could not then, nor can now, come up to them. And my reasons were, as they still are, because I see no reason to believe the Papists to be fools, whatever else we had occasion to think of them. I cannot, indeed, spare room to examine the weakness of the notion of a general massacre in England, where the Papists all over the kingdom are not five to a hundred, in some counties not one, and within the city hardly one to a thousand. But, 'tis plain, these notions prevailed to a strange excess, made our city blunderbusses to be all new burnished, hat and feathers, shoulder-belt, and all our military gew-gaws come in mode again, till the city trained-bands began to be so rampant, that, like other standing armies, they began to ride upon their masters, and trampled under foot the liberty of that very city they were raised to defend. They were made engines of oppression and disorder, disturbed meeting-houses, possessed the Guildhall, chose sheriffs, got drunk upon guard, abused the citizens upon their rounds, and their prodigal drunken sentinels murdered several people upon pretence they would not stand at their command. In a populous city, it was impossible but innocent people, either ignorant or perhaps in drink, might run themselves into danger, not imagining they had to do with brutes that would kill their fellow-citizens for such trifles, with the same severity as if in an enemy's country, or on the frontiers."

As there was nothing in the terrors of massacres and invasions; of burnings of London and of the shipping in the Thames; of Jesuits about to rule the land under the seal of the Pope,—too absurd for the multitude to credit; so there was no eminent person, however loyal and peaceable, who might not become a victim to the accusations of those men who had brought a whole nation into a condition of senseless panic. "All Oates' evidence," says Burnet, "was now so well believed that it was not safe for any man to doubt any part of it." He named peers to whom the Pope had sent over his commissions. He accused Wakeman, the queen's physician, of a project to poison his sovereign. Bedloe, a man of notorious evil life, surrendered himself at Bristol, pretending that he was cognisant of the murder of Godfrey, and could point out the murderers and instigators; and he then came forward in support of the accusations of Oates against certain peers who had been apprehended on Oates's charges. The consummation of the impudence of Oates was his attempt to involve the harmless queen in a charge of having concerted the murder of her husband. He told a story that the queen had sent for some Jesuits to Somerset House; that he went with them, and standing behind a door, heard one in a woman's voice, there being no other woman in the room than the queen, assure them that she would assist in taking off the king. North relates that Oates, at the bar of the House of Commons, said, "*Aye, Taitus* Oates, *accause* Catherine, *Quean of England, of Haigh Traison*." * Burnet has a curious relation of his own conversation with the king on this delicate subject. The good bishop's relations have been considered, though perhaps unjustly, a little open to doubt; but we are not entitled to question what he relates of his personal knowledge. "The king spoke much to me concerning Oates's accusing the queen, and acquainted me with the whole progress of it. He said she was a weak woman, and had some disagreeable humours; but was not capable of a wicked thing; and, considering his faultiness towards her in other things, he thought it a horrid thing to abandon her. He said he looked on falsehood and cruelty as the greatest crimes in the sight of God; he knew he had led a bad life, of which he spoke with some sense; but he was breaking himself of all his faults; and he would never do a base and a wicked thing. I spoke on all these subjects which I thought became me, which he took well; and I encouraged him much in his resolution of not exposing the queen to perish by false swearing."

We have thus shown some ludicrous aspects of this famous Plot. The

* Scott, from this hint, has given Oates his peculiar dialect in "Peveril of the Peak."

horrible realities connected with it present a fearful example of the atrocities that may be committed under the excitement of religious animosity. The trials of the accused persons commenced in November. Stayley, a Catholic banker, was first sacrificed, upon a ridiculous accusation brought forward by Carstairs, a Scotchman, who saw that the trade of false witness was prosperous. He swore that he heard the banker say, in French, that the king was a rogue, and that he himself would kill him, if nobody else would. Burnet gave offence by showing that Carstairs was an infamous character; and Shaftesbury, as the bishop relates, told him "that all those who undermined the credit of the witnesses were public enemies." The poor banker was tried and was hanged. Coleman was next brought to trial upon charges made against him by Oates and Bedloe. The evidence was very inconclusive; but his letters were against him, although he maintained that he had no idea of bringing in the Catholic religion, but by a general toleration. He was convicted of high treason, and executed. Three Jesuits, Ireland, Grove. and Pickering, were the next victims. Green and Hill, two Papists, and Berry, a Protestant, were then convicted of the murder of sir Edmondbury Godfrey, upon the testimony of Bedloe, and the pretended confession of Prance, a silversmith. The prisons were filled with hundreds of suspected traitors. Five peers were confined in the Tower under impeachment. Scroggs, the Chief Justice, conducted himself, in all the trials, with the most ferocious determination to procure a verdict against the prisoners. Oates in a few months was at the height of his greatness. "He walked about," says North, "with his guards assigned for fear of the Papists murdering him. He had lodgings in Whitehall, and 1200l. per annum pension: And no wonder, after he had the impudence to say to the House of Lords, in plain terms, that, if they would not help him to more money, he must be forced to help himself. He put on an episcopal garb, except the lawn sleeves; silk gown and cassock, great hat, satin hatband and rose, long scarf, and was called, or most blasphemously called himself, the Saviour of the Nation. Whoever he pointed at was taken up and committed; so that many people got out of his way, as from a blast, and glad they could prove their two last years' conversation. The very breath of him was pestilential, and if it brought not imprisonment, or death, over such on whom it fell, it surely poisoned reputation, and left good protestants arrant papists, and something worse than that, in danger of being put in the plot as traitors." *

We have dwelt at some length upon this Popish Plot; and in their order of time we shall have to give a few other details. It may be thought that such an occurrence might be more briefly related; but it is not only strikingly illustrative of the temper of the people, but was really pregnant with important consequences. Dr. Wellwood, who wrote his 'Memoirs' some twenty years after these events, has expressed, with tolerable impartiality, the view in which they were regarded after the Revolution :—"A great part of the Popish Plot, as it was then sworn to, will in all human probability lie among the darkest scenes of our English history. However, this is certain: the discovery of the Popish Plot had great and various effects upon the

* "Examen."

nation; and it's from this remarkable period of time we may justly reckon
a new era in the English account.   In the first place, it awakened the nation
out of a deep lethargy they had been in for nineteen years together; and
alarmed them with fears and jealousies that have been found to our sad experience but too well grounded.   In the next, it gave the rise to, at least
settled, that unhappy distinction of Whig and Tory among the people of England, that has since occasioned so many mischiefs.   And lastly, the discovery
of the Popish Plot began that open struggle between King Charles and his
people, that occasioned him not only to dissolve his first favourite parliament,
and the three others that succeeded; but likewise to call no more during
the rest of his reign.   All which made for bringing in question the Charters
of London, and other Corporations, with a great many dismal effects that
followed." *

* "Memoirs of the most material Transactions," &c. 1736, p. 111.

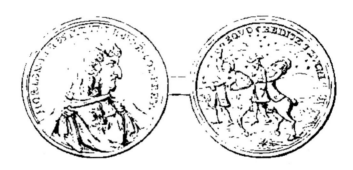

Bass Rock,—with the Prison of the Covenanters.

CHAPTER XXI.

THE political excitement of the Christmas time of 1678 had not been equalled since the early days of the Long Parliament. In the very height of the fever of the Popish Plot a discovery was made of the intrigues of the king with France, which very soon led to the ruin of the Lord Treasurer, Danby. In the secret treaty between Charles and Louis in May, 1678, it was agreed that the English army should be disbanded. The French ambassador, Barillon, pressed its reduction to 8000 men; which Charles as constantly evaded; and he is said to have exclaimed, " God's fish ! are all the king of France's promises to make me master of my subjects come to this ? or does he think that a matter to be done with 8000 men ? " Louis was out of humour with Charles, who appeared disposed to set up for a despot without his brother despot's aid; and he urged Ralph Montague, the English minister at Paris, to betray the secrets of their intrigues. Montague was also out of humour with his own government. He came home, and was elected a member of parliament. The Lord Treasurer dreaded Montague's disclosures; and ordered his papers to be seized, under pretence that he had held private conferences with the Pope's nuncio. A royal message to this effect was sent to the Commons. "But Montague," says Burnet, "understood the arts of a Court too well to be easily catched." He had put a box, in which certain letters were, "in sure hands, out of the way." The object in endeavouring to obtain possession of these papers was to destroy the evidence of the transactions of May, 1678. Montague, in his place in the House said, "I believe that the seizing my cabinets and papers was to get into their hands some papers of great consequence, that I have to produce, of the designs of a great minister of state." The box containing these was opened in the House; and Montague read two letters, one of which, signed Danby, empowered him to stipulate for a payment to the king of six hundred thousand livres annually for three years, as the price of his neutrality. At the bottom of the letter were these words: "This letter is writ by my order, C.R." Mr. Hallam has forcibly observed of the conduct of the king, as indicated by this letter, that it "bears date five days after an Act had absolutely passed to raise money for carrying on the war; a circumstance worthy of particular attention, as it both puts an end to every pretext or apology which the least scrupulous could venture to urge in behalf of this negotiation, and justifies the Whig party of England in an invincible distrust, an inexpiable hatred, of so perfidious a cozener." * There was a passage in this letter of instructions to Montague, which gave dire offence to those in the House of Commons who felt as Englishmen. Charles asked for the pension, "because it will be two or three years before he can hope to find his Parliament in humour to give him supplies, after your having made any peace with France." One member, Mr. Bennet, exclaimed, "I wonder the House sits so silent when they see themselves sold for six millions of livres to the French." Another, Mr. Harbord, said, "I hope now gentlemen's eyes are open, by the design on foot to destroy the government and our liberties." Sir Henry Capel, calling upon the House to impeach Danby of treason, said, "This minister has let the French king grow upon us, and let our king take money from him, to lay aside his people." † From this time the unity which the Lord Chancellor Finch so earnestly implored was impossible. The arts of the Court were met by counter-arts of the Opposition; the craft of the despot was resisted by the turbulence of the demagogue; the same foreign hand which had bribed the king to degrade his country now bribed the Parliament to contend against the king. It is a sickening spectacle. The only consolation is that ultimate good came out of the instant evil. Danby was impeached of high treason. He had reluctantly written this letter at the command of his unworthy master; but the penalty constitutionally fell upon the minister. He defended himself upon the plea that upon the matter of peace and war the king was the sole judge, and that he ought to be obeyed by his ministers of state, as by all his subjects. It is now well understood that the commands of the sovereign furnish no justification for evil measures of the Crown; that the minister must have the responsibility. Danby,

* "Constitutional History," chap. xiii.   † "Parl. Hist." vol. iv.

though a mere accomplice in guilt, was the one guilty minister; for the letter said "To the Secretary [sir W. Coventry] you must not mention one syllable of the money." The continuance of proceedings against the Lord Treasurer was interrupted by the prorogation of Parliament on the 21st of December, and by its dissolution on the 24th of January, 1679. This was the last Session of the Parliament that had continued since 1661. It commenced in a frenzy of loyalty; it ended in all the embitterment of discontent at the present, and in dread of the future.

Roger North says that the vacation of Parliament "was indeed a dismal one. . . . All populous places were made unquiet with artificial fears and jealousies. . . . All incidents were made wonders, and odd accidents right down prodigies." The Londoners were frightened, as if it were a terrible omen, by a great darkness in London on a Sunday morning, "so that the people in church could not read in their bibles." North asks a question which shows that our metropolitan atmosphere has not much changed during two hundred years. "To what end is this magnifying, so prodigiously, a common accident in London, there being seldom a winter without it; for when a common mist mixes with the coal-smoke it must be so; and out of town, where is no smoke, it is not half so much." * It was fortunate that the elections came to stir the people into real political action, instead of their yielding to vain delusions and idle fears. It seems, indeed, to have been a most stirring time. There is a striking picture of an election scene at Norwich, in sir Thomas Browne's letters. The return for the county of Norfolk was contested; and a new election took place: "I do not remember such a great poll. I could not but observe the great number of horses which were in the town; and conceive there might have been five or six thousand, which in time of need might serve for dragoon horses; besides a great number of coach-horses, and very good saddle-horses of the better sort. Wine we had none but sack and Rhenish, except some made provision thereof beforehand; but there was a strange consumption of beer, and bread, and cakes. Abundance of people slept in the market-place, and lay like flocks of sheep in and about the cross."† Evelyn laments that so many from the country came in to vote for his brother as knight of the shire for Surrey, "that I believe they ate and drank him out near to 2000l., by a most abominable custom." Burnet says, "The elections were carried with great heat, and went almost everywhere against the Court."

The duke of York, two days before the Parliament met on the 6th of March, was persuaded to go abroad. His absence might allay the heat which was manifested against him in the last Parliament, when there was a violent debate upon the proviso of the Lords, in the Bill for excluding Catholics from both Houses, that the duke should be exempted.‡ But the duke of York, before he left the country for a temporary exile, required that his interests in the succession to the Crown should be protected against the pretended claims of the duke of Monmouth. This supposed eldest of the many illegitimate children of Charles II. was born at Rotterdam, in 1649. James II. in his

* "Examen," p. 504.   † Sir T. Browne's Works, 1836, vol. i. p. 241.
‡ Catholics had been excluded from the Lower House previous to the statute of 1678 excluding peers.

" Advice to his Son" in the Stuart Papers, says, " All the knowing world, as well as myself, had many convincing reasons to think he was not the king's son, but Robert Sidney's." His mother, Lucy Waters, who was known as Mrs. Barlow, was a lady of somewhat disreputable life; but Charles seems to have clung to her with unusual fidelity. She lived on terms of friendly intercourse with the sister of Charles, the princess of Orange, who in writing to her brother says, " your wife desires me to present her humble duty to you." The term " wife " was probably used in jest by Charles's sister. Mrs. Barlow came to England with the boy in 1656; and is said to have been received by some Cavaliers with attentions paid to royalty. Cromwell had her, in the first place, apprehended, and then sent an order to the Lieutenant of the Tower to release " the lady of pleasure and the young heir." She went to Paris, and soon after died. The son was received with favour by the queen dowager, Henrietta Maria, and came with her to England in 1662. He was called Master Crofts, from having resided with lord Crofts, and is described by Evelyn as " a pretty spark." In 1663 he was created duke of Monmouth, and was ordered " to take place of all dukes." He was also married at the same time to the young countess of Buccleugh, a lady of immense fortune. Monmouth did not deserve " the finest lady in the three kingdoms," for he became an abandoned profligate. Charles appears to have been more constantly attached to him than to any other human being; and to this circumstance may be probably attributed the very general belief that the king had been married to his mother. The high offices bestowed upon Monmouth were far above his deserts or abilities; although he had exhibited bravery and judgment in the war of 1673, in which the English assisted Louis XIV. in his campaign. In 1677 he served on the other side, under the prince of Orange. The notion was either put into his head by the enemies of the duke of York, or he indulged in the delusion through some mysterious stories about documents in a black box, that he was the legitimate heir to the throne. The opinion was too general to be despised; and it is not surprising, therefore, that before the duke of York went abroad he should have required his brother to set the matter at rest by a solemn affirmation to the contrary. Charles, on the 3rd of March, declared to his Council, " in the presence of Almighty God, that he had never given or made any contract of marriage, nor was married to any woman whatsoever but his wife, queen Catherine, then living." James, with the duchess of York, then departed for Brussels.

The resumption of the impeachment against lord Danby, upon the meeting of Parliament, involved two great constitutional questions. One was, whether an impeachment by the Commons in one Parliament could be continued in another Parliament. The Lords resolved that " the dissolution of the last Parliament did not alter the state of the impeachments brought up by the Commons in that Parliament." * The other question was on the right of the king to grant a pardon pending an impeachment. Danby, when he saw the proceedings revived against him, obtained a pardon under the great seal, which the king affixed without the knowledge of the Chancellor. The Commons declared that a pardon to set aside an impeachment could not

---

* There were subsequent reversals of this decision; but in the impeachment of Warren Hastings, the resolution of 1679 was affirmed in 1791.

be pleaded. After various contests, Danby was committed to the Tower, and when a prorogation took place the impeachment fell to the ground.

After the fall of Danby, a great experiment in Administration was resolved upon, on the suggestion of sir William Temple. His notion was that any select body of ministers, such as was known then as a Cabal, and is now called a Cabinet, should not be the principal advisers of the king; that the Privy Council should be dissolved, and a Council smaller in number should be appointed, with which the management of affairs should be entrusted, the king pledging himself to submit all matters to their advice. This new Council was to consist of thirty members, fifteen being high officers of state, and fifteen noblemen and gentlemen of wealth and independence. The wealth was an essential condition in the notion of the projector. The thirty members were to possess estates or revenues amounting to £300,000, a sum equal to three-fourths of the income, as then estimated, of the whole House of Commons. The principle was evidently to interpose some great authority in the State between the king and the representatives of the people —something that would be a counterpoise to the vast development of the power of the Lower House.* As an administrative body it is evident that Temple's Council would prove a failure. It could not essentially differ from the old Privy Council; for thirty members would be as unfit for the united action of an executive as fifty. The Privy Council of Elizabeth and of James I., as in earlier times, gave orders and signed dispatches. When sovereigns were their own ministers, the inconvenience of a large executive body would interfere little with the rapid and secret conduct of affairs. There was a natural jealousy of Cabals or Cabinets; but they had become indispensable in the time of Charles II. The opinions of the Lord Keeper Guilford upon the Cabinet Council, are illustrative of this gradual change in the functions of Administration. Roger North says that his relative intended to describe the transactions of the Court, and the state of the empire, during his ministry as Lord Keeper: " He begins with the state of the Cabinet Council, that consisted of those great officers, and courtiers, whom the king relied upon for the interior dispatch of his affairs. . . . This council was derived from the Privy Council, which, originally, was the same thing, and derived out of the *magnum concilium*. . . . Assemblies at first reasonably constituted of a due number and temper for dispatch of affairs committed to them, by improvident increase came to be formal and troublesome, the certain consequence of multitude; and thereby a new institution becomes necessary; whereupon it is found easier and safer to substitute than to dissolve. Thus the Cabinet Council, which at first was but in the nature of a private conversation, came to be a formal Council, and had the direction of most transactions of the government foreign and domestic." † This opinion of Lord Guilford was formed subsequent to the experiment of 1679, and had no reference to the newly constituted advisers of the Crown. But it is clear that Temple's Council would have been as unmanageable as an executive body as the Privy Council, which had become unfit for dispatch of affairs " by improvident increase." Some of the popular leaders were of this new Council, such as

---

* The design of Temple is most ably elucidated in Lord Macaulay's " Essays," vol. iii.
† " Lives," vol. ii. p. 50.

Russell. Shaftesbury was proposed by the king, and was nominated president. There was great rejoicing at the formation of this Council. The people thought they should be better governed. The Parliament looked coldly upon the project. The ministers very soon formed into juntos. There was a Cabinet of four members within the Council. None of the hostility of the Commons to the duke of York was disarmed by this nominal union of men of conflicting opinions. The thirty had violent contentions; and in a short time Shaftesbury appeared in the anomalous character of President of the Council, and leader of the parliamentary Opposition. The conduct of the king in this Council is recorded by the great eulogist of the Court, with singular admiration of the royal cleverness. The rolls of justices were laid before the Council, in order to be reformed. ."It was pleasant to see with how much wit and good humour the king ordered affairs, to disappoint these reformers. He would not suffer the roll, that was begun with, to be out of his own hand, but pretended to mark the alterations upon it himself. Then, as many of the Council moved for alterations upon the account of good or bad men (terms of art, which for brevity, they used to signify such as the party liked, or would have put out, or not), if the king was content a man should out, he made a mark at his name; but, if he would not part with him, he found some jocular reason to let him stand; as that he was a good cocker, understood hunting, kept a good house, had good chines of beef, kept good fox-hounds, or some such indifferent matter, which it was ridiculous to contradict or dispute upon. And, in this manner, he frustrated all their intent as to removes." * With such a Council and such a sovereign, it is manifest there could be no abatement of a violent temper in Parliament. The confirmed hostility to the duke of York was manifested in a Bill for his exclusion from the succession to the throne. To prevent this passing, the Parliament was prorogued on the 26th of May to the 14th of August. The king took this step without communicating with his Council. The Exclusion Bill had passed a second reading of the Commons, and its clauses were being discussed in Committee. But there was a measure of greater importance to the real and permanent interests of the country than this premature attempt to disturb the Succession. A great legal reform had been carried through both Houses, and waited the Royal Assent. On that 26th of May Charles, however reluctantly, sanctioned the utterance of the three old words which make legislation law, when the Bill was presented to him, which now stands in our Statute Books as "An Act for the better securing the Liberty of the Subject, and for Preventing of Imprisonments beyond Seas." † This is the Habeas Corpus Act, the noble enactment which made that clause of the Great Charter which secures the personal liberty of every Englishman a living principle instead of a dead letter. By the Common Law no subject could be illegally imprisoned, for he might sue for the writ of Habeas Corpus, and be heard in open court. But judges, sheriffs, gaolers, used every art to refuse and to evade the writ. The Privy Council would cause men to be confined beyond seas, in the king's foreign dominions, out of the jurisdiction of the Courts of Justice. Political offences, real or pretended, were thus punished more severely than the laws could punish. Suspicion stood in the place of

* "Examen," p. 77.   † 31 Car. II. c. 2.

evidence. Unhappy men lingered out years in distant prisons; and their wrongs were never known except to their oppressors. The strictness and promptitude of the proceedings under the Habeas Corpus Act struck the old weapon of tyranny out of the hands of the powerful. To Shaftesbury, whatever may have been his demerits, we mainly owe the triumph of this great measure. On the same morning that the king gave his assent to the Habeas Corpus Act, he knocked off, perhaps unconsciously, the shackles of the Press. The Licensing Act of 1662 was to continue till the end of the next session of Parliament. All books had been under the control of the Licenser for seventeen years. By the prorogation of the 27th of May, that system came to a temporary close. There was many a struggle yet to be made before Englishmen could point to their own condition, and exultingly say,

> "This is true Liberty, when free-born men
> Having to advise the public, may speak free." *

The Parliament was dissolved by proclamation before the 14th of August, to which day it had been prorogued. The fourth Parliament of Charles II. met on the 7th of October, 1679, but it was prorogued, again and again, for more than a year. During the summer of 1679, the trials for the Popish Plot went forward, with no abatement of the popular outcry against the unhappy Roman Catholics. In June, two Jesuits, Whitbread and Fenwick, who had previously stood at the bar, and had been illegally remanded to prison in defect of evidence, were again indicted, with three others. The cross-swearing on these trials was astounding. The evidence of Oates went to prove a conspiracy of which he became cognizant in London in April 1678. Sixteen of the inmates of St. Omer's came over to the trial, and swore that Oates resided amongst them, uninterruptedly, from January to June. On the other side, eight persons swore that they had seen him in England at the beginning of May. The accused were all found guilty. Langhorne, a Catholic lawyer, was also tried and condemned. The six were executed on the 20th of June. The grossest partiality was manifested from the judgment seat in these trials. Scroggs, the Chief-Justice, kept no bounds of decency in urging the jury to convict. The other judges sat by his side, and interposed no opinion as to the credibility of the evidence. Roger North offers this excuse for his relative, and the rest of the ermined tools: "Nothing can qualify the silence, but the inconceivable fury and rage of the community, gentle and simple, at that time, and the consequences of an open opposition to the Chief, whose part it was to act, as he did, demanding no assistance of any of them; which opposition might have been fatal in many respects: for the credit of the witnesses must have been impeached, which the time would not bear; and it was not in their office to intermeddle; for, as to the fact, the jury is to answer. When it is so done by the co-assessors, it is for discretion, and not duty; the most cogent reason was, that the prejudice was so universal, and strong, that if an apostle had spoken against, no impression had taken place, nor had it done the prisoners any service; but on the other side, not only the rabble, but even the parliament itself, had flounced at it;

---

* Milton's motto to "Liberty of Unlicensed Printing," from Euripides.

which consideration turned the scales of the discretion, and made those judges rather let a vessel drive, which they could not stop, and reserve themselves for fairer opportunities, when such might happen, for them to do some good, without pretending to remove mountains." *

There was a stop at last to these disgraceful exhibitions. The English "rabble" are violent, but they are not blood-thirsty; and the executions of men who maintained their innocence to the last wrought pity and disgust even amongst the most prejudiced. The trial of sir George Wakeman, the queen's physician, came on in July. Oates and Bedloe were as positive in their testimony, as on former trials where they easily obtained convictions. But now, to their great astonishment, the bench allowed their assertions to be questioned; and thus, after Oates had gone through his course of bold accusations against Wakeman, the Clerk of the Privy Council came forward, and testified that when the confident witness was asked by the Lord Chancellor if he knew anything personally of the queen's physician, he lifted up his hands to heaven, and protested he did not. Three Benedictine monks were indicted as accomplices with Wakeman in the design to poison the king. After a trial of nine hours the whole were acquitted. The believers in the plot gradually diminished. "The witnesses," says Burnet, "saw they were blasted; and they were enraged on it, which they vented with much spite against Scroggs." The trials of common men were now laid aside. But Stafford and the four other lords were still in the Tower, waiting to be tried by their peers. The dissolution and repeated prorogations left their fate doubtful. In the meanwhile Oates and Bedloe were in comfortable quarters, and were receiving handsome gratuities, as well as Dugdale, another of their tribe. There are records of many payments to these worthies, under the heads of "free gift and royal bounty;" "for diet;" for "charges about several witnesses;" for "expenses about the plot;" for "maintaining witnesses in town about the plot;" for "a further discovery of the plot;" for "expenses in prosecuting;" for "discovering a Jesuit;" for "journeys;" for "discovering Papists harboured in Court;" for "lodgings in Whitehall;" extending over a period from March 30, 1679, to March 4, 1683. Of the previous payments to the "witnesses" during half a year, we have no record. We have made a careful analysis of about a hundred and twenty entries of payment to Oates, Bedloe, Tonge, and Dugdale, as they appear in the accounts of moneys paid for Secret Services; and we find that up to the 7th of September, 1681, Oates received 1660l. 8s. 10d.; Bedloe, to July 1680, received 804l.; Tonge, who died in January, 1681, received 344l., and for his funeral was also paid 50l.; and Dugdale, who kept drawing the wages of iniquity to the 4th of March, 1683, received 1138l. 15s. † After April, 1681, Oates and Dugdale, instead of being allowed to "sit at ten pounds a-week" like Falstaff, were reduced to a very ignoble two pounds for allowance. Dugdale seems to have held on, and received large sums, long after the supposed instigators of a pretended Plot—Shaftesbury and his friends—had lost power or parliamentary influence.

Whilst these fearful exhibitions of the dire effects of religious animosity

* "Life of Lord Keeper Guilford," vol. i. p. 327.
† "Moneys for Secret Services," Camden Society, pp. 3 to 67.

were passing in England, there were even more signal displays of the same spirit, though in an entirely opposite direction, manifested in Scotland. We turn with equal loathing from the corrupt judgments of Scroggs, to the brutal slaughters of Claverhouse. And yet these events must be recorded for instruction and for warning. Religious hatreds have not so entirely died out amongst us, that we can be quite sure that disputes about candles and flowers, about the Judaical observance of the Lord's day, about Jews in Parliament, about Maynooth, might be wholly settled by furious orators and writers, without the sword and the halter, unless the darkness which surrounds such controversies were somewhat dispersed by the light of History. Men can only effectually learn to be tolerant and loving, by seeing what monsters bigotry has made of their forefathers.

After the suppression of the insurrection of Covenanters, in 1666,[*] Scotland continued in an unquiet state; not openly resisting the government, but nourishing many elements of future disturbance. Archbishop Sharp was especially feared and hated by the stricter Presbyterians. The most fanatical believed him to be the enemy of God, and that his destruction would be an acceptable service. In July, 1668, as the archbishop was getting into his coach, he was shot at; and his companion, the bishop of Orkney, was wounded. No one attempted to seize the offender; but the archbishop had noted his features and general appearance. He wandered about the country for a long time, and then returned to Edinburgh. Six years afterwards, Sharp fancied that a shop-keeper who lived near him was the man who fired at him. His name was Mitchell. He was brought before the Council, and after a solemn promise that his life should be spared, he confessed his guilt. The Council doomed him to perpetual imprisonment on the Bass Rock, after having subjected him to the torture of the boot. Mitchell had been confined here three or four years when it was determined to bring him to trial, for his crime committed in 1668. Upon the duke of Lauderdale's becoming supreme in Scotland, in connexion with the Cabal ministry, he attempted to carry out the same policy of a compromise with non-conformists as was being attempted in England. Many Presbyterian ministers conformed under the Declaration of Indulgence. Burnet says that it was part of the plan to put "all the ousted ministers by couples in parishes;" but that Lauderdale, who governed by fits, "passing from hot to cold ones," neglected this precaution, and that many of the deprived ministers went about, holding conventicles. Very soon the principles of severity trampled down any disposition to moderate courses. Indeed the more violent of the Covenanters utterly despised any measure which would stop short of re-instating their church in triumphant domination. The Black Indulgence, as they termed the healing declaration, was denounced as a bait for the worldly-minded and ungodly. There were large assemblies in wild and solitary places, to which many came armed. The government went about the repression of these meetings with a frantic violence. To strike terror into the Covenanters they removed Mitchell from his wave-beaten rock in the Frith, and brought him to Edinburgh for trial. His own confession was urged against him. The promise upon which that confession was extorted was suppressed. The archbishop, who had first employed an

* Ante, p. 294.

agent to obtain this confession, denied any promise. The lords Lauderdale, Rothes, and Halton, swore that no such promise had been made by the Council. The Council books were not allowed to be produced; and the man was convicted. The distinct record of the promise was found in the Council books immediately after the conviction; and yet the man was executed. "This action," says Burnet, "with all concerned in it, was looked at by all people with horror; and it was such a complication of treachery, perjury, and cruelty, as the like had not perhaps been known." The Covenanters were not deterred by this manifestation of vindictiveness, but continued to assemble, particularly in the western counties. Lauderdale determined to act as if the whole district were in rebellion. He required all the land-owners to execute bonds, not only for their own conformity in attending the church service and avoiding conventicles, but for their servants, tenants, and residents on their property. They refused, and Lauderdale asked for authority to reduce them to submission by military force. Charles consented. The Highlanders were brought from their mountains to live at free quarters, and to plunder, in the devoted district. The inhabitants were disarmed. Lauderdale's excesses became at last too much even for the government of Charles to bear. The king could not wholly justify the acts of his minister. "But when May, the master of the privy purse, asked him in his familiar way, what he thought now of his Lauderdale, he answered, as May himself told me, that they had objected many damned things that he had done against them, but there was nothing objected that was against his service: such are the notions that many kings drink in, by which they set up an interest for themselves, in opposition to the interest of the people."* Hume terms the opinion of the king "a sentiment unworthy of a sovereign." It was a sentiment worthy of a captain of banditti.

There are no historical events with which the most cursory reader is more familiar, than the murder of archbishop Sharp, and the battles of Loudon Hill and Bothwell Bridge. The narratives of the atrocious tyranny which led to these events are sufficiently obscure, whether they issue from the perse-cuted or the persecutors; but they present a sufficiently distinct picture which scarcely requires the colouring of romance to command our interest. That ancient hunter of Covenanters, Captain John Creichton,—who was introduced by Swift to the notice of the world in 1731, as "a very honest and worthy man, but of the old stamp," and who himself laments over "the won-derful change of opinions,"—relates with the extremest glee his various· exploits in dispersing conventicles, in apprehending preachers, and in deliver-ing them to the proper authorities to be tortured and hanged. He attempts no sort of excuse for using deceptions, to find out his victims, quite unworthy of the fighting cavalier. He hunts "the rogues" as if he thoroughly enjoyed the chase. He cannot justify his "rashness" in such adventures, except that it manifests his loyalty to his prince, his zeal for the church, and his detesta-tion of all rebellious principles. These narratives of Creichton precede his account of the insurrection of 1679. It was in the western counties that "the booted apostles of prelacy" chiefly exercised their dragoonings. There the Covenanters were most numerous and most persevering. But in the

* Burnet. Book iii.

eastern districts there was the same spirit, though less openly displayed. In the county of Fife, a few religious enthusiasts, encouraging each other in their secret prayer-meetings, and accepting the stern denunciations of the Hebrew scriptures to smite the wicked as holy impulses to murder the enemies of their own form of worship, resolved upon the sacrifice of the archbishop of St. Andrew's, and of Carmichael, the commissioner of the Council. Ten of this band of fanatics went forth in search of their intended victims. John Balfour, known by the name of Burly, and his brother-in-law, Hackston of Rathillet, were the leaders in this design. Carmichael escaped. But they accidentally encountered archbishop Sharp; and at once considered, in their savage enthusiasm, that God had delivered their great enemy into their hands. Dragged from his carriage as he was passing, in company with his daughter, over Magus Muir, near St. Andrew's on the 3rd of May, 1679, he was inhumanly butchered, his unhappy child struggling with the murderers to save her aged father. The leaders fled into the west. Assembling some of the more violent of their own persuasion, their contempt of the civil government was manifested by their extinguishing the bonfires which had been lighted on the 29th of May, in honour of the king's restoration, in the burgh of Rutherglen. They also burnt the Acts of Parliament for restoring prelacy and suppressing conventicles. On the 1st of June, being Sunday, they held a field conventicle at Loudon Hill. John Graham, of Claverhouse, marched out from Glasgow with about a hundred and fifty cavalry, for the purpose of dispersing them. The number of the Covenanters had increased to five or six hundred; armed chiefly with pikes and pitchforks. They had a few horse amongst them. On a marshy ground near the village of Drumclog, Claverhouse charged this irregular force. He was utterly discomfited, and was compelled to retreat to Glasgow. The insurgents followed the fugitives, their ranks receiving constant accessions, not only of the Cameronians who would admit no compromise of the Solemn League and Covenant, but of moderate Presbyterians, who were indignant at the tyranny under which the country groaned. But their camp was divided into rival sects, each despising the other as much as they hated their common oppressor. At Glasgow they were repulsed, in their first attack, by Claverhouse, who had raised barricades within the city; but their numbers becoming more and more formidable, he withdrew his forces towards Edinburgh. What was at first the desperate revolt of a few became a vast tumultuous outbreak, approaching very nearly to a rebellion. The Council in London were in alarm. It was determined to send the Duke of Monmouth to Scotland to take the command of the government troops. There was no want of energy in the movements of Monmouth. He set out from London on the 18th of June. On the 22nd he was at the head of the royal army on Bothwell-moor, a few miles from Hamilton. The insurgents were encamped on the opposite side of the Clyde. They were dispirited and irresolute—neither prepared to fight nor to yield. A deputation from the more moderate had an audience of the duke; at which they limited their demands to the free exercise of their religion, and would submit all matters of difference to a free Parliament, and a General Assembly of the Church. The duke called upon them to lay down their arms, but refused to treat except after their implicit submission. Roger North

VOL. IV.—118.

has a curious relation of a secret arrangement for the employment of the duke as general of the forces, which appears to him a wonderful proof of the statesmanship of the duke of Lauderdale and of his royal master. Monmouth was first appointed with a latitude of power to fight, or treat, as he thought fit. The majority at the Council board "approved of such a trust in the General; for why, said they, should so much blood, and of these deluded miserables, be spilt, if they are willing to lay down their arms on fit terms?" None spoke to the contrary. "When the king rose from Council, the duke of Lauderdale followed him into the bed-chamber, where, having him alone, he asked his Majesty if he intended to follow his father? Why, said the king? Because, sir, said the duke, you have given the General orders to treat; the consequence of which is—encouraging and enlarging the rebellion in Scotland, and raising another, by concert, in England, and then you are lost. Therefore, if you do not change your orders, and send them positive to fight, and not to treat, the mischiefs that befell your father, in like case, will overtake you." These two worthies, according to North, then clandestinely altered the orders which had been approved in Council, and gave directions that they should not be opened but at a Council of War, and in sight of the enemy. "The event," says the sympathising chronicler of this duplicity, "sufficiently applauded this counsel."* That event was the slaughter at Bothwell Bridge. The Covenanters had exhibited one commendable point of strategy in guarding this passage of the Clyde. But Hackston of Rathillet, who defended the bridge, was not adequately supported. The mass of the insurgents were panic-stricken when they saw the king's troops advancing upon them, whilst the artillery from the opposite bank of the river was breaking their ill-formed ranks. They fled on every side, Claverhouse exhorting his men to avenge their defeat at Loudon Hill. All accounts agree that Monmouth laboured to stop the butchery that this worst of miscalled heroes commanded:—

> "Taking more pains when he beheld them yield,
> To save the fliers than to win the field." †

From the name of contempt which was bestowed upon the poor Western Covenanters was derived the great party name of *Whig*. The nicknames of opposite factions are necessarily obscure in their origin, and the attempts at their explanation partake of the same party character as the names themselves. The nicknames which will live for ever in English history had each a very humble origin. *Tory*, according to North, came in about a year before *Whig*. In 1679 the discussions on the Exclusion Bill were accompanied with great heats in Parliament, and "without doors, the debates among the populace were more fierce, and agitated with extremity of opposite talk." The use of opprobrious words became common. The anti-exclusionists were first called *Yorkists*. Then *Tantivy* became a bye-word against them. The duke and the Irish were for the most part in agreement; so the duke's supporters were first called *Bogtrotters;* and then "the word *Tory* was entertained, which signified the most despicable savages amongst the wild Irish." North says, that "according to the common laws of scolding," the loyalists now looked out for rival nicknames, "to clear scores." Their adversaries

* "Examen," p. 81.   † Waller.

were first called *True Blues*—not satisfied with the plain Protestant blue of the Church; then *Birmingham Protestants*, "alluding to false groats counterfeited at that place. That term was "not fluent enough for the hasty repartee; and, after divers changes, the lot fell upon *Whig*, which was very significative, as well as ready; being vernacular in Scotland, from whence it was borrowed, for corrupt and sour whey." * Defoe accepts this derivation of Whig; and says, the use of it began in Scotland "when the western men, called Cameronians, took arms frequently for their religion. . . . . It afterwards became a denomination to the poor harassed people of that part of the country." †

The further we advance in the history of this miserable reign, the more are we perplexed by intrigues and counter-intrigues, indicating the universal political corruption. After the dispersion of the Covenanters, the duke of Monmouth is suddenly sent for from Scotland. Sir John Reresby goes to meet him at Doncaster on the 9th of July. "It happened to be understood, that after his victory he was about laying a foundation whereon to succeed in that kingdom, and by the industry of his agents making himself popular.‡ Charles was ill at Windsor. Monmouth was about his sick bed. "He thought," says Reresby, "he had the king to himself." Suddenly the duke of York, who had travelled from Brussels in disguise, presented himself: The Court was in commotion. The king's brother, and the king's illegitimate son, had come to be considered as rivals for the succession. To preserve some tranquillity they were then both sent away—Monmouth to Flanders, James to Scotland, as Lord High Commissioner. At Edinburgh this Papist prince manifested the sincerity of his desires for general toleration, by superintending with the most anxious vigilance the punishment of the Covenanters. Charles reproached Monmouth for having given the government so much trouble with prisoners after the fight of Bothwell Bridge, and Monmouth answered, that he could not kill men in cold blood. James exhibited a worse trait of Stuart nature by presiding over the examinations of prisoners under torture. Under his administration the Presbyterians were subjected to the grossest violence of a licentious soldiery. The military despots had full power to exercise the privileges of the inquisition in the most summary manner. Do you renounce the Covenant? Do you admit that it was murder to kill the archbishop of St. Andrew's? Will you pray for the king? To hesitate was to incur not only imprisonment but instant death. This violation of every form of law and every principle of justice went on for several years. The story of John Brown, "the Christian carrier," has been honestly told by Scott, in spite of his lurking admiration of Claverhouse.§ The poor peasant, who had indeed been out with the insurgents of 1679, was again in his home. He is seized by dragoons as he is going to dig in some peat ground, and by the command of Claverhouse he is shot in the presence of his wife. To her the gallant butcher addressed himself: "What thinkest thou of thy husband now, woman?" She replied, "I thought ever much of him, and now as much as ever." He said, "It were but justice to lay thee beside him." She said, "If ye were permitted, I doubt not but your cruelty would go that

* "Examen," p. 32 a. † "Review," quoted in Wilson's "Life of Defoe," vol. i. p. 73.
‡ "Memoirs," p. 229.
§ Compare "Tales of a Grandfather," chapter lii., with "Old Mortality."

length; but how will ye make answer for this morning's work?" He said, "To man I can be answerable; and for God I will take him in my own hand." Such were the scenes that Scotland witnessed in these days of her desolation. Unquestionably the duke of York instigated the worst persecutions; and the wretched instruments of tyranny, such as Claverhouse, thought that their atrocities would best exhibit their love and loyalty. Whilst James was doing his congenial work in Scotland, the efforts of the faction opposed to his succession to the crown were conducted with few conscientious scruples. All the prejudices of the people were still stimulated into an unchristian hatred of Roman Catholics. The processions of the 17th of November were repeated, amidst the blaze of a thousand torches, lighting up the hideous representations of nuns, and priests, and cardinals; and the effigy of the pope was burnt at Temple Bar amidst the shouts of an enormous multitude, encouraged by men of rank, who huzzaed from the balcony of the King's Head Tavern. These were known as the King's Head Club; and then as the Green Ribbon Club. The annual pope-burnings were afterwards imitated at Edinburgh. The processions of Guy Fawkes on the 5th of November, and the processions of the pope on queen Elizabeth's coronation-day, kept alive the intolerant spirit towards Roman Catholics long after their original party-objects had passed away. Shaftesbury is represented as the grand contriver of these demonstrations of 1679 and 1680. But the demagogue contrives in vain unless he has popular materials to work with. No doubt he well handled the multitude, which at that period first acquired the name of *mob*. They were the *mobile vulgus* of these exhibitions. Shaftesbury had now been dismissed from the Presidency of the Council; and was the moving spirit of the popular party. On the 28th of November, Monmouth suddenly returned from Holland. The bells of the city welcomed his arrival. The bonfires were again lighted. Charles was angry, or affected to be so, at his son's disobedience. He deprived him of his offices. He ordered him to quit the kingdom, or incur the penalty of exclusion for ever from the royal presence. Monmouth obstinately remained. It was the policy of the king to prevent the Parliament assembling, for he had another scheme in hand to obtain a sum from the king of France, which would enable him to dispense with the advice of his troublesome subjects. The treaty failed; but Charles had boldly prorogued the Parliament on its meeting in October. The Country party now set on foot all the powerful machinery of petitioning. Grand Juries, Common Councils, provincial Corporations, were suddenly moved, as by one impulse, to petition the king that the Parliament should meet at the end of the first short prorogation. Charles became alarmed. He published a proclamation, vague and absurd enough, against subscribing petitions against the known laws of the land. What these laws were the proclamation did not set forth. But there was a re-action. The timid were alarmed; the servile were zealous. Men who stood aloof from parties dreaded the signs of another Civil War. They joined in declarations of *abhorrence* of petitions for the assembling of Parliament; and those who supported the king in what they considered his prerogative of calling a Parliament when he pleased, of acting without parliamentary advice, and without reference to public opinion, were denominated *abhorrers*. The name *abhorrer* soon became merged in that of *Tory*.

Tory—Whig—in a few years forgot that they each owed their birth to "the common laws of scolding." The Irish savage grew up into a fine gentleman; the sour whey became the richest cream. The names of opprobrium blossomed into names of honour. They flourished in full glory for about a century and a half; and then passed into other distinctive titles, not so "fluent for the hasty repartee." Whatever may be said for or against party distinctions—and there is a great deal to be said in either view of the question—one thing is clear: the invention of Tory and Whig has been a very pleasant boon for the writers upon politics and history. These once rival nicknames save many circuitous expletives; and, if they do not exactly define political principles, they answer as well as if one large section of public men and their followers had been called red, the other blue—or one big-endians, the other little-endians. The terms of Whig and Tory are vernacular; and we are thankful for their help in the labour that is before us.

Bothwell Bridge.

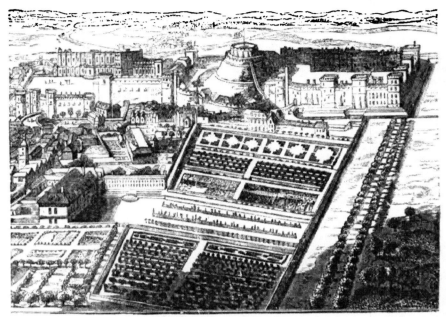

Windsor, in the time of Charles II.

CHAPTER XXII.

Charles the Second's alterations at Windsor—The Duke of York presented as a Romish Recusant
—Progress of the Duke of Monmouth—James leaves for Scotland—Parliament—The
Exclusion Bill—Trial and execution of Lord Stafford—The Parliament dissolved—The
Oxford Parliament—Its sudden dissolution—The King's Proclamation—The Whig Vindi-
cation—State Prosecutions—Stephen College—Shaftesbury indicted for high treason—The
Ignoramus—Court manœuvres for the choice of a sheriff of London—Shaftesbury flies to
Holland—Persecutions of the Scotch Covenanters.

WINDSOR CASTLE was now the summer residence of Charles II. In
August, 1678, Evelyn went with the duke of Norfolk to Windsor, "where
was a magnificent Court, it being the first time of his majesty removing
thither since it was repaired." Charles had changed the whole aspect of the
Castle. By his command the palatial fortress had been adapted for those
state-displays which were to rival the splendours of the Court of the great
Bourbon. A new building, forming the most imposing feature of the
north front, called the Star-building, had been erected from the plans of
Wren; and by the connexion of the suite of rooms thus obtained with the
older portion, that splendid series of state-apartments was produced which
terminated in St. George's Hall. But in these alterations the ancient cha-

racter of the proud dwelling of the Plantagenets was utterly destroyed. If Wren had not had a violent distaste of Gothic architecture; if his royal employer had not been wholly wanting in that patriotism which would have preserved the main features of the Windsor of Edward III. and of Elizabeth, as associated with the glorious days of the monarchy—his incongruous pile would not have remained for a century and a half a significant monument of the corrupt taste of the latter days of the Stuarts. To Frenchify Windsor Castle was worthy of the king who needed French gold to pay for his buildings and his mistresses; to reward Signor Verrio for seating him enthroned amongst the cardinal Virtues, or as the grand arbiter of the destinies of Europe. Catherine of Braganza sits in serene majesty, surrounded by the gods, on one of Verrio's ceilings. Mrs. Eleanor Gwynn had the more solid honour of dwelling within view of the Castle, at Burford House, so called after her son, lord Burford, afterwards the duke of St. Albans.* Windsor is as characteristic of the age as Whitehall. Reresby describes Charles in 1680 as living an unusually quiet life whilst Wren was building and Verrio painting: "The king shewed me a great deal of what he had done to the house, which was indeed very fine, and acquainted me with what he intended to do more; for then it was he was upon finishing that most majestic structure. He lived quite privately at this time; there was little or no resort to him; and his days he passed in fishing or walking in the park." †

Charles was thus "sauntering" at Windsor when the *denouement* of the great drama of his house was rapidly approaching. Evelyn has this record in his Diary, on the 24th of July, 1680: "Went with my wife and daughter to Windsor, to see that stately court, now nearly finished. There was erected in the court the king on horseback, lately cast in copper, and set on a rich pedestal of white marble, the work of Mr. Gibbons, at the expense of Toby Rustat, a page of the back stairs, who, by his wonderful frugality, had arrived to a great estate in money, and did many works of charity, as well as this of gratitude to his master, which cost him 1000*l*. He is a very simple, ignorant, but honest and loyal creature." There were many others of the simple, ignorant, honest, and loyal of Charles's subjects who would be ready to aver, with Toby Rustat, as the Latin inscription on the pedestal of this statue avers, that Charles II. was not only the most merciful of masters but the best of kings. The page of the back stairs who witnessed his never-failing urbanity would receive that quality as the evidence of every other merit. But from the more rational thinkers a severer judgment was to be expected. The duke of York "now reigned absolute in the king's affairs," writes Reresby.‡ Against the duke was all the Whig hostility now concentrated. The tale of Monmouth's legitimacy was revived. The king, on the 3rd of June, renewed his declaration that he was never married to any other than the queen. On the 26th of June, Shaftesbury, accompanied by several lords and commoners, came before the Grand Jury at Westminster, and presented the duke as a Popish recusant. The chief justice defeated this bold measure by

---

* Windsor has at length found fit chroniclers of its various subjects of historical interest, as well as of the minuter topographical details which illustrate manners and customs, in the elaborate work of Mr. Tighe and Mr. Davis—"Annals of Windsor," 2 vols. 1858.

† "Memoirs," p. 231. ‡ *Ibid.*, p. 232.

discharging the jury, whilst Shaftesbury was in consultation with some of the judges. The Parliament had been summoned to meet on the 21st of October. The great question of the exclusion of the duke of York from the succession to the throne was sure to be renewed. It was thought that the king could be gained over to consent to this departure from the principle of hereditary right. The duchess of Portsmouth had been induced by the Whig leaders, by threats and promises, to undertake the recommendation of the exclusion to the king, he having the right of naming his successor by will. He was to receive an ample grant of money; he might secure the power of naming his favourite son, Monmouth, to wear the crown after his decease. Burnet says that he was assured that the duchess of Portsmouth " once drew the king to consent to it." James in his Memoirs implies this, when he found that " his being sent away again began to be more discoursed of than ever." He suspected that " the king himself began to waver; and accordingly he soon found by discoveries on that subject that his majesty now doubted whether he could stand by him or no. The duke represented to him his constant and late engagement to the contrary, but found him so changed that it gave him great reason now at last to apprehend what he had been oft told, but never believed, that his majesty would abandon him in the end." * The day before the meeting of Parliament the duke of York sailed for Scotland. The French ambassador, Barillon, represents James as declaring that he would make his enemies repent—"as much as to say that he hopes to be able to excite troubles in Scotland and Ireland." Even in England his cause would not have been without supporters. " The papists lifted up their crest in great arrogance."† It was a moment of deep anxiety. Two of Charles's ministers, Godolphin and Sunderland, advised him to consent to a Bill of Exclusion. The duchess of Portsmouth had bribes and blandishments to mould that royal will upon whose consistency there could be no reliance. But the intrigue failed. The king wanted the vote of money to precede the Exclusion Bill. The Whig leaders wanted his assent to the Bill before the vote of money. The Session was opened on the 21st of October—that first meeting of the new Parliament which had been prorogued seven times. Charles in his speech promised to support the Protestant religion " against all the conspiracies of our enemies." He would concur " in any new remedies which shall be proposed, that may consist with preserving the succession of the Crown in its due and legal course of descent." On the 26th lord Russell moved " that we may resolve to take into our consideration how to suppress Popery, and to prevent a Popish successor." On the 2nd of November, the Bill of Exclusion was brought in.

With the projected exclusion of the duke of York was intimately associated the design to set up the duke of Monmouth as the future heir to the Crown. The king's declaration of his son's illegitimacy was little heeded by the people. " This duke, whom for distinction they called the Protestant duke, though the son of an abandoned woman, the people made their idol."‡ Dryden has painted Shaftesbury remonstrating with Monmouth on his doubts and apprehensions, when a crown was within his view:

* Clarke's " Life of James II."—Extract from James's " Memoirs," vol. i. p. 595.
     † Reresby, p. 232.   ‡ Evelyn, " Diary," November 28, 1679.

"Did you for this expose yourself to show,
And to the crowd bow popularly low ?
For this your glorious progress next ordain,
With chariots, horsemen, and a numerous train." *

The "glorious progress" of Monmouth was in the West of England, in August, 1680. The country people came from miles round to see him in his way to Longleat. At Ilchester the streets were strewed with flowers. At White Lackington House, near Ilminster, he was met by two thousand horsemen. A woman pressed upon him, and touched his hand, to be cured of the king's evil, as if he already sat in the chair of Edward the Confessor. A thousand young men, all clothed uniformly in white linen, went three miles out of Exeter to meet him, and preceded him, hand in hand, as he entered their city.† There were no riotous proceedings; but these demonstrations were very significant of the feelings of the middle classes towards the duke of York. The Protestant duke and the Papist duke were in direct antagonism. Monmouth understood how to keep alive this political cry. Ralph Thoresby went to see him at Whitehall after his progress. Being told "that we came from Leeds, the great clothing-place, he answered, with a smile, we were not for Popery there, no more than they in the West, alluding to his extraordinary kind entertainment there, as in the public news." ‡ There was no political dishonesty in thus appealing to popular opinion against the dreaded predominance of Popery. But to set up the son of Lucy Waters as a pretender to the Crown was a great mistake of some of the Whig statesmen—a mistake which inevitably tended to disgust the sober-minded, and to lead to that re-action which enabled Charles to walk once more in the old ways of despotism.

After many days' debate in the House of Commons, a Bill was passed on the 15th of November, "for securing of the Protestant religion, by disabling James, duke of York, to inherit the imperial Crown of England and Ireland, and the dominions and territories thereunto belonging." It was carried to the Peers by lord Russell. "A great number of members accompanied him and it; and as soon as it was delivered gave a mighty shout; which tumultuous and barbarous way of proceeding had, too great a resemblance of forty-one, not to convince all judicious persons that this would prove a prelude of the same tragedy, if not timely prevented." § The debate of the Lords was carried on with unusual heat. The two greatest orators, Shaftesbury and Halifax, were pitted against each other in this contest, although their general principles were the same. All accounts of this debate assign to Halifax the honour of having thrown out the Exclusion Bill, by his almost unexampled eloquence. It was rejected on the first reading by a majority of 33—63 dividing against 30. Halifax and others who opposed the exclusion of the duke of York, desired to enact limitations of the sovereign power, should he succeed to the Crown. The constitutional difference between these two propositions has been forcibly put by Mr. Fox, in his History of James the Second: "The question of what are to be the powers of the Crown is surely

* "Absalom and Achitophel."
† "Life of James, Duke of Monmouth." By George Roberts, vol. i. chapter vii.
‡ Thoresby's "Diary," vol. i. p. 66.
§ "Life of James II.," vol. i. p. 617.

of superior importance to that of who shall wear it ?   Those, at least, who consider the royal prerogative as vested in the king, not for his sake but for that of his subjects, must consider the one of these questions as much above the other in dignity, as the rights of the public are more valuable than those of an individual.   In this view, the prerogatives of the Crown are in substance and effect the rights of the people; and these rights of the people were not to be sacrificed to the purpose of preserving the succession to the most favoured prince, much less to one who, on account of his religious persuasion, was justly feared and suspected."

When Charles opened the Parliament on the 21st of October, he said, to give " the fullest satisfaction your hearts can wish for the security of the Protestant religion, I do recommend to you to pursue the further examination of the Plot, with a strict and an impartial inquiry. I do not think myself safe, nor you neither, till that matter be gone through with; and therefore it will be necessary that the lords in the Tower be brought to their speedy trial, that justice may be done."   In his private conversation at this period he expressed the utmost contempt of the witnesses for the Plot.   He " proved to a demonstration that many articles they had given in evidence were not only improbable but quite impossible."*   To turn the wrath of the Parliament against his brother to some humbler personages, there were victims in the Tower ready for the sacrifice.   The first and only victim selected from these prisoners was lord Stafford.   This nobleman, illustrious in the blood of the Howards, venerable for his age and infirmities, was impeached by the Commons, and brought to trial before his Peers on the 30th of November.   It was his sixty-ninth birthday.   Westminster Hall had been fitted up with a more than ordinary preparation.   Places were assigned to the king and queen, to the Peers, to the members of the House of Commons, to the managers of the impeachment, to the judges.   "I think it was the deepest solemnity I ever saw," writes Reresby.   The same forms were gone through, with the same arrangements, as when Pym confronted Strafford, and the father of the peer now accused presided as High Steward.   The forms and the arrangements of benches were the same ; but the spirit was essentially different.   It was not a trial which was to determine whether England was to be a free monarchy or an absolute monarchy.   It was the struggle of a faction for a temporary triumph, to assert a power which was unable to reach the great delinquent.   The witnesses against Stafford were Oates, and Dugdale, and Turberville.   The accused peer defended himself with unexpected ability.   He pointed out how unworthy Oates was of belief—one who pretended that he was never a Papist though he had gone over to the Church of Rome ; who avowed himself a spy at St. Omers, though he went through all the discipline of a proselyte. Evelyn, who was present, was much struck by this, and thought " such a man's testimony should not be taken against the life of a dog."   But Dugdale and others positively swore to Stafford's participation in a plot to assassinate the king.   The majority of the peers, eighty-six to fifty-five, pronounced him guilty, each giving his judgment, with his hand upon his breast, " upon my honour."   The unfortunate nobleman was condemned on the 7th of December, and he was executed on the 29th.   Though on the day of his trial he was

* Reresby, p. 234.

assailed by popular invective, when he protested his innocence on the scaffold the spectators cried, " We believe you, my lord—God bless you, my lord." The king, at the prayer of the House of Lords, had remitted that part of the sentence of a traitor upon which the most brutal could not look without disgust. The sheriffs raised a question, which they addressed to the House of Commons, whether the king could dispense with these barbarities. The House resolved that it was content that execution should be done upon lord Stafford by severing his head from his body. Lord Russell has been accused, upon the assertion of the historian Echard, of having sanctioned this interference with the dispensing power—of having, according to Hume, " seconded in the House the barbarous scruple of the sheriffs." There is no proof that Russell took any part in the debate upon the queries of the sheriffs. We scarcely think that lord John Russell, whatever impartiality he may thus show to the memory of his ancestor, is quite warranted in thinking the testimony of Echard sufficient to give probability to the assertion of a circumstance regarding Russell which is, " if true, the most to be lamented in his whole life."* In the reign of James the Second, a Bill was passed by the Peers, for reversing the attainder of Stafford. It was interrupted in the Commons by more urgent matters. It was not till the reign of George the Fourth, when religious animosities, if not wholly passed away, had lost their ancient character of vindictiveness, that by a special statute the attainder was annulled, and the descendants of lord Stafford were restored to the honours of their house. Whilst Stafford's blood was being shed upon evidence which the king considered that of false witnesses, he felt none of the qualms which his father felt when he consented to the death of the great earl who said " Put not your trust in princes." No one put any trust in the second Charles. Himself a Papist, he saw the Papist noble hunted to death without even a tear for his fate. On the 24th of December, says Reresby, " I was at the king's couchée, when there were but four present. His majesty was in a very good humour, and took up some time in displaying to us the fallacy and emptiness of those who pretend to a fuller measure of sanctity than their neighbours, and pronounced them to be, for the most part, abominable hypocrites and the most arrant knaves." Even mitred heads came in for the royal sarcasms. " He was that night two full hours in putting off his clothes, and it was half an hour past one before he went to bed. He seemed to be quite free from care and trouble; though one would have thought, at this time, he should have been overwhelmed therewith."† There was enough, indeed, to overwhelm a king who would take any matter seriously to heart. The levity of Charles was his shield and buckler. The Commons were not only resolute in their persistent hostility to the duke of York, but manifested an arbitrary violence in the arrest of some who had signed the declaration of " abhorrence." They exercised a more constitutional power in the impeachment of Chief Justice Scroggs for dismissing the Grand Jury when the duke of York was presented as a Romish recusant; for stopping the publication of a newspaper called " The Weekly Packet of Advice from Rome;" and for inflicting enormous fines upon publishers of news, and requiring excessive bail, declaring " he would have regard to persons and their principles in imposing of fines." The House at last

---

* " Life of William Lord Russell," vol. i. p. 235.　　　　† " Memoirs," p. 238.

resolved that until the duke of York was excluded from the succession, they would not grant any supply. This impracticable Parliament was dissolved on the 18th of January, 1681.

The distracted condition of public affairs at this juncture excited so great alarm, that superstitions, arising out of unwonted natural appearances, produced the same effect, even amongst the educated, as in the days before scientific knowledge, although of the humblest kind, had taught men to separate the aspects of the physical world from their supposed connexion with moral causes. On the 12th of December, 1680, Evelyn writes, " This evening, looking out of my chamber-window towards the west, I saw a meteor of an obscure bright colour, very much in shape like the blade of a sword, the rest of the sky very serene and clear. What this may portend God only knows. But such another phenomenon I remember to have seen in 1640, about the trial of the great earl of Strafford, preceding our bloody rebellion. I pray God avert his judgments." The danger of another Civil War was not altogether to be associated with popular credulity. That great danger seemed approaching when the new Parliament met at Oxford on the 21st of March. Some covert design on the part of the Crown was apprehended in thus departing from the ancient custom of assembling the Parliament at Westminster, except in times of the plague. The Oxford Parliament of Charles the First was no precedent for this meeting-place of a new Parliament elected by the general voice of the nation. The king went to Oxford surrounded by his guards. The Whig members went to Oxford accompanied by armed bands of retainers, wearing in their hats ribbons inscribed "no Popery, no slavery." Charles was indifferent as to the temper of the Parliament on the question of supplies. On the day that he went to Oxford he had concluded a treaty with Louis XIV. for a new subsidy of French gold. King James the Second records this transaction with the utmost *nonchalance*: " The king's necessities had been long so great, and the Parliament so refractory and insolent, that he had no way left of relieving one, without consenting to the unreasonable demands of the other, but by a private treaty with France. The duke first put the king in the way of it, which the French at first answered only by compliments and in general terms. But at last it was concluded they should give the king fifty thousand pounds every quarter, the first payment to be at the end of June, 1681, without any condition on the king's side but that of friendship, but promises on the French part not to disturb Flanders nor Holland."*

The Parliament of Oxford lasted seven days. The king and his Court were at Christchurch. The Commons sat in the Schools. Charles, in his opening speech, spoke in a bolder tone than had been his wont: " The unwarrantable proceedings of the last House of Commons were the occasion of my parting with the last Parliament; for I, who will never use arbitrary government myself, am resolved not to suffer it in others .... What I have formerly, and so often, declared touching the succession, I cannot depart from. But to remove all reasonable fears that may arise from the possibility of a Popish successor's coming to the Crown, if means can be found, that in such a case the administration of the government may remain in Protestants' hands, I

* " Life of James II.," p. 715.

shall be ready to hearken to any such expedient, by which the Religion might be preserved, and the Monarchy not destroyed."* The "expedient" which was proposed, with the sanction of the king, was to this effect—that the duke of York should be banished during his life to the distance of five hundred miles from the British dominions; that certain Roman Catholics of considerable estates should also be banished; that on the decease of the reigning monarch the duke should assume the title of king, but exercise no sovereign power, the government being administered by a regent—the princess of Orange being the first regent, and the lady Anne regent after the princess. The expedient was rejected. The Commons again resolved, "That a Bill be brought in to exclude James, duke of York, from inheriting the imperial crowns of England and Ireland, and the dominions and territories thereunto belonging." The refusal of the Commons to agree to the proposed compromise is regarded by some as factious, by others as imprudent. James himself thought the expedient, which originated with Halifax, "fully as pernicious" as the Bill of Exclusion.† The majority of the Parliament thought the expedient futile. In a "Vindication" which we shall presently notice, it was said, "The Parliament, observing the precedents of former ages, did wisely choose rather to exclude him, than to leave him the name, and place the power in a regent. For they could not but look upon it as folly to expect that one of his temper, bred up in such principles of politics as made him in love with arbitrary power, and bigoted in their religion which always propagates itself by blood, would patiently bear these shackles, which would be very disgustful unto a prince of the most meek disposition . . . . This would certainly have bred a contest; and these limitations of power proposed to keep up the government must unavoidably have destroyed it." During the eventful week of the Session at Oxford, the Commons were not only agitated by this great question of the succession, but the apple of discord was thrown between the two Houses, by the refusal of the Lords to entertain an impeachment by the Commons for high treason of an impudent spy and libeller, Fitzharris. The story of this man is merely the story of one of those miserable games of plot and counter-plot which disgraced these times. Being in the pay of the Court, he wrote a violent libel against the king, which it is conjectured that he intended to put into the pocket of some Whig leader, to implicate him in a treasonable design. Lady Russell, in writing to her husband, bids him look to his pockets. Fitzharris next pretended he had important discoveries to make of Court secrets; and the Whigs turned to him as a valuable auxiliary. The Attorney-General then having been ordered to prosecute him at law, the Whigs resolved to save him by an impeachment from the certain destruction of a trial at law. The Lords voted that Fitzharris should be left to the ordinary course of justice. The Commons asserted their right to impeach any peer or commoner for high-treason, and held that the refusal of the Lords to proceed upon this impeachment was a violation of the constitution of Parliament.‡ This dispute between the two Houses was a sufficient pretence for a dissolution. Charles

* "Parliamentary History," vol. iv. col. 1303.   † "Life of James II.," vol. i. p. 670.

‡ Mr. Hallam maintains that the "inadvertent position of Blackstone, that a commoner cannot be impeached for high treason, is contrary to the latest determination of the supreme tribunal." "Constitutional History," chap. xii. Lord Campbell is opposed to this opinion of Mr. Hallam; "Lives of the Chancellors," vol. ii. p. 257, edit. 1845.

accomplished this measure with a decision very unusual with him. The Theatre had been ordered to be fitted up for the Commons, who required more space than they found in the Schools. On Saturday, the 26th of March, the king was exceedingly busy amongst the workmen in the Theatre. On Sunday evening, he was describing to the circle about him how admirably his faithful Commons would be accommodated. On the Monday morning two sedan-chairs were moving out of Christchurch. At the door of the House of Lords the king got out of the first chair; his robes were taken out of the second chair. But "the Garter robes were put up instead of the robes of State; so the chair must go back, with an officer to bring the right." * A peer who saw the manœuvre was forcibly detained till the robes of State arrived. Then the king went into the chamber of the Peers; the Black Rod summoned the Commons; and these unexpected words came from the royal mouth: "My lords and gentlemen: That all the world may see to what a point we are come, that we are not like to have a good end when the divisions at the beginning are such, therefore, my Lord Chancellor, do as I have commanded you." My Lord Chancellor dissolved the Parliament. "The king immediately departed with all speed to London," says Reresby. "It was not to be expressed," writes North, "what clutter there was in town about getting off. The price of coaches mounted cent. per cent. in a quarter of an hour. It was the conceit of a foreign minister that the town looked as if it had been besieged, and just surrendered upon articles forthwith to remove." On the 8th of April the king published a Declaration of the causes for the dissolution of the two last Parliaments. Undutiful as was the behaviour of those Parliaments, his majesty declared, "That nothing should ever alter his affection to the Protestant religion as established by law, nor his love to Parliament: for he would still have frequent Parliaments." During the four remaining years of the life of Charles no other Parliament was summoned. The royal Declaration was answered in a very elaborate "Vindication of the proceedings of the two last Parliaments"—a calm and logical paper, which assumed the existence of a real conspiracy for the establishment of Popery.† The king's Declaration was read in the churches. The arguments of the Vindication, set forth by Sydney, Somers, and Jones, produced little effect. The terrors of the Popish plot had passed away. The danger of another Civil War excited, with few exceptions, an apprehension that the Whig leaders were looking beyond a constitutional resistance to arbitrary government and to a Popish successor. Addresses of attachment and confidence were now as unmeasured in their servility as in the days of the first James. Learned bodies sent their deputations to Whitehall to tell the king that he derived not his title from the people, but from God; that to God only are kings accountable; "that it belongs not to subjects either to create or censure, but to honour and obey their sovereign, who comes to be so by a fundamental hereditary right of succession, which no religion, no law, no fault, no forfeiture, can alter or diminish." ‡ Thus encouraged, it can scarcely appear surprising that the king should have followed up his triumph at Oxford—his *coup de maistre*, as

* North, "Examen," p. 104.
† It is printed in the "Parliamentary History," vol. iv. Appendix, No. xv.
‡ Address of the Vice Chancellor of Cambridge, quoted from Wilkins' "Concilia," by Dr. Lingard.

North terms the sudden dissolution,—by governing without Parliaments; and by calling in all the machinery of tyrannous judges and corrupt juries to crush the leaders of the Opposition; that he should have deprived adverse Corporations of their Charters; that he should have dispensed with the laws that interfered with his Papist brother; and have himself died with the avowal on his lips that contradicted the lie of his life,—the avowal that he belonged to the Romish Church.

The lawyers had ample business on their hands immediately after the dissolution of the Oxford Parliament. Fitzharris was put upon his trial in the Court of King's Bench. He pleaded his impeachment in bar of the jurisdiction of that court. The judges evaded the plea; and he was convicted of a treasonable libel, and was executed. Plunket, the titular archbishop of Armagh, was at the same time convicted of an Irish Popish plot. There is no infamy of the reign of Charles II. greater than this. The innocence of the Roman Catholic prelate was believed even by his persecutors; but he was sacrificed by the Court, that the popular suspicion of the Popish tendencies of the king might be removed by an ostentatious piece of blood-shedding. Thus far the law went in the old direction of religious intolerance. But the re-action of public opinion was not to be left unused. Some of the witnesses for the Plot were still in hand; and they were now as ready to give evidence against Protestants as they had been to swear away the lives of Papists. Stephen College, a London joiner, commonly known as "the Protestant Joiner," had been swaggering at Oxford with sword and pistol. He was accused of a treasonable attempt to seize the person of the king. The evidence against him was chiefly that of Dugdale. A London grand-jury ignored the indictment. College was then indicted in Oxfordshire, where a jury was more compliant. He was tried on the 17th of August, and on the trial Oates contradicted the evidence of Dugdale. We have shown the amount and duration of the payments to these witnesses.* It is to be observed that Oates ceased to be paid at this exact period. "To punish Oates for his conduct at this trial, his pension was taken from him, and he was turned out of his lodgings at Whitehall," says Dr. Lingard. The documents we referred to show that Dugdale received his wages for a year and a half longer. In spite of the contradictory evidence Stephen College was hanged; the Lord Chief-Justice Guilford having manifested his fitness for the dirty work of the government by intercepting the papers that were handed to the prisoner as materials for his defence, and withholding some that he asserted were libellous. "It had been a prime jest," says Roger North, "if, under the pretence of a defence, the criminal should be allowed to vent seditious libels, full of mutiny and reflection to amuse the people; and so to come forth and be published in print."† Burnet says of this trial, "North's behaviour in that whole matter was such, that, probably, if he had lived to see an impeaching Parliament, he might have felt the ill effects of it."

A man of far higher mark than "the Protestant Joiner" was now to be assailed through the great engine of the law. The Irish witnesses who came over to give testimony against the Roman Catholic primate had been believed

---

* *Ante,* p. 346.   † "Life of Lord Keeper Guilford," vol. i. p. 301.

by an English jury. Would they be less worthy of credit when they swore that they had been suborned by the earl of Shaftesbury to give false testimony against the queen, the duke of York, and other personages? Shaftesbury was sent to the Tower in July. In November he was indicted of high-treason before a London grand-jury, preparatory to a trial by his Peers in the Court of the High Steward. Had a true Bill been found Shaftesbury would unquestionably have finished his career on the scaffold, whether guilty or not. His judges would have been selected by the king; "his subsequent trial would have been mere matter of form, as much as after sentence the warrant to behead him." * During the five months of his imprisonment, Shaftesbury, through his counsel, repeatedly applied for the protection of his own Habeas Corpus Act. The judges evaded the application. His character was to be blasted, so that the indictment should come before a jury sufficiently prejudiced against the accused. Every weapon of abuse was employed against him. He was denounced from the pulpits as "the Apostle of Schism;" he was characterised, in doggrel verse which preceded Dryden's immortal satire, as Machiavel, as the devil's foster-brother, as Achitophel; the hint was taken, and a week before the indictment was presented at the Old Bailey, came out "Absalom and Achitophel." The king at this time "was more than usually serious, and seemingly under a greater weight of thought than had been observed of him on account of the most important business." Reresby, who notices this unusual demeanour of the king, says that Halifax maintained that it would be prudent to set Shaftesbury at liberty, upon terms; but that "the king was resolved to prosecute him to the utmost" was the information of one of the secretaries. On the 24th of November the indictment was presented to the Grand Jury at the Old Bailey. North and Pemberton sat on the Bench; and, contrary to all precedent, it was resolved that the examination of the witnesses should be in open court. The foreman of the jury contended that they were sworn to keep the king's counsel, their fellows' counsel, and their own, secret. North maintained that the king' could dispense with the secrecy. The object of these tools of power was to help out the witnesses in their contradictions, and to awe the jury. The evidence of the charge "for compassing and imagining the death of the king" was attempted to be supported by a paper, "containing no less than matter of high treason, which was sworn to have been found amongst the papers in his closet." † It was a plan of an association, not in his handwriting, and without a signature. "The witnesses," says Burnet, "swore many incredible things against him, mixed with other things that looked very like his extravagant way of talking." The jury retired for a short time, and brought back the indictment, with "*Ignoramus*" written on the back. A shout of joy went up in the hall, and was re-echoed through the streets. Bonfires were lighted. A medal was struck to celebrate the triumph. The king discoursed to the foreign ambassadors "on the subject of the hard measure dealt to *him* by Lord Shaftesbury's jury;" and, in a more sensible spirit, gave Dryden the hint for his poem of "The Medal." The poem made the Medal more popular; and men proclaimed their opinions by wearing it hanging at the button-hole.

* "Lives of Chancellors," vol. ii. p. 362. † Reresby, p. 252.

The refusal of the Grand Jury to find a true bill against Shaftesbury was imputed to the selection of jurymen by the Whig sheriffs.   To obtain obedient sheriffs who would summon pliant jurymen was now the great aim of the Court.   This scheme was carried into effect in a very remarkable manner.   The Lord Mayor of 1682, sir John Moor, was a more than average example of the weakness and vanity that sometimes clings to civic dignitaries. There was an old custom of the city which is thus described by Roger North. " At the Bridgehouse feast, which is sometime before the 24th of June, the day of the election at Guildhall, the Lord Mayor takes his time, and, out of a large gilt cup, drinks to some person he names by the title of Sheriff of London and Middlesex, for the year ensuing.   If the person be present, the cup is immediately borne to him, and he pledges my Lord-Mayor : if he be not present, then the cup is conveyed in the great coach, with the sword-bearer and officers, openly, and in state, to the house of the person drunk to, and the officer declaring the matter, presents the cup to him ; and then he is called my Lord Mayor's Sheriff, and not long after, he is summoned to the court of the Lord Mayor and Aldermen, and there, if he holds, he enters into bond to take upon him the office at the time ; and if he fines off, then, in a like method, the cup is sent to another, till the person is pitched upon that will hold : and this way of drinking and fining off is of great use to the city, for it brings money into the chamber ; and it is called going a birding for sheriffs.   At Midsummer-day, when the Common Hall meets for the election of sheriffs, and the Lord Mayor and Court of Aldermen are come upon the Suggestum, called the Hustings, the common sergeant, by the common crier, puts to the hall the question for confirming the Lord Mayor's sheriff, which used to pass affirmatively of course.   After that, the Lord Mayor and Aldermen rise and go up into the room they call the court of aldermen, leaving the floor or body of the livery men below to choose another sheriff by themselves, without their interposing or being concerned in the choice."   This is, in part, a misrepresentation.   For forty years the custom of nominating one of the sheriffs by the cup had been laid aside, and both sheriffs had been elected, without such nomination, by the Common Hall.   The Lord Mayor had been sent for by king Charles ; and " the king himself encouraged him, with expressions not only of protection but command ; and at last, after much hesitation, he determined roundly to conform, and all at once promised the king to send his cup to any citizen his majesty should nominate to him.   He was slow, but sure." *   Jeffreys, the recorder, suggested that there was a rich Turkey merchant recently arrived from Constantinople, who was the very man.   Dudley North, the brother of the Chief Justice, was a person of eminent ability, who had sounder notions of commerce and finance than most men of his time ; and it is painful to find one of such talent and knowledge listening to these arguments of his cunning and servile brother : " He was made to understand what an advantage such an opportunity was to oblige a king who had power to gratify by employment any fit persons, such as he was."†   And so the cup was sent, " in full parade and form " to Mr. Dudley North.   Midsummer Day, June 24, witnessed a tremendous uproar in Guildhall.   The refusal of the Lord Mayor's cup-sheriff was unmistakeable.   The Lord Mayor retired.

* " Examen," p. 600.   † Ibid., p. 601.

He came again and again to put the question, but with the same result. He then adjourned the Common Hall. It was contended that the adjournment was illegal. Counsel were brought on a subsequent day to argue the point, amidst the uproar of contending factions; "This was midsummer work indeed, extreme hot and dusty; and the partisans strongly disordered every way, with crowding, bawling, sweating, and dust; all full of anger, zeal, and filth in their faces. They ran about, up and down stairs, so that any one, not better informed, would have thought the place rather an huge Bedlam than a meeting for civil business. And yet, under such an awkward face of affairs as this was, the fate of the English government and monarchy depended but too much on the event of so decent an assembly." * Roger North, the encomiast of every measure that tended to convert the English monarchy into a pure despotism, has no hesitation in acknowledging that the fate of the existing government depended upon having a sheriff who would return corrupt jurymen. He says of the Court party, "If one good sheriff were gained, they did not fear what hurt the other alone could do; for both sheriffs made but one officer." The contest went on for several months. The city was in a continued fever. The Lord Mayor opened a poll at which North and another Court candidate were elected; the sheriffs opened a poll at which two popular candidates were elected. The Chief Justice and his tool Jeffreys bullied and intrigued: and in the end Dudley North and a fit coadjutor were sworn into office. It was clear that if another indictment had been presented against Shaftesbury, he would have had small chance of saving his head. He fled to Holland, accompanied by his constant friend, the famous John Locke. He died in the following year.

The duke of York, as High Commissioner in Scotland, had been manifesting the spirit in which he purposed to govern the two countries when the power should fall into his hands. He had put down an outburst of the puritan spirit in the followers of two ministers, Cargill and Cameron, known as Cameronians. The excess of fanaticism was met by the excess of tyranny; and women, refusing to cry "God bless the king," went to their deaths as martyrs. A Parliament was called. It voted that the succession to the Crown was indefeasible; it enacted a test, which, as altered by a compromise of opposite parties, asserted the king's supremacy, renounced the Covenant, inculcated the doctrine of passive obedience, and disclaimed any attempt to change the civil or religious establishments; but at the same time it expressed the adherence to the Protestant religion of the person taking the test. The courtiers proposed that all princes of the blood should be exempted from the oath. The earl of Argyle opposed this, and he was consequently marked for destruction. In taking the test himself, as a privy counsellor, he said that he did not mean to bind himself, in a lawful way, from wishing and endeavouring any alteration which he might think to the advantage of Church or State, and not repugnant to the Protestant religion and his own loyalty. A few days after he was arrested; was indicted for high treason; and was found guilty of treason and leasing-making. He contrived to escape to Holland. His estate was confiscated. Scotland was wholly under the feet of the tyrant. Judicial murders were committed in every district of the

* "Examen," p. 606.

southern and western counties. Hundreds were outlawed. A seditious declaration was published by the maddened Presbyterians, renouncing allegiance to Charles Stuart. To compel suspected persons to abjure the declaration was now the business of a lawless soldiery and slavish magistrates. The Scottish administration of the duke of York is thus complacently recorded : " He stifled at its first birth a commotion of the fanatical party which then happened to break out, whereof some were taken and made examples of, but many more were won over by the great esteem his presence had gained amongst them." * In his own Memoirs of this period, he wonders how men could apprehend danger from Popery, " while they overlooked the imminent danger of being swallowed up by Presbytery and Fanaticism." †

Congenial as his pursuits in Scotland were to the duke of York, he desired to return to England. He accomplished this object by enlisting the duchess of Portsmouth in his interest, by some secret arrangement for settling a pension upon her out of the income which he derived from the Post Office, upon which annuity she might raise a hundred thousand pounds. The affair could not be managed; but Charles gave the duchess 10,000*l.* quarterly out of his French pension, and she went abroad. The duke came to England for a short time, and then returned to Scotland, having narrowly escaped shipwreck in his passage. He again came to give that impulse to the schemes for arbitrary power which Charles had not resolution himself to carry out. Halifax and Seymour, two of the king's ministers, opposed the duke's return to London. Charles wanted his brother to fortify his resolves to take " those vigorous councils and resolute methods the duke had long pressed him to." ‡ The prince of Orange had been in England in 1681 ; and Charles then said to him that " he was confident, whenever the duke should come to reign, he would be so restless and violent that he could not hold it four years to an end." § Charles permitted the duke to try his hand in government before he " should come to reign." The duke's biographer says, " He shewed by his management in Scotland a good example of the doctrine he preached, which, when his majesty followed, it set him at rest for the remainder of his days."‖

* " Life of James II.," vol. i. p. 644.   † *Ibid.* p. 656.
‡ *Ibid.*, p. 799.   § Burnet.
          ‖ " Life of James II." p. 784.

The Rye-House.

CHAPTER XXIII.

The army establishment—Quo Warranto Information against the Corporation of London—Surrender of the Charters of other Corporations—The Rye-House Plot—Arrests of Russell, Essex, and Sidney—Trial of Russell—Russell's Execution—Trial of Sidney—Scottish persecution—The duke of York's power in England—Decree of the University of Oxford —Repeal of the Test Act—Death of Charles the· Second in the faith of the Romish Church—William Penn—Settlement of Pennsylvania—Penn's Treaty with the Indians.

The " rest for the remainder of his days " which Charles secured, through following the doctrine which the duke of York preached, was something very different from the ease which he enjoyed in the early years of the Restoration. There were to come, two years of a desperate struggle against the liberties of the people, the termination of which struggle was to be left to the greater energy of his successor. All the real power seemed now to lie in the hands of the Crown. London had lost its popular sheriffs; the choice of other sheriffs throughout the land was chiefly directed by the Court; the sheriffs could pack the jurymen upon state-trials; the jurymen would be duly exhorted from every pulpit to believe, upon the authority of the Scriptures, that, as all resistance to authority was a sin, the support of authority in all its desires was a virtue. When a subject stood at the bar, indicted for treason or misdemeanor at the king's command, it was necessary for the country's peace that the Crown should have its wished-for verdict. A trial was a ceremony at which good men should assist, by their unanimity of opinion with the king's judges and the king's attorney, to place the throne upon the solid foundation of the people's implicit obedience. There was now an army sufficient to make men understand the danger of insurrection. It was something more than two regiments of horse-guards, as in the recent days when the Parliament was jealous of a royal force, and relied for defence against external enemies upon a national militia. In addition to two regiments of household cavalry, there were two regiments of foot guards, a regiment of dragoons, and five other regiments of foot. There was no war to give employment to this small army. There was no foreign garrison to absorb any portion of that military strength which was available for the repression of sedition at home. Tangier, which, when it came to the English Crown as the dowry of queen Catherine, was held to be equivalent to Dunkirk, was abandoned in 1683, and the garrison was brought to England. Two millions had been expended upon the mole and fortifications. The Parliament had objected that the garrison was a nursery for a popish army. When the opinion of the Parliament had ceased to be regarded, Charles brought this army home; after the works of Tangier had been utterly destroyed, and the harbour blocked up with the rubbish. With an adequate military power about the Court, the lesser wheels of the machinery of government would be all in order. The rebellious city of London was now to be taught its duty. In the corporate franchises of the metropolis, and in those of other cities and towns, rested the chief force of the middle classes. The old puritan spirit was not dead. Liberty and Protestantism were names which stirred the most sluggish spirits into patriotism; and in the freedom of civic proceedings the temper of the people found a lawful right of assertion. Take away the charter of the city of London, advised the slavish lawyers, and break up that strong-hold of democracy. We are "the finest flour," said the courtiers; the common people are "the coarsest bran." * There was no precedent for a forfeiture of corporate privileges; but such forfeiture was to be accomplished now by the example of the surrender of the abbeys to Henry VIII. An Information, *quo warranto* technically called, was laid in the King's Bench against the Corporation of London for two misdemeanors—for having taken tolls under a by-law, and for having petitioned the king to assemble the Parliament, in 1679, which petition was published. On the 18th of June the lord mayor, sheriffs, and aldermen knelt before the king, and humbly petitioned that his majesty would not enter-up judgment against the City; and they were required to make no future election of mayor, sheriff, aldermen, recorder, or other officers, without the royal approbation; that if the king

* See Chamberlayne's "Present State of England," 1687, p. 87.

should disapprove of the mayor, they should proceed to re-election, when, upon a second disapproval, the mayor should be nominated by the king himself; that in the case of the sheriffs, if the king did not approve the first choice, he should at once nominate his own sheriffs. The Corporation, thus bound hand and foot, continued to be the slaves of the Court, till their shackles were knocked off by the Revolution of 1688. Other corporations were terrified into the surrender of their Charters. In 1684 the Lord Chief Justice, Jeffreys, did "great matters towards bringing in the Charters, as it was called," in his Northern circuit; and the king "was persuaded to present him with a ring, publicly taken from his own finger, in token of his majesty's acceptance of his most eminent services;" and thus encouraged, Jeffreys "went down into the country, as from the king *Legatus à Latere*, esteemed a mighty favourite; which, together with his lofty airs, made all the Charters, like the walls of Jericho, fall down before him; and he returned laden with surrenders, the spoils of towns." [*] There was little chance, after this, that a Parliament should be chosen in which the burgesses of England, who had fought the battles of freedom for four centuries, should have any due share of parliamentary representation. Prudent royalists were alarmed at such proceedings. Evelyn saw nothing but evil in "these violent transactions"—a learned recorder set aside to make way for an obscure lawyer—the Lord Mayor and two Sheriffs holding as *custodes*, at the king's pleasure. "The pomp and grandeur of the most august city in the world thus changed face in a moment: which gave great occasion of discourse, and thoughts of hearts, what all this would end in." [†] The Court judged that resistance to its behests was now utterly at an end. The king "at last subdued entirely that stubborn and rebellious city." [‡] The duke of York had a little private revenge to accomplish: "He thought it necessary to terrify others by making an example of the late sheriff, Pilkington; who having said, upon the duke's return, 'he had fired the city and was now come to cut their throats,' he caused him to be indicted, May 8, and the words being proved by two aldermen, the court assigned his royal highness a hundred thousand pounds for damages." [§] The royal influence could not only effect the utter ruin of a citizen for hasty words, but it had a year before shown that it could so manage the administration of justice that a detestable murderer should escape unpunished. Lady Ogle, a widow of fifteen, had, against her wish, become the wife of Thomas Thynne, of Longleat, called, on account of his great wealth, "Tom of Ten Thousand." The rich man and his bride were parted for a time; and she went abroad, where she had previously met Charles John, count Königsmark. The intimacy was probably renewed. On Sunday evening, the 12th of February, 1682, Thynne was passing in his coach along Pall Mall, and near a part then known as St. Alban's-street, where now stands the Opera-arcade, he was murdered by a mounted ruffian, attended by two others, who fired upon him with a blunderbuss loaded with four bullets. Thynne expired on the following morning. The assassin, George Borosky, a Pole, and his confederates, two Swedes, were apprehended. Count Königsmark was captured a week after, in endeavouring to escape from the country. The four were tried at Hicks's Hall, on the 28th,

* "Examen," p. 625.   † "Diary," October 4, 1683.
‡ "Life of James II." vol. i. p. 738.   § *Ibid.*

the count being indicted as an accessory before the fact. The Pole and the
two Swedes were found guilty and were hanged. The count was acquitted.
Sir John Reresby, who was very active in communicating with the king and
the council about this murder, says, "being at the king's couchée on the 21st,
I perceived by his majesty's discourse that he was willing the count should
get off." He was the first that carried the news of the count's acquittal to
the king, "who seemed to be not at all displeased at it; but the duke of
Monmouth's party, who all appeared to add weight to the prosecution, were
extremely dissatisfied that the count had so escaped." * Of Königsmark's
guilt there was not the slightest doubt.

Murder of Thynne.   From his Tomb in Westminster Abbey.

"Nothing," say the Memoirs of James, "now was wanting to make the
king perfectly easy in his affairs but the duke's assistance in the management of them. . . . . The discovery of a cursed conspiracy, which in
part they had already providentially escaped, but still in great measure hung
over their heads, hasted the duke's re-admission into business for their
mutual security." † The providential escape was from the assassination of
the king and the duke, which it was alleged was intended to be accomplished
at Rye-House, in Hertfordshire. Keeling, a vintner, communicated to one
of the Secretaries of State, that a plot had been devised for engaging forty
men to way-lay the king and his brother, as they returned from Newmarket,
at a farmhouse called the Rye, belonging to Rumbold, a maltster; that the
king returning sooner than was expected, that scheme was given up, and a
general insurrection was projected by certain eminent persons, amongst
whom were the duke of Monmouth, lord Essex, lord Howard of Escrick,
and lord William Russell. Some of the inferior persons accused were first
apprehended. The Rye-House Plot was in every mouth. The place was
not so well known to Londoners as at the present day, when hundreds of
summer holiday-folks go to make merry at the Rye-House on the pleasant
banks of the Lea. It was then described as " a place so convenient for such

* "Memoirs," p. 261-2.   † "Life of James II." vol. i. p. 733.

a villainy as scarce to be found in England; besides the closeness of the way over a river by a bridge, gates to pass, a strong hedge on one side, brick walls on the other." * The Rye-House Plot appears to have been a real conspiracy amongst obscure men. That the Whig leaders participated in the design of assassination was not considered probable even amongst royalists of the time. Upon the committal to the Tower of Russell, Essex, and Sidney, Evelyn writes, " The lords Essex and Russell were much deplored, few believing they had any evil intention against the king or the church. Some thought they were cunningly drawn in by their enemies, for not approving some late counsels and management relating to France, to Popery, to the persecution of the Dissenters, &c." The duke of Monmouth, lord Grey, sir Thomas Armstrong, and two others, for whose arrest a proclamation was made, escaped. The trials of three minor conspirators were hurried on, and they were convicted on the evidence of their associates. On the 13th of July, lord Russell was brought to trial. From the first he gave himself up for lost. As he entered the Tower he told his servant Taunton that he was sworn against, and that his enemies would have his life. Taunton hoped that his master's enemies had no such power. " Yes," said Russell, " the devil is loose ! " †

According to the political creeds of men of a past age, it has been customary to speak of Russell and Sidney as martyrs in the cause of liberty, or as scoundrels who had no just notions of government.‡ To regard the conduct and character of either of these eminent men with enthusiastic admiration is to us as impossible, as to consider them as selfish and ambitious intriguers, ready to plunge the nation into civil war for the advancement of a faction, or the advocacy of a wild theory of a republic. Their notions of political perfectibility were essentially different. Russell, the calm and practical representative of a great party, sought to attain freedom under a monarchy sufficiently checked by a Parliament, and to exercise religion under a Protestant establishment, tolerant to all forms of dissent but that of Roman Catholicism. Popery was his one great terror, and not unreasonably so. He was violent towards Papists, because he regarded Popery " as an idolatrous and bloody religion." He was their relentless and persecuting enemy when his party was all-powerful, for reasons which he thus expressed : "As for the share I had in the prosecution of the Popish plot, I take God to witness that I proceeded in it in the sincerity of my heart, being then really convinced, as I am still, that there was a conspiracy against the king, the nation, and the Protestant religion."§ The political principles of Algernon Sidney were essentially different. He was the last of the old Commonwealth-men, of the school of Vane. He hated the legitimate tyranny of Charles as much as he hated the usurped power of Cromwell. He disliked Popery rather with the dislike of the philosopher than that of the Christian. Neither Russell nor Sidney contemplated the removal of political evils by the assassination of the king. When Charles gave for his reason for denying mercy to Russell, "If I do not take his life he will soon have mine," he was thinking of his father's

---

* " Autobiography of Sir John Bramston," p. 182.
† " Life of William Lord Russell, by Lord John Russell," vol. ii. p. 25.
‡ The Tory opinion is thus delivered by the Tory Johnson, with his usual vehemence. See Boswell's " Johnson."
§ Russell's paper, delivered to the sheriff before his execution.

fate rather than of such danger as that of the Rye-House. He told Russell upon his first examination before the Council, that nobody suspected him of any design against his person, but that there was good evidence of his being in designs against his government. Russell was as conscious of his own political importance as Charles was aware that in removing him he removed the great obstacle to the designs which James now steadily advocated with the zeal of a bigot and the blindness of a despot. " Arbitrary government," said Russell to his chaplain, Mr. Johnson, " cannot be set up in England without wading through my blood."

The trial of Russell derives its chief interest from a circumstance which associates it with the tenderness, the devotion, the fortitude of woman. The day before the trial, lady Russell, the daughter of the earl of Southampton, wrote a note to her husband in these words : " Your friends believing I can do you some service at your trial, I am extremely willing to try ;—my resolution will hold out; pray let yours. But it may be the Court will not let me ; however, do you let me try." On the 13th of July the forms of indictment having been gone through, and the prisoner having in vain requested a postponement of the trial for a day, that he might produce witnesses not yet arrived, he said, " May I have somebody to write, to help my memory ? " " Yes, a servant," was the answer. " My wife is here to do it." And so, by her lord's side, sat that noble wife, calmly doing her office amidst the most exciting scenes. Lord Howard of Escrick appears. He was Russell's relative. To save himself, he offered to criminate his friends. He is put in the witness-box. His voice falters. " We cannot hear you, my lord," says one of the jury. Howard explains, " There is an unlucky accident happened which hath sunk my voice : I was but just now acquainted with the fate of my lord of Essex." The news ran through the court that Essex had committed suicide in the Tower. " This fatal news coming to Hicks's Hall upon the article of my lord Russell's trial, was said to have had no little influence on the jury and all the bench to his prejudice." * The Attorney-General said, " My lord Russell was one of the council for carrying on the plot with the earl of Essex, who hath this morning prevented the hand of justice upon himself." Men doubted whether Essex perished by his own hand. His head was so severed from his body " that an executioner could hardly have done more with an axe. There were odd reflections upon it."† The evidence of Howard and other witnesses went to show that Russell, before Shaftesbury left the country, had attended a meeting in the City, at which a rising was debated, and there was talk of the feebleness of the king's guard at Whitehall. Howard also asserted that there was a cabal of six persons, Monmouth, Essex, Russell, Sidney, Hampden, and himself; and that one of their objects was to draw the Scotch malcontents to join with them. Russell made a very short defence, in which he solemnly denied the charges imputed to him : " I have ever looked upon the assassination of any private person as an abominable, barbarous, and inhuman thing, tending to the destruction of all society. How much more the assassination of a prince, which cannot enter into my thoughts without horror and detestation ; especially considering him as my natural prince, and one upon whose death such dismal consequences are but

* Evelyn, "Diary." July 13. † Ibid.

too likely to ensue. . . .   As for going about to make or raise a rebellion, that, likewise, is a thing so wicked, and withal impracticable, that it never entered into my thoughts. Had I been disposed to it, I never found, by all my observation, that there was the least disposition or tendency to it in the people. And it is known, rebellion cannot be now made here, as in former times, by a few great men." *   And yet we cannot doubt that "a few great men" contemplated some coercion of the government, perhaps short of rebellion, despairing of "having things redressed in a legal parliamentary way." It is difficult to draw the line between legal and illegal resistance when men are hopeless of just government. Russell was convicted of treason, though certainly he was illegally convicted. He had committed no overt act, imagining the king's death, which had brought him within the Statute of Treasons of Edward the Third. The Act of William and Mary, annulling his attainder, says that he was, "by partial and unjust constructions of law, wrongfully convicted, attainted, and executed for high-treason." Russell went to his death with Christian fortitude. Extraordinary efforts were made to save his life, but Charles was not to be moved, even by the offer of a hundred thousand pounds. Russell was beheaded on the 21st of July, on a scaffold erected in Lincoln's Inn Fields. His parting with his noble wife had something more touching than sobs and tears. "This flesh you now feel, in a few hours must be cold," he said. They then kissed and separated, in eloquent silence.

The trial of Algernon Sidney was postponed till the 21st of November. Pemberton was Chief Justice when Russell was tried. He was removed to make room for Jeffreys. Lord Howard of Escrick was again the chief witness against the friend who had confided in the betrayer's professions of republicanism. Two witnesses were required by the Statute of Treasons. There was no second living witness against Sidney; that defect was supplied by a manuscript found amongst Sidney's papers, in which treasonable principles were held to be advocated. He approved of conspiracies against Nero and Caligula, and therefore was ready to compass the king's death. Howard's depositions were different from those which he gave on the trial of Russell. Sidney appealed to the jury whether any credit was due to a man who deceived and betrayed his friends—who had said he could not get his own pardon from the king till he had done "some other jobs." Of course Sidney was convicted in the utter absence of all legal evidence of treason. He was brought up for judgment on the 26th. When he heard his sentence he prayed God that, "if at any day the shedding of blood that is innocent must be revenged, let the weight of it fall only on those that maliciously persecute me for righteousness' sake." Jeffreys, although he had kept his brutal nature in some subjection to decency, then exclaimed, "I pray God to work in you a temper fit to go into the other world, for I see you are not fit for this." Sidney stretched out his arm, and said, "My lord, feel my pulse, and see if I am disordered." Evelyn records that on the 5th of December, he was at a wedding where he met Lord Chief Justice Jeffreys and Mr. Justice Withings. "These great men spent the rest of the afternoon, till eleven at night, in

* Lord John Russell's "Life," vol. ii. p. 60. From the MS. in Lord W. Russell's handwriting.

drinking healths, taking tobacco, and talking much beneath the gravity of judges; who had but a day or two before condemned Mr. Algernon Sidney, who was executed the 7th on Tower Hill, on the single witness of that monster of a man, lord Howard of Escrick, and some sheets of paper taken in Mr. Sidney's study, pretended to be written by him, but not fully proved." Sidney died with a simple courage and unostentatious composure worthy of his strength of mind. "When he came on the scaffold, instead of a speech, he told them only that he had made his peace with God; that he came not thither to talk, but to die; put a paper into the sheriff's hand, and another into a friend's; said one prayer as short as a grace; laid down his neck, and bid the executioner do his office." *

Connected with the other chief participators in the alleged conspiracy of 1683, we may mention that Monmouth was ultimately pardoned; and that sir Thomas Armstrong was given up by the States of Holland, and executed without a trial upon his sentence of outlawry. He had surrendered within the year, during which the law allows the accused to claim a trial. Jeffreys rudely resisted this legal demand of Armstrong.

The connexion of the English Whigs with the discontented in Scotland gave birth to a terrible persecution in that enslaved kingdom. In England, even a Jeffreys could not go beyond a certain point under the forms of law. In Scotland, those forms were utterly set at nought. Scotsmen, arrested in London, were sent to Edinburgh for their mock trials. Some eminent haters of the tyranny under which the land had fallen fled to Holland. Torture was administered to other suspected and accused persons with a ferocity exceeding even the times when the duke of York superintended the process of the boot. Sentences of forfeiture were lavishly pronounced, by which such tools as Graham of Claverhouse were enriched. The prisons were crowded with Covenanters. In England, James had openly succeeded to the chief administration of public affairs. He had not withheld his consent from the marriage of his daughter, Anne, to the Protestant prince George of Denmark. The king rewarded the duke by his restoration to his offices of High Admiral and Privy Councillor.† Titus Oates was indicted for *Scandalum Magnatum*, and damages of 100,000l. for a libel against the duke were awarded. The Rev. Samuel Johnson, chaplain to the late lord Russell, was summoned before the Council, to answer whether he was the author of a book called "Julian's Acts and Methods to undermine and extirpate Christianity." He acknowledged that he was. He was commanded to produce one of the books. He said that he had suppressed all the copies, "so that they were now his own private thoughts, for which he was not accountable to any power on earth." No copy could be obtained; and he was therefore prosecuted for writing a book called "Julian the Apostate." He was condemned in a fine of five hundred marks, which he was unable to pay; and was committed to prison. In prison he remained till the time when James had the regal power, and exercised it with a frantic violence, of which the barbarity perpetrated upon this exemplary clergyman, whose only fault was a love of his country's liberties, was one of the most hateful examples. ‡ Arbitrary

---

* Evelyn, "Diary."   † "Life of James II.," vol. i. p. 745.
‡ "Memorials of Mr. Samuel Johnson," prefixed to the folio volume of his works. 1710.

government had now its full swing. The Oxford divines came boldly forward to give their aid to degrade the free monarchy of England into an unmixed despotism. They published a decree against pernicious books and damnable doctrines. They anathematised the seditious and impious principle that civil authority is derived originally from the people; that there was any implied compact between a king and his people: passive obedience was the only concern of the subject with the government under which he lived. Sir George Mackenzie, the Lord Advocate of Scotland, published his treatise "Jus Regium," which he dedicated to the University of Oxford, in which he maintained that "whatever proves monarchy to be the best government, does, by the same reason, prove absolute monarchy to be the best government." Sir Robert Filmer's posthumous work, which had the honour of calling forth the refutation of its doctrines by Locke, went to the same extremes. Mr. Hallam truly says, "We can frame no adequate conception of the jeopardy in which our liberties stood under the Stuarts, especially in this particular period, without attending to this spirit of servility which had been so sedulously excited." The confidence of the ultra-royalists was un-bounded: "now the king had brought his affairs to a more happy situation than ever they had been since the Restoration. He saw his enemies at his feet, and the duke his brother at his side; whose indefatigableness in business took a great share of that burthen off his shoulders, which his indolent temper made uneasy to him." * Charles had his brother officially at his side through dispensing with the Test Act. Louis XIV. was carrying on his ambitious designs without any apprehension of the interference of England. By turns he bribed and he bullied the abject Charles. There were some even amongst Charles's advisers who felt the degradation. Halifax ventured to suggest the calling a Parliament. James was diametrically opposed to such a measure. Halifax advised that France should no longer dictate to England. James knew that the French alliance ratified the slavery of England. Charles was undecided—or pretended to be so. The great arbiter stepped in to settle many doubts and difficulties.

On Sunday evening, the 1st of February, 1685, Evelyn was at Whitehall. A week after he recorded his impressions of the scene which he there witnessed: "I can never forget the inexpressible luxury and profaneness, gaming, and all dissoluteness, and as it were total forgetfulness of God, it being Sunday evening. The king sitting and toying with his concubines, Portsmouth, Cleveland, and Mazarine, &c.: a French boy singing love songs in that glorious gallery; whilst above twenty of the great courtiers and other dissolute persons were at Basset around a large table, a bank of at least two thousand in gold before them." On Monday morning, the 2nd of February, the king was struck with apoplexy. On the Tuesday he had somewhat recovered. On the Thursday his case was considered hopeless. Two bishops came to him; he said he was sorry for what he had done amiss; heard the form of absolution; but declined to receive the sacrament. The duchess of Portsmouth, who had manifested a real grief, told Barillon, the French ambassador, that Charles was really a Roman Catholic; she urged Barillon to tell the duke that if any time were lost, his brother would die

* "Life of James II.," vol. i. p. 746.

out of the pale of his Church. James tells the result himself. The duke "asked him if he desired he should send for a priest to him ? to which the king immediately replied, 'for God's sake, brother, do, and please to lose no time.'. But then, reflecting on the consequences, added, 'But will you not expose yourself too much by doing it ?' The duke, who never thought of danger when the king's service called, though but in a temporal concern, much less in an eternal one, answered, 'Sir, though it cost me my life, I will bring one to you.'" * James found Father Huddleston, a Benedictine monk. The king confessed, received extreme unction; and then the Sacrament was administered by Huddleston. His natural children were called around the dying man's bed. Monmouth alone was absent, though his father had been privately reconciled to him. The queen sent to ask her husband's pardon for any offence she might have committed. "It is I that ought to ask her pardon," said Charles, with a passing remorse. "Do not let Nelly starve," he said to his brother. He apologised to the watchers around him for the trouble he was giving. The politeness of the gentleman remained with him to the last. Charles died at noon on Friday, the 6th of February. The people of London, odious as was the government of the king, lamented for the man. In that lament was probably mingled the fear that a worse king was coming.

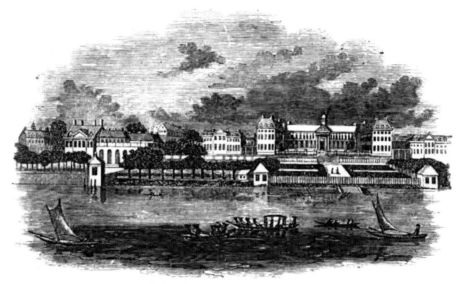

Chelsea Hospital.　Founded by Charles II.

About three years before the death of Charles the Second, an event took place which would then attract little of the regard of ·English courtiers and politicians, but which was fraught with important consequences never to be

* "Life of James II.," vol. i. p. 747.

forgotten in the history of the Anglo-Saxon race.   On the 5th of March, 1682, William Penn, who we last saw standing undaunted at the bar of the Old Bailey, was before the king in council at Whitehall.   His father, the admiral, had died in 1670, leaving his Quaker son a considerable property.   The duke of York, a friend of admiral Penn, had undertaken to be the young man's protector.   Two years after his father's death William Penn applied to James to use his influence to procure some remission of the persecution of the Quakers.   The duke made some of those professions of toleration which he had learnt to employ upon particular occasions.   He was kind to Penn; who became a person of consequence at Whitehall.   A considerable sum, about 16,000l., was due from the Treasury to Penn as his father's heir—the amount of money lent by the admiral, with accumulated interest.   He petitioned to have his claim settled, not by a money-payment, but by the grant of a large tract in America—a region of mountains and forests and prairies, accessible from the sea by the river Delaware.   During sixty years the colonisation of the great North American continent by Englishmen had gone steadily forward. The plantation of Virginia, the plantation of New England, in the reign of James I., laid the foundations of that mighty community whose present marvellous progress appears but the faint realisation of its ultimate destinies.[*] In the reign of Charles the Second, Carolina was also settled.   Maryland had been a previous acquisition; New Jersey had been conquered from the Dutch.   The commercial importance of the English North American settlements was stated by De Witt in 1669, when he wrote "The Interest of Holland."   He says, "The long persecution of Puritans in England has occasioned the planting of many English colonies in America, by which they drive a very considerable foreign trade thither."   Penn knew well that in the persecuted of his own sect he would find the best of settlers—men always remarkable for their industry and frugality.   Not so solicitous for worldly profit, as for a home for his followers beyond the reach of penal laws, Penn assiduously pressed his suit; and on the 5th of March, he stood before the king and council, to have his charter signed.   The name suggested for this mountainous and wooded region was first New Wales; and secondly, Sylvania.   The king prefixed Penn to Sylvania.   The Quaker legislator and his friend Algernon Sidney, the republican, drew up a constitution for the new colony.   It was essentially democratic.   Religious liberty was its great element, and with that was necessarily connected civil freedom.   There was to be an executive Council, of which Penn, the proprietor, or his deputy, was to be president; which Council was to consist of seventy-two persons.   There was to be an Assembly.   Both were to be chosen by universal suffrage.   It has been justly observed, that "as the proprietor and legislator of a province which, being almost uninhabited when it came into his possession, afforded a clear field for moral experiments, he had the rare good fortune of being able to carry his theories into practice without any compromises, and yet without any shock to existing institutions." [†]

The Welcome, a vessel of three hundred tons, in which Penn was to embark, set sail from Deal on the 1st of September, 1682.   There were a hundred passengers on board, of whom a third died of the small-pox during

* See *ante*, vol. iii., p. 343.   † Macaulay, "History," vol. i. 8vo, p. 507.

the voyage. On the 27th of October, the survivors, with their governor, landed at Newcastle, on the Delaware. The next day Penn assembled the inhabitants, consisting of families of various nations, Germans, Dutch, Swedes, English. He produced his charters. He explained his system of government. Penn's relation, Colonel Markham, had arrived before him, and had prepared the way for him, by calling an Assembly for the purposes of legislation. In three days, Penn's constitution was adopted; and supplementary laws were enacted to carry out its spirit. The industrial education of rich and poor was provided for; justice was to be cheaply administered; prisons were to be regulated with a view to the reformation of the criminal; death punishments, except for murder and treason, were to be abolished.

Treaty with the Indians; from West's picture.

The governor had much labour before him, but he went through it resolutely. The lands of the province were surveyed, and divided into lots for grant or purchase. Philadelphia was founded upon a plan which contemplated the growth of a magnificent city. In a year many houses had been built, and emigrants came in great numbers to become farmers or traders in a land where men could dwell without fear of oppression. Schools were founded. A Printing-Press was set up. A Post was established. The great outworks of civilisation were won. The principles of justice, upon which the new colony was founded, were to guide the conduct of the colonists towards the native Indians. The treaty with the red men—the only treaty that was never sworn to and never broken, says Voltaire—was one of friendship, and brotherhood, and mutual defence. An American has painted the scene, with the vagueness of his time as to portraiture and costume; but West's picture gives some notion of a solemn ceremony, in which the Great Spirit, the common Father of all, was appealed to in the pledge that the power of civilisation should not be abused by the exercise of force or injustice against the weakness of barbarism.[*]

[*] The interesting Biography of William Penn, by Mr. Hepworth Dixon, furnishes a very complete view of the settlement of Pennsylvania, of which ours is necessarily the briefest sketch.

Great Seal of James II.

CHAPTER XXIV.

THE chamber of death is closed. James retires for fifteen minutes to the privacy of his closet, and then comes forth as king to meet the Council. It was necessary that he should address the assembled counsellors. He declared that he would follow the example of his brother in his great clemency and tenderness to his people; he would preserve the government in Church and State as by law established; he knew that the principles of the Church of England were for monarchy, and that the members of it were good and loyal subjects, and therefore he should always have to defend and support it; he knew that the laws were sufficient to make the king as great a monarch as he could wish, and therefore, whilst he would never depart from the just rights and prerogatives of the Crown, he would never invade any man's property. Some members of the Council asked for copies of this "benign and gracious declaration." The king said that he had spoken from his heart without much premeditation, and had not his speech in writing. Finch, the Solicitor-General, stated that he thought he could write it down word for word. He did write a report; the king approved, and ordered it to be published. The biographer of James says that Finch worded the speech as strong as he could in favour of the established religion, and that James passed it over without reflection: "He was afterwards convinced it had been better expressed by assuring them he never would endeavour to alter the established religion, rather than he would endeavour to preserve it; and that he would rather support and defend the professors of it than the religion itself." * James the Second was proclaimed that same afternoon at Whitehall-gate, at Temple-bar, and at the Exchange. The Council, and other officers of State, accompanied the procession. On their return they all kissed the hands of the king and queen. "The queen," writes Evelyn, "was in bed in her apartment, but put forth her hand, seeming to be much afflicted, as I believe she was, having deported herself so decently upon all occasions since she came into England, which made her universally beloved." † Charles the

Maria Beatrix of Modena.

Second was buried on the 14th, "without any manner of pomp." This absence of the usual ceremonies is accounted for by the fact that the late king had died a Roman Catholic. That fact was not as yet public; and the people blamed the parsimony of James, or his want of the affection of a brother. The difficulty of conducting the funeral of Charles in accordance with "the greater ceremonies which must have been performed according to

* "Life of James II.," vol. ii., pp. 3 & 4.   † "Diary," February 6.

the rites of the church of England," * pressed with increased force when the Coronation-day arrived, on the 23rd of April. Some alterations were made in the ritual; and, "to the sorrow of the people, no Sacrament, as ought to have been." † The second Sunday after he came to the throne the king went openly to mass; and within a month of Charles' death the Romanists "were swarming at Court with greater confidence than had been ever seen in England since the Reformation, so that everybody grew jealous as to what this would tend." ‡

James had not been more than three days king, when his government committed an illegal act. The grant of customs for the life of the king expired on the death of Charles. A proclamation was issued ordering that the duties on merchandise should be levied as usual, till the royal revenue had been settled by Parliament. This was against the advice of the Lord Keeper, Guilford, who recommended that the duties should be collected and kept apart in the Exchequer, till the Parliament should dispose of them. "The temper of the public was, then, so propitious to the Crown, that almost anything would be borne with, which, in other times, would have raised a flame." § The counsellors chosen by the king for his especial confidence were his brother-in-law, Rochester; Sunderland, who had been Charles's Secretary of State; and Godolphin, who had been first lord of the Treasury: Halifax, who had held the Privy-seal, was appointed to the unimportant office of President of the Council. It was nominally a higher office, and therefore a witticism which he had used on the promotion of Rochester was applied to himself—he was kicked up-stairs. The king's other brother-in-law, Clarendon, was made Privy-Seal. Sunderland had voted for the Exclusion Bill, and therefore his continuance in office was a matter of surprise. But, if we are to credit the king's own assertion, this crafty minister saw the policy of connecting himself, however secretly, with the Roman Catholic party. James, in his own "Memoirs," says that in a consultation soon after his accession to the throne between lord Sunderland, Father Petre, Mr. Jermyn, and lord Tyrconnel, "it was agreed that Father Petre should be a Cardinal, lord Sunderland Lord Treasurer, lord Tyrconnel Lord Lieutenant of Ireland (who engaged to procure my lord Sunderland five thousand pounds per annum out of that kingdom, or fifty thousand pounds in money,) and that Mr. Henry Jermyn should be made a lord, and captain of the Horse Guards." ‖ Tyrconnel and Jermyn were Roman Catholics. The king did not stand alone in his inclination to tread a path beset with dangers.

The apologists of James have endeavoured to induce a belief that, soon after his accession, "he limited his views to the accomplishment of two objects, which he called liberty of conscience and freedom of worship, and which, had he been successful, would have benefited, not the Catholics only, but every class of religionists." Dr. Lingard expresses this opinion, after having stated that James "gave it in charge to the judges to discourage pro- secutions in matters of religion, and ordered by proclamation the discharge of

* "Life of James II.," vol. ii., p. 6.   † Evelyn, "Diary."
‡ Ibid. March 5th.   § North, "Life of Guilford," vol. ii., p. 118.
‖ "Life of James II.," vol. ii., p. 77.

all persons confined for the refusal of the oaths of allegiance and supremacy." • It is implied that " the dissenters " were relieved by this tolerant disposition. The relief extended only to Roman Catholics and Quakers. The Puritan dissenters—Presbyterians, or Independents, or Baptists,—had evinced no objection to the oath which renounced the authority of the Pope. Those who continued in prison were there for offences under the Conventicle Acts and the Five Mile Act. The Roman Catholics would not take the oath of supremacy; the Quakers would not take any oath. " I have not been able," says a high authority, " to find any proof that any person, not a Roman Catholic or a Quaker, regained his freedom under these orders." †   The orders, signed by Sunderland, were issued on the 19th of April. The relief to the Roman Catholics was a natural manifestation of the disposition of the government. The relief to Quakers was the result of a conviction that they were a harmless sect, who carefully abstained from all political action, and avoided even political conversation. The influence of William Penn, who had returned home from Pennsylvania, was laudably exercised to obtain this relief for the Society of which he was a member. The number of Quakers liberated was estimated at above fourteen hundred. Roman Catholics were liberated " to the amount of some thousands." ‡   The real disposition of the government towards Protestant dissenters was at that period amply manifested by the proceedings in the Scottish Parliament. The meeting of the Estates preceded that of the English Parliament by nearly a month. In obedience to a special letter from the king, calling for new penal laws against the Covenanters, it was enacted on the 8th of May, that the punishment of death, and confiscation of land and goods, should be awarded against those who should preach in a conventicle under a roof, or should attend a conventicle in the open air, either as preacher or auditor. The persecution of the times of Charles II. was continued with increased fury.§ The soldiery were let loose upon the districts where the Covenanters were still unsubdued, to kill and plunder. The tale of two unhappy women who were condemned to be drowned, and were tied to stakes when the tide had receded, there to await the lingering but certain death that would follow its return, is not a fiction. Romance has not imagined any cruelty so horrible as that perpetrated by the scoundrel Major Winram. Of the two women whose drowning he superintended, one was a girl of eighteen, of the name of Margaret Wilson. She had seen her elder friend perish. She was half dead herself when she was taken out of the water. " Dear Margaret," said her neighbours, " only say God save the king." Her answer was, " God save him, if he will, for it is his salvation I desire." Beyond this she refused to go. She would not abjure the cause of her religion, and consent to attend the episcopal worship; and she was again thrown into the engulphing waves. The old laws against nonconformists were severe enough, and were executed with sufficient ferocity, to justify any resistance, even without the addition of the infamous law which James caused to be passed against those who attended conventicles. The

* " History," 8vo edition, vol. xiv. p. 13.
† Macaulay, " History," vol. i. 8vo, p. 509. Note.   ‡ Lingard.
§ We anticipated the date of the murder of " The Christian Carrier," to indicate the mode of proceeding with the Covenanters by the sanguinary Claverhouse. See p. 351.

biographer of James thus explains the motives of the sovereign who desired, according to his panegyrists, "liberty of conscience and freedom of worship:" —"The king's earnestness to have the field conventicles suppressed was not from any spirit of persecution—though those wretches deserved no quarter— but from an apprehension of new troubles." * He made the Puritan religion a pretence for manifesting his hatred of the Puritan love of freedom.

The Parliament had been summoned to meet on the 19th of May. No one doubted that the House of Commons would exceed all former Parliaments in subserviency, looking to the influences which had been exercised in the returns of members. Burnet, the Whig, complains of "the injustice and violence used in elections, beyond what had been ever practised in former times." Evelyn, the Tory, writes, "Elections for the coming Parliament in England were thought to be very indirectly carried on in most places." † Again, he says, "There are many of the new members whose elections and returns were universally censured, many of them being persons of no condition, or interest in the nation or places for which they served." The boroughs were almost wholly in the hands of the Court; the old Charters having been superseded by new Charters, which placed the returns in the power of a corrupt few, nominated by the Crown. "It was reported that lord Bath carried down with him [into Cornwall] no fewer than fifteen Charters, so that some called him the Prince Elector." ‡ James had some ambitious projects floating in his mind, and especially exciting him to secure an obedient Parliament. The interference of the French king with the parliamentary system of England, during the reign of Charles, was perfectly known to his successor. James was not quite so abject as his brother; but nevertheless he was ready to receive the French livres, and to submit his policy to the wishes of his patron, till he could make himself sufficiently secure of a large revenue for life. Then he would manifest a real independence. Meanwhile he talked to foreign ministers about maintaining the balance of power in Europe. He aspired to vie with the Court of France in its ceremonial observances towards ambassadors. His pride made him bear his yoke somewhat impatiently. "He seemed resolved," says Burnet, "not to be governed by French counsels." He gave out that he would cultivate the friendship of the Prince of Orange and the United Provinces. The courtiers said that a prince now ruled who would make France as dependent on England as England had been dependent on France. Louis slily said that "for all the high things given out in his name, the king of England was willing to take his money, as well as his brother had done." §

The Parliament assembled on the 19th of May. Under the Stuarts there had been a vast increase of the Peerage. In the reign of James the Second there were fifteen dukes and duchesses, two marquises, sixty-seven earls and countesses, nine viscounts, and sixty-six barons and baronesses, making a total of one hundred and fifty-nine. Eighty years before, there was no duke, only one marquis, about nineteen earls, three or four viscounts, and forty lords.|| The learned Doctor of Laws, from whose Court Calendar we derive this information, estimates that through luxury, licentiousness, and want of fit educa-

---

* "Life of James II.," vol. ii., p. 12.   † "Diary." May 10.
  ‡ Ibid. May 22.   § Burnet.
  || Chamberlayne, "Present State of England," 1687, Part I. p. 285.

tion, " it was lately difficult to find, as some are bold to affirm, the courage, wisdom, justice, integrity, honour, sobriety, and courtesy of the ancient nobility." Of the riches of the Peerage he has no doubt. He computes the yearly revenue of all England to be about fourteen millions, and assigns one eleventh of the whole to the nobility. Including twenty-five spiritual Peers (the see of York was vacant), there were a hundred and eighty-one Lords of Parliament. The number of Members of the House of Commons was five hundred and thirteen.* From the printed List of Members, it appeared that there were not more than a hundred and thirty-five who had sat in former Parliaments.† The Whig majority was gone. The country gentlemen, whether Whig or Tory, who were returned for the Counties, were a weak minority compared with the representatives of the newly chartered Corporations. The composition of the House of Commons was such that it would have been difficult for the people to over-estimate the extent to which their so-called representatives would go in placing the property and liberty of the country at the feet of the king. The language of James, in his Speech from the Throne, argues an undoubting confidence in the machinery which he had procured for obtaining a large revenue, and for enforcing a due compliance with his projects for restoring the influence of his own religion. He repeated not only the substance, but the exact words, of the speech which he had addressed to the Privy Council on the day of his accession ; "the better," said the king, "to evidence to you that I spoke then not by chance." In demanding the settlement of the Revenue for his life, for the many weighty necessities of government, he added these words, "which I must not suffer to be precarious." Mr. Fox has pointed out that " in arguing for his demand, as he styles it, of revenue, he says, not that the *Parliament* ought not, but that *he* must not suffer the well-being of the government, depending upon such revenue, to be precarious ; whence it is evident, that he intended to have it understood that, if the Parliament did not grant, he purposed to levy a revenue without their consent." ‡ Think not, says the incipient despot, that you are to supply me with a little money from time to time, out of your inclination to frequent parliaments. " This would be a very improper method to take with me. The best way to engage me to meet you often is always to use me well." And the whole House of Commons, with one exception, were awed by the " vultus instantis tyranni "—and voted unanimously that the grant of revenue should be for life. The one bold member was sir Edward Seymour, a Cavalier of the staunchest breed. He did not oppose the grant, but he maintained that the first thing to do was to ascertain who were legal members of the House. This was more especially a duty, he said, when the laws and religion of England were in evident peril. No member dared to follow up this attack of a man whose high ancestry gave a special impulse to his proud courage. The members of this Parliament "were neither men of parts nor estates ; so there was no hope left of either working on their understandings, or of making them see their interest in not giving the king all at once. . . . There was no prospect of any strength in opposing anything that the king should ask of them." § An attempt was made a few days later,

* Chamberlayne, " Present State of England," 1687, Part II. p. 91.
† Evelyn, May 22.   ‡ Fox, " James II."
§ Burnet. The writer, David Hume, who has had the chief direction of the English histori-

to obtain some security in the matter of religion ; by passing a resolution in Committee " to assist and stand by his majesty, according to our duty and allegiance, for the support and defence of the reformed religion of the Church of England, as now by law established." This was a great deal more than his majesty desired. Nor was a concurrent resolution less unpalatable,—that the House be moved to make an humble Address to his majesty, to publish his royal Proclamation "for putting the laws in execution against all Dissenters whatsoever from the Church of England." Barillon, the French ambassador, writes that these votes gave great offence to the king and queen, and that orders were issued to the Court members to get rid of them. When the House had to decide upon the resolution of its Committee, the previous question was moved ; and it was resolved, unanimously, " That this House doth acquiesce, entirely rely, and rest wholly satisfied, in his majesty's gracious word, and repeated declaration, to support and defend the religion of the Church of England, as it is by law established, which is dearer to us than our lives."

There were two remarkable trials at this period, which must have had a considerable influence upon public opinion. The one was the prosecution of Titus Oates for perjury ; the other the prosecution of Richard Baxter for libel. Of the justice of the conviction of Oates there can be little doubt. The atrocious severity of his punishment was to gratify the revenge of the Roman Catholics, who crowded Westminster Hall on his trial, on the 7th of May. The chief witness to the Popish Plot had long been lying in prison, heavily ironed, in default of payment of the excessive fine imposed upon him on his conviction for libelling the duke of York. He had been accustomed to browbeat juries, and to be lauded to the skies by judges. He had now to bear all the tyrannous invective which judges thought it decent to use in state prosecutions ; and, what to his unabashed impudence was far more terrible, he was to be pilloried in Palace Yard, and at the Royal Exchange. He was to be whipped from Aldgate to Newgate on one day, and then again to be whipped from Newgate to Tyburn. He was to be imprisoned for life. He was to stand in the pillory five times every year. His conviction, says Reresby, " was a grateful hearing to the king." His majesty said " that Oates being thus convicted, the Popish Plot was dead." Reresby is proud of his ready reply : " I answering, that it had long since been dead, and that now it would be buried, his majesty so well approved of the turn, that going with him afterwards to the princess of Denmark, I heard him repeat it to her." * Whilst the small joke was circulating about the Court, the wretched Oates was tortured in a way which even the haters of his perjuries must have thought excessive. He was flogged at the cart's tail on the first day, almost to death. Intercession was made to the king to remit the second flogging. The answer was, " he shall go through with it, if he has breath in his body." He did go through with it, and survived even seventeen hundred lashes. It is clear that the judges meant him to be flogged to death. He could not be

cal mind for nearly a century, had the impudence to fabricate a debate in the House of Commons for this occasion, in which he makes the opposers of the grant use arguments well worthy of a free and enlightened assembly. Mr. Fox pointed out that this was a pure invention, utterly unsupported by any contemporary writers, or even by tradition.
* " Memoirs," p. 299.

executed for his offence; but he could be subjected to the torments of a lingering execution. Flogging, under the government of James the Second, became a favourite punishment. Another of the plot witnesses, Dangerfield, was scourged for a libel, and he died. His death was laid upon a violent man who struck him with a cane, injuring his eye, as he was carried in a coach back to Newgate after his flogging; and that man, Francis, was hanged for murder. The lacerated body of Dangerfield showed that the brutal assault of Francis was a secondary cause of Dangerfield's death.

If Titus Oates was unmercifully scourged for the satisfaction of the Papists, Richard Baxter was harassed, insulted, fined, and imprisoned, for the terror of the Puritans. Baxter was tried for a seditious libel, contained in his Paraphrase on the New Testament, in which he somewhat bitterly complained of the wrongs of the Dissenters. Baxter's counsel moved for a postponement of the trial. "I would not give him a minute more to save his life," exclaimed the brutal Chief Justice: "Yonder stands Oates in the pillory, and if Baxter stood by his side the two greatest rogues and rascals in England would be there." The trial, if trial it could be called, went on. The barristers who defended the venerable man, now in his seventieth year, were insulted by the ermined slave of the Crown. Baxter himself attempted to speak, and he was thus met by Jeffreys: "Richard, Richard! dost thou think we will hear thee poison the court? Richard, thou art an old fellow, an old knave; thou hast written books enough to load a cart; every one is as full of sedition (I might say treason), as an egg is full of meat; hadst thou been whipt out of thy writing trade forty years ago it had been happy. Thou pretendest to be a preacher of the gospel of peace, and thou hast one foot in the grave; it is time for thee to begin to think what account thou intendest to give; but leave thee to thyself, and I see thou wilt go on as thou hast begun; but, by the grace of God, I'll look after thee. I know thou hast a mighty party, and I see a great many of the brotherhood in corners, waiting to see what will become of the mighty Don; and a doctor of the party [looking to Dr. Bates] at your elbow, but by the grace of Almighty God I will crush you all." * The famous non-conformist,—he who, in the earnestness of his piety and the purity of his life, was unsurpassed by the greatest of the great divines of the English Church from which he differed so little,—was of course found guilty. He was surrounded by friends and admirers, who wept aloud. "Snivelling calves!" exclaimed Jeffreys. He was anxious, it was said, that the prisoner should be whipped at the cart's tail, but that was overruled by the three other judges. Baxter was unable to pay his fine of five hundred marks; and he remained in prison for eighteen months; when his pardon was obtained.

The king, in his Speech to the two Houses on the 23rd of May, informed them that he had received news that morning from Scotland, that Argyle had landed in the West Highlands, with men from Holland. The Houses sympathised with the king in his anger that Argyle had charged him with "usurpation and tyranny." The earl had been three years and a half in Holland, an exile under his unjust sentence. Many who had fled from the oppressions exercised upon the Presbyterians had gathered around him. He

* "State Trials."

was the natural leader in any open resistance; for five thousand of his vassals would immediately flock to his banner, and with the Covenanters in the western counties would form a considerable army. The duke of Monmouth had seen Argyle, and had been pressed by him to make a simultaneous attempt to raise an insurrection in England. Argyle was fully prepared with money and with arms. He had with him, to support the cause of his Church, men of rank and influence. Monmouth had made no preparations, and had very slight means of making any; and his supporters were not men on whom great reliance could be placed. But Monmouth's adherents had this advantage over the followers of Argyle—they were not jealous of entrusting authority to one hand; they were not distracted by minute differences, as the Covenanters had ever been distracted. Reresby says that at the beginning of May the government had "advice that a store of arms had been bought up in Holland and conveyed into Scotland;" and that Argyle and lord Grey, and even Monmouth, had gone with them. James had desired that the States of Holland should interfere to prevent any expedition sailing from their ports. The prince of Orange, it is alleged, was anxious to meet the wishes of his father-in-law, who had manifested some disposition to throw off his dependence upon France. But the authorities of the United Provinces were very slow in the exercise of their divided responsibilities; and three ships, in one of which Argyle was on board, sailed out of the Zuyder Zee on the 2nd of May. Monmouth and Grey were not with him. They remained to prepare for their own desperate adventure.

From the very first the expedition of Argyle was conducted with an imprudence which was the result of indecision. At Kirkwall, in the Orkneys, two men were allowed to go on shore. They were arrested; and the news of the armament quickly reached Edinburgh, whilst Argyle was lingering on the coast to obtain the release of his men. When he reached Lorn, and his son went on shore to summon the clans to gather round their chief, no person of mark came to join in the war-cry of the Campbells. Many humble vassals, however, assembled at Tarbet. Here the counsels of the insurgents became more dangerously opposed to any plan of concentrated action. Argyle wished to make a stand in his own Highlands. Sir Patrick Hume and Sir John Cochrane were for marching into the western Lowlands. The army divided. A squadron, bound for Ayrshire, sailed up the Clyde; and Cochrane, having landed at Greenock, was convinced of the hopelessness of an attempt to rouse the population into revolt. Argyle was now in the isle of Bute, and Cochrane returned to him. After various encounters with the king's troops, Argyle was marching upon Inverary, when the Lowlanders of his army refused to advance into the Highlands. He then, with a greatly reduced number of followers, moved to Dumbartonshire, intending to march for Glasgow. Meanwhile his ships had been taken, and the stores which he had disembarked were also lost. Disaster followed upon disaster. When the rebel army crossed the Leven they were surrounded by the royal troops. It was determined not to risk an engagement, but to advance upon Glasgow by a night march. They mistook their course. The little army was reduced by desertion to a few hundred men. Their leaders fled. Argyle, disguised as a peasant, was at last captured in the manner quaintly described by lord Fountainhall: "Argyle himself, being alone on a

little pony, was overtaken by two men of sir John Shaw's, who would have
had his pony to carry their baggage; whereupon he fired a pistol at them,
for he had three on him, whereof I have two, which I got from his son-in-law,
the second marquis of Lothian; and thereafter took the water of Inchinan.
But a webster, dwelling there, hearing the noise, came with a broadsword."
The weaver would not quit Argyle, though the other two men would have
let him go for gold; and finally "the webster gave him a great pelt over the
head with his sword, that he damped him so that he fell into the river, and in
the fall cried, 'Ah, the unfortunate Argyle!'" His fate was now sealed.
He was conducted to Glasgow, and thence to Edinburgh. The same humiliations were inflicted upon him as were inflicted upon Montrose. It was
determined to execute him, without any further trial, under the flagitious
sentence that had condemned him to death in 1681. All the innate noble-
ness of his character was developed in these his last hours of misery. He was
threatened with torture; but he refused to criminate any of his friends. He
made no supplications for mercy, but he prepared himself for the scaffold,
with the proud consciousness that he fell in a good cause, and with the calm
fortitude of an undoubting faith. The placid sleep of the prisoner as the
hour approached in which he was to die—that sleep which the apostate who
gazed upon him could scarcely hope again to enjoy—is a worthy subject for
the historical painter, and it has been worthily treated by a living artist.

On the 14th of June Evelyn makes the following entry in his 'Diary':—
"There was now certain intelligence of the duke of Monmouth landing at
Lyme in Dorsetshire." The fact had been communicated to Parliament the
day before. At daybreak of the 11th of June, three vessels were descried in
the deepest part of the bay; and at a creek five miles east of Lyme, three
persons landed, and proceeded to White Lackington House, near Ilminster.
This was the scene of Monmouth's first progress. The surveyor of the port
of Lyme, in the discharge of his official duty, put off in a boat to visit the
three vessels. He was conducted to the duke; was civilly treated; but was
not allowed to depart till late in the day. The surveyor belonged to a club,
who met weekly to play at bowls and to dine. The members grew alarmed
at their friend's absence. The post came in at five o'clock, and brought a
newspaper, giving an account of three ships having sailed from a port in
Holland. The alarm increased. The mayor and burgesses went on the
cliffs to watch the suspicious vessels. They talked of firing a great gun, but
they had no powder or shot. It was now near sunset; and the terrified
magistrates saw the king's revenue boat, with three other boats, filled with
men, rowing in-shore. The men landed. The few borough militia ran
away. Some of the townsmen cried "A Monmouth! A Monmouth! The
Protestant religion!" Before night-fall the duke's standard was set up in
the Market Place of Lyme, and a Declaration was read. Monmouth had
landed with only eighty-three followers.*

The alacrity of the two Houses of Parliament to support the king "against
James duke of Monmouth, his adherents and correspondents," was manifested
in a spirit of ultra-loyalty. Without the slightest evidence, beyond that of
the mayor of Lyme, who had posted to London with his news, they passed in

* From a MS. in the British Museum, written by Samuel Dassell, a Customhouse-officer of
Lyme, abstracted in Mr. Roberts' "Life of Monmouth," vol. i., p. 220.

one day a Bill of Attainder against Monmouth; and they passed another Bill "for the preservation of his majesty's royal person and government," in which, to assert the legitimacy of Monmouth, or to propose in Parliament any alteration of the succession to the crown, were made high treason. The duke's Declaration was ordered to be burnt by the common hangman. A supply was voted to the king to meet the charges attending this rebellion, and the Lords and Commons were dismissed to their respective counties, by adjournment. The Declaration issued by Monmouth asserted the great principle that "Government was originally instituted by God, and this or that form of it chosen and submitted to by men, for the peace, happiness, and security of the governed, and not for the private interest and personal greatness of those that rule." It accused the existing government of attempting to turn "our limited Monarchy into an open Tyranny," and to undermine "our Religion by Popish Councils." It declared that "the whole course and series of the life of the present Usurper hath been but one continued conspiracy against the reformed Religion and rights of the nation." It then accused the duke of York of having contrived the burning of London; of having fomented the Popish Plot; of having assassinated the earl of Essex; of having poisoned his own brother, the late king. It was not a wise Declaration. The violence which stimulated the passions of the ignorant was offensive to the reflecting and the moderate. There was no possibility of accommodation, when it was declared that the sword should not be sheathed till the reigning monarch was brought to condign punishment. In asserting his own legitimacy, and his consequent right to be king of England, the adventurer first said that he would leave his claims to be decided by a free Parliament. In a subsequent manifesto he took other ground. Rash and impolitic as were many parts of Monmouth's Declaration—"full of much black and dull malice," as Burnet describes it—there were others besides the clowns and mechanics of the western shires who regarded "the Protestant duke" as their deliverer. The Independents of Axminster recorded in their "Church Book" their hopes "that the day was come in the which the good old Cause of God and religion, that had lain as dead and buried for a long time, would revive again."* The fervid expectations excited by the landing of Monmouth were not entirely local in their character. Daniel Defoe, then twenty-four years of age, joined the blue banner of the duke, in the confidence that he came to do battle for civil and religious liberty. Defoe subsequently recorded some of the incidents of this short warfare—happily the last occasion in which Englishmen had to meet Englishmen in a deadly encounter for great principles.

A royalist force had collected at Bridport, and Monmouth resolved to attack them. He had landed from his ships four pieces of cannon. He had fifteen hundred suits of defensive armour, a small number of muskets, carbines, and pistols, and about a thousand swords and pikes. On the day after his landing, he had a thousand foot under his command, and a hundred and fifty horse. On that day dissension broke out amongst his followers. The celebrated Andrew Fletcher of Saltoun, who was in command of Monmouth's horse, had received an insult from Thomas Dare, one of Monmouth's

* Roberts, vol. i. p. 232.

followers, who had been a goldsmith at Taunton; and the fiery Scot shot the Englishman, who instantly died. Such summary vengeance was unsuited to the national character, and Fletcher was obliged to fly to Monmouth's ship. This was an ominous commencement. On the 14th lord Grey marched to Bridport; fought with the militia there; and then retreated in disorder to Lyme. In spite of quarrels and disasters numerous recruits flocked to Monmouth's head-quarters at the George inn at Lyme—an antique hostelry, which was burnt down about forty years ago. The duke of Albemarle, Lord Lieutenant of Devonshire, marched from Exeter, with four thousand of the train bands. On the 15th he was met at Axminster by a large body of the insurgents. He thought it judicious to retreat. His men were not staunch. They threw away their arms and clothes; and the road to Exeter was free to Monmouth. He was satisfied to march to Taunton, which he reached on the 18th of June. Situate in a valley of unrivalled fertility, and abundantly prosperous in its serge manufacture, Taunton had long been conspicuous for its resolute adherence to the old spirit of puritanism. Oppressed as was its dissenting population under the various Statutes against Non-conformists, the principle of resistance was not extinguished amongst them. Their pulpits were burnt; they evaded the statutory penalties for non-attendance at church, by joining in the Liturgy beneath the tower of St. Mary Magdalen. But this was only surface obedience. Monmouth approached the town, and found that the population had possessed themselves of the arms stored in the belfry of their church, ready for his service. Hundreds went out to meet their idol. They thronged around him in their narrow streets, every man with a green bough in his hat. The ways were strewed with flowers; the windows were hung with garlands; maidens of good families went in procession to offer him twenty-seven standards, which they had worked with their own hands. One of them was "The Golden Flag," embroidered with J. R. and a Crown. This reception at Taunton probably decided Monmouth to proclaim himself King. That resolve was not in accordance with his first Declaration. It was offensive to many of his followers, who cherished the notion of a republic. Welwood says, "Ambitious he was, but not to the degree of aspiring to the Crown, till after his landing in the West; and even then he was rather passive than active in assuming the title of King. It was importunity alone that prevailed with him to make that step; and he was inflexible, till it was told him, that the only way to provide against the ruin of those that should come in to his assistance, in case he failed in the attempt, was to declare himself king; that they might be sheltered by the Statute made in the reign of Henry VII., in favour of those that should obey a king de facto." * This forced application of the statute of Henry VII. was altogether fallacious. Monmouth was himself too ready to forget its real meaning. Had Monmouth been king de jure, James was king de facto. And yet Monmouth proclaimed the adherents of James as rebels and traitors. The assumption of the regal title secured Monmouth no real accession of strength. Not a nobleman joined him; not even any head of a rich and influential Whig family. His pretensions were ridiculed even by those of the higher classes who had

* "Memoirs," p. 148.

no affection for the existing government. He issued Proclamation after Proclamation, " from our camp at Taunton, in the first year of our reign." The Assembly sitting at Westminster, voting and acting as a Parliament under the usurper, James duke of York, were desired to disperse, under the penalties of treason. All who collected and levied taxes for James duke of York were declared to be rebels and traitors. Christopher, duke of Albemarle, and his adherents, " now in arms at Wellington," were to be pursued as rebels and traitors. Monmouth marched out of Taunton on the 22nd of June. Albemarle marched into Taunton on the 23rd. He immediately wrote a few brief words to Sunderland : " I came hither this night, where I found these several Proclamations, which I send to your lordship only for your diversion." *

Monmouth marched from Taunton to Bridgewater with six thousand men. Many were armed with scythes, fixed on upright handles. This rustic weapon was so important, that warrants were issued to tything-men " to search for, seize, and take all such scythes as can be found in your tything, paying a reasonable price for the same." † The large numbers that gathered round Monmouth's standard were rather an embarrassment than an aid. They could not be provided with arms. They were a burthen upon the country through which they marched. But the general disposition of the humbler ranks of people to join Monmouth is evident from this fact : the Lords Lieutenant were ordered to call out the Militia, not so much to oppose the duke, " as to hinder the country from flocking in to him ; for the king could have little confidence in the Militia of those parts, who were framed, to be sure, of the same mould and temper of their neighbours, who so readily had joined the invader." ‡ On the 22nd of June the insurgents marched to Glastonbury. The monastic ruins, and the churches, gave shelter to the wearied men, who had travelled through a swampy district under a drenching rain. The next day they had reached Shepton Mallet. The object of the march was to attack Bristol. On the 25th they crossed the Avon at Keynsham. The night before, a ship had taken fire at the quay at Bristol. It was afterwards alleged against the Bristowans that they had fired the ship as a signal to the rebels. They were suspected by the authorities, for the duke of Beaufort, having a considerable body of Gloucestershire train bands with him in Redcliffe Mead, threatened to fire the city if they afforded any aid to Monmouth. The king's forces now surrounded the insurgents. They became irresolute ; and marched away to Bath. Monmouth grew dejected. The large reward of five thousand pounds had been proclaimed for " any who should kill him." § He was deeply mortified at the manifest unwillingness of the country gentlemen to engage in his support. He expected some of the royal army to come over to him. He had himself commanded a regiment, and was personally beloved. But those who knew him best knew the weakness of his character. He was brave in the field ; but he had none of those high qualities which fitted him to contend, even with the enthusiastic support of large bodies of people, against the organised power of a government that was capable of inspiring dread if

* Ellis, " Original Letters," First Series, vol. iii. p. 340.
† Roberts, vol. i. p. 328.   ‡ " Life of James II." vol. ii. p. 29.
§ Evelyn.

it failed to secure affection. Monmouth made no attack upon Bath, which had a strong garrison. He marched to Philip's-Norton, half way between Bath and Frome. On the morning of the 27th the advanced guard of the king's army, under the earl of Feversham, was close to the insurgents. That guard was commanded by the duke of Grafton, the youngest of the illegitimate sons of Charles the Second. Through a narrow lane which led into Philip's-Norton, Grafton led his grenadiers against his eldest half-brother. A barricade stopped their progress; and Monmouth attacked them in flank. Grafton cut his way through; and got back to the main body of the royal army. There was fighting for several hours; and the cause of the insurgents was strengthened by the proof, that, raw and undisciplined as they were, they could stand up against regular troops. The royal army retreated to Bradford. Defoe says, that if Monmouth had pursued his advantage, he would have gained a complete victory. * The same night the insurgent army marched, under incessant rain, to Frome. This night-march, and the morning engagement, greatly reduced the number of Monmouth's followers. Many had thought of the glories of war,—of a pleasant march to London where their beloved duke would establish the liberties of his country, and reward his trusty friends. They had seen some of the dangers and miseries of real warfare, and they hastened to escape from them.

At Frome Monmouth heard of the defeat and capture of Argyle. At Frome there were no joyful congratulations as at Taunton; for the earl of Pembroke had a few days before put down a popular demonstration of those termed in the London Gazette "the rabble." The prospects of Monmouth became more and more dark. He was advised, according to some authorities, —he himself meditated, according to other accounts,—to leave his followers to their fate, and escape to some foreign place of refuge. He had a devoted mistress to fly to, lady Wentworth, whose passionate attachment might console him for all the disappointments of his ambition. Lord Grey opposed this dastardly hope of the unhappy man, and he remained for a last struggle. At Wells his army had become unmanageable. They lived at free quarters, and attempted to deface the cathedral. On the 2nd of July they marched on towards Bridgewater. A deputation from the people of Taunton came now to entreat Monmouth not to return to their town. There were symptoms enough that his cause was now desperate. He had marched out of Bridge-water with a confident army on the 22nd of June. He was again at Bridgewater with a broken and dispirited force on the 4th of July. In these eleven days he had accomplished nothing. On Sunday, the 5th, the earl of Feversham, at the head of the royal army, entered the great moor, called King's Sedgmoor, which stretches in a south-easterly direction from below Bridgewater to Somerton. He encamped on this morass, on the west side of which flows the river Parret, and whose deep and broad ditches, called Rhines, and high causeways, showed how gradually the labour of man had converted this dismal swamp into a region comparatively fertile. In this ancient region of waters Alfred had found refuge in its Isle of Athelney. The names of the villages, compounded of "Zoy"—zee, sea—showed the maritime origin of the district. Feversham's horse were quartered in the

---

* Wilson, "Life of Defoe," vol. i. p. 108. Philip's-Norton is erroneously called Chipping Norton, in the passage quoted by Wilson.

village of Weston Zoyland. His infantry were under canvas. On that Sunday the determination was taken by the insurgent leaders to attack the king's army at night, to anticipate the expected assault of Feversham. Monmouth, says Defoe, "went up to the top of the steeple, with some of his officers; and viewing the situation of the king's army, by the help of perspectives, he resolved to make an attempt upon them by way of prevention. He accordingly marched out of the town in the dead of the night to the attack." * Monmouth from the elevation of Bridgewater church could distinguish the regiment that he had once commanded. If he had these men with him, he exclaimed, he could not doubt of success. He had been told that the royal army was not entrenched. He saw a plain beneath him intersected by great ditches. He was promised to be led safely across them by guides. He would not take the direct road from Bridgewater to Weston Zoyland, but would advance along the Eastern Causeway, across the North Moor and the Langmoor, and surprise his sleeping enemies in their camp. By this circuitous route of six miles, Monmouth would avoid the royal artillery that commanded the direct road. But he had undertaken a night march of extraordinary difficulty. The biographer of Monmouth, whose local knowledge is evidently complete, says, "A guide was needed in the lanes, but was indispensable after the forces reached the open moor. Indeed, any person desirous of traversing the moor by daylight at the present time, would be glad of direction to make a way to the cradle bridges across the great drain or cut." † The front of the royal army was covered by this great drain or cut, called the Old Bussex Rhine. It was filled by the recent heavy rains. Defoe, who may be regarded as an actor in these events, says of Monmouth, "Had he not, either by the treachery or mistake of his guides, been brought to an impassable ditch where he could not get over—in the interval of which the king's troops took the alarm by the firing of a pistol amongst the duke's men, whether also by accident or treachery is not known—I say, had not these accidents and his own fate conspired to his defeat, he had certainly cut the lord Feversham's army all to pieces."

The report of the pistol was heard in the royal camp. The mist lay heavy upon the moor, but the moon was at the full; and in the uncertain light a body of men was seen approaching. The alarm was sounded by the beat of drum. Grey had advanced with the cavalry; Monmouth was following at the head of the infantry. Suddenly the great Bussex Rhine intercepted their progress. Concealment was no longer possible. King Monmouth! was shouted, with the old rallying word of the Puritans, "God with us!" The king's troops fired across the ditch; and the untrained cavalry horses of the insurgents were scattered about the peat-moor. Monmouth came up to the edge of the Rhine; and shots were exchanged across that impassable ditch for some time. The whole royal army was now roused. Passing along the Weston Zoyland road they could soon be in the open plain. The sun was rising as the Life Guards scoured the moor, and the foot-guards and other regiments advanced in compact ranks. Monmouth fled from the field when he saw that his horsemen and his waggons had gone. The king's artillery was brought up, the bishop of Winchester having applied his

---

* "Tour through Great Britain," quoted by Wilson.   † Roberts, vol. ii. p. 63.

carriage-horses to drag the guns along the Bridgewater road. Yet the peasants and cloth-workers made a brave stand with their scythes and pikes. Their muskets were useless, for in vain they shouted " For God's sake, Ammunition ! " Another race of hardy men stood their ground to the last. " The slain," says Evelyn, " were most of them Mendip miners, who did great execution with their tools, and sold their lives very dearly."

It is impossible to regard the fate of Monmouth without a large amount of commiseration. Bred up amidst all the follies and vices of a luxurious Court ; pampered with every indulgence by his imprudent father ; rendered independent at a very early age by marriage with a rich heiress ; raised to the highest honours and employments ; made the tool of a party, unqualified as he was for any consistent political action ; bewildered with popular applause ; he finally engaged in a desperate enterprise against a stern and relentless enemy. When he fled from the field of Sedgemoor, he had about him a pocketbook, in which there were certain entries which indicate that Charles the Second had a design to get rid of the control of the duke of York, and restore Monmouth to his former position. On the 16th of February is this expressive memorandum: " The sad news of his death, by L. O cruel Fate ! " * After his defeat there was no hope for Monmouth. The price set upon his head made escape from the kingdom almost impossible. Before four o'clock of that July morning the fugitives from the fatal moor were hiding in every ditch and every hovel from their pursuers. By six o'clock Monmouth, with Grey, and two or three others, was twenty miles from the field in which he had better have died fighting. They rode all day towards the New Forest, till their horses were exhausted. Disguised as countrymen they proceeded on foot. Parties of militia were on the look-out on every side. Grey was taken early on the morning of the 7th, near Ringwood. Two men had been seen entering some enclosed grounds, intersected with hedges, some of the fields affording the shelter of standing crops, and some overgrown with fern and brambles. The two men were Monmouth and Busse, a German. The place was surrounded all night with soldiers, after a fruitless search. Early on the morning of the 8th Busse was discovered. The soldiers were stimulated to greater exertion by the announcement that the reward offered for Monmouth's apprehension would be divided amongst his captors. The unhappy man, worn out with fatigue, starving, was found in a ditch, in the garb of a shepherd. The same pockets that had held the raw pease which had been his only food, contained the George with which Charles had invested his first-born son. The prisoner was conveyed to Ringwood, about six miles distant from the field now known as Monmouth's Close. The real character of him who had led so many devoted followers to ruin was now displayed. He did not rise out of misfortune a nobler man, as Argyle had risen. His first act was to write an abject letter to king James, expressive of remorse for the wrongs he had done him. He had assured the prince and princess of Orange that he would never stir against his majesty, but horrid people had led him away with false arguments. He could say many things to move compassion, but he only begged to have the happiness to speak to the king, for he had that to say which he hoped would give his

* Welwood's " Memoirs," Appendix xv.

majesty a long and happy reign. He had one word to say of too much consequence for him to write. After remaining at Ringwood two days,
Monmouth and Grey were conducted to London under a strong escort.
They were three days on the road. Monmouth was prostrated by his fears;
Grey was unmoved by his impending danger. Arrived at Whitehall, a scene
ensued which the French ambassador, Barillon, considered opposed to the
ordinary usage of other nations. The sovereign saw the prisoner whose life
he had determined not to spare. Monmouth was brought pinioned into his
uncle's presence. "He fell upon his knees, crawling upon them to embrace
those of his majesty ; and forgetting the character of a hero, which he had so
long pretended to, behaved himself with the greatest meanness and abjection
imaginable, omitting no humiliation or pretence of sorrow and repentance, to
move the king to compassion and mercy." This is the account given upon
the supposed authority of king James's papers. It is not contradicted by
other narratives. The mean motive of the king in granting an audience
which in ordinary cases implied a pardon, is exhibited in this statement:
"There appearing no great matters of discovery, there was no advantage
drawn to either side by this unseasonable interview." * The "one word," if
spoken, was of no avail to save the prisoner's life.
    Detailed narratives of executions for State offences occupy a considerable
portion of most English histories ; and, we presume, they are attractive
to the general reader. Whether those who died by the axe under Plantagenet, Tudor, or Stuart, were innocent or guilty, were of pure or corrupt
lives, the fortitude with which they looked death in the face—without shrink-
ing even from the disgusting preparations for the barbarities that accompanied death for high treason—is an almost universal characteristic of their
untimely ends. The abjectness which Monmouth displayed when he deluded
himself with hopes of life, appeared to the French ambassador very different
to the ordinary fortitude of Englishmen. Monmouth, however, recovered his
courage when the last great trial was at hand. He had seen his wife in the
presence of lord Clarendon, on the Monday when he was committed to the
Tower. He saw her again on the Wednesday of his execution. The nature
of these interviews is perhaps correctly given by Evelyn, who says that the
duke received his duchess "coldly, having lived dishonestly with the Lady
Henrietta Wentworth for two years." The duchess was far more affected
than her husband; but he showed a proper consideration for her future
safety by maintaining that she had been averse to his behaviour towards the
late king, and knew nothing of the circumstances of his recent attempt. In
his prison, and on the scaffold, Monmouth was attended by the bishop of Ely
and the bishop of Bath and Wells. The conduct of these prelates, Turner
and Ken, towards the unhappy man has been compared to that of "fathers
of the Inquisition." † On the other hand it has been said, "they appear to
have only discharged what they considered a sacred duty." ‡ They pressed
him to acknowledge the doctrine of Non-Resistance to be true, if he were of
the Church of England. He would do no more than acknowledge the doctrines of the Church of England, in general. Again and again he was
exhorted to a positive declaration upon this point. Upon one subject his

* "Life of James II." vol. ii. p. 36.   † Roberts.   ‡ Macaulay.

opinions were singularly illustrative of his defective moral training. He maintained that his intercourse with lady Wentworth was not sinful; for she had reclaimed him from licentiousness, and their mutual attachment was profound and enduring. His disrespect for the conjugal tie was considered by the prelates as a reason for not administering the Sacrament to one so imperfectly repentant. He was urged to speak to the soldiers, and say that he stood there, a sad example of rebellion. He was urged to entreat the soldiers and the people to be loyal and obedient to the king. His answer was emphatic: "I have said I will make no speeches: I will make no speeches: I come to die." His death was a horrible butchery, through the unskilfulness of the executioner. The multitude around, who, for the most part, regarded the duke as martyred for the Protestant religion, yelled with fury when they saw their idolised favourite thus mangled; and as they dipped their handkerchiefs in his blood, the thought must have crossed many minds that the day would still come when new Monmouths should arise, to uphold the Cause with happier results.

One of the dying man's answers to the questions with which he was assailed was expressive of his consistent humanity: "Have you not been guilty," he was asked, "of invasion, and of much blood which has been shed?" He replied, "I am sorry for invading the kingdom and for the blood that has been shed." Again pressed upon this matter, he said, "What I have done has been very ill; and I wish with all my heart it had never been. I never was a man that delighted in blood: I was very far from it." Could the soft-hearted Monmouth have looked forward to the slaughters that were still to be perpetrated upon his poor followers, he would have had still heavier reason for lamenting his brief career of civil warfare. It is horrible to know that a king sat upon the English throne, in times not barbarous, who could command and sanction the execution of nearly four hundred of his subjects for their rash participation in a sudden revolt. It is still more odious to know that, not two centuries ago, there was an English judge so eager for bloodshed, and English juries so awe-stricken, as to condemn three hundred and thirty-one persons to the death of traitors, during one terrible Assize. In addition to those who suffered the extreme penalty, eight hundred and forty-nine of the insurgents were transported; and thirty-three were fined or whipped. The record of such circumstances is chiefly valuable to show us the nature of the tyranny from which we have escaped. The professional atrocities of a colonel Kirke, however exaggerated, were natural results of the uncontrolled power of a brutal captain of a brutal soldiery. The calculating barbarities of a Chief Justice Jeffreys, under the forms of law, exhibit the excesses of an authority far more dangerous to freedom than the passing inflictions of drum-head tyranny. When Kirke and his officers sit carousing at the White Hart at Taunton; and at every toast of the drunken crew a prisoner was hanged up for their merriment, and the drums were ordered to beat to give the quivering limbs music for their dancing,— we trace the degradation of the unchristian warriors, who brought the habits of their warfare with barbarians to be the scourges of their own countrymen. But when the Chief Justice of England strains every faculty of his depraved intellect to procure the condemnation of a lady, whose only crime was giving a meal and a lodging to two fugitives, we may well believe that there is no more direct evidence of the fatal curse of arbitrary power than its capacity to make the sword of justice a far more terrible weapon of oppression than pike or gun, and to degrade the head of a learned and liberal profession to an office lower than that of the hangman. The lady Alice Lisle, then seventy years of age, calmly slept at the bar while Jeffreys charged the jury against her with the vehemence of an advocate; and she went to the scaffold with a composure which her furious judge must have resented as the proof of his impotence to kill the soul. Alice Lisle was his first victim, and the only one at Winchester. Every exertion was made to obtain her pardon, but king James was inexorable. It was nothing to the revengeful Stuart that the venerable lady had been illegally convicted as an accessory in concealing a traitor, before the trial and conviction of the said traitor himself. It was enough that she was the widow of John Lisle, the member of the Long Parliament and of the High Court of Justice. Jeffreys only fleshed his fangs upon Alice Lisle. In Dorsetshire he executed seventy-four persons. In Devonshire a mere thirteen were put to death. In Somersetshire two hundred and thirty-three suffered all the barbarous punishments of high-treason. The pitch cauldron was constantly boiling in the Assize towns, to preserve the heads and limbs from corruption that were to be distributed through the beautiful western country. As the leaves were dropping in that autumn of 1685, the great oak of many a village green was decorated with a mangled quarter. On every tower of the Somersetshire churches a ghastly head looked down upon those who gathered together for the worship of the God of love. The directing post for the traveller was elevated into a gibbet. The labourer returning home beneath the harvest moon hurried past the body suspended in its creaking gimmaces (chains). The eloquent historian of this reign of terror has attested from his own childish recollections, that "within the last forty years peasants, in some districts, well knew the accursed spots, and passed them unwillingly after sunset."[*]

The barbarous executions of this evil time can only be matched by the infamy of the great, in seeking to make a money advantage in proportion to the number of prisoners to be transported. It was calculated that a thousand of these unfortunates were to be distributed amongst certain favoured persons; and Sunderland, writing to Jeffreys by order of the king, says, "the queen has asked for a hundred more of the rebels." They were to be sold by these merchants in human flesh for field labour in Jamaica, Barbadoes, and the Leeward Islands. Jeffreys did not approve of this courtly generosity, that would assign to others the proper wages of the king and his instruments; and he writes to James, "I beseech your majesty that I may inform you that each prisoner will be worth ten pounds, if not fifteen pounds a-piece; and, Sir, if your majesty orders them as you have designed, persons that have not suffered in the service will run away with the booty."[†] The most notorious of these transactions was that of the claim of the Maids of Honour to make a profit out of the pardon of the young girls of Taunton, who had presented the embroidered banners to Monmouth on the day of his triumphal entry. More than two thousand pounds were paid to these ladies of the queen of England, to avert a prosecution of the innocent children who had

---

[*] Macaulay, vol. i. 8vo, p. 645.   [†] Roberts, vol. ii. p. 241.

graced the procession of the handsome duke whom they were told was their rightful king.

Jeffreys returned from his bloody Circuit to be rewarded with the Great Seal. He boasted that he had hanged more for high treason than all the judges of England since William the Conqueror. In his proceedings he had a double gratification. He had a pleasure in hanging, and a more solid delight in reprieving. He sold his pardons for enormous sums ; and he was enabled by his lawful earnings in this fattening time to purchase estates of the value of thirty-four thousand pounds.

Autograph of James II.

Crown. James II.

CHAPTER XXV.

WHEN the failure of Monmouth's expedition seemed almost inevitable, Louis the Fourteenth wrote to his ambassador in England, "there is every appearance that he will soon meet with the same fate as the earl of Argyle; and that his attempt will have served to render the king of England much more absolute in his kingdom than any of his predecessors." Louis made this incontrovertible deduction from the whole course of history. Tyranny never learns moderation from the resistance which is made to it. The resistance must be strong enough to crush the tyranny, or the second state of the enslaved people will be far worse than the first. The attempt of Monmouth was premature. The nation had vague fears of the disposition of the government, but those fears were not sufficient to justify insurrection. The system of James was not at that time fully developed. The man who undertook to attack that system in its infant strength had not the confidence of the best part of the nation. Yet his rallying cry of "The Protestant Religion" might have convinced any ruler less blind and obstinate than James, that the principle which was sufficient suddenly to raise the industrious people of the western counties into an army of cloth-workers and miners,—to make the train-bands throw away their uniforms, and to leave it doubtful whether the militia would fight,—would, if provoked beyond a certain point, convert the whole nation into the opponents of the king. Fortunate was it for the future destinies of England that James the Second, who would have been the most dangerous of rulers a century earlier, was the weakest of despots, in his utter ignorance of the new elements of society which had been called into real vitality during the struggles of his father.   He was not wanting in ability and in decision of character; he was capable of serious application to business; ne was not utterly prostrated by idleness and luxury as his brother was.   But his personal merits were as the fuel to nourish the fire of his intense egoism.   Every action of his life had reference to his personality.   James, the king, was the one power in the State, that was to counterbalance every other power.   If James, the king, could retain an Established Church, to proclaim his divine right to dispense with laws, and to share its honours and riches with the Romanists, till it should be wholly recovered to Rome, it were well.   If James, the king, could maintain a large standing army, by the voluntary contributions of the people, it were well. But if Parliament should refuse supplies; if the Church should preach of the supremacy of the law over the will of the sovereign; if the people should murmur under a hated military domination,—then, Parliament should be dismissed; a High Commission should again purge the Church of all disloyalty; the soldiers should familiarise burgess and yeoman with the benefits of free quarters.   James was not a man to accomplish such designs.   He ran straightforward, snapping as the mad-dog runs and snaps, and of course had the same mad-dog ending, as a public enemy.

The Parliament was to meet on the 9th of November.   Its meeting had been preceded by the dismissal of Halifax from his office of President of the Council.   The king could not induce the ablest man of his time to fall into his own views as to the removal of the Test Act.   The schemes of James were maturing; and he desired to be surrounded by ministers who would have no scruples in seconding them.   The removal of the barriers which opposed the admission of Roman Catholics to office; the repeal of the Habeas Corpus Act; and the establishment of a large Standing Army, were the objects to which the king devoted himself without reserve.   The Jesuits urged on the king, persuading him that "the present juncture is the most favourable one that can be hoped for," to strengthen his authority.   "But the opulent and settled Catholics are alarmed for the future, and apprehend a change which may ruin them."   So wrote Barillon, the French ambassador.   This juncture was not altogether the most favourable.   That persecution of the Protestants in France which was carried into effect by the Revocation of the Edict of Nantes, took place in October.   Under this Edict the Protestants had lived undisturbed in the exercise of their religion.   The Edict had been originally declared to be a perpetual and irrevocable law.   The most peaceful and industrious communities had flourished under this toleration; and now the law was suddenly abrogated at the will of a despotic king, to whom the people were no more than the beasts of the field.   Louis had long carried on a petty warfare against the Calvinists—interfering with education, seizing upon property, closing places of worship.   But now, the Protestant religion was to be extirpated in France at one blow.   The ministers of the reformed faith were suddenly banished or imprisoned; children were taken away from their parents; women were driven into nunneries; dragoons were let loose upon the people, to pillage and to destroy.   Burnet has described the horrible scenes of what he terms "one of the most violent persecutions that is to be found in history."   He says, "I went over the greatest part of France while it was in its hottest rage, from Marseilles to Montpelier, and from thence to Lyons, and so to Geneva. I saw and knew so many instances of their injustice and violence, that it exceeded even what could have been well imagined; for all men set their thoughts at work, to invent new methods of cruelty. In all the towns through which I passed, I heard the most dismal accounts of those things possible; but chiefly at Valence, where one Derapine seemed to exceed even the furies of inquisitors. One in the streets could have known the new converts, as they were passing by them, by a cloudy dejection that appeared in their looks and deportment. Such as endeavoured to make their escape, and were seized (for guards and secret agents were spread along the whole roads and frontier of France), were, if men, condemned to the galleys; and, if women, to monasteries. . . . The fury that appeared on this occasion did spread itself with a sort of contagion: for the intendants, and other officers, that had been mild and gentle in the former parts of their life, seemed now to have laid aside the compassion of Christians, the breeding of gentlemen, and the common impressions of humanity. The greatest part of the clergy, the regulars especially, were so transported with the zeal that their king shewed on this occasion, that their sermons were full of the most inflamed eloquence that they could invent, magnifying their king in strains too indecent and blasphemous to be mentioned by me." The persecuted families carried their industry to other countries. To England they brought their silk trade; and they taught us to make the hats which we had been accustomed to buy from France. "The tyrant's revenue," says Evelyn, "was exceedingly diminished; manufactures ceased." At the moment at which the Protestant refugees were pouring into England, James was labouring to attain the same power that Louis had so wantonly exercised. There was no concealment about the matter. Evelyn writes, "I was shewed the harangue which the bishop of Valentia, on Rhone, made in the name of the Clergy, celebrating the French king, as if he was a God, for persecuting the poor Protestants; with this expression in it: ' That as his victory over heresy was greater than all the conquests of Alexander and Cæsar, it was but what was wished in England; and that God seemed to raise the French king to this power and magnanimous action, that he might be in capacity to assist in doing the same here.' " *

The king opened the Parliament with a bold declaration. The rebellion, he said, was suppressed, but the Militia was insufficient for such services. "There is nothing but a good force of well-disciplined troops in constant pay, that can defend us from such as, either at home or abroad, are disposed to disturb us." He had increased the number of that army. He asked for a supply answerable to the expenses of that force. "Let no man take exception, that there are some officers in the army not qualified, according to the late Tests, for their employments. The gentlemen, I must tell you, are most of them well known to me; and having formerly served with me on several occasions, and always approved the loyalty of their principles by their practice, I think them now fit to be employed under me." He was afraid, he declared, that some men might be so wicked as to hope and expect that a difference through this might happen between the Parliament and himself; but he

* "Diary," November 3.

did not apprehend that any such misfortune could happen as a division, or even a coldness; nor anything to shake their steadiness and loyalty to him. Up to a certain point the House of Commons would have borne anything. All the Municipal Corporations of England might be destroyed; corrupt juries might be terrified into false verdicts; judicial massacres might be perpetrated without rebuke; au alderman of London, Cornish, might be hanged at this very time upon the revived story of the Rye-House Plot; a poor widow, Elizabeth Gaunt, might be burnt at Tyburn for giving shelter to a rebel, who afterwards betrayed her; there was no amount of Civil Despotism which a Parliament would not have sanctioned, and a Church declared righteous.—But to put the power of the sword into the hands of Popish officers, and to ask the Protestant Commons to pay for this dangerous army, was something more than could be borne. We have happily lived to see these distinctions abolished; but it may be a question if English Protestantism could have ultimately shown its capacity for doing a tardy justice to Roman Catholics, if its most violent prejudices had not been roused at this season, and had not acquired a real strength and dignity by finding that the Cause of religion was also the Cause of liberty. The House of Commons, however the majority was composed of the nominees of the Court, was still penetrated with the old instincts of freedom. It hesitated about voting supplies, before considering the king's address. It beat the Court in a division of 188 against 182. It then, cautiously and timidly, gave the king to understand that he had committed an illegal act in appointing officers without their taking the test; and humbly hoped that "he would be graciously pleased to give such directions that no apprehensions or jealousies may remain in the hearts of his majesty's good and faithful subjects." He frowned upon the Commons. He did not expect such an Address. He had warned them against fears and jealousies. The reputation which God had blessed him with in the world ought to have created a greater confidence in him. The Commons were awe-struck by the threatening brow of this poor inflated creature. A country gentleman, Cook, of Derbyshire, said, he supposed they were all Englishmen, and not to be frightened from their duty by a few high words. The new-born independence of the House was laid low; and Cook was committed to the Tower for daring to say a word of implied reproach. But the spirit of resistance began to spread. The Peers manifested a deeper indignation against the violation of the Test Acts avowed in the royal speech, than the Commons had dared to exhibit. The sarcasm of Halifax was supported by the zeal of Compton, the bishop of London, and by the boldness of lord Mordaunt, afterwards the famous earl of Peterborough. The king was present at a great debate. Jeffreys, the Chancellor, attempted to carry the brutality of the Bench to his new position on the Woolsack. The presence of his master was not sufficient to protect him from the indignation of the proudest nobility of Europe. The government dared not divide upon the motion to take the king's speech into consideration; and the next morning the Parliament was prorogued, without any supplies having been voted.

We have now come to the end of the first Act of the Drama of the English Revolution. The king's manifestation of a temper to govern despotically, and of a design to force an obnoxious creed upon the nation, had been gradually becoming more evident. The suppression of Monmouth's rebellion had made him presumptuous. He had a large hereditary revenue, and he had obtained the vote for life of the most important imposts. He had established a powerful Standing Army, and his provident expenditure, amounting almost to parsimony, would enable him to maintain it. The judges were his creatures. The Church might be awed or cajoled into any practical acceptation of its favourite doctrine of non-resistance. From the time of this first dissension with the most obsequious Parliament that had sat since the early years of the Restoration, James manifested the most perfect reliance upon his own self-sufficient power. His nature could brook no opposition. He held to his purpose with a firmness that would have been admirable, if it had been the result of any other principle than that proud stupidity which could see no danger and accept no warning. Having dismissed the Parliament, he had a little more judicial business to accomplish. He pardoned Grey for his part in Monmouth's rebellion, because he could induce him to play the betrayer, having bought his life at a heavy money payment and the heavier price of his forfeited honour. Lord Gerard of Brandon, and John Hampden, were tried for their participation in the Rye-House Plot, upon Grey's confession. Their lives were spared. The earl of Stamford had been indicted upon the same charge; but the prorogation of Parliament prevented his trial before his peers. Lord Delamere was tried before the Court of the High Steward. Jeffreys, who presided, had used every means to obtain a conviction, by the selection of the triers from men opposed in politics to the prisoner, and he conducted himself on the trial with his usual coarse partiality. But Delamere was acquitted. The most courtly began to feel that enough vengeance had been taken for past offences. Lady Rachel Russell expressed the general sentiment when she wrote to her friend, "I do bless God that he has caused some stop to be put to the shedding of blood in this poor land."

England was again to be governed without a Parliament. After the prorogation of the 20th of November, 1685, it was twice prorogued in 1686, and twice in 1687; and it was dissolved by proclamation on the 2nd of July in that year. The course of the government towards arbitrary power is a flood which has no constitutional barrier to prevent it devastating the land. Will the old sea-wall ever be built up again? A strong people is equal even to that work. A less vigorous race would have folded their hands, and have left their fairest possessions to the destroyer.

At the beginning of 1686, king James was steering his state-vessel, with a blind fatality, towards the inevitable Rapids. Prudent friends entreated him, while it was yet possible, to slacken sail; to tack; to veer round, or to seem to veer. Such counsel became offensive to him. His brothers-in-law, Clarendon and Rochester, were looked coldly upon, for they were stedfast in their adherence to their Protestant convictions. Sunderland became the prime adviser of the king, for he had consented to embrace Catholicism. Having impaired his fortune by habitual gambling, he shamelessly received a pension of twenty-five thousand crowns from the king of France to espouse his interests, and prevent the re-assembling of the Parliament. The minister and the king had now a common bond of union, in the purpose of degrading their country abroad and enslaving it at home. The Jesuits, with Father

Petre as their great director, were now paramount in the government of England. The moderate Roman Catholics looked with apprehension upon the rashness by which the habitual temper of the nation might easily be lashed into fury. The ostensible ministers of James were divided into two parties. The real power was with the secret cabal of Sunderland and Petre. It was determined to send an ostentatious embassy to the Pope, to replace the modest agency with which the diplomatic business with the Court of Rome had been previously conducted. Lord Castlemaine, the husband of the duchess of Cleveland, one of the late king's mistresses, was appointed to this mission. The pontiff, Innocent XI., was not favorable to the Jesuits, and was opposed to the measures of the French king. Castlemaine was instructed to listen to the counsels of the General of the Jesuits and of the ambassador of France. The Pope sympathised with the feelings of the moderate English Catholics, who were satisfied to be unmolested without hoping to be paramount. The Rector of the Jesuits' College at Rome congratulated Castlemaine that the flourishing Imperial Crown of England was at length added to the Papal Diadem.* The Pope's agent in England, Count d'Adda, had been instructed to solicit the intercession of James "with the French monarch, in favour of the French Protestants."† Although the king of England had at first exhibited some pity for the persecuted families who had sought shelter in his dominions, his real temper and views were now unmistakeably displayed. On the 5th of May, by the especial direction of the king in Council, and not without remonstrance from some of his counsellors, there was burnt at the Royal Exchange, by the common hangman, the translation of a small volume recently published on the continent. Evelyn describes this volume as "a translation of a book written by the famous Monsieur Claude, relating only matters of fact concerning the horrid massacres and barbarous proceedings of the French king against his Protestant subjects." The book was burned "without any refutation of any facts therein." Evelyn adds, "So mighty a power and ascendant here had the French ambassador, who was doubtless in great indignation at the pious and truly generous charity of all the nation, for the relief of those miserable sufferers who came over for shelter." The disposition of "the nation" never presented the slightest obstacle to the egoism of the Stuarts; and they always had abettors, in such antiquated idolaters of royalty as sir John Bramston, who, now in his seventy-fifth year, being told that Claude's book had in it "expressions scandalous to his majesty the king of France," says, "if so, it was fitly burned, for all kings ought to be careful of the honour and dignity of kings and princes."‡

The time was close at hand when the old cry of the Cavalier, "Church and King!" would be uttered "with bated breath." The king and the church were not unlikely to dissolve that partnership which Strafford and Laud attempted to perpetuate; and for the maintenance of which the first Charles struggled at the risk of his crown and his life. The bishops, who had never ceased to preach the doctrine of passive obedience and non-resistance, and some of whom had been suspected of inclinations towards Popery,

* Wellwood, "Memoirs," Appendix xviii.
† Lingard.   ‡ "Autobiography," p. 228.

were now alarmed at the tendencies of the king. A brief had been ordered in Council for collecting contributions for the French refugees. The collection was put off, under various pretexts. Previous to the publication of the brief, Ken, bishop of Bath and Wells, exerted his eloquence in expressing "detestation of the cruelties of the French, and exhorting to constancy in the Protestant religion. This sermon was the more acceptable, as it was unexpected from a bishop who had undergone the censure of being inclined to Popery." * Other bishops manifested the same spirit; which example was followed by many of the Anglican clergy. The king and his advisers would not be warned; but intimated to the archbishop of Canterbury that he must warn his clergy not to preach on the miseries which the bigotry of Louis had inflicted on his unhappy Protestant subjects. Such warning was a significant fact. The clergy were not propitiated by the intolerant resolution of the king that, in the distribution of alms to the refugees, the commissioners appointed to that duty should only relieve those who would conform to the Church of England, by receiving the sacrament according to its ritual. James was now resolved to bring to issue the question of the king's dispensing power—that is, of the right of the sovereign to abrogate express laws by the exercise of his prerogative. This prerogative had been exercised in the earliest times of the Constitution; but had gradually become more and more limited, as the legislative power had become more defined. It still continued to be exercised in matters of trifling import, and especially with regard to laws which had fallen into disuse. To admit this dispensing power as a general principle, applicable to all Statutes affecting the well-being of the community, would be to render the monarchy of England absolute. The Test Act had been passed, in direct opposition to the desire of Charles the Second, to prevent the admission of Roman Catholics to civil and military offices. James the Second openly proclaimed his design to render the Test Act nugatory by his dispensing power of admitting to all offices, secular or ecclesiastical. He had appointed sir Edward Hales, a Papist, to be governor of Dover Castle, and colonel of a regiment. He resolved to make an effort to have his dispensing power sanctioned by the Courts of Law. Four of the judges, although not opposed to the politics of the Court, remonstrated with the king on the illegality of his proposed measure; and they were dismissed from their offices. His Solicitor-General, Finch, held the same conviction; and he was also dismissed. Four subservient judges, and a crawling Solicitor, were appointed in their places. A collusive action was brought in the Court of King's Bench for the penalty incurred by sir Edward Hales, for not taking the Sacrament according to the Test Act. The information was laid by his own servant. The object of the action was to obtain an authoritative decision as to the legality of the plea of the defendant, that he was enabled to hold his commission by letters patent authorising him to do so notwithstanding the Test Act. The king's dispensing power was now solemnly confirmed. "The new, very young, Lord-Chief Justice Herbert, declared on the bench, that the government of England was entirely in the King; that the Crown was absolute; that penal laws were powers lodged in the Crown to enable the King to force the execution

* Evelyn, "Diary," March 14.

of the law, but were not bars to bind the king's power; that he could pardon all offences against the law, and forgive the penalties; and why could he not dispense with them? By which [judgment] the Test Act was abolished. Every one was astonished."* The Attorney-General, Sawyer, had refused to draw warrants, which the king required him to draw, by which members of the Church of Rome were authorised to hold benefices of the Church of England. The Solicitor-General was more obsequious. The warrants were issued. Under one, Edward Sclater, described by Evelyn as " an apostate curate of Putney," was enabled to hold two livings; and under another, Obadiah Walker, Master of University College, Oxford, who, from the accession of James, had been a declared Roman Catholic, and had been busily engaged in the work of conversion, was enabled to hold his office and his benefices. The king's design to sap the foundations, if not to destroy the whole edifice, of the Anglican Church, was now sufficiently manifest. One step remained to be taken. The powers of Ecclesiastical Supremacy which had been assumed at the Reformation for resisting the authority of Rome, were now to be adopted with renewed vigour for re-establishing that authority. James determined to create a Court of Ecclesiastical Commission —a Court modelled upon the Court of High Commission, which had been solemnly abolished at the Restoration.

The king, as the Head of the Church, had issued directions to the Clergy not to introduce into their pulpits any discussion upon doctrinal points which were matter of controversy. The whole question of the differences between the Anglican and the Roman Churches were to be excluded from the consideration of their congregations. A royal licence was granted to an apostate Protestant of the name of Hall, to be the King's Printer, for printing missals, lives of saints, and Roman Catholic tracts, whose publication was prohibited by various Acts of Parliament. The Protestant pulpit was to be silenced; the Papist pulpit was to be free. The Protestant press was to work under terror of venal judges and terrified juries; the Papist press was to be sanctioned by royal licence. A divine of high reputation, Sharp, Rector of St. Giles'-in-the-Fields and Dean of Norwich, refused to submit to the decree that the clergy were not to preach upon controversial topics. One of his parishioners earnestly begged to be informed of the reasons upon which the Church of England rested its claims to be a true national Church, in opposition to the universal pretensions of the see of Rome. He expounded, as he was requested to do, the essential differences of doctrine and practice between the two Churches. Compton, the bishop of London, was required to suspend Dr. Sharp. He declined to do so; but he requested the offending Dean to suspend his preaching for a season. The Ecclesiastical Commission was now in force. Jeffreys, the Chancellor, to whom all religious and moral principle was a matter of indifference, was its president. Sancroft, the archbishop, would not act. The bishops of Durham and Rochester were more compliant. Sunderland, the new convert to Rome, and Herbert, the advocate of the dispensing power, were two other commissioners. The Protestant convictions of Rochester, another of the commissioners, were not strong enough to lead him to risk his loss of place. Compton was called before

* Evelyn, "Diary," June 27.

this partial and illegal tribunal. Jeffreys bullied him; but the bishop was firm. The one question was, why he had disobeyed the king? Conscience, duty, were of no avail in this Court. He was suspended from his spiritual functions. The Crown did not dare to seize his revenues; for the Courts of Law must have restored them.

The king has himself recorded some of the manifestations of his open encouragement of Roman Catholicism, which gave deep offence. His kingdom, he says, "grumbled at his taking the chapel of St. James into his own hands, which then lay useless; though to avoid all reasonable cause of complaint he took care to leave the chapel of Whitehall to the Protestants, and built one there from the ground for his own use. He settled fourteen Benedictine monks in that of St. James, and gave leave to the Jesuits to build one in the Savoy, and settled a College there for the education of children, in which they had so good success that in a little time there was at least two hundred Catholic scholars, and about as many Protestants, who were no ways constrained in their religion, or required to assist at mass or any of their public devotions." * The chapel of Whitehall was opened with all the pageantry of the Romish ceremonial, at Christmas, 1686. A bishop was consecrated on the 29th of December. † He sat in his rich copes and wearing his mitre; Jesuits and priests stood around, "censing and adoring him;" the silver crozier was put in his hand, "with a world of mysterious ceremony." The worthy courtier, Evelyn, was astonished: "I could not have believed I should ever have seen such things in the king of England's palace." The Benedictine monks at St. James, the Jesuit's College in the Savoy, were only parts of a general system. The Franciscans had their chapel in Lincoln's Inn Fields; the Carmelites settled in the city. The streets presented the wondrous spectacle to English eyes of cowled and girdled friars mixing with the crowd; and exultingly telling the wonderers that "they hoped in a little time to walk in procession through Cheapside." ‡ Such things could not be, without exciting the violent dislike of a populace that regarded Popery with the traditional hatred of a hundred and fifty years. Riots took place in London. The priests were insulted in their worship in new chapels in the country. The school of the Jesuits in the Savoy, and the schools which they had set up in various towns, obtained little favour from their being opened to children of Protestant as well as of Catholic parents. The dread of proselytism assumed a practical shape, in the rapid establishment of those Charity-schools throughout the land, to which popular education was almost wholly confined during the eighteenth century. The Jesuits' school in the Savoy gave the first impulse to private endowments of those metropolitan schools for the poor, whose children of both sexes now annually gather beneath the dome of St. Paul's, to unite their five thousand voices in the simple hymns of a devotion well adapted to the national character. The side-aisles of the great Protestant cathedral were appendages which James compelled Wren to introduce into his plan, in the hope that they might resound with the chants of Palestrina as the host was borne along amongst kneeling worshippers. Fortunate for our country that our forefathers

* "Life," vol. ii. p. 79. "His Own Papers."   † Evelyn. "Diary."
‡ Welwood. "Memoirs," p. 178.

preferred to join in Luther's Hymn! The opposition of the Protestant mind of the latter years of the seventeenth century to the secular teaching of the Jesuits was natural and inevitable. No consideration of their ability as teachers could disarm the suspicion that they sought to make converts, under the guise of affording instruction adapted to all churches and sects. The same doubts of all religionists who profess to be merely secular teachers still linger amongst us under other forms; and they will continue to prevail between Protestant and Catholic, Churchman and Dissenter, until Christian worship rests upon a broader foundation of Christian love.

The measures of the king became day by day more clearly directed to the gradual advancement, and ultimate supremacy, of his own creed. The popular discontent was growing serious. When the first Roman Catholic chapel was opened in the city, the train-bands hesitated to disperse the mob that insulted the priests. When Mass was first celebrated at University College, Oxford, in a chapel opened by Obadiah Walker, the dangers of the Church were proclaimed from pulpits in which it had been recently proclaimed that there was no danger and no sin to be compared to that of resistance to the divine authority of kings. The formation of a great camp on Hounslow Heath was naturally considered to be for the purpose of coercing a sinful generation, that obstinately refused to accept the gracious invitation to come back to the creed of Gardiner and Bonner. The ponderous folio of "Acts and Monuments" was again brought out, and mothers gathered their children around their knees to hear the sad stories of Rowland Taylor and Anne Askew. The camp at Hounslow was supposed to be the evidence that another time of fiery trial was at hand. "There were many jealousies and discourses of what was the meaning of this encampment," writes Evelyn. The Reverend Samuel Johnson chose to interpret its meaning, in his own incautious fashion. He had been in prison since his conviction in 1683 for writing "Julian the Apostate." [*] A restless and dangerous man, Hugh Speke, was his fellow-prisoner; and in the spirit of mischief he excited Johnson to write an address to the troops encamped at Hounslow, which Speke undertook to get circulated. It was entitled "An humble and hearty address to all the Protestants in king James' army;" and, says the biographer of Mr. Johnson, "he exhorted the Protestant officers and soldiers not to serve as instruments to enslave their country, and to ruin the religion they professed." [†] Johnson was discovered as the author. He had the generosity not to implicate Speke, and he alone suffered. He was convicted, on the 16th of November, of a libellous publication, and was sentenced to stand three times in the pillory, and to be publicly whipped. According to one account, when sentence was pronounced he said, "You whip, upon my back, Acts of Parliament and the Church of England." [‡] According to another account, when told by the judge to be grateful to the Attorney-General that he was not tried for high treason, he exclaimed, "Am I, when my only crime is that I have defended the Church and the laws, to be grateful for being scourged like a dog, while Popish scribblers are suffered daily to insult the Church, and violate the laws with

* Ante, p. 375.　　　† "Memorials," p. xi.
‡ Bramston's "Autobiography," p. 249.

impunity ?" He was scourged like a dog; but previous to his punishment, he was stripped of his gown, by the bishops of Durham, Rochester, and Peterborough, Commissioners appointed for the diocese of London, during the suspension of Compton, the bishop. Johnson's cruel sentence was inflicted on the 1st of December, though strenuous endeavours were made to obtain a remission of the whipping. "The king was deaf to all entreaties: the answer was, that since Mr. Johnson had the spirit of martyrdom, 'tis fit he should suffer." * His biographer says of the courageous endurance of the suffering, "He observed afterwards to one of his most intimate friends, that this text of Scripture, which came suddenly into his mind, ' He endured the cross, and despised the shame,' so much animated and supported him in his bitter journey, that had he not thought it would have looked like vain-glory, he could have sung a psalm while the executioner was doing his office, with as much composure and cheerfulness as ever he had done in the church; though at the same time he had a quick sense of every stripe which was given him, with a whip of nine cords knotted, to the number of three hundred and seventeen."

In addressing the army of king James in a style which was an incentive to mutiny, Johnson went out of his province as a clergyman; and thus brought himself under the cognizance of a law which could scarcely be considered as arbitrary. The censorship of the press had been revived; and this Address to the Soldiers was one of the many publications that evaded all attempts at repression. One class of publications, however, the licensing system could not restrain—works of theological controversy. There were divines then in England who were fully equal to the task of defending their Church against the advocates of Rome, whose pamphlets, encouraged by the Court, and issued by its printer, were boldly denounced by Johnson upon his trial. In this controversy writers whose names live in honoured remembrance, ardently engaged—Sherlock and Tillotson, Stillingfleet and Prideaux. Such who filled the pulpits of London—others who were the ornaments of the Universities—had feeble opponents in the priests who addressed the learned in bad English, and sought to convert the multitude by legends of miracles, over which the shrewd artisan had his heartiest laugh. The government could not touch the controversial pamphlets, of which the Archbishop of Canterbury was the Licenser. Disputants without a professional privilege could be either punished or frightened away. At Amsterdam, the amusing John Dunton tells us, he had the good fortune to meet with Doctor Partridge, "whose Almanacks had been so sharp upon Popery that England was too hot to hold him." † But the contest soon grew beyond the skirmishes of a paper-war. Before the close of the year 1686, the king's determination to thrust Roman Catholics into the higher offices of the Church and the Universities, was manifested by the appointment of John Massey to the deanery of Christchurch, Oxford. This Romanist convert was installed without opposition, on the 20th of December. The success of this illegal act was encouraging. The fellowships of Oxford and Cambridge were as freeholds, held by Protestant tenure. No one could be admitted to a degree without taking those oaths which had been provided by Acts of Parliament to exclude Catholics from

---

* "Memorials," p. xii.
† Dunton's "Life and Errors," p. 210, 1705.

academical honours and offices. These Statutes king James resolved to violate. On the 7th of February a royal letter was sent to the authorities of the University of Cambridge, commanding that Alban Francis, a Benedictine monk, should be admitted to the degree of Master of Arts. The authorities required the Benedictine to take the oaths. He declined, and left Cambridge, hinting at the consequences of a refusal to submit to the sovereign will. There was an awkward precedent for granting degrees to foreigners. The Secretary to the Ambassador of Morocco, a Mahometan, had received the Master of Arts' degree. Burnet points out that a proper distinction was made between strangers, whose degree was merely honorary, and those who would have a vote in convocation, as the king's priests would have, if admitted upon the royal mandate. The University was twitted with the obvious remark that a Papist was treated worse than a Mahometan. John Pechell, the Vice-Chancellor, had to endure an agonising conflict between obedience to the Statutes and obedience to the king. Learned dignitaries had been preaching and writing in support of the king's absolute power, and they were now to have a practical lesson of the real meaning of their doctrine. The terrified Vice-Chancellor writes to our old friend Samuel Pepys, to relate his misery under his dread sovereign's frown: "Worthy sir, 'tis extraordinary distress and affliction to me, after so much endeavour and affection to his royal person, crown, and succession, I should at last, by the providence of God, in this my station, be exposed to his displeasure." * The "princely clemency" upon which the Vice-Chancellor desired to cast himself, was sought in vain. The Vice-Chancellor and the Senate were summoned before the Ecclesiastical Commission. Their judges were papists, or of papistical tendencies. Jeffreys, the Chancellor, to whom all principles were indifferent as long as he had the power to enforce arbitrary decrees by his own insolent demeanour, was the mouth-piece of this body. Pechell was frightened. The other delegates of the Senate in vain pleaded that they had acted in obedience to the laws. The Vice-Chancellor was deprived of his office, and suspended from the enjoyment of his revenue as Master of Magdalene College. The property-rights of the college, which were as sacred from any such interference as the estate which Jeffreys had bought out of the price of his swindling pardons during his Bloody Campaign, were thus as openly violated as the Statutes of the realm.

Cambridge was subjected to no further molestation. At Oxford it was concluded that the spirit of resistance might be easily kept down. Oxford had accepted a papist Dean of Christchurch. Oxford had suffered mass to be performed in two of its colleges. The noble institutions of Oxford might gradually be made as available for the advancement of Catholicism as the College of Douay, or the Jesuits' School in the Savoy. Had not Oxford, to use the words of Burnet, "asserted the king's prerogative in the highest strains of the most abject flattery possible, both in their addresses, and in a wild decree they had made but three years before this, in which they had laid together a set of such high-flown maxims as must establish an uncontrollable tyranny?" † Surely resistance would not come from Oxford,

* Letter of February 23,—in the Pepys' Correspondence.
† "Own Times," Oxford edit. vol. iii. p. 146.

whatever might happen. There were premonitory symptoms that the spirit of English gentlemen would at length be roused out of the sleep of slavery. Obadiah Walker was insulted and ridiculed in his popish seminary. The undergraduates had long believed, as Colley Cibber represented his own school-boy belief in 1684: "It was then a sort of school doctrine to regard our monarch as a deity; as in the former reign it was to insist he was accountable to this world, as well as to that above him." * The undergraduates of 1686 were a little veering round to this obsolete notion; and in spite of the Oxford deification of James II., it was necessary to quarter a troop of dragoons in that loyal city, to allow "Ave Maria" to be sung in more than one chapel without interruption from the scurrilous songs of the street. The crisis was at hand. The presidency of Magdalen College was vacant. It was rumoured that Anthony Farmer was to be recommended by a royal letter. This man was not qualified by the Statutes of the College, the presidency being limited to fellows of Magdalen or of New College; he was of notoriously immoral life; he had become a pervert to Rome. The fellows of Magdalen remonstrated in vain against the probability of this indecent choice. The royal letter came. In the hope of some compromise the election was postponed till it could be postponed no longer. John Hough, a man worthy of the office, was elected. The fellows were cited before the Ecclesiastical Commission. They produced such proofs of Farmer's unfitness, that no attempt was made to enforce his election; but that of Hough was declared void. In August, a royal recommendation of Parker, bishop of Oxford, arrived. The fellows justly held that the right of election was in themselves; that Hough was duly elected; that the presidency was not vacant. The king had set out on a progress. On the 3rd of September he reached Oxford. He lodged at the deanery of Christchurch, and heard Mass in a chapel fitted up by the dean. The fellows of Magdalen College were sent for. William Blathwayte, the Clerk of the Council, writes to Mr. Pepys an account of what took place at this audience: "His Majesty being informed that the fellows of Magdalen College had refused to admit the bishop of Oxford to be their president in the stead of Mr. Farmer, sent for them yesterday, after dinner, to his anti-chamber in Christ-Church College, where his majesty chid them very much for their disobedience, and with much a greater appearance of anger than ever I perceived in his majesty; who bade them go away immediately and choose the bishop of Oxford before this morning, or else they should certainly feel the weight of their sovereign's displeasure. The terms were to this effect; and yet I hear this morning they have not obeyed his majesty's commands, the consequences of which I cannot yet learn." † The consequences were more full of peril to the threatening tyrant, than to the fellows of Magdalen College. Resolute against the king's heaviest displeasure—unseduced by the arts of a man whose political faults all would willingly forget, but whose partial aberration from the path of duty can scarcely be disproved—the fellows of Magdalen College persisted in their right of election. Their legal president was ejected by a special commission,

* "Apology for the life of Colley Cibber,"—edit. 1756, p. 23.
† Pepys' "Correspondence," September 5th, 1687.

whose decrees were enforced by troops of cavalry. Hough refused to give up the keys of the college, and the doors were broken open. The bishop of Oxford was installed by proxy, only two fellows of the college giving their attendance. The other fellows at length consented to a modified submission to the authority which had been forced upon them. The king required a public acknowledgment that they had acted undutifully; and that the appointment of the bishop of Oxford was legal: they must sue for pardon. They one and all refused to submit to this humiliation. They were one and all ejected from their college, and declared incapable of holding any ecclesiastical appointment. The Ecclesiastical Commission, by which this edict was issued, forgot that a power might be raised again, as it had once been raised, before which High Commissioners might be swept away, and even the throne might totter to its base. The immediate object of the king was accomplished. Magdalen College soon became a college of Papists, with a Roman Catholic bishop at its head; for Parker, the bishop of Oxford, had enjoyed his dignity only during a few months, in which his authority was so openly resisted that he died, as men believed, of anxiety and mortification. A subscription was raised for the ejected fellows. All but the most bigoted saw that the ties which bound the Church to the Throne were so loosened, that upon one more violent strain the union might be utterly broken.

Town House. Hague.—Carriage of Prince of Orange—1686.

CHAPTER XXVI.

Fall of the Hydes—Tyrconnel Lord Deputy in Ireland—Declarations in Scotland and England for
Liberty of Conscience—Abolition of Penal Tests—Effects of the Declaration of Indulgence—
The camp at Hounslow Heath—The Papal Nuncio publicly received by the King—The
King's policy towards Dissenters—Dryden's Poem of "the Hind and the Panther"—The
Declaration commanded to be read in Churches—The Petition of the Seven Bishops—
They are committed to the Tower—The public sympathy—The trial and acquittal of the
Bishops—Birth of the Prince of Wales.

THE year 1687 opened with evil forebodings to those who were well-wishers
to the Monarchy and the Church.   One whose loyalty must have been sorely
shaken by the dangerous experiments upon the temper of the nation thus
records his impressions : " Lord Tyrconnel gone to succeed the Lord Lieutenant in Ireland, to the astonishment of all sober men, and to the evident
ruin of the Protestants in that kingdom, as well as of its great improvement
going on.   Much discourse that all the White-Staff officers and others should
be dismissed for adhering to their religion." *   The Lord Lieutenant, to

* Evelyn, "Diary," January 17.

whom Tyrconnel is to succeed, is Clarendon. The White-Staff officers are
to follow the dismissed Lord-Treasurer, Rochester. The fall of the two
Hydes, the brothers-in-law of the king, was of evil omen. It was seen that
the ties of relationship, of ancient friendship, of fidelity under adverse circumstances, were of no moment when the one dominant idea of the king was
to coerce all around him into his measures for forcing his creed upon a reluctant nation. From the highest minister of the Crown to the humblest
country magistrate, all appointments were to be made with reference to this
royal monomania : " Popish justices of the peace established in all counties,
of the meanest of the people ; judges ignorant of the law, and perverting it.
So furiously do the Jesuists drive, and even compel princes to violent courses,
and destruction of an excellent government both in Church and State." *
Tyrconnel, whose violence and rashness were objected to even by moderate
Catholics, was instructed to depress the English interest, and proportionately
to raise that of the Irish ; " to the end that Ireland might offer a secure asylum
to James and his friends, if by any subsequent revolution he should be driven
from the English throne." † But Tyrconnel, says Dr. Lingard, " had a further and more national object in view." He entered, with the sanction of
the king, into secret negotiations with Louis XIV., " to render his native
country independent of England, if James should die without male issue,
and the prince and princess of Orange should inherit the crown." Ireland
was then to become a dependency of France—a truly " national object."
Tyrconnel went about his work in a wild way. He displaced the Protestant
judges, and filled their seats with Catholics. He terrified the cities and
towns into surrender of their charters, and gave them new charters which
made parliamentary representation a mockery. He had a scheme for dispos-
sessing the English settlers of the property which they had acquired in the
forfeitures of half a century previous. His projects were opposed by grave
Catholic peers, who said that the Lord-Deputy was fool and madman enough
to ruin ten kingdoms. His character and that of his master, were ridiculed
in the famous ballad of Lilli-Burlero :

> " Dare was an old prophecy found in a bog,
>   Lilli burlero, bullen a-la ;
> Ireland shall be ruled by an ass and a dog,
>   Lilli burlero, bullen a-la."

James was the ass and Tyrconnel the dog. This ribaldry of Lord Wharton
was adapted to a spirited air of Purcell, published ten years before. " The
whole army," says Burnet, " and at last the people both in city and country,
were singing it perpetually." Wharton afterwards boasted that he had
rhymed James out of his dominions. He had produced a song, like many
other songs, of wondrous popularity, with little intrinsic merit. But those
whose conviviality, even in our own days, has been stirred by its fascinating
melody,‡ may well believe that it was whistled and sung in every street in
1689 ; and that it had charms for Corporal Trim, and his fellow soldiers in-

* Evelyn, " Diary," January 17.   † Lingard.

‡ " A very good song, and very well sung,
    Jolly companions, every one."

Flanders, when its satire upon the "new deputie" who "will cut de Englishman's troat," was utterly forgotten.

There is no error more common, even amongst educated persons, than to pronounce upon the opinions of a past age according to the lights of their own age. In February, 1687, James issued in Scotland a Declaration for Liberty of Conscience. In April, 1687, he issued a Declaration for Liberty of Conscience in England. Why, it is asked, were these declarations regarded with suspicion by Churchmen and by Dissenters? Why could not all sincere Christians, of whatever persuasion, have accepted the king's noble measures for the adoption of that tolerant principle which is now found to be perfectly compatible with the security of an Established Church. It was precisely because the principle has been slowly making its way during the contests of a hundred and fifty years, that it is now all but universally recognised as a safe and wholesome principle. It is out of the convictions resulting from our slow historical experience that all tests for admission to civil offices are now abolished for ever. Roman Catholic, Presbyterian, Quaker, Methodist, Independent, Unitarian, Jew, all stand upon the same common ground as the Churchman, of suffering no religious disqualification for the service of their country. But to imagine that such a result could have been effected by the interested will of a Papist king, who had himself been the fiercest of persecutors—who had adopted, to their fullest extent, the hatred of his family to every species of non-conformity,—is to imagine that the channels in which the great floods and little rills of religious opinion had long been flowing, were to be suddenly diverted into one mighty stream, for which time and wisdom had prepared no bed. King James announced to his people of Scotland that, "being resolved to unite the hearts and affections of his subjects, to God in religion, to himself in loyalty, and to their neighbours in Christian love and charity, he had therefore thought fit, by his sovereign authority, prerogative royal, and absolute power, which all his subjects were to obey without reserve, to give and grant his royal toleration to the several professors of the Christian religion after named." The moderate Presbyterians might meet in their houses; but field conventiclers were still to be resisted with the utmost severity. Quakers might meet and exercise their worship in any place. Above all, the various prohibitions and penalties against Roman Catholics were to be void; and all oaths and tests by which any subjects are incapacitated from holding place or office were remitted. The Council of Scotland made no hesitation about "sovereign authority" and "absolute power;" for they had told James at his accession that "we abhor and detest all principles and positions which are contrary or derogatory to the king's sacred, supreme, absolute power and authority." In Scotland, the experiment appeared to be successful. The successors of John Knox made no sign of resistance to a decree which gave honour to the image-worshippers. James now summoned his English Council to proclaim to them his new charter of religious liberty. Freedom of conscience was conducive to peace and quiet, to commerce and population; during four reigns conformity in religion had been vainly attempted. All penal laws should be suspended by the royal prerogative. "A Daniel come to judgment," cried some short-sighted Protestants of that day. "A wise and upright judge," cry some liberal philosophers of the nineteenth century.

lieth chiefly in a quick hand to cut off limbs; but she is the worst at healing of any that ever pretended to it." He warns the dissenters against the temptation to enjoy a freedom from which they had been so long restrained: "If the case then should be, that the price expected from you for this liberty is giving up your right in the laws, sure you will think twice before you go any further in such a losing bargain." * A large proportion of the Non-conformists held aloof from the blandishments of the Court, and ultimately made common cause with the Church. In his subsequent indignation against the relapse of churchmen into intolerance, Defoe exclaims, "Where had been the Church of England at this time, humanly speaking, if the dissenters had one and all joined in with the measures king James was taking to overthrow it?" The Church knew this, and made loud professions of brotherly regard to the separatists. The king and his papistical advisers, on the other hand, employed every device to manifest that the country was in favour of that dispensing power of a gracious king, which could bestow, not only toleration, but unlimited blessings of national glory and prosperity, which were not to be bestowed by old statutes or new enactments. Paternal government was the true remedy for all that was harsh and unequal in statutory laws. The corrupt Corporations sent up fulsome addresses of thanks to the king. In these some Protestant Non-conformists were induced to join. But the great body remained firm; and a common danger brought them nearer to that union with the Church, which the Stuarts, during four unhappy reigns, had done their best to render impracticable.

In the summer of 1687, a great Camp was again formed on Hounslow-heath. It was a military display of royal and aristocratic luxury, "the commanders profusely vying in the expense and magnificence of their tents." † The four troops of Horse Guards were commanded by the earl of Feversham, the duke of Northumberland, lord Churchill, lord Dover. The duke of Grafton commanded the first regiment of Foot Guards; the earl of Craven the second regiment. There were nine regiments of Horse commanded by the earls of Oxford, Peterborough, Plymouth, Arran, Shrewsbury, and Scarsdale; by sir John Lanier, general Warden, and sir John Talbot. There were three regiments of Dragoons, commanded by lord Cornbury, the duke of Somerset, and colonel Berkeley. Lastly, there were fourteen regiments of Foot, commanded by the marquis of Worcester; the earls of Dumbarton, Bath, Litchfield and Huntington: lord Dartmouth; and by colonels of the rank of commoners, amongst whom was the notorious colonel Kirke. The standing army had been trebled, as compared with its number in 1683.‡ The courtly habits of its commanders caused the people to regard this army as the instrument by which the king could accomplish his designs against their liberties and their religion. And yet in the hour of need this formidable army struck not a single blow; and most of his courtly officers deserted the king—a lesson which princes, who rely upon military force, have often been taught, however slow they may be to learn. The Londoners went out in holiday parties to look upon the magnificence of the

* This letter is reprinted in the "Somers' Tracts," and in "Parliamentary History," vol. iv.
† Evelyn, "Diary," June 6.
‡ For full details of the military force of 1687, see Chamberlayne's "Present State of England" for that year. Part i. p. 176; Part ii. p. 143.

camp at Hounslow. They mixed with the soldiers, who, with the exception of the household troops, were of their own rank as artisans and labourers. The temper of the nation was roused out of its apathy, to express itself with the freedom which Englishmen use when their political indignation is excited. A shrewd observer, then a very young man, thus describes this period : " It were almost incredible to tell you, at the latter end of king James' time—though the rod of arbitrary power was always shaking over us—with what freedom and contempt the common people, in the open streets, talked of his wild measures to make a whole Protestant nation Papists. And yet, in the height of our secure and wanton defiance of him, we of the vulgar, had no farther notion of any remedy for this evil, than a satisfied presumption that our numbers were too great to be mastered by his mere will and pleasure; that, though he might be too hard for our laws, he would never be able to get the better of our nature ; and that to drive all England into popery and slavery, he would find, would be teaching an old lion to dance." *

The camp at Hounslow was conveniently located between Whitehall and Windsor. It was at hand to suppress disturbances in the capital ; it could be speedily summoned to protect the king in the castle upon which his brother had lavished his adornments. Windsor was now to be the scene of a gorgeous ceremony, such as could scarcely have been exhibited without danger in the streets of Westminster. James had knelt at the feet of the papal Nuncio, who in the royal chapel of Whitehall had been consecrated bishop of Amasia. He was now to receive this ambassador of the Pope, with a pomp that belonged to past generations. It was resolved that a duke should introduce the Nuncio to the king. James proposed the honour to the duke of Somerset—the commander of the queen's regiment of dragoons, and a lord of the bed-chamber. This young nobleman, who afterwards obtained the distinction of being called " The proud duke of Somerset," behaved with a spirit on this occasion that wholly forfeited the royal favour: " He humbly desired of the king to be excused ; the king asked him his reason ; the duke told him he conceived it to be against law, to which the king said, he would pardon him. The duke replied, he was no very good lawyer, but he thought he had heard it said, that a pardon granted to a person offending, under the assurance of obtaining it, was void. This offended the king extremely. He said publicly, he wondered at his insolence ; and told the duke he would make him fear him, as well as the laws." † On the 3rd of July, Windsor was crowded with visitors. There was a procession to the castle of thirty-six coaches, each drawn by six horses. The Nuncio, robed in purple, was in the king's coach, with the duke of Grafton, who had agreed to introduce him. His own coaches followed with ten priests. Then came the coaches of the ministers of State, and great officers of the household ; and in that train of equipages were the coaches of the bishop of Durham and the bishop of Chester. The king and queen sat upon a throne in St. George's Hall.‡ The pensioner of France looked upon Verrio's painted walls, where the triumphs of the Black Prince were represented with no common skill. The devotee of Rome honoured its ambassador with manifestations of homage that reminded those who knew their country's

* " Life of Colley Cibber," vol. i. p. 48.
† Lord Lonsdale's Account. Note to Burnet, vol. iii. p. 178.
‡ Bramston's " Autobiography," p. 280.

history of the time when the ignoble John became "a gentle convertite." Although this outrage upon the popular feeling took place at Windsor, it was not done solely in the view of court attendants : "The town of Windsor was so full of all sorts of people, from all parts, that some of the inhabitants were astonished ; and it was very difficult to get provisions or room either for horse or man ; nay, many persons of quality, and others, were forced to sit in their coaches and calashes almost all the day." * As if to mark that England was entering upon a new era of government, on the 4th of July a Proclamation dissolving the Parliament appeared in the London Gazette.

In the autumn of 1687, the king made a progress through some parts of the West of England. One of his objects was to propitiate the Dissenters, who had taken so prominent a part in the insurrection of Monmouth. Storms and birds of prey had not yet cleared the gibbets of Somersetshire of the rags and bones of the victims of 1685, when James went amongst the scenes of Jeffreys' campaign, to promise not only spiritual liberty but civil honours to the relatives and friends of those who had fought the battle which they thought all good Protestants should fight. He gained little by his blandishments. The answer which was given to him by the rich non-conformist, William Kiffin, the grandfather of two youths who were treated with marked severity at the especial instance of the king, was perhaps not unknown in the West. "I have put you down, Mr. Kiffin, for an alderman of London," said James. "I am unfit to serve your Majesty, or the city," replied the old man : "I am worn out ; the death of my poor boys broke my heart." Others might have thought of their own bereavements ; and have felt a bitter contempt towards that king who had talked of his capricious favour as the "balsam for such sores." † The government had forced new charters upon London, and upon many of the municipal corporations throughout the country. Although the power of the Crown to nominate corporate functionaries, as well as to eject them, was disputed, the process of ejection was very summarily exercised. The supporters of Church and King were thrust out ; the Papists and the Independents were nominated. Non-conformists of different ranks of life were brought together in a way that offended the pride of the upper classes amongst them. Ralph Thoresby says, speaking of the Corporation of Leeds, "The places of such as were to be ejected were filled up with the most rigid Dissenters, who had put my name in the fag end of their reformed list, there being but one, a smith by trade, after me." ‡ The process of regulation, as it was called, was not successful. Many of the Charters were consequently attempted to be called in ; but the resistance carried on in the Law Courts by Corporations was almost general. All these arbitrary measures of the Crown had reference to the necessity which might arise of calling a Parliament, and to the readiest means of procuring a servile Parliament. Sir John Reresby tells us how, in his own case in 1688, this process was managed. The king commanded him to stand for York, in the event of an election. Reresby asked for his promise of more than ordinary support— "Whether he would assist me all he could to prevent my being baffled, and particularly by such means as I should propose to him. His answer was

---

* Relation of the Nuncio's public entry. Printed in 1687. Reprinted in the Somers' Tracts.
† See Macaulay. History, vol. ii. p. 230, 1st edition.   ‡ "Diary," vol. i. p. 186

Yes; and he gave immediate orders to the lords for purging of corporations, to make whatever change or alteration I desired in the city of York; and to put in or out, which the king it seems had reserved to himself by the last charter, just as I pleased." * In London, James had put in an Anabaptist Lord Mayor—"a very odd ignorant person," as Evelyn reports. When the sheriffs invited the king and queen, according to custom, to feast at Guild-hall, the king commanded them to invite the Nuncio. Burnet says the mayor and aldermen disowned the invitation, which much offended the king, who said, "he saw the dissenters were an ill-natured sort of people, that could not be gained." This opinion seems to have been that usually received at Court, if we may judge from the Court Calendar of this year, in which the dissenters are denounced as "the private, sullen, discontented, niggardly non-conformists." † At this time, Dryden published his famous poem of "The Hind and the Panther"—at a time of which he says, "The nation is in too high a ferment, for me to expect either fair war, or even so much as fair quarter, from a reader of the opposite party. All men are engaged either on this side or that; and though conscience is the common word which is given by both, yet if a writer fall among enemies, and cannot give the marks of their conscience, he is knocked down before the reasons of his own are heard." Dryden aims his satire at those he calls "the refractory and disobedient"—not against those "who have withdrawn themselves from the communion of the Panther, and embraced the gracious Indulgence of his majesty in regard to toleration." ‡ The great poet, however, does not attempt to propitiate the Sectaries. "The Panther"—the Church of England—is "sure the noblest, next the Hind"—the Church of Rome. But the "Independent beast" is typified by "the Bear;" the Anabaptist is "the bristled Boar" who "lurk'd in sects unseen;" the Presbyterian is "the insatiate Wolf" who "pricks up his predestinating ears;" "False Reynard" is the Socinian. The Papist Laureate of James did not bid for popularity, when he thus addressed the countries whose names had been hateful in English ears from the days of queen Mary:

> "Oh happy regions, Italy and Spain,
> Which never did those monsters entertain!"

We can now admire the beauty of his versification, and the energy of his reasoning, in this poem of a period when Dryden thought his cause was triumphant. It may be doubted whether it produced many converts to Romanism, or effected a wider separation of the Panther from the Bear, the Boar, and the Wolf. Many who would scarcely heed his musical polemics would recollect his own heedless sarcasm against the teaching of an infallible Church:

> "The priest continues what the nurse began,
> And thus the child imposes on the man."

The year 1688 is come. Men were thinking of the corresponding year of the previous century — of the glorious 1588, when the nation

---

* "Memoirs," p. 351.   † Chamberlayne's "Present State," p. 41.
‡ Dryden's Preface to the Poem.

rallied round the great Elizabeth, and the invaders who came, with the papal blessing, to destroy the heretical islanders perished in their pride. The contrast was humiliating. The king was now labouring to drive back the mind of England into the night of the fifteenth century. At this very time the great ally of this king was hunting his Protestant subjects to the death by his "dragoon missioners." Could any other consummation be expected from an illegal Declaration of Indulgence, which, abolishing the tests under pretence of universal toleration, thrust Romanists into the highest civil and military offices, seated Father Petre amongst the Privy Counsellors of the kingdom, and turning out the members of corporations who clung to a Protestant establishment, gave the municipal power to bigoted Papists or unscrupulous Dissenters. Thus reasoned the great body of Englishmen when this ominous year arrived. It was opened with "a solemn and particular office of thanksgiving for her majesty being with child." An heir to the throne had long ceased to be expected as the issue of James and his queen. The priests every where proclaimed that the king had put up his prayers for such an event at the Well of Saint Winifred; and that his supplications had been heard. The divines of the English Church were girding on their spiritual armour for a conflict. Whilst, at the beginning of April, mass was being performed at one chapel at Whitehall, the other chapel was crowded by eager multitudes, to hear bishop Ken describe the calamity of the reformed church of Judah under the Babylonian persecution. As God had delivered Judah upon the repentance of her sins, so should the new Reformed Church be delivered, wherever insulted and persecuted.* The princess Anne, the daughter of James, was amongst the hearers. The contest soon assumed a more formidable shape than in the eloquence of the pulpit or the arguments of the press. The king issued a second Declaration of Indulgence on the 27th of April. It was a repetition of the Declaration of 1687, with an avowal that his resolution was immutable, and that he would employ no servants, civil or military, who refused to concur with him. He would hold a Parliament in the following November; and he exhorted his people to choose representatives who would support him in his resolves. This proceeding was little regarded; for all knew what the king meant, and knew also the pride and obstinacy of his character. But his next step was something more exciting. By an Order in Council of the 4th of May, he commanded the Declaration to be read in all churches and chapels throughout the kingdom, on two successive Sundays, by the ministers of all persuasions. The Gazette of the 7th of May fixed the 20th of that month for the first reading in London and the neighbourhood. In the country, the first reading was to take place on the 3rd of June. There was short time to collect the opinions of ten thousand ministers of the Anglican Church. There were then very imperfect means of communication. The Gazette was wholly under the control of the government. Letters could not be sent through the post-office without the certainty that they would be opened, if suspected, and would be stopped, if their contents were displeasing. Country clergymen would peruse the Order of Council in the Gazette, and some might hear that it was considered by their brethren in London as an insult to their

* Evelyn, "Diary," April 1.

order. But to disobey was to incur the danger of deprivation by the Ecclesiastical Commission. The most eminent of the London clergy came to a resolution not to read the Declaration; and a large majority joined in the same pledge. On the 18th a great meeting of prelates and other divines took place at Lambeth, and a petition to the king was drawn up by the archbishop of Canterbury on behalf of himself, of divers of the suffragan bishops of his province, and of the inferior clergy of their dioceses. They professed their averseness to distribute and publish the king's Declaration for liberty of conscience, not from any want of duty and obedience,—for the loyalty of the Church of England was unquestionable,—" nor yet," they said, " from any want of tenderness to Dissenters, in relation to whom we are willing to come to such a temper as shall be thought fit, when the matter shall be considered and settled in Parliament and Convocation." Their averseness especially arose from the consideration that the Declaration was " founded upon such a dispensing power as hath been often declared illegal in Parliament." It was so declared, they said, in 1662, in 1672, and at the beginning of his majesty's reign; and therefore they could not in prudence, honour, or conscience make themselves parties to the Declaration, as the distribution and solemn publication of it in God's house would amount to. They therefore prayed the king not to insist upon their distributing and reading this Declaration. The archbishop and six suffragan bishops signed this petition. Sancroft was not received at Court; and therefore, without their head, bishops Lloyd, Turner, Lake, Ken, White, and Trelawney, immediately went to the king's palace, and were admitted to the royal closet. The king was unprepared for resistance to his mandate. When he read the petition he broke out into unseemly violence. " This is a standard of rebellion," he cried. Three bishops passionately disclaimed the imputation. " Did ever a good Churchman question the dispensing power before?" Ken answered, " We honour you, but we fear God." The final threat of the king that they should disobey him at their peril was met by " God's will be done " from the lips of Ken. The petition of the prelates was circulated through London on that Friday night. It was imputed to them that they were instrumental to this publication; but they denied it. There was but one copy, which the king kept. Burnet and Dalrymple intimate that some one was concerned in the publication, to whom the king had shown the original. A commentator on Burnet, Bevil Higgons, says, " All agreed that it must have been in the press, if not before, by the time it was delivered to the king, which was about five in the afternoon, and it came out that very night at twelve, and was so bawled and roared through the streets by hawkers, that people rose out of their beds to buy it." [*] Slow as were the operations of the printing press at that time, there was no necessity that the delivery of the petition, and the printing, should have occurred at the same hour of five, if not before, to allow of its circulation at midnight. The printers of that age had learnt to do their work with speed during the Civil War, when the broadside stood in the place of the newspaper, and a ballad was as effective as a leading article. On the Sunday following this memorable Friday, the reading of the Declaration " was almost universally forborne throughout London." [†] One exception to this disobedience shows

---

[*] Note to Burnet, Oxford edit. vol. iii. p. 220.   [†] Evelyn.

the direction of popular opinion. " I was then at Westminster school," says lord Dartmouth, " and heard it read in the Abbey. As soon as bishop Sprat, who was dean, gave order for reading it, there was so great a murmur and noise in the church that nobody could hear him; but before he had finished, there was none left but a few prebends in their stalls, the choristers, and Westminster scholars. The bishop could hardly hold the proclamation in his hands for trembling, and every body looked under a strange consternation." * In only four of the London churches was obedience yielded to the mandate of the king. Over all England, not above two hundred of the Clergy read the Declaration. " One, more pleasantly than gravely, told his people that, though he was obliged to read it, they were not obliged to hear it; and he stopped till they all went out, and then he read it to the walls." †

Sir John Reresby reports that he was told by lord Huntingdon, one of the Privy-council, " that had the king known how far the thing would have gone, he would never have laid the injunction he did, to have the Declaration read in churches." ‡ In its blind self-reliance, tyranny rarely sees how far the thing will go. It puts the match to the combustible matter, and is then astonished at the explosion. James had boasted that his past life ought to have convinced his people that he was not a man to recede from any course which he had once taken. In this case he took more than a week to look about him before he proceeded on his perilous way. Some of his more prudent counsellors recommended that he should issue a conciliatory proclamation, stating his deep mortification at the proceedings of the Clergy, but admitting that, as their scruples might have been conscientious, he was unwilling to treat them with the severity due to their disobedience. This advice was rejected. It was determined to prosecute the bishops for a seditious Libel. They were summoned to appear on the 8th of June before the king in council. During this interval, there had been no signs of submission in the metropolis or in the country. The archbishop of Canterbury, and his six suffragans, came into the royal presence at Whitehall on the appointed afternoon. They were asked if they acknowledged the petition to be theirs. They had received sound legal advice, and they refused to Criminate themselves. At length the archbishop said that if the king positively commanded him to answer he would do so, in the confidence that what he said in obedience to that command should not be brought in evidence against him. They were sent out, and upon their return the king gave the positive command. Sancroft and his brethen then acknowledged their hand-writing. They were immediately called upon to enter into recognizances to appear in the Court of King's Bench on a Criminal information for libel. They refused, maintaining that as peers they could not be so called upon. Their firmness irritated and embarrassed the misguided king. He must still proceed on his dangerous course. A warrant was made out for their committal to the Tower. Then was presented a spectacle which struck terror into the soul of the despot. The people of London had, in many a year of trouble, seen the state-barge leave Palace-yard stairs with some unhappy peer proceeding from Westminster Hall to his last prison. Often had they wept, as the axe was

* Note to Burnet, vol. iii. p. 218.　　　† Burnet, ibid.　　　‡ " Memoirs," p. 346.

borne before some popular favorite. But never had there been such an outburst of feeling as on this evening of the 8th of June. The seven prelates, surrounded by guards, passed through lines of weeping men and women, who prayed aloud for their safety, and knelt to ask their blessing. When they entered their barge, the river was sparkling in the setting sun, as the oars of a thousand wherries dashed up its silver waters. From Whitehall to the Tower, as the twilight stole on, the voices of the people were heard in one solemn cry of "God bless your lordships." There was something in their popular sympathy far more elevating and consoling than the favour of kings which the Church had so laboured to earn. The Church was now in its right attitude—the champion of the national faith and the national freedom. It seemed as if the old contests for minute differences of doctrine and discipline were at an end. To manifest respect towards them would be to secure the resentment of the king; but the feeling towards them received no abatement. Their very guards in the Tower would drink no other health than that of the bishops. Day by day, such numbers of persons flocked to them " for their blessing and to condole their hard usage," as Reresby relates, " that great and very extraordinary remarks were made both of persons and behaviour." The king saw with dismay, that his frown was powerless, even over a nobility that had been too long accustomed to fancy that the royal favour was their breath of life. Most indignant was James when ten nonconformist ministers—leading men amongst those whom he thought would be for ever at enmity with episcopacy,—visited the prelates in the Tower. " He sent for four of them to reprimand them; but their answer was, ' that they could not but adhere to the prisoners, as men constant and firm to the Protestant faith.' " *

The bishops remained a week in confinement. On the 15th of June they were brought before the Court of King's Bench. There was the same throng of spectators begging their blessing. They were called upon to plead, after legal objections against their commitment had been over-ruled. Their trial was fixed for the 27th, and they were then enlarged upon their own recognizances. The people fancied they were wholly released, and lighted up bonfires. The excitement went all through the land. The Dutch ambassador expected an insurrection in London. The miners of Cornwall would come to the rescue of their countryman, Trelawney, the bishop of Bristol, as the burden of the old ballad declares :—

> " And shall Trelawney die ?
> There's twenty thousand underground
> Will know the reason why." †

The day of trial came. Evelyn says there were " near sixty earls and lords on the bench." Westminster Hall and the whole neighbourhood were thronged with eager crowds. The trial lasted from nine in the morning till six in the evening. Every point was ably contested by the lawyers on each side—for a nation was looking on. No one could distinctly prove that the signatures to the petition were the hand-writing of the accused. The clerk

---

* Reresby, p. 347.
† In the quotation in Lord Macaulay's History, the words run, "thirty thousand Cornish boys." See " Quarterly Review," vol. cii. p. 313.

of the Privy Council, Blathwayte, was at last brought forward to swear that he had heard them confess that they had signed it. Then ensued a cross-examination which the counsel for the Crown tried in vain to stop; for it might implicate the king on an implied promise that the confession should not be used against the petitioners. The writing was thus proved. No evidence, however, could be obtained of the publication; till Sunderland came to swear that the bishops had told him of their intention to present a petition to the king. The subject matter of the petition was at last argued. It was maintained that the bishops were perfectly right when they held that the dispensing power was illegal. Amongst their counsel there was one, a young man, John Somers, who that day took the high position which he ever after maintained as the great constitutional lawyer and statesman of his time. The Chief-Justice, Wright, summed up that the petition was a libel. Justice Alibone held the same opinion. But the other two judges, Holloway and Powell, differed from them; and Powell affirmed that the dispensing power, as then administered, was an encroachment of the prerogative, and if not repressed, would put the whole legislative authority in the king. The jury were locked up all night. The king's brewer had fought stoutly for his royal customer; but he at last yielded; and at ten o'clock the verdict of " Not Guilty " was delivered. The shouts went from the benches and galleries of the Court to Westminster Hall; from the Hall to the streets and the river; from London to every suburb. They were echoed by the camp at Hounslow, when an express came there to James to tell him of his great failure. He left directly for London. " He was no sooner gone out of the camp than he was followed by an universal shouting, as if it had been a victory obtained." * The king asked the cause of the uproar. He was answered that it was nothing; the soldiers only rejoiced that the bishops were acquitted. " Do you call that nothing ? " said the baffled tyrant. He muttered some threat of " so much the worse for them "—for whom the threat was meant was not quite clear. He had one revenge. The two judges, Holloway and Powell, as soon as the term was over, were dismissed from their seats on a bench where independence and honesty were qualities not to be endured. On the night of the 30th of June, London was one blaze of bonfires and illuminations. The effigy of the pope again came forth to be burnt, as in the days of Shaftesbury. Pope-burners and bonfire-lighters were indicted at the Middlesex Sessions; " but," says Reresby, who was present as a justice, " the grand jury would find no bill, though they were sent out no less than three times; so generally did the love of the bishops and the Protestant cause prevail." The Declaration of Indulgence, and the Order in Council that the Clergy should publish it, appeared the climax of the king's determination to set his dispensing power above the law. The resistance of the Clergy brought the question to issue between the king and the people. It was shrewdly observed that " a solemn declaration that a king will not govern according to law seems a formal renouncing of any right he has by it; and when he has cut the bough he sat upon, he has little reason to be surprised if he falls to the ground." †

Two days after the seven bishops were sent to the Tower, the Council

---

* Burnet, vol. iii. p. 226.   † Lord Dartmouth's Note in Burnet. vol. iii. p. 228.

announced to the lords-lieutenant of counties that it had "pleased Almighty God, about ten o'clock of this morning, to bless his majesty and his royal consort the queen with the birth of a hopeful son, and his majesty's kingdoms and dominions with a prince."* In the language of the Council it was "so inestimable a blessing," that all the people would be called upon to unite in thanksgiving. Another language was held even by the staunch friends of the monarchy. Evelyn enters in his Diary of June 10th, "A young prince born, which will cause disputes." The legitimacy of this young prince was long disputed. This birth was as little a blessing to the house of Stuart as it promised to be to the weary subjects of that house. A large majority of the nation was convinced that this heir of the crown was supposititious. It was almost universally believed that imposture had been practised. The princess Anne did not give credit to the queen's alleged pregnancy. It was wholly disbelieved at the court of the prince of Orange. The birth arrived a month before it was said to be expected. The most ordinary precautions were not taken to put the fact beyond a doubt; for none but those in whom the people had little confidence were in attendance on the occasion. That there was no imposture is now matter of historical belief; but so convinced were many political partisans that there was no real son of James II., that, seventy years afterwards, Johnson drew the character of a violent Whig, who "has known those who saw the bed into which the Pretender was conveyed in a warming-pan." † Burnet devotes five or six pages of his folio volume to the various accounts of this pretended birth—stories which Swift properly ridicules. The belief in this story is the only blot in the subsequent Declaration of William of Orange to the English people; and James took the manly, though necessarily somewhat indelicate step, of instituting an inquiry and publishing all the evidence to refute the calumny. The most important influence of this birth upon the fortunes of England was, that the prospect of an heir to the Crown, born of a Catholic mother, and to be brought up in the bigoted school of a father who had cast aside Protestantism to be governed by Jesuits and apostates, precipitated the Revolution.

* Letter to the Earl of Rochester. Ellis. Series I. vol. iii. p. 339.   † "Idler," No. 10.

Medal of the Seven Bishops.

View of Lady Place, Hurley. 1832.

CHAPTER XXVII.

William, Prince of Orange—His character and position with regard to English affairs—The Princess Mary, and the Succession—Invitation to the Prince of Orange—Preparations of William—His Declaration—Hopes of the English people—Alarm of the king—William sails from Helvoetsluys—The voyage—Landing at Torbay—Public entry at Exeter—The king goes to the army at Salisbury—Desertions of his officers—The Prince of Denmark and the Princess Anne—James calls a Meeting of Peers—Commissioners to negotiate with the Prince of Orange—The queen and child sent to France—The king flies—Provisional Government—Riots—The Irish night—James brought back to London—The Dutch guards at Whitehall—The king again leaves London—The Prince of Orange enters—The Interregnum—The Convention—William and Mary King and Queen—The Revolution the commencement of a new era in English history.

At the village of Hurley, on the Berkshire side of the Thames between Henley and Maidenhead, stood, in 1836, an Elizabethan mansion called Lady Place, built on the site of a Benedictine monastery by sir Richard Lovelace, who was created a peer by Charles I. This building was the seat of lord Lovelace in the reigns of Charles II. and James II.,—a nobleman whose lavish hospitality and expensive tastes were rapidly wasting "the king of Spain's cloth of silver " * which his ancestor, one of Drake's privateering followers had won. The spacious hall opening to the Thames, the stately gallery

* " Worthies."

whose panels were covered with Italian landscapes, the terraced gardens— were ruined and neglected when we there meditated, some thirty years ago, upon the lessons of "Mutability." All the remains of past grandeur are now swept away. But beneath the Tudor building were the burial vaults of the house of " Our Lady," which seemed built for all time, and which, we believe, are still undisturbed. In these vaults was a modern inscription which recorded that the Monastery of Lady Place was founded at the time of the great Norman Revolution, and that " in this place, six hundred years afterwards, the Revolution of 1688 was begun." King William III., the tablet also recorded, visited this vault, and looked upon the " Recess," in which " several consultations for calling in the prince of Orange were held." During the four years in which James had been on the throne, the question of armed resistance had been constantly present to the minds of many Whigs ; and to the prince of Orange they looked for aid in some open attempt to change the policy of the government by force,—or, if necessary, to subvert it. The wife of the prince of Orange was the presumptive heir to the crown ; he was himself the nephew of the English king. His political and religious principles, and those of the republic of which he was the first magistrate, were diametrically opposed to those of his uncle. The chief enemy of his nation was the chief ally of king James. The one great purpose of the life of William of Orange was to resist the overwhelming ambition of Louis XIV. In 1688 he was thirty-eight years of age. When he was only in his twenty-second year, he had arrested the march of French conquest, and had saved his country. His uncle Charles had deserted his alliance, and had become the degraded pensioner of France. His uncle James equally crouched at the feet of the enemy of national independence, and of civil and religious liberty. William, under every difficulty, had in 1686 succeeded in forming the League of Augsburg, to hold in check this overwhelming ambition. His unrivalled sagacity and prudence had united rulers of Catholic as well as of Protestant states, in a determination that the Balance of Power in Europe should not be destroyed. James of England was content that his country should remain in the degraded position in which it had been left by his brother, provided that a continuance of that degradation would enable him to establish Jesuits and monks in the high places of the Church, and rule without Parliaments, by a power above the law. William of Orange must have long been convinced that this system could not endure. Holland was the refuge of many an Englishman who had fled from persecution, when dissenters were the objects of king James's hatred. They had no confidence in his pretended toleration, because it was based upon absolute authority. The public opinion of Englishmen at home was uniting in the same conclusion. A crisis was at hand, not only in England, but in the general policy of Europe. William had stood aloof from any connexion with plots in the later years of Charles, or of insurrections in the first year of James. His object was that in England there should be union between the Crown and the Parliament ; for then England would be strong, and capable of taking a part once more in such a joint system of action as was contemplated in the Triple Alliance. That hope was now utterly gone. It was clear that James and his people would never be at accord. It was equally clear that any bold and elevated foreign policy was hopeless. Unless he had determined wholly to separate himself from English affairs,

William of Orange would necessarily become associated with the leading men of England, who saw that the government was driving on to ruin. His original policy was to wait. The time might come when the princess of Orange would be queen, and then William would naturally be England's ruler. It was the desire of Mary that her husband, in that event, should be the real sovereign. Burnet relates this circumstance with some self-applause, but with evident truth : "I took the liberty, in a private conversation with the princess, to ask her what she intended the prince should be, if she came to the crown. She, who was new to all matters of that kind, did not understand my meaning, but fancied that whatever accrued to her would likewise accrue to him in the right of marriage. I told her it was not so. * * * I told her, a titular kingship was no acceptable thing to a man, especially if it was to depend on another's life : and such a nominal dignity might endanger the real one that the prince had in Holland. She desired me to propose a remedy. I told her, the remedy, if she could bring her mind to it, was, to be contented to be his wife, and to engage herself to him, that she would give him the real authority as soon as it came into her hands, and endeavour effectually to get it to be legally vested in him during life : this would lay the greatest obligation on him possible, and lay the foundation of a perfect union between them, which had been of late a little embroiled. * * * She presently answered me, she would take no time to consider of any thing by which she could express her regard and affection to the prince ; and ordered me to give him an account of all that I had laid before her, and to bring him to her, and I should hear what she would say upon it. * * * She promised him, he should always bear rule ; and she asked only, that he would obey the command of 'Husbands, love your wives,' as she should do that, 'Wives, be obedient to your husbands in all things.'" * Dartmouth conjectures that the prince ordered Burnet—whom he calls "a little Scotch priest"—to propose this to the princess, before he would engage in the attempt upon England. When the insane proceedings of James had rendered it more than probable that the event would happen which his brother Charles said should never happen to him—that he should be sent again upon his travels—the prince of Orange, with an ambition that was founded upon higher motives than mere personal advancement, might not unreasonably think that there was a shorter road to the English crown than by succession. At the very climax of the folly of James, a son, or a pretended son, was born. William and his wife believed that their just rights were attempted to be set aside by an imposture. The leading men of England believed the same. The quarrel between the king and the Church appeared to be irreconcilable ; and thus the most powerful influence over the people had ceased to be committed to the doctrine of non-resistance to arbitrary power. The time for decision was come in the summer of 1688. Edward Russell had been over to the Hague in May, to urge the prince of Orange to a bold interference with the affairs of England. "The prince spoke more positively to him than he had ever done before. He said, he must satisfy both his honour and conscience, before he could enter upon so great a design, which, if it miscarried, must bring ruin both on England and

---

* "Own Time," vol. iii. p. 129.

Holland : he protested, that no private ambition nor resentment of his own could ever prevail so far with him, as to make him break with so near a relation, or engage in a war, of which the consequences must be of the last importance both to the interests of Europe and of the protestant religion : therefore he expected formal and direct invitation. Russell laid before him the danger of trusting such a secret to great numbers. The prince said, if a considerable number of men, that might be supposed to understand the sense of the nation best, should do it, he would acquiesce in it." * Russell returned to England, and communicated with Henry Sidney, the brother of Algernon : with the earl of Shrewsbury ; the earl of Danby ; the earl of Devonshire ; and other peers. Compton, the suspended bishop of London, was also confided in. On the 30th of June, the great day of the acquittal of the seven bishops, an invitation to William of Orange, to appear in England, at the head of a body of troops, was sent by a messenger of rank ; admiral Herbert. It was signed in cipher, by Shrewsbury, Devonshire, Danby, Lumley, Compton, Russell, and Sidney. William took his determination. He resolved on a descent upon England. With a secrecy as remarkable as his energy, he set about the preparation of such a force as would ensure success, in conjunction with the expected rising of nineteen-twentieths of the people, to free themselves from an odious government.

In this eventful autumn there were dangers immediately surrounding the unhappy king of England, which were the almost inevitable results of a long career of government which had weakened, if not wholly extinguished, political honesty. The high public spirit, the true sense of honour, which had characterised the nobles and gentry of England during the Civil War, was lost in the selfishness, the meanness, the profligacy, of the twenty-eight years that succeeded the Restoration. Traitors were hatched in the sunshine of corruption. The basest expediency had been the governing principle of statesmen and lawyers ; the most abject servility had been the leading creed of divines. Loyalty always wore the livery of the menial. Patriotism was ever flaunting the badges of faction. The bulk of the people were unmoved by any proud resentments or eager hopes. They went on in their course of industrious occupation, without much caring whether they were under an absolute or a constitutional government, as long as they could eat, drink, and be merry. They had got rid of the puritan severity ; and if decency was outraged in the Court and laughed at on the stage, there was greater licence for popular indulgences. The one thing to be avoided was nonconformity, which was a very hard service, even when lawful ; and a very desperate sacrifice when it brought fine and imprisonment. Such was the temper of England at the accession of James. It was a temper fitted for any amount of national humiliation. It was a temper apt for slavery. But there was one latent spark of feeling which James blew into a flame. The English hated Popery with a passionate hatred. It was then seen by crafty politicians who had endured and even stimulated the bigotry of the king, that he had gone too far, and that he would not recede. Such a politician was Sunderland, who had even made a public profession of Romanism to retain his places. He became a Catholic to please the king in June. In August the breach between

* Burnet, vol. iii. p. 263.

the king and the Anglican Church had become so irreparable that Sunderland was in correspondence with the prince of Orange. The selfish instinct of such men was their storm-barometer. Sarah, duchess of Marlborough, says of this crisis: "It was evident to all the world, that as things were carried on by king James, everybody must be ruined, who would not become a Roman Catholic." * "Everybody" has a very limited signification in this lady's vocabulary. It included lord Churchill and a few others. The narrative which we have to pursue to the end of this chapter does not exhibit the nation in any very glorious light. The story of the Revolution of 1688 is not a great epic, full of heroism and magnanimity. There is only one real hero on the scene; and he is a cold, impassive man, stirring up no passionate enthusiasm—a hero, the very opposite of the fascinating Monmouth, who had crowds at his chariot-wheels. William of Orange goes steadily forward, flattering none, trusting few, suspecting most—a self-contained man, who will put his shoulder to the work to which he has been called, and if he fails, he fails. Such a man was wanted to re-construct the shattered edifice of English freedom upon solid foundations. A popular king, with an undoubted title, might have found a nation ready enough to be again manacled.

In the "Memoirs of king James" it is said, that he never gave any real credit to the belief that the preparations of the prince of Orange were designed against himself, till the middle of September; "for, besides the repeated assurances he had from the States, by their ambassadors and others, and even the prince of Orange himself, that these preparations were not designed against him, the earl of Sunderland, and some others about him whom he trusted most, used all imaginable arguments to persuade the king it was impossible the prince of Orange could go through with such an undertaking; and particularly my lord Sunderland turned any one to ridicule that did but seem to believe it." † Louis XIV. saw clearly the danger. He exhorted James; he remonstrated; he offered naval assistance. The envoy of France told the States that his king had taken the king of England under his protection, and that war against James would be war against Louis. James, in a spirit almost incomprehensible, despised the protection, and rejected the proffered aid. The intentions of the prince of Orange to come to England with an army were soon made manifest. A proclamation was prepared by the Grand Pensionary, Fagel; "who," says Burnet, "made a long and heavy draft, founded on the grounds of the civil law, and of the law of nations." Burnet translated it into English, and "got it to be much shortened, though it was still too long." It is, indeed, a long document; very little calculated for popular excitement. It set forth, in a calm and dispassionate tone, the violations of their laws, liberties, and customs, to which the people of England had been subjected. It detailed the various acts by which a religion opposed to that established by law had been attempted to be forced upon the nation. It alluded to the general belief that a pretended heir to the throne had been set up, against the rights of the princess of Orange. It declared that "since the English nation has ever testified a most particular affection and esteem, both to our dearest consort the princess, and to ourselves, we cannot excuse ourselves from espousing their interest in a

* "Authentick Memoirs," p. 52.   † "Life of James II." vol. ii. p. 177.

matter of such high consequence: and from contributing all that lies in us for the maintaining, both of the Protestant religion, and of the laws and liberties of those kingdoms, and for the securing to them the continual enjoyment of all their just rights; to the doing of which we are most earnestly solicited by a great many lords, both spiritual and temporal, and by many gentlemen, and other subjects of all ranks." For these reasons, the prince declares that he had thought fit to go over to England, and to carry with him a sufficient force to defend him from the violence of the king's evil counsellors. This expedition had no other design than to have a free Parliament called; of which the members should be lawfully chosen. "We, for our part, will concur in everything that may procure the peace and happiness of the nation, which a free and lawful Parliament shall determine, since we have nothing before our eyes, in this our undertaking, but the preservation of the Protestant religion, the covering of all men from persecution for their consciences, and the securing to the whole nation the free enjoyment of their laws, rights, and liberties, under a just and legal government." The Declaration is dated from the Hague on the 10th of October.

The expectation of the speedy arrival of the prince of Orange with his army was universal at the beginning of October. On the 7th Evelyn writes that the people "seemed passionately to long for and desire the landing of that prince, whom they looked on to be their deliverer from Popish tyranny; praying incessantly for an east wind, which was said to be the only hindrance of his expedition with a numerous army ready to make a descent." The king now endeavoured to put himself into a new attitude towards his people. He gave audience to the archbishop of Canterbury and some of the bishops. They represented to him the desirableness of revoking all the acts done under the dispensing power; of restoring the fellows of Magdalen College; of giving back their old franchises to the Corporations. The king did attend to some of these suggestions. He dissolved the Ecclesiastical Commission. He sent his Chancellor to deliver back to the Corporation of London their ancient charter; and he issued a proclamation restoring all the municipal corporations to their ancient franchises. He gave powers to the bishop of Winchester, which allowed him, as visitor, to re-instate the ejected fellows of Magdalen College. A sudden amendment of life under the influence of fear is not generally considered as likely to be permanent. A king's sudden redress of unjust acts, when one was at hand who could compel justice, was not likely to propitiate subjects whose confidence had been destroyed.

On the 16th of October, William, having taken a solemn leave of the States of Holland, set forward from the Hague to sail from Helvoetsluys. A fleet of fifty men of war, twenty-five frigates, many fire-ships, and four hundred transports, was there assembled. There were embarked four thousand horse and ten thousand foot soldiers. The command of the army was entrusted to marshal Schomberg. The van of the fleet was led by admiral Herbert. The prince of Orange embarked on the 19th. His ship bore a flag with the arms of England and Nassau, surrounded with the motto, "The Protestant Religion and Liberties of England." Underneath was the motto of the house of Orange, "Je maintiendrai." The equivocal device of his ancestry, "I will maintain," was now associated with a definite purpose, of unprecedented importance.

The east wind, which the people of London had been praying for, bore
the fleet of William prosperously towards the English shores. But it suddenly changed; and a strong western gale, which increased to a tempest,
compelled the Dutchmen to seek the refuge of their own havens. News

Embarkation of the Prince of Orange at Helvoetsluys.

reached the court of James that the damage had been so serious, that the
arrival of no hostile armament need now be dreaded. The Gazette announced
these tidings. But the damage was quickly repaired. On the evening of the
1st of November the fleet of William was again at sea. The east wind was
now full and strong. For some time an effort was made to steer northward;
but that course was at last abandoned; and about noon of the 2nd the order
was given to steer westward. The same wind that bore the Dutch fleet
towards our western shores kept the English fleet in the Thames. On the
3rd, midway between Dover and Calais, a Council of War was held. Rapin,
the historian, who accompanied the expedition, thus describes the unwonted
scene: "It is easy to imagine what a glorious show the fleet made. Five or
six hundred ships in so narrow a Channel, and both the English and French
shores covered with numberless spectators, are no common sight. For my
part, who was then on board the fleet, it struck me extremely." The 4th
of November was William's birth-day. He dedicated that Sunday to private
devotion, whilst the fleet rode past Portland, with the intention of anchoring
in Torbay. The prince's ship was in the van. The night was dark and
rainy; the wind was violent; the pilot mistook his course, and ran past
Torbay towards Plymouth. There was danger in attempting a landing at
that port, which was strongly garrisoned. But in the morning of the 5th
the wind became calm; and a southern breeze carried them back into the
magnificent bay. Here Napoleon, gazing on its shores from the deck of the

Bellerophon, exclaimed "What a beautiful country!" Here William saw
only hills shrouded in mist; and the huts of a fishing village. But Torbay
was, according to Rapin, "the most convenient place for landing horse, of any
in England." Before night the whole of the infantry was on shore. The
horse were landed the next morning. William and Schomberg were amongst
the first to land at Brixham. In the market-place of this prosperous fishing
town of narrow and dirty streets, there is a block of stone, with this inscription: "On this stone, and near this spot, William, prince of Orange, first
set foot on landing in England, 5th of November, 1688." Burnet says, "As
soon as I landed, I made what haste I could to the place where the prince
was; who took me heartily by the hand, and asked me if I would not now
believe predestination. I told him, I would never forget that providence of
God, which had appeared so signally in this occasion. He was cheerfuller
than ordinary. Yet he returned soon to his usual gravity." Rapin continues the narrative, with the graphic details of an eye-witness: "The
prince's army marched from Torbay, about noon the next day, in very rainy
weather, and bad roads. The soldiers, before they landed, were ordered to
bring three days' bread with them, and they carried their tents themselves. But the officers, even the most considerable, were in a very
uneasy situation, at their first encampment, being wet to the skin, and
having neither clothes for change, nor bread, nor horses, nor servants,
nor other bed than the earth all drenched with rain, their baggage being
yet in the ships." Burnet says, "It was not a cold night." After this
first disagreeable halt on English ground, the army, by noon the next
day, was on its march towards Exeter. It was the fourth day from the
landing before William made his public entry into the capital of the West.
Two hundred captains of the host, on Flanders steeds, clothed in complete
armour, each horse led by a negro; two hundred Finlanders, with beavers'
skins over their black armour; led horses; state coaches; the standard of the
deliverer who was to maintain the liberties of England; the prince himself,
with white ostrich feathers in his helmet; guards and pages,—volunteers;
and then a gallant army, bedabbled indeed with mud, and wearing the orange
uniform, strange enough in eyes accustomed to the English scarlet; twenty
pieces of cannon, then of enormous size; and, what was almost as potent,
waggons loaded with money—such was the spectacle upon which the people
of Exeter gazed, as the long procession moved through the steep streets, and
welcome was shouted from many a window of the old gabled houses. But
William had expected a reception more decisive—a welcome which should
give a greater assurance of success than a fleeting popular enthusiasm. No
man of rank, with troops of followers, was at Exeter to salute him. "The
clergy and magistrates of Exeter were very fearful and very backward. The
bishop and the dean ran away." Lord Dartmouth has a note upon this
passage of Burnet. Shrewsbury, he says, informed him, that the prince began
to suspect he was betrayed, and had some thoughts of returning; but Shrewsbury told William that "he believed the great difficulty amongst them was,
who should run the hazard of being the first; but if the ice were once broken,
they would be as much afraid of being the last." * It was a week from the

* Burnet, vol. iii. p. 314.

landing before any gentleman of Devonshire joined the prince. There was a king upon the throne whose vengeance would be even more terrible than in 1685, if another attempt against him should fail. But in that second week the feeling of confidence became more strong. Sir Edward Seymour arrived with " other gentlemen of quality and estate," and he organised an Association. The cloth workers and labourers, sufferers as they had been, had shown less calculating apathy than the " gentlemen of quality." " Whilst the prince stayed at Exeter," says Burnet, " the rabble of the people came to him in great numbers." He has no word of gratitude for their generous support. It was the fashion of that day, and long continued to be the fashion, to speak of the common people as " rabble " and " mob." William, in his cold way, looked upon this rabble of Exeter only as a soldier looks. He did not think it necessary to arm this undisciplined multitude, for he understood, from the temper of the royal army, that, if his cause were likely to prosper, the hired defenders of the throne would come over to him. He was not deceived.

From the time that the news arrived of the landing at Torbay, the metropolis was naturally the scene of the greatest excitement. A proclamation was issued, prohibiting all persons from reading the Declaration of the prince of Orange. Of course the desire to see that manifesto was increased. The king sends for the primate and three bishops, and shows them that passage in which the promised assistance of spiritual as well as temporal peers is set forth. They express a doubt whether the manifesto is genuine. The king upbraids them for their lukewarmness; they recapitulate their old injuries. He requires from them a declaration of abhorrence of the proceedings of William. They refuse to stand alone in such a declaration. The king in anger sent them away; and applied himself to touch for the evil, with a Jesuit and a Popish priest officiating.* A large force had been assembled at Salisbury. On the 15th, the king received the news that lord Cornbury, the eldest son of the earl of Clarendon, had marched from the camp, at the head of three regiments of cavalry. He did not carry through his design of joining the army of William, for his officers refused to proceed; but he arrived at the Dutch camp himself, and many of the men followed his example. The king was staggered at the treachery of a young man who had been bred up in the household of his own daughter Anne—of a favoured courtier, who was the son of his brother-in-law. James called the officers of the army to give him counsel. He exhorted them to preserve their loyalty as subjects and their honour as gentlemen. " They all seemed," says James in his Memoirs, " to be moved at this discourse; and vowed they would serve him to the last drop of their blood. The duke of Grafton, and my lord Churchill, were the first that made this attestation, and the first who, to their eternal infamy, broke it afterwards." † We can sympathise with the indignation of the unhappy king, without shutting our eyes to his errors and his crimes. Still more can we sympathise, when, ten days afterwards, he learnt that his son-in-law, George of Denmark, and his own daughter, Anne, had deserted him. He had set out for Salisbury, which he reached on the 19th. His agitation brought on a violent bleeding at the nose, which lasted three days. Meanwhile support was gathering round the prince of Orange

* Evelyn's "Diary."   † "Life," vol. ii. p. 219.

from every quarter. The northern counties were in arms. Nottingham was the rallying point for the assembling of large bodies of men, headed by Devonshire, and other great earls. On the 22nd, when the army of the prince of Orange was at a short distance from Salisbury, the earl of Feversham, the commander of the royal troops, intimated that there was defection in the camp, and advised arrests. James was still confident that no one could be a traitor to *him*. His prodigious self-esteem and self-confidence blinded him to signs of danger which were evident to all others. He began, however, to think of retreating. He called a council of war on the evening of the 24th. On the morning of the 25th Churchill and Grafton were in William's camp. All was alarm; and an immediate retreat was commanded by the king. At Andover, the prince of Denmark fled from him, with two noblemen. On the king's arrival in London on the evening of the 26th he found that his daughter, Anne, was gone. "God help me," exclaimed the wretched king, " my own children have forsaken me." Anne escaped from Whitehall, with the assistance of her friend, lady Churchill; and was taken by the bishop of London to Nottingham. "The king," writes the duchess of Marlborough, "went down to Salisbury to his army, and the prince of Denmark with him; but the news quickly came from thence that the prince of Denmark had left the king, and was gone over to the prince of Orange, and that the king was coming back to London. This put the princess into a great fright. She sent for me; told me her distress; and declared that rather than see her father she would jump out at the window." The crafty duchess says, " it was a thing sudden and unconcerted; nor had I any share in it, farther than obeying my mistress's orders, in the particulars I have mentioned; though indeed I had reason enough on my own account to get out of the way, lord Churchill having likewise at that time left the king, and gone over to the other party." *

James records his sense of his abandonment when he had come back to London: " The contagion was spread so universally that all parts of England furnished the same news of risings and defections; the only strife was who should be foremost in abandoning the king." † He had sent the infant prince of Wales to Portsmouth, to be conveyed to France, if there was no turn in affairs. Father Petre, and other obnoxious advisers, had fled. There was no manifestation of aid on the part of his Roman Catholic subjects—of those who had lighted bonfires, and madly danced around them when the unfortunate child was born. ‡ In his deep distress, James called a meeting of all the peers who remained in London. Nine spiritual lords, and between thirty and forty temporal lords, attended him at Whitehall on the 27th. He had received a petition, before he departed for Salisbury, entreating him to convoke a free parliament. At the meeting those who had signed it explained their views. But they further suggested that it would be desirable to send commissioners to treat with the prince of Orange. They also urged a general amnesty. Upon this point the king manifested some impotent anger; but he had provocations of treachery enough to irritate a wiser man; and he was goaded by words from Clarendon, which Burnet even characterises as "inso-

---

* " Authentick Memoirs," p. 80.   † "Life," p. 230—" Original Memoirs."
‡ At Carlisle; Story's Journal.

lent and indecent." Three commissioners, Halifax, Nottingham, and Godolphin, were appointed to treat with the prince. Godolphin told Evelyn that
" they had little power." A proclamation for a general amnesty was issued ;
writs were ordered to be sent out to call a parliament for the 13th of January.
But James, even in this moment of despairing concession, was insincere. He
told Barillon, the French ambassador, that a parliament would impose conditions on him that he could not bear. He must leave England. He would
take refuge in Ireland, or in Scotland, or he would seek aid in person from
the king of France, as soon as he had secured the safety of the queen and
his son. Dartmouth, the admiral of the fleet, refused to be a party to carry
the prince of Wales out of the country. The child was therefore brought
back to Whitehall. The commissioners proceeded to the camp of the prince
of Orange, who was steadily advancing towards the capital. On the 6th of
December he had reached Hungerford. A skirmish took place at Reading
between two hundred and fifty of his advanced guard, and six hundred Irish
troops who had entered the town. The inhabitants joined with the Dutch
troops in attacking the Irish, who were regarded by them as enemies. It
was the only serious affair of arms during this bloodless contest for a crown.
The memory of this Sunday fight was long celebrated in Reading, by ringing
the bells on the anniversary of the defeat of the " Papishes," who came to
destroy the town " in time of prayer," as a ballad records. At Hungerford,
the king's commissioners arrived on the 8th. William would not give them
a private audience. They announced to him, amidst a crowd of his supporters, that the proposition which they had to make was, that all matters
in dispute should be referred to the parliament, for which writs were being
issued ; and that in the interval the prince's army should not approach
within thirty miles of the capital. The prince retired, leaving the noblemen and gentlemen to consult together. The majority of his adherents
considered that the proposition . of the king should not be accepted.
William thought otherwise. But he required that if his troops were not
to approach London within the prescribed distance on the west, the
king's troops should be removed to an equal distance on the east. Whilst the
negotiation was proceeding at Hungerford, the queen and the prince were
privately conveyed down the river, and the vessel in which they were aboard
sailed with a fair wind for France. This was on the 10th of December. On
that day James wrote to lord Dartmouth, " Things having so very bad an
aspect, I could no longer defer securing the queen and my son, which I hope
I have done, and that to-morrow by noon they will be out of the reach of my
enemies. I am at ease now I have sent them away. I have not heard this
day, as I expected, from my commissioners with the prince of Orange, who I
believe will hardly be prevailed with to stop his march; so that I am in no
good condition, nay, in as bad a one as is possible." * When the king wrote
this letter, he was meditating his own flight. The true character of the man
was disclosed in his last hours of sovereignty. He sent for the great seal,
and for the writs to summon a parliament that had not gone out. He threw
the writs into the fire. He annulled those which had been issued. To no one
of his ministers did he reveal his intentions. He had announced to many

* " Pepys' Correspondence," vol. v. p. 147.

peers who had been invited by him to the palace, that he had sent his queen and his son away, but that he should himself remain at his post. At three o'clock of the morning of the 11th he stole out of Whitehall by a secret passage ; entered a hackney coach provided by sir Edward Hales; crossed the Thames in a wherry, and threw the great seal into the river. Before London was awake, he was far on the road towards Sheerness.

England was without a government. Her king, who would not rule according to law, left his people to the terrible chances of anarchy. In a great metropolis like London, there are marauders always ready to take advantage of any public commotion. James had commanded the earl of Feversham, by letter, to disband his troops ; and they were let loose without any of the restraints of discipline. In an emergency like this it was necessary that some decided resolution should be instantly taken, to prevent universal confusion. Seven spiritual lords, with Sancroft as their head, and twenty-two temporal peers, drew up a declaration that the flight of the king having destroyed the hope of a parliamentary settlement of affairs, they had determined to join the prince of Orange, and until his arrival to preserve order by their own authority. Never was some authority more necessary. The night came, and a fierce multitude, amidst the cry of No Popery, burnt Roman Catholic chapels, and attacked the houses of ambassadors from Roman Catholic states. But no lives were sacrificed. The next day the trainbands were under arms ; and tumults were kept down by some troops of cavalry. On that day, the hated lord Chancellor, Jeffreys, was discovered in the disguise of a sailor, in a public house at Wapping. He was saved from a fierce mob by the trainbands, but not without severe injury, and was taken before the Lord Mayor. It was mercy to the terrified judge, who had carried terror into so many families, to send him to the Tower by an order from the peers at Whitehall.

The night of the 12th was long memorable in London as "the Irish night." The rioters had gone home. The city was peaceful. But a rumour was spread that the Irish troops of Feversham's disbanded army were marching on London. Every citizen came forth with pike and musket to fight for life and property, whilst every window was lighted up, and barricades were hastily constructed in every leading thoroughfare. The alarm was altogether false. But by some unknown agency the same consternation was excited throughout the country. Thoresby has left a vivid picture of a night scene at Leeds. A fearful cry went through the town of "Horse and arms, horse and arms ! the enemy are upon us." The drums beat, the bells rang backward, the women shrieked. Thousands of lighted candles were there also placed in the windows. Aged people who remembered the Civil Wars, said they never knew anything like it.* When the panic was over, men felt ashamed of their fears. If the agents in spreading this shameful delusion had expected to excite the people against the depressed Roman Catholics, they were greatly mistaken. The exaggerated terror showed how little there was really to apprehend in a country in which nine-tenths of the people were Protestants. The poor Irish soldiers, wandering through the towns and villages, begged for food, but they neither massacred nor plundered. They were soon required to deliver up their arms, and were provided with sufficient necessaries.

* Thoresby. "Diary," vol. i. p. 190.

On the third day from the flight of James, it became known in London that he had not left the country. He had gone on board a hoy near Sheerness. But the vessel was detained by the state of the tide; and the news had come that the king had absconded. The hoy was about to sail at night, when she was boarded by fishermen, who had heard that some persons, dressed as gentlemen, had taken their passage in her. They roughly treated the king, who they fancied was Father Petre, and they carried him and sir Edward Hales ashore to Sheerness. James was recognised by the crowd around the inn to which he was taken; but although they treated him with respect, they refused to let him go. The Council in London were assembled, when a messenger arrived from the king, bringing a paper calling upon all good Englishmen to rescue him. A troop of Life Guards was immediately sent off; and when Feversham, their commander, arrived, he found the king guarded by militia, and surrounded by Whig gentlemen of Kent, who thought it would be an acceptable service to detain him. He was now moved to Rochester. William learnt at Windsor that the flight of James was thus unluckily interrupted. On Sunday, the 16th, the king had been persuaded by his friends to return to Whitehall. Pity, amongst many, had taken the place of hatred. He was received by the people with shows of kindness that misled him. He instantly put on the attitude that had so alienated his subjects. He "goes to mass, dines in public, a Jesuit saying grace." Evelyn adds, "I was present." He called the lords before him who had saved the country from confusion, and haughtily blamed their presumption in taking upon themselves the government. The next day, the 17th, a Council of Lords was held at Windsor. It was determined that the king should not remain at Whitehall. A message was sent to recommend him to move to Ham House, near Richmond. Meanwhile the army of William was advancing. On the night of that Monday, Whitehall was guarded by Dutch troops. The lords from Windsor arrived. James declined to go to Ham. He would prefer Rochester. A messenger was sent to William, who had reached Sion, and returned in a few hours with his approval. One entry from Evelyn's diary briefly tells the great event of the next morning: "I saw the king take barge to Gravesend at twelve o'clock—a sad sight." That night the prince of Orange slept in St. James' palace.

WILLIAM & MARY.

Medal struck at the Revolution. William and Mary.

The reign of James II. is held to have terminated on the 11th of December, when he secretly departed from Whitehall, with the intention of leaving the kingdom. The reign of William and Mary is determined by Statute to have commenced on the 13th of February, 1689, "the day on which their majesties accepted the crown and royal dignity of king and queen of England." The interval of about two months is called by historians

THE INTERREGNUM.

On the 19th of December the prince of Orange held a court at St. James's. Thither came the Corporation of London in state. All the prelates were there, with the exception of the archbishop of Canterbury. The London Clergy were not wanting in their tribute of respect. Non-conformist divines also attended in a body. "Old Sergeant Maynard came with the men of the law. He was then near ninety, and yet he said the liveliest thing that was heard of on that occasion. The prince took notice of his great age, and said, that he had outlived all the men of the law of his time: he answered, he had like to have outlived the law itself, if his highness had not come over." * Amidst this throng William stood "stately, serious, and reserved." † His position was one of exceeding difficulty. He was urged to take the crown, as Henry VII. had taken it, by right of conquest. He rejected the advice. Such a claim would have been a violation of his own promises. It would have justly irritated a proud and sensitive people, who already looked with suspicion upon the orange uniform of his guards. He resolved to assemble, provisionally, two bodies that should represent the Lords and Commons of England. He invited the Peers to attend him; he invited also those who had sat in the House of Commons during the reign of

* Burnet, vol. iii. p. 341. Swift has a characteristic note on this passage, "He was an old rogue, for all that."
† Evelyn.

Charles II., and with them the aldermen of London, and a deputation from the Common Council. He begged them to consider the state of the country, and communicate to him the result of their deliberations. The two bodies met in separate chambers; and they each finally agreed to present to William addresses, to request that he would issue letters to summon a Convention of the Estates of the realm, and in the mean time take upon himself the administration of government. These resolutions were agreed to with less hesitation when it was known that James, after staying a week at Rochester, had gone over to France. William applied himself with all the energy of his character to extricate the nation out of its confusion. The exchequer was almost empty. Such was the confidence in him that, upon his word alone, two hundred thousand pounds were immediately placed in his hands by the Common Council of London, as a loan subscribed by the merchants. The nation felt, generally, that it was under a temporary ruler who would respect the law, and maintain order and security. The letters for calling the Convention were sent out; the old charters had been restored; and the elections proceeded without any interference with the freedom of the electors, by the influence of the servants of the government. The prince of Orange had also been requested to proceed in the same manner in regard to Scotland as in England—to take on himself the provisional administration, and to call a Convention of the Estates.

On the 22nd of January the Convention met. The composition of the House of Commons was such that there was not likely to be any serious difference of opinion upon the fundamental principles of a settlement of the nation. But there were great difficulties to be overcome. Evelyn has related the discussions at a dinner on the 15th, at the palace of the archbishop of Canterbury, where he met five bishops and several peers: "Sorry I was to find there was as yet no accord in the judgments of the Lords and Commons who were to convene. Some would have the princess made queen without any more dispute; others were for a Regency; there was a Tory party, then so called, who were for inviting his majesty again upon conditions; and there were Republicans, who would make the prince of Orange like a Stadtholder." The bishops, he adds, "were all for a Regency, thereby to salve their oaths, and so all public matters to proceed in his majesty's name." The most important of these differences was encountered and settled by the Commons, in their great vote of the 28th of January: "Resolved, That king James the Second, having endeavoured to subvert the Constitution of the Kingdom, by breaking the original Contract between king and people, and, by the advice of Jesuits, and other wicked persons, having violated the fundamental Laws, and having withdrawn himself out of the Kingdom, has abdicated the Government, and that the Throne is thereby become vacant." On the 29th they passed another resolution: "That it hath been found, by experience, to be inconsistent with the safety and welfare of this Protestant kingdom, to be governed by a Popish Prince." The Lords, on receiving the Resolution of the Commons that the throne was vacant, to which their concurrence was desired, entered upon long and serious debates, having concurred in the Resolution that the kingdom ought not to be governed by a Popish Prince. The great question by them discussed was, whether a Regency, under which the royal power should be administered in the name of king James II. during his life, was not the best and safest way to preserve the laws and the Protestant religion. This motion was only lost by a majority of two, fifty-one to forty-nine. They then proceeded to the discussion of the abstract question, whether or no there was an original contract between king and people. This brought into conflict the assertors of divine right, and the assertors that all power originally belonged to the community, the power of the king being by mutual compact. This latter position, which rejected the notions of absolute authority which had been so servilely maintained since the Restoration, was carried by fifty-three votes against forty-six. It was then resolved, that king James had broken the contract; and then the substitution of the word "deserted" for "abdicated" in the Resolution of the Commons was agreed to. But the great point of discussion was, "Whether king James, having broken that original contract between him and his people, and deserted the government, the throne was vacant." The negative was decided by a majority of fifty-five to forty-one. The Lords and Commons were now at issue upon a great principle. The majority maintained that in the monarchy of England the throne could never be vacant; that upon the demise of the crown the right of the heir was complete; any other principle would make the monarchy elective. A conference between the two Houses was carried on with remarkable ability; but the firmness of the Commons, intent as they were upon a practical result, led the Lords to agree, the day after the Conference, to the Resolution of the Commons, without alteration; and further to resolve, that the prince and princess of Orange should be declared king and queen of England and all the dominions thereunto belonging. The Commons had resolved, on the 29th of January, that "before the Committee proceed to fill the throne now vacant, they will proceed to secure our religion, laws, and liberties." They accomplished this in the memorable document known as "THE DECLARATION OF RIGHTS." On the 13th of February, the two Houses of the Convention went in a body to Whitehall. The princess of Orange, who had arrived from Holland on the previous day, sat with her husband, under a canopy in the Banqueting-House. Halifax, the Speaker of the Lords, addressed their highnesses, and said that both Houses had issued a Declaration, which was then read by the Clerk of the House of Lords:

"Whereas the late king James, by the assistance of divers evil counsellors, judges, and ministers employed by him, did endeavour to subvert and extirpate the Protestant religion, and the laws and liberties of this kingdom : By assuming and exercising a power of dispensing with, and suspending of laws, and the execution of laws, without consent of Parliament : By committing and prosecuting divers worthy prelates, for humbly petitioning to be excused from concurring to the said assumed power : By issuing and causing to be executed, a commissioner under the great seal, for erecting a Court called 'The Court of Commissione for Ecclesiastical Causes :' By levying money for and to the use of the Crown, by pretence of prerogative, for other time, and in other manner, than the same was granted by parliament : By raising and keeping a standing army within this kingdom in time of peace, without consent of parliament ; and quartering soldiers contrary to law : By causing divers good subjects, being Protestants, to be disarmed, at the same time when Papists were both armed and employed contrary to law : By violating the freedom of election of members to serve in parliament : By prosecutions in the Court of King's Bench for matters and causes recognizable only in parliament ; and by divers other arbitrary and illegal courses. And whereas of late years, partial, corrupt, and unqualified persons, have been returned and served on juries in trials, and particularly divers juries in trials for High Treason, which were not freeholders : and excessive bail hath been required of persons committed in criminal cases, to elude the benefit of the laws made for the liberty of the subjects : and excessive fines have been imposed, and illegal and cruel punishments inflicted : and several grants and promises made of fines and forfeitures, before any conviction or judgment against the persons upon whom the same were to be levied : All which are utterly and directly contrary to the known laws and statutes, and freedom of this realm.   And whereas the said late king James II. having abdicated the government, and the throne being thereby vacant, his highness the prince of Orange (whom it hath pleased Almighty God to make the glorious instrument of delivering this kingdom from Popery and arbitrary power) did (by the advice of the Lords spiritual and temporal, and divers principal persons of the Commons) cause letters to be written to the Lords spiritual and temporal, being Protestants, and other letters to the several counties, cities, universities, boroughs, and cinque-ports, for the choosing of such persons to represent them as were of right to be sent to parliament, to meet and sit at Westminster upon the 22nd day of January in this year 1688, [1689] in order to such an establishment, as that their religion, laws, and liberties, might not again be in danger of being subverted : Upon which letters, elections having been accordingly made ; and thereupon the Lords spiritual and temporal, and Commons, pursuant to their several letters and elections, being now assembled in a full and free representative of this nation, taking into their most serious consideration the best means for attaining the end aforesaid, do in the first place (as their ancestors in like case have usually done) for vindicating and asserting their ancient rights and liberties, declare : That the pretended power of suspending the laws, or the execution of laws, by royal authority, without consent of parliament, is illegal : That the pretended power of dispensing with laws, or the execution of laws, by royal authority, as it hath been assumed and exercised of late, is illegal : That the commission for erecting the late Court of Commissioners for Ecclesiastical Causes, and all other commission and courts of the like nature, are illegal and pernicious : That levying money for or to the use of the crown, by pretence of prerogative, without grant of parliament, for longer time, or in any other manner than the same is or shall be granted, is illegal : That it is the right of the subjects to petition the king, and all commitments and prosecutions for such petitioning, are illegal : That the raising or keeping a standing army within the kingdom in time of peace, unless it be with consent of parliament, is against law : That the subjects, which are Protestants, may have arms for their defence suitable to their condition, and as allowed by law : That elections of members of parliament ought to be free : That the freedom of speech, and debates, or proceedings in parliament, ought not to be impeached or questioned in any court or place out of parliament : That excessive bail ought not to be required, nor excessive fines imposed, nor cruel and unusual punishments inflicted : That jurors ought to be duly empanelled and returned ; and jurors, which pass upon men in trials of high-treason, ought to be freeholders : That all grants, and promises of fines, and forfeitures of particular persons, before conviction, are illegal and void : And that for redress of all grievances, and for the amending, strengthening, and preserving of the laws, parliaments ought to be held frequently.   And they do claim, demand, and insist, upon all and singular the premises, as their undoubted rights and liberties ; and no declarations, judgments, doings or proceedings, to the prejudice of the people in any of the said premises, ought in any wise to be drawn hereafter into consequence or example.   To which demand of their rights they are particularly encouraged by the declaration of his highness the prince of Orange, as being the only means for obtaining a full redress and remedy therein. Having therefore an entire confidence that his said highness, the prince of Orange will perfect the deliverance so far advanced by him, and will still preserve them from the violation of their rights, which they have here asserted, and from all other attempts upon their religion, rights, and liberties; the said lords spiritual and temporal, and commons, assembled at Westminster, do resolve, That William and Mary, prince and princess of Orange, be, and be declared king and queen of England, France, and Ireland, and the dominions thereunto belonging, to hold the crown and royal dignity of the said kingdoms and dominions, to them, the said prince and princess during their lives, and the life of the survivor of them; and that the sole and full exercise of the royal power be only in, and executed by the said prince of Orange, in the names of the said prince and princess during their joint lives; and after their deceases the said crown and royal dignity of the said kingdoms and dominions to be to the heirs of the body of the said princess; and for default of such issue to the princess Anne of Denmark, and the heirs of her body; and for default of such issue, to the heirs of the body of the said prince of Orange. And the said lords spiritual and temporal, and commons do pray the said prince and princess of Orange, to accept the same accordingly: And that the oaths hereafter mentioned be taken by all persons of whom the oaths of allegiance and supremacy might be required by law, instead of them; and that the said oaths of allegiance and supremacy be abrogated: 'I, A. B., do sincerely promise and swear, that I will be faithful, and bear true allegiance to their majesties, king William and queen Mary. So help me God. I, A. B., do swear That I do from my heart abhor, detest, and abjure, as impious and heretical, this damnable doctrine and position, That princes excommunicated or deprived by the pope, or any authority of the see of Rome, may be deposed or murdered by their subjects, or any other whatsoever. And I do declare, that no foreign prince, person, prelate, state, or potentate, hath or ought to have, any jurisdiction, power, superiority, pre-eminence, or authority, ecclesiastical, or spiritual, within this realm. So help me God.'"

When the reading of the Declaration was concluded, lord Halifax, in the name of all the Estates of the realm, requested the prince and princess to accept the Crown. "We thankfully accept," said William, "what you have offered us." A few words of assurance from those undemonstrative lips, that the laws should be the rule of his life, that he would endeavour to promote the kingdom's welfare, and that he would constantly seek the advice of the two Houses of Parliament, concluded this memorable transfer of the Crown. Amidst the shouts of the people, the Prince and Princess of Orange were proclaimed King and Queen of England. The Revolution was accomplished.

The Revolution of 1688 is the commencement of a new era in English history. It was not a great popular victory over an absolute king or an intolerant priesthood. Such a victory had been achieved by the Long Parliament; but the change from a Monarchy to a Commonwealth, from Episcopacy to Puritanism, was too extreme, and too sudden, to be permanent. The re-action brought back the evil theories of Strafford and Laud; but the time was past when any successful attempt could be made to carry them out to their extreme consequences. The time was also past when resistance to oppression and corruption would contemplate the overthrow of the Crown and Mitre. The opposition to the measures of the two successors of Charles the First was narrowed by limits which did not circumscribe the contest with their father. When the insane passion of James the Second, to thrust an obnoxious religion upon the nation, was to be carried through by his own illegal assumption of power,—when chartered privileges were violated —when justice was corrupted at its fountain head—the desire to substitute some other form of government in the place of the ancient monarchy was gone. The republican enthusiasm of Vane and Ludlow had given place to the safe Constitutionalism of Halifax and Somers. When the Church of England was roused by its own danger into a contest with the absolute king, whose right-divine to unlimited obedience it had so strenuously maintained, the Non-conformists did not reproach the Church for its inconsistency, or make common cause with its enemies, in the hope of its downfall. The zealotry of Peters, and the fanaticism of Venner, had been succeeded by the moderation of Howe and the peace-making of Penn. Hence, in the Revolu-lution of 1688, there was scarcely a manifestation that the leaders of the movement contemplated any violent change in the institutions of the country. It was by no means clear that the most influential among them contemplated the removal of their obnoxious sovereign. They sought to curb his illegal proceedings, through the power of a foreign prince, whose interest in the welfare of the kingdom gave a semblance of legality to his invasion, and whose sagacity and courage were the pledges that his attempt would not miscarry for the want of the necessary qualities to carry it through. From the same cause that had rendered the resistance to the government a policy rather than an impulse, the support which the government still retained was a calculation rather than a feeling. That Loyalty was gone, which regarded the king as the supreme arbiter of a nation's destiny, to be served without any limitation, and to be obeyed without any doubt. With the Roundheads of the Civil War, resistance to this irresponsible power was a principle. With the Cavaliers, the defence of all royal power was a sentiment. Charles the Second destroyed the sentiment when it became incompatible with respect for the possessor of the crown. James the Second completed its destruction, when he cast off those allies who had attempted to found implicit obedience upon the divine command. From the inevitable changes of national feeling in the past half century, whose lessons of experience had been so harsh and yet so salutary, it resulted that the Revolution of 1688 was not a great emotional change, in which the evil might be feared as much as the good—a convulsion which should overthrow many right things which ought to be pre-served as well as the bad things which ought to be swept away. That convulsion had taken place in the previous generation. It was scarcely necessary now to do more than preserve what had been won ; to restore what had then been destroyed ; and to render any future attempts impossible to bring back the period of misrule that preceded the great catastrophe of the Monarchy. But to accomplish this amount of good effectually and securely, it was the first condition of success that the Monarchy should be preserved. The great difficulty of effecting this preservation, and yet changing the occupier of the throne, is the natural explanation of the inconsistency of the theory upon which James was set aside. The practical necessity over-rode the abstract incongruity. There was to be sovereignty ; but the legitimate sovereign was cast out and the heir passed by. And yet the elective principle was not absolutely maintained. But at the same time the right divine, upon which the claim to absolute power had been built, was rejected ; the compact between king and people was recognised. There was still the Monarchy, with all its ancient dignity and possessions, but the title rested no longer upon slavish theories. The title of William and Mary was irrevocably associated with the Declaration of Rights. When, on the thirteenth of February, William, prince of Orange, said to the Peers and Commons who tendered him the Crown in conjunction with his wife—" We thankfully accept what you have offered us "—their recognition of the gift also recognised the conditions of the gift,—that the Rights and Liberties of the People, and the legal prerogatives of the Sovereign, were thenceforth to be inseparable.

The broad foundation upon which the Rights and Liberties of the People were to be restored, kept up, extended if necessary, was that of a free Parliament,—freely elected, free in its proceedings, without whose consent no taxes could be levied, and no standing army maintained—a Parliament frequently meeting, " for redress of all grievances, and for the amending, strengthening, and preserving of the Laws." Upon Parliamentary Representation was the Revolution based. It is for this reason, especially, that the Revolution may be considered the commencement of a new era. The Parliament was thus to be a great integral part of the Constitution, without which no act of government could have a real vitality. During the whole unhappy time of the Stuarts, their great struggle had been to govern without Parliaments. During the Civil War and the earlier years of the Commonwealth, the attempt of the legislative power to govern without the monarchical, was found to be full of danger and insecurity. The sagacity of Cromwell saw that a Monarchy, or " something like a Monarchy," in conjunction with a Parliament, was best adapted to the whole structure of the English laws, and best suited to the character of the English people. What Cromwell in vain aimed at was accomplished without difficulty, by a prince who much resembled him in some of the great qualities that belong to a ruler of men. In 1689, the Constitution was established through the principle of Resistance, not upon any new theories, but upon fundamental laws, many of which were of an older date than that of the oldest oak which stood upon English ground. For this reason, it has never again been necessary to call in the principle of Resistance. A time would come, when the government of England, being so essentially a Parliamentary government, the struggles of Parties would have more regard to the possession of power than to the interests of the.nation. But it was the essential consequence of these very strifes of Party, that, whatever the influence of oligarchs or demagogues, a controlling public opinion was constantly growing and strengthening. The power that distinguished the century following the Revolution from all other centuries, was the power of the Press, and especially the power of Journalism. Rude and incomplete as were its first efforts against, and often for, corrupt and unpatriotic administrations, it gradually rendered public opinion so active and concentrated, that statesmen could no longer affect to despise its admonitions. The Press ceased to be controlled by a licenser. It ceased to be awed by the fear of state prosecutions, when its security rested upon the verdict of twelve men. The tampering with Juries was one of the most crying evils of the period which preceded the Revolution. The doctrine which had been so often violated was solemnly asserted in 1689, that "Jurors ought to be duly empanelled and returned." Chiefly through the influence of public opinion, kept in vigorous order by the Press,—and let it always be borne in mind that the Press was essentially controversial, and always will be so,—extreme opinions became less and less. In the same degree the union of Classes became closer. The representatives of the old great families approached the commonalty, not as a "rabble," but as fellow-citizens. The commonalty looked upon the aristocracy, not as a hateful caste of oppressors, but as their natural leaders. The Revolution of 1688 has been despised by some as an aristocratic Revolution. Happy for us that it was not born of that "violent and unextinguishable hatred of inequality," that fierce desire "to raze to their foundations all that remained of the institutions of the Middle Ages;" * which, chiefly, have made the Revolutions of another great nation so unstable.

* De Tocqueville.

Obverse of Medal, struck at the Revolution.

	ENGLAND.	FRANCE.	GERMANY.	PAPAL STATES.	SPAIN.	RUSSIA.
1625	Charles I.	Louis XIII.	Ferdinand II.	Urban VIII.	Philip III.	Michael Federowitch.
1637			Ferdinand III.			
1643		Louis XIV.				
1644				Innocent X.		
1645						Alexei Michaelowitch.
1649	{ Charles II., King de jure. Commonwealth.					
1655				Alexander VII.		
1658			Leopold I.			
1660	Charles II., King de facto.					
1665					Charles II.	
1667				Clement IX.		
1670				Clement X.		
1676				Innocent XI.		Feodore II.
1682						Ivan Alexandrowitch,
1685	James II.					Peter the Great.
1689	William and Mary.			Alexander VIII.		

LONDON:
PRINTED BY WILLIAM CLOWES AND SONS,
STAMFORD STREET AND CHARING CROSS.

LaVergne, TN USA
11 April 2011
223737LV00006B/28/P